Knowledge-Based Development for Cities and Societies:
Integrated Multi-Level Approaches

Kostas Metaxiotis
University of Piraeus, Greece

Francisco Javier Carrillo
Tecnologico de Monterrey, Mexico

Tan Yigitcanlar
Queensland University of Technology, Australia

INFORMATION SCIENCE REFERENCE
Hershey · New York

Director of Editorial Content: Kristin Klinger
Director of Book Publications: Julia Mosemann
Acquisitions Editor: Lindsay Johnston
Development Editor: Joel Gamon
Publishing Assistant: Sean Woznicki
Typesetter: Deanna Zombro
Quality control: Jamie Snavely
Cover Design: Lisa Tosheff
Printed at: Yurchak Printing Inc.

Published in the United States of America by
Information Science Reference (an imprint of IGI Global)
701 E. Chocolate Avenue
Hershey PA 17033
Tel: 717-533-8845
Fax: 717-533-8661
E-mail: cust@igi-global.com
Web site: http://www.igi-global.com/reference

Library of Congress Cataloging-in-Publication Data

Knowledge-based development for cities and societies : integrated multi-level approaches / Kostas Metaxiotis, Francisco Javier Carrillo and Tan Yigitcanlar, editors.
p. cm.

Includes bibliographical references.
Summary: "This book presents a better knowledge and understanding of applying knowledge-based development policies, contributing to the theorizing of knowledge-based development and creation of knowledge societies"--Provided by publisher.

ISBN 978-1-61520-721-3 (hbk.) -- ISBN 978-1-61520-722-0 (ebook) 1. City planning. 2. Knowledge management. 3. Intellectual capital. 4. Information technology--Social aspects. 5. Information society. I. Metaxiotis, Kostas. II. Carrillo, Francisco Javier. III. Yigitcanlar, Tan.
HT166.K59 2010
307.1'16--dc22

2009048636

British Cataloguing in Publication Data
A Cataloguing in Publication record for this book is available from the British Library.

Dedication

This book is dedicated to the rapidly and surely emerging global knowledge based development community, and our beloved families.

List of Reviewers

Table of Contents

Foreword xvii

Preface xxii

Section 1
Concepts, Foundations and Frameworks of Knowledge-Based Development

Chapter 1
Knowledge-Based Value Generation 1
Francisco Javier Carrillo, Center for Knowledge Systems, and The World Capital Institute, Mexico

Chapter 2
Building Successful Knowledge Cities in the Context of the Knowledge-Based Economy: A Modern Strategic Framework 17
Emmanouil Ergazakis, National Technical University of Athens, Greece
Kostas Ergazakis, National Technical University of Athens, Greece
Kostas Metaxiotis, University of Piraeus, Greece

Chapter 3
Attracting and Retaining Knowledge Workers: The Impact of Quality of Place in the Case of Montreal 42
Sébastien Darchen, York University, Canada
Diane-Gabrielle Tremblay, Télé-Université (UQÀM), Canada

Chapter 4
The Impact of Proximity Dimensions on the Knowledge Diffusion Process 59
Antonio Messeni Petruzzelli, Politecnico di Bari, Italy

Chapter 5
The Interaction between Local and Regional Knowledge-Based Development: Towards a Quadruple Helix Model 81
Tooran Alizadeh, University of Sydney, Australia

Chapter 6
Making Space and Place for Knowledge Production: Socio-Spatial Development of Knowledge Community Precincts 99
Tan Yigitcanlar, Queensland University of Technology, Australia
Cristina Martinez-Fernandez, University of Western Sydney, Australia

Chapter 7
Essentials for Developing a Prosperous Knowledge City 118
Rabee M. Reffat, King Fahd University of Petroleum and Minerals, Saudi Arabia

Section 2
Multi-Level Approaches of Knowledge-Based Development

Chapter 8
Personal Knowledge Management by the Knowledge Citizen: The Generation Aspect of Organizational and Social Knowledge-Based Development 131
América Martínez Sánchez, Instituto Tecnológico y de Estudios Superiores de Monterrey, México

Chapter 9
Deep Knowledge as the Core of Sustainable Societies 141
Alex Bennet, Mountain Quest Institute, USA
David Bennet, Mountain Quest Institute, USA

Chapter 10
Knowledge Worker Profile: A Framework to Clarify Expectations 162
Gulgun Kayakutlu, Istanbul Technical University, Turkey

Chapter 11
Up the Junction? Exploiting Knowledge-Based Development through Supply Chain and SME Cluster Interactions 179
Tim Donnet, Queensland University of Technology, Australia
Robyn Keast, Queensland University of Technology, Australia
David Pickernell, University of Glamorgan Business School, UK

Chapter 12
Creativity and Knowledge-Based Urban Development in a Nordic Welfare State: Combining Tradition and Development in the Helsinki Metropolitan Area 196
Tommi Inkinen, University of Helsinki, Finland
Mari Vaattovaara, University of Helsinki, Finland

Chapter 13
The Role of the Built Environment in the Creation, Cultivation and Acquisition of a Knowledge-Base 211
Kristine Peta Jerome, Queensland University of Technology, Australia

Chapter 14
Using Communities of Practice to Share Knowledge in a Knowledge City 222
Sheryl Buckley, University of Johannesburg, South Africa
Apostolos Giannakopoulos, University of Johannesburg, South Africa

Section 3
Global Best Practices of Knowledge-Based Development

Chapter 15
Singapore: A Model for Knowledge-Based City 255
Caroline Wong, The University of Queensland, Australia

Chapter 16
Israel: A Knowledge Region Case Study 272
Edna Pasher, Edna Pasher Ph.D & Associates, Israel
Sigal Shachar, Edna Pasher Ph.D & Associates, Israel

Chapter 17
Orchestrating Knowledge-Based Urban Development: Lessons from Multimedia Super Corridor, Malaysia 281
Tan Yigitcanlar, Queensland University of Technology, Australia
Muna Sarimin, Queensland University of Technology, Australia

Chapter 18
Rising Northern Light: A Systems Outlook on Manchester's Knowledge-Based Capitals 296
Blanca C. Garcia, Colegio de la Frontera Norte/Colef., Mexico

Chapter 19
Knowledge Management Orientation and Business Performance: The Malaysian Manufacturing and Service Industries Perspective 315
Baharom Abdul Rahman, Universiti Sains Malaysia, Malaysia
Norizan Mat Saad, Universiti Sains Malaysia, Malaysia
Mahmod Sabri Harun, Universiti Sains Malaysia, Malaysia

Afterword
The Way Forward: Theorizing Knowledge-Based Development? 329
J.C. Spender, Lund University, Sweden

Compilation of References 340

About the Contributors 380

Index 388

Detailed Table of Contents

Foreword xvii

Preface xxii

Section 1
Concepts, Foundations and Frameworks of Knowledge-Based Development

Chapter 1
Knowledge-Based Value Generation 1
Francisco Javier Carrillo, Center for Knowledge Systems, and The World Capital Institute, Mexico

This chapter aims to characterize Knowledge Based Development (KBD) from the perspective of value systems. After an introduction to its purpose and scope, the chapter is divided into five sections. The first section looks into the distinctive aspects of human knowledge-based or represented experience as the rationale for both Knowledge Management and Knowledge Based Development. The concept of KBD is introduced as a distinctive category and as the basis of a new social paradigm of special significance in view of both the current stage of human evolution and our impact on other Earth systems. In the second section the emergence and evolution of KBD as a field of study and practice is overviewed. Thirdly, the received perspective of knowledge capital as instrumental to increasing monetary growth and accumulation is contrasted with an integrated approach where all value elements relevant to a group are balanced into a unified system of categories. Such *radical* approach to KBD recaptures the essence of human value production and allows the redesign of accountacy and management practices at the organizational level, as well as of cultural and political practices at the communitary and global levels. Next, a review of some of the most visible KBD research agendas shows the trends in the evolution of this area and suggests the viability of a global R&D agenda. Finally, the possible contribution of KBD as a language to articulate national and international consesus-building on the most urgent issues is discussed as a conclusion.

Chapter 2
Building Successful Knowledge Cities in the Context of the Knowledge-Based Economy: A Modern Strategic Framework 17
Emmanouil Ergazakis, National Technical University of Athens, Greece
Kostas Ergazakis, National Technical University of Athens, Greece
Kostas Metaxiotis, University of Piraeus, Greece

The topics of Knowledge-Based Development (KBD) and especially of Knowledge Cities (KCs) have attracted the interest of many researchers and practitioners during the last years. In a previous research work of the authors, a set of hypotheses for the design, development and operation of successful KCs had been proposed and validated through the analytical study of KCs cases' support to these hypotheses, resulting to a related Framework. However, the rapid changes in the field render more than necessary today to re-examine the elements which had leaded to the formulation of the Framework, so as to update it and conclude on a modern strategic framework. The methodology followed is based on the examination of the already identified KCs and the inclusion of five additional KCs cases. For the new set of KCs, the authors examine at which degree each case supports the hypotheses. Modifications in the set of hypotheses are proposed. The hypotheses that continue to be valid are considered as dominant, thus leading to the modern strategic Framework. Among the main findings is that all cities previously examined continue to actively support their KBD, through a series of strategies and appropriate actions. The majority of the hypotheses continue to be valid, while three of them need to slightly change so as to adapt to prevailing current conditions.

Chapter 3
Attracting and Retaining Knowledge Workers: The Impact of Quality of Place in the Case of Montreal 42
Sébastien Darchen, York University, Canada
Diane-Gabrielle Tremblay, Télé-Université (UQÀM), Canada

A concentration of knowledge workers, including scientists and engineers, has been identified by recent works as an element fostering economic growth in metropolitan areas. The authors' aim in this chapter is to study the factors influencing the mobility of graduate students in science and technology. The creative class thesis has emphasized the fact that criteria related to the quality of place have a positive impact on the attraction of *talents* and on economic development. This thesis was the basis for the authors' research. In this paper, they assimilate the workforce in science and technology to the concept of knowledge workers. They authors compared the influence of criteria related to the quality of place on the mobility of students with other criteria related to career opportunities and to the social network. They collected the data through an on-line questionnaire and we also proceeded to interviews with students in science and technology. The authors present in this chapter the results of their research for Montreal. With a quantitative analysis, they show that while Montreal is often considered as a very attractive place, the criteria related to the quality of place play a secondary role in the attraction and retention of the population studied, while those related to the career opportunities dominate. This leads to nuance the theories that highlight the importance of place versus job opportunities, and shows that while the quality of place may be important, job opportunities dominate.

Chapter 4
The Impact of Proximity Dimensions on the Knowledge Diffusion Process 59
Antonio Messeni Petruzzelli, Politecnico di Bari, Italy

The purpose of this research is to explore how proximity dimensions can favour the diffusion of knowledge between economic actors, focusing on the knowledge relationships established by a knowledge gatekeeper. In particular, the authors formulate several hypotheses regarding the role of proximity dimensions (i.e. geographical, organizational, and technological) in affecting the establishment of gatekeepers' knowledge relationships, taking into account their collaborative-non collaborative type and exploitative-explorative nature. Adopting a patent-based analysis, the authors test their hypotheses on a research sample constituted by 527 knowledge relationships established by two distinct types of knowledge gatekeeper, i.e. an university and a firm.

Chapter 5
The Interaction between Local and Regional Knowledge-Based Development: Towards a Quadruple Helix Model 81
Tooran Alizadeh, University of Sydney, Australia

By the turn of the 21st century, the significance of knowledge to be the key factor in urban and regional development is well established. However, it has been only recently that attempts have been made to identify the specific mechanism and institutional relationships, through which knowledge-based development takes place. In this regard, very little consideration has been given to the ways that different levels of knowledge-based development communicate to each other. This chapter examines the mutual interaction between knowledge-based development in local and regional level in two different sections. The first section builds upon the third wave of economic development supporting the growth of cluster of related firms and relates it to an empirical case study of knowledge-based community development in Queensland- Australia. It concludes that knowledge-based local developments do not evolve without a regional support network. The second section reviews the "Triple Helix" of university–industry–government collaboration as the basis of knowledge-based regional development in the investigated case study. This review determines the central role of local community as an innovation base for the interaction among the key factors, and suggests a promotion for a Quadruple Helix Model where community works alongside business, university and government in the new economy.

Chapter 6
Making Space and Place for Knowledge Production: Socio-Spatial Development of Knowledge Community Precincts 99
Tan Yigitcanlar, Queensland University of Technology, Australia
Cristina Martinez-Fernandez, University of Western Sydney, Australia

In the knowledge era the importance of making space and place for knowledge production is clearly understood worldwide by many city administrations that are keen on restructuring their cities as highly competitive and creative places. Consequently, knowledge-based urban development and socio-spatial development of knowledge community precincts have taken their places among the emerging agendas of the urban planning and development practice. This chapter explores these emerging issues and scrutinizes the development of knowledge community precincts that have important economic, social and cultural dimensions on the formation of competitive and creative urban regions. The chapter also sheds light on the new challenges for planning discipline, and discusses the need for and some specifics of a new planning paradigm suitable for dealing with 21st Century's socio-economic development and urbanization problems.

Chapter 7
Essentials for Developing a Prosperous Knowledge City 118
Rabee M. Reffat, King Fahd University of Petroleum and Minerals, Saudi Arabia

The essentials and challenges of the 21st century's economy include knowledge and innovation. Both are the key in order for a city to calmly race forward and safely ride out in the ever changing global economy. Knowledge and innovation could be viewed as the true hard currency of the future and corner stones in developing a prosperous knowledge city. This chapter introduces a model for developing a prosperous knowledge city through knowledge and innovation. The model consists of five components that are most important for cities pursuing towards prosperous Knowledge Cities including: developing creative environments, knowledge creation, skills, collaboration/partnership, and leadership. The chapter focuses on articulating the primary components of the proposed model and identifying how they will contribute to achieving prosperous Knowledge Cities and innovative knowledge regions.

Section 2
Multi-Level Approaches of Knowledge-Based Development

Chapter 8
Personal Knowledge Management by the Knowledge Citizen: The Generation Aspect of Organizational and Social Knowledge-Based Development 131
América Martínez Sánchez, Instituto Tecnológico y de Estudios Superiores de Monterrey, México

The discipline of Personal Knowledge Management (PKM) is depicted in this chapter as a dimension that has been implicitly present within the scope and evolution of the Knowledge Management (KM) movement. Moreover, it is recognized as the dimension that brought forth Knowledge-based Development (KBD) schemes at organizational and societal levels. Hence, this piece of research work aims to develop parallel paths between Knowledge Management moments and generations and the PKM movement. KM will be depicted as a reference framework for a state-of-the-art review of PKM. A number of PKM authors and models are identified and categorized within the KM key moments and generations according to their characteristics and core statements. Moreover, this chapter shows a glimpse of the knowledge citizen's PKM as an aspect with strong impact on his/her competencies profile; which in turn drives his/her influence and value-adding capacity within knowledge-based schemes at organizational and societal levels. In this sense, the competencies profile of the knowledge citizen is of essence. Competencies are understood as the individual performance of the knowledge citizen interacting with others in a given value context. The chapter concludes with some considerations on the individual development that enables PKM to become a key element in the knowledge citizen's profile, such as the building block or living cell that triggers Knowledge-based Development at organizational and societal levels.

Chapter 9
Deep Knowledge as the Core of Sustainable Societies 141
Alex Bennet, Mountain Quest Institute, USA
David Bennet, Mountain Quest Institute, USA

Knowledge-based social communities are critical to sustain economic levels and quality environments for community members. The pace of change, rising uncertainty, exponentially increasing complexity and the resulting anxiety (CUCA) have made competition among nations, cities and communities greater and more fierce. As economies look from industry to knowledge for their prime income generator, the role of knowledge and its supporting infrastructure become critical to economic and social health. In this chapter the authors focus on what deep knowledge is and the environment needed to maximize its contribution to the health and growth of societies. They also introduce knowledge attractor network teams as sources of power for community sustainability.

Chapter 10
Knowledge Worker Profile: A Framework to Clarify Expectations.. 162
Gulgun Kayakutlu, Istanbul Technical University, Turkey

One of the major reasons for economic crisis of 2008-2009 is determined as value delivery. Major resource of value creation is the knowledge worker who works at different levels of an organisation. This study analyses knowledge worker studies in diverse disciplines, in order to determine the requests. The goal of the study is to propose a framework to clarify the skill requirements by integrating the requests at operational, team, organisational and inter-organisational levels with drivers provided by educating, attracting, motivating and retaining strategies. The framework facilitates employing the right employee for the right post while balancing the requests and the performance measures. This new vision will be beneficial for managers, human resource experts, and educators.

Chapter 11
Up the Junction? Exploiting Knowledge-Based Development through Supply Chain and SME Cluster Interactions 179
Tim Donnet, Queensland University of Technology, Australia
Robyn Keast, Queensland University of Technology, Australia
David Pickernell, University of Glamorgan Business School, UK

Maximisation of Knowledge-Based Development (KBD) benefits requires effective dissemination and utilisation mechanisms to accompany the initial knowledge creation process. This work highlights the potential for interactions between Supply Chains (SCs) and Small and Medium sized Enterprise Clusters (SMECs), (including via 'junction' firms which are members of both networks), to facilitate such effective dissemination and utilisation of knowledge. In both these network types there are firms that readily utilise their relationships and ties for ongoing business success through innovation. The following chapter highlights the potential for such beneficial interactions between SCs and SMECs in key elements of KBD, particularly knowledge management, innovation and technology transfer. Because there has been little focus on the interactions between SCs and SMECs, particularly when firms simultaneously belong to both, this chapter examines the conduits through which information and knowledge can be transferred and utilised. It shows that each network type has its own distinct advantages in the types of information searched for and transferred amongst network member firms. Comparing and contrasting these advantages shows opportunities for both networks to leverage the knowledge sharing strengths of each other, through these 'junctions' to address their own weaknesses, allowing implications to be drawn concerning new ways of utilising relationships for mutual network gains.

Chapter 12
Creativity and Knowledge-Based Urban Development in a Nordic Welfare State: Combining Tradition and Development in the Helsinki Metropolitan Area 196
Tommi Inkinen, University of Helsinki, Finland
Mari Vaattovaara, University of Helsinki, Finland

This chapter addresses the provision and condition of the knowledge-based development in the Helsinki metropolitan area, Finland. This chapter looks at linkages between regional (urban) development and welfare state elements supported by local and national policies. the authors concentrate on one hand on urban and regional policy tools, and on the other to education, because together they provide a platform for building a knowledge-based society. The authors also explore the current condition of selected creative and knowledge-intensive employment in the Helsinki metropolitan area.

Chapter 13
The Role of the Built Environment in the Creation, Cultivation and Acquisition of a Knowledge-Base 211
Kristine Peta Jerome, Queensland University of Technology, Australia

This chapter explores the role of the built environment in the creation, cultivation and acquisition of a knowledge base by people populating the urban landscape. It examines McDonald's restaurants as a way to comprehend the relevance of the physical design in the diffusion of codified and tacit knowledge at an everyday level. Through an examination of space at a localised level, this chapter describes the synergies of space and the significance of this relationship in navigating the global landscape.

Chapter 14
Using Communities of Practice to Share Knowledge in a Knowledge City 222
Sheryl Buckley, University of Johannesburg, South Africa
Apostolos Giannakopoulos, University of Johannesburg, South Africa

When it comes to a formal CoP, be it face-to-face or virtual, its success or failure will depend on a number of factors. For this reason it is necessary to investigate its nature, functions, aims and reasons for existence. Then the true value of communities, both for the individual participants and the supporting organisation, will come from the ongoing interaction and work of the group. To sustain that value, organisations should quickly move into a sustaining-and-evolving mode to match ever-changing member needs and business goals (Vestal, 2006). In a knowledge based development approach to modern societies as suggested by Ergazakis, Metaxiotis & Psarras (2006), CoPs can be used as the originators of change and innovation for a 'knowledge city'. This chapter will address the role that CoPs can play in the development of a 'knowledge city'.

Section 3
Global Best Practices of Knowledge-Based Development

Chapter 15
Singapore: A Model for Knowledge-Based City 255
Caroline Wong, The University of Queensland, Australia

Singapore's commitment to knowledge-based economy (KBE) development in the past decade has enabled it to make a rapid and successful transition to knowledge-based city. This chapter focuses on how Singapore government has forged an environment that is conducive to innovations, new discoveries and the creation of new knowledge. In the process, Singapore has emerged as one of the top knowledge-based cities in the world through various frameworks used globally. In this period, Singapore strengthened its engagement with the global knowledge economy developing a creative industries development strategy which endorsed the importance of creative industries. The Singapore experience represents one of few examples of how knowledge can become the driving force of economic growth and transformation. It provides valuable insight into how public policies have successfully negotiated the current global network economy to suit economic changes. Although Singapore's developmental model has created benefits in many ways, it had also negatively constrained its development particularly in the area of knowledge creation and application to entrepreneurship and creativity.

Chapter 16
Israel: A Knowledge Region Case Study 272
Edna Pasher, Edna Pasher Ph.D & Associates, Israel
Sigal Shachar, Edna Pasher Ph.D & Associates, Israel

Israel, a small country in the Middle East, is a very unique case of a knowledge based region. The authors have extensively studied Israel as an innovative region in different contexts. Since 1998 they published three Israel Intellectual Capital Reports for the Israeli Government. During 2007 the authors led a study for the European Commission focused on regional innovation systems. This study has aimed to measure the effectiveness of participation in ICT (Information Communication Technology) EU projects on the EU innovation system at the regional level. Israel was selected as a regional best practice though it is a nation state and not a region since it is as small as a region, and since the authors had good relevant data from the previous IC reports and since Israel is consistently recognized as one of the most innovative countries in the world. The authors discovered that an Intellectual Capital audit is a powerful and useful framework to understand the effectiveness of regional innovation systems, offering the possibility for evidence-based future policies rather than retrospective performance analyses. This chapter demonstrates the case of Israel as a knowledge-based region, as well as critical success factors for regional innovation systems.

Chapter 17
Orchestrating Knowledge-Based Urban Development: Lessons from Multimedia
Super Corridor, Malaysia 281
Tan Yigitcanlar, Queensland University of Technology, Australia
Muna Sarimin, Queensland University of Technology, Australia

In the era of knowledge economy, cities and regions have started increasingly investing on their physical, social and knowledge infrastructures so as to foster, attract and retain global talent and investment. Knowledge-based urban development as a new paradigm in urban planning and development is being implemented across the globe in order to increase the competitiveness of cities and regions. This chapter provides an overview of the lessons from Multimedia Super Corridor, Malaysia as one of the first large scale manifestations of knowledge-based urban development in South East Asia. The chapter investigates the application of the knowledge-based urban development concept within the Malaysian context, and, particularly, scrutinises the development and evolution of Multimedia Super Corridor by focusing on strategies, implementation policies, infrastructural implications, and agencies involved in the development and management of the corridor. In the light of the literature and case findings, the chapter provides generic recommendations, on the orchestration of knowledge-based urban development, for other cities and regions seeking such development.

Chapter 18

Rising Northern Light: A Systems Outlook on Manchester's Knowledge-Based Capitals................ 296

Blanca C. Garcia, Colegio de la Frontera Norte/Colef., Mexico

One of the difficulties in creating and sustaining knowledge cities is the lack of benchmarks to identify those cities and regions that are generating knowledge-driven initiatives, triggering development and collective value. One of such benchmarks is the value-based *Generic Capital System* (GCS) taxonomy. The rigorous application of GCS to cities in European contexts has already yielded its initial fruits, with Manchester as one of the cities in which a deeper perspective can be gained through the GCS lens. In this chapter, the authors aim to introduce GCS as an integrative system of capitals for the case of the Greater Manchester city-region and its journey into developing its knowledge capitals. Through the lens of the GCS generic KC capital system taxonomy, some of Manchester's *systems of information*, *systems of learning* and *systems of knowledge* are expected to emerge as a comprehensive meta system articulated by the extensive life-long learning initiatives implemented by Manchester's development-based Knowledge-City schemes. The GCS lens will be introduced within the different system layers interacting in the city in the aim to discover how they tie the City's learning, communicating and reflecting dynamics together in the emerging context of knowledge-based development initiatives. The chapter will attempt to highlight how ICT connectivity systems (managing information) could be viewed as closely linked to skill development (managing learning) and people's management of tacit and explicit knowledge (knowing), with visible regional aspirations for development. Such *systems* view aims to cover a wider (although still limited) range of the instrumental, human and meta capitals observable in the city in a simultaneously rich mosaic of different layers. The chapter will explore how to build a systematic account of capitals for the Greater Manchester city-region in the context of a demanding knowledge-intensive policy-making. The city's traditional and knowledge-intensive hubs, its communications and infrastructure, its identity, traditions and cultural diversity have seemingly thrust Manchester into a leading position in the new Knowledge-revolution era, as this chapter will attempt to demonstrate.

Chapter 19
Knowledge Management Orientation and Business Performance: The Malaysian Manufacturing and Service Industries Perspective 315
Baharom Abdul Rahman, Universiti Sains Malaysia, Malaysia
Norizan Mat Saad, Universiti Sains Malaysia, Malaysia
Mahmod Sabri Harun, Universiti Sains Malaysia, Malaysia

Even though knowledge has been recognized as a crucial strategic resource in most organizations, Malaysian companies are still at infancy stage of knowledge management. Research and academic writing dealing with knowledge management implementation among Malaysian companies are still scarce. Previous research on the knowledge management efforts among Malaysian companies indicated that these local companies are rather slow in its implementation and still largely rely on the physical aspects of production. This study investigates the level of knowledge management implementation among Malaysian manufacturing and service companies and further explores the effects of such implementation on their overall business performance. The findings suggest that these companies emphasize the dissemination and utilization of knowledge over the creation of new knowledge, thus subjecting them to continuously becoming copiers and adaptors of knowledge.

Afterword
The Way Forward: Theorizing Knowledge-Based Development? 329
J.C. Spender, Lund University, Sweden

Compilation of References 340

About the Contributors 380

Index 388

Foreword

UNDERSTANDING AND CULTIVATING SOCIAL KNOWLEDGE

Just imagine that you are sitting in an historical coffee house in Vienna, Austria, or a modern Starbuck´s coffee bar in New York, USA. Just sense the ambience and smell. Observe the conversations. It is the same social effects that were at hand in the old coffee shops on Through Morton Street, London some 150 years back. It was in this social context the London Stock Exchange as well as Lloyd's insurance was emerging.

It illustrates the importance of social context and networking for value creating. And here we might find the core of the City as well as Society Knowledge Development. This might be the community effect of 1+1=11, or in other words that the cumulative result of networks shape a higher value. This is also sometimes referred to as the Law of Increasing Marginal Utility as developed by the pioneering economists Brian Arthur and Paul Romer, USA.

"Cities of the Future" is the title of a well appreciated report from Price Waterhouse Coopers 2007. Here they are identifying some interesting City cases as well as a way to address the value creating components. It is mainly based on the core components of Intellectual Capital, human capital, relational and structural capital, but refined into more components, among others Social Capital (see www.pwc.com). Major critical elements of value creating systems as well as the language for Knowledge Based Development is further explored in this book.

The City emerged as a place for mainly defense or security as well as exchange of goods in the old days. Today the City is becoming a place for exchange of Knowledge and Networks, by so called Knowledge Workers. This means people working with value creation through more and more intangible dimensions. The City is then becoming a critical contextual platform as structural capital for shaping and leveraging human capital into collective intellectual capital. Therefore Urban design is becoming a more and more an essential challenge for Social Knowledge Innovations, especially as the world migration into cities is so immense.

Today more than 50% of our global population is in cities and the global talents seem to gather in fewer and fewer so called mega cities. Architecture and urban design will become critical for knowledge based development of communities. Especially this relates to quality of place, socio-spatial design and the emerging new requirements for a New Welfare City State, as described later on in this book.

But the traditional perception and function of the urban design evolution has more been about suburbs, roads or specific objects. This way of designing cities for the future is often starting on an engineering desk, by drawings, of streets, with well defined separating areas, of residence, office and work, as well as city areas versus suburbs. This separation process is an old science approach, called fragmentation.

Perhaps for a modern sustainable knowledge city, the opposite approach should be explored, i.e. as a quest of shaping for *intelligent social integration and interactivity*. This might be especially essential for attracting the migrating knowledge workers, as important value creators. For this we need to focus more on the intangible dimensions of understanding and cultivating the social knowledge. A long time ago this was actually also prototyped in case of the city Ragusa.

Let me first give some background on Ragusa. This city was shaped more than 1000 years back, in the Mediterranean area. It became a very successful city state, well ahead of its time. It flourished with a continuously growing wealth for more than 600 years, up to 1806. It was surrounded by envious enemies for a long time, trying to conquer the city and its growing wealth. In spite of not having a traditional military force Ragusa sustained.

What was the recipe for this sustainability and growing wealth? Research on the recipe and findings is highlighted in a book titled: Ragusa Intelligence & Security (RIS) - A Model for the 21st Century, by late professor Stevan Dedijer active among others at Lund University, Sweden. Ragusa focused on shaping knowledge ecology and specific knowledge recipes, around 3 pillars of Education, Diplomacy and Trade/Networking. Today this is called social intelligence.

The urban design of Ragusa was full of very explicit as well as implicit ideas. On the explicit side was e.g. to design the city to be ventilated by its own streets, as a kind of City air conditioning. On the implicit side was to appoint the City Leader or Mayor with the title of Rector/Dean. The meaning of this was among others to amplify the role of Knowledge Leadership. Furthermore this position was rotated every 13 month to another person. When visiting the Rector's palace in Ragusa's Senate you will find above the entrance a motto: "Forget private interests (as you) manage public ones." The name of the city today is Dubrovnik, Croatia, located along the Adriatic Coast line of the Mediterranean.

Ragusa is a very unique example which managed to combine relational, human and structural capital. Even the word "Libertas" on their ships' flags, which means freedom, enhances this pioneering mind set. Now since 2007 and every year a special group of excellent students from Zagreb is organizing a special conference – trying to find the deeper roots of these knowledge recipes (See more on http://www.youtube.com/watch?v=-0M9cUBgMVI).

Knowledge Based Development is valid both for the developing nations, cities and regions acting in a global competition for talents. In this the educational investments or the intangible investments is a CSF. The core of this evolution seems to be in the urban shaping to include both the tangible, for example the street design, as well as the intangible aspects, such as the social integration of multi talents. The streets are becoming important tools as flow channels. Not just for traffic, but also for personal interactions and so called proximity dimensions, as described later in this book. In the Old Italian design of villages there was a special concept called Vincinato, an open small space outside the house for social interactions. Open space on a University campus area is today becoming such an area for the mindfulness of social and societal volunteers. Other types of such space are the coffee shop or knowledge café as described initially.

Networking activities are on a macro level social capital, and on another micro level neuro science. today this is also called relational capital. to manage these social and networking knowledge flows requires a special type of leadership, a kind of cultivator role. the focus of this society leadership should be on social dynamics and cultivation.

Today the City of Melbourne in Australia has such an Office of Knowledge Capital. Barcelona was perhaps the very first city in modern time to appoint a Chief Knowledge Officer already around late

1990´s. The City of Manchester has also today a special organization for the intangibles called Manchester Knowledge Capital.

These networking activities can be showing the roads of connectivity among people. A new type of mapping is emerging, called Social Networking Analyses. With modern software tools there are special possibilities to visualize as well as simulate this Social Networking, with highlighting connections, roles and activities especially for Regional innovation (see www.valuenetworks.com).

So the recipe for the City as a Knowledge Tool is becoming a very important subject, especially in a quest for value delivery by its citizens. I wrote about this already in 2006 (see www.corporatelongitude.com). In simplified terms or the taxonomy of Intellectual Capital it is about refining the offer of structural capital to the human capital or citizens of both today and tomorrow.

Today we know more and more about the impact of urban design on the attractiveness as well as mental/brain health of citizens. This might be called Knowledge Policy development or Knowledge Politics. Especially it is about refining the recipe for the flow of relationships and knowledge ergonomics. Already in 2003 Dr. Debra Amidon launched the concept of special KIZ-knowledge Zones. KIZ is a geographic region, product/service/industry segment or community of practice in which knowledge flows from the point of origin to the point of need or opportunity (see www.inthekzone.com).

The research by Richard Florida and Charlotte Melander on Wealth of Places and birth of Mega places is highlighting the importance of the Creative Class. In one of the chapters in the book this is explained more in detail. They are characterized by the same pillars as Intellectual Capital, but instead of calling it Human capital, Relational Capital and Structural Capital, it is called Talent, Tolerance and Technology. In their research is highlighted a growing competition between some 100 key cities that attract the Talents or the Creative Class. These are attracted by among others such factors as esthetics, quality of schools, meeting spaces, low frictions, quality of life, security, and easy communications. The critical mass or the density of brains seems to be one of the interesting factors. Brains attract other brains. But more important than the individual, seems to be the structural context capital aspects for quality of life.

The magazine Monocle, in July-August issue 2009, ranks cities around the world based on a number of such quality elements for where to live and work. This is then summarized into The Most Liveable Cities Index. The top 10 list is this year:

- Zurich
- Copenhagen
- Tokyo
- Munich
- Helsinki
- Stockholm
- Vienna
- Paris
- Melbourne
- Berlin

These intangible dimensions of cities are either leveraged and multiplied by good urban design or hampered, with huge friction costs. The forthcoming Expo 2010 in Shanghai has even the focus of a City Life in Harmony. It is about quality of life factors, often very immaterial. The City of Helsingborg in Sweden is therefore now looking into how to shape a special Mind Zone. This Mind Zone is a specific area of the City. The purpose of the Mind Zone is to support and cultivate the Urban Capital of the City. It will be characterized by among others offering both mind progression as well as mind retreat, a place for sustainable lifestyle which renews and reinvent itself over time. Mind Zone is both a way of thinking for Urban Design as well as a way of interacting in the City to enhance the Urban Capital. It might be the opposite of a traditional Shopping Center or Mall area and its transaction focus.

Tomorrow will challenge our thought patterns and over focus on savings and traditional economics. For the knowledge navigation into the Future we need to invest into intangibles such as relationships, social media, and knowledge flow and joy. The traditional focus on governance by cost accounting of tangibles has to replace by focus on renewal and organic flows. The future is not about knowledge as an object but knowing as a relationship. Politicians have to be more of Paradigm Pioneers, the Administration more of Welfare and Value developers and the Chairman as Chief Endorphin Officer. So the leadership is about understanding the weak or strong signals of social interactions and getting the social mandate of power for the knowledge navigation into the future – as social intercultural intelligence.

This is resulting in growing Intelligent Regions, Metropolitan Mega Cities or Collaborative Social Communities. They are characterized by among others Social Renewal based on Social innovations, Futurizing, Volunteers and Digital Collective Commons. Some traditional cases are Oxford, Boston Singapore as well as the State of Israel. More recent ones might be MMSC- Multimedia Super Corridor in Kuala Lumpur, Malaysia, as well as the Oresund Region between Denmark and Sweden. Such borderline zones or Twilight Zones are evidently cultivating platforms for the flow.

An interesting recent case to look into more is Shenzhen, in China, on the borderline to Hong Kong. This city was declared the very first SEZ- Special Economic Zone in China, in 1989 by Deng Xiaoping. At that time the city was more of a fishing village with some 40.000 citizens. In about only 30 years Shenzhen has evolved into a modern Knowledge Based City with some 12 million citizens. That is also where the Second World Knowledge City summit is taking place in November 2009 (see www.kcsummit2009.com).

However we can also see, not only an aging of citizens around the world, but also see how many of the old institutions of societies are eroding, like the hospitals, schools, harbors, customs etc. This structural capital becomes either museum of the past or critical leveraging instruments for the future. We evidently now need radical innovations to reinvent the public sector.

In Sweden the government has in 2008 allocated funds through its Knowledge Foundation to a special nine year program for exploring the research, education and piloting of societal entrepreneurship. It is an initiative aimed at improving that which is missing or not working in the social structure: new solutions that create a sustainable society – economically, socially and ecologically. Societal entrepreneurship exists when people take their own initiative to improve that which they believe is missing or not working in society. It may be a matter of skateboard ramps, regional development or Fairtrade-labelled clothing. In the same way that traditional entrepreneurs are necessary to renew business and industry, their cousins – societal entrepreneurs – are needed as volunteers to develop public-welfare services and societal functions (see www.kks.se).

A new book was also launched 2009 in Denmark , called Speed up the Citizens, implying the need for getting the volunteers to be involved as drivers in a bottom up process for social innovation impact. In Denmark there is now also a special task force on the subject. In UK Tony Blair was initiating such programs many years, among others a prototyping center called NESTA (see www.NESTA.org.uk). Today there are special labs for the Social Innovations. Recently, President Obama in the USA initiated an Office for Social Innovation. Volunteers seem to be very dependent on networking, legitimacy and structural capital support. The drive and thrust is coming from within.

The tool for this renewal and transformation is sometimes referred to as Future Center, a lab concept and special environment for the organizational design of intangibles. I shaped the very first one in the world in 1996, as Skandia Future Center in Sweden. Today there are more than 30 such labs around the world, such as in Denmark the Mind Lab or COK, exploring the Future of Social Design, in in the Netherlands the LEF by the Ministry of Transportation or Studio BliQ in the City Oss, in UK NESTA as the Innovation Imperative, as well as in Japan Fuji Xerox KDI Future Centers.

This book about KBD-Knowledge Based Development, which consists of 19 well-written chapters, is a further stimulating reading of multi perspectives of the new urban landscape. It addresses among others KBD as a language, quality of places, proximity dimensions, socio-spatial developments for prosperous cities, generic capital system and local communities as innovation bases. it highlights very interesting cases such as the cities of Manchester and Helsinki, as well as cases from Israel, Singapore and Malaysia.

This book is pointing to the many important elements of shaping of knowledge cities as the larger ecological and intangible structural capital, for our own future value creation as well as coming generations.

Happy future.

Leif Edvinsson
The World'S First Professor of Intellectual Capital
Lund University, the Hong Kong Polytechnic University

Leif Edvinsson *is a key pioneering contributor to both the theory and practice of Intellectual Capital. As the world's first director of IC in 1991 he initiated the creation of the world's first public corporate Intellectual Capital Annual Report 1994, and inspired the development ever since on IC metrics. He was parallel to that prototyping the Skandia Future Center as a Lab for Organisational design, one of the very first in the World in 1996, and inspired many to be followed. During 1996 he was recognised with awards from the American Productivity and Quality Centre, USA and Business Intelligence, UK. In January 1998, Leif received the prestigious Brain Trust "Brain of the Year" award, UK. for his pioneering work on IC. In 1999 noted as Most Admired Knowledge Award on Knowledge Leadership. He was also awarded The KEN Practitioner of the Year 2004, from Entovation International, where he also is an E 100. In 2006 also listed in a book by London Business Press, as one of The 50 Most influential Thinkers in the World. In March 1997, together with Michael S. Malone, he launched one of the very first books on Intellectual Capital.*

Preface

Over the past twenty years, there have been intensive discussions about the importance of knowledge management in the business world. In recent years the conventional knowledge management approach has evolved into a strategic management approach that has also spread into other fields. As a result the new strategic management approach has found application ground and opportunities not only in the business world but also in other areas such as education, urban planning and development, governance and healthcare, and so on. The fact that major international organizations – such as the European Commission, the World Bank, the United Nations Organization, and the OECD – have adopted knowledge management frameworks in their strategic directions focusing on global development, is a clear indication that a strong link is established between knowledge management and knowledge-based development.

This new link created an appropriate environment for the advent of a new concept in the scientific and practitioners' communities, the concept of so called *"Knowledge City"*. At the moment, the theme of knowledge city is an important focus of interest, discussion and research for many disciplines. When the concept of Knowledge City naturally expanded into city-regions and nations the wider concept of *Knowledge-based Development (KBD)* became prominent, giving room to the variation of Knowledge-based Urban (or regional / national/) Development.

The field of knowledge-based development faces, nowadays, the big challenge of making concrete and relevant contributions to the amelioration of societies (i.e. creating a Knowledge Society) and not solely to the promotion of competitive advantage for businesses. The momentum in the field of KBD becomes evident through the wealth of initiatives that an urban (e.g. Singapore, Barcelona), regional (e.g. Veneto Valley, Basque Country), national (Denmark, New Zealand) and supranational (European Union) levels flourish day by day. Every initiative sets its own limits as long as it corresponds to some of the levels mentioned above and reaches those limits as it develops the required capacities.

With the publication of the *International Journal of Knowledge-Based Development* (2009), which aims at bridging the theoretical and technical contributions of KBD and increasing the awareness of the role of knowledge cities and knowledge societies in the knowledge era, and the special issues of the *Journal of Knowledge Management,* the new field became a field of advanced study on its own accord.

Knowledge-Based Development for Cities and Societies: Integrated Multi-Level Approaches is a book aimed at enlightening the above concepts and challenges and therefore at enhancing the expertise and knowledge of scholars, researchers, practitioners, managers and urban developers in the development of successful knowledge-based development policies, creation of knowledge cities and prosperous knowledge societies. In particular, its specific purposes are:

- To create a large knowledge base for scholars, researchers, practitioners, managers and urban developers by introducing them to multi-level aspects of knowledge-based development and indicating other areas of fertile research;
- To develop scholars', researchers', practitioners', managers' and urban developers' capacity in the design, implementation and application of knowledge-based development concepts, models, methods, policies for the creation of modern knowledge societies and cities; and
- To increase the awareness of the role of knowledge cities and knowledge societies in the knowledge era, as well as of the challenges and opportunities for future research.

The book presents insights gained by leading professionals from the practice, research, academic, and consulting side in the field. This is why it should be useful to a variety of target groups, which are interested in the interrelationships between knowledge management, knowledge-based development and urban development. The Foreword is written by a well-known and key pioneering contributor to both the theory and practice of intellectual capital and knowledge leadership Dr. Leif Edvinsson of Lund University, Sweden. The Afterword is written by a well-respected researcher and consultant Knowledge Management and Corporate Strategy Dr. J.C. Spender of ESADE, Spain and Lund University, Sweden. The book is divided into three sections, each one dealing with selected aspects of knowledge-based development.

SECTION 1: CONCEPTS, FOUNDATIONS AND FRAMEWORKS OF KNOWLEDGE-BASED DEVELOPMENT

The seven chapters in Section 1 present advanced theories and modern concepts in several fields of knowledge-based development. Chapter 1 aims to characterize KBD from the perspective of value systems. This chapter looks into the distinctive aspects of human knowledge-based or represented experience as the rationale for both Knowledge Management and Knowledge Based Development. The concept of KBD is introduced as a distinctive category and as the basis of a new social paradigm of special significance in view of both the current stage of human evolution and our impact on other Earth systems. The emergence and evolution of KBD as a field of study and practice is also overviewed.

Chapter 2 presents an advanced strategic framework for the development of successful Knowledge Cities (KCs). A set of hypotheses for the design, development and operation of successful KCs is proposed and validated through the analytical study of KCs cases' support to these hypotheses, resulting to a strategic framework.

Chapter 3 assimilates the workforce in science and technology to the concept of knowledge workers. The authors compared the influence of criteria related to the quality of place on the mobility of students with other criteria related to career opportunities and to the social network. They collected the data through an on-line questionnaire and also proceeded to interviews with students in science and technology. The chapter presents the results of this research for Montreal.

Chapter 4 explores how proximity dimensions can favour the diffusion of knowledge between economic actors, focusing on the knowledge relationships established by a knowledge gatekeeper. In particular, the author formulated several hypotheses regarding the role of proximity dimensions (i.e. geographical, organizational, and technological) in affecting the establishment of gatekeepers' knowledge relationships, taking into account their collaborative-non collaborative type and exploitative-explorative nature. Adopting a patent-based analysis, the author tested the hypotheses on a research sample constituted by 527 knowledge relationships established by two distinct types of knowledge gatekeeper, i.e. a university and a firm.

Chapter 5 examines the mutual interaction between knowledge-based development in local and regional level in two different sections. The first section builds upon the third wave of economic development supporting the growth of cluster of related firms and relates it to an empirical case study of knowledge-based community development in Queensland, Australia. It concludes that knowledge-based local developments do not evolve without a regional support network. The second section reviews the "Triple Helix" of university–industry–government collaboration as the basis of knowledge-based regional development in the investigated case study.

Chapter 6 explores the emerging issue of knowledge-based urban development and scrutinizes the development of knowledge community precincts that have important economic, social and cultural dimensions on the formation of competitive and creative urban regions. The chapter also sheds light on the new challenges for planning discipline, and discusses the need for and some specifics of a new planning paradigm suitable for dealing with 21st Century's socio-economic development and urbanization problems.

Chapter 7 introduces a model for developing a prosperous knowledge city through knowledge and innovation. The model consists of five components that are most important for cities pursuing towards prosperous Knowledge Cities including: developing creative environments, knowledge creation, skills, collaboration/partnership, and leadership.

SECTION 2: MULTI-LEVEL APPROACHES OF KNOWLEDGE-BASED DEVELOPMENT

The second part of this book moves from a more theoretical focus to consider practical multi-level approaches of knowledge-based development.

The first chapter in this section, Chapter 8, discusses the discipline of Personal Knowledge Management (PKM) as a dimension that has been implicitly present within the scope and evolution of the Knowledge Management movement. Moreover, it is recognized as the dimension that brought forth Knowledge-based Development schemes at organizational and societal levels. The chapter concludes with some considerations on the individual development that enables PKM to become a key element in the knowledge citizen's profile, such as the building block or living cell that triggers KBD at organizational and societal levels.

Chapter 9 focus on what deep knowledge is and the environment needed to maximize its contribution to the health and growth of societies. It introduces knowledge attractor network teams as sources of power for community sustainability.

Chapter 10 analyses knowledge worker studies in diverse disciplines, in order to determine the requests. The author proposes a framework to clarify the skill requirements by integrating the requests at operational, team, organisational and inter-organisational levels with drivers provided by educating, attracting, motivating and retaining strategies. The framework facilitates employing the right employee for the right post while balancing the requests and the performance measures.

Maximisation of Knowledge-Based Development (KBD) benefits requires effective dissemination and utilization mechanisms to accompany the initial knowledge creation process. Chapter 11 highlights the potential for interactions between Supply Chains (SCs) and Small and Medium sized Enterprise Clusters (SMECs), including via 'junction' firms which are members of both networks, in key elements of KBD, in order to facilitate such effective dissemination and utilization of knowledge.

Chapter 12 addresses the provisions and conditions of the knowledge-based development in the Helsinki metropolitan area, Finland. It looks at linkages between regional (urban) development and welfare state elements supported by local and national policies. The authors concentrate on one hand on urban and regional policy tools, and on the other to education, because together they provide a platform for building a knowledge-based society. They also explore the current condition of selected creative and knowledge-intensive employment in the Helsinki metropolitan area.

Chapter 13 explores the role of the built environment in the creation, cultivation and acquisition of a knowledge base by people populating the urban landscape. It examines McDonald's restaurants as a way to comprehend the relevance of the physical design in the diffusion of codified and tacit knowledge at an everyday level. Through an examination of space at a localised level, this chapter describes the synergies of space and the significance of this relationship in navigating the global landscape.

Chapter 14 discusses the role Communities of Practice (CoPs) to share knowledge in a knowledge city. In a knowledge based development approach to modernise societies, CoPs can be used as the originators of change and innovation for a knowledge city.

SECTION 3: GLOBAL BEST PRACTICES OF KNOWLEDGE-BASED DEVELOPMENT

The final part of this book considers some case studies and best practices of knowledge-based development.

Singapore's commitment to knowledge-based economy (KBE) development in the past decade has enabled it to make a rapid and successful transition to knowledge-based city. Chapter 15 focuses on how Singapore government has forged an environment that is conducive to innovations, new discoveries and the creation of new knowledge. In the process, Singapore has emerged as one of the top knowledge-based cities in the world through various frameworks used globally.

Chapter 16 presents the case of Israel as a knowledge-based region, as well as critical success factors for regional innovation systems. Based on Israel's experience, the authors discuss key issues related to regional innovation systems, knowledge creation, and intellectual capital audits.

Chapter 17 provides an overview of the lessons from Multimedia Super Corridor, Malaysia as one of the first large scale manifestations of knowledge-based urban development in South East Asia. The chapter investigates the application of the knowledge-based urban development concept within the Malaysian context, and, particularly, scrutinises the development and evolution of Multimedia Super Corridor by focusing on strategies, implementation policies, infrastructural implications, and agencies involved in the development and management of the corridor.

One of the difficulties in creating and sustaining knowledge cities is the lack of benchmarks to identify those cities and regions that are generating knowledge-driven initiatives, triggering development and collective value. One of such benchmarks is the value-based Generic Capital System (GCS) taxonomy. The rigorous application of GCS to cities in European contexts has already yielded its initial fruits, with Manchester as one of the cities in which a deeper perspective can be gained through the GCS lens. In chapter 18, the author aims at introducing GCS as an integrative system of capitals for the case of the Greater Manchester city-region and its journey into developing its knowledge capitals.

The final chapter 19 investigates the level of knowledge management implementation among Malaysian manufacturing and service companies and further explores the effects of such implementation on their overall business performance in the knowledge economy.

The work presented in this book has been made possible through the hard work of the contributors who kept the deadlines and were always enthusiastic. The editors would like to thank all the contributors and hope that this book will increase the awareness of the role of knowledge cities and knowledge societies in the knowledge era, and will encourage the reader to keep strengthening the design and application knowledge-based development policies.

Kostas Metaxiotis
Francisco Javier Carrillo
Tan Yigitcanlar
Editors

Section 1
Concepts, Foundations and Frameworks of Knowledge-Based Development

Chapter 1
Knowledge-Based Value Generation

Francisco Javier Carrillo
Center for Knowledge Systems and The World Capital Institute, Mexico

ABSTRACT

This chapter aims to characterize Knowledge Based Development (KBD) from the perspective of value systems. After an introduction to its purpose and scope, the chapter is divided into five sections. The first section looks into the distinctive aspects of human knowledge-based or represented experience as the rationale for both Knowledge Management and Knowledge Based Development. The concept of KBD is introduced as a distinctive category and as the basis of a new social paradigm of special significance in view of both the current stage of human evolution and our impact on other Earth systems. In the second section the emergence and evolution of KBD as a field of study and practice is overviewed. Thirdly, the received perspective of knowledge capital as instrumental to increasing monetary growth and accumulation is contrasted with an integrated approach where all value elements relevant to a group are balanced into a unified system of categories. Such radical approach to KBD recaptures the essence of human value production and allows the redesign of accountacy and management practices at the organizational level, as well as of cultural and political practices at the communitary and global levels. Next, a review of some of the most visible KBD research agendas shows the trends in the evolution of this area and suggests the viability of a global R&D agenda. Finally, the possible contribution of KBD as a language to articulate national and international consesus-building on the most urgent issues is discussed as a conclusion.

INTRODUCTION

The global economic crisis that started in 2007, exploded in 2008 and continues to shake the foundations of the whole financial establishment, seems an adequate context to put the received developmental and economic paradigms in perspective. As mortgage and investment institutions collapse, corporate capitalization vaporizes, stock value

DOI: 10.4018/978-1-61520-721-3.ch001

Figure 1. Dominant factors of major productive systems

	Production type	Input	Process: Agent	Process: Instrument	Output
Physical Era	Hunting-gathering	Natural habitat	Human and animal	Hands and primitive tools and techniques	Game, fish and collected natural goods
Physical Era	Agricultural	Land, water, seeds, fertilizers	Human and animal	Agricultural equipment and techniques	Agricultural goods
Physical Era	Extractive	Natural deposits	Human and animal	Mining equipment and techniques	Stones, metals, minerals
Physical Era	Industrial	Raw materials and enery	Human and automata	Industrial machinery, equipment and techniques	Manufactured goods and industrialized products
Physical Era	Physical-based production	Matter and energy	Muscular strength and sensory-muscular dexterity	Physical tools, equipment and techniques	Physical goods
Knowledge Era	Knowledge-based production	(Relative) lower-level K-input	Rationality and Emotion	K-processing tools, systems and networks	(Relative) higher-level K-output

fjcarrillo, 2000

plunges, Fortune 500 icons get bankrupt, credit sharply contracts, banks are nationalized and the first global recession unfolds, the current financial establishment and world economic system are seriously brought into question while claims for a new world order gain support. But a different configuration of players, financial centers, banking institutions or even global regulatory and supervision schemes might not be enough. Also, a new language to articulate collective preferences and priorities, public participation and social accountability seems necessary.

From a particular reinterpretation of both economic and knowledge acts, a historical deconstruction of the relationship between the values of a community, its social organization, its cultural products, and its knowledge base becomes relevant. Such reinterpretation is founded on the acknowledgement of an experiential evolution from material reality to represented or knowledge-based reality (cfr. Figure 1). This means that rather than material objects (all manifestations of matter and energy generating a sensory record) are the representations of these objects (ideas, emotions, etc.) what dominate individual and collective human experience. This substitution process[1] is at the core of psychological life, knowledge-based behavior and culture.

Under such perspective, the transition of adaptive and cultural patterns from nomadic societies of hunters-gatherers, through agricultural and industrial societies, up to the emerging knowledge societies can be observed. Under this social evolution process, it becomes apparent that while major transformations in social, economic and cultural organization have occurred throughout history, it might be precisely at the current transition from matter-based[2] to knowledge-based societies (roughly around the year 2000) when human experience is qualitatively leveraged and with it the realm of possibilities for social organization.

The fundamental realization behind this perspective consists in the qualitative difference between the natural principles describing the behavior of objects (mainly physics, chemistry and biology) and the natural principles describing the behavior of ideas and emotions as well as the subsequent impact such difference has on the social and economic possibilities of each domain. For example, insofar as the products of human activity upon matter and energy are regulated by space-time constraints, social norms regulating their production, distribution and ownership are restricted by physical posession, resulting in property laws. Likewise, thermodynamics determines the wasting of production lines, resulting in diminishing returns. A basic contention of this chapter is that while it is now generally accepted that knowledge is a leveraging factor of economic growth and that it has some special properties such as partial excludability, non-rivalry and increasing returns (Romer, 1994), we are still far from understanding the nature and harnessing the potential of knowledge-based value dynamics.

Thus, physical reality contains a universe of possibilities that determines the nature of physics-based value dynamics. Economic theory, accountancy systems, management practices and policy making have been up to now, by far, dominated by the immediate weight of physical realities. Certainly, knowledge-based realities have been present since the dawn of mankind, i.e., the origin of distinctively "human" psychological events. Private and public administration have been always inevitably marked by the unescapable and often masked intervention of individual and social behavioral dimensions. Nevertheless, these realities have not been granted so far an ontological status equivalent to that of material and monetary units. The later two dimensions remain by far the limits to the language -and in Wittgenstein's criterion the limits to the world- of economics, accountancy and administration.

Only insfoar as these limits continue to be challenged by realizations from ouside and contradictions from within established practices, alternative paradigm have begun to emerge. It is the increasing recognition of behavioral realities and the acceptance of their natural weight in all human affairs what has open the door of formal economics, management and politics to knowledge-based events.

Human creation and innovation out of ideas and emotions has a natural dynamics of its own but it lacks the same physical constraints and is therefore ubicuous in space and time, does not waste with use, can be infinitely reproduced and its posession creates no rivalry, amongst other peculiarities. Far from having understood these realities, we do have strong leads to expect that the principles of value production and its consequences on social organization and culture have radically changed with the dawn of the new millenium. We can also reasonably expect that the options for subsequent human history -or its mere viability- depend upon our capacity to understand these distinctively human dynamics as well as upon our capacity to redesign our patterns of coexistence amongst ourselves and with the rest of the planet.

When talking about KBD then, we should not be restricted to talking *only* about subjects such as competitiveness, education, science, technology, intellectual property and innovation (particularly with regard to categories such as science parks, industry clusters, technopoles, business incubators and accelerators, technology transfer centers, innovation regions and so forth). Important as these are, each has a distinctive meaning and applies to well-demarcated realities, all in use by the 1980s, before the concept of KBD took off at the turn of the century. If Knowledge Based Development could be reduced to any of these or even to the sum of all of these, then it would prove redundant: we should do away with it.

The urging need to capture and codify the systemic unity of all value created by human societies as well as the apparent incapacity of current economic theories for doing that, motivates the search for an integrated understanding and management of human value systems. Therefore, KBD has to be founded on an economic system that allows the recording, visualization, dimensioning and management of the total value which is product of human activity. That shall include forms of knowledge capital such as those related to education, technology and innovation which are often associated firstly with the term KBD, but also other less obvious such as identity, intelligence, cohesion, attractiveness, etc.

Within this context, paradigmatic roles and institutions of modernity and their reexpresions and contradictions in the turbulence of posmodernity shall be revised. In the light of these considerations, it is urgent to redraw the tacit contract inherited from 20th Century industrial societies. Economic categories in force can be seen as coins of a value universe whose structural and functional legitimacy tends to depretiate, as the challenges and opportunities of the new knowledge-based social contracts begin to draw organization and innovation alternatives in the new political and economic worldmap of ideas and emotions.

This ongoing evolutionary process can be illustrated with some transition options such as distributed work and learning, knowledge-citizenship, value networks, competencies and technology brokerage, expertise markets, talent auctions, etc. Beyond these, more distinctive knowledge dynamics such as ubiquity, virtuality and dematerialization reconfigure the boundaries of the economically possible and the terms of the social contract.

¿What is then the conceptual demarcation of KBD? ¿Can it be differentiated as a study of field and practice? ¿Are increases in economic productiviy and competitiveness the distinctive KBD outcomes? ¿What are its mains R&D issues? ¿Is there a special significance of KBD to the global financial crisis? ¿To human evolution? These are question we will be addressing throughout the chapter.

The chapter is divided into five sections. The first section looks into the distinctive aspects of human knowledge-based experience. Second, the emergence and evolution of KBD as a field of study and practice is overviewed. Thirdly, the transitional perspective of knowledge capital is contrasted with a radical approach. Next, a review of some of the most visible KBD research agendas follows. Finally, the possible contribution of KBD to the most urgent issues is discussed.

KBD AS A DISTINCTIVE CATEGORY

Knowledge Based Development (KBD) is a theoretical and technical field derived from the convergence of a scientific field and a management movement. The field of origin is that part of Economic Science traditionally known as Growth Theory (GT). GT focuses on the understanding of macroeconomic principles determining increases in total production of countries and regions. The movement of origin is Knowledge Management (KM), primarily emerged in business administration as a response to the need of identifying, valuing and capitalizing all factors of value creation, prominently knowledge-based factors. As the KM movement evolved, it extended from the organizational domain to both the individual (Personal Knowledge Management) and social (Knowledge Based Development) domains.

GT, as a formal branch of Economic Theory, has an evolution parallel to the discipline as a whole and to its main schools of thought. Major theories have made their respective explanatory claims on growth dynamics and had reached their respective impacts upon national and international policies until the end of the Cold War. The turn-of-century identification of a new value dynamics in economic growth led to the emergence of a "new" or "Endogenous" Growth Theory (NGT). The "endogenous" or "from within" character of NGT derives from a constant awareness of a faster production growth than what could be attributed to traditionally accounted factors. Hence, the novel assumption was entered that growth rate could depend on the preferences –that is, on the value system- of productive agents. This awareness has awakened GT from its relative stagnation of the seventies and early eighties, to a boom parallel to KM emergence. Contributions by economists such as Gary Becker on Human Capital, Robert Solow on the role of Technological Progress, Amartya Sen on Welfare Economics, Paul Romer on Endogenous Knowledge, Daniel Kahneman on Behavioral Economics and Paul Krugman on Globalized Trade and Urbanization, amongs many others, set GT, specifically NGT, in a benign collision course with Knowledge Management.

After World War II an increasing number of industries and regions started to show for the first time in history a preponderance in productivity of knowledge-based factors, creating the conditions for KM emergence in the eighties. In the early nineties, the KM movement gathered momentum thanks to the confluence of three major economic drivers[3]: a) the constraints of industrial business models to capitalize on Information and Communication Technologies –also known as "productivity paradox", b) the increasing acceleration of the obsolescence rate of productive competencies, and c) particularly, the urge to identify, measure, understand and capitalize on "intangible" (or knowledge) assets contributing to wealth generation and to social development at large. From organizational KM to Government KM to KBD the new perspective spread rapidly. Thus, Knowledge Based Development became the response of Economic and Management Sciences to the emergence of Knowledge Societies.

Large international development agencies refocused their efforts, just as the century was closing to an end, moving from financial investment in physical infrastructure towards knowledge-based programs. The KM movement, in turn, had gone in a swift take-off, from being the fastest-growing business consultancy field in the 90's[4], to becoming a major factor in development policies throughout countries such as Japan, Singapore, Canada, and regions such as Australasia, Scandinavia and the European Union as a whole. More recently major re-emerging Asian economies such as China and India are joining this trend. The specific topic of Knowledge Cities -due perhaps to its more recognizable and appealing nature- has attracted substantial interest. The formal consummation of the marriage between GT and KM happened from 2000 onwards. In 2002, the *Journal of Knowledge Management* published a first Special Issue on Knowledge Based Development (Vol. 6, No. 4) that became an annual issue since 2006. This special issue aimed at bridging the theoretical and technical contributions of GT and KM granting a birth certificate to KBD. Other publications soon continued to lay the foundations for the new field (Bounfour and Edvinsson, 2005; Carrillo, 2005; Yigitcanlar, Velibeyoglu and Baum, 2008). After an initial decade, the present volume concurs with the inaugural issue of the first dedicated journal to this field: The *International Journal of Knowledge Based Development*.

Three Levels of KBD

KBD, just like KM, has rapidly evolved. The numerous KM approaches as well as major KBD programs can be distinguished on the basis of the focus of their development actions, i.e., how the economic act and the knowledge act are each understood, leading to a KBD definition[5]. Basically, knowledge tends to be understood either as an *object accumulation* (content) in most cases, or with increasing frequency as a *capacity transfer* (flow) or else, in state-of-the-art KM, as a *value allignment* (context). While several parallels can be drawn between these three levels of Knowledge Based Development and the three main views on the dynamics of the knowledge economy: knowledge-as-asset, knowledge-as-relation, and knowledge-as-capability (Eliasson G. 2005; Dolfsma, W. and Soete, L. 2005; Fagerberg and Srholec, 2008), these two distinctions move on different planes. The received attempts to characterize the knowledge economy from within economic science have focused in identifying the functional relationships between factors of production. These have advanced in characterizing the dynamics of value creation when incorporating distinctive knowledge-based factors such as education, R&D, ITC and how these combine in leveraging endogenous capabilities. Recent comprehensive views (e.g., Dang and Umemoto, 2009) come close to the sort of systemic, dynamic, strategic, future-value oriented development of knowledge capitals proposed next and their contributions are complementary to the KBD characterization constructed here. However, it has proved difficult for economic science to come to terms with the qualitative difference of represented or

Table 1. Three KBD levels

Concept	Level		
	Level I: Object - centered	*Level III: Agent - centered*	*Level III: Context - centered*
Knowledge	Information content	Flow capacity	Value allignment
Development	Accumulate and retain stock	Facilitate and increase circulation	Dynamically adjust to sustainable balance
KBD	KBD is an ***infrastructure*** to increase social knowledge stock	KBD is a ***policy*** for facilitating the social flow of knowledge	KBD is a ***strategy*** for the dynamic balance of all common capital
			© F.J. Carrillo, 1999

knowledge-based realities as discussed above. In fact, no extensive practice in development programs, policy making or public administration that accounts in an integrated manner for both monetary and knowledge-based capital is visible in the public domain.

Table 1 shows, for each of three KBD levels, the knowledge concept assumed, the development concept enabled and finally, the resulting KBD approach.

Level I KBD: Social Knowledge Infrastructure

A majority of KBD programs start focusing on the most immediate area of impact: the instrumental base that leverages the capacities of productive agents, particularly ICTs and other infrastructure. An example of this approach is the World Bank's Global Knowledge Partnership, which focuses on the multiplication of information, experiences and resources through ICTs. These sort of experiences, which have already accumulated a decade of lessons learnt, are well documented and are often a good departure point. However, there is a growing consensus that ICTs and social knowledge infrastructure in general (universities, libraries, R&D centers, technoparks, etc.) constitute a necessary but not sufficient condition for generating development. Several infrastructural efforts have produced rather poor results relative to investments. There is a growing trend to manage these resources within broader social value frameworks (Sharma, Ng, Dharmawirya and Lee, 2008).

Level II KBD: Human Capital Programs

After the constraints of the infrastructural approach became evident, there has been a shift towards facilitating self-development in natural agents. KBD policies centred on human capital development are now strongly favoured by NGT. Self-directed learning, leveraged by self-esteem and entrepreneurship virtuous circles, articulation of communities of practice, integration of talent bases, establishment of knowledge clusters, construction of knowledge support networks and of regional innovation systems, are some of its more common manifestations. Examples are the United Nations STDev Net (Science and Technology for Development Network) and the World Bank GDLN (Global Development Learning Network). Highly focused on knowledge flows amongst natural agents, these kind of programs get replicated within communities and organizations, particularly those having a virtual or distributed nature. Even if lessons learnt at this level are preliminary, a clear one is that the mere multiplication of flows does not necessarily produce a social or organizational improvement. The issue of value or context of significance emerges hence as fundamental. KBD begins to unfold as a qualitative matter, as an issue of social transformation and not sheer accumulation (Fagerberg and Srholec, 2008).

Level III KBD: Capital System Strategies

The leading KBD thought goes beyond the multiplication of both, knowledge objects and knowledge flows, thus focusing on *knowledge-based value systems.* These systems are human collectives deliberately pursuing a complete and sustainable development with particular emphasis on intangible or knowledge value. Such values include in principle all meaningful dimensions of experience and therefore, all potential human fulfillments. Under this perspective, an improvement in the human condition (the value dimension) recovers its purposive nature, while knowledge stock or k-capital recovers its instrumental character as the most powerful mean for such purpose. Also, Level III KBD reaches a strategic meaning, since the capital system aims to capture the quintessential expression of a community's identity and purpose, as well as of the human competencies and tools to accomplish them. The main tasks deriving from this approach are: i) the articulation of the set of social capitals under a complete, consistent and homogeneous system, ii) the operationalization and metrics of such system, iii) the identification of strategic gaps, iv) the undertaking of initiatives to narrow those gaps, v) the feedback and adjustment of such initiatives (e.g., Mutius, 2005).

There are enough examples of efforts moving in this new direction amongst national governments (e.g., Finland, Israel, Canada, India), cities (e.g., Barcelona, Boston, Ottawa, Manchester, Munich, Melbourne, Valencia) and international agencies (e.g., UN, World Bank, OECD), as well as numerous private and public organizations (World Capital Institute, New Club of Paris, Ibero-American Community for Knowledge Systems). Most of these involve a strategy rationale increasingly approaching Level III and are based in the measurements of intellectual capital elements. Nevertheless, few of their social capital systems can yet satisfy the requirements of consistency, completeness and homogeneity. Existing frameworks still tend to consist of inductive aggregates of knowledge capitals, but lack an integrated value taxonomy.

Efforts are underway for articulating social capital which are based precisely on the identification and consolidation of value systems in order to subsequently align all productive capitals. Also, there are some efforts to develop global KBD platforms, such as the UNDP initiative to build an inventory of "Global Public Goods" and the World Capital Institute goals to determine alternative global capital structures and assessing the impact that major agents such as military and trade superpowers, large transnational corporations and the main international agencies have upon the *Global State of Capitals.*

KBD AS A FIELD OF STUDY AND PRACTICE

Interdisciplinarity is key to sustaining Knowledge Based Development as an emerging field by contributing to attract the relevant R&D talent. The convergence of New Growth Theory and Knowledge Management in the early 1980s has already been mentioned. Other fields such as Sociology and Anthropology have been gaining presence in Social and Economic Development, insofar as these disciplines had developed decades before the conceptual and analytical tools for handling dimensions such as identity, cohesion, belongness, etc. On the other hand, Urban Studies and Urban Planning were engaged with cities as development units long before the distinctive opportunities for knowledge-based urban development became evident; while Regional Development studies have done the corresponding at the mezzo-level. Geography has been another significant contributing discipline, opening new areas within itself such as Knowledge Geography based on the former Economic and Social Geography. The whole spectrum of "Sciences of Knowledge" –an evolution from the earlier "Sciences of Science" Movement of the 1970s- has also been involved, including the History, Sociology, Psychology and Political Economy of Science. In particular, psychological research has become a major foundation to KM and KBD for it deals with the very core of knowledge: the processes by which our behavior realm interplays between sensory stimuli and represented stimuli such as those involved in thinking, language, memory, learning, cognition and motivation -the knowledge stuff. The recent convergence between Behavioral Science and Economic Science, as well as the new grounds covered by Evolutionary Psychology have a significant role to play in the understanding and management of knowledge societies.

Conceptual and methodological variety seems also indispensable to KBD. From epistemological grounds to research techniques, a number of different approaches are required to tackle each of the social components of knowledge value dynamics. There is no assumption that conceptual and methodological eclecticism will per se obtain a plausible synthesis. But it seems inevitable that any alternative frameworks claiming to provide a satisfactory account of KBD will have to include and articulate theoretical and methodological resources able to include all the sciences and techniques of knowledge.

Indeed, the pattern of activities signaling the institutionalization of a new discipline (Ben-David, 1972) can be recognized in recent KBD activities worldwide such as scientific organizations, dedicated publications, international conferences, professional associations, etc. Some of these signs are evident in aspects such as the affluents, the issues, the cases, the sources, the events, the organizations and the initiatives showing the vitality of KBD. This includes the broader realities of policy making and development governance of knowledge-based communities as well as the planning and management of knowledge cities, regions and nations. Each of these elements is exemplified next.

KBD **affluents** have already been discussed and will only be summarized. These can be traced back to renewal movements within stablished disciplines such as Economics (*New* or *Endogenous* Growth Theory, Knowledge-based production, Behavioral and Evolutionary Economics, *New* Theory of the Firm), Urban Studies and Planning (*New* Urbanism and Urban Environmentalism) as well as Regional Development Studies, Geography (Human Geography, knowledge flows and territoriality), Neuroscience (including the Artificial Intelligence and Nanotechnology convergence), Psychology of Science and Technology (from cognition through accelerated innovation), Anthropology and Sociology of Knowledge (identity and cohesion), Social Studies of Science, Political Economy of Knowledge and Technology, Innovation Management and, of course, Knowledge Management.

The city and nation **cases,** also previously mentioned, are exemplified by cities such as Manchester, Singapore, Boston, Sidney, Barcelona, Holon, Montreal, Bilbao, as well as by countries such as Austria, Japan, Finland, New Zealand, Denmark, Ireland, Costa Rica and Sweden. All these, deliberate attempts at KBD policies and arguably some of the leading indications of lessons to be learned in KBD conceptualization and implementation.

Some of the **sources** indicative of advances in the field are: the *Urban Studies Journal*, specially Knight (1995) and the Special Issue of 2002 on Knowledge Cities; Bounfour and Edvinsson' (eds.) *Intellectual Capital for Communities* (2005); Richard Florida's *Cities and the Creative Class* (2005); Carrillo (ed.) *Knowledge Cities* (2006); R&B Consulting' *Knowledge Management Austria* (2006); PriceWaterhouseCoopers' *Cities of Knowledge Report* (2007); Pirjo Stahle' (ed.) *Five Steps for Finland's Future* (2007); Yigitcanlar, Velibeyoglu and Baum' *Knowledge-based Urban*

Development (2008) and the upcoming *International Journal of Knowledge Based Development (Inderscience,* inaugural issue January 2010). In terms of electronic sources, websites such as *The Knowledge Cities Clearinghouse, Learning City/regions Resources,* The *INK Research Center* at SPRU, The *Metropolitan New Economy Index* and *Knowledgeboard* are good examples.

Being **events** such as conferences, symposia and congresses a well-established scientific socialization practice, it is worth noticing KBD specialized ones such as the annual *Assembly and Conference of the Ibero-American Community for Knowledge Systems* (2000--), the *World Summit on the Information Society* (UN/ITU: 2003--); the *International Symposium on Knowledge Cities* (AUDIAUDI: 2005--), the annual *Intellectual Capital for Communities Conference* (U. Paris-Sud/NCP: 2005--), the Eurocities *Knowledge Societies Forum* (EUROCITIESEUROCITIES: 2007--), and prominently, the annual *Knowledge Cities World Summit* (2007--).

All of the above are conducted by **organizations** directly concerned with KBD. Some are established institutions that became deeply concerned with the Knowledge Society such as the *European Commission, UNESCO,* the *World Bank,* the *OECD,* while others are purpose-created such as the *Center for Development Research (ZEF), University of Bonn,* the *New Club of Paris,* the *World Capital Institute, Knowledge Desert Australia,* the *Ibero-American Community for Knowledge Systems,* the *Entovation-100 Network,* the *Creative Cities Network,* the *Cities Alliance, TeleCities,* and many others. These organizations also produce some distinctive initiatives such as the *Human Development Report* (UN) the *Knowledge for Development Program* (WB), the *RICARDIS Report* (NCP), the *European Regions KB Innovation Network* (ERIK) and the *Most Admired Knowledge City Awards* (Teleos/WCI).

TRANSITIONAL VS. RADICAL APPROACH

Shortly after its birth, KBD is at a crossroads: whether continuing to sustain the received transitional view under which knowledge is considered as a resource, relation or capability particularly suited to leverage economic growth in a way that may eventually bring social prosperity. This view is instrumental, incremental and focused on the growth of the monetary base. An alternative view is one where social capital accounts become an instrument for balanced, equitable and sustainable development. This view, in contrast, is purposeful, systemic and focused on the balance of collective capital, both intellectual (such as identity and relational capitals) and traditional (material+financial).

A strategic KBD perspective seems necessary to realize its explanatory and transformational promise. Since around the year 2000, contributions to KBD have ranged from the instrumental or object-centered, through the human or subject-centered, to the strategic or context-centered epistemology, as described above. Much like happens in KM, the 1st and 2nd generations of KBD are rather widespread while the 3rd seems to be embrionary. This can be described as a **transitional** phase of KBD.

Nevertheless, an increasing awareness about the necessity to bring KM and KBD to their full strategic perspective can be documented. Such perspective involves, basically, an acknowledgment that the concepts and tools deviced to explain, account and manage the material-based value processes underlying the industrial economy are not sufficient to deal with the simbolic-based value processes underlying the knowledge society. A straightforward implication of this realization is that a new axiological, epistemological and political platform may be required to build the foundations for KBD, one in which we are capable of mapping, accounting and organising not just the economic impact of knowledge factors, but the universe of social value dimensions as a complete and consistent system. This can be described in turn as the **radical** phase of KBD.

As argued before, a transitional KBD perspective may be rendered useless if it is not clearly distinct from the technology and innovation categories it is often reduced to. Left to this level, KBD would become a redundant neologism. On the other hand, a radical approach to KBD is necessary to differentiate a contribution to the explanation and management of distinctive knowledge-based value creation and distribution processes. Such approach becomes more critical as the economic paradigm on which the world financial establishment is founded is in urgent need of a major redesign.

R&D AGENDAS ON KBD

After the initial years of a 'variation phase' in KBD literature, is it now time to start moving into a more mature 'selection phase'? Can some fundamental components to all KBD research and innovation be distinguished at this point? Could such components be of significance to the international KBD community of interest and practice? Is there already a global KBD research and innovation agenda?

The huge diversity of human experiences, mounting sustainability concerns such as biosphere degradation and climate change, energy and food shortages, financial instabilities, demographic dynamics, urban agglomerations, extensive poverty, response to natural disasters and pandemias, etc., as well as new options for urban design, regional innovation, economic growth and social renewal, multiply the conceivable meanings of KBD. To identify common threads of a collective effort to understand and manage the leveraging potential of knowledge seems necessary.

Meanwhile, a KBD agenda is taking shape in the form of R&D and application programs. Implicit agendas can be reconstructed from policies, research areas, publications, events, curricula, etc. at universities, international agencies, government units and other organizations concerned with expanding the field of KBD. Some such agendas are already explicit, even if in preliminary forms. The following is a sample of the most prominent KBD agendas.

The KBD global agenda exercise carried out at the Global KBD Week 2007[6] by means of an Open Space session, where delegates from thirty-one countries contributed to this result[7]. The main categories identified were:

- Paradigm shift from financial to human capital
- Value and values shift
- Organizational and social innovation
- New collaboration designs
- Social k-distribution and computing
- Knowledge sciences and human organization
- Social learning and new ITC platforms
- Voids in k-dissemination
- Knowledge inclusion
- Urban k-voids
- New participation mechanisms
- Social intelligence
- Knowledge and intelligence for sustainability
- Intelligent regions: fusing old and new logics
- Ecological and hapiness urban dimension
- Management of Virtual Communities
- Open Society and Intellectual Capital

The emphasis on the human dimension is prominent in this exercise. It should be pointed out that this conference was marked by a collective sensitivity to this dimension. Somehow, a reflective condition resulted by which accounts of social Intellectual Capital issues (signified by the integration of tangible and intangible value dimensions) captured not only the conventional objective and detached rational perspectives of many delegates, but to some extent the emotional and subjective ones as well.

A KBD agenda has also been generated by The New Club of Paris. The NCP is "an association of scientists and 'intellect entrepreneurs' dedicated to research and promotion of the idea of supporting the transformation of our society and economy into a knowledge society and a knowledge economy"[8]. It has recently proposed a series of R&D topics[9], organized into two major sets, as in the following abridged version[10]:

- Microeconomic / corporate
- IC of large groups, SMEs, specific administrations
- IC ratings per sector, country, region
- International reporting standard and new approaches
- IC at functional level
- Incentive systems and organizational design
- Entrepreneurship and IC building
- Meso / macroeconomic / societal
- GDP and the symmetry dimension for IC
- Demography, innovation and social likns
- Fiscal aspects
- IPRs regimes: copyrights, copylefts, hybrid forms
- Nations, cities and regions IC management / rating
- Dinamic capabilities / renewability
- Regional benchmarking
- Optimal performance size / other criteria
- IC/KBD politics

It should be noted that this is still a preliminary agenda, but it shows that the NCP is also engaged in identifying and structuring a meaningful and manageable set of KBD topics.

Another selection of KBD R&D issues is provided by the 2nd Halle Forum on Urban Economic Growth[11]. As its Call for Papers pointed out "... many larger and middle-sized cities dispose of a considerable potential of institutions creating and disseminating knowledge. This kind of endowment seems to be especially valuable in an upcoming knowledge-based economy. Recent strategic concepts and competitions referring to 'knowledge-based urban development', 'knowledge city', 'creative city', or 'science city' indicate that urban planners and politicians are beginning to search for strategies to take advantage and to make use of this potential"[12].

A condensed list of topics of the 2nd Halle Forum on urban KBD is as follows[13],

- Empirical and theoretical advances in agglomeration economies,
- Entrepreneurship, innovation and urban economic growth,
- The impact of networks and milieus on urban economic growth,
- Knowledge spillover and technology transfer in urban innovation systems,
- Urban business development and local public policies,
- New patterns in hierarchies of cities,
- Urban sprawl and integration of migrants.

Naturally, this selection bears a knowledge-urbanist perspective that clearly overlaps with more generic KBD issues. A different point of view is provided by knowledge-geographers focusing on the spatial dimensions of knowledge, such as the Heidelberg University 'Knowledge and Space' research group, who has published the rationale of its agenda. A sample of questions relevant to KBD is provided in the general outline of its next symposium on "Knowledge and Economy":

- Under what conditions does knowledge become an economic product in different cultures? What types of knowledge can be turned into economic products?
- What are the societal consequences if knowledge becomes an economic product and if it does not?

- Research and industry in historical perspective.
- Knowledge transfer between universities and economic institutions and vice versa?
- The recruitment of scientists and top managers in various types of firms.
- Evolution of technologies in time and space.
- Knowledge, technologies and regional competitiveness.
- The effects of technological change on regional development.
- Innovations and regional development.
- How can we define and measure spatial disparities of innovativeness?
- Which factors contribute to regional disparities of innovativeness?
- Knowledge in economic theory. Is rationality enough?

A deliberate attempt to capture the state of the art in KBD is the list of topics regularly included in the Call for Papers for the *Journal of Knowledge Management* annual Special Issue on KBD:

- Dynamics of social knowledge-based value creation
- Identification, measurement and strategic development of social intellectual capital
- National, regional and urban KBD planning and development
- Knowledge Cities concepts and models
- Descriptions and assessments of implementation cases
- Metrics, benchmarkings and comparative analyses
- Social accounting and strategy deployment
- Social learning networks and social knowledge bases
- Knowledge citizenship, access to information and distributed participation
- ITCs and social bases of instrumental capital
- KBD policy and cultural issues
- Global marginalization and the knowledge divide
- Systems perspectives on KBD
- Radical KBD as a strategic and disruptive paradigm

To finish this account of R&D agendas related to KBD in the search of a common, global KBD agenda, the broader categories of the first dedicated periodical publication, the upcoming *International Journal of Knowledge Based Development* are listed as follows,

- Knowledge-based value generation
- Knowledge-based economy
- Knowledge-based urban development
- Knowledge cities and regions
- Knowledge societies
- Multi-level approach to Knowledge Based Development
- Global best practices in Knowledge Based Development
- Knowledge and innovation clusters
- Knowledge-economy, assets and capital systems
- Knowledge-intensive service activities

By looking at the diversity and richness of KBD perspectives on the one had, and the synergies and convergencies on the other, we may be able to evolve into a more integrated and collaborative global agenda. The growing attention given to KBD by groups from many different disciplines, geographic regions, professional fields, government offices, international organizations and local communities, widen its perspective and multiply its reach.

RESTARTING HUMAN HISTORY

Certainly, if human collective experience throughout history has been substantially different from the dominant daily lifestyle of the 20th Century, it is conceivable that it might become unlike any of the social design possibilities that humans have so far explored . The Knowledge Society is by itself a redefinition of the collective significant and the humanely possible. KBD challenges the limits of human imagination and innovation.

We live now in a different world from that in which this book was conceived only some months ago. On the one hand, the first global financial crisis and first global pandemia were acknowledged as this volume took shape. On the other hand, a number of signs all around the world seem to indicate deep upcoming transformations in international institutions, economic policies, role of the state, corporate governance and accountability, risk management, consuming patterns, social preferences, e-socialization and participation, political organization and other manifestations of people's preferences, i.e., values. Value reconfiguration not only in terms of geopolitical distribution and economic cycles but also in terms of cultural evolution and supranational coordination.

KBD has to do above all with value identification, visualization, measurement, understanding and development. How knowledge-based realities expand the realm of the possible and how these can be capitalized for building equitable and sustainable futures for organizations and societies is the core rationale for KBD.

Although the current global economic crisis has been largely anticipated, it had not (it hasn't as of the Winter of 2009) shown its true transformative reach. Beyond cyclical economic patterns (other than Kondratiev's waves), the World will probably never go back to what it was just two years ago. Lack of regulation and supervision in high-end financial speculation; massive self-replication of a global monetary mass with little or no exchange value; extensive greed pervading from investment institutions, to company treasuries, to family budgets; generalized consumption patterns overcoming the realistic possibilities of individual and social wealth generation; energy and matter utilization rates well beyond what renewable sources can provide; all are coming to a sudden hault.

Adding to global recession, the first global pandemia has also occurred. Even if long anticipated by epidemiologists and international organizations, the outbreaks of human influenza A H1/N1 virus seem to have taken everybody by surprise. No doubt, earlier efforts to build an international response capacity coordinated by the WHI contributed largely to regain control within a few days. But the unexpected mutations of the influenza viruses, the novelty of the human A H1/N1 stem, the consequent lack of vaccine, its uncharacteristic dead toll on young healty adults, and the fast spread of cases accross countries and continents, generated confusion the world over. Under these circumstances, misinformation, ignorance and prejudices travelled fastest and might have been more harmful than the virus itself at the early stages of the outbreak. This experience has underscored how urgent it is learning to act globally for supranational challenges of systemic planetary reach such as global warming, ignorance, poverty and disease.

If crises are times of opportunity, this moment demands that we reinvent production, consumption, international organization, political participation, and in short, the whole globalized industrial culture of the 20th Century. And we will need new knowledge -and perhaps also some ancient wisdom- to do just that. We have extensive knowledge about industrial production and distribution; we need new knowledge about k-based creation and transfer. We have learnt something about material innovation processes, we now need to learn more about social innovation and participation. We accumulated knowledge about centralized power; we urgently need to understand distributed decision-making. We know about imperial centers, we must now discover global democracy. We have documented corporate control, we need to experience value networks. We can tell about capital accumulation, we are urged to implement balanced and sustainable capital systems. We need a new value system for opening to the next generations the very possibility of survival and we do not have yet the knowledge for securing that.

While the many challenges to human survival might seem powerful enough to reconsider the whole way of life received from the Twentieth Century industrial culture, there are even more significant drives in redrawing our futures. A human culture consciously developed at the level of knowlege-based experience is a scenario worth pursuing. For that, we need to begin by recognising our historical incompetence and by increasing our knowledge about what we value.

REFERENCES

Ben-David, J. (1972). The Profession of Science and its Powers . *Minerva*, 10.

Borja, J. (2003). *La ciudad conquistada*. Madrid: Alianza Editorial.

Bounfour, A., & Edvinsson, L. (Eds.). (2005). *Intellectual capital for communities –Nations, regions and cities*. New York: Elsevier Butterworth/Heinemann.

Carrillo, F. J. (2001, January). Meta-KM: A Program and a Plea. *Knowledge and Innovation: Journal of the KMCI, 1*(2), 27–54.

Carrillo, F. J. (2002, October). Capital Systems: Implications for a Global Knowledge Agenda. *Journal of Knowledge Management, 6*(4), 379–399. doi:10.1108/13673270210440884

Carrillo, F. J. (2004, October). Capital Cities: A taxonomy of capital accounts for knowledge cities. *Journal of Knowledge Management, 8*(5), 28–46. doi:10.1108/1367327041058738

Carrillo, F. J. (Ed.). (2005). *Knowledge cities: Approaches, experiences and perspectives*. New York: Elsevier Butterworth/Heinemann.

Carrillo, F. J. (2006). From Transitional to Radical Knowledge-based Development. *Journal of Knowledge Management, 10*(5), 3–5. doi:10.1108/13673270610691125

Carrillo, F. J. (2007). The coming of age of Knowledge-based Development. *Journal of Knowledge Management, 11*(5), 3–5. doi:10.1108/13673270710819753

Carrillo, F. J. (2008). Towards a global Knowledge Based Development agenda. *Journal of Knowledge Management, 12*(5). doi:10.1108/13673270810902894

Dang, D., & Umemoto, K. (2009). Modelling the development toward the knowledge economy: a national capability approach. *Journal of Knowledge Management, 13*(5). doi:10.1108/13673270910988169

Dolfsma, W., & Soete, L. (2005). Dynamics of a knowledge economy: introduction . In Dolfsma, W., & Soete, L. (Eds.), *Understanding the Dynamics of a Knowledge Economy* (pp. 1–6). Northampton, MA: Edward Elgar.

Eliasson, G. (2005). The nature of economic change and management in a new knowledge based information economy. *Information Economics and Policy, 17*, 428–456. doi:10.1016/j.infoecopol.2005.02.002

Fagerberg, J., & Srholec, M. (2008). National innovation system, capabilities and economic development. *Research Policy, 37*, 1417–1435. doi:10.1016/j.respol.2008.06.003

Florida, R. (2005). *Cities and the creative class*. New York: Routledge.

INK Research Center at SPRU. (n.d.). Retrieved March 4, 2009, from http://www.sussex.ac.uk/spru/1-4-9-1-1-2.html

Knight, R. (1995). Knowledge-based Development: policy and planning implications for cities. *Urban Studies (Edinburgh, Scotland)*, *32*(2), 225–260. doi:10.1080/00420989550013068

Knowledgboard. (n.d.). Retrieved March 4, 2009, from http://www.knowledgeboard.com/

Knowledge Cities Clearinghouse. (n.d.). Retrieved March 4, 2009, from http://www.knowledgecities.com

Learning City/regions resources. (n.d.). Retrieved March 4, 2009, from http://www.learningcities.net/services/Links/displaycat.cfm?CatIdd=340

Liedloff, J. (1985). *The continuum concept: Allowing human nature to work successfully*. Reading, MA: Addison-Wesley.

Metropolitan New Economy Index. (n.d.). Retrieved March 4, 2009, from http://www.neweconomyindex.org/metro/

Mutius, B. V. (2005). Rethinking leadership in the knowledge society, learning from others: how to integrate intellectual and social capital and established a new balance of value and values. In A. Bounfour & L. Edvinsson (Ed.), Intellectual capital for communities: nations, regions, and cities (pp. 151-163). Tokyo: Elsevier Butterworth-Heinemann. R&B Consulting (Eds.). (2006). Knowledge management Austria, Assess, Wien.

Romer, P. M. (1994). The origins of endogenous growth. *The Journal of Economic Perspectives*, *8*(1), 3–22.

Saul, J. R. (2006, March). The Collapse of Globalism. *Harper's*, *308*(1846), 33-43.

Sharma, R., Ng, E., Dharmawirya, M., & Lee, C. (2008). Beyond the Digital Divide: A Conceptual Framework for Analyzing Knowledge Societies. *Journal of Knowledge Management*, *12*(5), 151–164. doi:10.1108/13673270810903000

Simmie, J., & Lever, W. F. (Eds.). (2002). Special Issue on 'The Knowledge-based City.' . *Urban Studies (Edinburgh, Scotland)*, *39*(5-6).

Small, M. (1995). Rethinking Human Nature (Again). *Natural History*, *104*(9), 8–24.

Stahle, P. (Ed.). (2007). *Five steps for Finland's future*. Helsinki, Finland: TEKES.

Wilson, E. O. (1998). The Biological Basis of Morality. *Atlantic Monthly*, *281*(4), 53–70.

Yigitcanlar, T., Velibeyoglu, K., & Baum, S. (2008). *Knowledge-based Urban Development: planning and applications in the information era*. New York: Information Science Reference.

ENDNOTES

1 "Responding to x in the absence of x" according to B. F. Skinner's parsimonious expression.

2 In describing new realities, we are constrained by the limits of our language as often pointed out in the past by Philosophers such as A. J. Ayer and scientists such as B. F. Skinner. It is paradoxical than in trying to assert the preeminence of knowledge-based experience we should resort to a contrast with "physical", or "matter-based" reality, risking the implication of a dualistic worldview. Quite on the contrary, a knowledge-based perspective -certainly the one presented here- supposes a monistic perspective as a fundamental tenant. The radical approach to KBD thus emphasizes the continuity of natural phenomena and hence the fundamental homogeneity of all value systems (cfr. Liedloff, J., 1985, on the continuum concept). In consistency, the domain of economics is now dissociated from a purely monetary base -as much as business results become dissociated from purely financial outcomes- to deal with

all objects (material as well as represented) of human preference. Monetary systems are in fact primitive knowledge economies insofar as they rely on first-order (e.g., metal coins) to n^{th}-order (e.g., futures and derivatives) representations.

3 Carrillo, Francisco J. "The Knowledge Management Movement: Current Drives and Future Scenarios". Proceedings of *The 3rd International Conference on Technology, Policy and Innovation: Global Knowledge Partnerships: Creating Value for the 21st Century*. Austin, University of Texas. August 30-September 2, 1999.

4 IDC: *US and Worldwide KM Market Forcast 2005* y GARTNER: *Hype Cycle for KM 2003*

5 Carrillo, F. J., (2001) La Evolución de las Especies de Gestión del Conocimiento: Un reporte expedicionario de los nuevos territorios, "Entorno empresarial del Siglo XXI. Cinco años del Cluster de Conocimiento" Parque tecnológico de Zamudio. Bilbao, Spain, June 2001; and (2002), p. 390

6 http://globalkbdweek.mty.itesm.mx/ Consulted March 4, 2009.

7 Joloy, Carlos: Knowledge-based development initiatives: the agenda (trans. from Spanish by Blanca García). *Science, Knowledge & Technology Journal*, Nuevo Leon Science & Technology Council. No. 65. 26 October 2007.

8 http://www.the-new-club-of-paris.org/ Consulted March 4, 2009.

9 Bounfour, Ahmed. Structure of Scientific Topics. The New Club of Paris. Research Agenda - 1st Draft. *Unpublished document.*

10 Carrillo, Francisco J. The MAKCi Awards and the global KBD agenda. *4th World Conference on Intellectual Capital: Intellectual Capital for Communities in the Knowledge Economy: Nations, Regions, Cities and Emerging Communities*. Paris, May 22 and 23, 2008.

11 Organized by The Halle Institute for Economic Research (IWH) Halle, Germany, November 23, 2006.

12 Hartung, Annete. 2nd Halle Forum on Urban Economic Growth. Call for Papers. *Personal communication*, February 19, 2008.

13 http://www.socialcapitalgateway.org/eng-halle.htm Consulted March 4, 2009.

Chapter 2
Building Successful Knowledge Cities in the Context of the Knowledge-Based Economy: A Modern Strategic Framework

Emmanouil Ergazakis
National Technical University of Athens, Greece

Kostas Ergazakis
National Technical University of Athens, Greece

Kostas Metaxiotis
University of Piraeus, Greece

ABSTRACT

The topics of Knowledge-Based Development (KBD) and especially of Knowledge Cities (KCs) have attracted the interest of many researchers and practitioners during the last years. In a previous research work of the authors, a set of hypotheses for the design, development and operation of successful KCs had been proposed and validated through the analytical study of KCs cases' support to these hypotheses, resulting to a related Framework. However, the rapid changes in the field render more than necessary today to re-examine the elements which had leaded to the formulation of the Framework, so as to update it and conclude on a modern strategic framework. The methodology followed is based on the examination of the already identified KCs and the inclusion of five additional KCs cases. For the new set of KCs, the authors examine at which degree each case supports the hypotheses. Modifications in the set of hypotheses are proposed. The hypotheses that continue to be valid are considered as dominant, thus leading to the modern strategic Framework. Among the main findings is that all cities previously examined continue to actively support their KBD, through a series of strategies and appropriate actions. The majority of the hypotheses continue to be valid, while three of them need to slightly change so as to adapt to prevailing current conditions

DOI: 10.4018/978-1-61520-721-3.ch002

INTRODUCTION

The theme of Knowledge Cities (KCs), as a subfield of Knowledge-Based Development (KBD) has attracted the interest of researchers and practitioners during the last years. In this direction, back on 2005, the authors have proposed a set of hypotheses for the design, development and operation of successful KCs (Ergazakis et al., 2005; Ergazakis et al., 2006). They conducted an empirical evaluation of several successful KCs cases and assessed the support of each case to each hypothesis. The key findings of this assessment were the core for the formulation of a coherent framework for the development and operation of successful KCs.

However, it should be noted that this framework was produced in an era that the theme of KC had been recently introduced in the scientific community· it still was in its infancy. Since then, rapid and significant changes have taken place concerning KCs as well as KBD in general, thus formulating a new landscape. Currently there are many new methodologies, approaches and insights, new concepts & views, many new contributions from various scientific fields, new Information and Communication Technology (ICT) tools etc. These changes had impacts not only in the research community but also in the real-life approaches of KCs.

For all these reasons, it is understood that now it becomes more than relevant (if not necessary) to update the framework initially introduced: this can be accomplished by examining again the elements which had leaded to the formulation of the framework, through the examination of KCs' progress. In this respect, in this chapter:

- The progress of each already identified KC is examined and especially if it continues to be developed in knowledge–based ways and if it still can be considered as a KC. Potentially new KCs are also identified.
- For the new set of KCs, it is examined whether and at which degree theses cities continue to support or not the hypotheses that had leaded to the formulation of the framework.
- It is examined if the hypotheses themselves need any modifications / changes so as to better reflect the existing reality. In this way, an updated set of validated hypotheses which can be considered as dominant is concluded.
- The updated strategic framework for the design and development of KCs is settled down.

The proposed strategic framework in this chapter can be considered reliable and accurate enough, as its validity has been evaluated again after the major changes of latest years. This remaining part of the chapter is structured is as follows: Next section presents the progress of the already identified KCs and presents the case of another successful case (Singapore). The following section analytically examines the support of each case for each one of the hypotheses. A synthesis of the results of the previous analysis and the strategic framework are then presented. The last section proposes issues for further research and discusses the main conclusions.

CASE STUDIES: SUCCESSFUL KCS

Barcelona (Barcelona, 2005, 2008)

In Barcelona there are a number of key elements rendering the city a major knowledge economy centre. The city has eight universities, with one of the largest university communities in Europe· it hosts many R&D and technology centres and a scientific park network that is home to companies working in the technology and engineering fields. Telecommunications infrastructures are of high quality˙ talented, qualified human capital is attracted and sustained in the city due to the high standard of living that it offers. The region's companies working in high and medium-high technology industries and those that offer knowledge-based services account for 28.55% of the Spanish total. Barcelona and its metropolitan area have attracted manufacturers of electronic equipment and offices of leading companies that play a major role in the development and use of ICTs in Spain.

The city has become a reference point in Spain due to projects ranging from the 22@Barcelona district – the technology and innovation district for excellence – to an extensive network of leading services companies, a deeply rooted entrepreneurial spirit and longstanding educational and business tradition in telecommunications. The city is home to prestigious universities, state-of-the-art research centres, R&D laboratories, and intermediary institutions that encourage the development of technological projects to attract new initiatives in the digital industry by means of knowledge transfer. According to a study conducted by the Universitat Autònoma de Barcelona, Barcelona has a high degree of specialisation in knowledge-intensive areas: 45% of employment, 26.6% of businesses, 38.1% of production, 79.5% of manufacturing exports, 33.9% of professionals employed in science and technology sectors and 28.3% of the working-age population with tertiary education.

Barcelona sufficiently covered the objectives of the first Strategic Metropolitan Business Plan (SMBP) while it has already developed the second SMBP. Specifically issues that have been considered are:

- The education, training and preparation of human capital. Connection between research and educational centres and the production sectors.
- Globalisation of competition and innovation.
- Growing use of strategic planning schemes by the most dynamic metropolises with public-private cooperative systems, leadership and territorial governability.
- Concentration of creativity-related strategies (whereas before it seems more emphasis was placed on isolated specific sectors).

The concept of KC is still a dominant characteristic in the strategic choices of the city. "Barcelona Knowledge City" is a strong brand name and it is obvious that the city authorities and citizens are proud of it.

Stockholm (Centre for International Competitiveness, 2008)

Stockholm is the 6th most competitive knowledge economy in the world according to World Knowledge Competitiveness Index 2008 (WKCI) while is the only European region among the top ten, otherwise dominated by North America. Stockholm has also climbed two places from last year's study, which is conducted by Centre for International Competitiveness at the University of Wales Institute. "Stockholm region is one of the global frontrunners in the knowledge economy, especially within sectors such as ICT, life sciences and finance. WKCI 2008 is yet another proof of that", said Sten Nordin, mayor of Stockholm.

The top rating is based upon gains across a range of indicators, in particular business R&D spending, biotechnology employment and higher educational spending. The city of Stockholm has as its mission to develop and market Stockholm as a destination of choice for new businesses and visitors. Some important strategic choices of the city concern:

- Development of fast regional growing high-tech sectors
- Improvement of its importance as a strong financial market

- Development of growing market for construction and high-tech infrastructures for companies
- Attraction of highly educated and skilled work force
- Provision of high-quality everyday life

The city also pays great attention to the development of knowledge zones in its premises. An example is the

Stockholm Business Alliance:

- It is formed by 43 municipalities in the Stockholm-Mälar region
- It has over 3 million inhabitants
- It provides more than 50% of Sweden's total R&D capacity
- It represents 25% of the Swedish economy
- It is a leading financial centre
- It is the site of the Nobel prize

Moreover, the city possesses a very strong knowledge base, including 6 universities, 18 university colleges; 6000 scientists, 8900 PhD students, more than 110,000 students; world-known research institutes; innovation with world-class ICT; one of Europe's biggest biotech clusters etc.

Based on the above, it is obvious that the city's authorities continue to actively support the KBD of the city and their strategic choices are characterized by this philosophy.

Montréal (Montréal 2002, 2007)

City of Montréal conducted the first strategic plan for sustainable development (2007-2009). The goal of drawing up an initial strategic plan for KBD emerged from the Montréal Summit held in June 2002. During the Summit there was strong consensus around the need to position Montréal as KC on the international scene. Many organizations interested in KBD committed themselves to working in collaboration with the city and promised to carry out specific actions. Montréal's First Strategic Plan for KBD was adopted by the Montréal Executive Committee on April 20, 2005, and is spread out over a five-year period. The main characteristic of this plan lies in the collective commitment of partner organizations, associated with the city administration, to use the KC concept as a foundation on which to build Montréal. The participation by a growing number of organizations in carrying out actions under this plan is a proof of the growing interest and willingness on the part of socio-economic players to be part of a combined effort devoted to achieving sustainable KBD.

On 2008, Montréal International released the 3rd edition of its publication, *Attractiveness Indicators*, which presents Greater Montréal's advantages. Among the main location factors considered by foreign investors, this research confirms the Montréal metropolitan area's power of attraction compared to its leading North American rivals. According to the study, Greater Montréal's business climate is highly favourable to foreign investment and ranks, among North America's major metropolitan areas. Thus, Montréal ranks: 1st for the number of university students per capita; 1st for the competitiveness of total business operating costs in the R&D sectors; 3rd for high technology job growth; 1st for overall R&D performance of businesses and universities; 1st for the number of university enrollments and degrees awarded; 1st for the number of patents held etc.

City of Montréal also conducted the "Imagining – Building Montréal 2025" that sets Montréal as a city of knowledge, creativity and innovation with main strategic choices being:

- Implement complementary measures to keep students in school and raise Montréalers' graduation rate
- Support initiatives to encourage young people to choose scientific careers
- Work to eliminate the underfunding of institutions of higher learning

- Develop university infrastructure
- Promote the integration of foreign students by creating a Montréal international university district
- Foster industrial research and innovation by supporting
- Accelerate university research by supporting initiatives for sharing scientific equipment

It is obvious that Montréal continues to support the KC theme and the KBD while planning the future.

Munich (Munich, 2005; Eller, 2006)

Munich occupies a prime position within the knowledge society: Knowledge is available in the city as a social and cultural resource and is the prime mover of industrial development. Knowledge as a resource can be acquired by the city's population through education and life-long learning. Knowledge generates opportunities for participating in social life and is a precondition of skilled employment. Besides, technological and scientific knowledge in the city gives a leading edge in knowledge to be successful in the competition among cities and regions. Knowledge is imbued with life in an environment ready to embrace it, exciting to advance into areas that are new and unknown.

The desire for knowledge has a long tradition in Munich: To educate oneself, learn and acquire knowledge are all elements of historic development. Urban knowledge society builds on a diversified school system, renowned institutions for continuing education and adult education, universities and technical colleges. These institutions provide broad general education and also communicate intensive technical and expert knowledge. Research activities in companies, universities, colleges and numerous research institutions generate innovation in the product and processes sectors of technology-intensive industries and thus improve the city's stance. Industries such as medical equipment, biotechnology, information and communication technology, environmental technology, the media, and financial services are the prime movers of the knowledge-intensive urban economy. They attract investment and provide high-skill jobs and define the future fields of growth of this city.

A special feature of the urban economy of Munich is the variety of production clusters. The successful placement of high-tech industries in the world market is due to the regional concentration of innovation activities in clusters. Clusters while attracting new high-technology businesses and industries facilitate the actors in an interlinked network of relations access to technological know-how in the process of innovation. Such networks with actors in universities, research institutions and companies of any size often emerge around research, supporting and qualification establishments and with pioneering firms as nucleus. Based on trust, mutual benefit and frequent communication, these innovative environments are not mobile in space at random and are therefore crucial factors in the regional competition of sites. Even in the age of communication technologies, the exchange of knowledge among individuals remains an important component of cooperation also in the knowledge society. Fast and direct contact is an essential precondition for it.

An open approach to knowledge as a resource and an inspiring climate are important conditions to attract creative people and cause them to feel loyal to the city. This keynote is felt in places such as libraries, museums or theatres. They promote the culture of meeting knowledge and make people want to know more. Strategies and an action plan for improving Munich as city of knowledge are presented at the study "Munich city of knowledge" (Munich, 2005). In terms of economic power and quality of life, the Bavarian capital can regularly be found among the top performers in Germany in most different city ranking lists. Also, virtually all statistics with information on the innovation and competition capabilities of regions and their positions in the knowledge society, Munich is invariably among the best.

Dublin (Dublin 2004, 2008)

Since Dublin Chamber of Commerce published its Dublin 2010 Vision seven years ago, there have been remarkable changes to Dublin. High quality employment is now a realistic option for most people, the fabric of the city has improved immeasurably, visitors are flocking from overseas countries, and there is a new confidence among young people. All cities have life cycles. Dublin is emerging from a successful period of growth – but still there is need to continue and sustain that development.

Dublin recognizes that there is need to build on their strengths in knowledge-based employment, and to tap the resource of schools and colleges. Dublin Chamber of Commerce has taken this initiative in order to set an agenda for a new and improved city. The working group included a cross section of interests from business, development agencies, property and consultants groups, with great assistance from the Futures Academy at Dublin Institute of Technology (DIT). They identified key themes and policy measures to make Dublin a KC that is internationally competitive. They set out proposals for a governance and political leadership structure that a major European capital needs if it is to work effectively.

Dublin 2020 is a "knowledge city" that generates, attracts and retains high quality skills. Dublin's education strengths come from its people. Creative and innovative thinking is a natural part of living in Dublin. Dublin has the capacity to create new knowledge in a culture of research activity excellence. Universities of the highest international standards attract talented young people from all over the world and generate active and highly skilled people in the workforce. The national policy is to support connections between different knowledge clusters in the city. The third level institutions collaborate with each other in order to fulfil market needs and educational aspirations of students. The strong links with business allow for the development of R&D centres of excellence, which form an important sector of the city's economy. This creates a business environment, which is both collaborative and competitive. The value of small indigenous companies is well recognised and entrepreneurship is highly promoted and supported. Well-developed physical infrastructure and a high quality living environment sustain merging of knowledge, society and commercial activities in Dublin.

Connectivity, an essential feature of the city, is facilitated by broadband services that are accessible equally for organisations and individuals at all rungs of the economic ladder. Everybody has access to Internet services and training in basic computer literacy. Community groups receive support for training activities and computer equipment. Dublin chamber of commerce plays a crucial role in showing the way Dublin will be establish as a KC. It has recently set an action plan for 2012 in which the following actions (with sub-actions) are set as high priority:

- Developing, attracting and retaining entrepreneurial, skilled and creative workforce
- Embedding a next generation IT infrastructure
- Branding the Greater Dublin Area as a KC region

Delft (Delft, 2009)

In the decades of 1970s and 1980s the difficulties that the industrial companies that resulted in a significant drop of employment in the industrial sector led local authorities to develop a plan for development. Nowadays Delft economy is strongly based on knowledge and tourism. Delft Knowledge City is a cooperation of the so-called four O's:

- Onderwijs [Education]
- Onderzoeksinstelling [Research Institute]
- Ondernemers [Entrepreneurs]
- Overheid [Government]

The main pillars of Delft's strategy are:

- *Active Involvement of Businesses / Institutions.* There are various enterprises / institutions involved in this cooperation: TU Delft (University of Technology), two HBO (Higher Vocational Education) establishments, the TNO (Netherlands Organization for Applied Scientific Research), Delft Municipality, Chamber of Commerce in Haaglanden, three Delft enterprise networks and VNO-NCW West (The Confederation of Netherlands Industry and Employers). The council chairmen have a seat on the Advisory Board. The executive committee of the Delft Knowledge City institution cooperates with the employees of "The Knowledge Alliance" of South Holland.
- *Knowledge Economy.* The knowledge economy is running at full speed. Approximately half of all Delft jobs are knowledge-intensive. The 13,000 students at the Delft University of Technology ensure a constant circulation of high-quality personnel. They also ensure the establishment of dozens of new enterprises each year, including many techno start-ups.
- *No Local Economy.* The Delft knowledge economy is not a local economy. The world is the market for many enterprises and knowledge institutions. Cooperative agreements are being concluded on a national level more often. After working within the Delft Knowledge City for ten years, projects that are being stimulated have been expanded to a provincial level. The Delft Knowledge City institution has therefore played a large role in the establishment of the "Knowledge Alliance" of South Holland.
- *Support.* The Delft Knowledge City institution focuses on bringing the many projects and products that the city delivers into the spotlight. In this way, Delft will be able to reveal its character as a Centre of Technology to the world.

Eindhoven (Eindhoven, 2006; Horizon Programme, 2008)

At the end of 2001 the Eindhoven Regional Government (SRE) took the initiative to set up the Regional Opportunities Committee after becoming aware of an economic downturn in key economic sectors in the Eindhoven Region. The composition of the Committee, chaired by Dr H.G.J. de Wilt, was sympathetic to the needs of the business world, education and knowledge institutes as well as the government. The Committee's purpose was to draw up a strategic action plan to strengthen the economic structure of the region over the medium term. In June 2002 this resulted in the presentation of the Horizon Programme. On 19 September 2002 the principles and aims of the Horizon Programme were approved by the SRE's regional board, which also approved the financial contributions for the programme agency and the catalyst fund. The Horizon Programme agency was launched on 1 October 2002. The mission of the Horizon Programme was to change the city from industrial mainport to top technology region, with the emphasis on people and technology. Its objectives were:

- To reduce and solve structural shortages in the labour market
- To increase the return on knowledge by strengthening innovation and market competencies
- To reduce sensitivity to market fluctuations through diversification
- To improve international profile

The Brainport Navigator 2013 strategic programme of action builds on the successful Horizon Programme and focuses on creating a continuum for economic and social development. The subgoals are to:

- Create balance in the employment market
- Bring knowledge and skill to bear
- Facilitate diversification in economic activity
- Create a stimulating climate for location
- Strengthen the international image

Some indicative strategic directions included in the programme are:

- **Focus on knowledge intensity.** The programme's focus lies in the further development of knowledge-intensive manufacturing. Traditionally, the regions have strong roots in engineering, research and knowledge development. The Brainport Navigator 2013 programme wants to see the region build on this solid base and create a region with an innovative climate capable of competing globally. That requires not only measures for sustainable strengthening of the economic structure – investment in the engineering structure – but also initiative and action in the field of spatial physics and the social structure. Brainport Navigator 2013 therefore works on four domains: people, technology, business and basics.
- **Cross-border collaboration.** In 2013 the 'Regions of Knowledge' in Europe will take on a key role. To be able to excel as a top technology region, achieving the Barcelona standard from the Lisbon objectives – as is now the case in Brainport – is insufficient. It needs to be a doubling (R&D = 5-6%). This makes critical mass vital. To achieve this Brainport Eindhoven is working together in the ELAt programme (Eindhoven-Leuven-Aachen triangle) and participating in the international agreements that the Ministry of Economic Affairs has with Flanders and Nordrhein-Westfalen. This cross-border collaboration boosts the European prospects of Brainport Eindhoven.
- **Investing in a balanced social-economic development.** There is a strong mutual relationship, Europe teaches us, between economic development, poverty and social inequality. The connection between social and economic dimensions is crucial for a dynamic and competitive knowledge economy and for the knowledge economy of Brainport.
- **Experimental garden.** In the projects being developed by the region within the four domains, Brainport Eindhoven acts in many cases as an experimental garden. Brainport can provide a test environment for dynamic traffic management (Phileas) or a regulation-free zone for the knowledge industry (Knowledge Zone). Being an experimental garden means that failure is allowed in Brainport and may even be necessary in order to learn.
- **Pride.** The human factor is central to all programme components. Brainport Eindhoven aims to earn the pride of its population. People and companies should be conscious of the position and importance of Brainport Eindhoven in the Netherlands.

Melbourne (City of Melbourne, 2005; Yigitcanlar et al., 2008; Melbourne Vice-Chancellors' Forum, 2007)

Melbourne city has already developed a strategic plan (2004-2008) in which several developing axes were settled. City Plan 2010 is Melbourne City Council's primary planning strategy. It sets out what it is believed that must be happened over the next 10 years aiming at the vision of the

City of Melbourne in 2010. The vision is for the City of Melbourne to be a thriving and sustainable city. Melbourne City Council will work with all who have a stake in the City of Melbourne's future to realise this vision and will simultaneously pursue:

- Economic prosperity
- Social equity; and
- Environmental quality.

The path to achieving sustainability is long and will take many years to travel. However, by 2010, there will have been taken many significant steps. There will have been made many positive changes to the natural and physical environment, to the City's culture, to the way business is done, and to how community is valued. Council has adopted a set of strategic directions to realise this vision. These directions are organised around four themes:

- Theme 1: Connection and accessibility
- Theme 2: Innovation and business vitality
- Theme 3: Inclusiveness and engagement
- Theme 4: Environmental responsibility

The vision of City Plan 2010 is for Melbourne to be a thriving and sustainable City that simultaneously pursues economic prosperity, social equity and environmental quality. Council understands that realising the vision will require the cooperation of all those who have a stake in the City of Melbourne's future. Council will develop and maintain strong relationships with Victorian Government, the business and wider community, and other key stakeholders to take opportunities to achieve our vision. Council will contribute by providing:

- strong capital city governance;
- leadership, support and education;
- delivery of a range of key city services;
- maintenance of city infrastructure and assets (for example, its heritage, parks, gardens, roads, and social infrastructure);
- an efficient and effective integrated regulatory environment;
- marketing of the city's culture, characteristics, advantages and abilities;
- innovative and integrated strategic and corporate planning;
- advocacy on the needs of the residential and business communities;
- networks of businesses, agencies and community groups;
- partnerships, brokering agreements and alliances with key stakeholders; and
- sponsorship of events, businesses, festivals and other initiatives.

The main way to achieve the vision is by delivering works programmes, services and daily activities, and by continuing to find ways to use sustainable products and processes in construction, maintenance and service programs.

Council has developed an Integrated Planning Framework to ensure that all of the actions Council undertakes, and policies and strategies that are developed, work towards the achievement of the vision for the City expressed in City Plan 2010. The Integrated Planning Framework is made up of a series of corporate and strategic planning tools to implement the vision. It includes:

- City Plan 2010 — Council's most important strategic document that provides broad based objectives and strategic directions for the City.
- The Council Plan — Council's four-year corporate plan containing actions derived from City Plan 2010.
- The Annual Plan and Budget — a business resource allocation plan. It identifies all of Council's services and the key initiatives to be delivered over the financial year.

The Framework also includes strategies such as the Municipal Strategic Statement – the strategic land use policy and development framework for the municipality – which assist the delivery of City Plan's Strategic Directions.

Bilbao

Metropolitan Bilbao has no doubts about its role in Europe and the World. To maintain the leadership it has enjoyed throughout its history, Bilbao knows that it must work together with institutions and companies in planning the future of the city. Following the drafting of the Revitalisation Plan in 1992, the Association focused its activities on furthering the launch of the revitalisation process through public-private partnership.

In the decade of the 90's, a new scenario emerged for Metropolitan Bilbao, with globalisation, the transformation of social and economic structures, information and communications technologies and the emergence of a multicultural society. In order to provide a suitable response to these challenges, in 1999 the Association's efforts were consolidated in the project "Bilbao 2010: Strategic Reflection", presented on 25 November 1999.

Subsequently, and with a view to channelling the strategic reflection, its key areas and core aspects towards projects that will enable Bilbao to make the most of the change already undertaken, projecting the metropolis as an international world-class city in the Knowledge Society, on 4 April 2001 the Association presented the strategic plan called "Bilbao 2010: The Strategy".

The Association "Bilbao Metropoli-30" has been formed to carry out planning, research and promotion projects, headed towards the recuperation and revitalization of Metropolitan Bilbao (defined as a social and economic reality without precise geographical limits and whose existence has been projected throughout its regional and international environment). The Association for the Revitalization of Metropolitan Bilbao is an association of promotion and research, with full legal and patrimonial responsibility, established in May. Its headquarters were established in Bilbao with the aim of carrying out investigation and promotion work for the revitalization of Metropolitan Bilbao, this last being mainly its territorial scope:

- Principally, the Association drives the implementation of the Strategic Plan for the Revitalization of the Metropolitan Bilbao.
- Secondly, the Association undertakes any type of actions derived from the Strategic Plan which are entrusted to its responsibility, and particularly, of those whose aim is the improvement of the external and internal image of Metropolitan Bilbao.
- The Association, in third place, carries out study and research projects related to Metropolitan Bilbao, as well as other metropolis that, due to its circumstances, can provide useful knowledge.
- In fourth place, the Association fosters the cooperation between public sector and private sector with the aim of finding joint solutions to problems of mutual interest that affect Metropolitan Bilbao

Strategy 2010 is founded on three basic elements: people, activities and the appeal of the metropolis. And at their core, as a supporting structure and strategic reference, lie innovation and knowledge.

- People: they have the knowledge and the Plan is made by and for people. For high value added business initiatives to take shape it is necessary for the role of leaders to be reinforced in developing Metropolitan Bilbao and to design mechanisms for training, keeping and attracting professionals.
- Activity in the City: high added-value business activities are the motor force of the metropolitan system. To encourage these

activities a suitable environment must be created providing immediate Internet access, support policies for innovative initiatives and the creation of intelligent infrastructures (IT systems, equipment for laboratories and areas of research, etc).

- The Appeal of the Metropolis: the Association Bilbao Metropoli-30 starts off from the premise that the city is a vital space, an inhabited place that must be liveable in, where the priority is to shape an environment in which human beings may find an atmosphere conducive to harmonious development where the personal and the social come together in solidarity.

Among the top priority projects, which would require substantial budgetary commitment to get them moving, four stand out in particular: the creation of a "city for innovation and knowledge", for which Zorrozaurre is an evident candidate as one of the suitable locations; the holding of a Universal Exhibition as a way of projecting Bilbao internationally and acting as a catalyst for a score of public and private initiatives; the urban regeneration of the Old quarter of Bilbao to consolidate its role as a space for citizens to get together, with leisure, trade and culture as its foundation; the cleaning and recovery of the River and its banks, transforming it into the articulating axis for an open multicultural society, and making it an identifiable and unmistakeable symbol of Bilbao City and of the socioeconomic dynamism of the areas through which it flows.

Manchester

Manchester has been one of the most forward thinking cities in the UK when it comes to the knowledge economy. The city, at the heart of one of the biggest economic regions outside London1, has a Knowledge Capital programme, aiming to increase investment; innovation and technology transfer around seven elemental themes. It is one of the designated 'Science Cities' and is using this opportunity to create public / private partnerships building on research strengths. Manchester explicitly aims to work with neighbouring local authorities, the sub-region and other Northern Core Cities to "build upon distinctive strengths to deliver mutual benefit and a powerful economic hub". Knowledge is at the heart of Manchester's current strategies and future vision and the diverse stakeholders share this vision and are optimistic about its success. This puts Manchester in a strong position to deliver on many of its aspirations.

Manchester: Knowledge Capital is a dynamic force for innovation and economic transformation, built around a highly competitive combination of knowledge assets across the Manchester city region. Through a partnership of all ten Greater Manchester authorities, four universities, the strategic health authority, other key public agencies and leading businesses, Manchester: Knowledge Capital is working to secure substantial and sustainable growth which benefits all the people of Manchester and makes a major contribution to the Northwest, the North of England and the UK's future prosperity.

Manchester: Knowledge Capital is unlocking opportunity through action in four areas:

- Stimulating and supporting increased business innovation from research, science and knowledge;
- Engaging with the people of Manchester in securing this future, through dialogue, debate, education and employment;
- Supporting the growth of a city-region environment which facilitates business success, provides an outstanding quality of life and is open to all;
- Championing and trying new ideas and new ways of living and working.

Established in 2002, Manchester: Knowledge Capital has a small Executive Team, taking the lead on implementing the various programmes of activity. The Executive Team reports to the Manchester: Knowledge Capital Board - a high level, predominantly private sector group that meets once a quarter to steer ongoing strategy. Current programmes of activity and innovation led by Manchester: Knowledge Capital (M:KC), include:

- *Science City*: Gordon Brown designated Manchester one of six science cities across England. M:KC leads Manchester's Science City activity, establishing Innovation Partnerships, encouraging public engagement with science and technology,

Table 1.

Barcelona		
Hypothesis	**Support Level**	**Explanation**
Design and development		
H1. Political and social will is indispensable	+	The strong political and social support that the KC development initiative initially met, it still exists. In addition, there is a specific strategy committee being responsible for the overall management of the initiative, aiming at continuing the efforts.
H2. Strategy and development plan is crucial	+	The First Metropolitan strategic Plan of Barcelona was approved on 2003. Until today, Barcelona has sufficiently covered the objectives of the 1st SMBP while through its evaluation they stepped forward, developing a 2nd SMBP with horizon until 2010.
H3. Financial support and strong investments are necessary	+	The projects' financing, like in the 1st SMBP, comes from the local administration, private and public companies and banks. The infrastructure of the city is still reinforced as it is considered as a top priority.
H4. Setting-up of agencies to promote the development of knowledge-based regions is essential	+	"BarcelonaActiva" and "22@Barcelona Society" are the main organizations responsible to promote KBD in the city.
H5. International, multi-ethnic character of the city and open, inclusive society is necessary	+	The promotion of specific cooperation strategies with other regions (Asia, Latin America etc.), the creative coexistence of different groups of people among the city and the metropolitan plan for the accommodation of immigrants are some of the 1st SMBP objectives successfully covered and continue to be present in the 2nd SMBP.
H6. Metropolitan web site is very important	+	The City continues to pay great attention to the design and functionality of the metropolitan web-page. It contains a plethora of content and provides a series of services so as to be useful for all citizens.
H7. Value creation to citizens is indispensable	+	Many initiatives aim to provide services and solutions that will add value in everyday life for the citizens and for the companies operation as well.
H8. Creation of urban innovation engines is significant	+	Innovation is a key point for Barcelona as the knowledge that is produced in universities, research centres and by the human capital is being used by high technology industries and incorporated in knowledge-based services.
H9. Assurance of knowledge society rights of citizens is substantial	+	Barcelona sufficiently covered the objectives that were set in the Charter of Rights of Citizens in the Information Society. In the 2nd SMBP this is still an important issue.
Operation		
H10. Low cost access to advanced communication networks is imperative	+	Barcelona was one of the first cities which established free (Wi-Fi) and low-cost access in advanced broadband networks to its citizens.
H11. Research excellence is indispensable	+	The city has eight universities, with one of the largest university communities in Europe' it is a host of R&D and technology centres and a scientific park network that is home to companies working in the technology and engineering fields.
H12. Existence of network of public libraries is necessary	+	Due to the fact that there are so many students and university programs in Barcelona, there are excellent education resources and specialized libraries all over the city, offering a significant part of their material online. Moreover, the cost is significant low or free.

and developing an innovation ecosystem that nurtures growing businesses. The Manchester Science Festival, which has just enjoyed its second successful year, is a cornerstone of Manchester Science City's "Real World Science" programme for public engagement.

- *Manchester Is My Planet (MIMP)*: Formerly the Manchester Green Energy Revolution, this programme is a partnership between the local authorities of the Manchester city region and Sustainability Northwest to convince large organisations, businesses and households to radically reduce emissions and secure economic benefit through the innovations developed to do so. Recent sub-projects include learning from Swedish expertise on planning for

Table 2.

Stockholm		
Hypothesis	**Support Level**	**Explanation**
Design and development		
H1	+	Citizens' overall attitude and opinion towards knowledge-based initiatives is currently more mature and favourable. Local Administration has already gained great experience in managing KBD projects and initiatives and, thus, continues to plan accordingly for the future.
H2	+	Stockholm is already one of the most competitive knowledge economies in the world. Moreover, Stockholm's stakeholders are still conducting strategy plans to develop and market Stockholm as a top KC in the region of North Europe.
H3	+	Significant amount of the overall city budget supports the KC strategy and the relative initiatives and actions.
H4	~	There are not specific organizations supporting KBD initiatives. These responsibilities are lying only in the local administration.
H5	+	Stockholm has always had as a top priority, to establish the international character of the city. Many scientific and research initiatives have international dimensions. Moreover, Stockholm has one of the best immigrant adoption systems.
H6	+	Stockholm owns one of the best and fully functional web pages. It integrates many e-services and modules addressed to citizens and companies as well.
H7	+	Stockholm citizens can be proud of the every-day services that are being offered to them by the local administration, in the framework of its KBD strategy, which takes strongly into account issues regarding citizen services such as: access into ICT technologies, entrepreneurship and innovation support, benefits to specific target groups (students, immigrants, mothers, etc.), etc.
H8	+	Stockholm with 6 universities, 18 university colleges, 6000 scientists, 8900 PhD students, 110,000 students and World-known research institutes, is considered itself as a global innovation centre. Moreover among Stockholm's targets, is to interconnect innovation with every-day life in the city.
H9	+	Stockholm's local administration provides citizens with all necessary knowledge/information about the city in a friendly and transparent way. Moreover, in many cases, citizens have an active role in the decision making process.
Operation		
H10	+	Stockholm has passed the era that broadband services provided to the citizens at low-cost. The new trend is to expand the network of free Wi-Fi hotspots so as citizens have free access to Internet everywhere in the city.
H11	+	See H8.
H12	+	There is an advanced network of libraries with academic and general bibliography, offered also online in many cases.

energy supply, climate change work with young people in Wythenshawe and initiating the recent 'Mini-Stern' for Manchester work to assess the economic impact of climate change legislation on the city region.

- *Innovation Manchester*: An initiative aimed at catalysing innovation across the Manchester city region. This initiative has engaged with over 70 private sector leaders and has levered in substantial resources from the National Endowment for Science Technology and the Arts (Nesta) and the North West Development Agency.

Singapore (Singapore, 2009; World Capital Institute, 2009)

The World Capital Institute (WCI), in association with Teleos, have announced the winners of the inaugural Most Admired Knowledge City Awards 2007 (MAKCi, 2007). Singapore has been recognized as this year's MAKCi Winner, followed by Boston and Barcelona. Singapore is regarded as the premier regional hub to attract foreign Multinational Corporations (MNCs) and local enterprises to use it as a production base for high value added products and to provide manufacturing related services for their subsidiaries in the region. This south-Asian city-nation has attracted key MNCs headquarter services to the region.

The Singaporean government also recognizes the need to nurture small and medium local enterprises and to build up a core of world-class companies with core competencies, which can compete in the global economy. As such, the Economic Development Board (EDB) of Singapore has launched a knowledge-based 10-year plan to develop Singapore into a vibrant and robust global hub of knowledge-driven industries in manufacturing and traded services with emphasis on technology, innovation and capabilities.

The idea is to encourage MNCs to locate more of their key knowledge-intensive activities in Singapore and for local companies to embrace more knowledge-intensive activities and become world-class players. Such plan envisions integrating Singapore into the global economy to leverage on international talent, knowledge and technology, by providing an entrepreneurial environment that embraces innovation to generate new business and growth and grooming world-class local and foreign companies in niche areas. Additionally, Singapore

Figure 1. The Strategic Framework

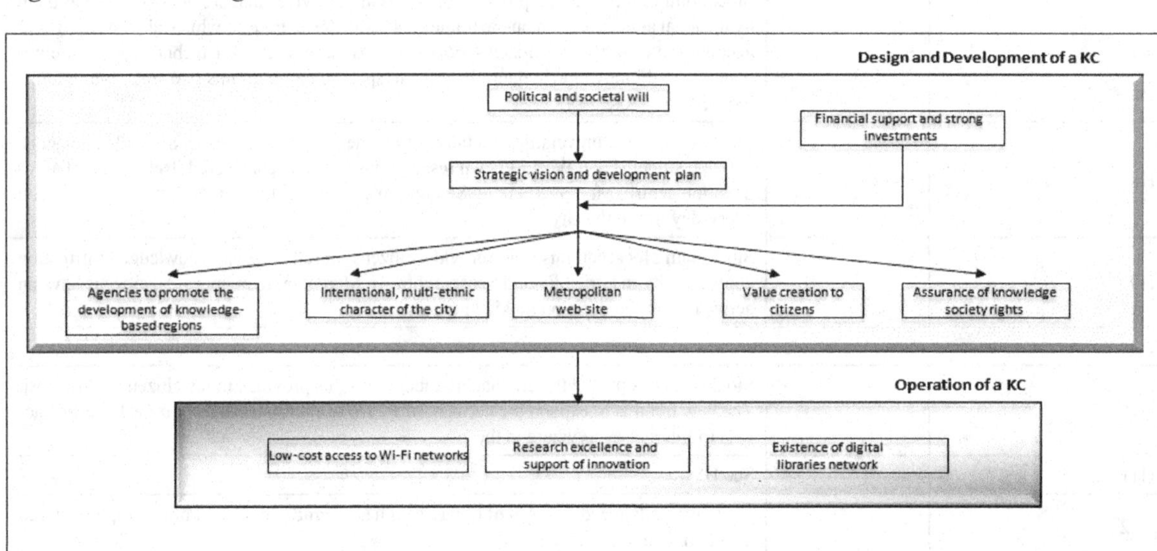

Table 3.

Montréal		
Hypothesis	**Support Level**	**Explanation**
Design and development		
H1	+	It is clear that policy makers and the society support the city to establish itself as a KC. Montréal can be proud that its citizens are aware of the benefits that a KC can offer.
H2	+	The Montréal Executive Committee has already conducted and continues to conduct strategic plan, having as main pillar KBD.
H3	+	A significant element of the strategic plan is the identification and proposal of various ways so as to secure financial support for the its initiatives/projects.
H4	+	The Montréal Executive Committee promotes sufficiently the KBD concept and related initiatives.
H5	+	Montréal Executive Committee considers that the international character and openness of the society are very important factors for the KC initiative and takes into account this in the design of its projects/initiatives.
H6	+	The City's metropolitan site is attractive in its design, provides access to important amount of knowledge/information at a friendly way and offers various e-services to citizens.
H7	+	The creation of added value to everyday life of citizens is an important dimension of the City's strategic plan.
H8	+	Among Canada's major metropolitan areas, Greater Montréal ranks 1st for: overall R&D performance of businesses and universities; number of university enrolments and degrees awarded; number of patents held; number if university students per capita;
H9	–	There is no clear indication that the reinforcement of citizens' knowledge society rights is among the city's strategic objectives.
Operation		
H10	+	There is low-cost access in broadband networks while efforts are currently concentrated to expand the Wi-Fi network.
H11	+	World-class research institutes are operating in the City. Reinforcement of research is a key strategic priority.
H12	+	There is sufficient network of libraries all over the city, offering a series of advanced services (e-services as well).

has engaged now in an effort to nurture its cultural base and to develop other social capitals.

In the last decade, Singapore has successfully grown its R&D base, drawn top scientific and creative talent and nurtured R&D collaborations between the public sector and private enterprise. Today, Singapore holds global leadership positions in areas of manufacturing such as electronics and petrochemicals. The city-state remains an attractive base for complex manufacturing activities, in tandem with its move towards a more knowledge-centric and research-based economy. This emphasis on innovation and capital-intensive activities and a globalised workforce has shaped Singapore into a city-state where Chinese and Indian companies can internationalise, where American and European companies make their entry into Asia, and where views on the future of this dynamic and fast-evolving region can be forged

SUPPORT TO THE HYPOTHESES

The set of proposed hypotheses and their description can be found in the previous related research work of the authors. In this section we examine whether the cities with the new facts and conditions still support the hypotheses and in what

Table 4.

Munich		
Hypothesis	**Support Level**	**Explanation**
Design and development		
H1	~	Many public organisations in the city are involved in KM processes taking place in the city as well as in the KC initiatives. However, it is not clear at which degree simple citizens are involved.
H2	+	There is specific strategy and an action plan for improving the position of Munich as city of knowledge.
H3	+	The City is a financial centre of the country. Many investments are directed to the implementation of the KC strategy.
H4	~	There are many organizations related to knowledge management and KBD but there is not a specific authority to promote KBD, except from the local administration.
H5	+	Munich has already become a city of the world with its multi-national and multi-cultural character. Almost 25% of its inhabitants have not the German nationality. The local administration has managed to avoid the creation of ghettos. The intense cultural life (many museums, galleries, art scenes etc) reinforce even more its multi-ethnic character.
H6	+	The City's web-page is attractive and offers a variety of e-services.
H7	+	Citizens are offered a variety of knowledge-related services in their everyday life, from public organisations, institutes, companies etc.
H8	+	The City is considered as a centre for the implementation of innovative and business ideas. Based on the number of patents, Munich's companies are among the first in Germany. Moreover, the percentage of employees working in companies' R&D departments is among the highest in the country. Finally, there are many important universities and research institutes.
H9	+	An important target of local administration's policy is the equal citizens' participation to broadband networks, to transparent public information and knowledge as well as to education and training services.
Operation		
H10	+	Last years, Munich invests in the development of Wi-Fi network. The percentage of citizens with access to broadband connection is the highest in the country.
H11	+	Research conducted in universities and companies' R&D departments is of particular high-quality
H12	+	There is a network of more than 700 libraries, offering various advanced services.

way. For this purpose, a table is provided for each city. The hypotheses are in the first column of the table. The level of support is demonstrated in the second column, using three levels:

- "+" means full support of the hypothesis.
- "~" means partially support.
- "-" means deficiency in support.

Finally, there is a short explanation of the way that the case of the city supports the hypothesis (or not). There is a different city for each table (Tables 2-11).

The following tables provide a general picture of the level of support of each case study to the hypotheses.

REVISED HYPOTHESES AND THE STRATEGIC FRAMEWORK

From the previous analysis, it is obvious that the majority of the hypotheses are still supported by the cities cases. Thus, these hypotheses can be considered as dominant and can be incorporated in the proposed framework for designing, developing

Table 5.

Dublin		
Hypothesis	**Support Level**	**Explanation**
Design and development		
H1	+	Dublin local government recognizes the need to build on their strengths and to be developed in a knowledge-based way. In this effort, there are combined synergies among the political stakeholders and the local society as well.
H2	+	The Knowledge City initiative stakeholders identified strategic priorities and policy measures to render Dublin an internationally competitive KC. Dublin chamber of commerce plays a crucial role in showing the way Dublin will be established as a KC. It has set a vision and strategic plan until 2012
H3	+	Dublin city supports the initiative with its own resources but in parallel they also efficiently absorbed the EU structural funds.
H4	+	Dublin Chamber of Commerce has taken the initiative to define the KC agenda. The working group included representatives from business sector, development agencies, property and consultants groups, with great assistance from the Futures Academy at DIT.
H5	+	The City is particularly open to variety and has many inter-cultural communities and immigrants. It also accepts many visitors and has a lot of museums, theme parks, expositions and cultural centres.
H6	+	Dublin city's web-site is user-friendly with a variety of useful services.
H7	+	Well-developed physical infrastructure and a high quality living environment sustain merging of knowledge, society and commercial activities in Dublin.
H8	+	Dublin's education strengths come from its people. Nobody leaves the learning cycle, but everybody develops their personal, professional and civic abilities continuously. Creative and innovative thinking is a natural part of living in Dublin. The policy for innovation is formulated by the Irish Council for Science, Technology and Innovation.
H9	+	City of Dublin has as a top priority that everyone has equal knowledge society rights.
Operation		
H10	+	Everybody has low-cost access to broadband networks as well as to training in basic computer literacy. The development of the Wi-Fi network is currently a major priority.
H11	+	The third level institutions collaborate in order to fulfil market research needs and educational aspirations of students. Strong links with the business sector allow for the development of R&D centres of excellence, which form an important sector of the city's economy.
H12	+	Dublin has a well-developed network of libraries. A major amount of available content is offered online.

and operating a successful KC. However, there are some hypotheses which can be modified so as to better reflect prevailing conditions:

- There is a strong correlation between H8 "Creation of urban innovation engines is significant" and H11 "Research excellence is indispensable". Most of the cities consider these topics similar, invest and promote innovation and research excellence simultaneously. It seems so that there is no reason to have two hypotheses, and they can be mixed to "Research excellence and support of innovation it is indispensable", under the category "Operation", since it is a factor related to the operation of a KC.
- The other conclusion concerns the H10 "Low cost access to advanced communication networks is imperative". Low cost access to broadband network seems to be a reality not only for cases examined but for many other cities globally. The new trend

Table 6.

Delft		
Hypothesis	**Support Level**	**Explanation**
Design and development		
H1	+	Difficulties faced by the industrial sector in the decades of 70s and 80s resulted in a significant drop of employment and led local authorities to develop a KBD plan. This plan had the support of the entire society. The effort has been successful and all cities' stakeholders continue to support initiative for the reinforcement of the city as a KC
H2	+	The local government has the responsibility to develop KC strategy, involving local business, the university, research institutions etc. as partners.
H3	+	Important funds are made available for the implementation of projects of the strategic plan.
H4	+	There are various enterprises / institutions involved in the promotion of the KBD: TU Delft (University of Technology), two HBO (Higher Vocational Education) establishments, the TNO (Netherlands Organization for Applied Scientific Research), Delft Municipality, Chamber of Commerce in Haaglanden, three Delft enterprise networks and VNO-NCW West (The Confederation of Netherlands Industry and Employers)
H5	+	The Delft knowledge economy is not a local economy. The world is the market for many enterprises and knowledge institutions. Cooperative agreements are being concluded on a national level more often. Moreover, Delft has a beautiful historical city centre that attracts many tourists. The city is open to people with different backgrounds.
H6	+	The metropolitan web page is complete and integrates a variety of e-services.
H7	+	The city, though its knowledge-based strategy managed to overcome important problems and continues to offer a series of advantages for its citizens in their everyday-life.
H8	+	In the KC strategy, innovation and research play vital role. A special centre, devoted to innovation is operating in the city
H9	–	There is no clear evidence that the strengthening of the accessibility and participation rights of the citizens in one of the city's strategic goals
Operation		
H10	+	Wi-Fi networks are the next step for broadband services in Delft.
H11	+	Recently it was decided to develop a Research & Development park for high tech companies at the Technical University campus
H12	+	Delft has a very well developed network of libraries.

is the expansion of free Wi-Fi networks. This exactly can be currently considered the distinguishing feature of KCs. From the analysis above, it is concluded that the majority of cases examined support this trend. So the hypothesis can be change to "Low-cost access to Wi-Fi networks"

- Finally, regarding the H12 "Existence of network of public libraries is necessary" one basic conclusion is that the majority of cities cases currently offer the possibility to citizens to access a big bulk of the available libraries' material online. In this respect, it can be said that libraries are "digital". Thus, the hypothesis can be changed to "Existence of digital libraries network".

Figure 1 depicts the strategic Framework.

Table 7.

Eindhoven		
Hypothesis	**Support Level**	**Explanation**
Design and development		
1. Political and social will is indispensable	+	The Eindhoven Regional Government (SRE) took the initiative to set up the Regional Opportunities Committee after becoming aware of an economic downturn in key economic sectors in the Eindhoven Region. This initiative was the trigger for the city to begin its transformation to a KC and it was supported by the entire society.
2. Strategy and development plan is crucial	+	On 2002 the principles and aims of the Horizon Programme were approved by the SRE's regional board, which also approved the financial contributions for the programme agency and the catalyst fund. The Horizon Programme agency was launched the same year. The Brainport Navigator 2013 strategic programme builds on the successful Horizon Programme and focuses on creating a continuum for knowledge-based economic and social development
3. Financial support and strong investments are necessary	+	The funds for this initiative are mainly covered by the regional budget, but there are other sources as well.
4. Setting-up of agencies to promote the development of knowledge-based regions is essential	+	The Eindhoven Regional Government in cooperation with the organisation NV Rede are mainly responsible to draw up strategic plans regarding KBD
5. International, multi-ethnic character of the city and open, inclusive society is necessary	+	A basic objective of the KC strategy was to promote social cohesion and the smooth integration of people from various backgrounds into city's social and economical life.
6. Metropolitan web site is very important	+	Eindhoven's web-page has attractive design, well-organised knowledge and information and offers a plethora of web-services.
7. Value creation to citizens is indispensable	+	Another basic objective of the KC strategy was the re-engineering of administrative processes of local government so as to offer advanced and added-value services to citizens.
8. Creation of urban innovation engines is significant	+	The City's is focused in the further development of knowledge-intensive manufacturing. The Brainport Navigator 2013 programme targets to build on this solid base and create a region with an innovative climate capable of competing globally.
9. Assurance of knowledge society rights of citizens is substantial	+	The enhancement of equal access and participation rights of citizens is among the strategic objectives. This is expressed by the main strategic pillar which refers to the improvement of social cohesion.
Operation		
10. Low cost access to advanced communication networks is imperative	+	The City offers low-cost access to broadband networks. Wi-Fi network development is the new trend.
11. Research excellence is indispensable	+	The existence of technology parks reinforces significantly the research conducted in the city.
12. Existence of network of public libraries is necessary	+	There is a well-developed network of libraries.

FEATURE RESEARCH CHALLENGES AND CONCLUSIONS

The main objective of this chapter has been to update the initial framework proposed by the authors on 2005, for the design, development and operation of successful KCs. For this purpose, the current status of KCs cases has been re-examined and the level of support of each cases to the hypotheses has been re-assessed. One conclusion is

Table 8.

Melbourne		
Hypothesis	**Support Level**	**Explanation**
Design and development		
1. Political and social will is indispensable	+	The vision for the development of the City as a KC is the result of the cooperation of City Council with the leadership of local government. Society actively supports the related strategy.
2. Strategy and development plan is crucial	+	Melbourne is distinguished for its qualitative and integrated strategic planning concerning its development targets. In this respect, in relation to its development as a KC, specific and well-defined targets and priorities have been described.
3. Financial support and strong investments are necessary	+	In the city's strategic plan there is a special axis referred to the necessity of responsible and effective management of City's financial resources, the financing of its strategy and the attraction of private funds and other financing forms.
4. Setting-up of agencies to promote the development of knowledge-based regions is essential	+	The local government and the City's Council are the organisations responsible to define the KC strategic objectives, to monitor their progress and to implement many of the related interventions.
5. International, multi-ethnic character of the city and open, inclusive society is necessary	+	There is separate axis in the City's strategic plan regarding social equity and cohesion and smooth social and economic integration of immigrants.
6. Metropolitan web site is very important	+	Melbourne city web-page is integrated and well-designed.
7. Value creation to citizens is indispensable	+	Another axis of the strategic plan is related to the design, development and provision of modern/innovative services to citizens and companies through the use of advanced ICT.
8. Creation of urban innovation engines is significant	+	An important strategic objective is the reinforcement of networks among city's actors so as to promote innovation culture in the business sector as well as in everyday life.
9. Assurance of knowledge society rights of citizens is substantial	+	Although it is not referred as specific objective, many of the other objectives defined in the strategic plan contribute to the assurance of knowledge society citizens rights.
Operation		
10. Low cost access to advanced communication networks is imperative	+	Access in broadband networks is low-cost and many free Wi-Fi hotspots are already installed across the city.
11. Research excellence is indispensable	+	The reinforcement of investments in research is an important objective.
12. Existence of network of public libraries is necessary	+	The City of Melbourne has three public libraries. The libraries offer a wide range of facilities, services and resources, including books, CDs, DVDs, magazines, journals and newspapers in a range of languages as well as electronic publications. Library membership is free and open to anyone.

Table 9.

Bilbao		
Hypothesis	**Support Level**	**Explanation**
Design and development		
1. Political and social will is indispensable	+	In the decade of 80's the City faced many difficulties. The local government in cooperation with other actors of local society set the city's development goals and created a KDB plan which has been successfully implemented. Through this procedure, the basis has been set so as even today the development priorities are defined based on a participatory approach which has political and social support.
2. Strategy and development plan is crucial	+	With a view to channelling the strategic reflection, its key areas and core aspects towards projects/initiatives that will enable Bilbao to enhance its position as an international world-class city in the Knowledge Society, the City has defined a strategic plan called "Bilbao 2010: The Strategy"
3. Financial support and strong investments are necessary	+	Local administration funds the initiative with the support of public organizations and private companies.
4. Setting-up of agencies to promote the development of knowledge-based regions is essential	+	The Association "Bilbao Metropoli-30" has been formed on 1991 by public actors, important companies and city's universities so as to be responsible for the implementation and evaluation of the city's development plan. This organisation has continued since then, through participative procedures, to set the strategic development targets. Today the strategy that it promotes it is knowledge-based
5. International, multi-ethnic character of the city and open, inclusive society is necessary	+	The reinforcement of social cohesion and a society open to minorities is described in the latest development plan as a basic factor for the success of the KBD strategy
6. Metropolitan web site is very important	+	Bilbao metropolitan web-page is well-developed.
7. Value creation to citizens is indispensable	+	The added value in every-day life of citizens is in top of the priorities of the strategy.
8. Creation of urban innovation engines is significant	+	Among the top priorities is the creation of a "city for innovation and knowledge". To achieve this target, a suitable environment has to be created providing internet access for all, supporting policies for innovative initiatives and developing intelligent infrastructures (IT systems, equipment for laboratories and areas of research, etc).
9. Assurance of knowledge society rights of citizens is substantial	+	Even it is not referred explicitly as specific strategic objective, many of the other objectives in the strategic plan are contributing to the assurance of knowledge society rights of citizens.
Operation		
10. Low cost access to advanced communication networks is imperative	~	Although the improvement of telecommunications infrastructure of the city is among the targets, the objective of offering low cost access to all is not fully achieved yet.
11. Research excellence is indispensable	+	The reinforcement of research conducted in the city is a priority.
12. Existence of network of public libraries is necessary	~	The city has many libraries but additional actions are needed so as to be better networked and offer online services.

Table 10.

Manchester		
Hypothesis	**Support Level**	**Explanation**
Design and development		
1. Political and social will is indispensable	+	Manchester: Knowledge Capital is a dynamic force for innovation and economic transformation, built around a highly competitive combination of knowledge assets across the Manchester city region. Through a partnership of all ten Greater Manchester authorities, four universities, the strategic health authority, other key public agencies and leading businesses, Manchester: Knowledge Capital is working to secure substantial and sustainable growth
2. Strategy and development plan is crucial	+	Manchester Knowledge Capital has already conducted a strategic plan visioning the future and setting the priority areas that the city should support.
3. Financial support and strong investments are necessary	+	The finance of the actions and projects comes from public and private investments.
4. Setting-up of agencies to promote the development of knowledge-based regions is essential	+	Manchester: Knowledge Capital has a small Executive taking the lead on implementing the various programmes of activity. The Executive Team reports to the Manchester: Knowledge Capital Board - a high level, predominantly private sector group that meets once a quarter to steer ongoing strategy.
5. International, multi-ethnic character of the city and open, inclusive society is necessary	+	Supporting the development of a city-region environment which facilitates business success, provides an outstanding quality of life and is open to all, is one of the first priorities in the Manchester: Knowledge Capital strategy.
6. Metropolitan web site is very important	+	Manchester has seriously upgraded its web-page and now it is fully functional providing e-services to its citizens.
7. Value creation to citizens is indispensable	+	The majority of the selected actions and projects aiming at improving the every-day life of the Manchester citizens.
8. Creation of urban innovation engines is significant	+	The first priority in the Manchester City is Stimulating and supporting increased business innovation from research, science and knowledge. For example "Innovation Manchester" is an initiative aimed at catalysing innovation across the Manchester city region. This initiative has engaged with over 70 private sector leaders and has levered in substantial resources from the National Endowment for Science Technology and the Arts (Nesta) and the North West Development Agency.
9. Assurance of knowledge society rights of citizens is substantial	+	Even it is not referred explicitly as specific strategic objective, many of the objectives in the strategic plan are contributing to the assurance of knowledge society rights of citizens.
Operation		
10. Low cost access to advanced communication networks is imperative	+	Manchester already has a low-cost broadband network while the Wi-Fi network is expanding.
11. Research excellence is indispensable	+	The status with the research is similar with that in innovation (hypothesis 8) while there are public investments in research centres such as: Wellcome Clinical Research Facility, North West Genetic Knowledge Park, UK Biobank Hub.
12. Existence of network of public libraries is necessary	+	There is an extended library network while in parallel most of them provide 24hour access through their on-line versions.

Table 11.

Singapore		
Hypothesis	**Support Level**	**Explanation**
Design and development		
H1	+	The Singaporean government has recognized the need to be developed on a knowledge-based way. Moreover, it seems that citizens and local society fully supports this vision.
H2	+	The Economic Development Board (EDB) of Singapore has launched a knowledge-based 10-year plan to develop Singapore into a vibrant and robust global hub of knowledge-driven industries in manufacturing and traded services with emphasis on technology, innovation and capabilities.
H3	+	The initiative is mainly self-funded by private investments and partially by local administrations' funds.
H4	+	The Economic Development Board (EDB) of Singapore in co-operation with the city's local government are responsible to formulate the strategy.
H5	+	Singapore is regarded as the premier regional hub to attract foreign Multinational Corporations (MNCs) and local enterprises to use it as a production base for high value added products and to provide manufacturing related services for their subsidiaries in the region. Moreover, the city is particularly open to citizens from other nations.
H6	+	Singapore holds an advanced web-page offering access to various services.
H7	+	The provision of services that add value to the everyday life of citizens is among the strategic priorities.
H8	+	The target of EDB is to encourage MNCs to locate more of their key knowledge-intensive activities in Singapore and for local companies to embrace more knowledge-intensive activities and become world-class players, by providing an entrepreneurial environment that embraces innovation.
H9	~	It is not clear if the re-assurance of knowledge society rights of citizens is among the strategic priorities.
Operation		
H10	+	Singapore not-only has a plurality in low-cost internet providers but in free Wi-Fi networks as well.
H11	+	See H8.
H12	+	There is an extended network of libraries, which offer many online services.

that all of cities cases examined on 2005, continue to actively support their KBD through a series of strategies and appropriate actions. Moreover, the majority of the hypotheses continue to be valid, while three of them need to slightly change so as to adapt to prevailing current conditions. Additional KCs cases have been identified.

In terms of future research, it seems that among the most important challenges is to identify and categorize best practices used by KCs leaders so as to be developed in knowledge-based ways. This could contribute to the creation of a global knowledge base of KCs best practices. Furthermore, another challenge is to develop methodologies (based on the proposed strategic framework) which will effectively support local cities' identify the most appropriate best practices for their development as KCs, and adapt them accordingly to their cities.

Table 12.

Total results												
Hypoth-eses	**Evidence of our case study**	**Barce-lona**	**Stock-holm**	**Mon-tréal**	**Mu-nich**	**Dub-lin**	**Delft**	**Eind-hoven**	**Mel-bourne**	**Bil-bao**	**Man-chester**	**Singapore**
Design and development												
H1	Mixed	+	+	+	~	+	+	+	+	+	+	+
H2	Full	+	+	+	+	+	+	+	+	+	+	+
H3	Full	+	+	+	+	+	+	+	+	+	+	+
H4	Mixed	+	~	+	~	+	+	+	+	+	+	+
H5	Full	+	+	+	+	+	+	+	+	+	+	+
H6	Full	+	+	+	+	+	+	+	+	+	+	+
H7	Full	+	+	+	+	+	+	+	+	+	+	+
H8	Full	+	+	+	+	+	+	+	+	+	+	+
H9	Mixed	+	+	–	+	+	–	+	+	+	+	~
Operation												
H10	Full	+	+	+	+	+	+	+	+	~	+	+
H11	Full	+	+	+	+	+	+	+	+	+	+	+
H12	Full	+	+	+	+	+	+	+	+	~	+	+

REFERENCES

Barcelona. (2005). *Metropolitan Strategic Plan of Barcelona Phase 2006/2010.* Retrieved December 9, 2008, from http://www.bcn2000.es/en/publicacions-jornades/publicacions-del-pla-estrategic.aspx?_gIdTema=50&idioma=EN&_gIdContexto=1

Barcelona. (2008). *Barcelona Data Sheet 2008.* Retrieved December 9, 2008, from Ajuntament de Barcelona.Web site: http://w3.bcn.es/V44/Home/V44PublicacionsHomeCanalCtl/0,3729,71420027_75408511_3,00.html

Centre for International Competitiveness. (2008). *World Knowledge Competitiveness Index 2008.* Cardiff: Cardiff School of Management, University of Wales Institute.

City of Melbourne. (2005). *City Plan 2010: Towards a Thriving and Sustainable City. Delft.* (2009). Retrieved January 9, 2009, from http://www.delft.nl/

Dublin Chamber of Commerce. (2004). *Dublin 2020: Our vision for the future of the city.* Retrieved January 9, 2009 from http://www.dublinchamber.ie/Uploads/2020%20Vision.pdf

Dublin Chamber of Commerce. (2008). *Developing a Knowledge City Region A TEN POINT PLAN.* Retrieved January 9, 2009, from http://www.dubchamber.ie/uploads/Knowledge_City_Region.pdf

Eindhoven. (2006). *Brainport Navigator 2013: Beyond Lisbon!* Brainport. Retrieved January 9, 2009, from http://www.brainport.nl/Brainport_C01/ShowDocument.asp?OriginCode=H&OriginComID=32&OriginModID=2099&OriginItemID=1020&CustID=354&ComID=32&DocID=77&SessionID=~SessionID~&Download=true&Ext=.pdf

Eller, B. (2006). *Creativity strategies in Munich, Creative Industries – The impact of creative industries on City- Region competitiveness.* Retrieved January 9, 2009, from www.compete-eu.org/events/barcelona1/6_BERNHARD_ELLER.pps

Ergazakis, K., Metaxiotis, K., & Psarras, J. (2005). An Emerging Pattern of Successful Knowledge Cities' Main Features . In Carrillo, F. (Ed.), *Knowledge Cities: Approaches, Experiences and Perspectives*. Amsterdam: Elsevier.

Ergazakis, K., Metaxiotis, K., & Psarras, J. (2006). A Coherent Framework for Building Successful Knowledge Cities in the Context of the Knowledge-Based Economy. *Knowledge Management Research & Practice*, *4*, 46–59. doi:10.1057/palgrave.kmrp.8500089

Horizon Programme. (2008). Retrieved December 11, 2008, from http://www.programmahorizon.nl

Melbourne Vice-Chancellors' Forum. (2007). *Melbourne Australia's knowledge capital.* City of Melbourne. Retrieved January 10, 2009, from http://www.melbourne.vic.gov.au/rsrc/Publications/KnowledgeCapital/3030-Uni_study_screen.pdf

Montréal. (2002). *Imagining Building Montréal 2025: A World of Creativity and Opportunities*. Retrieved January 10, 2009, from http://ville.montreal.qc.ca/pls/portal/docs/page/montreal2025_en/media/Documents/Montreal_2025_Summary.pdf

Montréal. (2007). *Montréal's First Strategic Plan for Sustainable Development 2007- 2009 Phase*. Retrieved January 10, 2009, http://ville.montréal.qc.ca/portal/page?_pageid=4176,4738953&_dad=portal&_schema=PORTAL

Munich. (2005). *Munich – City of Knowledge*. Department of Labor and Economic Development. Retrieved January 10, 2009 from http://www.compete-eu.org/publications/Munich_cityofknowledge_2005.pdf

Singapore. (2009). *Singapore Economic Development Board*. Retrieved January 10, 2009, from http://www.edb.gov.sg/edb/sg/en_uk/index.html

World Capital Institute. (2009). Retrieved December 11, 2008, from http://www.worldcapitalinstitute.org/makci.html

Yigitcanlar, T., O'Connor, K., & Westerman, C. (2008). The making of knowledge cities: Melbourne's knowledge-based urban development experience. *Cities Journal*, *25*, 63–72. doi:10.1016/j.cities.2008.01.001

ENDNOTES

1. Available at http://www.bm30.es/plan/pri_uk.html
2. Available at http://www.bm30.es/plan/estrategia_uk.html
3. Available at http://www.bm30.es/plan/estrategia_uk.html
4. Based on material available at http://www.manchester-enterprises.com/fundingprogrammes/nwregional/nwrap_index.htm

Chapter 3
Attracting and Retaining Knowledge Workers:
The Impact of Quality of Place in the Case of Montreal

Sébastien Darchen
York University, Canada

Diane-Gabrielle Tremblay
Télé-Université (UQÀM), Canada

ABSTRACT

A concentration of knowledge workers, including scientists and engineers, has been identified by recent works as an element fostering economic growth in metropolitan areas. The authors' aim in this chapter is to study the factors influencing the mobility of graduate students in science and technology. The creative class thesis has emphasized the fact that criteria related to the quality of place have a positive impact on the attraction of talents and on economic development. This thesis was the basis for the authors' research. In this paper, they assimilate the workforce in science and technology to the concept of knowledge workers. The authors compared the influence of criteria related to the quality of place on the mobility of students with other criteria related to career opportunities and to the social network. They collected the data through an on-line questionnaire and they also proceeded to interviews with students in science and technology. The authors present in this chapter the results of their research for Montreal. With a quantitative analysis, they show that while Montreal is often considered as a very attractive place, the criteria related to the quality of place play a secondary role in the attraction and retention of the population studied, while those related to the career opportunities dominate. This leads to nuance the theories that highlight the importance of place versus job opportunities, and shows that while the quality of place may have an influence on the mobility patterns of knowledge workers, job opportunities have more impact on the attraction/retention of this professional category.

DOI: 10.4018/978-1-61520-721-3.ch003

INTRODUCTION

Recent research has demonstrated that the concentration of scientists and engineers are an asset for the economic growth of metropolitan areas (Beckstead & Brown, 2006; Beckstead, Brown & Gellatly, 2008). These works are inspired by both the human capital theory and by the creative class thesis. The creative class thesis has emphasized some criteria related to the quality of place which we used in the construction of our questionnaire (the lifestyle, the social and cultural activities, the level of tolerance or the openness to creativity) to test if they would have an impact on the attraction and retention of *talents*. We took the workforce in science and technology as an example of a professional category which is part of the group of the professionals of the creative class; in this paper we also explain why this professional category can also be considered as being part of the group of knowledge workers. We tested the criteria on a population of students in science and technology; while this group may not be perfectly equivalent to the actual knowledge workers in the field, they appear to be a very good approximation, since they intend to work in this field. In the questionnaire, we asked them what would be their career objectives and where they intend to realize them. Our objective here is to gain a better understanding of the criteria influencing the mobility of students in science and technology once they have graduated and to conclude on the consequences for the design of policies regarding knowledge-based development. We present in this paper the quantitative analysis of the results for the students who answered the questionnaire in Montreal. We are adding to this quantitative analysis some qualitative material based on interviews realized with students in science and technology between September 2007 and January 2008. In the first part of the chapter, we present briefly the principles of the creative class thesis and we compare it with the human capital theory. We then present the results of our research for Montreal and our conclusion on the relevance of the criteria related to the quality of place regarding the attraction and retention of students in science and technology, as a proxy for knowledge workers.

BACKGROUND

Research in urban economics has demonstrated that a concentration of human capital has a positive impact on economic growth (Shapiro, 2003; Simon, 1998) and that the level of human capital (in terms of the population's level of education) constitutes a competitive advantage (Glaeser & Saiz, 2003; Glaeser, Sheinkmen & Sheifer, 1995; Shapiro, 2005). Therefore, the capacity of cities to attract a qualified and high-skilled workforce such as engineers and scientists is an asset regarding economic growth and urban competitiveness. Students in science and technology are supposed, once they graduate, to be part of the creative class and also according to recent research, the workforce in science and technology as a professional occupation is supposed to have a major impact on regional development (Beckstead and Brown, 2006). This workforce can also be assimilated to the concept of knowledge workers, which refers to a workforce with a high level of education and which can be defined according to their professional activity; this includes engineers but also professionals in the financial domain, amongst others. Peter Drucker (1994) coined this term and refers to knowledge workers as professionals with a high education background who apply their knowledge to the development of new products and services; this type of workforce is considered as a key component of success in the present economic context.

Florida, Mellender and Stolarick (2008) as well as Florida (2002a) have suggested an alternative measure of human capital based on the professional occupations which are described in the acronym TAPE (Technology and Innovation,

Arts and Culture, Professionals and Management, Education). Florida's work on the creative class has many similarities to the human-capital model but is also related to the urban-amenities model; Florida presented his approach to economic development (the creative-capital perspective) as an improved approach compared with the human capital model (Manning Thomas & Darnton, 2006). Florida (2003, p. 8) differentiates his theory of creative capital from the human capital model in two respects: 1. It identifies a type of human capital, creative people, as being key to economic growth; 2. It identifies the underlying factors that shape the location decisions of these people.

Florida's approach is part of the third model of metropolitan economic development identified by Manning Thomas & Darnton (2006) - the two other models being the social capital and the human capital models - which is based on the human capital model with an emphasis on urban amenities. The work of Clark (2004) also emphasizes the fact that the quality of place is a necessary condition to attract talented people. As mentioned by Manning Thomas & Darnton (2006), the work of Jane Jacobs already focused on the link between the attractiveness of a neighbourhood and the attraction of talented people. The creative class thesis has mainly contributed to emphasize the relevance of urban amenities and criteria related to the quality of place (level of tolerance, openness to creativity, lifestyle, etc.) in the attraction of human capital. However, no consensus has been reached yet regarding the effect of urban amenities on the attraction of human capital. Recent works have shown that we can predict economic growth according to the concentration of human capital; however, this was not necessarily linked to urban amenities since metropolitan areas have experienced rising wages with or without urban amenities (Glaeser, Kolko & Saiz, 2001; Glaeser & Saiz, 2003). Beckstead and Brown (2006) indicate that a combination of human capital remains a better indicator to predict than urban amenities. Beckstead and Brown (2006) have also demonstrated that there is a link between the size of the city and the part of employment in science and technology as well as its prospect of growing with time. Bigger cities have a larger number of firms which require more specialised types of human capital like scientists and engineers (Beckstead & Brown, 2006). Therefore, it appeared necessary to evaluate if various characteristics of cities have an influence on the attraction of scientists and engineers. With the results of our quantitative analysis, we show that the criteria related to the quality of place play a secondary role compared with criteria regarding career opportunities, even for a city such as Montreal, generally considered quite attractive, even in Florida's work (Stolarick, Florida & Musante, 2005). We complete the results with an analysis of interviews which shows that the criteria related to the quality of place play a part in the decision of choosing a place to work but these criteria alone cannot explain the attraction or retention of graduate students in science and technology.

ISSUES AND CONTROVERSIES

The creative class thesis has generated a number of criticisms since its publication (Darchen & Tremblay, 2008a). We synthesize these criticisms here. Some mention that the creative class includes different professional categories which could have very different tastes, especially regarding the urban environment they wish to live in (Markusen, 2006). Using the concept of class is therefore problematic because the author is not presenting a class defined by criteria of class interest, outlook or social patterning of behaviours (Markusen, 2006). Therefore, it could be risky to frame policies regarding urban development based solely on this thesis of economic development. Florida (2005, 2002b) has emphasised the fact that creative workers are considering other factors than the salary or criteria related to career opportunities in their choice of a city to live in;

for example, cultural and recreational amenities appealing to young professionals are supposed to contribute to the attraction of professionals from the 'creative class'. However, some research has also stressed the importance of family ties, social networks and familiarity with a particular location regarding labor mobility (Cherry & Tsournos, 2001). Economic research has also demonstrated that wage levels in a city or region can compensate for the absence of amenities (Dumond, Hirsch & MacPherson, 1999). In a study concerning Pittsburgh, researchers showed that salary and access to continuing education (criteria related to career opportunities) were each more than three times as important as amenities to explain the retention of students (Hansen, Ban & Huggins, 2003). As we see, there is not yet a clear consensus on the factors which motivate graduate students in their job search process. In terms of knowledge-based development, the creative class thesis can serve as a base to the development of policies for the attraction of knowledge workers and this is why we address this issue.

Our objective in this chapter is to find out if the students in science and technology (as a future professional category part of the group of knowledge workers) consider the quality of place (the criteria emphasized in the creative class thesis) as an important component in their choice of a place to work once they have graduated, compared with criteria related to career opportunities. We thus measured the importance of two criteria related to career opportunities (the quality of work and the level of salary) as well as that of the criteria concerning the quality of place in the quantitative analysis of data collected with our questionnaire.

METHODOLOGY

Our method of data collection is based on the use of an on-line questionnaire which was filled by students in science and technology. Our sampling is composed of 529 students from programs in science and technology of francophone universities in Montreal: UQÀM, Université de Montréal, ETS (École de Technologie Supérieure), École Polytechnique de Montréal. We developed the questionnaire in order to evaluate the criteria influencing the mobility of students once they have graduated. Therefore, we asked them to anticipate some of the decisions they would take regarding their career orientation once they had graduated (regarding the place of work and the factors influencing this choice). The questionnaire aims at analyzing the following issues: the criteria influencing the attractiveness of Montreal as a place to study; the retention factors for graduate students, the factors influencing the attraction of the workforce, the influence of the lifestyle in Montreal as a retention factor, the issue related to the place of living in the metropolitan area (city-centre vs. suburbs), the destination once graduated and the factors influencing this choice. Regarding the criteria used in the questionnaire, we propose the following definitions:

- *Quality of the university*: this refers to the quality of the university as an institution and also to the quality of the programs available in science and technology.
- *Quality of work*: this refers to a work which is stimulating and which corresponds to the academic background of the student and to his or her career objectives.
- *Quality of life*: this refers to characteristics like the level of security, the social welfare, the quality of the urban environment, the quality of public transport, etc.
- *Level of tolerance*: this refers to low barriers of entry to human capital (e.g: ethnic and cultural diversity are elements having a positive impact on the level of tolerance of a city according to the creative class thesis).
- *Lifestyle*: this refers to the elements offered by a city in terms of lifestyle. It includes the possibility to have access to cultural

and social activities. In our questionnaire, we refer to the following characteristics: international festivals, a diversity in terms of restaurants, the nightlife and art galleries.

- *Openness to creativity*: this criteria is linked to the level of tolerance of a city. According to Florida (2003), places gain a creativity advantage from their ability to attract people from a wide range of backgrounds.
- *Authenticity of the urban milieu*: this refers to the capacity of the urban milieu to offer a variety of opportunities in terms of entertainment, nightlife, and cultural activities.
- *Social network*: it refers to the social environment of the students; the social relationships developed by the students in the city (family ties or other social relationships)

Regarding the method of data analysis, we used SPSS 16 software and we proceeded to statistical tests (using the non-parametric Wilcoxon tests) to determine the order of ranking for the different criteria used in the questionnaire. We also evaluated the size of the difference between the criteria using the scale of Cohen's standard. Criteria are ranked in the tables according to their level of relevance. We present in the tables the means regarding the ranks and we discuss the results according to the two types of tests presented in this paper. However, tables 1, 7, 8 and 11 present the results using percentages.

We also did nine interviews, and we used a thematic analysis using NVIVO8 software. We explored the following themes: the choice of Montreal as a place to study, the criteria influencing the choice of a destination once graduated (criteria related to career opportunities, the social network and criteria related to the quality of place), the attractiveness of Montreal as a place to live.

EMPIRICAL FINDINGS

The theory of human capital or of the creative capital implies that the workforce in science and technology is mobile and according to Florida (2002), looking for cities which offer urban environments with characteristics appealing to creative workers. In our sample, however, all the students do not consider themselves as a mobile workforce.

We found that approximately half of the students had already an idea of the place where they intended to realize their career objectives. We considered these students as non-mobile since they have a clear idea of the place where they intend to work once they graduate. The part which is considered as mobile has not yet (when answering the questionnaire) a clear idea where it wishes to work once graduated and is still hesitating between different destinations.

Table 1 shows that approximately half of the students considered themselves as non-mobile, or less influenced by the criteria related to different places in the process of looking for a first employment. Table 2 shows that students from abroad and born in Montreal tend to be more in the category of the non-mobile in comparison with students coming from the rest of the province of Quebec, who have a tendency to be less mobile (or have already a clear idea where they intend to realize their career objectives).

Table 1. Mobility according to the origins of students (%)

	Montreal (n=115)	Quebec (n=252)	Abroad (n=116)	Total (n=483)
Mobile	59.1	46.8	59.5	53.2
Non- mobile	40.9	53.2	40.5	46.8

Source: Our research questionnaire.

Table 2. Montreal as a place to study

	Montreal (n=529)
Quality of the university	1.36
Quality of life	1.97
Level of tolerance	2.66

(scale: 1= very important; 2= somewhat important; 3= not so important)
Source: Our research questionnaire.

The first question concerns the factors influencing the attraction to Montreal as a place to study. Students were asked to rank three factors: the quality of the university and of the programs available in Montreal in science and technology, the quality of life and finally, the level of tolerance. The results of the Wilcoxon tests show that there is a significant difference between the three factors proposed in Question 1. The quality of the university is more important than the quality of life ($T = 105\ 328$, $p < 0.05$, $r = 0.33$)[1] and the quality of life is more important than the level of tolerance ($T = 110\ 658.5$, $p < 0.05$, $r = 0.38$). The effect sizes of the differences are considered to be small[2]. Moreover, the quality of the university is also more important than the level of tolerance ($T = 129\ 046.5$, $p < 0.05$, $r = 0.54$), and the effect size is medium. Our conclusion is that the quality of the university is fairly more important than the level of tolerance and is a bit more important than the quality of life according to our analysis; based on the scale of Cohen's standard.

Students have thus emphasised the criteria of the quality of the university and much less the criteria related to the quality of place. Criteria of the quality of the city of Montreal (the quality of life and the level of tolerance) have less impact on the attraction of students.

The nine interviews done with students involved in programs of science and technology in Montreal confirm the results of the questionnaire on the relevance of the criteria related to the university/program in science and technology as the main criteria regarding the decision of choosing Montreal as a place to study (Interview 1, 2, 3, 4, 5, 7). The issue of proximity and of the social network is also present (Interview 5, 9). One of the students mentioned that his decision is linked to personal reasons (social network) combined with the proximity of the program of studies (Interview 9). We can mention that none of the students interviewed mentioned elements related to the quality of the urban environment as a criteria in their choice to study in Montreal.

Table 3 shows the results regarding the factors influencing the retention of students in Montreal once they have graduated. Students were asked to rank five factors: the quality of work, the social network, the lifestyle, the quality of life and the cost of living. According to the Wilcoxon tests, we have significant differences between these factors. The quality of work is more important than the social network ($T = 92\ 888$, $p < 0.05$, $r = 0.21$) but the effect size of the difference is considered to be small according to Cohen's standard (based on the number of respondents). The quality of work is also more important than the lifestyle ($T = 105\ 505.5$, $p < 0.05$, $r = 0.32$) and than the quality of life ($T = 111\ 328$, $p < 0.05$, $r = 0.37$) and these differences are considered to be small. The quality of work is also more important than the criteria related to the cost of living ($T = 123\ 917$, $p < 0.05$, $r = 0.49$) and this effect size of the difference is small but close to medium size. The criteria of the social network is also more important than the criteria related to the quality of place (lifestyle and quality of life) ($T = 82\ 839$, $p < 0.05$, $r = 0.12$) and ($T = 90\ 073$, $p < 0.05$, $r = 0.18$) and the effect sizes

Table 3. Montreal as a place to work: retention factors

	Montreal (n=525)
Quality of work	2.02
Social network	2.69
Lifestyle	3.09
Quality of life	3.30
Cost of living	3.88

(scale: 1= very important; 2= important; 3= somewhat important; 4= not so important; 5= not at all important)
Source: Our research questionnaire

of the differences are considered o be small. We can also mention that the criteria of the lifestyle is more important than the criteria related to the quality of life (T = 77 454, $p < 0.05$, r = 0.07) but the effect size of the difference is extremely small between the two criteria.

The criteria regarding the quality of place (the lifestyle and the quality of life) are thus less important than the quality of work or of the social network; however those criteria are more important than the criteria of the cost of living (T = 123 917, $p < 0.05$, r = 0.25); (T = 94 396.5, $p < 0.05$, r = 0.23) and the effect sizes of the differences are considered to be small in this last case.

The interviews confirm that the quality of work is the most important criteria related to their decision of staying in Montreal once they graduate. The students also reckon that they often compromise and that they are considering different elements in their choice of staying in Montreal once they graduate. They prioritize the criteria related to the quality of work but they also consider the quality of Montreal as a place to live in (in terms of ethnic diversity, cultural activities and social interactions) (Interview 3, 4, 6, 7, 8, 9). The interviews thus confirm that the quality of work (a work related to their program of studies and to their career objectives) would be the main criteria. The social network is also mentioned in the interviews (Interview 3, 4, 9). When mentioned to explain the choice of staying, the characteristics of the city (e.g: cultural activities, or ethnic diversity) are considered as contributing to the quality of life but the students mentioning them are also evaluating their career opportunities in Montreal at the same time (Interview 1, 2, 3, 4, 6, 7, 8, 9). To summarize, students interviewed balance the different criteria (social network, career opportunities, criteria related to the quality of place) in their choice of staying in Montreal and elements related to the quality of place are part of this decision, but these criteria alone are not significant to explain the decision of choosing Montreal rather than another place to work once graduated.

We asked the students, if they were not living in Montreal, what would attract them in this city as a place to live. They were asked to rank four factors: the quality of work, the level of salary, the openness to creativity and the level of tolerance. The criteria related to the quality of work is more important than the level of salary (T = 110 226.5, $p < 0.05$, r = 0.37) but the effect size of the difference is considered to be small. The criteria related to the quality of work is also more important than the criteria related to the quality of place (openness to creativity, level of tolerance) (T = 122 624, $p < 0.05$, r = 0.47); (T = 127 628.5, $p < 0.05$, r = 0.51) and the effect size of the difference is small (close to medium) in the case of the openness to creativity and of medium size in the case of the level of tolerance. The criteria of the level of salary is more important than the criteria related to the quality of place (openness

Table 4. Montreal as a place to work: attraction factors

	Montreal (n=528)
Quality of work	1.53
Level of salary	2.35
Openness to creativity	2.82
Level of tolerance	3.28

(scale: 1= important; 2= somewhat important; 3= not so important; 4= not at all important)
Source: Our research questionnaire

to creativity and the level of tolerance) ($T = 90640.5$, $p < 0.05$, $r = 0.18$); ($T = 106\ 560$, $p < 0.05$, $r = 0.32$) but the size of the differences are considered to be small.

We can conclude that the quality of work is more important than the criteria related to the quality of place and that this difference is fairly important when we compare with the criteria of the level of tolerance. The interviews confirm that the quality of work (as defined in the methodology section) is more significant than the level of salary to explain the attraction of students in Montreal; this criteria is mentioned in two interviews but the criteria is compared with the quality of work and the latest remains a priority (Interview 1, 3). The openness to creativity is mentioned twice in the interviews, students refer to it as a characteristic which is linked to social interactions in the urban environment and contributing to a better productivity at work (Interview 5, 7). The level of tolerance is mentioned in three interviews and is understood as the capacity of a city to welcome newcomers (Interview 5, 6, 8). Regarding this point, the ethnic diversity and the two cultures (francophone and anglophone) characterising Montreal are perceived as an asset (Interview 8).

The students were asked to rank four factors regarding what would attract them in a city in general once they graduate: the quality of work, the level of salary, the authenticity of the urban milieu and the level of tolerance. According to the Wilcoxon tests, there are significant differences between the four factors proposed. The criteria related to the quality of work is more important than the criteria related to the level of salary ($T = 111808.5$, $p < 0.05$, $r = 0.4$) and the effect size of the difference is considered to be small but close to medium size. The criteria related to the quality of work is also more important than the criteria related to the quality of place (authenticity of the urban milieu and the level of tolerance) ($T = 96\ 603$, $p < 0.05$, $r = 0.51$); ($T = 132\ 647$, $p < 0.05$, $r = 0.57$) and the effect sizes of the differences are medium. The level of salary is more important than the criteria related to the quality of place (authenticity of the urban milieu and the level of tolerance) ($T = 96\ 603$, $p < 0.05$, $r = 0.25$); ($T = 118\ 517.5$, $p < 0.05$, $r = 0.44$).

The results shown in table 5 confirm that the criteria related to the quality of work is the most important to explain the attraction of graduate students in a city; however, if the level of salary is more important than the criteria related to the quality of place, the effect size of the difference is smaller between the level of salary and the authenticity of the urban milieu than between the quality of work and the level of salary.

The authenticity of the urban milieu is never mentioned directly in the interviews, but students refer to the lifestyle characterising Montreal, and mention that ethnic and cultural diversity contribute to create a vibrant living environment which we do not find necessarily if staying outside of the city (Quebec regions) (Interview 5, 9). The lifestyle of Montreal is viewed as an asset because it is easy to find all kinds of entertaining activities

Table 5. A city as a place to work: attraction factors

	Montreal (n=525)
Quality of work	1.44
Level of salary	2.22
Authenticity of the urban milieu	2.86
Level of tolerance	3.46

(scale: 1= important; 2= somewhat important; 3= not so important; 4= not at all important)
Source: Our research questionnaire

(Interview 5). However a student mentions that you can find social activities anywhere and that you do not have to be in an urban environment to find entertainment (Interview 8).

We asked the students to rank various activities regarding their contribution to the quality of the lifestyle as shown in table 6. Students in science and technology estimated that the criteria related to international festivals are more important than the variety of restaurants ($T = 78\ 848.5$, $p < 0.05$, $r = 0.09$); the effect size of the differences between the criteria are small. This criteria of the international festivals is also more important than the ones regarding the nightlife and art galleries ($T = 91\ 372$, $p < 0.05$, $r = 0.2$); ($T = 117\ 751$, $p < 0.05$, $r = 0.44$) and the effect sizes of the differences are small.

Our aim was also to measure if these activities could have an impact on the retention of students compared with career opportunities available in another city. We then asked the students if a lack of these activities in another city but with better career opportunities could make them hesitate to leave Montreal. They had four choices: Yes (they would hesitate); It is likely (that they would hesitate); It is unlikely (that they would hesitate); No (they will not hesitate).

As shown in table 7, career opportunities still dominate; indeed, a majority of students (62.8%) considers that it is unlikely or that they would not hesitate to leave Montreal for better career opportunities. However, table 7 also shows that these activities contribute to the quality of the lifestyle and would have an impact on their decision for 37.2% of the students (the respondents considering that they would hesitate or likely hesitate to leave Montreal for better career opportunities). This confirms partly that the lifestyle characterising Montreal is an asset regarding the retention of students but that career opportunities have a stronger impact on the attraction of students.

We also asked the students where they would rather live once they have graduated: in the suburbs or in the city-centre. We wanted to see if, in line with the theories presented above, the workforce in science and technology is attracted towards an urban living environment.

Table 6. Activities contributing to the quality of the lifestyle

	Montreal (n=524)
International festivals	2.03
Variety of restaurants	2.24
Nightlife	2.56
Art galleries	3.15

(scale: 1= important; 2= somewhat important; 3= not so important; 4= not at all important)
Source: Our research questionnaire

Table 7. Impact of social and cultural activities on the retention of students in Montreal compared with career opportunities in another city (%)

Montreal (n=524)	Yes	Likely	Unlikely	No
Activities	13.5	23.7	38.5	24.3

Source: Our research questionnaire

Table 8. Choice regarding the place of living (%)

	Montreal (n=521)
Suburbs	62.8
City-centre	37.2

Source: Our research questionnaire

Almost two third of the students would rather live in the suburbs of Montreal rather than in the city-centre. This confirms that students in science and technology are not necessarily looking for vibrant living environments to live in, even if they appreciate the lifestyle of Montreal; and this somewhat contradicts what the creative class thesis puts forward.

Regarding the reasons for choosing the suburbs as a place of living, students had to rank three criteria: the space available, the lifestyle and the cost of living. According to the Wilcoxon tests, we have significant differences between the criteria. The space available in the suburbs is significantly more important than the lifestyle ($T = 34\ 153$, $p < 0.05$, $r = 0.18$) but the size effect of the difference is small; this criteria is also more important than the cost of living ($T = 44\ 322$, $p < 0.05$, $r = 0.42$) and the effect size of the difference is close to medium.

The Wilcoxon tests show that there are significant differences between the three factors, the criteria of the lifestyle being significantly more important than the criteria of the proximity of commercial activities ($T = 15\ 200$, $p < 0.05$, $r = 0.48$) and of the level of tolerance ($T = 16\ 478$, $p < 0.05$, $r = 0.48$); the size effect of the difference is considered to be small but close to a medium size effect. The criteria of the proximity of commercial activities is significantly more important than the criteria of the level of tolerance ($T = 11\ 290$, $p < 0.05$, $r = 0.47$) and the size of the difference is considered to be small. Lifestyle is the main criteria for choosing to live in the city-centre but the results of table 8 confirm that a majority of students are not necessarily attracted by urban environments to live in.

In a way, this contradicts the assertion of Florida regarding the fact that creative workers find urban lifestyles more appealing than the lifestyle characterising the suburban way of life. This also confirms the findings of Markusen (2006) about the fact that the creative class includes professional categories with different tastes regarding their ways of living.

In the interviews, students mention the fact that living in the city-centre offers better opportunities regarding the accessibility to transportation and cultural activities (Interview 5, 7, 8, 9). Living in a suburban environment is also considered as an environment which is not encouraging social interactions (Interview 7). Regarding the choice of living in the suburbs, a student mentions that this living environment is more residential and more appropriate for raising a family (Interview 6).

A majority of our respondents choose a city in Quebec rather than a city in Canada or in Europe, and a city in the U.S in the least chosen destination.

Table 9. Reasons for choosing the suburbs

	Montreal (n=326)
Space available	1.58
Lifestyle	1.91
Cost of living	2.5

Source: Our research questionnaire

Table 10. Reasons for choosing the city-centre

	Montreal (n=195)
Lifestyle	1.4
Proximity of commercial activities	2.07
Level of tolerance	2.69

Source: Our research questionnaire

This choice is probably due to the fact that we have a majority of students who come from the province of Quebec and these students tend to prefer a city in Quebec (74.9%). Students coming from abroad are choosing a city in Canada or in Europe rather than in Quebec. Students born in Montreal would choose a city in Quebec or in Europe and then a city in Canada. The francophone culture could be an element to explain that students born in the province (from Quebec and from Montreal) tend to be less mobile and would rather remain in Quebec for their first employment.

The last question concerns the factors which would influence the choice of another city than Montreal once the students have graduated. The students were asked to rank four factors: the quality of work, the quality of life, the level of salary and the level of tolerance. According to the Wilcoxon tests, there are significant differences between the four factors proposed. The criteria related to the quality of life is more important than the criteria of the quality of work ($T = 115\ 010$, $p < 0.05$, $r = 0.007$) but the effect size of the difference is extremely small. The criteria of the quality of life is more important than the level of salary and than the level of tolerance ($T = 97\ 626$, $p < 0.05$, $r = 0.26$); ($T = 127\ 739$, $p < 0.05$, $r = 0.43$) and the effect sizes of differences are considered to be small. The criteria of the quality of work is more important than the level of salary ($T = 102\ 742$, $p < 0.05$, $r = 0.32$) and the size of the difference is considered to be small. The criteria of the quality of work is more important than the criteria of the level of tolerance ($T = 127\ 877$, $p < 0.05$, $r = 0.54$) and the effect size of the difference is considered to be medium.

We thus observe that the students in science and technology would leave Montreal for a city which offers a better quality of life, this criteria is slightly more important than the quality of work (although the effect size of the difference is very small). The criteria regarding the level of salary and the level of tolerance are secondary to explain the choice of leaving Montreal for another city. We can explain the results of Table 12 by the fact that our respondents are not necessarily satisfied with the quality of life in Montreal and might be attracted by a better quality of life in another city once they have graduated. The fact that we have a majority of respondents coming from the Quebec regions could also be an explanation to these results.

Table 11. Destination once graduated according to the origins of students (%)

	Montreal (n=108)	Quebec (n=247)	Abroad (n=102)	Total (n=457)
A city in Quebec	51.9	74.9	16.7	55.8
A city in Canada	14.8	10.5	41.2	18.7
A city in Europe	27.8	11.3	26.5	18.7
A city in the U.S	5.5	3.3	15.6	6.8

Source: Our research questionnaire

Table 12. Criteria influencing the choice to leave Montreal for another city

	Montreal (n=522)
Quality of life	1.87
Quality of work	1.9
Level of salary	2.58
Level of tolerance	3.64

(scale: 1= important; 2= somewhat important; 3= not so important; 4= not at all important)
Source: Our research questionnaire

DISCUSSION

Our results show that the criteria related to the quality of work is the most relevant to understand the mobility of students in science and technology once they have graduated: graduate students would go where they will find a work corresponding to their career objectives. This can also be considered an indicator of the factors influencing the mobility of knowledge workers. We have different results in table 12, the criteria related to the quality of work is in second position in the ranking behind the criteria of the quality of life. This is due to the fact that we are asking our respondents about the criteria influencing their decision to leave Montreal and in that case the quality of life is a concern for the students.

Although the level of salary has an influence, it has a lesser influence on the mobility of students than the quality of work (as defined in the methodology section). Although the effect size of the difference is small, the criteria related to the quality of place are less relevant than the criteria related to work opportunities to explain the mobility of students once they graduate.

In the case of the retention of students, as shown in table 2, the criteria related to the quality of work and to the social network are more relevant to explain the retention of students in Montreal than the criteria related to the quality of place (lifestyle and quality of life). Moreover, regarding the retention of students, activities contributing to the quality of the lifestyle are not considered by a majority of students (62.8%) as having a major impact on their decision of leaving Montreal if they had better career opportunities elsewhere.

We also observed that a majority of students in science and technology would rather live in the suburbs. It is a clear indication that students in science and technology are not necessarily looking for vibrant urban environments to live in. Our research also shows that other criteria may influence the mobility of graduate students. In fact, students coming from the province of Quebec tend to be less mobile than the rest of the sample (table 1). This group is less mobile geographically than the two other groups (table 10). The origins of students may have an influence on the results and it is likely that for most of the respondents from the Quebec regions, the destination of Montreal is not necessarily a choice bur largely determined by the offer of programs, although we need to investigate this point further.

LIMITS AND FUTURE RESEARCH DIRECTIONS

Our research has analyzed the intentions of students who will soon be part of the creative class and the group of knowledge workers, as scientists and engineers are considered to be part of these caterogories[3]; of course a research on students' aspirations may be different from actual behaviours of these students in the future. Nevertheless, our results present a first exploratory analysis of the impact of criteria related to the quality of place in the decision process of these professional categories when choosing a place to work. We are also aware that our research analyzes the mobility of a given professional category of the creative class, and not all of it.

We have shown in this chapter that the origin of students has an influence on the results concerning the mobility and regarding the place of destination once the students have graduated. The results obtained for Montreal could also be compared with another city. We have collected the same kind of data for Ottawa and we will soon compare the results on these two cities.

CONCLUSION

Our aim in this chapter was to compare the relevance of the criteria related to the quality of place with criteria concerning career opportunities. We found that criteria related to the quality of place are generally less relevant. The interviews also confirm that students take into consideration criteria related to the quality of place but this remains secondary in their decision, and those criteria are always balanced with criteria related to career opportunities (quality of work) or to the social network.

Criteria related to the quality of place do not appear to have a major impact on the retention of students. Moreover, a criteria like the social network has more impact on the retention of graduate students. Students in science and technology also have a preference for suburban living environments and the main reason mentioned is the space available. It is therefore important to make a distinction between professional categories within the creative class as all of them are not necessarily striving for urban living environments.

Our results also show that our respondents would leave Montreal for a better quality of life and this can be explained by the fact that the students in science and technology did not necessarily chose to come and study in Montreal; we are thinking of the students coming from the Quebec regions for whom coming to study in Montreal is not necessarily a choice. Our results also show that it would be rather risky to base policies aiming at the retention of graduate students in science and technology solely on the principles of the creative thesis of economic development as these results may vary according to the origins of students, as has been shown here and elsewhere (Darchen and Tremblay, 2008b).

The main findings of this research is therefore that from a practical point of view, the implementation of policies with an emphasis only on criteria related to the quality of place would not necessarily have an impact on the attraction and retention of knowledge workers as this professional category is considering other criteria in the decision to settle or to stay in a place. In particular, the criteria related to the social network and to career opportunities have more influence on the mobility of this workforce; in the case of Montreal for example a better quality of place will not necessarily change the fact that Montreal will continue to attract students and therefore knowledge workers from the rest of the province of Quebec; as we mentioned, the influence of criteria related to the quality of place needs to be discussed with other criteria. A policy regarding knowledge-based development and aiming at the attraction/retention of knowledge workers cannot solely be based on criteria related to the quality of place as it is emphasised in the creative class thesis, since the development of career opportunities (employment related to the aspirations of graduate students) has more influence on the attraction/retention of this professional category as was shown here.

Our research has thus not only theoretical implications since it leads to nuance the creative class thesis and its indications concerning the mobility of knowledge workers, but it also has practical implications, in terms of the types of policies that cities can put forward to attract these professional categories. It also shows that this professional group is not uniform, since the origin of the students (Montreal, Québec or abroad) makes a difference in some of the elements regarding choice of localization, choice of work and the factors that attract students and future knowledge workers to a given city. The research needs to be pursued, but we have here clear indications that not all members of the knowledge workers' group will react the same way to a given city's amenities and, more importantly, that job opportunities are extremely important. We saw that while Montreal is often considered a very attractive place, the criteria related to the quality of place play a secondary role in the attraction and retention of the population studied, while those related to the career opportunities dominate. This leads to nuance the theories that highlight the importance of place versus job opportunities, and shows that while quality of place may be important, job opportunities dominate. All this has important practical consequences in terms of what can be done and what cannot be done – or will have no impact – as regards the attraction and retention of knowledge workers in Montreal, but possibly even more so for cities which do not even have the "quality of place" elements which Montreal has.

INTERVIEWS

- Interview 1. Student, computer science program (UQÀM), September 7th, 2007.
- Interview 2. Student, electrical engineering program (ETS), September 11th, 2007.
- Interview 3. Student, biochemistry program (UQÀM), September 12th, 2007.
- Interview 4. Student, biology program (UQÀM), September 25th, 2007.
- Interview 5. Student, computer science program (UQÀM), November 9th, 2007.
- Interview 6. Student, biochemistry program (UQÀM), November 16th, 2007.
- Interview 7. Student, mechanical engineering program (ETS), November 29th, 2007.
- Interview 8. Graduate student in engineering working in Montreal, December 5th, 2007.
- Interview 9. Student, biology program (UQÀM), January 30th, 2008.

REFERENCES

Beckstead, D., & Brown, W. M. (2006). *Capacité d'innovation: l'emploi en sciences et en génie dans les villes canadiennes et américaines*. Ottawa, Canada: Statistique Canada.

Beckstead, D., Brown, W. M., & Gellatly, G. (2008). *Villes et croissance: le cerveau gauche des villes nord-américaines: scientifique et ingénieurs et croissance urbaine*. Ottawa, Canada: Statistique Canada.

Cherry, T. L., & Tsournos, P. T. (2001). Family ties, labor mobility, and interregional wage differences. *Journal of Regional Analysis and Policy, 31*(1), 23–33.

Clark, T. N. (Ed.). (2004). *The city as an entertainment machine*. Oxford, UK: Elsevier.

Darchen, S., & Tremblay, D.-G. (2008a). La thèse de la «classe créative»: son incidence sur l'analyse des facteurs d'attraction et de la compétitivité urbaine. *Interventions Économiques,* (37).

Darchen, S., & Tremblay, D.-G. (2008b, May 20-24). *The attraction and retention of students in science and technology, an analysis based on the "Creative Class" thesis: the case of Montreal.* Paper presented at the Annual Meeting of the Association of Canadian Geographers, Quebec City.

Drucker, P. E. (1994). The Age of Social Transformation. *Atlantic Monthly, 274*, 53–80.

Dumond, M. J., Hirsh, B. T., & MacPherson, D. A. (1999). Wage differentials across labor markets and workers: does cost of living matter? *Economic Inquiry, 37*(4), 577–598. doi:10.1111/j.1465-7295.1999.tb01449.x

Florida, R. (2002a). The economic geography of talent. *Annals of the Association of American Geographers. Association of American Geographers, 92*(4), 743–755. doi:10.1111/1467-8306.00314

Florida, R. (2002b). *The rise of the creative class and how it's transforming work, leisure, community and everyday life*. New York: Basic Books.

Florida, R. (2003). Cities and the creative class. *City & Community, 2*(1), 3–19. doi:10.1111/1540-6040.00034

Florida, R. (2005). *Cities and the creative class*. New York, London: Routledge.

Florida, R., Mellander, C., & Stolarick, K. (2008). Inside the black box of regional development-human capital, the creative class and tolerance. *Journal of Economic Geography, 8*(5), 615–649. doi:10.1093/jeg/lbn023

Glaeser, E. L., Kolko, J., & Saiz, A. (2001). Consumer city. *Journal of Economic Geography, 1*(1), 27–50. doi:10.1093/jeg/1.1.27

Glaeser, E. L., & Saiz, A. (2003). The rise of the skilled city. *Brookings-Wharton Papers on Urban Affairs,* (5), 47-94.

Glaeser, E. L., Sheinkman, J. A., & Shleifer, A. (1995). Economic growth in a cross-section of cities. *Journal of Monetary Economics, 36*(1), 117–143. doi:10.1016/0304-3932(95)01206-2

Hansen, S. B., Ban, C., & Huggins, L. (2003). Explaining the «brain drain» from older industrial cities: the Pittsburgh region. *Economic Development Quarterly, 17*(2), 132–147. doi:10.1177/0891242403017002002

Maning Thomas, J., & Darnton, J. (2006). Social diversity and economic development in the metropolis. *Journal of Planning Literature, 21*(2), 153–168. doi:10.1177/0885412206292259

Markusen, A. (2006). Urban development and the politics of a creative class. *Environment and Planning, 38*(10), 1921-1940.

Shapiro, J. M. (2003). *Smart cities: explaining the relationship between city growth and human capital*. Unpublished manuscript.

Shapiro, J. M. (2005). *Smart cities: quality of life, productivity and the growth effects of human capital*. National Bureau of Economic Research.

Simon, C. J. (1998). Human capital and metropolitan employment growth. *Journal of Urban Economics, 43*(2), 223–243. doi:10.1006/juec.1997.2048

Stolarick, K., Florida, R., & Musante, L. (Cartographer). (2005). *Montreal's capacity for creative connectivity: outlook and opportunities.* Catalix.

ADDITIONAL READING

Andersson, A. E. (1985). Creativity and regional development. *Papers / Regional Science Association. Regional Science Association. Meeting*, (56): 5–20. doi:10.1007/BF01887900

Darchen, S., & Tremblay, D.-G. (2008). *L'attraction et la rétention des étudiants dans le domaine des sciences et de la technologie: le cas de Montréal.* Rimouski, Association de science régionale de langue française, 25-28 août 2008. Retrieved from http://asrdlf2008.uqar.qc.ca/Papiers%20en%20ligne/DARCHEN-TREMBLAY.pdf

Donald, B. (2006). From growth machine to ideas machine. The new politics of local economic development in the high-skilled city . In Tremblay, D.-G., & Tremblay, R. (Eds.), *La compétitivité urbaine à l'ère de la nouvelle économie: enjeux et défis* (pp. 269–284).

Fainstein, S. S. (2005). Cities and diversity. Should we want it? Can we plan for it? *Urban Affairs Review*, *41*(1), 3–19. doi:10.1177/1078087405278968

Florida, R. (2005). *The flight of the creative class: the new global competition for talent.* New York: Harper Business.

Florida, R., Gates, G., Knudsen, B., & Stolarick, K. (2006). *The university and the creative economy.* Retrieved from http://creativeclass.com/rfcgdb/articles/univ_creative_economy082406.pdf

Gertler, M. S., Florida, R., Gates, G., & Vinodrai, T. (2002). *Competing on creativity: placing Ontario's cities in North American context.*

Glaeser, E. L. (2005). Review of Richard Florida's the rise of the creative class. *Regional Science and Urban Economics*, *35*(5), 593–596. doi:10.1016/j.regsciurbeco.2005.01.005

Hansen, H. K., & Niedomysl, T. (2008). Migration of the creative class: evidence from Sweden. *Journal of Economic Geography*, *9*(2), 191–206. doi:10.1093/jeg/lbn046

Krätke, S. (2004). City of talents? Berlin's regional economy, socio-spatial fabric and 'worst practice' urban governance. *International Journal of Urban and Regional Research*, *28*(3), 511–529. doi:10.1111/j.0309-1317.2004.00533.x

Lewis, A. W. (1955). *The theory of economic growth.* London: Allen & Unwin.

Lösh, A. (1940). *The economics of location.* Jena: Fisher.

Malanga, S. (2004). The curse of the creative class. *City Journal (New York, N.Y.)*, *14*(1).

Malanga, S. (2005). Florida daze. *City Journal (New York, N.Y.)*, *15*(2).

Marcuse, Peter. (2003). Review of the rise of the creative class by Richard Florida. *Urban Land*, (62), 40-41.

Marlet, G., & Van Woerkens, C. (2004). *Skills and creativity in a cross-section of Dutch cities.* Universiteit Utrecht, Utrecht School of Economics: Tjalling C Koopmans Research Institute, Discussion Paper Series, 04-29.

Mathur, V. K. (1999). Human capital-based strategy for regional economic development. *Economic Development Quarterly*, *13*(3), 203–216. doi:10.1177/089124249901300301

Peck, J. (2005). Struggling with the creative class. *International Journal of Urban and Regional Research*, *29*(4), 740–770. doi:10.1111/j.1468-2427.2005.00620.x

Rausch, S., & Negrey, C. (2006). Does the creative engine run? A consideration of the effect of creative class on economic strength and growth. *Journal of Urban Affairs*, *28*(5), 473–489. doi:10.1111/j.1467-9906.2006.00310.x

Sawicki, D. (2003). The rise of the creative class: and how it's transforming work, leisure, community and everyday life (Book Review). *Journal of the American Planning Association. American Planning Association*, *69*(1), 90–92.

Stolarick, K., & Florida, R. (2006). Creativity connections and innovation: a study of linkages in the Montreal region. *Environment & Planning A*, *38*(10), 1799–1817. doi:10.1068/a3874

Törnqvist, G. E., & Butttimer, A. e. (1983). Creativity and the renewal of regional life. In Creativity and Context: A Seminar Report (Lund Studies in Geography. B Human Geography, No 50 (pp. 91-112). Lund, Sweden: Gleerup.

Tremblay, D.-G. (2005). Virtual communities of practice: explaining different effects in two organizational contexts. *Canadian Journal of Communication*, *30*(3), 367–382.

Tremblay, D.-G., Doray, P., & Landry, C. (2005). Cooperation as a new mode of regulation of training: the sectoral councils in Quebec. *Socio-economic Review*, *3*(3), 517–543. doi:10.1093/SER/mwi022

Tremblay, D.-G., & Pilati, T. (2008). The Tohu and artist-run centers: contributions to the creative city? *The Canadian Journal of Regional Science*, *30*(2), 337–356.

ENDNOTES

1. T corresponds to the sum of ranks (negative ranks or positive ranks) related to the Wilcoxon tests, p corresponds to the p-value (probability value) of the significance of the Wilcoxon test, r is the effect size of the difference between the two criteria.
2. The Wilcoxon tests are created specifically to calculate the differences between groups for ordinal variables and they also enable to calculate the importance of an effect. It is important to note that the level of significance is not sufficient to qualify a difference between groups as small, medium or large, especially with a big sample size. The results of the analysis using Cohen's method are based on the variance explained by the relations between the variables. It is thus possible to differentiate the importance of two significant differences. Consequently, using the effect size, this analysis takes into account the number of respondents and offers an opportunity to qualify the differences between the criteria.
3. Although we must reckon that all the respondents of our questionnaire would not necessarily be part of this group depending on the first employment chosen once they have graduated.

Chapter 4
The Impact of Proximity Dimensions on the Knowledge Diffusion Process

Antonio Messeni Petruzzelli
Politecnico di Bari, Italy

ABSTRACT

The purpose of this research is to explore how proximity dimensions can favour the diffusion of knowledge between economic actors, focusing on the knowledge relationships established by a knowledge gatekeeper. In particular, the authors formulate several hypotheses regarding the role of proximity dimensions (i.e. geographical, organizational, and technological) in affecting the establishment of gatekeepers' knowledge relationships, taking into account their collaborative-non collaborative type and exploitative-explorative nature. Adopting a patent-based analysis, the authors test their hypotheses on a research sample constituted by 527 knowledge relationships established by two distinct types of knowledge gatekeeper, i.e. an university and a firm.

1. INTRODUCTION

Nowadays, it is generally recognized that the creation of knowledge and its efficient and effective use are fundamental for the development of innovations and high value-added activities, then representing the core of firms and nations' strategies for growth (see also Hamel and Prahalad, 1994; Tallman et al., 2004). The creation of new knowledge and its implementation into innovations can be conceived as an open system which combines pieces of knowledge and information both internal and external to the organizations (Katz and Kahn, 1996). This depends on the fact that organizations are more and more specialized and hence, seldom have all the required resources internally.

Shifting the focus from single organizations to regions or districts, scholars have underlined the importance of knowledge sources external to the geographical areas. In fact, they can "open" these areas through the establishment of global relationships, so avoiding cognitive locking situations at the local level (see also Camagni, 1991; Breschi, 2000; Pouder and John, 1996).

DOI: 10.4018/978-1-61520-721-3.ch004

The process of inter-organizations knowledge transfer is often performed by networks, which can be seen as hybrid organizational structures, alternative to both market and hierarchy (Lambooy and Boschma, 2001; Powell et al., 1996; Williamson, 1999). Networks consist of three components: i) nodes, as individuals or organizations, ii) connections, as communication channels, and iii) the intensity of the transfer of knowledge, in terms of strong or weak ties (Granovetter, 1973; Krackhardt, 1992). In general, it can be contended that these structures perform two main functions. First, they support the co-ordination of decisions made by separate nodes of the network and second the transmission of data, information, and knowledge (Lambooy, 2004). With this regard, nodes can establish relationships aimed at exchanging knowledge (knowledge relationships) based on different types of learning processes, such as interaction and imitation ones (e.g. Malerba, 1992). In particular, processes of learning by interaction are related both to the interaction with upstream/downstream sources of knowledge (such as suppliers, and customers) and to the collaboration with other firms and scientific organizations (such as universities and research centres). On the contrary, processes of learning by imitation are based on the observation of what competitors and other organizations are doing and on the absorption of their developments in science and technology. On the basis of this distinction, it is possible to recognize two main types of knowledge relationships between nodes, such as collaborative and non collaborative ones, created through interaction and imitation learning processes, respectively. In particular, I identify collaborative (non collaborative) knowledge relationships according to the direct (indirect) participation and involvement of two or more actors in designing and/or producing a product or process (see also Polenske, 2004).

Moreover, knowledge relationships can be further distinguished on the basis of their exploitative or explorative nature (Levinthal & March, 1993; March, 1991). The difference between exploration and exploitation has been defined referring to the different type of learning adopted or to the presence/absence of learning. In particular, some scholars have shown that both exploration and exploitation are associated with learning and innovation, albeit of different types. In fact, exploration refers to a learning performed through variation and experimentation processes, involving a shift towards new technological trajectories, whereas exploitation refers to a learning performed through experimental refinement, selection, and reuse of existing routines, reinforcing existing technological trajectories (see also Baum et al., 2000; Gupta et al., 2006; He and Wong, 2004). Differently, other studies (e.g., Rosenkopf and Nerkar, 2001; Vassolo et al., 2004) appear to treat all activities associated with learning and innovation as instances of exploration and to reserve the term exploitation for activities in which the central goal is using past knowledge rather than moving down any type of learning trajectories. Regarding the difference between exploration and exploitation, several works have shown their complementarity and the importance of their balance to fruitfully develop innovations (see also Gilsing and Nootebbom, 2006; McNamara and Baden-Fuller, 1999; Katila and Ahujia, 2002). In fact, explorative activities are important to discover new knowledge domains and opportunities, access to new sources and activate renewal mechanisms. However, once the new knowledge has been acquired, an efficient exploiting capability plays a fundamental role for an effective use of the results of this knowledge searching activity and for the generation of economic returns.

Studies carried out in the field of network theory have clearly shown that nodes can assume different roles, according to their position inside networks (e.g. Dhanaraj and Parkhe, 2006; Hargadon and Sutton, 1997;). With this regard, nodes characterised by a high degree of centrality (Bell, 2005) and absorptive capacity (Cohen and Levinthal, 1990; Giuliani and Bell, 2005), generally known as knowledge gatekeepers (see also Allen, 1977; Hargadorn and Sutton, 1997; Tushman, 1997), have received an increasing consideration, since they can have access to and collect a great amount of knowledge, hence playing a focal role in local and global innovation networks (e.g. McEvily and Zaheer, 1999). The role of knowledge gatekeepers has been extensively analysed in the literature, both at the individual (e.g. Tushman and Katz, 1980; Burt, 2004) and organizational level (e.g. Howells, 2006; Boschma and ter Wal, 2007). Nevertheless, much more researches need to be undertaken into the nature of the relationships and knowledge flows exchanged by gatekeepers. In fact, most of the discussion about this type of actors has been in the context of their function and not of their network relationships. In particular, which factors can favour and support the transfer of knowledge between the gatekeeper and the other nodes of the network should be investigated.

With this regard, the research intends to analyse how geographical, organizational, and technological proximity can affect the exchange of knowledge between the gatekeeper and the other nodes involved in its network. In particular, geographical proximity strictly refers to the spatial or physical distance between economic actors (e.g. Boschma, 2005; Torre and Gilly, 2000; Torre and Rallet, 2005), while organizational proximity can be defined as the extent to which relationships are shared in an organizational arrangement, either within or between organizations (e.g. Boschma, 2005; Davenport, 2005; Knoben and Oerlemans, 2006). On the basis of these definitions, it is assumed that geographical and organizational proximity play a major role in the establishment of collaborative knowledge relationships, and collaborative and exploitative ones, respectively. Regarding technological proximity, considered as the degree of overlapping between actors' shared technological experiences and knowledge bases (see also Nooteboom, 2000; Schamp et al., 2004), it is argued that it plays a positive role in the creation of collaborative and exploitative knowledge relationships.

In the research the knowledge relationships of two knowledge gatekeepers are analysed, represented by an Italian university (the Polytechnic University of Milan) and an Italian firm (ST Microelectronics Italy). These organizations represent the Italian university and firm best performing as knowledge gatekeepers. In fact, they have been selected since their knowledge diffusion capability, in terms of knowledge relationships established.

In particular, these relationships are distinguished as collaborative and non collaborative, and analysed through the gatekeeper's patent joint-developments and citations. Furthermore, their exploitative or explorative nature is identified investigating the scientific/technological fields in which the gatekeeper patents. Finally, for each knowledge relationship the geographical, organizational, and technological proximity between the gatekeeper and the actors involved in its network are measured.

This study is structured as follows. In the next Section the theoretical background is presented and several hypotheses about the effect of proximity dimensions on gatekeepers' knowledge diffusion processes are formulate. Then, in Section 3 the research framework for identifying the gatekeepers' knowledge relationships and measuring the three proximity dimensions is provided. Successively, Section 4 presents the case studies and the empirical analysis. In Section 5, discussions are provided. Finally, limitations, future researches, and conclusions are reported (Sections 6 and 7).

2. THEORETICAL BACKGROUND

In this section, on the basis of the literature review, several hypotheses about the role of geographical, organizational and technological proximity on the establishment of knowledge relationships with knowledge gatekeepers are identified.

2.1. Geographical Proximity and Knowledge Relationships

According to some scholars, organizations involved in knowledge intensive activities tend to geographically co-locate, since they benefit from positive cognitive externalities and then, increase the effectiveness of their external learning processes (see also Alcacer, 2006; Audretsch and Feldman, 1996; Lublinski, 2003). With this regard, although previous studies have documented geographical localization of knowledge flows (e.g. Jaffe et al, 1993), other works raise theoretical and methodological concerns that could have lead to the overestimation of this phenomenon (e.g. Breschi and Lissoni, 2001; Thompson and Fox-Kean, 2005). Therefore, it has been tested how geographical proximity between the knowledge gatekeeper and the nodes of its network differently affects the transfer and diffusion of knowledge, according to the collaborative/non collaborative type of the relationships established. In fact, it has been assumed that collaborative activities, requiring frequent interactions and face-to-face contacts, are notably favoured by the agglomeration of the actors in the same geographically bounded area. On the contrary, non collaborative relationships mainly concern the exchange and acquisition of codified and explicit knowledge, which does not necessarily require spatial closeness for an effective transfer (e.g. Breschi, 2000).

This leads to the formulation of the following hypothesis:

Hypothesis 1. Geographical proximity between the knowledge gatekeeper and the other actors of its network is positively related to the establishment of collaborative knowledge relationships.

2.2. Organizational Proximity and Knowledge Relationships

As previously explained, the notion of organizational proximity is related to the existence of organizational arrangements connecting actors. Moreover, on the basis of the strength or weakness of these arrangements, a high or low organizational proximity between actors can be identified.

Stronger organizational arrangements greater act as mechanisms that coordinate transactions (Cooke and Morgan, 1998; Davenport, 2005). Therefore, they have a positive effect mainly on the interactive learning processes, such as collaborative knowledge relationships, whose effectiveness and efficiency strictly depends on the capability to coordinate the different partners to acquire and collect the complementary pieces of knowledge (Inkpen and Tsang, 2005; Powell et al., 1996). Furthermore, the important role played by organizational arrangements in collaborative relationships is related to the uncertainty and opportunistic behaviours associated to the development and creation of new knowledge. In fact, to reduce these, formal control mechanisms are required, hence ensuring ownership rights and sufficient rewards for own investments in new technologies. Finally, as stated by Nooteboom (1999), detailed formal contracting makes more difficult to change the terms and conditions of the agreements, so preventing actions that can hinder the development and implementation of novelties. On the contrary, the diffusion of knowledge through non collaborative relationships mainly occurs through unintentional and uncontrolled mechanisms, such as learning by imitation, and can also produce negative externalities for the competitiveness of the spilled actor (see also Kalnins and Chung, 2004; Shaver and Flyer, 2000). Thus, it is assumed that these relationships mainly take place between actors that have not established strong organizational arrangement for the governance of their relationships.

Accordingly, it is possible to hypothesize that:

Hypothesis 2. Organizational proximity between the knowledge gatekeeper and other actors of its network is positively related to the establishment of collaborative knowledge relationships.

Scholars have largely debated about the role of strong or weak organizational ties as channels to exchange and transfer knowledge. With this regard, Granovetter (1973) has argued that new knowledge is obtained through weak ties rather than strong ones, since they enable the discovery of new opportunities, serving as bridges to new and different information. Nevertheless, other scholars have claimed the importance to establish strong organizational arrangements (Krackhardt, 1992), since they can offer steady flows of new ideas and technological innovations, encourage reciprocity and joint problem-solving arrangements, and stimulate knowledge transfer and protection in inter-organizational settings (Dyer and Nobeoka, 2000; Uzzi, 1997).

The results of these studies lead to the idea that strong and weak organizational arrangements cannot be considered as alternative or substitute channels, but rather as complementary ones in order to fully gain the benefits arising from both exploitative and explorative activities. In fact, in order to expand its technological base and explore new opportunities, a knowledge gatekeeper has to establish relationships with a great number of various and different partners (e.g. Capaldo, 2007; Reagans and McEvily, 2003). However, their great number and heterogeneity make difficult to commit a high level of resources to the relationships and, then, to establish strong ties. Moreover, a high organizational proximity can hinder the organizational flexibility required by explorative innovations. In fact, the tighter and more dependent are the relationships in an organizational arrangement, the less initiatives may be undertaken, with a negative effect on the exploration of new technological opportunities. In addition, exploration is, by definition, uncertain and associated with radical changes, which make difficult to specify outcomes upfront and, then, to identify and create strong arrangements (Nooteboom, 2004). In contrast with exploration, exploitation concerns an increase in specialization, that entails more specific and codified knowledge on a narrower range of issues and a consolidation into a dominant design. Hence, exploitative relationships need a less variety and variability of partners, permitting ad hoc relational investments in the organization of production and distribution, and in durability, to guarantee a stable, efficient division of labour, and a quick pay-back (Gilsing and Nooteboom, 2006). Furthermore, being exploitation activities needed to survive in the short term, strong organizational arrangements can allow to ensure an effective and efficient transfer of knowledge in order to reduce the time necessary to the innovations development (see also Hansen, 1999).

These considerations suggest the following third hypothesis:

Hypothesis 3. Organizational proximity between the knowledge gatekeeper and other actors of its network is positively related to the establishment of exploitative knowledge relationships.

2.3. Technological Proximity and Knowledge Relationships

The role of technological proximity as an enabler for the establishment of collaborative relationships has been largely debated by the literature. In particular, some scholars (e.g. Mowery et al., 1998; Williamson, 1999) have underlined the importance to restrict the technological distance between organizations in order to reduce the transaction costs arising from contractual hazards and the related coordination costs. In fact, the uncertainty concerning contingencies of collaboration entails limited opportunities for monitoring and, then, ex ante measures of governance are seldom complete and need to be supplemented with ex post adaptation for effectively coordinate the different partners and decrease the risks of opportunistic behaviours. Moreover, following a learning perspective, organizations characterised by similar technological bases, increase their capability to understand and absorb partners' knowledge, and, thus, their mutual learning (e.g. Cohen and Levinthal, 1990; Dyer and Singh, 1998).

Nevertheless, following the competence perspective (Grant, 1996; Hodgson, 1998; Teece et al., 1997), other works have shown that organizations tend to collaborate with actors characterised by different technological bases. In fact, this permits to acquire new capabilities and competencies, in order to achieve a sustainable competitive advantage (Colombo, 2003). Furthermore, an high degree of technological similarity between organizations can improve the transaction costs arising from appropriability hazards, since involuntary and uncontrolled knowledge spillovers are more easy and frequent (Williamson, 1999). Finally, scholars (e.g. Nooteboom, 1999; 2004; Nooteboom et al., 2007) have argued that mutual learning is most beneficial when the knowledge distance between partners is sufficiently large to favour novelty and innovations rise.

Therefore, on the basis of these contrasting findings I test if:

Hypothesis 4. Technological proximity between the knowledge gatekeeper and the other actors of its network is positively related to the establishment of collaborative knowledge relationships.

In Section 1 the distinction between exploitative and explorative knowledge relationships has been discussed. As previously stated, exploitation can be characterized as routinized learning, which adds to the existing knowledge base and competence set of firms without changing the basic nature of activities (Hagedoorn and Duysters, 2002; Rowley et al., 2000). Therefore, this requires a strong mutual understanding of the firms involved, in order to coordinate rapidly and without errors. In fact, a certain similarity in terms of technological knowledge bases is a necessary condition for the development and the exploitation of innovations, since common technological bases are important for identifying the appropriate partner for this type of relationships, creating a common language, and, then, reducing the time necessary for the innovation development and its commercial application (Mowery et al., 1998; Nooteboom et al., 2007; Wuyts et al., 2005).

Instead, exploration can be generally characterized as a break with an existing dominant design and a shift away from existing rules, norms, routines, activities, etc., to allow for Schumpeterian novel combinations. This connects with the idea that firms have to move beyond local search by reaching novel contexts in order to overcome the limitations of contextually localized search (Almeida and Kogut, 1999; Pouder and John, 1996; Rosenkopf and Almeida, 2003). By its nature exploration is an uncertain process that deals with searching for new, technology-based business opportunities (Hagedoorn and Duysters, 2002; Nooteboom, 2000). This requires access to and absorption of new insights and knowledge that are, by definition, at a larger technological distance. In fact, more distant technological bases can represent an opportunity for investigating new research fields and, then, different and heterogeneous partners are generally involved in this type of activities in order to stimulate creativity and "cross-fertilization".

These considerations suggest the following hypothesis:

Hypothesis 5. Technological proximity between the knowledge gatekeeper and the other actors of its network is positively related to the establishment of exploitative knowledge relationships.

3. RESEARCH FRAMEWORK

As stated in Section 1, a knowledge gatekeeper can be identified on the basis of its capability to move knowledge, i.e. to establish knowledge relationships with other economic actors. As a consequence, greater is the number of knowledge relationships established, more a specific actor is expected to behave as a knowledge gatekeeper. Once identified and recognized the gatekeepers' knowledge relationships, the second step of this research is devoted to analyse the impact of geographical, organizational, and technological proximity on the knowledge spread by the gatekeepers inside their networks.

3.1. Measuring Knowledge Relationships

In this research knowledge relationships are recognized adopting patent analysis. The use of patents as a means by which identifying knowledge flows and relationships between actors has been largely adopted in the literature (see also Alcacer and Gittleman, 2006; Audretsch and Feldman, 1996; Jaffe et al., 1993; Pavitt, 1985). Several factors can explain their intensive use (Ratanawaraha and Polenske, 2007). First, patent data are readily available in most countries. Second, the extensiveness of patent data enables researchers to conduct both cross-sectional and longitudinal analysis. Third, patent data contain detailed useful information, such as the technological fields, the assignees, the inventors, and some other market features.

Then, the knowledge gatekeeper's network has been mapped by identifying the actors: i) cited in the patent of the knowledge gatekeeper, and/or ii) citing the patent of the knowledge gatekeeper, and/or iii) developing a patent together with the knowledge gatekeeper. Hence, knowledge relationships are distinguished as collaborative, described by the patent joint-developments between the gatekeeper and other economic actors (co-applicant actors), or non collaborative, described by the gatekeeper patent citations (both cited and citing actors).

Nevertheless, the use of patents as a proxy for knowledge relationships presents also some restrictions. In particular, patents are effective means to protect innovations and intellectual property rights only in some industries and sectors, characterised by high-technology activities (e.g. Hagedoorn, 2006; Wartburg et al., 2005). In fact, in these contests knowledge is strongly codified and explicit. Therefore, patents can effectively describe and represent inter-organizational knowledge flows and innovations development.

Indeed, the exploitative or explorative nature of these relationships is also investigated analysing the gatekeeper's technological knowledge base. In fact, I identify a vector f_g, whose components are constituted by the number of patents registered by the gatekeeper (g) and allocated to the patent class i (n_i). This vector represents its technological portfolio. With this regard, I have considered the patents registered at the European Patent Office (EPO) and the related International Patent Classification (IPC). Therefore, evaluating the average number (m) of patents registered by g in each class, it is possible to identify the technological fields in which it is specialized. In fact, if the number of patent assigned to the generic class i (n_i) is greater than m, then, I assume that the class i represents a specialization field for g, otherwise it is not specialized in that specific field.

Thus, being each relationship associated to a specific patent and, hence, to a specific IPC class, it has been assumed that analysing the gatekeeper's specialization fields, the exploitative or explorative nature of its relationships can be derived (see also Nooteboom et al., 2007). In particular, if the gatekeeper is specialized in the specific class concerning a certain knowledge relationship, this is considered as exploitative, otherwise as explorative.

3.2. Measuring Geographical Proximity

Geographical proximity is adopted for taking into account the spatial distance (Torre and Rallet, 2005) between the gatekeeper and the actors involved in its knowledge-based network. The importance to geographically characterise the actors is strictly related to the investigation of

Table 1. Organizational proximity and inter-organizational ties (Rowley et al., 2000)

Relationship	Low organizational proximity	High organizational proximity
Equity alliances		•
Joint ventures		•
Non equity R&D cooperative ventures		•
Marketing agreements	•	
Licensing agreements	•	
Patent agreements	•	

the role played by the knowledge gatekeepers in fostering the innovative capability of the local area in which they are located. In fact, the total amount of knowledge spread by an organization inside its network is a necessary, but not a sufficient condition for considering the organizations as a knowledge gatekeeper for the regions in which it is located (Giuliani and Bell, 2005). Only a certain level of balancing between local and global actors forming the network may guarantee that the organization favours knowledge creation, diffusion, and sharing inside its region, effectively acting as a knowledge gatekeeper at the local level.

Geographical proximity is analysed calculating the actual geographic distance (expressed in kilometres) between the knowledge gatekeeper and the actors involved in its cognitive network: in particular, it has been used *City Distance Tool*[1] application, provided by Geobytes®.

3.3. Measuring Organizational Proximity

In this research the organizational proximity between the knowledge gatekeeper and the actors involved in its knowledge-based network is assessed considering the presence of formal organizational arrangements between them. In particular, following the distinction made by Rowley et al. (2000) between strong and weak ties it is possible to identify actors low or high organizational proximate to the gatekeeper. In fact, the authors identify three types of strong inter-organizational links (such as equity alliances, joint ventures, non equity cooperative R&D ventures) and three types of weak ones (such as marketing, licensing, and patent agreements) on the basis of the frequency of interaction between partners and the level of resource commitment to the relationships. This classification well addresses the distinction between the different degrees of organizational proximity given by Boschma (2005) and Knoben and Oerlemans (2006).

Thus, these considerations permit to state that: i) if the gatekeeper and the other actors have not established any organizational arrangements, they are not organizational proximate; ii) if they have established weak ties, they are low organizational proximate; iii) if they have established strong ties, they are high organizational proximate (Table 1).

In particular, in order to study the effects of the low and high organizational proximity on the knowledge mobility, I have mapped the ties existing between the knowledge gatekeeper and the external actors before the registration date of the patents and distinguished those ties into strong and weak.

To investigate the existence of inter-organizational ties, between the gatekeepers and the other actors, multiple sources have been consulted, which also provide an opportunity to verify the data. One valuable source is CMP Media Inc.'s web site[2]. CMP is a publishing firm with about 15 magazines dedicated to reporting information on firms and events related to computers, electronics, information technology, and the Internet. Moreover, the Il Sole 24 Ore database[3], the web site of the Italian Ministry of University and Research (MIUR)[4], and other major publications and press releases are adopted. Finally, public and corporate reports available on the web sites of the two selected knowledge gatekeepers and the other actors involved in their networks are analysed.

3.2. Measuring Technological Proximity

In the literature, technological proximity between actors is generally measured analysing their technological knowledge bases, in terms of scientific/technological fields in which they patent (Cincera, 2005; Trajtenberg, 2001). In particular, in this research the technological proximity is evaluated following the measure proposed by Jaffe (1986), who uses the patent technological class information to construct a measure of the closeness between two actors in the technology space. In this case the technology space is represented by 129 patent classes (two-digit) assigned by the IPC. Then, the technological proximity is evaluated as:

$$Tprox_{g,i} = \frac{f_g f_i^{'}}{\sqrt{\left(f_g f_g^{'}\right)\left(f_i f_i^{'}\right)}},$$

where the vectors f_g and f_i (apex indicates the transposed vector) are constituted by all the patents registered by the gatekeeper (*g*) and the generic actor (*i*) at the EPO (esp@cenet® has been queried), respectively, and allocated to the patent class *n* (*n*=1,…,129). Thus, the gatekeeper's patent portfolio is compared to the patent portfolio of each actor who has established a relationship with it.

$Tprox_{g,i}$, which represents the uncentered correlation between the two vectors, assumes value 1, if *g* and *i*'s patent activities perfectly coincide ($f_g = f_i$). On the contrary if they do not overlap at all, i.e. the two vectors are orthogonal, it assumes value 0.

4. EMPIRICAL ANALYSIS

In this section, the selection of the two knowledge gatekeeper and the sample data are described. Then, the variables characterizing the logit regression models are presented.

4.1. Sample Data

The role played by geographical, organizational and technological proximity is investigated studying the knowledge relationships established by two different gatekeepers. In particular, they are represented by the university and firm best performing as knowledge gatekeepers in Italy. Selecting the actors best performing as knowledge gatekeepers permits to well describe the phenomenon, having an extensive number of knowledge relationships on which testing the hypotheses. In addition, I chose to investigate the knowledge relationships established by different types of gatekeepers in order to analyse how institutional differences may affect knowledge management strategies. Specifically, it has been largely demonstrated that universities and firms significantly differ in terms of economic and scientific goals (e.g. Beckers, 1984; Nelson, 2004; Lacetera, forthcoming), that, on turn, may influence the use of proximity dimensions, as well as the type (collaborative and non collaborative) and nature (explorative and exploitative) of knowledge relationships. Thereby, testing the hypotheses on two different settings, it is possible to provide a better understanding of how proximities promote gatekeepers' knowledge flows. Previous works have adopted an analogous methodology. For instance, Santamaria et al. (2009) investigate the impact of innovation activities (training, design, and formal R&D) on the

Table 2. The best university and firm acting as knowledge gatekeepers in Italy

Knowledge Gatekeeper	Knowledge Mobility	Type	Region
Polytechnic University of Milan	145	University	Lombardy
ST Microelectronics Italy	382	Firm	Sicily

innovative performance of firms, analysing how results differ if companies operate in medium-low or high technology industries.

The two knowledge gatekeepers are the Polytechnic University of Milan and the ST Microelectronics Italy, which have been selected on the basis their knowledge mobility, in terms of overall number of their knowledge relationships (see Table 2).

In the specific, the knowledge mobility has been calculated studying the knowledge gatekeepers' granted patents at the EPO database and, hence, identifying, for each registered patent, the relative knowledge relationships: collaborative (patent joint development), and non collaborative (forward and backward citations)[5]. This analysis has been carried out on all Italian universities and on the principal multinationals with headquarter in Italy. In particular, they have been identified by analysing the Italian technological clusters, as reported by the MIUR' database[6]. Hence, the sample data are represented by 145 and 382 knowledge relationships established by the Polytechnic Universities of Milan and ST Microelectronics Italy, respectively. Finally, each established relationships have been distinguished by type (collaborative/non collaborative) and by nature (exploitative/explorative), as respectively reported in Table 3 and 4, respectively.

Data reveal that both the gatekeepers mainly establish non collaborative knowledge relationships. On the contrary, regarding the exploitative or explorative nature, different results emerge. In particular, the Polytechnic University of Milan shows a certain balance between the two types of relationships, whereas the ST Microelectronics Italy mainly creates exploitative knowledge relationships. This finding is strictly coherent with the different nature and activities characterising the two gatekeepers. In fact, firms are generally more specialized than universities and, hence, tend to develop innovations along well known technological trajectories, deepening their knowledge bases on specific topics, rather than explore and search new technological opportunities.

4.2. Results

Logit regression models have been adopted to test the hypotheses: in particular, one model has been used to test the hypotheses on the type of knowledge relationship (collaborative/non collaborative) and the other one has been applied for the hypotheses on the nature of the knowledge relationship (exploitative/explorative). In the specific, the dependent variable is represented by the knowledge relationships, assuming value 1 if the relationship is col-

Table 3. The gatekeepers' collaborative/non collaborative knowledge relationships

Knowledge Gatekeeper	Knowledge Relationships	
	Collaborative	Non collaborative
Polytechnic University of Milan	17	128
ST Microelectronics Italy	53	329

Table 4. The gatekeepers' exploitative/explorative knowledge relationships

Knowledge Gatekeeper	Knowledge Relationships	
	Exploitative	Explorative
Polytechnic University of Milan	87	58
ST Microelectronics Italy	318	64

laborative (exploitative) or value 0 if it is non collaborative (explorative).

Instead, the independent variables are represented by the three chosen dimension of proximity. Hence, the geographical proximity is evaluated by the distance (expressed in kilometres) between the gatekeepers and the other actors. The organizational proximity can assume value 0 (no inter-organizational ties are established between the gatekeeper and the other actors), 1 (weak inter-organizational ties are established between the gatekeeper and the other actors), and 2 (strong inter-organizational ties are established between the gatekeeper and the other actors). Finally, regarding the technological proximity its value depends on $Tprox_{g,i}$ and can range from 0 to 1.

In Table 5 and Table 6, the hypotheses on the type and nature of knowledge relationship have been tested; in particular, Model 1 and Model 2 refer to the case of the Polytechnic University of Milan and the ST Microelectronics Italy, respectively.

The first hypothesis is partially confirmed. In fact, the Polytechnic University of Milan establishes collaborative knowledge relationships with actors geographically proximate, whereas, for the ST Microelectronics Italy, data indicate that geographical proximity is not a relevant condition for the transfer of knowledge through collaborative relationships.

On the basis of this analysis, the second hypothesis is confirmed for both the gatekeepers: in fact, the presence of organizational arrangements linking the gatekeepers and the actors, i.e. the organizational proximity between them, increases the likelihood to establish collaborative knowledge relationships. On the contrary, results reveal that the third hypothesis is confirmed only for the firm acting as a knowledge gatekeeper. In particular, in this case the organizational proximity between the gatekeeper and the other actors positively affect the establishment of exploitative knowledge relationships. On the contrary, the university creates exploitative and explorative relationships with actors both organizationally proximate and not.

Table 5. Hypotheses test on type of knowledge relationship

Variable	Type of knowledge relationships	
	Model 1	Model 2
Geographical proximity	-.008 (2.66)*	0.001 (.002)
Organizational proximity	.707 (10.6)***	1.03 (11.3)***
Technological proximity	-.046 (.036)	1.49 (3.89)**
The values of the Wald chi-square test statistics are in parentheses. *p < .10; **p < .05; ***p < .01		

Table 6. Hypotheses test on nature of knowledge relationship

Variable	Nature of knowledge relationships	
	Model 1	Model 2
Geographical proximity	-	-
Organizational proximity	.133 (.002)	.062 (2.87)*
Technological proximity	1.03 (11.3)***	1.50 (13.7)***
The values of the Wald chi-square test statistics are in parentheses. *ρ < .10; **ρ < .05; ***ρ < .01		

Results show that the fourth hypothesis is confirmed only for the firm acting as a knowledge gatekeeper, since technological proximity can be considered as an enabler for the creation of relationships based on interactive learning mechanisms. On the contrary, the university does not select its collaborative partners on the basis of their technological overlap.

Finally, the fifth hypothesis is confirmed both for the university and the firm. In fact, in both the cases technological proximity affects the establishment of exploitative knowledge relationships. Thus, the knowledge gatekeepers seem to select the partners for exploitative or explorative activities on the basis of their technological similarity.

5. DISCUSSION

This section aims at analysing the findings emerging from the present work, in order to develop a theoretical framework for explaining how geographical, organizational and technological proximity can affect the gatekeepers' knowledge diffusion patterns. Even if only two knowledge gatekeepers have been analysed, the unit of analysis of the present study is represented by knowledge relationships. Therefore, their extensive number (527), as well as the national and international relevance of the two actors and their partners heterogeneity, assure a certain confidence to consider the results not strictly dependent on the two cases' specific characteristics.

Referring to the establishment of collaborative knowledge relationships interesting results emerge on the basis of the knowledge gatekeeper's type. In particular, geographical proximity appears to be an important condition mainly in the case of Polytechnic University of Milan. In fact, ST Microelectronics Italy creates these relationships with actors characterised by a lower degree of spatial closeness. Therefore, only Polytechnic University of Milan exploits geographical proximity as a communication resource for activating collaborative learning and innovation processes. This explains the different role that the two actors can play in diffusing knowledge at the local level. In fact, universities, showing a greater degree of local connectedness and involvement, are more oriented to the building and enhancement of the local innovative capabilities, hence assuming a central role in regional innovation systems (e.g. Link and Scott, 2005; Moulaert and Sekia, 2003; Rothaermel and Thursby, 2005). Whereas, firms seem to present a major attention to the external environment, since they are more oriented to select the necessary complementary knowledge assets for improving their own innovative capabilities.

Furthermore, the analysis reveals that organizational proximity is likewise exploited in all the gatekeepers to create and exchange knowledge through collaborative mechanisms. In fact, both the Polytechnic University of Milan and the ST Microelectronics Italy have established organizational arrangements (such as equity alliances, joint-ventures, non equity cooperation R&D, marketing, licensing, and patent agreements) with partners of collaborative knowledge relationships. The reasoning behind the importance of organizational proximity for collaborations is that these are more efficient and lead to better results when the organizational context of both the interacting partners is similar due the fact that this similarity facilitates mutual understanding (Knoben and Oerlemans, 2006). This notion is strictly related to the Granovetter's (1973) idea of embeddedness, i.e. the extent in which economic actions and organizations' outcomes are affected by dyadic relationships and by the structure of the overall network of relationships. Embeddedness performs several functions in the context of innovations, such as allowing the confrontation of different fields of knowledge, the coordination of partners, and the mobilization of external knowledge resources (Kogut and Zander, 1992; Lundvall, 1992; McEvily and Zaheer, 1999).

Moreover, the important role played by organizational arrangements in collaborative learning and innovation processes is related to the uncertainty and opportunistic behaviours associated to the development and creation of new knowledge. Hence, to reduce these, formal control mechanisms are required in order to ensure ownership rights and sufficient rewards for own investments in new technologies. As stated by Nooteboom (1999), detailed formal contracting makes more difficult to change the terms and conditions of the agreements, so preventing actions that can hinder the development and implementation of novelties. Often, markets cannot offer this because it would involve too high transaction costs. Furthermore, the transfer of complex knowledge requires strong relationships (high organizational proximity) because of the need of feedbacks. With this regard, Hansen (1999) showed that strong rather than weak ties between units in a multiunit organization stimulate the transfer of complex knowledge in collaborative development projects.

Referring to technological proximity, it is differently exploited by Polytechnic University of Milan and ST Microelectronics Italy. In fact, on the basis of the data collected, it is possible to notice that Polytechnic University of Milan tends to create collaborative knowledge relationships with partners having both close and distant technological bases. This results suggest how universities are also involved in R&D collaborations with partners having complementary knowledge and operating in different fields to investigate new scientific opportunities, stimulating creativity and "cross-fertilization". It may depend on the same nature of this type of knowledge gatekeeper which is not generally involved in a market competition and, then, can devote its effort to the exploration of new and uncertain technological opportunities. On the contrary, ST Microelectronics Italy founds their success and survival on the quick innovations development and thus, the similarity in knowledge bases and common technological language are key conditions for identifying the right partners and reducing the time necessary for the innovation development and its commercial application (Hagedoorn and Duysters, 2002; Mowery et al., 1998; Nooteboom et al., 2007). In fact, technological proximity between actors favours the acquisition and development of technological knowledge and technologies, affecting their absorptive capacity (Cohen and Levinthal, 1990). It depends on the fact that, partners' technological bases should be close enough in order to reduce the time necessary to communicate, understand and apply the new knowledge.

As well as for collaborative knowledge relationships, the analysis provides also interesting results about the creation of non collaborative knowledge relationships by gatekeepers. Regarding geographical proximity, it does not seem to be relevant for the establishment of this type of relationship in any of the two considered cases. In fact, non collaborative knowledge relationships mainly concern the exchange of codified and explicit knowledge (as in the case of patent citations), which does not require spatial closeness for an effective transfer. In particular, factors such the extensive use of ICT and the creation of common codes and rules, as in the case of the scientific communities, can explain this result, since they permit to transfer knowledge despite of the geographical distance between the actors. This result sheds further light about the studies on the localised nature of knowledge spillovers (see also Breschi and Lissoni, 2001; Maruseth and Verspagen, 2002). In fact, it seems to be possible to argue that knowledge spillovers, associated to non collaborative relationships between knowledge gatekeepers and other economic actors are mainly not localised.

In all the two distinct types of knowledge gatekeeper analysed, non collaborative relationships are mainly established with actors not organizationally connected with them. This result can be strictly dependent on the nature of this type of relationships, which are generally related to unintentional and uncontrolled spillovers and can be also negative for the competitiveness of the spilled actor (see also Alcacer and Chung, 2007; Kalnins and Chung, 2004; Shaver and Flyer, 2000). In fact, non collaborative knowledge relationships are often related to imitative learning mechanisms, which entail unidirectional knowledge flows, undermining the competitive capabilities and competences of the actors. For instance, organizations with strong knowledge bases, technologies, human capital, and training programs can have a lot to lose establishing organizational relationships with weak actors, since, so doing, these can easily access to their distinctive resources and skills. Hence, it seems to be reasonable to state that these relationships mainly take place between actors that have not established any formal and stable organizational arrangement for the governance of their relationships.

The codified and explicit nature of the knowledge transferred by means of non collaborative relationships can explain also the influence of technological proximity on these types of relationship. In fact, the empirical analysis has shown that the degree of technological overlapping is not relevant for the creation of non collaborative knowledge relationships, since this knowledge can be exchanged also between actors characterised by a low degree of technological similarity (Jensen et al., 2007).

Furthermore, the present research has investigated the role of proximity referring to the exploitative or explorative intent of the knowledge relationships. Results have shown how, also in this case, the different nature of the knowledge gatekeepers differently affects the use of proximity dimensions, i.e. organizational and technological. With regard to exploitative knowledge relationships, the analysis has revealed that organizational proximity plays a significant role only for ST Microelectronics Italy. In fact, Polytechnic University of Milan does not seem to create exploitative knowledge relationships on the basis of the existence of organizational ties with their partners. This result can be well explained taking into account the same meaning of exploitation and the different nature of the two knowledge gatekeepers. In fact, exploitation refers to the "refinement, choice, production, efficiency, selection, implementation, and execution" of knowledge (March, 1991, p. 71.) and it concerns its commercialization for generating economic benefits, mainly in the short term. Nevertheless, this capability, generally known as appropriability (e.g. Saviotti, 1998), can be challenged by opportunistic behaviours of their partners, such as competitors, in terms of utilization and management of the innovation results. Therefore, to prevent these problems and create a trustworthy atmosphere with their partners, firms need to establish organizational relationships and formal and structured governance arrangements aimed at defining the rules and norms for their conduct.

Referring to Polytechnic University of Milan, the different result can be analysed considering its nature. In fact, it has different strategic aims respect to ST Microelectronics Italy, in fact, it is characterised by a more long term perspective and it is not involved in market competitions. Thus, this entails that universities are not forced to establish organizational arrangements with their partners (both profit and no profit organizations) and to sustain the consequent costs, since the lack of the appropriability hazards (Agrawal, 2001; Tijssen, 2006; Zucker et al., 2002).

Analogous results emerge for both university and firm case, when explorative knowledge relationships are studied. In fact, organizational proximity does not seem to positively affect the likelihood to establish explorative knowledge relationships. This result depends on the fact that tight inter-organizational links may evolve into closed and inward-locking systems. In fact, strong links may limit access to various sources of novel information and knowledge, because search for novelty often requires going out of the established channels. Furthermore, exploration activities require an organizational flexibility, which can be hindered by formal governance structures (see also Boschma, 2005).

The findings about the relationship between organizational proximity and exploitative/explorative activities is strongly related to the scientific debate about the role of strong or weak ties (see also Capaldo, 2007). In fact, scholars have shown that weak ties, such as in loosely coupled system, can favour and support the discover of new scientific and technological opportunities, as well demonstrated in the study of Hansen (1999).

Finally, the relationship between technological proximity and the creation of exploitative knowledge relationships has been also investigated. With this regard, the analysis has shown that both the Polytechnic University of Milan and ST Microelectronics Italy use technological proximity as a communication resource for the establishment of these relationships. This result indicates that a certain similarity in terms of technological knowledge bases is a necessary condition for the development and the exploitation of innovations. In fact, common technological bases are important for identifying the appropriate partners for these relationships, creating a common language, and then, reducing the time necessary for the innovation development and its commercial application (Wuyts et al., 2005). Moreover, as previously stated, exploitation involves learning mechanisms aimed at reinforcing competences and knowledge bases and, thus, it moves along well known technological trajectories (see also Lavie and Rosenkopf, 2006). This requires that partners have to be specialized in the same knowledge and technological areas, in order to provide a similar understanding on some specific topics. Moreover, technological proximity contributes also to guarantee the same deepening on these issues, so permitting to notably improve their alignment and capabilities to quickly create innovative and exploitable results.

On the contrary, technological proximity does not appear to be critical for the establishment of explorative knowledge relationships between gatekeepers and other economic actors, regardless of their nature. As previously stated, exploration refers to a learning performed through variation and experimentation, aimed at searching and discovering new competencies and knowledge (see also Gilsing and Nootebbom, 2006). Therefore, by its definition, it seems to be reasonable that more distant technological bases can represent an opportunity for investigating new research fields and, thus, different and heterogeneous partners are generally involved in these activities (e.g. Felin and Hesterly, 2007). In fact, the current economic scenario presents actors more and more specialized and focalised on their own competencies, that rarely have all the required knowledge resources to shift towards new technological trajectories.

6. LIMITATIONS AND FUTURE RESEARCH DIRECTIONS

The study investigates only two distinct knowledge gatekeepers. Therefore, an extension of the sample could lead to achieve more general results. Furthermore, this research uses patents to describe knowledge relationships. However, they capture only a subset of the potential knowledge relationships. An extension could be to supplement patent collaboration data with additional data sources (e.g. collaboration on research publications and projects), in order to analyse more completely the role of proximity dimensions. Moreover, the investigation of the gatekeeper's knowledge relationships is based on three proximity dimensions. Thus, further researches could focus on how other proximity dimensions, such as social institutional, and cultural, can affect the gatekeepers' knowledge diffusion patterns. Finally, another interesting direction of research would be exploring the behaviour of other different knowledge gatekeepers, distinguished by type and country, in order to study the role played by the institutional contest in the gatekeepers' knowledge diffusion patterns.

7. CONCLUSION

The present research has investigated if and how geographical, organizational and technological proximity can affect the diffusion and transfer of knowledge between knowledge gatekeepers and other economic actors of its network. In particular, two different types of gatekeeper have been considered (university and firm) to evaluate how they differently exploit the three proximity dimensions. Some hypotheses about the role of proximity dimensions for establishing collaborative/non collaborative and exploitative/explorative knowledge relationships have been formulated and tested on a sample of 527 knowledge relationships, adopting logit regression models.

The analysis reveals that only the university acting as a gatekeeper creates collaborative knowledge relationships with actors located in short distance areas. This result seems to show how universities present a greater degree of local connectedness and involvement, being more oriented to the building and enhancement of the local innovative capabilities. On the contrary, firms seem to present a major attention to the external environment, being more oriented to select the necessary complementary knowledge assets for improving their own innovative capabilities.

Moreover, from the study it emerges that both the university and the firm acting as gatekeepers tend to exchange knowledge through collaborative mechanisms with actors that have previously created organizational arrangements with them. In this way the uncertainty and the opportunistic behaviours associated with the innovations joint-development can be prevented. Furthermore, results suggest that the organizational proximity between the firm acting as a gatekeeper and their partners strongly affect the type of knowledge relationship established. In fact, a high degree of organizational proximity with their partners leads the gatekeeper to create relationships aimed at developing more exploitative innovations rather than explorative ones.

Data show that the firm establishes collaborative relationships mainly with actors characterised by a high degree of technological proximity. It may depend on the fact that firms found their success and survival on the fast development of innovations and, thus, the similarity in knowledge bases is a key condition for creating a common technological language and reducing the time necessary for the innovation development and its commercial application.

Finally, results reveal that the technological proximity between the gatekeepers (both the firm and the university) and their partners strongly affect the type of knowledge relationship established. In fact, a high degree of technological similarity with their partners leads the gatekeepers to create relationships aimed at developing more exploitative innovations rather than explorative ones.

The present research provides some interesting implications. First, it contributes to explain how knowledge gatekeepers, on the basis of their nature, differently use proximity dimensions to exchange knowledge, through collaborative and non collaborative relationships, and develop exploitative and explorative innovations. Second, recognizing the importance of knowledge gatekeepers as knowledge sources, this work allows economic actors to identify which proximity dimensions assume a relevant role for activating collaborative knowledge relationships with them. Moreover, with this regard, policy makers can leverage the proximity dimensions between gatekeepers and local actors in order to favour and support the exchange of knowledge, hence improving the innovative capability, competitiveness, and attractiveness of regional areas.

REFERENCES

Agrawal, A. (2001). University-to-industry knowledge transfer: literature review and unanswered questions. *International Journal of Management Reviews*, *3*, 285–302. doi:10.1111/1468-2370.00069

Alcacer, J. (2006). Location choices across the value chain: how activity and capability influence collocation. *Management Science*, *52*, 1457–1471. doi:10.1287/mnsc.1060.0658

Alcacer, J., & Chung, W. (2007). Location strategies and knowledge spillovers. *Management Science*, *53*, 760–776. doi:10.1287/mnsc.1060.0637

Alcacer, J., & Gittelman, M. (2006). Patent citations as a measure of knowledge flows: the influence of examiner citations. *The Review of Economics and Statistics*, *88*, 774–779. doi:10.1162/rest.88.4.774

Allen, T. J. (1977). *Managing the Flow of Technology*. Cambridge, MA: MIT press.

Almeida, P., & Kogut, B. (1999). Localization of knowledge and the mobility of engineers in regional networks. *Management Science*, *45*, 905–917. doi:10.1287/mnsc.45.7.905

Audretsch, D. B., & Feldman, M. (1996). R&D spillovers and the geography of innovation and production. *The American Economic Review*, *86*, 630–640.

Baum, J. A. C., Li, S. X., & Usher, J. M. (2000). Making the next move: how experiential and vicarious learning shape the locations of chains' acquisitions. *Administrative Science Quarterly*, *45*, 766–801. doi:10.2307/2667019

Beckers, H. L. (1984). The role of industry . In Fusfeld, H. I., & Haklisch, C. S. (Eds.), *University - Industry Research Interactions*. London: Pergamon Press.

Bell, G. G. (2005). Clusters, networks, and firms innovativeness. *Strategic Management Journal*, *26*, 287–295. doi:10.1002/smj.448

Boschma, R. A. (2005). Proximity and innovation: a critical assessment. *Regional Studies*, *39*, 61–74. doi:10.1080/0034340052000320887

Boschma, R. A., & ter Wal, A. L. J. (2007). Knowledge networks and innovative performance in an industrial district. The case of a footwear district in the South of Italy. *Industry and Innovation*, *14*, 177–199. doi:10.1080/13662710701253441

Breschi, S. (2000). The geography of innovation: a cross sector analysis . *Regional Studies*, *34*, 213–229. doi:10.1080/00343400050015069

Breschi, S., & Lissoni, F. (2001). Knowledge spillovers and local innovation systems: a critical survey. *Industrial and Corporate Change*, *10*, 975–1005. doi:10.1093/icc/10.4.975

Burt, R. S. (2004). Structural holes and good ideas. *American Journal of Sociology*, *110*, 349–399. doi:10.1086/421787

Camagni, R. (1991). *Innovation Networks. Spatial Perspectives*. London: Bellhaven.

Cantwell, J., & Piscitello, L. (2005). Recent location of foreign-owned research and development activities by large multinational corporations in the European regions: the role of spillovers and externalities. *Regional Studies*, *39*, 1–16. doi:10.1080/0034340052000320824

Capaldo, A. (2007). Network structure and innovation: the leveraging of a dual network distinctive relational capability. *Strategic Management Journal*, *28*, 585–608. doi:10.1002/smj.621

Cincera, M. (2005). Firms' productivity growth and R&D spillovers: an analysis of alternative technological proximity measures. *Economics of Innovation and New Technology*, *14*, 657–682. doi:10.1080/10438590500056768

Cohen, W. M., & Levinthal, D. A. (1990). Absorptive capacity: a new perspective on learning and innovation. *Administrative Science Quarterly*, *35*, 128–152. doi:10.2307/2393553

Colombo, M. G. (2003). Alliance form: a test of the contractual and competence perspective. *Strategic Management Journal*, *24*, 1209–1229. doi:10.1002/smj.353

Cooke, P., & Morgan, K. (1998). *The associational Economy. Firms, Regions, and Innovation*. Oxford, UK: Oxford University Press.

Davenport, S. (2005). Exploring the role of proximity in SME knowledge-acquisition. *Research Policy*, *34*, 683–701. doi:10.1016/j.respol.2005.03.006

DeBresson, C., & Anesse, F. (1991). Networks of innovators: a review and introduction to the issue. *Research Policy*, *20*, 363–379. doi:10.1016/0048-7333(91)90063-V

Dhanaraj, C., & Parkhe, A. (2006). Orchestrating innovation networks. *Academy of Management Review*, *31*, 659–669.

Dyer, J. H., & Singh, H. (1998). The relational view: cooperative strategy and sources of interorganizational competitive advantage. *Academy of Management Journal*, *23*, 660–679.

Felin, T., & Hesterly, W. S. (2007). The knowledge-based view, and new value creation: philosophical considerations on the locus of knowledge. *Academy of Management Review*, *32*, 195–218.

Gilsing, V., & Nooteboom, B. (2006). Exploration and exploitation in innovation systems: the case of pharmaceutical biotechnology. *Research Policy*, *35*, 1–23. doi:10.1016/j.respol.2005.06.007

Giuliani, E., & Bell, M. (2005). The micro-determinants of meso-level learning and innovation: evidence from a Chilean wine cluster. *Research Policy*, *34*, 47–68. doi:10.1016/j.respol.2004.10.008

Gomes-Casseres, B., Hagedoorn, J., & Jaffe, A. B. (2006). Do alliances promote knowledge flows. *Journal of Financial Economics*, *80*, 5–33. doi:10.1016/j.jfineco.2004.08.011

Granovetter, M. (1973). The strength of weak ties. *American Journal of Sociology*, *78*, 1360–1380. doi:10.1086/225469

Grant, R. M. (1996). Toward a knowledge-based theory of the firm. *Strategic Management Journal*, *17*, 109–122.

Gupta, A. K., Smith, K. G., & Shalley, C. E. (2006). The interplay between exploration and exploitation. *Academy of Management Journal*, *49*, 693–706.

Hagedoorn, J., & Duysters, G. (2002). External sources of innovative capabilities: the preferences for strategic alliances or mergers and acquisitions. *Journal of Management Studies*, *39*, 167–188. doi:10.1111/1467-6486.00287

Hamel, G., & Prahalad, C. K. (1994). *Competing For The Future*. Cambridge: Harvard Business School Press.

Hansen, M. (1999). The search transfer problem: the role of weak ties in sharing knowledge across organization subunits. *Administrative Science Quarterly*, *44*, 82–111. doi:10.2307/2667032

Hargadon, A. B., & Sutton, R. I. (1997). Technology brokering and innovation in a product development firm. *Administrative Science Quarterly*, *42*, 716–749. doi:10.2307/2393655

He, Z.-L., & Wong, P. K. (2004). Exploration vs. exploitation: An empirical test of the ambidexterity hypothesis. *Organization Science*, *15*, 481–494. doi:10.1287/orsc.1040.0078

Hodgson, G. M. (1998). Competence and contract in the theory of the firm. *Journal of Economic Behavior & Organization*, *35*, 179–201. doi:10.1016/S0167-2681(98)00053-5

Howells, J. (2006). Intermediation and the role of intermediaries in innovation. *Research Policy*, *35*, 715–728. doi:10.1016/j.respol.2006.03.005

Inkpen, A. C., & Tsang, E. W. K. (2005). Social capital, networks, and knowledge transfer. *Academy of Management Review*, *30*, 146–165.

Jaffe, A. B. (1986). Technological opportunity and spillovers of R&D: evidence from firms' patents, profits, and market values. *The American Economic Review*, *76*, 984–1001.

Jaffe, A. B., Trajtenberg, M., & Henderson, R. (1993). Geographic localization and knowledge spillovers as evidence by patent citations. *The Quarterly Journal of Economics*, *108*, 577–598. doi:10.2307/2118401

Jensen, M. B., Johnson, B., Lorenz, E., & Lundvall, B. A. (2007). Forms of knowledge and modes of innovation. *Research Policy*, *36*, 680–693. doi:10.1016/j.respol.2007.01.006

Kalnins, A., & Chung, W. (2004). Resource-seeking agglomeration: a study of market entry in the lodging industry. *Strategic Management Journal*, *25*, 689–699. doi:10.1002/smj.403

Katila, R., & Ahuja, G. (2002). Something old, something new: A longitudinal study of search behaviour and new product introduction. *Academy of Management Journal*, *45*, 1183–1194. doi:10.2307/3069433

Katz, D., & Kahn, R. (1996). *The Social Psychology of Organizations*. New York: Wiley.

Knoben, J., & Oelremans, L. A. G. (2006). Proximity and inter-organizational collaboration: a literature review. *International Journal of Management Reviews*, *8*, 71–89. doi:10.1111/j.1468-2370.2006.00121.x

Kogut, B., & Zander, U. (1992). Knowledge of the firm, combinative capabilities, and the replication of technology. *Organization Science*, *3*, 383–397. doi:10.1287/orsc.3.3.383

Krackardt, D. (1992). The strength of strong ties . In Nohria, N., & Eccles, R. G. (Eds.), *Networks and Organizations*. Cambridge, MA: Harvard Business School Press.

Lacetera, N. (forthcoming). Different mission and commitment power in R&D organization: theory and evidence on industry-university alliances. *Organization Science*.

Lambooy, J. G. (2004). The transmission of knowledge, emerging networks, and the role of universities: an evolutionary approach. *European Planning Studies*, *12*, 643–657. doi:10.1080/0965431042000219996

Lambooy, J. G., & Boschma, R. (2001). Evolutionary economics and regional policy. *The Annals of Regional Science*, *35*, 113–131. doi:10.1007/s001680000033

Lavie, D., & Rosenkopf, L. (2006). Balancing exploration and exploitation in alliance formation. *Academy of Management Journal*, *49*, 797–818.

Levinthal, D., & March, J. (1993). The myopia of learning. *Strategic Management Journal*, *14*, 95–112. doi:10.1002/smj.4250141009

Link, A. N., & Scott, J. T. (2005). Universities as partners in U.S. research joint ventures. *Research Policy*, *34*, 385–393. doi:10.1016/j.respol.2005.01.013

Lublinski, A. E. (2003). Does geographic proximity matter? Evidence from clustered and non-clustered aeronautic firms in Germany. *Regional Studies*, *37*, 453–467. doi:10.1080/0034340032000089031

Lundvall, B. A. (1992). *National Systems of Innovations: Towards a Theory of Innovation and Interactive Learning*. London: Printer Publisher.

Malerba, F. (1992). Learning by firms and incremental technical change. *The Economic Journal*, *102*, 845–859. doi:10.2307/2234581

March, J. (1991). Exploration and exploitation in organizational learning. *Organization Science*, *2*, 71–87. doi:10.1287/orsc.2.1.71

Maruseth, P. B., & Verspagen, B. (2002). Knowledge-spillovers in Europe: a patent citation analysis. *The Scandinavian Journal of Economics*, *104*, 531–545. doi:10.1111/1467-9442.00300

McEvily, B., & Zaheer, A. (1999). Bridging ties: a source of firm heterogeneity in competitive capabilities. *Strategic Management Journal*, *20*, 1133–1156. doi:10.1002/(SICI)1097-0266(199912)20:12<1133::AID-SMJ74>3.0.CO;2-7

McNamara, P., & Baden-Fuller, C. (1999). Lessons from the Celltech case: balancing knowledge exploration and exploitation in organizational renewal. *British Journal of Management*, *10*, 291–307. doi:10.1111/1467-8551.00140

Moulart, F., & Sekia, F. (2003). Territorial innovation models: a critical survey. *Regional Studies*, *37*, 289–302. doi:10.1080/0034340032000065442

Mowery, D. C., Oxley, J. E., & Silverman, B. S. (1998). Technological overlap and interfirm cooperation: implications for the resource-based view of the firm. *Research Policy*, *27*, 507–523. doi:10.1016/S0048-7333(98)00066-3

Nelson, R. (2004). The Market economy and the scientific commons. *Research Policy*, *33*, 455–471. doi:10.1016/j.respol.2003.09.008

Nooteboom, B. (1999). Innovation and inter-firm linkages: new implications for policy. *Research Policy*, *28*, 793–805. doi:10.1016/S0048-7333(99)00022-0

Nooteboom, B. (2000). *Learning and Innovation in Organizations and Economies*. Oxford, UK: Oxford University Press.

Nooteboom, B. (2004). *Interfirm Collaboration, Learning and Networks, an Integrated Approach*. London: Routledge.

Nooteboom, B., Van Haverbeke, W., Duysters, G., Gilsing, V., & van den Oord, A. (2007). Optimal cognitive distance and absorptive capacity. *Research Policy*, *36*, 1016–1034. doi:10.1016/j.respol.2007.04.003

Pavitt, K. (1985). Patent statistics as indicators of innovative activities: possibilities and problems. *Scientometrics*, *7*, 77–99. doi:10.1007/BF02020142

Polenske, K. R. (2004). Competition, collaboration and cooperation: an uneasy triangle in networks of firms and regions. *Regional Studies*, *38*, 1029–1043. doi:10.1080/0034340042000292629

Pouder, R., & John, C. H. S. (1996). Hot spots and blind spots: geographical clusters of firms and innovation. *Academy of Management Review*, *21*, 1192–1225. doi:10.2307/259168

Powell, W. W., Koput, K. W., & Smith-Doerr, L. (1996). Interorganizational collaboration and the locus of innovation: networks of learning in biotechnology. *Administrative Science Quarterly*, *41*, 116–145. doi:10.2307/2393988

Ratanawaraha, A., & Polenske, K. R. (2007). Measuring the geography of innovation: a literature review . In Polenske, K. P. (Ed.), *The Economic Geography of Innovation*. Cambridge, UK: Cambridge University Press. doi:10.1017/CBO9780511493386.004

Reagans, R., & McEvily, B. (2003). Network structure and knowledge transfer: the effects of cohesion and range. *Administrative Science Quarterly*, *48*, 240–267. doi:10.2307/3556658

Rosenkopf, L., & Almeida, P. (2003). Overcoming local search through alliances and mobility. *Management Science*, *49*, 751–766. doi:10.1287/mnsc.49.6.751.16026

Rothaermel, F. T., & Thursby, M. (2005). Incubator firm failure or graduation? The role of university linkages. *Research Policy*, *34*, 1076–1090. doi:10.1016/j.respol.2005.05.012

Rowley, T., Behrens, D., & Krackhardt, D. (2000). Redundant governance structures: an analysis of structural and relational embeddedness in the steel and semiconductor industries. *Strategic Management Journal*, *21*, 369–386. doi:10.1002/(SICI)1097-0266(200003)21:3<369::AID-SMJ93>3.0.CO;2-M

Santamaria, L., Nieto, M. J., & Barge-Gil, A. (2009). Beyond formal R&D: taking advantage of other sources of innovation in low- and medium-technology industries. *Research Policy*, *38*, 507–517. doi:10.1016/j.respol.2008.10.004

Saviotti, P. P. (1998). On the dynamics of appropriability, of tacit and of codified knowledge. *Research Policy*, *26*, 843–856. doi:10.1016/S0048-7333(97)00066-8

Schamp, E. W., Rentmeister, B., & Lo, V. (2004). Dimensions of proximity in knowledge-based networks: the cases of investment banking and automobile design. *European Planning Studies*, *12*, 607–624. doi:10.1080/0965431042000219978

Shaver, J. M., & Flyer, F. (2000). Agglomeration economies, firm heterogeneity, and foreign direct investment in the United States. *Strategic Management Journal*, *21*, 1175–1193. doi:10.1002/1097-0266(200012)21:12<1175::AID-SMJ139>3.0.CO;2-Q

Siggelkow, N., & Levinthal, D. A. (2003). Temporarily divide to conquer: Centralized, decentralized, and reintegrated organizational approaches to exploration and adaptation. *Organization Science*, *14*, 650–669.

Tallman, S., Jenkins, M., Henry, N., & Pinch, S. (2004). Knowledge, clusters and competitive advantage . *Academy of Management Review*, *29*, 258–271.

Teece, D. J., Pisano, G., & Shuen, A. (1997). Dynamic capabilities and strategic management. *Strategic Management Journal*, *18*, 509–533. doi:10.1002/(SICI)1097-0266(199708)18:7<509::AID-SMJ882>3.0.CO;2-Z

Thompson, P., & Fox-Kean, M. (2005). Patent citations and the geography of knowledge spillovers: a reassessment. *The American Economic Review*, *95*, 450–460. doi:10.1257/0002828053828509

Tijssen, R. J. W. (2006). Universities and industrially relevant science: towards measurement models and indicators of entrepreneurial orientation. *Research Policy*, *35*, 1569–1585. doi:10.1016/j.respol.2006.09.025

Torre, A., & Gilly, J. P. (2000). On the analytical dimension of proximity dynamics. *Regional Studies*, *34*, 169–180. doi:10.1080/00343400050006087

Torre, A., & Rallet, A. (2005). Proximity and localization. *Regional Studies*, *39*, 47–59. doi:10.1080/0034340052000320842

Trajtenberg, M. (2001). Innovation in Israel 1968-97: a comparative analysis using patent data. *Research Policy*, *30*, 363–390. doi:10.1016/S0048-7333(00)00089-5

Tushman, M. L. (1997). Special boundary roles in the innovation process. *Administrative Science Quarterly*, *22*, 587–605. doi:10.2307/2392402

Tushman, M. L., & Katz, R. (1980). External communication and project performance: an investigation into the role of gatekeepers. *Management Science*, *26*, 1071–1085. doi:10.1287/mnsc.26.11.1071

Uzzi, B. (1997). Social structure and competition in interfirm networks: the paradox of embeddedness. *Administrative Science Quarterly*, *42*, 37–69.

Vassolo, R. S., Anand, J., & Folta, T. (2004). Non-additivity in portfolios of exploration activities: a real options-based analysis of equity alliances in biotechnology. *Strategic Management Journal*, *25*, 1045–1061. doi:10.1002/smj.414

Wartburg, I. V., Teichert, T., & Rost, K. (2005). Inventive progress measured by multi-stage patent citation analysis. *Research Policy*, *34*, 1591–1607. doi:10.1016/j.respol.2005.08.001

Williamson, O. E. (1999). Strategy research: governance and competence perspectives. *Strategic Management Journal*, *20*, 1087–1108. doi:10.1002/(SICI)1097-0266(199912)20:12<1087::AID-SMJ71>3.0.CO;2-Z

Wuyts, S., Colombo, M. G., Dutta, S., & Noteboom, B. (2005). Empirical tests of optimal cognitive distance. *Journal of Economic Behavior & Organization*, *58*, 277–302. doi:10.1016/j.jebo.2004.03.019

Zucker, L. G., Darby, M. R., & Armstrong, J. S. (2002). Commercializing knowledge: university, science, knowledge capture, and firm performance in biotechnology. *Management Science*, *48*, 138–153. doi:10.1287/mnsc.48.1.138.14274

ENDNOTES

1. City Distance Tool: http://www.geobytes.com/CityDistanceTool.htm
2. CPM Media Inc.: www.techweb.com
3. Il Sole 24 Ore: http://www.ilsole24ore.com
4. Italian Ministry of University and Research (MIUR): http://www.miur.it
5. European Patent Office limits the number of consultable patents to 500, then for Italian universities all patents has been studying, because they have not more than 500 registered patents; instead, for the principal multinationals with headquarter in Italy, only the last 500 registered patents has been investigated.
6. MIUR's database on Italian technological clusters: http://www.ricercaitaliana.it/

Chapter 5
The Interaction between Local and Regional Knowledge-Based Development:
Towards a Quadruple Helix Model

Tooran Alizadeh
University of Sydney, Australia

ABSTRACT

By the turn of the 21st century, the significance of knowledge to be the key factor in urban and regional development is well established. However, it has been only recently that attempts have been made to identify the specific mechanism and institutional relationships, through which knowledge-based development takes place. In this regard, very little consideration has been given to the ways that different levels of knowledge-based development communicate to each other. This chapter examines the mutual interaction between knowledge-based development in local and regional level in two different sections. The first section builds upon the third wave of economic development supporting the growth of cluster of related firms and relates it to an empirical case study of knowledge-based community development in Queensland- Australia. It concludes that knowledge-based local developments do not evolve without a regional support network. The second section reviews the "Triple Helix" of university–industry–government collaboration as the basis of knowledge-based regional development in the investigated case study. This review determines the central role of local community as an innovation base for the interaction among the key factors, and suggests a promotion for a Quadruple Helix Model where community works alongside business, university and government in the new economy.

INTRODUCTION

The digital revolution at the end of 20th century has provided great opportunities for communities to play aggressive roles in the new economy and take active part in the process of knowledge production and distribution. The growing number of home-based teleworkers, e-entrepreneurs and high-rank information workers who are very selective on their residential communities heralds a new era that has already been celebrated (Florida, 2002). Scholars, admitting each community to be a unique instance

DOI: 10.4018/978-1-61520-721-3.ch005

with its special characteristics, search for some general elements that can be adjusted to different knowledge-based local and regional development projects. Here, the common objective of every level of knowledge-based development efforts is the creation of an innovating base to adopt the new technological paradigm and get renewed. To achieve this common objective, different levels of knowledge-based development may adopt atypical mechanisms that are enforced by different scales offering contrasting resources and capabilities. In this regard, very little knowledge has been produced on the effects that different levels of knowledge-based development have on each other. This chapter specifically examines the interaction between knowledge-based development in the local[1] and regional level. It includes two main sections where different sides of the mutual relation between local and regional development is examined. This two-sided elaboration is to guarantee that the benefit of each level - local and regional- is carefully considered.

The first section investigates the progress of knowledge-based local development in conventional larger regions. It presents some empirical data collected from a case study of knowledge-based community development in Queensland, and reviews infrastructural and institutional challenges experienced based on lack of awareness in the regional level. The finding is consistent with the third wave of economic development theory (Blakely, 2001; Herbers, 1990; Ross & Friedman, 1990) that emphasizes on a cluster of related firms as the key factor for prosperity in the new economy. This section notes that local communities may start separately using the powerful mediators like a thoughtful developer, an ambitious local authority and so on. Yet, a long-term knowledge-based progress is impossible unless the larger region realizes the opportunities provided by different communities and supports the growth of specified clusters of related firms at the regional strategy making level. It concludes that knowledge-based local development will not evolve unless a regional network of knowledge-based firms/communities gets established and works together.

On the other hand, the second section investigates the process of knowledge-based development in larger regions. It reviews the "Triple Helix Model" (Etzkowitz, 2008; Etzkowitz & Klofsten, 2005; Etzkowitz & Leydesdorff, 2000) where university, business and government have been introduced as the key factors behind any knowledge-based regional development. This section examines the role of the "Triple Helix" in the progress of the investigated case study and determines the central role of the community as an innovation base for the interaction among these main factors. It suggests a promotion for a Quadruple Helix Model where community – as innovation base- is as important as business, university and government in the new economy. It concludes that regional knowledge-based developments will not sustain unless all four factors- community, business, university, government- work together.

There is a dearth of articulated/empirical data on the characteristics of knowledge-based developments in Australia. This was the incentive for a study that this chapter is reviewing some of its preliminary finding regarding the relation between local and regional knowledge-based development. This finding is based on in-depth interviews and participatory observation in a case study of knowledge-based development in Queensland namely Varsity Lakes that has been planned as a smart mixed-use residential community offering live/work opportunities to the residents through the telecommunication technologies (Bajracharya & Allison, 2008). This study conducted interviews with a purposeful sample of residents and key informants at the community. The interviews were done with people representing main stakeholders and institutional spheres in the community such as office park and incubator directors, Lend Lease (the developer), Bond University, Gold Coast City Council, private firms, small business support networks, and residents' community groups. The resident interviewees also have been chosen based on their work-type to cover a reasonable variety of the people involved with the community. The study also investigated strategic documents such as Varsity Lakes Development Plans, Regional Development Plans and internal reports.

This chapter, investigating Varsity Lakes, searches for some general themes that can be adjusted to different knowledge-based local and regional development projects. It builds upon previous studies of similar case studies in Europe and USA and promotes the theoretical framework suggested by them based on the new empirical finding. This chapter aims to develop a theoretical understanding of how and under what conditions local and regional knowledge-based development projects do communicate to each other.

KNOWLEDGE-BASED LOCAL DEVELOPMENT

The evolution of new information communication technologies follows three main trends in the literature. The first trend arises with the classic and popular studies that posit the decline of cities as the new technologies make it possible to replace the face-to-face activities that occur in central cities (Garreau, 1992; Gordon & Richardson, 1997; Negroponte, 1995). The second trend accuses the first one of being shallow and declares that the information technologies develop the complexity of cities by increasing the number and type of interactions among individuals, firms and technical systems (Audirac & Fitzgerald, 2003; Castells, 1996, 2004; Graham & Marvin, 1996; Mitchell, 1996, 1999). In this trend, the authors refer to the empirical data from the forerunner cities in the digital age and note that telecommunication leads to both the centralization and decentralization of economic activities. They argue that the once clear distinctions between city and suburb, countryside and metropolis are now diminishing and there are both successful and unsuccessful places of every type in the new era (Clifford, 2002; Kotkin, 2000). This provides the foundation of the third trend- still emerging- that emphasizes the concept of "quality of life" (Florida, 2002; Lloyd & Clark, 2001) and considers it as the main reason for location decision in the digital era. This new trend encourages communities to reassess their firm attraction efforts and reorient them towards people attraction. This approach has been particularly effective in the communities where the "quality of life" factor attracting knowledge workers shapes incubators for high-technology firms. This is interesting that the successful hubs could be as different as urban "creative centers" and elite rural areas.

Apart from some scholarly disagreements in the new trend, it seems that different studies are talking about a similar concept using different terms like digital neighborhood, wired community, broadband community, creative centre, information district, computer mediated community and so on. Here, authors introduce "knowledge-based local development" to be the best localities that attract information workers, emphasize on the productive side of residential communities and finally boost the regional prosperities. The knowledge-based local development is presented as technology-based mixed-use residential communities that can accept different urban and rural forms to offer the desired life style to information workers. A growing body of literature (Kotkin, 2000; Mitchell, 1999) describes these new settlement patterns of the twenty-first century as live/work dwellings and 24-hour pedestrian-scale neighborhoods that recreate what was best about old-style small towns in the digital era.

There is no real consensus on the urban form of knowledge-based neighborhoods. However, from a social science perspective, there is a relatively long list of promises that are to be addressed. Several studies suggest that these communities reduce the digital divide (Graham, 2002; Malina & Macintosh, 2004); others emphasize that the local web network increases the interaction among residential home computer users, helps them to arrange in-person get-togethers and form real neighborhoods as social units (Hampton, 2002; Krouk, Pitkin, & Richman, 2000; Loader, Hague, & Eagle, 2000). There is even a common theme throughout some studies to explore the ways in which the communities apply ICT to build a better and more sustainable future for all sections of their local society (Gurstein, 2000). Also, some research refers to the potential impact of knowledge-based local developments on travel behavior, energy consumption and air pollution though telecommunications (Illegems & Verbeke, 2003).

All of this so far shows that growing number of scholars support knowledge-based local developments to reconcile urban environments and the new economy in the digital age. Yet, little knowledge has been produced on the ways these forerunner communities communicate with the larger region. In this regard attempts have been made to introduce a glocal (global-local) approach to address the dispute between highly globalized regions and specific localities. This new approach argues that new theories and representations of spatial models are needed to clarify the new setting (Brenner, 1998; Martins & Álvarez, 2007; Thornton, 2000). The following has a review on the theoretical base of local economic development to illustrate the progress that has led to a glocal approach. It then describes the empirical finding from a case study in Queensland-Australia to explore the role of these new communities in the larger region.

The Third Wave: Economic Development in Perspective

A consistent theme in the scholarly literature (Blakely & Bradshaw, 2002; Herbers, 1990; Ross & Friedman, 1990) describes three waves of economic development practice. Despite all the differences, for the first two waves local economic development has been based on the notion that a locality can provide all of the resources to build and sustain an economic base. They use tax inducement and provide expansion loans to either attract new businesses or retain existing ones. However, it is unclear in the digital age whether any resources that local authorities control are germane for economic development. It is also increasingly evident that the new economy is being formed more by global than by local forces. As a result of this the third wave is emerging. Third wave argues that as global hub centres arises, the communities that build the infrastructure to connect to this network will thrive.

This new wave (Blakely, 2001), introducing a glocal approach, states that economic development has to redesign development tools and see which firms are likely to establish hubs. There is actually an emphasis on the technology-based globalization as the new paradigm in the notion of this wave. It then notes that for a community to be competitive as a hub, technological infrastructure and human resource capacity are essential. Third wave suggests a link between education and industry as a continuum in regional collaboration and creates context for better relations among firms. It introduces a critical role for the local government in forging new partnerships across sectors, so that a new incubating environment can be created in every community across the nation. The third wave places the greatest emphasis on technological infrastructure that supports *a cluster of related industries*, not just single firms. It, rather than dealing with firms one by one, supports the growth of specified clusters of related firms to achieve the local and also regional development.

These "industry clusters" are not actually dissimilar to quasi-firm residential communities seeking for productive roles in the new economy. This characteristic encourages the present chapter to examine knowledge-based local developments in the light of third wave to understand their interaction with related firms. The following describes the progress of a mixed-use residential community- Varsity Lakes- that originally has been planned to work with the global cluster/network.

However, the lack of related firms/infrastructures in the region is retarding its progress.

The Emergence of Varsity Lakes

Varsity Lakes is a master planned community covering 343 hectares of land including 80 hectares of lakes and waterways and 56 hectares of open space. The community is located on Queensland's Gold Coast (*Figure 1, 2*) adjacent to Bond University and close proximity to golf courses, North Burleigh Beach and a number of canal residential estates. Development of the community commenced in 1999 and is expected to be completed by late 2010. The built out population will be approximately 7,800 residents. The community has already attracted more than 6200 people.

Varsity Lakes contains a mixed-use residential community, business land uses, a range of green spaces and beautiful walking paths. The Varsity Lakes town centre, "Varsity Central" is the business and innovation hub of Varsity Lakes with 150000 sq m. of commercial space and the employment of over 5000 people[2]. The town centre contains two precincts, namely, Varsity Central and Market Square. The Varsity Central precinct (which continues along Varsity Parade axis) immediately adjoins the university and contains office park, mixed-use developments, and education facilities. The range of businesses located in Varsity Central include those with expertise in areas such as ICT, law, finance, education, professional services, medicine and general business services. The Market Square precinct backs on to the lakes and contains a small local shopping centre, dining and entertainment facilities. Much of the early development of Varsity Lakes centred on detached dwellings as well as the Varsity Central business precinct. The more recent stages of residential development are more focused on medium density dwellings and mixed-use developments. The future stage will include the second town centre which will fulfil more entertainment/shopping facilities and the community centre to empower the sense of community.

Varsity Lakes is a popular residential community for very different groups with different backgrounds due to its built form, provision of natural amenities and business parks. The community also has a strong focus on business and offices within the development. Broadly efforts have been made to attract e-entrepreneurship and information work through equipping co-work[3] places (Johnson, 2003) and office parks with high-speed fibre optic Internet. There is an emphasis to encourage ICT related industries and telework opportunities as part of the efforts to create a fully integrated live/work community. The greatest emphasis to offer live/work experience to the residents occurs in the town centre area where SOHO units evoke the memory of old European cities where people could live on top of their local shops. Here though the businesses connect to the bigger world through telecommunication and do not depend only on local customers. This does not mean that work opportunities (telework, e-entrepreneurial etc.) are limited to Varsity Central. Planning regulations in Varsity Lakes are generally very welcoming to home-based businesses as residents are allowed to employ 4-10 people – in different parts of the community- for their home businesses which has resulted in many active home offices.

There is no index of small businesses spread out in the whole community working from co-work offices, incubator facilities, home offices and street shops. "Varsity Central Business Association" that represents the business activities in the community estimates that at least 250 small and medium businesses function in the community. However, this study has collected a preliminary/non-inclusive list of about 120 small businesses including: 30 high-rank business services that function in areas such as law, finance, accounting, taxation, medical support, corporate branding, travel agencies and planning; 35 ICT related offices that are involved with web design, website development, web hosting, web-based advertising, printing services, video conferencing, Internet, phone and mobile support services; 15 technology-based entertainment businesses such as graphic design, digital photography, animation, and movie production; and finally 4 banking and financial system related offices. It is also interesting to see that the different lifestyle of information workers who actually live/work in the community has attracted a number of retail service businesses that actually have helped the diversity and liveability of the community. This includes more than 10 café and restaurants; 8 health and fitness services with specialities in areas such as surf coaching and Tai Chi instruction; 2 temporary residential units (hotel apartment); 18 Retail businesses (chemist, supermarket, gift shops, cloth shops, florist, hair and beauty saloon, babysitting service).

The growing number of small businesses in the Varsity Lakes has cultivated an active/liveable base that is impressive for a young community. However, this characteristic impacts on an area certainly broader that Varsity Lakes borders. The following describes some of the opportunities and challenges experienced in the interaction between the community and larger region. It also relates to the third wave of local economy development to further our understanding of the future progress of knowledge-based development in Varsity Lakes.

Varsity Lakes in the Region

In Varsity Lakes the natural amenities, IT facilities and the liveability and diversity of the community offer "quality of life" that seems to be the key to success in the new economy. These opportunities have not only attracted professional information-workers to live/work in the community but also created a large number of high and medium ranked knowledge-related jobs for the larger region. The existence of regional office of big companies such as IBM Australia, MaxSoft Group, On the Net, go talk, Conics and Minter Ellison Lawyers that each and every one of them employ between 15- 300 people in the vicinity of Varsity Lakes shows how much the larger region benefits from the community. Yet, there are some problems in Varsity Lakes related to a lack of regional awareness on what could be done through such communities as technology nodes for the development of the whole region. Most of the problems are beyond the control of the developer, and regional or even national authorities are needed to address them. Some problems also simply refer to the fact that Varsity Lakes seems to be the only one of this type in the nearby area. These problems threaten different aspects of knowledge-based development in Varsity Lakes. The following represents three main points, revealed during the in-depth interviews, in relation to lack of proper infrastructure and institutional relationship with related firms in the larger region which decrease the quality of life in the community and hinder the community development:

- The main issue that Varsity Lakes is inheriting from the regional/national agenda is the non-competitive nature of IT infrastructure industry in Australia. As it was mentioned, Varsity Lakes provides high-speed internet through fibre optic in the Varsity Central which is the town centre and embeds business parks, office areas and the core of activities. Yet, the Internet provider company is unable, in spite of its size and dominance in the market, to provide enough broadband access points for the home offices scattered in different residential parts of the community. In other words, the idea behind Varsity Lakes to attract information work at different levels is not fully achieved for people to operate from their home offices because of poor Internet connections in some parts of the community.
- The notion of network in the digital age puts a great emphasis on the relation between universities and knowledge-based

developments. Universities are the institutions that provide the human resource and direct the entrepreneurial spirit. However, the complexity of the relation between Bond University and Varsity Lakes has been problematic over the past few years. Needless to say there is a very powerful spiritual bond between some individual academics in Bond University and business groups in Varsity Lakes. The synergy between these two supports the entrepreneurial research environment with very direct benefits for the prosperity of community economic development. Also, half of 3000 students in the university are international and around 600 units in the community are occupied by the university students and staff. Yet, it seems that the university leadership is not really involved with the progress of Varsity Lakes. This study's investigation reveals that the unfriendly institutional relationship between university and the community is strained by underlying tensions over land ownership in the past two decades. More recently the university put a lot of time and effort to be physically separated from the very immediate community of Varsity Lakes through new traffic arrangements that have even banned one of two main entrances of the community that passes through the university land. Unfortunately, these ongoing tensions impede constructive collaborations between these two related firms that could benefit a lot from each other.

- Telecommunication facilities in knowledge-based neighbourhoods could impact on travel behaviour of the residents. In Varsity Lakes, this opportunity has been used to offer a better quality of life to people who live, work and play in the same locality. Availability of a network of walking paths including 2 km walking path besides the lake and bike paths encourage a culture of sustainable transport within the community. Though these green networks are connected to nowhere out of the community and whenever people need to leave the community all the sustainable options disappear. This is actually more important when you consider the number of people who work in Varsity Lakes and live nearby. The highway network just out of the community is designed as auto dominated movement system. This simply leads to the next regional problem in southern Queensland which is the lack of reliable frequent enough public transport. This is the last straw that stops any other options but private cars for all external access in or out of the community. In other words, one of the community attempts to offer a better quality of life through sustainable solutions to information workers is not fully attained due to the lack of infrastructure in the larger region.

It is evident that the up to now impressive progress of Varsity Lakes could be hindered because of the institutional and infrastructural challenges that have not been fully addressed in the regional level. Varsity Lakes represents the smart communities that play a quasi-firm role seeking for productive roles in the knowledge economy, and declares that the resources provided by a single community are not sufficient to sustain the long term knowledge-based development. This evokes the third wave's emphasis on a cluster of related industries- not just single firms- as the main key to local community development. This emphasis could be nicely implemented in Varsity Lakes where the lack of institutional and infrastructural support network retards its progress. In fact, the future progress of knowledge-based development in Varsity Lakes needs support network of a cluster of related firms (transport system, universities,

IT infrastructure providers etc.) that have to get founded or reformed -through existing firms- in the regional strategy making level.

It is time to investigate the other side of mutual interaction between different levels of knowledge-based development. While the first section showed that the continuity of local knowledge-based development depends on the regional support network, the following section attempts to review the process of regional knowledge-based development in theory and practice to understand the role of local communities in the prosperity of larger regions.

KNOWLEDGE-BASED REGIONAL DEVELOPMENT

There is an extensive body of literature emphasising on the role of knowledge in the regional economy development. Here knowledge has been introduced as the primary source of power in the creation of innovating regions, and the economic prosperity of the areas that seek for active roles in the global network. Yet, it has been recently and in only a few studies that attempts have been made to explain the specific mechanism and institutional relationships, through which knowledge-based regional developments actually takes place. These studies review the successful case studies of knowledge based development and argue that the conditions for creating continuous high-tech social and economic growth can be identified. The earlier studies in this group (Lundvall, 1992; Nelson, 1993) mostly consider the firm or government as having the leading role in innovating regions. However, Triple Helix- which will be presented in this chapter- has a broader and more historical perspective to understand the development of a whole region. The following reviews the basis of Triple Helix to understand the ins and outs of collaboration network that actually leads Varsity Lakes' knowledge-based development within the larger region.

Towards the Theory of Triple Helix

The Triple Helix Model was initially derived from an analysis of the renewal of Boston economy through a university–industry–government collaboration in the 1930s (Etzkowitz, 2008). Later on the initial case study based model developed through utilizing longitudinal data from a Swedish region, and international comparisons. The current model builds upon studies of different regions in Europe and the US collecting data to explore the development and transformation of knowledge-based regions (Jones-Evans, Klofsten, Andwerson, & Pandya, 1999; Klofsten & Jones-Evans, 1996; Klofsten & Jones-Evans, 2000).

The Triple Helix introduces a model of knowledge-based regional development through collaboration among business, government and university. This model comprises three basic elements (Etzkowitz, 2008). First, it presumes a more prominent role for the university, alongside industry and government. In this model the universities that played only a supporting role move into centre stage accepting a new entrepreneurial role. Second, there is a movement towards collaborative relationships among the three major institutional spheres in which regional development strategy is increasingly an outcome of interaction rather than a prescription from government. Thirdly, the new role of each institutional base is a combination of their traditional functions plus some of the role of others. An entrepreneurial business group (industry), being open to take some of the traditional roles of government could enhance the progress of an innovating region.

This model describes the knowledge-based development as a gradual process and identifies four stages of development: Inception, Implementation, Consolidation and Renewal (Etzkowitz & Klofsten, 2005). The first stage- Inception- develops the idea of a new regional model. The second- Implementation- starts new activities that actually could get consolidated or adjusted in the third stage, and then the last stage of renewal includes the self-sustaining growth. The key event- in these four stages- is the creation of an entrepreneurial university which creates a support network- together with government and industry- for firm formation and regional growth. The result of this collaboration is a self-sustaining dynamic region in which the role of university and government recede as industrial actors come to the fore and a network of knowledge-based firms is created. Nevertheless, as one technological paradigm is exhausted and another base for innovation is needed, the role of university and government comes to the fore again in creating the conditions for the next wave of innovation.

The Triple Helix describes three different institutional arrangements that industry-university-government interact to one another (Etzkowitz & Leydesdorff, 2000). These three different levels of interaction actually have different impact on the process of knowledge-based development (*Figure 3)*. Triple Helix I shows a statist model of government that leads university and industry, and directs the relations between them. This configuration is mostly known as a failed developmental model with too little room for "bottom up" initiatives. On the other hand, Triple Helix II refers to Laissez-faire model with industry, academia and government interacting only modestly across strong boundaries. This policy nowadays is also advocated as shock therapy to reduce the role of government in the Triple Helix I. Triple Helix III represents a triad of equal and overlapping collaboration among university-government-Industry. This configuration that is known as the Triple Helix of Innovation is not expected to be stable. This also could be described through the biological metaphor in which each strand may relate to the other two to develop an emerging overlay of communications and networks among the helices. The collaboration among the Triple Helix in this configuration is no longer a pre-given order, and has the flexibility to adopt an endless transition which is the key to self-sustainability of knowledge-based development.

The Triple Helix is a flexible framework that acknowledges the challenges that different areas taking off for knowledge-based development could be struggling with. It also understands the different starting points that different communities within a region choose to be parts of innovation hub. However, it identifies the collaboration between three main institutional spheres- university, industry and government- to be the foundation of success in every region. Even if not present in the beginning, they likely appear at a later phase to fill gaps between local and regional level of knowledge-based development.

Australian Context

It is interesting to know that the larger region in the investigated case study (Varsity Lakes) which is South Eastern Queensland is an important part of the "Smart Strategy Plan" proposed for Queensland. More specifically, there is an emphasis on innovation in Gold Coast City Council through introducing "Pacific Innovation Corridor". The following reviews the progress of these regional knowledge-based development plans to identify the links with Triple Helix Model.

Queensland: Smart State Strategy

In 1998 Queensland Government defined a vision for Queensland to be the Smart State where knowledge, creativity and innovation would drive economic growth (Queensland Government, 2006). In August 2003, the government released the Smart State Strategy prospectus (Queensland Government, 2004). The prospectus outlined the government's commitment to achieve the vision. Later on, in 2004 the government undertook a consultation process to inform development of this vision. The next report of Smart State Strategy was published in 2005 when Queensland Government introduced a mid-term plan (2005-2012) to achieve knowledge-based regional development (Queensland Government, 2005). The statistics in this report indicate an impressive performance from the inception of the Smart State Vision. The latest progress report on Smart State was recently published in 2008 (Queensland Government, 2008). This report reviews the progress of the strategy and introduces a new direction for the future that includes a new emphasis on fulfilling the skill shortage that is challenging the future of Queensland.

The Smart State Strategy describes its own objective to put Queensland competitively on the world stage as a place of great inspiration and achievement. The strategy outlines Queensland's short to mid-term investment program, with funding concentrated in innovation, new technologies and industries, research and development infrastructure, education and training reforms. The latest report on the progress of the strategy (Queensland Government, 2008) actually indicates that over the last decade $3.4 billion was invested in R&D and innovation, resulting in 36 new research institutes and creating 60000 jobs in industries such as aviation, biotechnology and creative industries. The highlight of the 2008 strategy report is the introduction of a new direction for the future of plan that includes a trebling of investment in creative people including: $23.3 million to attract experts in science and industry through the Innovation Skills Fund, and $25 million to attract leading clinical researchers via the Health and Medical Research Program.

Queensland Government is using its influence to promote the importance of knowledge, creativity and innovation at different levels. However, the government directing everything leads to a Triple Helix I where a statist government control university and industry. In other word, knowledge-based development in Queensland seems to be mostly based on the earlier studies that emphasize on the role of government to establish a support system that creates new firms through universities. This configuration is mostly known as a controversial developmental model that discourages bottom-up innovation. The Triple Helix explicitly warns that by the time that a self-sustained collaboration environment among university-government- industry does not exist a region with a cluster of firms- rooted in a particular technological paradigm- is in danger of decline once that paradigm runs out.

On the other hand, Queensland is still learning from its progress in the last decade and if we remember the progressive nature of knowledge-based development in the Triple Helix we can see that the region is just in the second stage of development. The first stage of development that includes developing the idea of a new regional model started 10 years ago and as the model illustrates -as a result of that- Queensland has enjoyed remarkable improvements in its economic prospects (Queensland Government, 2005). Economic growth has averaged five per cent per year compared with the Australian average of 3.7 per cent. Labor productivity in Queensland has also grown faster, at 2.9 per cent, than the Australian average of 2.3 per cent. The current stage that government is investing in new activities and fulfilling the skill shortage is considered as the second stage. This means that to achieve a sustainable knowledge-based development the region has to be ready for the consolidation and adjustment stage that could facilitate the fourth stage of self-sustaining growth. This long way ahead leads to the point made by few studies (Yigitcanlar & Velibeyoglu, 2008) that explicitly examined the progress of Smart State Strategy in Queensland: it is still early to comment as there is plenty of room to improve.

Pacific Innovation Corridor

The Pacific Innovation Corridor (PIC) is one of Gold Coast City Council's long term economic development plans (Gold Coast City Council, 2008). PIC has been proposed to create globally capable geographical and economic focused precincts. These focus precincts on the corridor are characterized by the availability of research and development, innovation and international interaction. Gold Coast City Council prioritizes the hard 'telecommunications' infrastructure delivery to focus precincts. It also promotes the clustering of related firms and industry sectors within specific focused precincts to enhance the knowledge-based development.

There are a total of ten such PIC focused precincts on the Gold Coast including Beenleigh, Yatala, Coomera, Oxenford, Southport, Nerang, Surfer's Paradise, Varsity, Burleigh, Coolangatta. The role of each precinct supports the geographic and cultural nature of these areas. Among these, Varsity Lakes- with a focus on Varsity Central- has been proposed as the "Technology Precinct" on the Pacific innovation corridor. The main reasons behind this choice are: emerging a cluster of hi-tech companies- big and small- in Varsity Lakes, close proximity to Bond University, and the (smart) mixed-use nature of the community.

It is important to remember that Varsity Lakes is competing with some old/well-known areas like Southport and Surfer's Paradise on the Pacific Innovation Corridors. This encourages this chapter to review the progress of Varsity Lakes over the last decade in the new light of the Triple Helix. It will help us understand how three main spheres of university-industry-government have been working together, and actually the role of communities like Varsity Lakes in the knowledge-based development of the larger region

Triple Helix in Varsity Lakes

The development of Varsity Lakes could be approached in two different ways. The simplistic approach probably presumes that what has happened in Varsity Lakes is underpinned by a partnership between the Queensland State Government, Gold Coast City Council and Delfin Lend Lease (the developer). This joined public-private collaboration formed a dual helix that combined different sources -of social and education providers, ICT specialists, general business and so on- to ensure that the innovative economic development strategy succeeds.

On the other hand, the more complicated approach argues that the initial public-private partnership formed an "innovation organizer" that designed new initiatives to foster economic and social development. This partnership facilitated IT infrastructure and negotiated with new economy industries to move in to the community. Also, a few individuals -as the Triple Helix Model points out- were crucial at the beginning phase of the process. These people are called "extrapreneurs" (Etzkowitz & Klofsten, 2005) and described as who project a future vision and go beyond the boundaries of their organization to create entrepreneurial spirit in the larger region. In Varsity Lakes we can trace back extrapreneurs in many different areas. The extrapreneurs in the developer side who created co-work places and SOHOs cultivated the base for innovation success, and the ones in government side (Gold Coast City Council) pushing green transport options for the community developed the desire life-style of information workers. However, the progress of knowledge-based development in Varsity Lakes is not limited to this, as extrapreneurs per se are not able to guarantee the self-sustainability of innovation. The development of Varsity Lakes is the result of a complicated collaboration among different stakeholders that even go beyond the Triple Helix Model.

To investigate the collaboration between different spheres of the Triple Helix in Varsity Lakes, it is necessary to understand that as the theoretical model has illustrated the current network of collaboration in Varsity Lakes is the outcome of a gradual process. For example in regard to the relation between industry and government, collaboration commenced when Gold Coast City Council approved new planning regulation that supports the idea of a mixed-use development vs. a pure residential one. More specifically the very significant change in regulatory environment allowed home-offices to have employees. These simple but important changes encouraged the prosperity of small and medium sized firms and cultivated an attractive base for the niche players to move in to the community.

As mentioned before there are some institutional problems that restrict the official role of university in the progress of Varsity Lakes. Contrary to the theoretical model, university was not involved with the initial "innovation organizer" that put forward the initiatives for the knowledge-based development of the community and its role in the larger region. Yet, in reality there is actually a strong connection between the university and industry in the community. The growing number of entrepreneurial research projects in Bond University focusing on small businesses, and academics who are involved with business activities in the community empower the innovation base. Currently local business groups mediate the interaction between university and business/industry. The collaboration between representatives of these two spheres support and potentially lead the prosperity of the economic development of Varsity lakes.

The Triple Helix Model suggests that when university fails to play a leading role in the progress of knowledge-based development it is often because a broader institutional coalition to encourage this role is lacking (Etzkowitz, 2008). This seems to be true for Varsity Lakes, as the relation between university and government in this case study is very unclear. Although governmental reports always support the existence of the biggest private university of Australia in the area, they do not encourage any institutional leading role for the university in the development of nearby communities.

To sum up, the initial success of Varsity Lakes could be traced back to the existence of the extrapreneurs in different spheres of Triple Helix who create initiatives for the prosperity of the area. However, the continuity of the progress is a result of a complicated network in the community that is even ready to take over some of the responsibilities of the initial "innovation organizer". The network groups who represent residents and businesses involved in the community have already formed a forum of all stakeholders to lead the future progress of Varsity Lakes. This forum protects the mixed-use identity of the community that has been able to create growing small and medium sized firms, attract niche players, and generate additional clusters through a desired life-style.

Lessons Learnt in Varsity Lakes- Quadruple Helix Model

Varsity Lakes is a noteworthy case study as it allows us to examine the conditions under which a double helix is transformed into a more complicated network of collaboration among different stakeholders. The Triple Helix Model (Etzkowitz & Klofsten, 2005) hypothesizes that the involvement of an entrepreneurial university is the key to the transition from starting point of a government–industry double helix. However, our investigation shows that this has not happened in Varsity Lakes, as still university has not taken the centre stage and is playing mostly a supportive role through some entrepreneurial academic members. So, what is behind the ongoing transition in Varsity Lakes?

Varsity Lakes is successful because what the "innovation organizer" initiated could renew and self-sustain. This would not happen unless for the creation of a "local community" that absorbed extrapreneurs from the Triple Helix, and actually established a local identity around them. The local community is an amalgamation of all the people from different spheres of the Triple Helix who cultivate an innovation base. The people in the developer side who -having big plans in mind- encourage small businesses to form an attractive business environment for niche players; individual academics and community business groups who go beyond the institutional conflicts and create an ongoing entrepreneurial spirit in the community; and finally every one who work/live in Varsity Lakes took their part in the progress of this knowledge-based community.

In other words, the local community in Varsity Lakes followed the initiatives presented by the "innovation organizer" and facilitated its transition through a local identity. Here the dual helix of public-private partnership has transformed to a collaboration network through the community that has absorbed all the organic potential in absence of strong institutional relationship. It is actually difficult to identify the knowledge-based development model of Varsity Lakes among three suggested configurations of Triple Helix. The overlap among three different institutional spheres in the Triple Helix III could be similar to the notion of community (*Figure 4*). Although this configuration is unable to illustrate the organic relations through community that empower the institutional collaboration among Triple Helix spheres, it could promote to a Quadruple Helix Model where four strands of university-community-government-industry work together (*Figure 5*). This model is able to explain the development of case studies like Varsity Lakes where "the community" forms an organic collaboration among other institutional spheres in a dynamic configuration.

Introducing the concept of community in the knowledge-based development model of Varsity Lakes opens some new doors for larger regions. They can enhance the development process through the local communities that shape some organic links between different stakeholders involved with the Triple Helix Model. This specifically helps when some institutional sectors hesitate to take active part in the knowledge-based development in the beginning phase. This also facilitates the renewal stage as the common "sense of belonging" to the communities could sustain the continuity of the collaboration. In fact, the puzzle of participation in the Quadruple Helix has a large room for bottom-up initiatives that expedite the knowledge-based development through constructive collaboration between local communities and larger region.

CONCLUSION

Varsity Lakes as a smart mixed-used residential community locating in South Eastern Queensland, the so called Smart State, is an interesting case to investigate the interaction between local and regional level of knowledge-based development. This chapter benefited from well-known theoretical frameworks that attempt to model the local and regional economic development in the new era, and related them to the empirical findings in Varsity Lakes which shows that:

Firstly, communities may start their local development plans separately using powerful mediators-such as a thoughtful developer, supportive local authorities and so on. Yet, the resources provided by a single community are not sufficient to sustain the long term knowledge-based development. This could be re-interpreted through the important basis of the third wave of community economic development emphasising on a cluster of related industries- not just single firms. The lessons learnt in Varsity Lakes note that knowledge-based local development does not evolve unless a regional support network of related firms gets established and works together.

Secondly, the knowledge-based development of Varsity Lakes introduces a promotion of the Triple Helix Model where community on a par with government, business and university are the key factors. In this Quadruple Helix Model the creation of a local community goes beyond some institutional conflicts and builds a dynamic network of collaboration. More specifically, in Varsity Lakes the Quadruple Helix follows an organic configuration where community actually relates university and industry through connection of entrepreneurial academics and local business groups. It evolves the notion of innovation through renewing the organic – and not just institutional-collaboration between different factors within the local community and larger region. This opens some new doors for larger regions to pursue the local identity of smart communities to enhance the knowledge-based developments in both local and regional level.

FUTURE RESEARCH DIRECTION

To date, there has been limited research on the interaction between different levels of knowledge-based development. Introducing the notion of local community to the regional knowledge-based development model, this study has contributed to this neglected research area. Yet, the Quadruple Helix is a young model that could be corroborated in the future research. Specifically there is a demand for longitudinal research in the investigated case study- Varsity Lakes- to examine the future progress of the knowledge-based local development and the role of community in the long term alongside with university, government and industry. More generally, more case study research need to be conducted to test the Quadruple Helix Model in different situations for communities with different starting points and in different institutional environments. Last but not least, there is a dearth of spatially integrated research on the progress of knowledge-based development in Australia. To compete on the global level, Australian academia needs to have a better understanding of the attempts undertaken by different levels of policy making and compare them with the progress of the key players on the world stage. Further research that focuses on these neglected areas to determine the best future direction needs to be undertaken.

ACKNOWLEDGMENT

I would like to express my gratitude to Crighton Properties for their financial support that facilitated the progress of this study.

REFERENCES

Audirac, I., & Fitzgerald, J. (2003). Information Technology (IT) and Urban Form: An Annotated Bibliography of the Urban Deconcentration and Economic Restructuring Literatures. *Journal of Planning Literature*, *17*(4), 480–511.

Bajracharya, B., & Allison, J. (2008). Emerging Role of ICT in the Development of Knowledge-Based Master Planned Communities . In Yigitcanlar, T., Velibeyoglu, K., & Baum, S. (Eds.), *Knowledge-Based Urban Development: Planning and Applications in the Information Era* (pp. 279–295). New York: Information Science Reference.

Blakely, E. (2001). Competitive Advantage for the 21st-Century City. *Journal of the American Planning Association. American Planning Association*, *67*(2), 133–145.

Blakely, E., & Bradshaw, T. (2002). *Planning Local Economic Development: Theory and Practice*. Thousand Oaks, CA: Sage Publications.

Brenner, N. (1998). Global Cities, Glocal States: Global City Formation and State Territorial Restructuring in Contemporary Europe. *Review of International Political Economy*, *5*(1), 1–37.

Castells, M. (1996). *The Information Age: The Rise of the Network Society*. Boston, MA: Blackwell Publishers.

Castells, M. (Ed.). (2004). *The Network Society (A Cross-Cultural Perspective)*. Cheltenham, UK: Edward Elgar Publishing Limited.

Clifford, J. S. (2002). *Transcending Locality-Driven Lifestyle: The Potential of the Internet to Redefine our Neighbourhood Patterns*. Cambridge, MA: Harvard University.

Etzkowitz, H. (2008). *The Triple Helix: University-Industry-Government Innovation in Action*. London: Routledge.

Etzkowitz, H., & Klofsten, M. (2005). The Innovating Region: Toward a Theory of Knowledge-Based Regional Development. *R & D Management, 35*(3), 243–255.

Etzkowitz, H., & Leydesdorff, L. (2000). The Dynamics of Innovation: From National Systems and "Mode 2" to a Triple Helix of University–Industry–Government Relations. *Research Policy, 29*(2), 109–123.

Florida, R. (2002). *The Rise of the Creative Class*. New York: Basic Books.

Garreau, J. (1992). *Edge City: Life on the New Frontier*. New York: Anchor Books.

Gold Coast City Council. (2008). *Business Precincts: Delivering a Balanced, Connected and Prosperous Economy*. Retrieved March 2, 2008, from http://businessgc.com.au/index.php?page=gc-precincts

Gordon, P., & Richardson, H. W. (1997). Are Compact Cities a Desirable Planning Goal? *Journal of the American Planning Association. American Planning Association, 63*(1), 95–106.

Graham, S. (2002). Bridging Urban Digital Divides? Urban Polarisation and Information and Communications Technologies (ICTs). *Urban Studies (Edinburgh, Scotland), 39*(1), 33–56.

Graham, S., & Marvin, S. (1996). *Telecommunications and the City: Electronic Spaces, Urban Places*. London, New York: Routledge.

Gurstein, M. (Ed.). (2000). *Community Informatics: Enabling Communities with Information and Communication Technologies*. Hershey, PA: Idea Group Publishing.

Hampton, K. (2002). Place-Based and IT Mediated 'Community. *Planning Theory & Practice, 3*(2), 228–231.

Herbers, J. (1990). A Third Wave of Economic Development. *Governing, 9*(3), 43–50.

Illegems, V., & Verbeke, A. (2003). *Moving Towards the Virtual Workplace*. Cheltenham, UK: Edward Elgar Publishing.

Johnson, L. C. (2003). *The Co-Workplace: Teleworking in the Neighbourhood*. Vancouver, Canada: UBC Press.

Jones-Evans, D., Klofsten, M., Andwerson, E., & Pandya, D. (1999). Creating a Bridge between University and Industry in Small European Countries: The Role of the Industrial Liaison Office. *R & D Management, 29*(1), 47–56.

Klofsten, M., & Jones-Evans, D. (1996). Stimulation of Technology-Based Small Firms - A Case Study of University-Industry Co-Operation. *Technovation, 16*(4), 187–193.

Klofsten, M., & Jones-Evans, D. (2000). Comparing Academic Entrepreneurship in Europe: The Case of Sweden and Ireland. *Small Business Economics, 14*, 299–309.

Kotkin, J. (2000). *The New Geography: How the Digital Revolution Is Reshaping the American Landscape*. New York: Random House.

Krouk, D., Pitkin, B., & Richman, N. (2000). Internet-Based Neighbourhood Information Systems: A Comparative Analysis . In Gurstein, M. (Ed.), *Community Informatics: Enabling Communities with Information and Communication Technologies*. Hershey, PA: Idea Group Publishing.

Lloyd, R., & Clark, T. N. (2001). The City as an Entertainment Machine . In Gotham, K. F. (Ed.), *Critical Perspectives on Urban Development* (*Vol. 6*, pp. 357–378). Oxford, UK: Elsevier.

Loader, B. D., Hague, B., & Eagle, D. (2000). Embedding the Net: Community Empowerment in the Age of Information . In Gurstein, M. (Ed.), *Community Informatics: Enabling Communities with Information and Communication Technologies*. Hershey, PA: Idea Group Publishing.

Lundvall, B. (Ed.). (1992). *National Systems of Innovation*. London: Pinter.

Malina, A., & Macintosh, A. (2004). Bridging the Digital Divide: Developments in Scotland . In Mälkiä, M., Anttiroiko, A. V., & Savolainen, R. (Eds.), *eTransformation in governance: new directions in government and politic* (pp. 255–271). Hershey, PA: IGI Publishing.

Martins, L., & Álvarez, J. M. R. (2007). Towards Glocal Leadership: Taking up the Challenge of New Local Governance in Europe? *Government and Policy*, *25*(3), 391–409.

Mitchell, W. J. (1996). *City of bits*. Cambridge, MA: The MIT Press.

Mitchell, W. J. (1999). *E-topia*. Cambridge, MA: The MIT Press.

Negroponte, N. (1995). *Being Digital*. New York: Knopf.

Nelson, R. R. (Ed.). (1993). *National Innovation Systems: A Comparative Study*. New York: Oxford University Press.

Queensland Government. (2004). *Smart Strategy Progress 2004*. Brisbane: Smart State Council.

Queensland Government. (2005). *Smart Queensland: Smart State Strategy 2005–2015*. Brisbane: Smart State Council.

Queensland Government. (2006). *Smart Regions: Characteristics of Globally Successful Regions and Implications for Queensland*. Brisbane: Smart State Council.

Queensland Government. (2008). *Smart State Strategy 2008-2012*. Brisbane: Smart State Council.

Ross, D., & Friedman, R. E. (1990). The Emerging Third Wave: New Economic Development Strategies. *Entrepreneurial Economy Review*, *90*, 3–11.

Thornton, W. H. (2000). Mapping the `Glocal' Village: The Political Limits of `Glocalization'. *Journal of Media & Cultural Studies*, *14*(1).

Yigitcanlar, T., & Velibeyoglu, K. (2008). Queensland's Smart State Initiative: A Successful Knowledge-Based Urban Development Strategy? In Yigitcanlar, T., Velibeyoglu, K., & Baum, S. (Eds.), *Knowledge-Based Urban Development: Planning and Applications in the information Era* (pp. 116–131). New York: Information Science Reference.

ADDITIONAL READING

Aurigi, A. (2005). *Making the Digital City: The Early Shaping of Urban Internet Space*. New York: Ashgate Publishing.

Batten, D. F. (1995). Network cities: Creative Urban Agglomerations for the 21st Century. *Urban Studies (Edinburgh, Scotland)*, *32*(2), 313–327.

Bradshaw, T., & Blakely, E. (1999). What Are "Third Wave" State Economic Development Efforts? From Incentives to Industrial Policy. *Economic Development*, *13*(3), 229–244.

Brooks, D. (2000). *Bo Bos in Paradise*. New York: Simon & Schuster.

Bussing, A. (1998). Teleworking and Quality of life. In P. Jackson & J. v. d. Wielen (Eds.), Teleworking, International Perspectives from Telecommuting to the Virtual Organization (pp. 144-165). London: Routledge.

Caplan, S. E., Perse, E. M., & Gennaria, J. E. (2007). Computer-Mediated Technology and Social Interaction . In Lin, C. A., & Atkin, D. J. (Eds.), *Communication Technology and Social Change*. London: Lawrence Erlbaum Associates.

Castells, M. (1998). *The Information Edge: End of Millennium*. Boston, MA: Blackwell Publishers.

Corey, K. (2000). Intelligent Corridors: Outcomes of Electronic Space Policies. *Journal of Urban Technology*, *7*(2), 1–22.

Couchman, P. K., McLoughlin, I., & Charles, D. R. (2008). Lost in Translation? Building Science and Innovation City Strategies in Australia and the UK. *Innovation: Management . Policy & Practice*, *10*(2-3), 211–223.

David, P. A., & Foray, D. (2002). An Introduction to the Economy of the Knowledge Society. *International Social Science Journal*, *54*(171), 9–23.

Dunning, J. (Ed.). (2000). *Regions, Globalization and the Knowledge-Based Economy*. Oxford, UK: Oxford University Press.

Etzkowitz, H. (2002). *MIT and the Rise of Entrepreneurial Science*. London: Routledge.

Florida, R. (2005a). *Cities and the Creative Class*. London: Routledge.

Florida, R. (2005b). *The Flight of the Creative Class*. New York: Harper Business.

Giles, S. L., & Blakely, E. J. (2001). *Fundamentals of Economic Development Finance*. London: Sage Publications.

Gillespie, A. (1992). Communications Technologies and the Future of the City . In Breheny, M. (Ed.), *Sustainable Development and Urban Form* (pp. 67–77). London: Pion.

Knight, R. (1995). Knowledge-Based Development: Policy and Planning Implications for Cities. *Urban Studies (Edinburgh, Scotland)*, *32*(2), 225–260.

Knight, R. V. (1989). City Development and Urbanization: Building the Knowledge Based City . In Knight, R. V., & Gappert, G. (Eds.), *Cities in a Global Society* (pp. 223–242). London: SAGE Publication.

Kotval, Z. (1999). Telecommunications, A Realistic Strategy for the Revitalization of American Cities. *Cities (London, England)*, *16*(1), 33–41.

Landry, C. (2000). *The Creative City*. London: Earthscan Publication.

Leydesdorff, L., & Meyer, M. (2003). The Triple Helix of University- Industry- Government Relations. *Scientometrics*, *58*(2), 191–203.

Mitchell, W. J. (2003). *Me*. Cambridge, MA: The MIT Press.

Riva, G. (2002). The Socio-Cognitive Psychology of Computer-Mediated Communication: The Present and Future of Technology-Based Interaction. *Cyberpsychology & Behavior*, *5*(6), 581–598.

Rogerson, R. J. (1999). Quality of Life and City Competitiveness. *Urban Studies (Edinburgh, Scotland)*, *36*(5-6), 969–985.

Sakaiya, T. (1991). *The Knowledge Value Revolution or a History of the Future*. New York: Kodansha.

Segedy, J. A. (1997). How Important is "Quality of Life" in Location Decisions and Local Economic Development? In R. D. Birmingham (Ed.), Dilemmas of Urban Economic Development. London: Sage Publications.

Van Sell, M., & Jacobs, S. M. (1994). Telecommunicating and Quality of Life: A Review of the Literature and a Model for Research. *Telematics and Informatics*, *11*(2), 81–95.

Wheeler, J. O., Aoyama, Y., & Warf, B. (Eds.). (2000). *Cities in the Telecommunications Age: The Fracturing of Geographies*. New York, London: Routledge.

Yigitcanlar, T., Velibeyoglu, K., & Baum, S. (Eds.). (2008). *Knowledge Based- Urban Development: Planning and Applications in the Information Era*. New York: Information Science Reference.

ENDNOTES

1 Local scale in this paper refers to a new mixed-use residential community development project that covers two third of the local government area.

2 This is more than the original agreement between the developer and the council (4500) and shows just the long term employment (Short-term construction employment is not included).

3 Co-work offices or co-work places (Johnson, 2003) are common centres in a community where people could rent office spaces and share some common facilities like administrative and technological services.

Chapter 6
Making Space and Place for Knowledge Production:
Socio-Spatial Development of Knowledge Community Precincts

Tan Yigitcanlar
Queensland University of Technology, Australia

Cristina Martinez-Fernandez
University of Western Sydney, Australia

ABSTRACT

In the knowledge era the importance of making space and place for knowledge production is clearly understood worldwide by many city administrations that are keen on restructuring their cities as highly competitive and creative places. Consequently, knowledge-based urban development and socio-spatial development of knowledge community precincts have taken their places among the emerging agendas of the urban planning and development practice. This chapter explores these emerging issues and scrutinizes the development of knowledge community precincts that have important economic, social and cultural dimensions on the formation of competitive and creative urban regions. The chapter also sheds light on the new challenges for planning discipline, and discusses the need for and some specifics of a new planning paradigm suitable for dealing with 21st Century's socio-economic development and urbanization problems.

INTRODUCTION

The economic and social importance of knowledge production is clear, if not precise (Westlund, 2006). Insofar as it is an emerging social phenomenon and research agenda in the urban planning discipline. The impact of what has been broadly labeled as the 'knowledge economy' has, however, been such that even absent precise measurement it is the undoubted dynamo of the contemporary global market and an essential part of any global 'knowledge city' (Clarke, 2001; Carrillo, 2006). Advanced urban economies all across the world are now moving, if not already, from a period of sweeping change in the structure of their industries. The enterprises, their activities and their importance to the economy differ significantly from the position three decades ago and show radical

DOI: 10.4018/978-1-61520-721-3.ch006

changes from the position that existed at the early 20th Century. This change can be seen as a shift from manual to mental labor. At the beginning of the 20th Century manual labor was a massive social presence. In the advanced economies of the 1950s people employed to make or move things were still in the majority. By 1990 they had shrunk to one-fifth of the workforce. By 2010 they will form no-more than one-tenth. On the other hand, in the same year it is projected that broadly defined 'knowledge workers' will comprise 20 percent of the total workforce (Drucker, 1993).

It is against a background of growing economic and social importance that one of the important research agendas of the 21st Century is to investigate socio-spatial development for the production of knowledge. In recent years not only in the fields of urban planning and development but also in the field of economic geography, under the influence of knowledge economy, a different approach is developed that deals with the geography of R&D and innovation (Vence-Deza and Gonzalez-Lopez 2008). Several research have shown that academic research and R&D are key components for the production of both codified and tacit knowledge and they tend to be geographically concentrated mainly in the creative urban regions (i.e. Feldman, 1994; Baum et al., 2008). During the past decade knowledge-based development has been a key in order to boost knowledge production for developing globally competitive urban economies (Yigitcanlar et al., 2008c). The raison d'être for the recent strong spatial urban development focus of the knowledge-based development policies is that spatially speaking knowledge production is an urban phenomenon. This important spatial focus has caused the birth of a new development approach so called 'knowledge-based urban development' (Yigitcanlar et al., 2008a). However, this development approach is not integrated into the urban planning process, mainly because of the incapability of modernist planning doctrines dealing with the socio-spatial changes of the 21st Century. Hence at that very point in the knowledge era, planning is still searching for its new paradigm or in other words its new identity.

As cities and their economies become competitive, knowledge production and knowledge-based urban development are becoming more important for success in the though global competition, particularly for attracting and retaining knowledge workers and industries (Florida, 2005). The immediate object of analysis of knowledge production and knowledge-based urban development, therefore, is the urban 'knowledge community precinct', which is a magnet place for global talent and investment. Borrowing from Henry and Pinch (2000) and Baum et al. (2007) a knowledge community precinct can be described as an integrated centre of knowledge creation, learning, commercialization and lifestyle that is created through a cooperative partnership of all tiers of government, the education community, private sector operators, a group of highly talented people and the general public. Knowledge community precincts distinctively differ from what have been developed as business parks, technology parks and industry clusters where the emphasis has been much more on the advantages of business co-location (Yigitcanlar et al., 2008d).

The broad aim of this paper is to explore the role of knowledge-based urban development, as one of the key research agendas of urban planning, in making space and place for knowledge production. The socio-spatial development of knowledge community precincts, as the nexus of knowledge-based urban development, has important economic, social and cultural dimensions, all of which contain surprisingly novel features. Therefore, the specific aims of the paper include to: scrutinize socio-spatial development of knowledge community precincts; contribute to the discussions on knowledge production and urban spatial transformation; and underline the importance of further investigating this new form of development, knowledge-based urban development.

STRATEGISING URBAN SPATIAL TRANSFORMATION FOR KNOWLEDGE PRODUCTION VIA KNOWLEDGE-BASED URBAN DEVELOPMENT

Since the industrial revolution social production had been primarily understood and shaped by the neo-classical economic thought that recognized only three key factors of production: land, labor and capital. Neo-classical theory considered knowledge, education, and intellectual capacity as secondary, if not incidental, parameters of production (Li et al., 1998). Human capital was assumed to be either embedded in labor or just one of numerous categories of capital. Nevertheless, during the last two decades it has become apparent that knowledge in and of itself is sufficiently important for production, and the new growth theory and the new economic geography recognized knowledge as the fourth factor of production (Romer, 1990; Sheehan and Grewal 1998). These theories also attempt to understand the role of knowledge, technology and education in driving productivity and economic growth, where investments in R&D, education, training, and new managerial work structures are keys for success (OECD, 2001).

Knowledge, both codified and tacit, encompasses the full range of human experience (Howells, 2002). Knowledge is a vital resource for creating and sustaining a strong economy, society and culture. In the business world, knowledge is considered as one of the most valuable assets of an enterprise that has to be managed efficiently and effectively in order to gain a competitive advantage in the knowledge era (Ergazakis et al., 2006). As Gibbons et al. (1994) point out the new production of knowledge that comprises the interaction of many disciplines and actors within a network of mutual reactions and feedback. The new mode of knowledge production challenges the traditional notion of innovation as the outcome of successive inputs linked in a chain of development. It requires, amongst other things, an examination of the trilateral relationships between academic institutions, government and industry, so called the triple-helix model (Etzkowitz and Leydesdorff, 1997).

In the global knowledge economy endogenous dynamism, most notably technological innovation and change, plays a crucial role and the production of knowledge is the main source of growth (Cooke, 2001). In the knowledge economy growth occurs primarily via continuous waves of innovation and knowledge production (Hearn and Rooney, 2008). It is an inevitable result of such circumstances that urban structures are transformed into new forms to become highly competitive. Lever (2002) stresses that in knowledge economies knowledge and information and the social and technological settings for their production and communication are keys to sustainable development and economic prosperity. According to the new growth theory a nation or city's capacity to take advantage of the knowledge economy depends on how quickly it can form a 'knowledge community', a community that in which the creation, distribution, diffusion, use, and manipulation of knowledge is a significant economic, political, and cultural activity. Idea-driven innovation cycles in the knowledge economy determine an economy's position in the global hierarchy, mainly by providing support for expanded investment and commitment to human capital (Jaffee, 1998).

Although knowledge has always been at the core of urban development, it is only recently that knowledge has been recognized as a primary factor that drives urban development (Knight, 2008:16). Traditionally cities have always been centers of production, development and civilization, in other words centers for economic and social opportunity. In the rapidly growing knowledge economy talent and creativity of communities are becoming increasingly decisive in shaping both economic opportunity and urban spatial transformation. As urban regions have become the localities of key knowledge community precincts (KCPs) across the globe, the link between a range of new planning approaches and the development of creative urban regions has come to the fore. Creative urban regions provide vast opportunities for knowledge production and spillover, which lead to the formation of knowledge cities (Landry, 2006; Yigitcanlar et al., 2008b).

Understanding the social complexity of urban development and the need for a new planning paradigm for 21st Century urbanization and development have become forefront of recent discussions in the literature. Smith and Kelly (2003), like many others, advocate the vital role of knowledge, technical expertise and the human environment in order to develop better urbanization policies. However with modernist planning doctrine and tools it is not easy to achieve sound planning outcomes, addressing social, economic and environmental issues, particularly in complex urban regions. Law and Urry (2004) argue that the call for knowledge-production and reforms in urban development stems from the growing awareness that modernist modes of decision-making do not meet the complexity of urban realities in the 21st Century. On this matter Van Wezemael (2008:2) states that "[a] world that renders instable what accounts for proper 'knowledge' in an increasingly high pace and that calls for more adaptive and generative organizations in both economy and administration. The experience of insufficient concepts is also echoed from practice, where a linear or modernist worldview is faced with a variety of anomalies: identical interventions in allegedly similar situations produce very different results. The application of [modernist approaches in] urban planning does not meet up with the increasing complexity in urban development. It becomes clear that in order to address 'knowledge' in the 21st Century urban development we must be able to deal with social complexity".

Cities worldwide have undergone major transformations in the 21st Century, an era in which the role of knowledge in wealth creation becomes a critical issue for the success of cities. Many urban administrations started to explore new approaches to harness the considerable opportunities of knowledge production to compete globally. Knowledge is produced by cultures and most cultures producing knowledge are concentrated in creative urban regions that are also recently undergoing constant spatial transformations (Yigitcanlar et al., 2008a). In the knowledge era as an inevitable result of the changes in production, economy, lifestyles and urban spatial transformations the planning profession faces major challenges. Benneworth and Hospers (2007) see global knowledge economy, emerging new urban hierarchy and emergence of disconnected cities and regions amongst the 21st Century's biggest challenges for planners. According to Corey and Wilson (2006:34) these new conditions and challenges in cities and regions also include "changes in production, with the shift away from manufacturing to services, and also toward advanced services and knowledge work; the impact of [ICT] on how and where services are produced, and how people interact; implications for social justice of uneven access to ICT; and the potential change associated with ICT and globalization".

During the last two decades knowledge-based development has become a powerful strategy for economic growth and the post-industrial development of cities and nations to participate in the knowledge economy (Laszlo and Laszlo, 2006). Knowledge-based development is an emerging field of study and practice, and principally it is about new processes of knowledge production. Knowledge-based development involves contemporary understanding and management of value dynamics for which traditional economic thinking and tools as well as traditional categories to describe production, capital, business, government, civic organization, urban life, urban development, community participation, civilization and culture have proven limited. It has two purposes. The first one is, it is an economic development strategy that codifies technical knowledge for the innovation of products and services, market knowledge for understanding changes in consumer choices and tastes, financial knowledge to measure the inputs and outputs of production and development processes, and human knowledge in the form of skills and creativity, within an economic model (Lever, 2002). The later one is that, it indicates the intention to increase the skills and knowledge of people as a means for individual and social development (Gonzalez et. al., 2005). Knowledge-based development policies include: developing and adopting the state of art technologies, distributing instrumental capital, investing on human and intellectual capitals, and developing capital systems (Carrillo, 2004).

To compete nationally and internationally cities need knowledge infrastructures; a concentration of well-educated people; technological, mainly electronic, infrastructure; and connections to the global knowledge economy (Yigitcanlar, 2008c). Almost a decade into the new century the economic success of the knowledge-based development policies in a number of cities have led urbanists to think of whether similar policies could be applicable for the knowledge-based development of urban regions. During the last few years the concept of 'knowledge-based urban development' (KBUD) has started to gain acceptance among the planning scholars. Parallel to this recognition, KBUD has become an emerging area of research interest which links interests of planners, geographers, economists and social scientists. Despite this growing interest in KBUD as an approach to transform urban environments into creative urban regions, it still remains in its infancy (Yigitcanlar et al., 2008a).

Silicon Valley has inspired KBUD around the world in the belief it is a royal road to competitive advantage and economic development (Ku et al., 2005). Such successful KBUD policy implementation in the US has exposed that creative urban regions can be engineered by promoting knowledge-based and high-tech precinct developments (Yigitcanlar et al., 2008b). According to Saxenian (1994:2) the success of Silicon Valley was originated from its "regional network-based industrial system that promotes collective learning and flexible adjustment among specialist producers of a complex of related technologies [and] [t]he region's dense social networks and open labor markets encourage experimentation and entrepreneurship". There is an agreement in the literature that engineering a creative urban region is a challenging task and factors related to the culture of the place and government priorities might have a large influence on economic success (Yigitcanlar and Velibeyoglu 2008b). Even ideal regions such as Silicon Valley are now shrinking and adjusting to a new business environment.

KBUD transcends many areas of economic, social and urban policy. Yigitcanlar and Velibeyoglu (2008a) distinct KBUD from other spatial development strategies because of its successful holistic approach for development. Economic development strategy of KBUD aims a local economic development that is competitive and integrated with the global knowledge-based economy. Social development strategy of KBUD aims to increase the quality of life by investing on intellectual, human and social capital systems and providing necessary services for societal development. Urban development strategy of KBUD aims to build a strong spatial relationship among urban development clusters for augmenting the knowledge spill-over effect that contributes significantly to the establishment and expansion of creative urban regions. KBUD also aims an ecologically sensitive and sustainable urban development (Figure 1).

Perry (2008) identifies three dimensions of KBUD as: process, product or acquisition-driven. She writes (p:17) that "in the process driven [KBUD]: knowledge is central and subject to change as a result of external pressures, whilst in the acquisition-driven [KBUD], knowledge itself

Figure 1. Three pillars of knowledge-based urban development (Yigitcanlar and Velibeyoglu, 2008c)

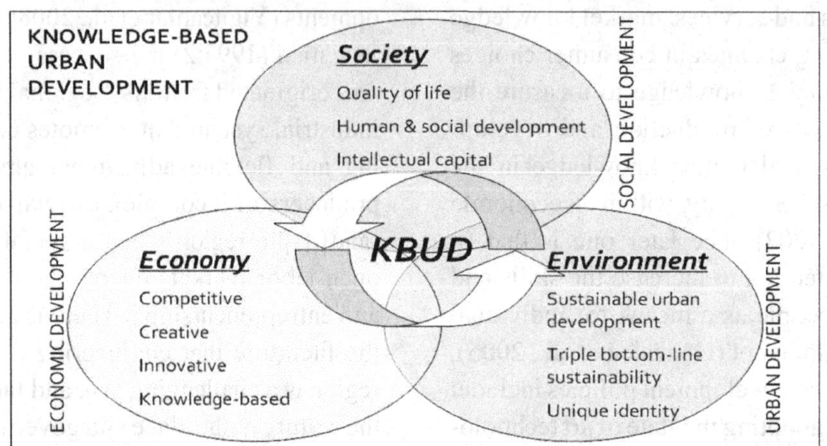

is only a small part of the processes, embedded in a wider set of economic, social and cultural processes. Similarly, while the 'urban' is only implied and peripheral in process, or product-driven [KBUD], 'place' is central to the concept of the 'ideopolis' in which local authorities themselves take a central role". She (p:27) then concludes that "only through a combination of all three dimensions into a more holistic [KBUD] vision can the expected benefits of the knowledge economy be delivered".

In a broader perspective, Knight (1995) describes KBUD as a social learning process, as a way for citizens of a city to inform and become informed about the nature of changes occurring in their city. He suggests that a particular attention must be paid to the nature of their knowledge resources, how cultures in the city produce knowledge and how this knowledge is used to create wealth that is transformed into local economic development. Most importantly in his recent research Knight (2008:xvii) emphasizes on that "this type of learning does not occur spontaneously or through established channels; if it is to occur, it has to be carefully orchestrated".

FROM 'FIRM' TO 'URBAN' KNOWLEDGE PRODUCTION SPACES

Any discussion on knowledge production needs to look into the discourse of 'the firm' and the understanding that the key to business competitiveness is innovation activity (OECD, 2001). The sophistication of business environments have prompted enterprises to focus on their learning space, their alliances and opportunities to get innovative ideas. There is enough evidences of the positive effects of designing knowledge-rich-environments on business innovation activity. Recent studies have shown how services industries are reorganizing themselves into 'networks of production' where they use formal and informal services from the private and public sector to boost their innovation outcomes (Martinez-Fernandez and Miles, 2006). The empirical studies suggest that the network space of the firm has a significant role to play in their learning and innovation processes, and that this role might be more significant than the role attributed to formal transactions with 'knowledge-intensive business services' (KIBS) and 'research and technology organizations' (RTOs). These studies also suggest that service firms are proactive organizations in the search of knowledge, that they overcome market barriers due to their small size or revenue through the use of network sources of expertise closely related to their services, and that knowledge is co-produced from both formal and informal sources leading to change and innovation. Results of the studies also indicate that in order to build firm capabilities for innovation, knowledge management needs to differentiate formal and informal processes of co-production of knowledge, as these different types of knowledge require specific strategies for their selection, acquisition, integration and final adoption within the firm. Thus, in theory, KCPs may well represent an ideal seed environment and an ideal local innovation system for knowledge production. These elements in business knowledge production space and their application to urban KCPs are explored below.

The key point stressed, by a recent OECD study on 'knowledge-intensive service activities' (KISA) (OECD, 2006), is that innovation is not just produced by R&D organizations and R&D expenditure but that innovation is the result of a series of activities that can be sector specific or core to the innovation process and that these activities occur in a certain knowledge space where the firm operates. Most important, the OECD study found that those activities many times come from the network space of the firm where formal and informal knowledge transactions are performed with all sort of organizations and actors. KISA are defined as the activities originated by the production and integration of knowledge-intensive services crucial for the innovation process of the firm. Typical examples of KISA include: R&D services, management consulting, ICT services, human resource management services, legal services, accounting, financing, and marketing services (Martinez-Fernandez and Martinez-Solano, 2006). Such activities, oriented to the use and integration of knowledge, are instrumental for building and maintaining a firm's innovation capability. In practice, KISA in a firm is achieved by the use of in-house, or the combination of in-house and external expertise. The capacity of the firm to perform these KISA more effectively may indeed be what differentiates a firm from its competitors. However, the interaction of these different KISA remains an ad-hoc, and largely informal process that firms are not totally aware of (Martinez-Fernandez and Miles, 2006). Understanding how firms access and employs the variety of innovation-related KISA available to them in different industries, in different spaces, and at different times, is itself a new research agenda chiefly pursued by the OECD and the European Union. This emerging agenda gives greater attention to the external, informal, community interactions in the co-production of knowledge than it has previously happened.

The context of KISA in firms is shaped by this co-production of knowledge and innovative activity. Currently, the major players may link in different ways at different spatial levels through activities, such as R&D provided through public and/or private enterprises, or through the development and use of management and other business-related skills including expertise. The focus on this wider space in which the firm operates has brought more understanding of the elements involved in the co-production of knowledge by different actors. The main formal external intermediaries of knowledge linked to firm-innovation, and capability building that act as functions in the co-production of knowledge are KIBS, public, and hybrid RTOs. The influence of these intermediaries in the co-production of knowledge in firms is best understood through the study of the knowledge-intensive services they provide, which can be characterized as 'activities' or 'KISA' due to the level of sophistication of these services. But then, an important area of provision of knowledge is added to these formal organizations. They are the informal actors from the network space of the firm: competitors, customers and other organizations from their own industry sector or from other sectors that share problems with them, contacts made through professional and standards-setting

Figure 2. Knowledge-production space of a firm in the co-production of knowledge

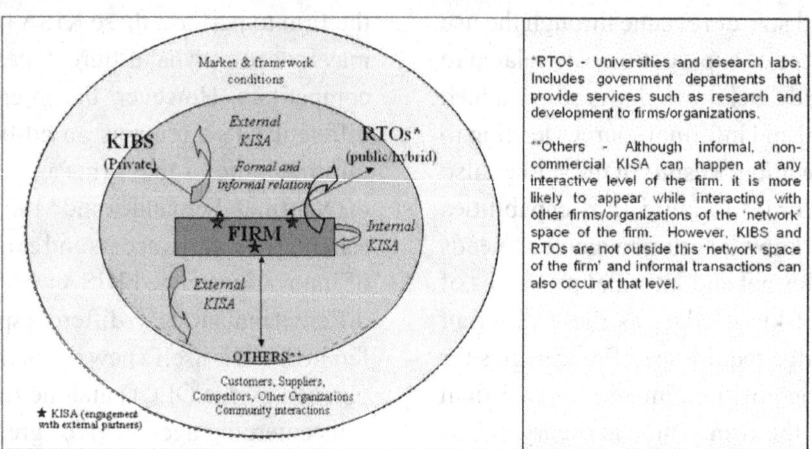

associations. KISA can also come from more organized network sources through business networks, and industry clusters or industry associations but these informal activities are chiefly responsible for that 'innovative space' characterizing knowledge communities or knowledge spaces important in building and maintaining their innovation capability (Martinez-Fernandez and Miles, 2006). Furthermore, the analysis of how firms create wealth today within their production space suggest that there are grounds for thinking that the existing literature may have overestimated the importance of KIBS and RTOs compared to the use of informal transactions from organizations and community actors within the firm's network space. Figure 2 illustrates the knowledge-production space of the firm and the engagement of KISA with intermediaries of knowledge: KIBS, RTOs, and other organizations in their network space. KISA can take place in any of the engagement activities that the firm has with other organizations. KISA can then be developed as a formal transaction or informal or internally to the firm's innovation process.

The KISA studies show the significance of this network space of a firm in terms of co-production of knowledge. The application of these findings to an urban knowledge production space, such as KCP, has not yet been undertaken despite the strong support of knowledge as the driver of economic and innovative activity. This also differs from research agendas on business parks, technology parks, and industry clusters where the role of the community and the residential component is often not part of the analysis (Martinez-Fernandez, 1998; Porter, 2001).

Early elaborations of knowledge communities within urban spaces refer to the organization of knowledge and its effects in cities and regions. There is an agreement in the literature that it is often important for firms and organizations to locate close to universities, research institutes, co-operative research centers or government scientific and industrial research organization to maximize their access to information concerning products and services developed by local knowledge-intensive institutions. This is also important for knowledge institutions so that the knowledge they generate is used and transformed into new knowledge. The equation is not easy because most knowledge travels through networks and, in fact, some knowledge producers might be more close to users at the other end of the planet than to those next door within the same building or precinct. This means that geographic proximity does not automatically imply that the different parts of the local innovation system will produce, share, transform and adopt knowledge. Strategic planning and policy measures might be needed to ensure that knowledge circulates through the system, creating new opportunities for players that otherwise would not have access to specialized information, skills or technology. Most importantly this points out to the issue of relevance of knowledge and how best knowledge producing organizations can co-produce the knowledge that is needed in a particular space (Martinez-Fernandez and Sharpe, 2008).

Aforementioned spatial organization of knowledge has been labeled as a 'knowledge hub'. This may be defined as an ensemble of knowledge-intensive organizations located in both public and private sectors. Some are research-intensive knowledge producers, such as research institutes or universities. Others are demanding knowledge users, including firms but also service providers such as hospitals or airports (Marceau et al., 2005). The intensity of the knowledge produced and transmitted makes the hub a 'system of activities' and while the boundaries are not limited at the geographical level, the organization at the core of the hub does need to be in geographic proximity (Acs, 2003). These studies have analyzed broader spaces such as regions or states or even countries. Cities have also been analyzed in terms of knowledge concentrations and this has formed the bases of important policy documents in Global Cities such as the Sydney Metropolitan Strategy (DPNR, 2005) where pockets of knowledge were identified across the Greater Sydney Region. Organizations identified include university campuses, scientific and industrial research organization units, hospital and medical research units and co-operative research center headquarters. There are clear concentrations of knowledge producing institutions in the eastern and central suburbs of Sydney. These are also areas of high concentration in terms of the number of ICT companies (Searle and Pritchard, 2004) presenting the conditions of a 'knowledge corridor' across different suburbs of the North-West of Sydney (Figure 3).

As shown in Figure 3 the organization of knowledge production in Australia's most global city, Sydney, the central business district acts as a magnet attracting knowledge workers and institutions. For example few knowledge institutions are located in the west side of the Sydney corridor despite the growing population in Western Sydney and therefore this creates a disadvantage in accessing knowledge to both a significant part of the population and to important contributing industries to the state and the nation. If the geography of knowledge producers and users matters for the development of cities and for the attraction of talent then knowledge strategies need to be linked to the development and planning priorities in the local area or region so that support policies can be more effectively designed.

In the particular case of Australia, the knowledge precinct policy dates back to early 1980s (Joseph, 1997), and resulted in so far more than 30 knowledge precinct developments across the country which only a few of them could be called a KCP (i.e. The Macquarie Technology Business Precinct in Sydney, The La Trobe Research and Development Precinct in Melbourne, Kelvin Grove Urban Village in Brisbane). And analyzing if the conditions for knowledge hubs to emerge can be replicated and engineered into small scale KCPs where residential, recreation and business spaces co-exist is highly useful. There is not, however, a clear understanding of what a KCP actually needs to include for generating those highly innovative knowledge flows and innovation outputs produced by the famous Silicon Valley (Saxenian, 1994). On one hand is the issue of having high-tech designed buildings in closed precincts where the separation from the rest of the suburb is evident through gates and security enforcement. On the other hand is the open urban space where the 'living space' is integrated with the working space but probably better represented by the new 'techno(su)burbs' emerging across rapid transit corridors such as the new M4 and M7 motorways in Sydney's Western

Figure 3. Sydney's knowledge hub locations (DPNR, 2005:11-12)

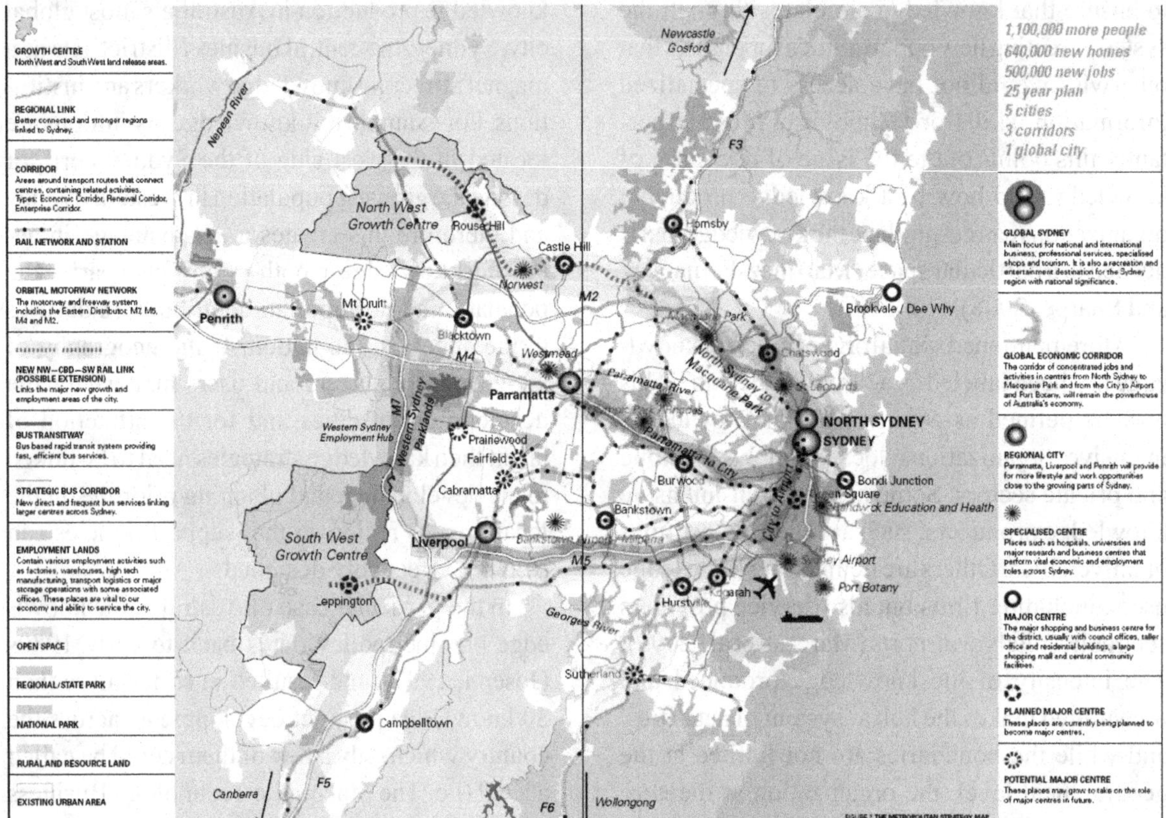

suburbs. Both concepts imply a very different planning system and the strategies for residential and commercial development and land use would also be very different.

Although very few attempts exist to specify the elements of a KCP, there are three functions of knowledge that can be considered as indicators: transmission, production and transfer of knowledge plus the issue of relevance of knowledge to the particular space of production. The way these three elements are combined is dictated by the talent involved and the environments where this talent results in innovation activity and commercialization of knowledge production. Three elements can be targeted: type of knowledge workers to be attracted, type of industries rich on KISA, and type of knowledge-based occupations of major revenue in terms of knowledge.

Building physical infrastructure with state of the art offices surrounded of research centers or industry incubators is not sufficient to foster knowledge and commercial innovations unless a functional understanding of the dynamics of knowledge forms part of the equation. For example, universities today are magnets of specialized knowledge and much knowledge migrates with the scientific and research staff of universities; this alone is a strategic tool for policy aimed at bringing knowledge into a city or urban region. It is then necessary to ensure that this knowledge melts and expands through participation in networks. Policy makers also need to be aware of the science and technology conditions operating in our world today. There is an increasing competition from other regions to attract scientists and industry talent; knowledge carriers are often targeted by other players to move institutions and knowledge bases. There is also a danger on focusing on a particular type of technology or picking a winning knowledge base occupation. For instance government regulations in favoring certain knowledge fields can hamper other forms of new knowledge resulting on decline in knowledge attraction and, maybe, urging scientists or other knowledge workers to emigrate.

Planning strategies can certainly be structured to directly enhance the relevance of knowledge co-produced in a certain space, but the conditions for high intensity of knowledge traffic are much more complicated than traditional planning domains such as land use. A different set of skills are needed to develop knowledge networks where ideas can be trialed and discussed. Government policies, also at the local level, have a critical role to play in fostering the conditions where intellectual vitality is made up of intensive collaboration networks that attracts and retain knowledge carriers in a certain production space. It is in this social complexity that the analysis of KCPs is taking place as a new realm of planning practice.

SOCIO-SPATIAL DEVELOPMENT OF KNOWLEDGE COMMUNITY PRECINCTS

In the knowledge era, knowledge production is considered as an urban phenomenon, and its object of analysis, in the planning perspective, is an urban KCP. At the most general level such a precinct is an urban complex of production, residential, retail, recreation, education and transport activities (Baum et al., 2007). This close weave of different land uses is unusual in an urban context that since the 19th Century, and the massing of industrial labor, had required the segregation of consolidated activities into separate places. Knowledge work needs mass organization. Indeed insofar as knowledge work is produced and used in global networks the massing of labor in the 21st Century is at a level not before seen in human history. Much of the organization of this work however occurs in virtual space thus eroding the need for the spatial consolidation of work. In this context a new possibility exists for the re-integration of work space and domestic places and the reversal of an historic urban trend of land use segregation.

Such re-integration of work space and domestic places established a new community, 'knowledge community', and in the last few years these communities have been the subject of considerable international writing (Florida, 2005; Peck, 2005; Nathan and Urwin, 2006). Interest has been sharpened by the suggestion of knowledge community is not merely knowledge workers at rest and play but an important dynamic in the production of knowledge itself. The community, in classic terms, is a factor of production. Here we see a common motif in all the literature on the knowledge economy/society or community/precinct, the juxtaposition of activities previously seen as quite separate, in this case 'live', 'play' and 'work'. A possible set of common themes, values and indicators of KCP developments is presented in Figure 4 (see Yigitcanlar et al., 2008d).

According to Felsenstein (1994) KCPs were generally established with two primary objectives in mind. The first objective of a KCP is to be a seedbed and an enclave for technology, and to play an incubator role, nurturing the development and growth of new, small, high-tech firms, facilitating the transfer of university know-how to tenant companies, encouraging the development of faculty-based spin-offs and stimulating the development of innovative products and processes. The second objective is to act as a catalyst for regional economic development or revitalization and to promote economic growth, while providing working, playing and living spaces to knowledge workers. Conceptually KCPs do not foster innovation for itself but apply innovation and innovative/knowledge production.

Figure 4. Common themes, values and indicators of KCP developments (Yigitcanlar et al., 2008d)

KNOWLEDGE WORKERS	RICH KISA ENVIRONMENTS	KNOWLEDGE-BASED OCCUPATIONS
- Information & Communication Technologies - Business & Financial Services - Managers (general & specialists) - Technical Workers - Scientists - Engineers	- Business Services - Banking - Finance - Insurance - Marketing - Education - Health	- Engineering & Building - Scientific - Business & Information - Craft & Trades - General Management
THEMES	**VALUES**	**EXAMPLES**
LIVING AND WORKING (mixed-use environments)	BUSINESS, REAL ESTATE VALUE: Real-estate and technology capitals are very active in shaping knowledge precincts (i.e. Nokia in Helsinki). Hence, commercial success has a great value. This means the end of rigid separation of working and living environments of so-called knowledge workers.	Helsinki Digital Village, Brisbane Kelvin Grove Urban Village
CENTRALITY (proximity, clustering, premium access to different infrastructures, services, and amenities, place quality)	ECONOMIC VALUE, DEVELOPMENT VALUE: Formation of knowledge precincts has become a new urban policy tool for the revitalisation of environmentally degraded former industrial sites or inner city urban districts.	Helsinki Digital Village, 22@bcn Barcelona
BRANDING (symbol for branding a city as a knowledge city)	SYMBOLIC VALUE, DESIGN VALUE: A regeneration strategy for creating successful knowledge cities or formation of new niche markets. Marking the name of the emerging knowledge city with a landmark development.	22@bcn Barcelona, Taipei 101
LEARNING AND PLAYING (interactive environments, living laboratories, experience of place)	LEARNING VALUE, EXPERIMENTAL VALUE: Urban playfield of cutting-edge technological innovation and creativity, places of interaction, knowledge hubs-such as universities.	Copenhagen Crossroads, Zaragoza Digital Mile
CONNECTIVITY (social networking, places of interaction, pedestrian orientation, face-to-face contact)	SOCIAL VALUE: Face-to-face contact, tacit knowledge transfer, place identity.	One-North Singapore, Kelvin Grove Urban Village Brisbane

The implicit assumption, that the social form of the KCP is an aggregation of creative individuals/class, is worth examining. The pattern of contemporary knowledge production argues against this essentially innocent formulation. The literature suggests the culture of the knowledge community be seen as complementary to material conditions of their work (Nathan, 2008). Such culture would be a mirror image, as it were, of conditions of production. Thus, if the abstract work of knowledge production increasingly marginalizes the human body, the spatio-culture of knowledge workers requires opportunities for its display. Similarly, if the industrial organization of knowledge production on a global scale puts more and more time pressure on workers, compensatory cultural dynamics can be expected in the knowledge community. The literature also notes the desire manifest in existing knowledge communities for 24/7 urban development; and, further, the demand for art spaces, museums and authentic forms and experiences (Yigitcanlar et al., 2007; Yigitcanlar et al. 2008d).

Baum et al. (2007) portray an ideal KCP as "a networked space of many places – a stimulating, disjunctive environment that both echoes the multiplicity of contemporary knowledge production while, in its physical quality, compensating for the abstract nature of such work" (p.69). They also point out the most critical aspect of such development as the constant change. "Change is fundamental to this environment: it continually refreshes experience – it is the medium of the new. If the nature of the contemporary knowledge [community] precinct can be summed up in phrase it is: excessive change. The challenge before policy is to provide for such change in space and through time" (p.69). They also stress that creating and managing 'dynamism and change' are the two major challenges for the socio-spatial development of KCPs. Figure 5 summarizes the basic principles of the development of an ideal KCP.

Figure 5. Development principles of a knowledge community precinct (derived from Baum et al., 2007)

Social desire and the precinct	The precinct is the social gravitational constant of the contemporary knowledge environment.
Building long-term institutional and financial support	The emergence of business leadership in the creation of a knowledge community precinct.
Building of a base of knowledge production	A world class research and development with networks constructed at different scales.
Making produced knowledge useful	Profitable economic use of knowledge.
Integration of work and life	Where and when possible integrated work and life in the knowledge community precinct.
Housing knowledge community	Higher densities of housing development in the knowledge community precinct than that of the traditional suburb.
Retail in the precinct	The knowledge community precinct reflects the spending capacity of its residents, and requires adequate retail rich space.
Recreation in the precinct	24/7 recreation intensive knowledge community precinct – in space and time.
Nature in the precinct	Natural places to provide islands of tranquility in a space of intense activity.
Physical transport in the precinct	Good and sustainable connection with the wider urban region and, in particular, the metropolitan/city centre.
Virtual communication and the precinct	ICT is at the heart of the knowledge community precinct where contemporary knowledge flows through these virtual arterials.
Aesthetic values of the precinct	A post-modern look with a style of eclecticism, ready borrowing, and pastiche, all executed with a certain machined or technological exactitude.
Quality of place as force of knowledge production	The knowledge community precinct as a space of many qualities.

Like Florida (2005)Jacobs (2004) too insists on the importance of KCPs for socio-economic development. However different than Florida she sees such developments as the unplanned chaos of the urban environment that is the driving force behind our welfare and well-being. One-North KCP in Singapore is an example that falsifies her point on unplanned nature of such precincts. Clearly, the concept and design of One-North as a KCP has been influenced by Florida's understanding of the importance of attracting creative talent with, and retaining it in, a total knowledge environment to become the 'knowledge capital' of South East Asia (Baum et al., 2007). The success of One-North is coming from its uniqueness by choosing not to replicate other global best practices. In her book on 'cities of knowledge' O'Mara (2005) discusses many failed efforts to imitate Silicon Valley. She scrutinizes the relationship between knowledge production and metropolitan development including debates about urban and regional planning. O'Mara concludes that creative urban regions are not simply accidental market creations but planned communities of knowledge production that were shaped and subsidized by the venture capitalist.

NEW CHALLENGES FOR URBAN PLANNING DISCIPLINE

As the finite opportunities of globalized knowledge production are taken up on an ever-widening scale elsewhere, KBUD is gaining reputation in forming urban spaces for knowledge production. However, the primary challenge here is where to place KBUD in the planning theory or how to link it with the planning paradigm, especially while planning discipline has been in the seek of a new paradigm, possibly a multi-disciplinary theory, for quite sometime (Thompson, 2000; Castells, 2004).

Planning for KBUD is a difficult task. Sanyal (2000:317) states that in the knowledge era "the planning profession needs to: integrate spatial and socioeconomic planning; re-justify government intervention; and construct new planning theories to meet the needs of planning profession". One of the main reasons of planning not being able to keep up with the speed of the socioeconomic and technological changes is its lack of dynamic visioning ability (Corey and Wilson, 2006). Similar to this statement Sanyal (2000:332) points out the most important challenge as to create a mindset that "require[s] strong commitment to social progress and a worldview that government, market and civil society must complement each other in moving forward toward the goal. How to create such a mindset, not only among planners but among all citizens, remains [an] important challenge for the planning profession".

Yigitcanlar (2007) contributes to this discussion by criticizing the static nature of statutory planning and the slow pace of participatory planning processes. In the knowledge era so far planning could not meet the complexity of urban realities and neglected to penetrate into the realm of business and management disciplines. Therefore, when we look at the creative urban regions worldwide, we observe that the structuring most of these regions has proceeded organically: in essence, as a dependent and derivative effect of global market forces. Urban planning has either responded slowly or not responded at all to the challenges and the opportunities of the new knowledge-intensive urban activities (Yigitcanlar, 2007). Van Wezemael (2008) links the failure of urban planning in the knowledge era with the 'linear perspective' of the modernist worldview and 'hierarchic government' -based modes of urban decision-making'.

There is a growing appearance of rich and diverse planning theory discussions in the literature that were stimulated by the new and dynamic circumstances of the global knowledge economy (Baum, 1996; Plummer and Taylor, 2003). Most of these discussions focused on the necessity of a new planning paradigm or an approach responsive to KBUD. Until recently, there was little in the way of theory that urban planners could use to form their global knowledge economy responsive planning strategies. In this regard the 'relational theory' is a rising one. Corey and Wilson (2006:214) note that relational theorizing is "congruent with the complex, multi-layered functions and flows of today's global knowledge economy and network society... [And it] can serve to stimulate our imagination and free up our collective and conventional neoclassical economic and locational perspectives of the world, and our approach to planning". Graham and Marvin (2001:202) also support the relational theorizing in planning, they identify relational theory as "a broad swathe of recent theoretical writing about cities and social change". Basically a relational perspective views cities and urban regions as agglomerations of heterogeneity, which are locked into a multitude of relational networks of varying geographical reach (Amin, 2002).

How to operationalize the relational theory for planning practice is still uncertain. Graham and Healey (1999:19-20) argue the prerequisite of translation of several interrelated points for an effective contemporary planning practice with relational thinking: "consider relations and processes rather than objects and forms; stress the multiple meanings of space and time; represent places as multiple layers of relational assets and resources which generate a distinctive power geometry of places; and planning practice [to] recognize how the relations within and between the layers of the power geometries of place are actively negotiated by the power of agency".

Although the relational theory has not been fully matured to become a panacea for the 21st Century urbanization imbalances and problems, this theory is still very important. According to Wilson and Corey (2008:86) "it enables one to order more effectively, and therefore to plan better, the highly complex new mix of influences such as globalization, information and networking technologies and socio-economic functions that play out today and in the future at the scale of urban and regional areas". While waiting planning theoreticians to construct the next planning paradigm, as Knight (2008) suggests, we, planners, still have to do our best in orchestrating social learning and KBUD processes.

CONCLUSION

Knowledge is the primary source of development power for cities. Although it seems to be cities' knowledge base is a result of their economic strength, KBUD is founded on different set of values and attributes than solely economic oriented ones. Predominantly cultures and social development facilitate as the building blocks of cities' knowledge bases. And KBUD provides a process in which citizens collectively shape the development of their city by enhancing cultures for producing knowledge in the city. The spatial nucleus of KBUD is a KCP, where these precincts play a significant role in knowledge production. Therefore, socio-spatial development of KCPs is crucial for strengthening the knowledge-based development of cities. KCPs are emerging forms of development in competitive global cities' creative urban regions and further development of the broad policies on their socio-spatial development is needed. Such policies will need to account for the substantial spatio-technical parameters of the different land uses. Equally important, however, is the wider social context of public or policy intervention. Such parameters are considered as the structure of governance, urban politics, the urban land market and the role of corporate partners. Along with these parameters the close connection between the political economy of urban development and revitalization, and high-tech economic development are worth taking into consideration.

Making space and place for knowledge production, such as KCP developments, has become a challenge for the planning profession. As Zolnik (2008) indicates just putting all of the high-technology pieces into a place does not assure a KCP will ever experience the long-term benefits from strategic investments in the highly competitive global knowledge-based economy. Therefore, the following issues are worth considering. The first issue is that the spaces of traditionally separated, 'residential space', 'recreation space' and 'business space', are now coming together for the production of urban knowledge spaces, and how to best structure these spaces is still a big mystery to planners. The second one is that many of the issues, traditionally in the realm of business and management disciplines, are now calling for the planning profession to step in and lead the design of better knowledge production spaces that are no longer solely dependent on the firm as the entity where innovation occurs. And the last issue is the limitations of the linear planning perspective and the complexity of, as the relational theory suggests, planning for KBUD with a non-linear perspective and heterarchic governance network-based modes with negotiation logic. These challenges and the evidence from the literature reveal that further investigation is necessary in order to configure how to best socio-spatially develop our urban environments as spaces and places for the production of knowledge and creative urban regions.

REFERENCES

Acs, Z. (2002). *Innovation and the growth of cities*. London: Edward Elgar.

Amin, A. (2002). Spatialities of globalisation. *Environment & Planning A*, *34*, 385–399. doi:10.1068/a3439

Baum, H. (1996). Practicing planning theory in a political world . In Mandelbaum, I., Mazza, L., & Burchell, R. (Eds.), *Explorations in planning theory*. New Brunswick, NJ: Rutgers.

Baum, S., Yigitcanlar, T., Horton, S., Velibeyoglu, K., & Gleeson, B. (2007). *The role of community and lifestyle in the making of a knowledge city*. Brisbane: Urban Research Program.

Baum, S., Yigitcanlar, T., & O'Connor, K. (2008). Creative industries and the urban hierarchy: the position of lower tier cities and regions in the knowledge economy? In Yigitcanlar, T., Velibeyoglu, K., & Baum, S. (Eds.), *Knowledge-Based Urban Development: Planning and Applications in the Information Era* (pp. 42–57). London: Information Science Reference.

Benneworth, P., & Hospers, G. (2007). Urban competitiveness in the knowledge economy . *Progress in Planning, 67*, 105–197. doi:10.1016/j.progress.2007.02.003

Carrillo, F. (2004). Capital cities. *Journal of Knowledge Management, 8*(5), 28–46. doi:10.1108/13673270410558738

Carrillo, F. (Ed.). (2006). *Knowledge cities*. New York: Butterworth–Heinemann.

Castells, M. (2004). The information city, the new economy, and the network society . In Webster, F. (Ed.), *The Information Society Reader* (pp. 150–164). London: Routledge.

Clarke, T. (2001). The knowledge economy. *Education + Training, 43*(4/5), 189–196. doi:10.1108/00400910110399184

Cooke, P. (2001). *Knowledge economies*. New York: Routledge. doi:10.4324/9780203445402

Corey, K., & Wilson, M. (2006). *Urban and regional technology planning*. New York: Routledge.

DPNR. (2005). *Metropolitan strategy, economy and employment*. Sydney: Department of Planning and Natural Resources.

Drucker, P. (1993). *Post-capitalist society*. New York: Harper Business.

Ergazakis, K., Metaxiotis, K., & Psarras, J. (2006). Knowledge cities. *Journal of Information and Knowledge Management Systems, 36*(1), 67–81.

Etzkowitz, H., & Leydesdorff, L. (1997). (Eds.) Universities and the global knowledge economy. London: Pinter.

Feldman, M. (1994). *The geography of innovation*. Dordrecht: Kluwer Academic Publishers.

Felsenstein, D. (1994). University-related science parks. *Technovation, 14*(2), 93–110. doi:10.1016/0166-4972(94)90099-X

Florida, R. (2005). *The flight of the creative class*. London: Harper Collins.

Gibbons, M., Limoges, C., Nowotny, H., Schwartzman, S., Scott, P., & Trow, M. (1994). *The new production of knowledge*. London: Sage.

Gonzalez, M., Alvarado, J., & Martinez, S. (2005). A compilation of resources on knowledge cities and knowledge-based development. *Journal of Knowledge Management, 8*(5), 107–127.

Graham, S., & Healey, P. (1999). Relational concepts of space and place. *European Planning Studies, 7*(5), 623–646.

Graham, S., & Marvin, S. (2001). *Splintering urbanism*. London: Routledge. doi:10.4324/9780203452202

Hearn, G., & Rooney, D. (Eds.). (2008). *Knowledge policy*. Northampton, UK: Edward Elgar.

Henry, N., & Pinch, P. (2000). The industrial agglomeration . In Bryson, J., Daniels, P., Henry, N., & Pollard, J. (Eds.), *Knowledge space economy* (pp. 120–141). London: Routledge.

Howells, J. (2002). Tacit knowledge, innovation and economic geography. *Urban Studies (Edinburgh, Scotland), 39*(5/6), 871–884. doi:10.1080/00420980220128354

Jacobs, J. (2004). *Dark age ahead*. Toronto: Random House.

Jaffee, D. (1998). *Levels of socio-economic development theory*. London: Praeger.

Joseph, R. (1997). Political myth, high technology and the information superhighway. *Telematics and Informatics, 14*(3), 289–301. doi:10.1016/S0736-5853(97)00004-X

Knight, R. (1995). Knowledge–based development. *Urban Studies (Edinburgh, Scotland), 32*(2), 225–260. doi:10.1080/00420989550013068

Knight, R. (2008). Knowledge-based development . In Yigitcanlar, T., Velibeyoglu, K., & Baum, S. (Eds.), *Knowledge-Based Urban Development* (pp. 14–19). Hershey, PA: Information Science Reference.

Ku, Y., Liau, S., & Hsing, W. (2005). The high-tech milieu and innovation-oriented development. *Technovation, 25*, 145–153. doi:10.1016/S0166-4972(03)00074-9

Landry, C. (2006). *The art of city making*. London: Earthscan.

Laszlo, K., & Laszlo, A. (2006). Fostering a sustainable learning society through knowledge based development. In *50th ISSS Conference*, 9-14 July 2006, California.

Law, J., & Urry, J. (2004). Enacting the social. *Economy and Society, 33*(3), 390–410. doi:10.1080/0308514042000225716

Lever, W. (2002). Correlating the knowledge-base of cities with economic growth. *Urban Studies (Edinburgh, Scotland), 39*(5/6), 859–870. doi:10.1080/00420980220128345

Li, H., Zinand, L., & Rebelo, I. (1998). Testing the neoclassical theory of economic growth. *Economics of Planning, 32*, 117–132. doi:10.1023/A:1003571107706

Marceau, J., Martinez-Fernandez, C., Rerceretnam, M., Hanna, B., Davidson, K., & Wixted, B. (2005). *Stocktake of NSW as a potential knowledge hub*. Sydney, Australia: UWS.

Martinez-Fernandez, C. (1998). *Industry clusters*. Newcastle, Australia: HURDO.

Martinez-Fernandez, C., & Martinez-Solano, L. (2006). Knowledge-intensive service activities in software innovation. *International Journal Services Technology and Management, 7*(2), 109–174.

Martinez-Fernandez, C., & Miles, I. (2006). Inside the software firm. *International Journal Services Technology and Management, 7*(2), 115–125.

Martinez-Fernandez, C., & Sharpe, S. (2008). Intellectual assets and knowledge vitality in urban regions . In Yigitcanlar, T., Velibeyoglu, K., & Baum, S. (Eds.), *Creative urban regions* (pp. 48–64). Hershey, PA: Information Science Reference.

Nathan, M. (2008). Creative class theory and economic performance in UK cities . In Yigitcanlar, T., Velibeyoglu, K., & Baum, S. (Eds.), *Creative urban regions* (pp. 80–94). Hershey, PA: Information Science Reference.

Nathan, M., & Urwin, C. (2006). *City people*. London: IPPR.

O'Mara, M. (2005). *Cities of knowledge*. Princeton, NJ: Princeton University Press.

OECD. (2001). *Benchmarking knowledge-based economies*. Paris: OECD Press.

OECD. (2006). *The role of knowledge-intensive service activities in innovation*. Paris: OECD Press.

Peck, J. (2005). Struggling with the creative class. *International Journal of Urban and Regional Research, 29*(4), 740–770. doi:10.1111/j.1468-2427.2005.00620.x

Perry, B. (2008). Academic knowledge and urban development . In Yigitcanlar, T., Velibeyoglu, K., & Baum, S. (Eds.), *Knowledge-Based Urban Development* (pp. 21–41). Hershey, PA: Information Science Reference.

Plummer, P., & Taylor, M. (2003). Theory and praxis in economic geography. *Environment and Planning C*, 21, 633-649.

Porter, M. (2001). Regions and the new economics of competition . In Scott, A. (Ed.), *Global city regions* (pp. 139–157). New York: Oxford University Press.

Romer, P. (1990). Endogenous technological change. *The Journal of Political Economy*, *98*(5), 71–102. doi:10.1086/261725

Sanyal, B. (2000). Planning's three challenges . In Rodwin, L., & Sanyal, B. (Eds.), *The profession of city planning*. New Brunswick, NJ: Rutgers.

Saxenian, A. (1994). *Regional advantage*. Cambridge, MA: Harvard University Press.

Searle, G., & Pritchard, B. (2004). *To cluster or not to cluster*? ANZRSAI Annual Conference, Sydney.

Sheehan, P., & Tegart, G. (Eds.). (1998). *Working for the future*. Melbourne: Victoria University Press.

Smith, W., & Kelly, S. (2003). Science, technical expertise and the human environment. *Progress in Planning*, *60*, 321–394. doi:10.1016/S0305-9006(02)00119-8

Thompson, R. (2000). Re-defining planning . *Planning Theory & Practice*, *1*(1), 126–133. doi:10.1080/14649350050135248

Van Wezemael, J. (2008). Knowledge creation in urban development praxis . In Yigitcanlar, T., Velibeyoglu, K., & Baum, S. (Eds.), *Knowledge-Based Urban Development* (pp. 1–20). Hershey, PA: Information Science Reference.

Vence-Deza, X., & Gonzalez-Lopez, M. (2008). Regional concentration of the knowledge-based economy in the EU: towards a renewed oligocentric model? *European Planning Studies*, *16*(4), 557–578. doi:10.1080/09654310801983472

Westlund, H. (2006). *Social capital in the knowledge economy*. Berlin: Springer-Verlag.

Wilson, M., & Corey, K. (2008). The alert model . In Yigitcanlar, T., Velibeyoglu, K., & Baum, S. (Eds.), *Knowledge-Based Urban Development* (pp. 82–100). Hershey, PA: Information Science Reference.

Yigitcanlar, T. (2007). The making of urban spaces for the knowledge economy . In Al-Furaih, I., & Sahab, A. (Eds.), *Knowledge cities* (pp. 73–97). Selangor, Malaysia: Scholar Press.

Yigitcanlar, T., Baum, S., & Horton, S. (2007). Attracting and retaining knowledge workers in knowledge cities. *Journal of Knowledge Management*, *11*(5), 6–17. doi:10.1108/13673270710819762

Yigitcanlar, T., O'Connor, K., & Westerman, C. (2008c). The making of knowledge cities: Melbourne's knowledge-based urban development experience. *Cities (London, England)*, *25*(2), 63–72. doi:10.1016/j.cities.2008.01.001

Yigitcanlar, T., & Velibeyoglu, K. (2008a). Knowledge-based urban development: local economic development path of Brisbane, Australia. *Local Economy*, *23*(3), 197–209. doi:10.1080/02690940802197358

Yigitcanlar, T., & Velibeyoglu, K. (2008b). Knowledge-based strategic planning: harnessing (in)tangible assets of city-regions. In *Proceedings of the 3rd International Forum on Knowledge Asset Dynamics*, 26-27 June 2008, Matera, Italy (pp. 296-306).

Yigitcanlar, T., & Velibeyoglu, K. (2008c). Engineering creative urban regions for knowledge city formation: knowledge-based urban development experience of Brisbane, Australia. In *the Proceedings of the 3rd International Symposium on Knowledge Cities*, 17-19 Nov 2008, Istanbul, Turkey.

Yigitcanlar, T., Velibeyoglu, K., & Baum, S. (Eds.). (2008a). *Knowledge-based urban development: planning and applications in the information era*. Hershey, PA: Information Science Reference.

Yigitcanlar, T., Velibeyoglu, K., & Baum, S. (Eds.). (2008b). *Creative urban regions: harnessing urban technologies to support knowledge city initiatives*. Hershey, PA: Information Science Reference.

Yigitcanlar, T., Velibeyoglu, K., & Martinez-Fernandez, C. (2008d). Rising knowledge cities: the role of urban knowledge precincts. *Journal of Knowledge Management, 12*(5), 6–17. doi:10.1108/13673270810902902

Zolnik, E. (2008). Biotechnology and knowledge-based urban development in DNA Valley . In Yigitcanlar, T., Velibeyoglu, K., & Baum, S. (Eds.), *Knowledge-Based Urban Development* (pp. 171–184). Hershey, PA: Information Science Reference.

Chapter 7
Essentials for Developing a Prosperous Knowledge City

Rabee M. Reffat
King Fahd University of Petroleum and Minerals, Saudi Arabia

ABSTRACT

The essentials and challenges of the 21st century's economy include knowledge and innovation. Both are the key in order for a city to calmly race forward and safely ride out in the ever changing global economy. Knowledge and innovation could be viewed as the true hard currency of the future and corner stones in developing a prosperous knowledge city. This chapter introduces a model for developing a prosperous knowledge city through knowledge and innovation. The model consists of five components that are most important for cities pursuing towards prosperous Knowledge Cities including: developing creative environments, knowledge creation, skills, collaboration/partnership, and leadership. The chapter focuses on articulating the primary components of the proposed model and identifying how they will contribute to achieving prosperous Knowledge Cities and innovative knowledge regions.

1. INTRODUCTION

In the recent years a new theme of Knowledge Cities is brought to the forefront through having science, technology, supporting activities as well as normal city functions to stand side by side and be organically integrated. The research, innovation and commercial activities are expected to be imbedded in an environment that has all the functions of a global city. The local knowledge infrastructure includes economic, social and cultural knowledge networks of the city that are particularly place-specific knowledge resources. Accordingly, there are two kinds of understanding the models of Knowledge Cities, the model of real world and the model of virtual Knowledge Cities. The former includes the geographical components, technical facilities, and people. The latter includes the technological and social networks and knowledge resources (Wang & Pan, 2005).

The emerging notion of Knowledge Cities attracts considerable interest from city policy makers

DOI: 10.4018/978-1-61520-721-3.ch007

and researchers in the domains of knowledge management and knowledge based development. Knowledge Cities are economically focused on innovation and pushed forward by science and engineering employment. Knowledge Cities are incubators of knowledge and culture forming a rich and dynamic blend of theory and practice within their boundaries and are driven by knowledge workers through a strong knowledge production (Work Foundation, 2002). Edvinsson (2003) describes a Knowledge City as a city that was purposefully designed to encourage the nurturing of knowledge. Knowledge Cities are introduced by Ergazakis et al (2004) as cities that aim at a knowledge-based development, by encouraging the continuous creation, sharing, evaluation, renewal and update of knowledge. Furthermore, Knowledge Cities are cities that possess an economy driven by high value-added exports created through research, technology, and brainpower (Carrillo, 2006). There are several complementary perspectives from which to consider the concept of Knowledge Cities, such as: Information Technology Technopolis (Smilor et al, 1988), (Komnions, 2002), Knowledge-based Clusters (Arbonies & Moso, 2002), Urban Capital Systems (Carrillo, 2004), Ideopolis (Garcia, 2004), Knowledge Corridors, Knowledge Harbors, Knowledge Villages, and 'knowledge regions' (Dvir & Pasher, 2004), and Regional Intellectual Capital (Bounfour & Edvinsson, 2005).

Knowledge Cities are cities in which both the private and the public sectors value knowledge, nurture knowledge, spend money on supporting knowledge dissemination and discovery and harness knowledge to create products and services that add value and create wealth. Today's potential Knowledge Cities, such as Shanghai, Seoul, Singapore and San Francisco, are investing in the future and spending billions on infrastructure and human capital (people's skills and abilities), to position themselves for the global economy. These cities focus on developing quality housing, smart communities, creative education, challenging work opportunities, and livable environments for its residents. Furthermore, they provide advanced telecommunications, freight and goods movement systems that are the base for creating new, good jobs for a more diverse population. Therefore, prosperous Knowledge Cities must invest in the future and deal with several myths that are holding other cities back. Some of these myths for example include: let the market do the planning, and cannot afford the infrastructure (Blakely, 2005).

- *Let the market do the planning*: The market is scarcely an infallible tool for urban planning. In most cases, the market delivers needed infrastructure only when demand is clear, which can create long delays in needed services.
- *Cannot afford the infrastructure*: Cities must invest in the future. There is a continuous need to provide better housing and better community amenities to improve people lifestyles and be attractive for coming generations.

Knowledge Cities represent a new concept and "the field still lacks a consensus regarding appropriate conceptual and methodological frameworks" (Carrillo 2006). Not surprisingly, there is no unified methodology for either the articulation or implementation of Knowledge Cities. Nevertheless, there are certain characteristics of the knowledge city that seem to resonate in the literature. Dvir (2006) introduced a Knowledge City model wherein a Knowledge Moment happens at the intersection of People, Places, Processes and Purposes. In this model Knowledge Cities trigger and enable an intensive, ongoing, rich, diverse and complex flow of Knowledge Moments. A Knowledge Moment is a spontaneous or planned human experience in which knowledge is discovered, created, nourished, exchanged, and transformed into a new form. This model connects Knowledge Cities to the daily experiences of the citizen. The fundamental idea behind this model is based on the principles of co-evolution–through the dense stream of Knowledge Moments, all actors acting in the city co-evolve towards sustainability. Yigitcanlar et al (2008) through a literature investigation of Knowledge Cities identified a number of broad components that form a Knowledge City with the realization that every Knowledge City is different and requires different knowledge qualities to grow. These fundamental components for the creation of Knowledge Cities include technology and communication; creativity and culture; human capital; knowledge workers, and urban development clusters and their spatial relationships.

The rapid expansion of knowledge throughout the world's advanced societies generates a strong culture of creativity. For a knowledge city in the 21st century to be able to properly position itself in the fields of knowledge and at the crossroads of new modes of economic development it must build a unique character so as to attract and retain knowledge workers, promote exchanges of knowledge, and maintain a climate conducive to creativity and innovation. Therefore, knowledge and innovation capacities are at the core of the knowledge economy. Today the knowledge, skills, experience and innovation potential of talented individuals have greater value than capital equipment or even the capital itself. Talented individuals are highly mobile and can reward those regions that attract them. The creation of new knowledge mainly takes place in cities, where knowledge is produced, processed, exchanged and marketed. Hence, today's cities striving to achieve a knowledge-based economy are in need for adopting a useful model to attain their goals. Therefore, this chapter provides a coherent model for achieving a successful shift towards the knowledge-based economy and prosperous knowledge-cities. The chapter targets decision and policy makers and provides them with a workable model to be implemented with measures to remark its success.

2. SUCCESS FACTORS OF KNOWLEDGE CITIES

Cities around the world are taking steps to ensure their success in the knowledge era. These cities range from cities with an international stature such as Boston, London and Singapore, to medium-sized cities like Lyon, Munich and Stockholm and smaller ones including Waterloo, Ontario, Bilbao, Spain and Portland. Some of these cities clearly stand out today as high Knowledge Cities, at the forefront of new scientific developments, e.g. Boston. Others have undertaken considerable efforts to transform their industrial structures and invest in high technology, e.g. Dublin. Others have built on their specific cultural and artistic assets to assert themselves in the knowledge era, Barcelona among them. The direction taken by cities in the knowledge era generally takes the form of a mix of science and high technology investments, traditional infrastructure investments, and strategic investments in the arts and culture. Each city is distinctive in its particular mix of investments and implementation mode. For instance, Chicago opted for a position as a platform for knowledge exchange by building on its centralized geographical location, availability of large real estate sites that can house convention and conference centers, and its first rate transportation infrastructure. Chicago pursued a goal of attracting conventions, professional events and meetings in all areas of knowledge, from design to high technology to the bio-medical industries. The hosting of such events not only generates immediate economic benefits but ensures the periodic presence of communities of professionals in dynamic knowledge fields. The majority of the cities that seek to position themselves as Knowledge Cities go through the stages of in-depth analysis of the situation, definition of a vision and strategy, implementation of action plan with particular attention paid to fundamental aspects such as regeneration of traditional infrastructures

Table 1. Conditions for success that distinguish the Knowledge Cities [extracted from Michaud & Tcheremenska (2003)]

Conditions for success shared by existing Knowledge Cities		Examples
1.	***A sense of urgency and belief in the necessity for change***	• Sense of urgency was due to: decline of key industries, scarcity of local resources, and depreciation of the downtown core in favor of the metro region
2.	***Frontline role assumed by local players***	• Example cities include Stockholm, Lyon and Barcelona
3.	***Targeting opportunities and consistency in the implementation of strategies*** • Targeting a few sectors only and setting ambitious goals for each and aiming at nothing less than global leadership • Balancing the interests of chosen sectors against available resources and competitiveness of the metropolitan area	• Dublin: any new initiative must dovetail with the urban strategy • Stockholm: all new development projects must be in line with one of the four key sectors in which the community has chosen to excel (information technologies, new media and the Internet, biotechnology and biomedicine, and environmental technologies)
4.	***Strong financial investments and sustained pursuit of goals***	• Denver invested US$3 billion to redevelop its downtown core, while Boston spent US$60 billion in urban renewal and global-connectivity improvements to its mass-transit system • Massive investments have been made over the past several years by Barcelona, Lyon and Dublin
5.	***Ensuring that day-to-day existence in the transformed city is efficient and pleasant***	• In Barcelona and Boston, particular care has been taken to preserve the distinctive character of heritage districts

and investment in technology infrastructures. But there are some specific conditions for success that are shared by cities that have undertaken major repositioning efforts in the knowledge era as illustrated in Table 1 that is extracted from Michaud & Tcheremenska (2003).

3. A MODEL FOR DEVELOPING A PROSPEROUS KNOWLEDGE CITY

This chapter introduces a model for developing prosperous Knowledge Cities through innovation and knowledge. This model consists of five essential components that are most important for cities pursuing towards prosperous Knowledge Cities: developing creative environments, knowledge creation, skills, collaboration/partnership, and leadership. The primary components in the proposed model are illustrated in Figure 1 and are articulated in the following subsections.

3.1 Developing Creative Environments

There is a need for investing in developing creative environments that foster gradual and incremental innovations. Research centers, businesses, skilled workers should be the driving force for these creative environments. This may also involve strengths in the creative and cultural sectors, which in turn can impact on economic success. With the rise of competition for mobile highly qualified knowledge workers and the positive economic impact of this new class more attention is now being paid to individuals who decide where knowledge will be developed. This attention to the knowledge workers and their inclinations has been given new momentum and popularity by Florida (2002 and 2005) on his successful works, "The Rise of the Creative Class" and "The Flight of the Creative Class" respectively. This made an impact by consulting a wide range of cities on the conditions and potential of raising their attractiveness in the eyes of the creative class, i.e. the knowledge workers. According to Florida,

Figure 1. The proposed model consists of the most essential five components and their interrelationships for developing a prosperous Knowledge City

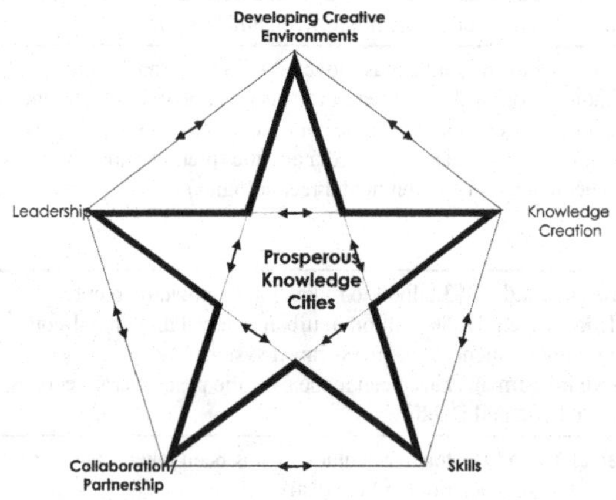

Knowledge Cities compete on their capacity to attract, retain and integrate talented individuals who place value on creativity. This capacity relies on the quality of local culture, the presence of local amenities as well the existence of a thick labor market offering the possibility of lateral moves for knowledge workers who are looking for new challenges. A knowledge-based economy is characterized by a range of networks of creative institutions, businesses and individuals who initiate and implement technological, economic, social and cultural innovation. Florida emphasizes the attempt to optimize such relational capacity which constitutes a key area for regional policy attention. According to Florida, the success factors of a knowledge city comprise:

- Abundance of places and events valued by knowledge workers
- Citizens actively involved in development of their city and its identity
- Culture of knowledge
- Open flow of information
- Pronounced support for creative activities
- Significant growth in leading edge service and ground-breaking economic sectors
- Significant proportion of the labor force working in creative positions
- Strong dynamics of innovation across all sectors, within all institutions.
- Strong link between arts/culture and scientific/technological knowledge

Since infrastructural development is one of the core competences of any regional administration, urban planning is a natural focus area for city-regional development. In relation to knowledge development urban planning receives additional weight and a challenge in which scientific infrastructure has to be flexibly adaptable to changing scientific needs. Investments in major scientific facilities have to be justified by benefiting a community of users and by being associated with reliable long-term scientific strengths of the local institutions. Infrastructures for knowledge-intensive businesses, universities and related agencies have to foster networking and chance encounters that may give rise to unusual innovative ideas for new projects and products. In addition, the expansion of knowledge city-regions warrants supportive actions in the shape of additional infrastructural connections, housing and recreation zones. All of these features have to be part of a sustainable development plan which will allow the expanded city to maintain its attractiveness. Therefore, urban planners and architects need to combine these perspectives and live up to the demands of creative environments. Interestingly, these challenges seem to result in the re-emergence of an old genre of international architectural creativity. The design of campuses, science cities, and urban renewal for new mixes of knowledge workers and creative persons leads to designing spaces which lend themselves to spontaneous communication and chance encounters of the diverse groups of knowledge workers. Knowledge Cities are sufficiently self-aware to invest considerable sums in the creation of such spaces (Reichert, 2006). Others dimensions of creative innovative environments that help fostering the development of Knowledge Cities include (Haselmayer, 2005):

- Innovation Drivers which involve dynamic relationship between Science-Industry-Government and Entrepreneurial Culture; innovation by combining intentions, strategies and projects; and focus on interaction among dynamic players leading to seemingly endless transitions.
- Urban Dynamics: Innovation Environments that include providing interdisciplinary, creative, interactive innovation resources; urban life style; public, private or scientific partnerships/participation; availability of externalized knowledge resources; localize global resources; and speed, efficiency, and international standards.

3.2 Knowledge Creation

There is an urgent need for cities to focus on the creation of knowledge of their distinctiveness; knowledge that has added value and that boosts the economy. A knowledge city is notable primarily for the intensity and constancy of its dynamics of knowledge creation. Beyond the sheer volume of knowledge produced, a city's capacity to rapidly transform that knowledge capital into innovative products, processes and services is paramount. In this regard, there are three main components that determine the intensity of knowledge in a city: its degree of knowledge production, the pace of assimilation and use of new knowledge types, and the scope of knowledge circulation (Michaud & Tcheremenska, 2003).

(a) ***Degree of knowledge production:*** One way in which a city stands apart is by the wealth of its acquired knowledge. Knowledge production proceeds largely from what are known as city's engines of economic development that include: Universities (and their affiliated research centers and teaching hospitals); Research centers (public and private); Business firms; and Creators (e.g. artists, fashion designers). The dynamics within and across these four pillars are what gives a city its knowledge production and transformation quotient. The more a significant proportion of the city's labor force is busy creating and inventing new knowledge, products and services in the fields of science, technology and the arts, the greater the city's development of knowledge capital. A strong flow of knowledge in a city is therefore conducive to various types of innovation including technological, organizational and/or institutional. A continuous stream of innovation drives competitiveness, high-tech startups, and emergence of key innovative projects.

(b) ***Pace of assimilation and use of new knowledge types:*** It is not enough to simply produce knowledge. One must have the capacity to extract economic and social wealth from it. Hence, one of the distinguishing factors for a knowledge city to prosper is the ability to consistently reap the benefits of new knowledge types and new expertise whether home-grown or imported. There are various factors that may influence the pace at which a city assimilates and uses these knowledge types. These include: ease of access to knowledge, understanding of the new knowledge types available, and the ability to integrate them into the activities of organizations likely to extract value from them. This ability is directly related to the competencies of the city's labor force. It relies upon individuals' scientific, technological and artistic know-how and talent, and their capacity to join creative networks of knowledge made up of diverse individuals and institutions.

(c) ***Scope of knowledge circulation:*** The amount of dissemination and sharing of knowledge whether among individuals or organizations, across industry segments or geographical regions is another benchmark for quality in a knowledge city. Knowledge circulation that is directly related to circulation of individuals is essential for a city to consistently revisit its perspectives and its innovation pool. Therefore, a city must have the capabilities and determination to constantly push the frontiers of knowledge whereby great discoveries and promising developments may happen. In this way, the city is able to constantly renew its wealth of knowledge, ideas and practices and assert itself as a knowledge city.

For knowledge city to be prosperous there is a need for an intensive knowledge production from the primary four components (Universities, Research Centers, Business Firms, and Creators) associated with both a good pace of assimilation and a high scope of knowledge circulation. Goodness of the pace of assimilation is measured in terms of achieving an integration of new types of knowledge, converting them into activities, and extracting economic values. The high scope of knowledge circulation is measured in terms of the amount of knowledge dissemination and sharing of knowledge between individuals and organization. The success of achieving a good leap in these three dimensions will potentially lead to a prosperous knowledge city as depicted in Figure 2.

3.3 Skills

Cities need to invest in skills appropriate to their key sectors and can benefit from the innovation associated with higher skills as well as the spin-off benefits of educational institutions. Skills matter to cities for the same reasons they matter to countries since skills support higher productivity and better social outcomes for individuals. The UK Leitch Review of Skills (2006) highlighted that skills are important due to: (a) individuals without skills are much more likely to be unemployed, which has an impact not only on their income and physical and mental health but potentially on that of their family; (b) low levels of skills constrain growth and innovation in firms; (c) demand in developed countries is increasing for skilled or knowledge workers; (d) firms employing skilled individuals are likely to be more productive; and (e) countries

Figure 2. Achieving a prosperous knowledge through intensive knowledge production associated with both a good pace of assimilation and a high scope of knowledge circulation

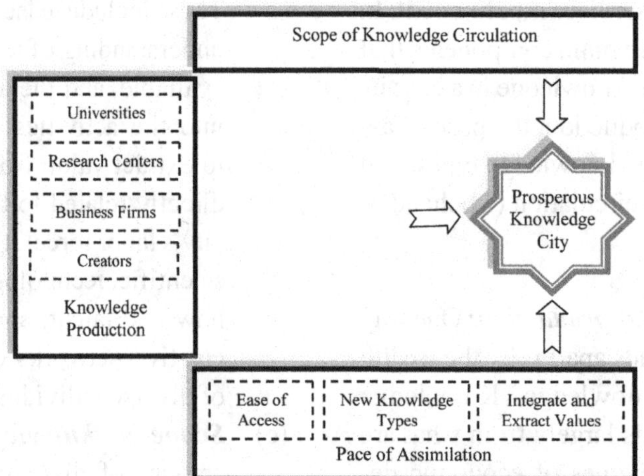

that have high numbers of skilled individuals are more likely to be affluent. Whilst skills policy may seem a soft issue that has no tangible outcome, there are clear benefits not only to national economies but also to cities' ability to respond to the changing economy and provide both production and consumption benefits to businesses and individuals. Specifically, investment in skills and educational institutions will mean that cities can (Hutton, 2007):

- Have a labor market with skills that respond to the needs of the knowledge economy, making that city a more attractive place to locate to it and increasing the likelihood of successful businesses (production benefit),
- Have educational institutions that are embedded within the city and can contribute to the innovation required in knowledge intensive firms (production benefit) and generate their own economic activity through student demand (production and consumption benefit), and
- Have improved social inclusion and healthier residents because of the non-economic outcomes of investment in education.

The growth of knowledge industries and knowledge jobs is creating demand for higher levels of skills, and cities that can provide those skills are thriving because it is a response to the growing demand for high levels of skills and high value work. Research consistently links the average level of qualifications in a city with economic growth, with considerable evidence existing that the highly skilled are more productive. Glaeser & Saiz (2003) draw on US evidence and suggest that this may be in large part due to the ability of skilled cities to adapt to economic change. However, whilst cities that have high levels of skills reap clear benefits, there is also evidence that the changing economy demands that cities have a good mix of skills. Successful cities not only need highly skilled knowledge workers but also people with the skills to work in other growing areas of the economy that respond to rising affluence, consumer demand and the marketization of domestic and personal services. Many cities, however, struggle to respond to demand for this mix of skills.

3.4 Collaboration/Partnership

Different cities have different strengths, but frequently these are complementary and working together can enhance the offer that both cities can make to businesses and to workers. For example, a large city could find it easier to employ workers if a nearby city offers a high quality of place where they can live with their families. Collaboration may be particularly important for cities where the core industry has declined. There is increasing interest in collaboration as cities become more entrepreneurial and begin to recognize the role that their position in the wider economic geography of their country plays in the way they can respond to wider economic change. Therefore, for achieving better collaboration/partnership cities should (Hutton, 2007):

- Build realistic and genuine links with other cities. If city authorities acknowledge both their position in an urban system, and the economic and social flows which run through them, the potential for city collaboration becomes clear. Links with other cities must have clear objectives; however, with consensus about what the links are for and how they will work. At a local level, this might be about identifying mutually beneficial collaboration on specific issues in order to respond to economic and social change. However, links should not only be restricted to nearby cities. Links between different regions or with international cities can be highly beneficial and generate real economic activity and exchanges of ideas.

- Have national governance structures that support strategic decision-making across cities. Where cities collaborate, there is an opportunity to have a more strategic conversation that moves beyond competitiveness or very local issues to take decisions about how to enhance the economic success and quality of life across a wider area and for a wider pool of people. This may require difficult decisions about investing in one place rather than another. Governance structures should support cities to work together in a way that generates trust, acknowledges their interdependence, and enables decisions to be taken in a transparent way, with consideration for how all areas may benefit from success. Governance structures should also try to support decision-making with an eye to the short, medium and longer term.

3.5 Leadership

If cities are to change direction, they need strong leadership to work with key stakeholders and generate a sense of shared purpose. Successful cities have strong leadership around a clear vision of how the economy is changing, how the city should respond and what the future of the city might look like. Meaningful networks and partnerships support this leadership vision, enabling it to have a real impact on how the city works and how it responds to changing business and consumer demands. The role that leadership plays in enabling a city to respond to changes in the economy and society will also vary according to the individual circumstances of a city. Successful cities may need leadership less to enable them to respond to changing demand, and more to be able to manage the consequences of success. For example, the city of Cambridge in the UK is a highly successful knowledge intensive city that has benefited from university and business leadership, but is now struggling with the consequences of its economic success, such as congestion and pressure on public services. It already has strong leadership from the private sector, but has a growing need for more leadership from the public sector. In contrast, the strong public sector leadership in Sheffield is helping the city to find its feet after the substantial decline of its core industries but there is a growing need for more business leadership there.

Despite the variation in the role that it plays in different cities, leadership remains a key driver of success in the knowledge economy. Particular benefits of leadership are (Hutton, 2007):

- It creates a clear vision of the city and how it will respond to the changing economy and society. This acts as a framework for decision-making and helps to attract knowledge intensive businesses and workers, providing production benefits.
- It brings together different stakeholders – local authorities, local community bodies, businesses, and the university – in strong networks that have a clear purpose and can enable ideas to be shared.
- It improves clarity for businesses about where decisions are made and who makes them.
- It helps to engage key stakeholders by being clear about the benefits of engaging in discussions about how the city should develop.

4. GUIDELINES FOR THE APPLICATION OF THE PROPOSED MODEL

The five essential components (of the proposed model for developing prosperous Knowledge Cities), articulated in the previous Section are strongly interrelated and their interrelationships are vital for the successful application of the proposed model. For a city to successfully progress towards being a prosperous knowledge city, there is a need for its authorities or local government to develop a strategic plan considering these five essential components. These components must be planned to be concurrently implemented. These components should not be viewed as sequential factors where one follows the other or be considered as less important than the other. Put it simply, if a prosperous knowledge city can be depicted as a bounded pentagon shape (as illustrated in Figure 1), then the five components of the proposed model are the necessary and sufficient nodes to constitute the bounded pentagon shape. The edges connecting these nodes (interrelationships between the five components) are vital to constitute a bounded pentagon shape, i.e. vital to develop a prosperous knowledge city. Accordingly, the presence and success of these five components and their interrelationships (both ways arrows in Figure 1), are mandatory for the success of developing prosperous Knowledge Cities. At the same time, these interrelationships can also be viewed as interconnectedness and interdependencies between the five components. For instance, it is not enough to develop creative environments; it is impartial to establish collaboration and partnership. Both have to be associated with intensive knowledge creation from skilled people supported with a strong leadership that has a clear vision. The dynamic interrelationship between these five components provides a framework to realize the transformation of a city to a prosperous knowledge city.

The successful application of the proposed model by cities' authorities or local government is initially dependent on adopting an interconnected and interdependent view of the five essential components (developing creative environments, knowledge creation, skills, collaboration/partnership, and leadership) within a strategic plan. This strategic plan should include: (a) Conducting SWOT analysis (Strengths, Weaknesses, Opportunities, and Threats) of these five components in the target city; (b) Articulation of the specific desired status of the city; (c) Identification of gap between the current status and desired status of the city; (d) Developing strategic initiatives that can potentially lead to the desired status; (e) Transforming the strategic initiatives into strategic projects; (f) Developing a work plan for implementing these projects; and (g) Establishing performance measures and indicators for evaluating the success of these projects. The development of this strategic plan is the first and most important corner stone for the successful application of the proposed model for developing a prosperous knowledge city.

5. DISCUSSION

In recent years, many cities around the world have embarked on initiatives that involve discussions, collaborative efforts and establishment of strategies aimed at sharpening their competitive edge on the national, continental and international scale. In several respects, the initiatives undertaken by these cities are in keeping with the development thrusts for Knowledge Cities including:

- Building on a vigorous knowledge-based economy,
- Developing a pervasive knowledge culture, and
- Investing in an attractive, stimulating urban dynamics.

The transformation of the world economy over the last two decades offered a mix of opportunities and challenges for the cities in which the effects of this change are most being felt. Therefore, there is a need for a shift in policy to recognize the importance of place to realizing desired outcomes, and for national, regional and local policymakers to work together, across boundaries, to ensure that places support the knowledge economy, and benefit from its growth. This chapter has introduced a model that consists of five components that are most important for cities pursuing towards prosperous Knowledge Cities including: knowledge creation, creative environments, skills, collaboration/partnership, and leadership. These primary components are articulated and their role to contribute in achieving prosperous Knowledge Cities and innovative knowledge regions are identified. This model provides a roadmap for policy and decision makers and provides a workable model to be implemented with measures to remark its success. On the other hand, policy and decision makers should be aware of other important issues that are considered drivers for failure while pursuing the development of Knowledge Cities including (Michaud & Tcheremenska, 2003):

- Artificial nature of redesigned districts, e.g. focus is solely on tourism and not knowledge.
- Artificial nature of the new infrastructures aimed at promoting technology clusters, e.g. spaces shared by people who are not conducting the same type of research and development or working on similar strategic issues.
- Excessive attention to infrastructures of the past, such as sports stadiums.
- Too little focus on the intensity and quality of knowledge flow.
- Excessive focus on attracting businesses while too little on attracting knowledge workers.

Considering these drivers of failure to avoid is quite important while adopting the proposed model in order to boost the process of achieving a prosperous knowledge city. Furthermore, while the primary components of the proposed model might be generically applicable, they should be thoroughly elaborated to each city aiming for a prosperous knowledge city based on critical analysis of its current situation.

REFERENCES

Arbonies, A., & Moso, M. (2002). Basque Country: the knowledge cluster. *Journal of Knowledge Management*, *6*(4), 347–355. doi:10.1108/13673270210440857

Blakely, E. (2005). *Do the Myths: Now is Time to Create the Knowledge City*. Australia: University of Sydney.

Bounfour, A., & Edvinsson, L. (2005). *Intellectual Capital for Communities: Nations, Regions, and Cities*. Boston: Butterworth-Heinemann.

Carrillo, F. (2004). Capital Cities: A taxonomy of capital accounts for knowledge cities. *Journal of Knowledge Management*, *8*(5), 28–46. doi:10.1108/1367327041058738

Carrillo, F. (2006). Knowledge Cities: Approaches, Experiences and Perspectives. Burlington, MA: Butterworth-Heinemann (Elsevier).

Dvir, R. (2006). Knowledge city, seen as a collage of human knowledge moments. In Carrillo, F.J. (Eds.), Knowledge Cities: Approaches, Experiences and Perspectives (pp. 245-272). Burlington, MA: Butterworth-Heinemann (Elsevier).

Dvir, R., & Pasher, E. (2004). Innovative engines for knowledge cities: an innovation ecology perspective. *Journal of Knowledge Management*, *8*(5), 16–27. doi:10.1108/13673270410558756

Edvinsson, L. (2003). *Introduction to Issues in Knowledge Management*. Oxfordshire, UK: Henley Knowledge Management Forum.

Ergazakis, K., Metaxiotis, K., & Psarras, J. (2004). Towards Knowledge Cities: Conceptual Analysis and Success Stories. *Journal of Knowledge Management*, *8*(5), 5–15. doi:10.1108/13673270410558747

Florida, R. (2002). *The Rise of the Creative Class: And How It's Transforming Work, Leisure and Community*. New York: Basic Books.

Florida, R. (2005). *The Flight of the Creative Class*. New York: Harper Collins.

Garcia, B. (2004). Developing futures: a knowledge-based capital for Manchester. *Journal of Knowledge Management*, *8*(5), 47–60. doi:10.1108/13673270410558774

Glaeser, E., & Saiz, A. (2003). *The Rise of the Skilled City*. Discussion Paper Number 2025, Harvard Institute of Economic Research, Harvard University, Cambridge, MA.

Haselmayer, S. (2005). *The Intelligent Place: Foundations for a Knowledge City*. Interlace-invent ApS. Retrieved February 5, 2009 from Http://www.localret.net/jornades/materials/gsc/T4_eGovern_Haselmayer.pdf

Hutton, W. (2007). Building Successful Cities in the Knowledge Economy: The Role of Soft Policy Instruments. In *Proceedings of the OECD International Conference: What Policies for Globalizing Cities? Rethinking the Urban Policy Agenda*, Madrid, Spain.

Komninos, N. (2002). *Intelligent Cities: Innovation, knowledge systems and digital spaces*. London: Sponpress.

Leitch, U. K. Review of Skills. (2006). Prosperity for all in the global economy - world class skills. Norwich, UK: Crown.

Michaud, P., & Tcheremenska, A. (2003). *Montréal Knowledge City*. Montréal: Report of the Montréal, Knowledge City Advisory Committee.

Reichert, S. (2006). *The Rise of Knowledge Regions: Emerging properties and Challenges for Universities*. Brussels: European University Association.

Smilor, R., Gibson, D., & Kozmetsky, G. (1988). Creating the Technopolis: High-technology Development in Austin. *Journal of Business Venturing*, *4*, 49–67. doi:10.1016/0883-9026(89)90033-5

Wang, Z., & Pan, D. (2005). Framework for Virtual Knowledge City: A Case of City Dalian, China. In *Proceedings of the First World Congress of the International Federation for Systems Research: The New Roles of Systems Sciences For a Knowledge-based Society*, Kobe, Japan.

Work Foundation. (2002). *Manchester: Ideopolis?* London: The Work Foundation.

Yigitcanlar, T., OConnor, K., & Westerman, C. (2008). The making of knowledge cities: Melbourne's knowledge-based urban development experience. *Cities (London, England)*, *25*(2), 63–72. doi:10.1016/j.cities.2008.01.001

Section 2
Multi-Level Approaches of Knowledge-Based Development

Chapter 8
Personal Knowledge Management by the Knowledge Citizen:
The Generation Aspect of Organizational and Social Knowledge-Based Development

América Martínez Sánchez
Instituto Tecnológico y de Estudios Superiores de Monterrey, México

ABSTRACT

The discipline of Personal Knowledge Management (PKM) is depicted in this chapter as a dimension that has been implicitly present within the scope and evolution of the Knowledge Management (KM) movement. Moreover, it is recognized as the dimension that brought forth Knowledge-based Development (KBD) schemes at organizational and societal levels. Hence, this piece of research work aims to develop parallel paths between Knowledge Management moments and generations and the PKM movement. KM will be depicted as a reference framework for a state-of-the-art review of PKM. A number of PKM authors and models are identified and categorized within the KM key moments and generations according to their characteristics and core statements. Moreover, this chapter shows a glimpse of the knowledge citizen's PKM as an aspect with strong impact on his/her competencies profile; which in turn drives his/her influence and value-adding capacity within knowledge-based schemes at organizational and societal levels. In this sense, the competencies profile of the knowledge citizen is of essence. Competencies are understood as the individual performance of the knowledge citizen interacting with others in a given value context. The chapter concludes with some considerations on the individual development that enables PKM to become a key element in the knowledge citizen's profile, such as the building block or living cell that triggers Knowledge-based Development at organizational and societal levels.

DOI: 10.4018/978-1-61520-721-3.ch008

INTRODUCTION

It is widely recognized in the context of knowledge economy (Carrillo, 2001,2002) that people are a highly valuable asset, and the most relevant and strategic differentiation, resides in the people that make up any human entity (Martínez, 2007). In this chapter, segment "A" addresses the personal dimension of knowledge management, which considers the origin and starting point of the Knowledge-Based Development (KBD) schemes at organizational and societal levels. The state of the art in PKM is determined on the basis of a review of the moments and generations in the evolution of KM. Likewise; the author identifies the knowledge-based Value Systems approach (KBVS) (Carrillo, 1996), as a reference framework for PKM. Thus, PKM is located within an integral and strategic conception that is based, on one hand, on its relation with the societal, organizational, and chiefly individual dimensions; and on the other on the KM processes (management of capital systems, of human capital and of instrumental capital).

In segment "B", the basic elements managed in Personal Knowledge Management are defined using as reference the fractal relation between the knowledge-based Value Systems. Concurrently, different background data are discussed as they address strategic performances in the profile of the knowledge citizen, from an individual standpoint in interaction and into a context (competencies), and the concept of Knowledge Citizen (Carrillo, 2005) is defined.

In segment "C", the conclusions relate to some considerations on individual development that enables PKM to become a key element in the knowledge citizen's profile.

STATE-OF-THE-ART PKM

Indeed, the PKM notions and concepts have grown in emphasis and popularity in recent years. As this Chapter develops, some of the key elements considered stem from Carrillo's work (Carrillo, 1996, 2001a, 2001b, 2002; CSC, 2001, 2002; Martinez, 1999) based in his concepts on KM perspectives. However, it should be acknowledged (Carrillo, 1996) that in the onset of the movement the personal/individual dimension of KM received scarce attention from researchers and practitioners. Although Personal Knowledge Management concepts are mainly used today within the KM field, such notions have an earlier foundational background rooted in a number of disciplines related to individual human development; such as philosophy, psychology and sociology. More recently, the same notions have been used to support considerations such as the Emotional Intelligence approach developed (among others) by Goleman (1995) and Frand and Hixon (1999), and Personal Intellectual Capital (Carrillo, 2002).

The KM movement where PKM resides has evolved significantly from a scattered condition to professionalization and consolidation. Carrillo has identified and put together the features of the developmental moments in the field of KM (Carrillo, 2001b, 2002). The most relevant features of the developmental moments in the KM field (Carrillo, 2001) are described below. In its first moment –scattering–, knowledge is understood as an object, and consequently stresses building information stock and solutions based on information systems, as well as documenting and codifying management. In the second moment –professionalizing KM–, knowledge is defined as a process and the presence of an emerging community of professionals who study this discipline is acknowledged. There is likewise a presence of groups specialized serving this field professionally, there are relevant actions in KM research and education. In the third KM moment –consolidation–, understanding of knowledge emphasizes value alignment and balance and the emergence of alternate approaches built on value systems knowledge; and accounting practices based on the chief pivot –called the capitals system– are widely spread.

Table 1. Parallelism between relevant elements in KM and PKM

Generation	KM	PKM
First	Tool oriented to save and accumulate information stock	Stresses handling and management of personal information
Second	Method to facilitate and circulate information	Stresses personal information interconnections Awareness of the interpersonal information flow and the flow of what others know and what the person knows Use of the personal information
Third	Strategy oriented to achieve a value balance	Emphasizes the personal value system as the basis for decision-making and personal development

In line with the stages of evolution of the KM movement, Carrillo (2001a) recognizes three KM generations, differentiated by the level of knowledge integration they elicit, which in turn determines the level of knowledge they manage. A parallelism can therefore be observed between KM and the developmental stages of PKM. The characteristics of the three generations of KM are described below.

In the first generation the concept of knowledge pivots on records and capitalization is achieved by their containment, and KM is understood as a tool to identify, safeguard, order and exploit the organizational knowledge base. In the second generation, knowledge is defined as a flow, and therefore it is capitalized by spreading it and KM is defined as a method to identify, codify, structure, store, retrieve, and spread knowledge. Third-generation knowledge is understood as the net future value and capitalized by balancing value; while KM is defined as a strategy to identify, systemize, and develop the universe of capitals in the organization. In short, the first generation pivots on the object, the second on the agent, and the third on the context (Carrillo, 2002).

Consequently, it may be concluded that the essence of the third generation (Carrillo, 2002) is the creation of value starting from the entity's Value System and its corresponding operationalization in a capitals system, contrary to the first and second generations, which stress and focus on accumulation and flow of knowledge, respectively.

The following table shows the recognized concurrence of KM and the stages of PKM development. Table 1: *Parallelism between relevant elements in KM and PKM* shows the correspondence of emphases in one and the other, according to their stage of development.

Within the first KM generation (Carrillo, 2001b) the core aim is to collect and store information, in the same way that PKM defines its first moment of conceptualization. Not surprisingly, PKM has been widely used in the KM field from an instrumental standpoint: emphasis on the use of methods and technologies to manage information at a personal level. More particularly, the use of information technology is privileged in order to support the individual's capacity to manage large amounts of information. Clearly, this KM generation pays considerable attention to the handling and use of information on a personal basis. Researchers that assume PKM from this perspective and illustrate this instrumental principle within PKM at different degrees of intensity are, amongst others: Boyd (2001), Frand and Hixon (1991), and Sidoli (2000). These authors recognize in KM a clear inclination to the personal dimension. They emphasize that KM initiatives in an organization are constructed starting from the individuals that make it up; yet, they still show an emphasis on knowledge only as an object and a process. Boyd (2001) makes a reference to knowledge management through documentation of what employees know; and this contemplates the transformation of tacit knowledge into explicit knowledge by means of documents, charts, and the like. Frand and Hixon (1991) highlight the importance of initiatives to capture information by focusing support technology on *just in time* knowledge.

On the other hand, Kaplan (2000) has introduced the notion of *personal management effectiveness* into the PKM perspective. His definition incorporated the process through which individuals integrate experience into their daily lives, and by doing so he went a step beyond the first PKM generation. However, Kaplan (2000) made this attempt from an original emphasis on information management and the assimilation of tools to foster *personal management effectiveness*. He identified his advancements as CUEOD, an acronym for the key actions undertaken in each of the cycle stages he proposed: C for *Capture*, U for *Understand*, E for *Evaluate*, OR for *Organize* and D for *Deploy*. Also, some contributing elements to the PKM second generation such as fostering Knowledge flows can be recognized in Sidoli (2000). In this case, features of a third generation PKM may be found in Carrillo's (2002) perspective, as he recognized and stressed the significance that information may have for the individual, that is, the articulation and sense a person makes of the information.

Additionally, authors such as Ash (2002) advanced a more integral perspective beyond first generation PKM. The author emphasized the relevance of knowledge of workers' competencies in a context of continuous and swift change, and the relevance of developing such competencies. Ash and the team involved in the *Association of Knowledge* (2002) have worked around notions of how to take advantage of the individual's personal knowledge so that s/he takes the lead of his/hers own personal development, and focuses on factors that allow an individual's self-development from his/her own knowledge. In Ashes' initiative, an inclination to appreciate knowledge beyond the instruments and tools of personal information management is clearly observed. Some of the greater categories he proposes that seem to match an integral scope for PKM are: collaboration, performance, learning, and strategy, among others.

Barth (2000) addressed a wider concept of PKM condidering that the economy of knowledge value in the organization derives from the intellectual capital of its knowledge workers. Barth emphasized the concept of self-organization that relates to the personal dimension where a fundamental issue is the *self* as the basic unit and critical ingredient in the creation of the ecology of knowledge where a balance and congruence are key issues.

Sidoli (2000) also brought a more integrative PKM scope and highlighted the relevance of the individual's values, since these orient his/her behavior. He advanced an audit in terms of PKM, starting from some of the key elements found in third-generation KM, such as values and key targets, as well as *core competencies* and personal strengths within a network interaction. He also highlighted the existing correspondence between the strategic elements within the individual, his/her behavior, and his/her development.

Likewise, Sidoli (2000) established, as significant PKM elements, learning acquired throughout the life span plus a plan for living and working, and proposed the promotion of a feedback loop between such plan, values, and lifelong learning, so that each one briefs the other in an enveloping fashion.

Other parallel elements Sidoli contributed to a the construction of PKM are, for instance, that Goleman's (1995) approach of emotional intelligence as paraphrased by Ricardo (2000) constitutes a source for the foundations of PKM. Sidoli considers that the skills of emotional intelligence and cognitive skills are necessary and synergetic. The competencies of emotional intelligence are the keys to personal and professional success. Competencies in emotional intelligence contributed to PKM are, for instance: empathy, self-discipline, initiative, personal competency, emotional awareness, self-regulation, reliability, integrity, adaptability, commitment, innovation, motivation, and optimism.

A psychology background that contributes to the foundations of PKM is from Erickson (in Woolfolk, 1990), and specifically refers to the construction of an identity emphasizing the psycho-social dimension in this process and the significance of the family and cultural environment where the individual evolves. Identity is a fundamental element in the overall perspective of PKM, as it constitutes the starting line from which each individual, as an integrated entity, recognizes himself, and vis-à-vis others. Likewise, Hoffman (in Woolfolk, 1990) spots the stages of the process where the concept of *others* develops in an individual. This process goes from an initial stage of total personal non-differentiation regarding the other, to a final stage where the individual gains awareness and understands that other people have their own identity, history, and future. Otero (2000) addressed the subject of alterity noting that *others* are recognized as similar to *us,* and concurrently *external and* agree that the relation between *oneself* and the *other* is not only total reciprocity and empathy, but also the notion that *he/she is not I.* It is thus that the incorporation of the foundations of alterity constitute a significant input in the construction of the PKM concept.

PKM AND ITS FRACTAL RELATION WITH KNOWLEDGE-BASED VALUE SYSTEMS MODEL: PROFILE OF THE KNOWLEDGE CITIZEN COMPETENCIES

In this chapter, the Knowledge-Based Value Systems Model (KBVS) submitted by Carrillo (1996) constitutes the frame of reference that provides leverage to PKM. The KBVS model is made up of both the KM dimensions and the key KM processes.

The KBVS model contemplates three dimensions where the individual dimension resides, besides the social and organizational dimensions (Carrillo, 2002). The individual dimension is clearly oriented to the individual's potential and self-management (Carrillo, 1996, 2002). Individual development is considered to be the building block or living cell of a development based on organizational and social knowledge (Carrillo, 2002). He concretes conceptual elements and applications made (CSC, 2001; Martínez, 2001) that include a value basis that provides the foundation of application of PKM by means of individual and group self-management from a human perspective. This model is strongly related with an approach of PKM, as it is based on the recognition of human potential and the conviction that each individual has cad guide the course of his/her life. It likewise ranks as fundamental those attitudes and values that favor people's involvement and growth in a self-managed learning environment. It considers that four competencies are required for self-management as an element of personal knowledge management; namely: self-esteem, self-knowledge, self-evaluation, and self-teaching (Martínez, 1999; CSC, 2001). It also contemplates, as basic elements: self-confidence, risk-taking, tolerance for ambiguity, internal orientation (or internal control locus), recognition of strengths and weaknesses, questioning, will power, and conscience; including two large meta dimensions, one related to the cognitive domain and the other to the emotional domain.

In parallel, meta cognition is recognized as the ability to deliberately direct the cognitive activity of the self to accomplish successful results from learning (Martínez, 1999). This implies that the individual should be able to ponder about the cognitive process and control it "from outside". The meta mood (Goleman, 1995) refers to awareness of the emotional state and the conscious, continuous attention to this state. It involves pondering emotional processes and is emotional competency

Figure 1. Relationship among KM dimensions and processes

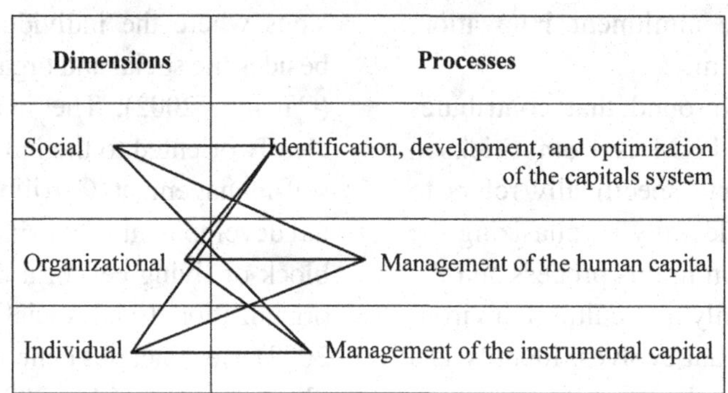

in trems of the knowledge of the self's mood and thinking about it. The meta mood is a factor that, similarly to meta cognition, is incorporated to the comprehensive self-management model of Knowledge System Center.

In turn, the key KM (2001) processes are identification, development, and optimization of the capitals system (universe of entity value); the administration of the human capital (alignment and optimization of those internal elements of individuals that allow them a competent performance given a value context) and the instrumental capital (alignment and optimization of those external elements that provide leverage for their performance given a value context).

Dimensions and processes in the Knowledge-based Value Systems model are incorporated in such a manner to a relation that, in each particular dimension, the three processes that ensure knowledge is being managed strategically in each setting –personal, organizational and social– are applied. Figure 1 shows this relation between KM dimensions and processes.

Thus, regarding relationship among its dimensions, particularly the individual and the three processes, the KBVS, allows derivation of a relationship between PKM and a profile of the knowledge citizen. This profile is made up of significant competencies and strategies in a value context representative of the economy of knowledge, specifically, the city of knowledge.

The individual perspective in the KBVS approach allows approaching and focusing on the completeness of performances required in the personal setting and recognizing that the primary aspect to consider in this sense refers to identification, development, and optimization of the Individual capitals system, as well as management of the Individual Agent Capital (or individual Competency Capital) and, finally, management of the Individual Instrumental Capital. On Table 2. *Fractal relation among the dimensions in the* KBVS *model and PKM: manageable elements*, shows the major elements to manage in the PKM approach from an all-embracing perspective of KBVS (Carrillo, 1996). It is called fractal because the basic structure of KBVS is repeated in a parallel fashion matching a different scale in the individual setting, which is constituted as PKM. It is thus that the elements to be managed are specifically identified when we are in the field of PKM.

It is thus that, from an integral perspective and based on the KBVS proposal, PKM involves an explicitation of the value systems of the individual entity, its operationalization and the respective explicitation in a personal capitals system. From the latter, one may foresee the determination of the capitals gap by comparing the actual status and the ideal status of each capital and its evolution according to the entity's strategic elements (CSC, 2003).

Table 2. Fractal relation among the dimensions in the KBVS model and PKM: manageable elements

KBVS	PKM
Identification, development, and optimization of the capitals system	Individual capitals system: identification, explicitation, ordering, systematizing, categorizing, and operationalizing the Personal Value System
Management of the human capital	Individual Agent Capital (or Individual Competence Capital): package of competencies that make up the offer of personal value
Management of the instrument capital	Individual Instrument Capital: set of external resources and processes available to and usable by the individual

Thus we may derive the need of a differentiated competencies profile for the knowledge citizen. A forerunner of this is the Taxonomy of competencies in the profile of the knowledge citizen (Martínez, 2005), as constituted by both the specific and the general competency categories, in which performances expected from the knowledge citizen are specified. For the specific ones, expectations include performances related to the development of internal and external referents (Development of Referents), to the articulation of significant personal relationships and relations with significant contexts (Articulation), and with an implementation directed to the concretion of actions that lead to personal and community development (Deployment). Likewise, the general competencies category refers to the use of interaction instruments (Instrumentation for Interaction).

An additional forerunner in this same line of thought contains the proposal of building the profile of the knowledge citizen on the basis of the abundant advancements in the democratic citizen's competencies and the proposal of complementarity and ensurance of competencies of the knowledge citizen, since the development of both competencies does not occur in an isolated manner, but in a dynamic interaction (Buendía, Martínez, Martínez, 2005; Martínez, 2006). Such competencies include, among other thingss: generating new forms of value contribution through the application of knowledge management processes from a strategic perspective; developing an innovative attitude as an agent in the context where the citizen evolves, relating the contribution of personal value to city, community, nation, region, and world needs; aligning personal values to personal strategic definitions and to the strategic definitions of the city, community, nation, region, and world; identifying and defining the total dimensions of personal value, operationalizing and developing them; cultivating relations that are significant to personal value dimensions, as well as city, national, and regional values. These competencies enable the individual to diagnose, design, apply, and evaluate initiatives from a comprehensive perspective that considers all the value elements in a given context, and to participate as well in their construction, explicitation, and development.

On the other hand, a very congruent profile (Martínez, 2007) is found that strengthens the connection between PKM and the profile of a knowledge citizen, one that considers competencies that are critical in a context of interaction among people who have common objectives and aspects they consider vital: the practice community. It is an inherent concept and reality in a city of knowledge where the citizen evolves. The profile of the members identified in entities emerging in cities of knowledge is made up of: cognitive competence (an awareness of own thinking that allows self-knowledge and self-control); ethical competence (reaching a decision to act or refrain from acting as a result of a clarification and planning process focused on what is to be achieved, the why and the criteria, considering the wellbeing of those involved); vision competence: (analyzing and understanding global trends and issues on the basis of knowledge of the world-wide context); articulation competence (taking action to facilitate the process of shaping/building a community and generating a self-managed community process; identifying common aspects that will generate rapport/affinities and encourage interaction among the members to generate and transfer knowledge); management competence (facilitating and ensuring the construction process for strategic or guiding elements in the community and congruence between decisions and actions).

It is thus that the approaches that focus and delve into the strategic performances (competencies) involved in the profile of the knowledge citizen from an individual perspective in interaction with the context; inherent aspects of PKM. PKM is thus recognized as a fundamental element in the profile of the knowledge citizen and natural congruence is found between the PKM approach and the essence of people who are members of a city of knowledge.

It should be noted that, for the purpose of this chapter, profile is understood as the set of competencies that characterize the performance potential of citizens in the cities of knowledge; and competencies (Martínez, 2007) such as the individual performance that involves an indivisible set of concepts, skills, attitudes, and values that come into play when the citizen interacts with others in the city context.

Likewise, the connection between PKM and the knowledge citizen should be leveraged considering the definition of city of knowledge and knowledge citizen. According to Carrillo (2005), city of knowledge is understood as an arrangement of a given value that induces preference for a congregation of people and its permanence. This implies a deliberate, systematic action to generate a sustainable balance of the universe of capitals that becomes attractive for people who recognize an exchange of productive value. This interaction involves an ongoing mutual construction performed by the citizen and the city. Knowledge citizen is defined as an agent who establishes and develops a relationship where productive value is exchanged, in a value-based context (city of knowledge) and capable of self-managing his/her knowledge, concurrently contributing to manage knowledge in his/her city.

CONCLUSION

On the basis of developing this chapter and furthering its purpose, it may be concluded that there are significant advancements and contributions around PKM and that the framework of its KM moments and generations, constitutes a sound referent to order and analyze them, thus allowing identification of the state-of-the-art PKM.

Likewise, we may conclude that the KBVS model, with its dimensions and processes, is a robust conceptual foundation that allows for derivation of an integral and strategic comprehension of PKM and, further yet, assuming that the individual is interacting with his/her context, he/she is the most important strategic asset in human organizations; in this case, particularly in cities of knowledge. Therefore PKM, from an integral and strategic perspective, and the viewpoint of its particular components (competencies such as individual performance when interacting in a given value context), are found to be fundamental for the development of potential in the individuals themselves, as well as for the respective development of more extensive contexts (i.e.: organizational and social).

Thus, PKM is considered a building block or living cell in a development based on organizational and social knowledge, in the extent that it boosts the influence and added value of an individual development based on organizational and social knowledge. From this standpoint, the knowledge citizen is constituted as an agent of change, with a vision and a mission that target on personal balance and social value with identify and define his/her own personal value accounts, as well as those pertaining to the city of which he/she is part and parcel.

The construction of PKM needs to continue; as it is a powerful subject, highly relevant in the development and wellbeing of knowledge citizens and their living space. The study and shaping of PKM should endure as a specific field of knowledge; whereas it is a fundamental subject in the present context as well as in the context built in the future, a future shaped as of now with each and every building block used.

REFERENCES

Ash, J. (2002). Personal Knowledge, analyzing and visualizing Knowledge Domains.

Barth, S. (2000). *The Power of One*. Retrieved March,2009, from http://www.quantum3.co.za/KMM%20Article%20Dec2000.htm

Boyd, S. (2001). Rethinking Knowledge Management: This Time It`s Personal. *Knowledge Capital Group*. Recuperado Marzo, 2009, de http://www.crmodyssey.com/Documentation/Documentation_PDF/Rethinking_Knowledge_Management.pdf

Buendía, A., Martinez, A., & Martinez, S. (2005). Competencias del Ciudadano en la City de Conocimiento . In Mujica Alberdi, A. (Ed.), *Conocimiento para el Desarrollo* (pp. 215–236). San Sebastián, Spain: Universidad de Deusto.

Carrillo, F. J. (1996). The Ways of Knowledge Management. In *Proceedings of the 1996 National Business Conference: The management of intellectual capital and innovation*. Hamilton, Ontario: McMaster University.

Carrillo, F. J. (2001a). El Futuro de la Gestión del Conocimiento: tres incógnitas, tres fases y tres escenarios . In Arboníes, Á. (Ed.), *Cómo evitar la miopía en la Administración del Conocimiento*. Bilbao, Spain: Cluster de Conocimiento.

Carrillo, F. J. (2001b). Un reporte expedicionario de los nuevos territorios . In *Entorno empresarial del Siglo XXI. Cinco años del Cluster de Conocimiento, Technology park of Zamudio*. Bilbao, Spain: La Evolución de Las Especies de Gestión de Conocimiento.

Carrillo, F. J. (2002). Capital Systems: Implications for Knowledge Agenda. *Journal of Knowledge Management*, *6*(4), 3–5. doi:10.1108/13673270210440884

Carrillo, F. J. (2005). Ciudades de Conocimiento: el estado del arte y el espacio de posibilidades. *Transferencia*, *18*(69), 26–28.

Centro de Sistemas de Conocimiento. (2001). *Manual General de Referencia modalidad electrónica. Documento Integrado de Identidad del CSC. Internal document*. México: Tecnológico de Monterrey.

Centro de Sistemas de Conocimiento. (2002). *Macromodelo Conceptual de los Sistemas de Conocimiento. Internal document*. México: Tecnológico de Monterrey.

Centro de Sistemas de Conocimiento. (2003). *Procesos Clave del KM. Modelo del CSC. Internal document*. México: Tecnológico de Monterrey.

Frand, J., & Hixon, C. (1999). *Personal Knowledge Management: Who, What, Why, When, Where, How?* Retrieved March, 2009, from http://www.anderson.ucla.edu/faculty/jason.frand/researcher/speeches/PKM.htm

Goleman, D. (1995). *Emotional Intelligence: Why it can matter more than IQ*. New York: Bantam Books.

Kaplan, R. (2000). *Randy Kaplan on PKM, Tools for personal Knowledge Effectiveness.*

Martínez, A. (1999). *Modelo integral de autogestión en grupos de aprendizaje de adultos.* Universidad Virtual. Master's Thesis, Instituto tecnológico y de Estudios Superiores de Monterrey.

Martínez, A. (2001). Un Modelo de Procesos Clave de Administración de Conocimiento. *Transferencia, 14*, 28–29.

Martínez, A. (2005). Knowledge Citizens: A Competence Profile . In Carrillo, F. J. (Ed.), *Knowledge Cities* (pp. 233–244). New York: Elsevier.

Martínez, A. (2006 September). El conocimiento de las personas. Factor clave en la Gestión del Conocimiento. *La Revista Sociedad y Conocimiento*.

Martínez, A. (2007). *Competencias de los integrantes de una comunidad de práctica.* Universidad Virtual. Tesis Doctoral, Instituto tecnológico y de Estudios Superiores de Monterrey.

Martínez, A., & Buendía, A. (2006). Las Competencias del Ciudadano de Conocimiento como base para ejercer sus derechos y responsabilidades . In Mariñez, F. (Ed.), *Ciudadanos, decisiones públicas y calidad de la democracia*. Ciudad de México, México: Limusa Noriega Editores.

Otero, B. A. (2000). *The African Past in America as a Bakhtinian and Levinasian other. 'Rememory' as Solution in Toni Morrison's 'Beloved.'* Retrieved March, 2009, from http://dialnet.unirioja.es/servlet/oaiart?codigo=193823 and http://eprints.upc.es/rebiun/index.php/record/view/11860

Ricardo, S. (2000). *Inteligencia Emocional en la Práctica: Resumen*. CapitalEmocional.com. Retrieved March, 2009, from http://www.capitalemocional.com/articulos/iemo.htm

Sidoli, J. (2000). *Think Like an Owner! Personal Knowledge Networking*. Retrieved March, 2009, from http://www.actlikeanowner.com/articles/default.asp

Woolfolk, E. A. (1990). *Psicología Educativa*. Ciudad de México, México: Prentice Hall Hispanoamericana.

Chapter 9
Deep Knowledge as the Core of Sustainable Societies

Alex Bennet
Mountain Quest Institute, USA

David Bennet
Mountain Quest Institute, USA

ABSTRACT

Knowledge-based social communities are critical to sustain economic levels and quality environments for community members. The pace of change, rising uncertainty, exponentially increasing complexity and the resulting anxiety (CUCA) have made competition among nations, cities and communities greater and more fierce. As economies look from industry to knowledge for their prime income generator, the role of knowledge and its supporting infrastructure become critical to economic and social health. In this chapter the authors focus on what deep knowledge is and the environment needed to maximize its contribution to the health and growth of societies. They also introduce knowledge attractor network teams as sources of power for community sustainability.

THE STARTING POINT

Society is taken to be all of the conditions and actions of a social community, both inter-connected and inter-dependent. A social community is a bounded group of people living together in the same locality under the same governing structure, with conditions from which emerge a culture and related behaviors. Further, a social community is a complex system which must adapt quickly to opportunities to develop knowledge-based solutions while at the same time implementing solutions for value creation and maintaining learning efficacy. When these occur the social community is behaving as an intelligent complex adaptive system. This perspective is consistent with the perception forwarded by Garcia (2006) describing cities as connected (Huysman and Wulf, 2005) complex systems of values (Carrillo, 2004), meanings (Tuomi, 2005) and conversations (Dvir, 2006).

Consistent with our previous work, **information** is considered the result of organization expressed by a non-random pattern or set of patterns (Bennet and Bennet, 2007b, 2008a, 2008b, 2008c, 2008d, 2009a;

DOI: 10.4018/978-1-61520-721-3.ch009

Stonier, 1990, 1997). Information is represented in the brain by patterns of neuron connections and the strength of those connections. Data (a form of information) is simple patterns, and data and information are both patterns but have no meaning until some organism recognizes and interprets the patterns. As a functional definition grounded in the natural world, **knowledge** is *the capacity (potential or actual) to take effective action in varied and uncertain situations* (Bennet, 2005; Bennet and Bennet, 2004, 2007b).

This definition highlights knowledge as a creation of the human mind. It exists in the human brain in the form of stored or expressed neuronal patterns that may be selected, activated, mixed and/or reflected upon through thought. From this mixing process (associative patterning) new patterns are created that may represent understanding, meaning and the capacity to anticipate (to various degrees) the results of potential actions. Through these processes the mind is continuously growing, restructuring and creating increased organization (information) and knowledge (Bennet and Bennet, 2006, 2008b, 2009a).

Recognizing that knowledge is the result of associative patterning in the mind/brain, we choose to consider knowledge as comprised of two parts: knowledge (informing) and knowledge (proceeding) (Bennet and Bennet, 2008b, 2008c, 2009a, 2009b, 2009d). This builds on the distinction made by Ryle (1949) between "knowing that" and "knowing how". **Knowledge (informing)** is the *information* part of knowledge and represents understanding, meaning, insights, expectations, theories and principles that support or lead to effective action. **Knowledge (proceeding)** represents the *process and action* part of knowledge. In other words, it is the *process* of selecting and associating the relevant information—knowledge (informing)—from which specific actions can be identified and implemented, that is, actions that result in the desired outcome.

It is also useful to think of knowledge in terms of surface, shallow and deep (Bennet and Bennet, 2008d, 2009b). **Surface knowledge** is predominantly, but not exclusively, information. Surface knowledge answers the question of *what*, *when*, *where* and *who*, is primarily explicit, representing visible choices that require minimum understanding. Further, it is more of an awareness on the part of the receiver of *what is* and only minimal action is typically required. Surface knowledge in the form of information can be stored in books, computers, and the mind/brain. Much of our everyday life such as light conversations, descriptions and even top-level self-reflection could be considered surface thinking and learning that creates surface knowledge. A large amount of what is taught in schools falls into this descriptive category. For example, the National Research Council expressed concern that the U.S. education system teaches students science using a mile wide and inch deep approach (National Research Council, 2000; Oakes & Lipton, 1999).

Shallow knowledge is information that represents deeper levels of understanding, meaning and sense-making. To understand is to comprehend some level of meaning, with meaning typically relating to a specific individual, organization or situation, and implying some level of action. To interpret meaning requires context. Thus shallow knowledge requires a level of understanding and meaning such that the user can—utilizing logic, analysis, observation, reflection, and even to some extent prediction—identify cohesion and integration of the information in a manner that makes sense (Bennet and Bennet, 2008d).

Deep knowledge is the development and integration of six components: understanding, meaning, insight, creativity, judgment, and the ability to anticipate the outcome of one's actions (Bennet and Bennet, 2004, 2007). Deep knowledge represents the ability to shift your frame of reference as the context and situation shift. The unconscious plays a large role in this area. The source of deep knowledge lies in an individual's creativity, intuition, forecasting experience, pattern recognition, and use of theories (also important in shallow situations) (Bennet and Bennet, 2008d). This is the realm of the expert. During the lengthy period of practice needed to develop deep knowledge, the expert has often developed an internal theory that guides knowledge (proceeding). The unconscious mind of the expert has learned to detect patterns and evaluate the importance of those patterns in order to anticipate the behavior of situations that are too complex for the conscious mind to understand (Ross, 2006; Bennet and Bennet, 2008b, 2009d).

The three levels of knowledge described above are not actual levels. Knowledge is a continuum of the depth of understanding and meaning. We suggest three levels in order to be able to discuss the variations of understanding, learning and action related to different depths of knowledge. For example, to share knowledge at each level requires a different approach. Surface knowledge can be shared by normal conversations and communication via the Internet, etc. Shallow knowledge is best shared in a social context, that is, through clear and careful communication and context that allows the receiver to re-create the knowledge of the sender (Bennet and Bennet, 2007a, 2008d). Dialogue is extremely useful in such situations (Ellinor and Gerard, 1998). Deep knowledge takes much more time to develop, and requires learning over time in situations such as mentoring, shadowing and practice under the guidance of an expert (Bennet and Bennet, 2007, 2009a).

In his 1995 book, Karl Wiig, one of the original founders of KM (Bennet, 2005), introduced the concept of the knowledge proficiency dimension as seven levels from beginner to grandmaster (Wiig, 1995). While there is not a one-to-one correspondence with our definitions of surface, shallow and deep levels of knowledge, Wiig's seven levels roughly correspond as follows: surface knowledge is a beginner; shallow knowledge includes advanced beginner, competent performer and proficient performer; and deep knowledge includes the expert, master and grandmaster.

CONNECTIONS, RELATIONSHIPS AND INFORMATION FLOWS

It is assumed that the community has (1) identified and decided upon the desired vision and direction needed to become a knowledge-based society; and (2) developed support systems such as infrastructure (for example, educational and medical facilities), and financial resources to attract and keep knowledge-based individuals. As suggested by the extensive diversity of—and described in—the papers introduced in the special *Journal of Knowledge Management* issues on knowledge based development (2002, 2004, 2006, 2007, 2008) and the first book published on knowledge cities (Carrillo, 2006), all levels of knowledge are needed for effective knowledge-based development. For example, street vendors and purchasers use surface knowledge continuously throughout the day; professionals who design, build and support the infrastructure require shallow knowledge; and decision-makers with the creative thinking abilities to solve complex issues and challenging problems need deep knowledge.

The major characteristics of a social community are connections, relationships and information flows built on a practice of continuous learning (see Figure 1). Connections are seen as the option for seamless and interlinked communication among interested parties (Yigitcanlar, et al., 2008). Relationships represent a *particular type of connection* among people who are related or are having dealings with each other (American Heritage Dictionary, 2006). As a working definition, we take information flows to mean the timely and efficient movement of information between and among individuals and organizations in support of effective decision-making and actions. Together, these characteristics represent the culture needed to support and sustain *knowledge flows*. The intersection of these three factors forms the foundation for transforming a community into a knowledge-based society.

Figure 1. The major characteristics of a social community are connections, relationships and information flows built on a practice of continuous learning

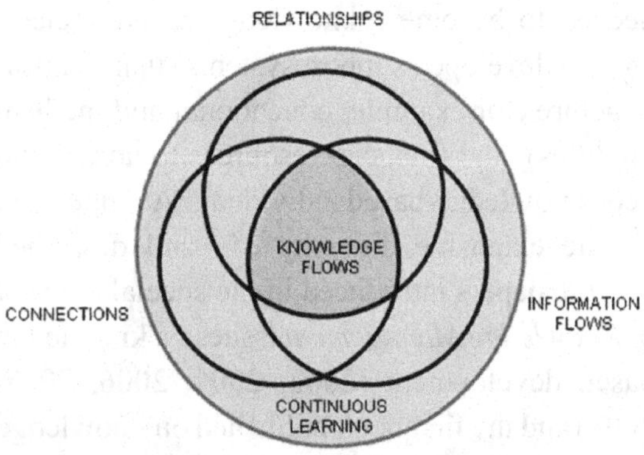

Connections that occur throughout the day and night are based on movement and living patterns. Living in the midst of work, home and community requirements, people have a tendency to develop repetitive patterns of actions. For example, one individual may catch the metro at 6:55 AM, work from 8 AM to 5 PM (generally going to lunch with the same group of colleagues), catch the 5:20 PM metro for home, stop by the gym for a 45 minute workout, and then spend the evening preparing, eating and cleaning up after dinner; taking a shower; and getting ready for the next day of work. This pattern goes on for five days, then another pattern begins on Saturday that may include getting together with friends or family, and still a different behavior on Sunday. In the midst of all this activity, while moving from place to place and performing the functions required in each place, this individual is continuously developing connections, building relationships, exchanging information with others, and learning at some level.

In a given community, virtual connections begin at the infrastructure level, that is, ensuring technology availability that supports the interactions of citizens and their organizations— private, public, not-for-profit, and personal (family, friends, collegial, etc.)—as well as the interactions of individuals and organizations via the Internet across the larger global-based society. For example, is fast Internet connectivity available to all areas of the community? Are computers with Internet connectivity available locally for those who do not own personal computers? Are members of the community aware of the benefit of information literacy in support of their personal needs and knowledge-based development? Is there a source of learning available to the community to spread information literacy?

Information literacy is an integrative competency for all members of a knowledge-based society (Porter, et al., 2002; Bennet and Bennet, 2004). It is a set of information and knowledge age skills that enable individuals to recognize when information is and is not needed, and how to locate, evaluate, integrate, use and effectively communicate information in a virtual environment. These skills are critical to citizens in dealing with the daily barrage of information; and the broad array of tools to search, organize and analyze results, and communicate and integrate them for decision-making. For example, the basic goals or standards for information literacy competency are the ability to (1) determine the nature and extent of the information needed; (2) access needed information effectively and efficiently; (3) evaluate information and its sources critically, and incorporate selected information into your knowledge base and value system; (4) use information effectively to accomplish a specific purpose; and (5) understand the economic, legal, ethical and social issues surrounding the use of information and act accordingly.

Information flows occur 24 hours a day 7 days a week as each individual's senses receive information from the external environment, complex it with what they have previously learned or experienced, and use it as a basis for interacting with the world. Information flows across a social community occur whenever one individual interacts with another by sharing thoughts and feelings.

Although all information flows represent surface level knowledge flows, they can contribute to development of shallow or deep knowledge flows as well (Bennet and Bennet, 2008d). Continuous learning built on these information flows occurs on two levels. Any time we converse with others or observe activities, or get involved in situations, we absorb new information and experiences which remain in our memories and may influence our future behavior. The second way we experientially learn is to repeatedly and deliberately question and think about our most important experiences and thereby develop insights and a deeper understanding of those experiences. This second way—sometimes called *effortful learning*—leads to a deeper knowledge base that grows over time (Ross, 2006).

Virtual information flows can be thought of in terms of availability, access and desire. Availability refers to information content and how it is stored. For example, is the information available that is needed by citizens to meet every-day life society norms such as the what's and how's for medical, commerce, government and community services? Access includes (1) having the information virtually available in various formats; (2) the ability of citizens to obtain that information, that is, citizen information literacy; and (3) the capacity of citizens to understand and act on that information, that is, their ability to create knowledge from available information. Desire refers to the incentives individuals have to access available information and convert it into knowledge that helps them take effective action. For example, a tax filing date may serve as an incentive for accessing virtually-available tax information or an awareness of a circus coming to down can serve as an incentive for purchasing e-tickets. Desire also refers to sharing information (and knowledge) with others. For example, filling out personal information in a virtual dating system, or helping a senior citizen apply for social security benefits.

Relationships come into play in every aspect of connection and information flows. While humans have always been social creatures, we are just waking up to the complexity of our own brains and how they are linked together, that "all of our biologies are interwoven" (Cozolino, 2006, p. 3). People are in continuous, two-way interaction with those around them—with a great deal of this communication occurring in the unconscious (Bennet and Bennet, 2007a). Concurrently, *the brain* is continuously changing in response to these interactions. When a secure, bonding relationship in which trust has been established occurs, there is "a cascade of biochemical processes, stimulating and enhancing the growth and connectivity of neural networks throughout the brain" (Shore, 1994). This process promotes neural growth and learning, and facilitates organization and integration within the brain (Cozolino, 2002). Both of these authors based this activity on a relationship involving trust, which carries an emotional tag, that is, the stronger the emotion attached to the experience, the longer it will be remembered and the easier it will be to recall, thereby enhancing learning.

Relationships can be characterized in many different ways; for example, in terms of collaborative or exploitative, or in terms of geographical, organizational or technological proximity (Petruzzelli, 2008). However, whether virtual or face-to-face, relationships arc ultimately about people and the way they interact with each other over time. Every individual is part of a relationship network made up of those people with whom the individual interacts—or has interacted with in the past—and with whom there is a connection or significant association (Bennet & Bennet, 2004); in short, all those people with whom you have some common ground and repeated conversations. A social network is people (representing nodes) connected to exchange information (Bennet and Bennet, 2004), which are "the fabric of most complex systems" (Barabasi, 2002, p. 222). As social networks, relationship networks are an important element of citizen engagement (Putnam, et al, 1993) as they support the exchange of information and knowledge (Boschma, 2005; Knoben and Oerlemans, 2006; Albino et al., 2007a).

Relationship network management is based on the recognition that everyday conversations lay the groundwork for the decisions you make in the future. When we recognize the value of our relationship network, we can learn to consciously manage and support it. For example, by (1) identifying the people with whom you interact regularly; (2) consciously choosing to develop, expand, and actively sustain those positive relationships in terms of thought, feelings, knowledge, and actions; and (3) staying open to sharing and learning through your professional and personal relationship networks.

Successful relationship network management has a number of basic characteristics (Bennet & Bennet, 2004). These include the *flow* of data, information and knowledge; *equitability* in terms of fairness and reasonableness (with both sides getting something of value out of the relationship); *trust* based on integrity and consistency over time, saying what you mean (and following through on what you say); *openness* (directly related to trust and a willingness to share); and *interdependency* (a state of mutual reliance, confidence, and trust).

But what about relationships and trust in the new paradigm of virtual social networking? This demands a shift in perception, and a further shift from relationship-based interactions to idea-based interactions, that is, relationships based on ideas. Virtual networking primarily relies on the resonance of ideas to develop a level of trust. Those that connect build up a level of trust over time based on the responses of those with whom they interact. Further, there is the phenomenon of sequential linkages that comes into play and supports our willingness to trust. If I know someone that you know who was a close colleague of someone else who owns a company that another individual is a partner in, then we have a starting place for building some level of trust. For example, in a military organization if two individuals have served on the same ship at some point in their career, or if they have experienced service in the same region of conflict, there is a common bond on which to begin an exchange.

Wikis and blogs provide opportunities for individuals to virtually build trust. Because there are minimal pre-developed mental or emotional barriers to communication among strangers, exchanges that occur virtually are generally open and often frank, providing a good criteria upon which to build a relationship based on ideas. However, this may get out of control. As pointed out by Donald Tapscott in his 2009 book, virtual social networking can lead to issues of privacy since in the course of open exchange with unknown individuals personal details are often shared. He warns that the net generation is "giving away their personal information on social networks and elsewhere and in doing so are undermining their future privacy" (Tapscott, 2009, p. 7).

While all relationships support surface knowledge sharing, to share shallow and deep knowledge requires increased context which means more interactions and more sharing, thus stronger relationships (Bennet and Bennet, 2007a, 2008d). The *efficient* sharing of shallow knowledge requires a social attunement, that is, trust and resonance (based on a common language, background, experiences, etc.) between the participants (Johnson and Taylor, 2006).

KNOWLEDGE FLOWS

As information flows across connections built on relationships, knowledge emerges. For a deeper discussion of this phenomenon see Bennet and Bennet (2004) page 67 through 71. From a neuroscience perspective all knowledge is emergent. Recall that information informs knowledge and is selected, combined and reshaped to take effective action—the basis of Knowledge (Informing) and Knowledge (Proceeding). Thus knowledge—a product of the human mind—*emerges* in response to a specific issue or intention and for a specific context, whether its solving a problem or planning for the future. The flow or sharing of *knowledge* (the capacity to take effective action) is highly dependent on an understanding of the context and situation related to that knowledge. Describing eight areas of context that affect the flow of knowledge, Bennet and Bennet (2007a) forward that the higher the number of related (relevant) context patterns involved in communication, the greater resonance between the source and the perceiver and the higher the amount of shared understanding. The eight areas of context are:

- *Context 1*: Information **content**, that is, the specific nouns and verbs selected, and the adjectives and adverbs used in the primary expression, and structure of sentence that supports content).
- *Context 2*: The **setting or situation** surrounding the information.
- *Context 3*: Silent attention/presence; that of which we are aware but is not expressed, not available.
- *Context 4*: **Non-verbal**, non-voiced communications patterns; associated information signals (emphasis and tone). In face-to-face interactions this would include body expressions, attitude and physical appearance, as well as other sensory inputs.
- *Context 5*: System of shared context. **Mutually shared common information/ patterns** with meaning such as culture, environment history, etc.
- *Context 6*: Personal context. Internal **beliefs, values, experiences and feelings** that emerge into conscious awareness (6 and 7 work together).
- *Context 7*: Impact of **unconscious processes**, memories and feelings on context 3, 4, 5 and 6. Can be thought of in terms of (1) the unconscious, (2) experiences and feelings (memories) not in conscious awareness, and (3) empathetic process that can mirror behavior.
- *Context 8*: Overarching pattern context. **Higher levels of patterns of significance** that emerge in the mind. (Bennet & Bennet, 2007a, p. 43).

The context and situation could be considered meta-knowledge, that is, knowledge about knowledge. See Bennet and Bennet (2007a) for additional information on context.

In the community setting, knowledge flows are facilitated through the nurturing of knowledge moments. Ron Dvir (with the Futures Center in Tel-Aviv, Israel) describes the knowledge city as a collage of human knowledge moments, connecting the daily experiences of citizens as they create, nourish, share and transform knowledge for their individual and collective purposes (Dvir, 2006). These moments happen as individuals move through their lives, occurring at the intersection of people, places, processes and purpose. Since a city or community—whether a place or a group of linked individuals—is always *co-evolving* with its environment, the quantity of these planned and spontaneous exchanges increases the potential for quality and impact, and thus sustainability.

Since knowledge is the capacity to take effective action, knowledge moments refer to exchanges that provide the potential for, or lead to, effective action. The behavior of a community is driven by the result of the interaction of all decisions made and actions taken based on the knowledge moments of every individual in the community. Similar to the butterfly concept in chaos theory, there is the potential for success or failure based on knowledge moments which cannot be specifically identified or tied directly to that success or failure! This new frame of reference lays the groundwork for understanding knowledge mobilization. The *nurturing and facilitating of knowledge moments* is one objective of knowledge mobilization.

Knowledge mobilization (KMb) is the process of generating value or a value stream through the creation, assimilation, leveraging, sharing and application of focused knowledge to a bounded community (Bennet and Bennet, 2007b). In communities and cities this concerns the creating, moving and tailoring of knowledge from its source in universities and individual experts to practitioners, community leaders and larger stakeholder groups such that consequent actions are effective and sustainable.

Thus KMb is the process—or a program comprised of a number of specific processes—of applying knowledge to a specific objective. For a simple issue or problem, the KMb process may end when the issue is solved, but for a more complex problem the process may continue as long as the action sequence is needed to achieve the objective. In a social setting new thoughts and behaviors emerge from other thoughts and behaviors of those citizens and organizations involved in the issue. These new ideas are then mixed with yet another set of thoughts and behaviors from the larger stakeholder community, and so on. We call this mixing and entwining set of unpredictable associations the process of *collaborative entanglement*.

The knowledge mobilization process in a community—moving bounded knowledge into the community—works very much as does the human mind. All the living and learning of an individual is recorded in the brain, stored among some hundred billion neurons that are continuously moving between firing and idling, creating and re-creating patterns. Information coming in through the senses may resonate with stored patterns that have strong synaptic connections and emotional tags. When this resonance occurs, the incoming information is consistent with the individual's frame of reference and belief systems. As this incoming information is complexed (the associative patterning process) it connects with, and to some degree may bring into conscious awareness, deep knowledge. The unconscious continues this process 24/7, with new knowledge sometimes emerging at the conscious level.

Collaborative entanglement can be used to purposely and consistently develop and support approaches and processes that combine the sources of knowledge (in our example university researchers) and the beneficiaries of that knowledge (in our example local communities) to move toward a common direction, such as meeting an identified community need. Beyond decision-making, collaborative entanglement includes the execution and actions that build value for all stakeholders, engaging social responsibility and providing a platform for knowledge mobilization. The collaborative entanglement model is highly participative, with permeable and porous (unclear and continuously reshaping) boundaries between the source of knowledge and knowledge beneficiary as well as between the knowledge and its application in a continuous learning cycle. See Figure 2. Lee and Garvin contend that to be effective, knowledge exchange depends on multi-directional, participatory communication among stakeholders (Lee and Garvin, 2003). *The collaborative entanglement model moves beyond knowledge exchange to the creation of shared understanding that results in collaborative advantage and increased value.*

In the collaborative entanglement model, individuals and groups are continuously interacting as new information comes through their senses. For example, they might: (1) recognize a problem or issue and/or solution, (2) see new indicators that bode well or poorly for the community, or (3) see new events occur that affect an on-going project or community effort. From these interactions and others—often related to strong emotional feelings which increase the importance and strength of their meaning—new knowledge emerges. As new knowledge is created by experts and applied by community decision-makers an iterative loop of collective learning occurs. As part of this process a large amount of tacit knowledge (embodied, affective, intuitive and spiritual) is created beyond that which visibly affects the community. This tacit knowledge then forms the grounding (state-of-the-art thinking) for future incoming information that will be associated with these patterns and thereby create new knowledge. In other words,

Figure 2. The collaborative entanglement model is highly participative, with permeable and porous boundaries between the source of knowledge and knowledge beneficiary as well as between the knowledge and its application in a continuous learning cycle (Bennet & Bennet, 2007b) (used with permission)

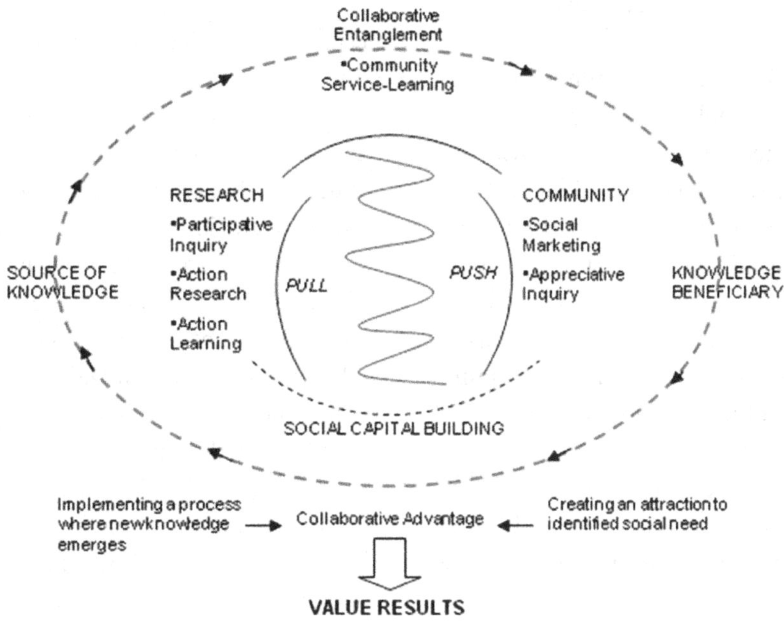

the process of collaborative entanglement among experts and stakeholders not only helps provide a specific solution to a current issue, but seeds the ground for continuous community improvement, collaboration, and sustainability.

Two modes of nurturing collaborative entanglement are appreciative inquiry and social marketing. To appreciate is to value, to recognize the best in people and the things around us; and to inquire is the act of exploration and discovery and asking questions. Based on the simple premise that communities grow in the direction of what they are repeatedly asked questions about and therefore focus their attention on (Srivastva & Cooperrider, 1990), **appreciative inquiry** is an approach that discovers and promotes the best in people and those things around us. Hammond and Hall describe it as a way of thinking, seeing and acting to bring about purposeful change (Hammond & Hall, 1996). They translate the principles of appreciative inquiry into the following assumptions:

1. In every society, organization or group, something works.
2. What we focus on becomes our reality.
3. Reality is created in the moment and there are multiple realities.
4. The act of asking questions of an organization or group influences the group in some way.
5. People have more confidence and comfort to journey to the future (the unknown) when they carry forward parts of the past (the known).
6. If we carry parts of the past forward, they should be what is best about the past.
7. It is important to value differences.
8. The language we use creates our reality. (Hammond & Hall, 1996, pp 2-3)

The appreciative inquiry approach has been successfully used in community development (Bennet & Bennet, 2007b). As the focus in organizations and communities moves back to people and the knowledge they create, share and use, the empowering aspects of the appreciative inquiry approach can build self-confidence in—and receptivity to—new ideas and accelerate behavior change.

Social marketing utilizes commercial marketing concepts and tools to support programs specifically designed *to influence behavior* to improve the well-being and health of individuals and society (Kotler, et al., 2002; Kotler and Roberto, 1989). Social marketing is customer-driven, seeking to increase the acceptability of an idea, cause, or practice in a specific community based on identified needs of that community. Combining business and social objectives, ideas and attitudes are marketed in order to bring about social change. For example, the objective may be to produce understanding (such as the health issues related to smoking); to bring about a one-time action (free chest X-rays); to bring about a behavior change (wearing seat belts); or to change a basic belief (the movement from a control-oriented bureaucracy to a collaborative work environment). Whether local or global, the focus is on learning what people want and need, and proactively responding to those wants and needs in terms of "selling" ideas, attitudes and behavior change (Bennet & Bennet, 2007b).

Social marketing differs from traditional marketing only with respect to the objectives (Andreasen, 1995). Some of the same ideas used to sell products can be used to sell ideas, attitudes and behaviors. For example, following a normal marketing approach, the social change objective would first be defined; then the attitudes, beliefs, values and behavior of the targeted audience analyzed. This is followed by development of a marketing plan, either building a marketing group or hiring a marketing organization to do so, and, once the plan is underway, continuously evaluating, adjusting and readjusting the program to ensure effectiveness. While in a sense all marketing is the marketing of ideas, social marketing is specifically under-girded by the intent to move toward the greater good of society.

DEEP KNOWLEDGE FLOWS

Recall the distinction between surface, shallow and deep knowledge. Because of their complexity, situations that require deep knowledge are often the most difficult to successfully navigate, yet such situations often have the potential for a high value payoff. Easier payoff situations would likely have already been recognized and addressed. In other words, it typically takes deep knowledge to create the highest value. Thus we now focus on deep knowledge flows.

As discussed earlier, deep knowledge consists of understanding, meaning, insight, creativity, judgment and the ability to anticipate the outcome of actions, and requires the capability to shift frames of reference as the context and situation shift. Each learning experience builds on its predecessor by broadening the sources of knowledge creation and the capacity to create knowledge in different ways. When an individual has deep knowledge, more and more of their learning will continuously build up in the unconscious. In other words, in the area of focus, knowledge begets knowledge. The more that is understood, the more that can be created and understood.

The development of deep knowledge is not an easy process. It takes an intense and persistent interest and dedication to a specific area of learning, knowledge and action. An individual must "live" within their field of expertise and at the same time focus on the details and contexts of every specific experience, asking questions and analyzing what went right, what went wrong and why such actions lead to uncovering relationships and patterns that over time become the unconscious bedrock of deep knowledge. Gathering relevant information and combining it into hierarchical chunks builds a wide range of patterns from which to draw when encountering a new or unusual situation. Gathered through what is called *effortful practice*, much of this knowledge resides within the unconscious and surfaces only when the individual takes an action or makes a decision based on "feel" or "intuition." Nevertheless, deep knowledge usually provides the best solution to emerging problem. See Ericsson et al. (2006) for a thorough and up-to-date review of expertise and expert performance.

To create deep knowledge flows requires more than surface-level conversations or even shallow-level dialogue. Since deep knowledge is largely unconscious, coaching, mentoring and significant learning through experience are needed. For example, in the field of medicine deep knowledge flows are planned into the education process through well-designed intern and residency programs. An industry example is development of career paths in which high potential employees are given specific, challenging career assignments as they progress up the ladder.

Stories can connect at the unconscious level and thereby facilitate deep knowledge flows across a society. For purposes of this paper, stories are considered accounts or recitals of an event or series of events which may be real or fictional. Stories can communicate values, ideas, modes of thinking, frames of reference, and be guides for action, providing an effective way to share understanding of both simple and complex systems (Bennet & Bennet, 2007c; Snowden, 1999). When embedded in a surrounding context, they can provide the key ideas of systems, relationships and boundaries. Because stories can convey multiple levels of meaning, they are able to introduce, illuminate and explain complex issues and phenomena, thus offering a way to break through complex issues, making visible underlying patterns of foundational concepts that often lay hidden by the flow of events or the multiple chains of causality.

Thus stories provide numerous ways of communicating that can not only convey a message and its underlying context, but also spread quickly and—because of their potential emotional power—can significantly influence listeners. Carefully crafted stories can convey levels of meaning that are effective in influencing cultures and sharing understanding throughout a targeted group or environment. For example, negative stories can push an emotional response in a community that leads to the formation of activist groups. Conversely, the hero's story can be highly effective in garnering support for societal change while simultaneously providing a role model for that change.

Joseph Campbell is one of the best-known sources for exploring the subtext of the hero's story. For Campbell (1949), myth is a philosophical text—one in which truths are revealed symbolically during a three-phased adventure. In phase one (departure), the mythological hero sets forth from his common home (or a castle), and is lured, carried away, or else voluntarily proceeds to the threshold of adventure. In phase two (initiation), he encounters a shadow presence that guards the passage. At this point the hero either defeats or conciliates this power and goes, either dead or alive, through a world of unfamiliar yet strangely intimate forces. In phase three (return), he undergoes a supreme ordeal and gains his reward.

While these myths continue today, Campbell points out that in the stories of today the hero's journeys are no longer undertaken in the mystical and symbolic context of cosmic law—in bright moments of the tribe's great victories—but in the silences of personal despair. Campbell sees the mythical journey of man today as understanding man, coming to terms with himself, with the hero playing a larger role in the universal cycle of growth, dissolution and redemption that is part of every man's life. Ultimately, we each move from the microcosm of the individual to the macrocosm of the universe, with the hero's journey opening us to the unalterable truths of human existence—its joys and sorrows, its pains and pleasures—which are the same for all people (Campbell, 1949).

Stories built around the hero's journey abound at all levels of society, resonating with societal values and modeling the cultural ideal. They are about everyday hero's. For example, in a local community this may be the story of a successful soup kitchen for the homeless; a fireman who saved the beloved family dog; or a local businessman who decides to sponsor a little league team. At a city level, the story may be about a politician who goes up against the mafia to expose payoffs in the city police department; or a group of concerned citizens that stand up against an "unfair" city ordinance; or a pilot whose quick thinking and expertise saves the lives of 71 passengers.

The telling of stories is part of a complex adaptive system, that is, a system made up of the storyteller, the story, the audience, the environment, and all the relationships among these. For example, the storyteller brings personal objectives, experiences, memories and frames of reference. Along with his telling comes nonverbal signals related to spirituality, emotion, language, mannerisms and timing. The story itself has a purpose, message, and persona built on patterns relating actions and values over time. Characteristics of the audience include goals, experiences, values, frames of reference (habits of the mind and viewpoints), memories, interest and learning states (spiritual, somatic, emotional, and intellectual). An example of relationships would be the history of past interactions between the storyteller and the audience. Similarly, the generation and application of deep knowledge is unique to each situation.

In the unconscious mind the association of incoming information with internal information is a powerful form of continuous learning (Bennet & Bennet 2008a). As people move through their daily lives, there is *a range* of shifting conceptual and sensory information and images that the mind uses to make sense of a situation or event that is encountered (Hodgkin, 1991). In other words, the unconscious is creating and "sculpting" information and knowledge to apply to the situation at hand. Significant gains can be made in the effectiveness of problem solving and decision-making through understanding and stimulating this process of story sculpting and telling.

Knowledge sculpting begins with identifying what is significant and the deliberate removal or modification of all information and knowledge that is not relevant to a specific problem or situation. The purpose of the sculpting process is to identify and apply only that knowledge and information that is directly applicable to the context and content of the situation, modifying the language of the "story" to build and support that which is most significant. This assures that the minimum necessary and sufficient information and knowledge are available and utilized in the resolution of problems or situations. It also minimizes the danger of information overload.

Stories can powerfully transmit deep knowledge through their values and the unconscious sharing of meaning and insight. Their power does not come from telling the listener what is good or bad, what to believe or not to believe. What happens is that the listener (or reader) hears (or reads) the story and from their personal reflection creates the meaning and knowledge that lies within the story. This allows the listener to *own* the meaning and knowledge within the story because they have created it themselves. Such ownership means that they will act on their knowledge, perhaps without even knowing why. Thus stories represent a powerful way to generate and maintain deep knowledge flows.

THE KNOWLEDGE PROCESSES

We propose that the application of knowledge will normally be connected to the major processes of creativity, problem-solving, decision-making and implementation. Throughout any society—by every individual and in every organization—these four processes are used continuously, although often they are unconscious, invisible, or merged together. For example, many actions are taken without realizing that a decision was made before taking the action, and often decisions are so natural that there is no problem-solving needed. However, in an unstable environment all four processes are generally fully engaged.

Creativity, problem-solving, decision-making and implementation together constitute a procedure for ensuring all aspects of a situation are taken into account.

Most creativity comes from the unconscious. Often a long time has been spent thinking about a given field or subject, and gathering considerable experience through living with that subject. This is the incubation phase of the creative process introduced by Poincare (2001) prior to illumination, when creative thoughts burst through the unconscious stirring of incubation into the conscious stream of thought, where they can be explored and tested (Bennet & Bennet, 2004; Sternberg and Davidson, 1995). As discussed earlier, over time experiences—and the unconscious activities related to those experiences—create a depth of knowledge and understanding that is expertise. For any society to keep up with world progress it must offer significant contributions through new ideas and inventions, both requiring the continuous creation of deep knowledge. Without the capacity to create deep knowledge, companies and perhaps even governments will look outside their society for such talent, or, worse, they will move their research departments to foreign soil where deep knowledge is readily available (Augustine, 2008).

Problem-solving is one of the most important processes, that is, taking inputs from past experience and the creative process as needed and linking ideas, problems and decisions. A problem can be viewed as an undesirable situation, with ideally its solution becoming a new, desirable situation. This process of finding ways to change an undesirable situation into a desirable one is the creative part of problem-solving, or the process of gap analysis. The output of the problem-solving process is a solution set of alternatives that provide ways to achieve a desired situation or problem solution, that is, anticipation of a future result. For the most complex problems it is often impossible to "change the situation." What is more likely is a solution that includes influencing the problem and changing/adapting internal actions to accommodate an adjustment in the relationships between the external environment and the community. For example, the building of a new airport would cause traffic problems for the city. To resolve this problem, the city might have to change current traffic patterns, invoke their right of eminent domain, and provide funding vehicles to enable building a new metro line to the airport.

Decision-making refers to the selection of one or more alternatives generated by the problem-solving process. Most day-to-day decisions and their follow-on actions are based on local facts and needs, thus requiring only surface and/or shallow knowledge. These facts are commonly available and when connected with logical and causal relationships (usually unknowingly filtered by our emotional feelings), the decision is made. This process works well for a large percentage of decisions made with any society. However, it does not work for decisions that relate to the distant future where information and facts are only useful if they can be extrapolated into the future. Deep knowledge can both magnify economic productivity and improve decision-making in many fields of social experience and societal health. For example, in the areas of strategic thinking and management, deep knowledge is essential for guiding decisions at all levels of society. As the world surges into complexity, it becomes essential that effective decisions dealing with the future are based on a combination of historic decision processes coupled with the *competency to recognize patterns*, those existing today and those that will carry us into the future. These guiding patterns—often buried in the unconscious mind, or tacit—can result in good decisions through the decision-maker's intuition, gut feel or judgment. However, these decisions cannot happen without some conscious explanation and justification to colleagues and constituents. Thus the relevant facts and logic must be developed to provide a rational explanation of the decision, requiring surface, shallow and deep knowledge.

A society's growth and success depends upon a myriad of strategic decisions—from education to economic investments, to culture and health and welfare, to politics and defense—and how they are implemented. Actions and results make the difference. Making high-quality decisions is essential to getting good results, but it is not enough. Implementation is the most situation-dependent of the major processes, that is, the details of the actions required to achieve the desired results cannot be generalized. Undoubtedly, the outcome of such strategic decisions will depend upon the existence and quality of a large number of individuals with the deep knowledge to make the right strategic choices that will successfully guide society's movements into the future. Success is also dependent on the ability of these leaders to share understanding built on deep knowledge at the surface and shallow levels.

COMMUNITY SUSTAINABILITY

Sustainability is not a constant, but rather comes from continuous learning and re-learning—creating, re-creating and adapting knowledge—as we co-evolve with our environment. For our communities and cities, as well as for each of us as individuals, the objective is no longer a stable, secure environment. Sustainable communities and cities are those engaged in the continuous process of collaborative entanglement (complexing and associative patterning) and mutual adaptation from which we can learn, grow and thrive (Bennet & Bennet, 2008b). Summarizing, to successfully influence and adapt to a complex world requires the capacity and capability to: (1) continuously create a wide range of options (ideas, strategies, and actions), (2) select from that range those options that appear to solve the specific complex problems at hand, (3) take action on the selection options, and (4) observe the results, amplifying successful approaches and filtering out failures. This is a somewhat trial-and-error approach driven by the dynamic complexity of the environment but ameliorated by surface, shallow and deep knowledge and an understanding of complexity.

Deep knowledge supports sustainability, that is, the recognition and capacity to create effective solutions to complex and difficult problems. In 2005 Mountain Quest Institute surveyed 200 senior executives in the U.S. Federal sector regarding the ability of their organizations to effectively function under the conditions of CUCA. The eight sustainability factors that emerged are as follows:

- **Continuous learning** = having a mindset and a self-directed program to continuously learn, create and apply knowledge.
- **Quick response** = capable of reacting/responding quickly when needed.
- **Robustness** = the ability to respond to a broad range of tasks or problems.
- **Resiliency** = the ability to recover from setbacks and to resume high performance.
- **Flexibility** = keeping an open mind and attitude, willing to change positions and direction, adopt new perspectives and try new things.
- **Adaptability** = the ability to change the internal structure of an organization or society; changing habits, beliefs, and values as necessary to maintain performance in a changing environment.
- **Stakeholder satisfaction** = providing value that satisfies stakeholders.
- **Alignment** = the capacity to maintain internal and personal consistency and cohesion while simultaneously staying flexible and adaptable to a changing environment.

Societies are continuously exposed to (and threatened by) external and internal wicked problems, or what Russel Ackoff (1978) calls "messes". These are situations where one knows there is a problem but does not know exactly what the problem is, nor whether a good solution exists. Examples might be (1) military and political threats from neighboring societies; (2) internal discontent or uprising; (3) internally corrupt politicians; (4) increasing economic spreads between the rich and the poor within the society; (5) loss of competitiveness in international trade; (6) decay of social values; and (7) members of society becoming satisfied with the status quo and thereby unwilling or incapable of keeping up with beneficial world advances. All too often decision-makers simplify wicked problems or messes and assume simple solutions based on previous experience. This can prove to be extremely dangerous or even deadly giving rise to the dictum "before you simplify something you had better understand its complexity."

Further, as a society evolves to a higher level of knowledge and sophistication, it will likely become a more desirable target for economic, social or political disruptions. Deep knowledge plays an important role in responding or reacting to complex external threat. Resiliency and flexibility require immediately available resources, including deep knowledge, and the capacity to rapidly collect and use those resources. In other words, a society must prepare ahead of time to counter or adapt to potential external forces that are often unknown in an uncertain and complex world. Such preparation requires a broad base of deep knowledge in many areas, and the willingness to learn and expend the time, energy and funds to ensure such knowledge is available when it is needed. This would include the availability of experts with a deep understanding of the external world.

Deep knowledge supports the understanding of problems, situations and opportunities that surface and shallow knowledge does not. Such knowledge provides insights and meaning that have the potential to create new ideas, better ways of doing things or perhaps even maximizing knowledge flows that can move a society or community to a higher quality of life or a better way of dealing with poverty. The questions of how to deal with the most difficult social problems such as crime, education or equal opportunity are extremely complex and require not only deep knowledge for finding the answers but also deep knowledge that can guide successful implementation and societal change.

A recent and unfortunate example of the role (or lack of) deep knowledge is provided via a statement before the Democratic Steering and Policy Committee of the U.S. House of Representatives by Norman R. Augustine, retired Chairman and Chief Executive Officer of the Lockheed Martin Corporation. In his testimony to Congress, Augustine noted a number of factors that were affecting America's declining competitiveness. Among these were a declining educational system. In particular, he noted that, "America is widely acknowledged as having one of the worst K-12 education systems in the world, yet spends more on it per student than all but two other nations" (Augustine, 2009, p. 3).

Unfortunately such a system represents negative knowledge-based development. Where is the deep knowledge that has the depth of understanding and experience to change educational policies and their current stifling approaches to education? Two other areas mentioned by Augustine were science and engineering talent and investment and research—both associated with the creation and application of deep knowledge—yet both declining, and thereby reducing the amount and efficacy of deep knowledge available to support societal growth and sustainability.

THE KNOWLEDGE ATTRACTOR NETWORK TEAM

Ultimately, communities, cities and nations can only be as effective as their leaders and constituents. Every decision-maker—which at some level includes every individual in the community—has the responsibility to pursue sustainability in the domains of knowledge they influence or that influences them. This process starts with the active involvement of all community members in knowledge mobilization processes, connecting through whatever ways each individual best learns and can best contribute, whether that is involvement in formal learning processes or spending time reading, reflecting, and engaging in community dialogues and events.

Deep knowledge, however, requires continuous learning as the area of expertise shifts with economic, social and political changes. If these changes are slow and only mildly complex, people with surface or shallow knowledge may understand and resolve issues before there are any undue consequences. If the sources of the changes are not understood because of their complexity, it will take the best experts in the field to uncover, explain and suggest actions to redirect energy and circumvent serious social disruption. A breadth of deep expertise is also needed to sustain knowledge-based development and value creation when the environment becomes turbulent and the community is faced with a broad range of setbacks or unpredictable threats.

Although no single expert may know the answer, a Knowledge Attractor Network Team (KANT) with deep and broad expertise in relevant areas can provide rapid and unbiased explanations and insights to social and political leaders. A prime mover for growing and nurturing a social community's knowledge-based resources, a KANT is composed of experts with deep knowledge in a diversity of disciplines working cooperatively and synergistically together. They are flexible, quick reacting, adaptable and able to create and respond to opportunities and rebuff threats. To achieve this capability, they are previously identified sources of deep knowledge and are connected through overlapping relationship networks. They meet periodically and communicate regularly via virtual community platforms. In addition, each KANT member belongs to communities of practice in their specialty area(s) and has an active professional social network to draw upon. The creation, maintenance and nurturing of this powerful community resource is an amplifier of individual expertise and an integrator of diverse disciplines.

A knowledge-based society may have many hierarchal levels of nested knowledge attractor network teams, with each level of the hierarchy having strong connections to related network teams at the next lower level. In a hierarchy the dominant structural element may be a central point such as in a circular structure, or have an axial symmetry. Wherever the central point (dominant structure) is located, each part is determined by where it is located in relation to the central point. Most hierarchies consist of groups and subordinate hierarchies who in turn have groups of subordinate hierarchies, with each group having its own particular relation to the dominant center point (Kuntz, 1968). The dominant center point in a society is the senior level decision-making body. For example, while the general manager of a drinking water utility may report to the city council, the deep knowledge needed to solve complex water issues would normally reside in the utility or in experts external to the city. Similarly, while hierarchical in nature, each team brings a specific focus level of expertise where the deep knowledge to make the best decision resides.

The mesh is one example of a KANT. Meshes are special networks of individuals that have a deep knowledge of specific areas and are available on short notice. These people come to the mesh with a high level of community context and an understanding of the community's vision and purpose. Meshes are created for rapid response situations, thus the relationships among mesh members have already been developed in terms of knowledge, communication, collaboration and trust. As illustrated in Figure 3, members of meshes are drawn primarily out of ongoing communities composed of internal and external knowledge workers who have experience and expertise in specific areas of immediate interest to the community. When expertise is needed beyond internal resources, meshes may need to draw from extended silent networks that could include retired employees under an "as needed" consulting contract with the government, knowledgeable individuals from partnering organizations, or experts who have had some previous relationship with the situation at hand. A mesh is often comprised of individuals from government, not-for-profit and private sectors. While these individuals are usually aware of the potential need, an extended mesh network is most often invisible until called upon to handle a significant situation requiring knowledge and experience related to a specific problem or opportunity.

The mesh is designed to meet mandated response criteria. For example, when an event occurs that may significantly impact the community, a combination of virtual and face-to-face mesh meetings are called within 24 hours of the event or emergency. Relevant material is sent to all mesh members within six hours of such event. After a fast exploration and development of context, and building an understanding of the problem or opportunity, the mesh self-organizes, selects a leader and drafts a short charter before commencing work—all of these accomplished in a timeline of approximately four hours. Previously developed administrative procedures, resources, internal working agreements, etc. are automatically activated, providing full support to the process. The identification of expertise, pre-organization and pre-commitment, and the development of formal relationships and operating responsibilities and procedures have been completed prior to the need for response. After completing the task and transitioning any further work to its governing organization, the mesh prepares an after-action report and then disbands as an active team, with members of the mesh continuing to provide insights and guidance on an individual basis as needed. Members of the mesh are also charged with continuing interaction in their community and team settings to disseminate information and champion implementation of measures as required.

In summary, meshes are intended to be transient teams that specialize in connecting broad areas of expertise (deep knowledge) with a quick response capability. Their members know and are known to community leaders, and have their trust and

Figure 3. While individuals represented in the mesh are loosely connected in overlapping relationship networks, they come to life as a fully-functioning KANT when needed (Bennet, 2000; Bennet & Bennet, 2004)

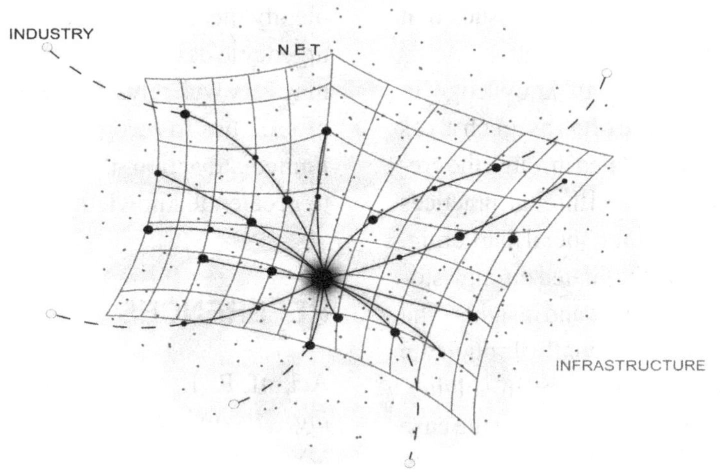

respect. Most of them are full-time employees in positions scattered throughout the community who stay cognizant in their area of expertise as well as how it relates to community direction, vision, tactics, and culture. Because they are active participants in their professional organizations, functional areas and the communities in which they live, they have built-in relationship networks. Thus members of the mesh can be viewed the emergency crew that works with the local knowledge workers, coming in to generate quick-response actions, then returning to their normal responsibilities.

FINAL THOUGHTS

At the societal level, successful knowledge-based development is a never-ending process. It entails not only the continuous development of knowledge at all three levels—surface, shallow and deep—but also specific mechanisms to ensure connectivity, help citizens build trusting relationships, and facilitate the flow of information. The resulting knowledge flows are essential to maintain the continuous learning and knowledge development necessary for sustaining a society in an increasingly uncertain and complex environment. While all levels of knowledge are important to sustainability, deep knowledge is perhaps the most critical because of the difficulty of comprehending and making decisions on highly complex issues that emerge in this environment.

Because of the sensitivity of knowledge to context, knowledge flows are often as much art as science. Such flows are facilitated through the creation of knowledge moments and through practices such as appreciative inquiry and social marketing. Deep knowledge flows are facilitated through storytelling that incorporates values and insights. The application of knowledge is normally through the classical processes of creativity, problem-solving, decision-making and implementation. In the case of deep knowledge, creativity plays a particularly important role through the generation of new ideas or solutions to highly complex problems. Where challenging problems exist, problem-solving and decision-making require a deep understanding of the situation in order to anticipate the outcome of specific decisions.

Community or society sustainability is essential for long-term health and knowledge growth. Sustainability requires a number of capabilities to withstand or respond to changes either internally or externally. For most perturbations, surface and/or shallow knowledge would be sufficient to identify and implement the responses. However, for complex issues a knowledge-based society needs deep knowledge to ensure its response capacity in terms robustness, resiliency, flexibility and adaptability. Thus we introduce the idea of the Knowledge Attractor Network Team, specifically focusing on the mesh, a special network of individuals that have deep knowledge of specific areas and previously-developed relationships that support the leveraging of team knowledge.

Since deep knowledge is at the core of sustainable societies, it is clear that knowledge-based development requires continuous learning over time in areas relevant to their goals and vision. Thus the investment in education and continuous learning—together with an infrastructure that supports connections, relationships and information flows—is foundational to knowledge development. Further, as change, uncertainty and complexity increase exponentially there is a growing urgency to develop deep knowledge. Sustainability may very well rely on the willingness and capacity of societies to recognize this challenge and take immediate action, that is, invest in their citizens to accelerate knowledge development.

REFERENCES

Ackoff, R. L. (1978). *The Art of Problem Solving: Accompanied by Ackoff's Fables*. Songs, NY: John Wiley.

Albino, V., Carbonara, N., & Messeni-Petruzzelli, A. (2007). Proximity as a communication resource for competitiveness: a rationale for technology clusters. *International Journal of Learning and Intellectual Capital*, *4*, 430–452. doi:10.1504/IJLIC.2007.016337

(2006). *American Heritage Dictionary of The English Language* (4th ed.). Boston, MA: Houghton Mifflin Company.

Andreasen, A. R. (1995). *Marketing Social Change: Changing Behavior to Promote Health, Social Development, and the Environment*. San Francisco: Jossey-Bass.

Augustine, N. (2009, January 7). *America's competitiveness*. Testimony before the Democratic Steering and Policy Committee, U.S. House of Representatives.

Barabasi, A. L. (2002). *Linked: The New Science of Networks*. Cambridge, MA: Perseus Publishing.

Bennet, A. (2005). *Exploring Aspects of Knowledge Management that Contribute to the Passion Expressed by Its Thought Leaders*. Retrieved from http://www.mountainquestinstitute.com

Bennet, A., & Bennet, D. (2004). *Organizational Survival in the New World: The Intelligent Complex Adaptive System*. Burlington, MA: Elsevier.

Bennet, A., & Bennet, D. (2007a). CONTEXT: The shared knowledge enigma. *VINE . The Journal of Information and Knowledge Management Systems*, *37*(1), 27–40.

Bennet, A., & Bennet, D. (2007b). Knowledge Mobilization in the Social Sciences and Humanities: Moving From Research to Action. Frost, WV: MQIPress.

Bennet, A., & Bennet, D. (2007c). From stories to strategy: Putting organizational learning to work. *VINE: The Journal of Information and Knowledge Systems*, *37*(4), 404–409.

Bennet, A., & Bennet, D. (2008a). The decision-making process for complex situations in a complex environment . In Burstein, F., & Holsapple, C. W. (Eds.), *Handbook on Decision Support Systems 1: Basic Themes* (pp. 3–20). New York: Springer-Verlag. doi:10.1007/978-3-540-48713-5_1

Bennet, A., & Bennet, D. (2008c). The fallacy of knowledge reuse: Building sustainable knowledge. [Special Issue on Knowledge Based Development]. *Journal of Knowledge Management*, 21–33. doi:10.1108/13673270810902911

Bennet, A., & Bennet, D. (2009b). Meta-knowledge: Understanding the knowledge that drives our actions . In Batra, S., & Carrillo, F. J. (Eds.), *Knowledge Management and Intellectual Capital: Emerging Perspectives* (pp. 411–434). New Delhi: Allied Publishers.

Bennet, A., & Bennet, D. (2009c). Managing self in troubled times: Banking on self-efficacy . In *Effective Executive* (pp. 56–82). Hyderabad, India: The ICFAI University Press.

Bennet, A., & Bennet, D. (2009d). Leaders, decisions, and the neuro-knowledge system . In Wallis, S. (Ed.), *Cybernetics and Systems Theory in Management: Tools, Views and Advancements*. Hershey, PA: IGI Global.

Bennet, D., & Bennet, A. (2008a). Engaging tacit knowledge in support of organizational learning. *VINE: The Journal of Information and Knowledge Systems*, *38*(1), 72–94.

Bennet, D., & Bennet, A. (2008c). The depth of knowledge: Surface, shallow or deep? *VINE: The Journal of Information and Knowledge Management Systems*, *38*(4), 405–420.

Bennet, D., & Bennet, A. (2009a). Associative patterning: The unconscious life of an organization . In Girard, J. (Ed.), *Building Organizational Memories* (pp. 201–224). Hershey, PA: IGI Global.

Boschma, R. A. (2005). Social capital and regional development: An empirical analysis of the Third Italy . In Boschma, R. A., & Kloosterman, R. C. (Eds.), *Learning from Clusters: A Critical Assessment from an Economic-Geographical Perspective*. Dordrecht, The Netherlands: Springer-Verlag.

Campbell, J. (1949). *The Hero With a Thousand Faces*. New York: MJF Books.

Carrillo, F. J. (2004). Capital cities: A taxonomy of capital accounts for knowledge cities. *Journal of Knowledge Management*, *8*(5), 28–46. doi:10.1108/13673270410587386

Cozolino, L. (2002). *The Neuroscience of Psychotherapy: Building and Rebuilding the Human Brain*. New York: Norton.

Cozolino, L. (2006). *The Neuroscience of Human Relationships: Attachment and the Developing Social Brain*. New York: Norton & Company.

Dvir, R. (2006). Knowledge city, seen as a collage of human knowledge moments . In Carrillo, F. J. (Ed.), *Knowledge Cities: Approaches, Experiences, and Perspectives*. Oxford, UK: Butterworth Heinemann Elsevier.

Ellinor, L., & Gerard, G. (1998). *Dialogue: Creating and Sustaining Collaborative Partnerships at Work*. New York: John Wiley & Sons.

Ericsson, K. A., Charness, N., Feltovich, P. J., & Hoffman, R. R. (Eds.). (2006). *The Cambridge Handbook of Expertise and Expert Performance*. Cambridge, UK: Cambridge University Press.

Garcia, B. C. (2006). Learning conversations: Knowledge, meanings and learning networks in Greater Manchester. *Journal of Knowledge Management: Knowledge Cities*, *10*(5), 99–109.

Hammond, S. A., & Hall, J. (1996). *What is Appreciative Inquiry?* Retrieved September 2006, from http://www.thinbook.com

Hodgkin, R. (1991, September 27). Michael Polanyi—Profit of life, the universe, and everything. *Times Higher Education Supplement*, 15.

Huysman, M. H., & Wulf, V. (2005). The role of information technology in building and sustaining the relational base of communities. *The Information Society*, *21*, 81–89. doi:10.1080/01972240590925285

Johnson, S., & Taylor, K. (2006). *The Neuroscience of Adult Learning: New Directions for Adult and Continuing Education*. San Francisco: Jossey-Bass.

Knoben, J., & Oerlemans, L. A. G. (2006). Proximity and inter-organizational collaboration: a literature review. *International Journal of Management Reviews*, *8*, 71–89. doi:10.1111/j.1468-2370.2006.00121.x

Kotler, P., Roberto, N., & Lee, N. (2002). *Social Marketing: Improving the Quality of Life*. New York: Sage.

Kotler, P., & Roberto, W. (1989). *Social Marketing: Strategies for Changing Public Behavior*. New York: The Free Press.

Kuntz, P. G. (1968). *The Concept of Order*. Seattle, WA: University of Washington Press.

Lee, R. G., & Garvin, T. (2003). Moving from information transfer to information exchange in health and health care. *Social Science & Medicine*, *56*, 449–464. doi:10.1016/S0277-9536(02)00045-X

National Research Council. (2000). *How People Learn: Brain, Mind, Experience, and School*. Washington, DC: National Academy Press.

Oakes, J., & Lipton, M. (1999). *Teaching to Change the World*. Boston: McGraw-Hill College.

Poincare, H. (2001). *The Foundations of Science: Science and Hypothesis, The Value of Science, Science and Method*. New York: Modern Library.

Porter, D. E., Bennet, A., Turner, R., & Wennergren, D. (2003). *The Power of Team: The Making of a CIO*. Alexandria, VA: U.S. Department of the Navy.

Putnam, R. D., Leonardi, R., & Nanetti, R. Y. (1993). *Making Democracy Work*. Princeton, NJ: Princeton University Press.

Ross, P. E. (2006, August). The expert mind. *Scientific American*, 64–71. doi:10.1038/scientificamerican0806-64

Ryle, G. (1949). *The Concept of Mind*. London: Hutchinson.

Shore, A. (1994). *Affect Regulation and the Origin of the Self: The Neurobiology of Emotional Development*. Mahway, NJ: Erlbaum.

Snowden, D. (1999, November). The paradox of story: Simplicity and complexity in strategy. *Journal of Strategy & Scenario Planning*.

Srivastva, S., & Cooperrider, D. L. (Eds.). (1990). *Appreciative Management and Leadership*. San Francisco: Jossey-Bass.

Sternberg, R. J., & Davidson, J. E. (Eds.). (1995). *The Nature of Insight*. Cambridge, MA: The MIT Press.

Stonier, T. (1990). *Information and the Internal Structure of the Universe: An Introduction into Information Physics*. New York: Springer-Verlag.

Stonier, T. (1997). *Information and Meaning: An Evolutionary Perspective*. New York: Springer.

Tapscot, D. (2009). *Grown Up Digital*. New York: McGraw-Hill.

Tuomi, I. (2004). *Future challenges of the European knowledge society*. Discussion paper presented at Institute for Prospective Technological Studies, IPTS, 11 August 2004. Retrieved from http://www.meaningprocessing.com/personalPages/tuomi/articles/TheFutureOfLearningInTheKnowledgeSociety.pdf

Wiig, K. M. (1995). *Knowledge Management Methods: Practical Approaches to Managing Knowledge*. Arlington, TX: Schema Press.

Yigitcanlar, T., Velibeyoglu, K., & Martinez-Fernandez, C. (2008). Rising knowledge cities: The role of urban knowledge precincts. *Journal of Knowledge Management: Towards a global knowledge-based development agenda, 12*(5), 8-20.

Chapter 10
Knowledge Worker Profile:
A Framework to Clarify Expectations

Gulgun Kayakutlu
Istanbul Technical University, Turkey

ABSTRACT

One of the major reasons for economic crisis of 2008-2009 is determined as value delivery. Major resource of value creation is the knowledge worker who works at different levels of an organisation. This study analyses knowledge worker studies in diverse disciplines, in order to determine the requests. The goal of the study is to propose a framework to clarify the skill requirements by integrating the requests at operational, team, organisational and inter-organisational levels with drivers provided by educating, attracting, motivating and retaining strategies. The framework facilitates employing the right employee for the right post while balancing the requests and the performance measures. This new vision will be beneficial for managers, human resource experts, and educators.

INTRODUCTION

Global economic crisis in 2008-2009 hit the service companies as well as the manufacturing enterprises. One of the major reasons of failure is seen as the lack of full-value delivery from the existing resources expressed in finance and intellectual capital (Hsiao & Lee, 2008). Politicians, CEOs and Managers are warned to have new mechanisms to institutionalise organisational systems and are invited to be rational on the critical resources rather than following the footprints of brand owners (Arvidsson, 2009). Economists suggest solutions by focusing on system innovations instead of technology and product innovations (Mavrotas et al., 2007). The attention is drawn to knowledge workers who are accepted as the major resource of innovation and competitiveness (Chen, 2008). Contrary to cost-focused approach to employ less skilled but increasingly global and virtual knowledge workers (Tucker et al., 2005), the skill revolution is observed while moving into a more demanding cognitive age (Brooks, 2008). New economic models are in process for proposing sustainable frameworks, guardianship of intellec-

DOI: 10.4018/978-1-61520-721-3.ch010

tual property, impact of intellectual quality, more knowledge production based on more reliable performance of knowledge workers.

Wider range of skills is to be recognised and supported for knowledge workers in new business models. The challenge of developing sustainable models in value chains request more than just higher education and more company-based training. The impact of intellectual quality is to be enhanced (Cope & Kazantsis, 2009); person-to-person skills or soft skills are to be developed (Warhurst, 2008). Individual knowledge facilitators are to be motivated and retained in order to achieve effective collaboration (Garcia, 2007). As an impact of all these improvements, not only individuals will be more innovative but the entire system within a company, within a city, a region or nation as Helbrecht (2004) has stated. Besides, knowledge workers are the main organizational asset that cannot be imitated and therefore create a sustainable competence (Livanage et al., 2008).

This study aims to propose a conceptual framework to define realistic expectations from a knowledge worker within the new business models. The proposed model will integrate the achievements of the previous research in diverse fields and complete a vision of a whole. The study is based on analysis of expectations in operational, team, organisational and inter-organisational work levels driven by education, attraction, motivation and retention. Requests and contributions are combined to determine the competence created in terms of personal, relational, technical and professional skills.

This chapter is so organised that next section will define the knowledge worker and summarise expectations and drivers in different dimensions. The third chapter will present the proposed framework. Final section will be the conclusion and suggestions for further studies. This new vision will open a new dimension for managers, human resource experts and educators.

BACKGROUND

Studies on knowledge worker take place mainly in information technology and management fields. In order to define a new profile for the knowledge worker, analysis in education, epistemology, psychology, economics and political science fields are reviewed as well. Previous research will be analysed grouped in common focus.

Definition of Knowledge Worker

The term Knowledge Worker was first used by Peter Drucker in his 1959 book, *Landmarks of Tomorrow* to identify the workers in the information technology fields. Today, anyone who works for a living at the tasks of developing or using knowledge is named to be a knowledge worker. Davenport has summarised the background and the operations of the post: "Knowledge workers have high degrees of expertise, education or experience, and the primary purpose of their jobs involves the creation, distribution or application of knowledge. One third to two thirds of any company workforce are included in this definition" (McKellar, 2005). This definition includes tasks of planning, acquiring, searching, analyzing, organizing, storing, programming, distributing and marketing goods and services in addition to transformation and commerce of data, information and knowledge. Hence, the term includes lawyers, teachers, scientists of all kinds in addition to programmers, system analysts, technical writers, academic professionals, researchers.

A knowledge worker is a participant of the knowledge economy where intangible products are as important as the tangible objects with raw material and physical goods. To create, produce and disseminate intangibles, knowledge workers are expected to have high level skills and high technology literacy. Greene (2006) adds characteristics like high cognitive power and abstract reasoning as well as new perspectives and insights. Gurteen (2006) mentions the responsibility feature in the following words: "Knowledge workers are those people who have taken responsibility for their work lives. They continually strive to understand the world about them and modify their work practices and behaviours to better meet their personal and organisational objectives. They are self-motivated. Knowledge workers cannot be coerced, bribed, manipulated or rewarded and no amount of money or fancy technology will incentivise them to do a better job. Knowledge workers see the benefits of working differently for themselves. They are not wage slaves; they take responsibility for their work and drive improvement."

These unique features cause the knowledge workers to be the ones to find and solve difficult problems. They use the books, web and their network effectively to design solutions. They use the knowledge support to take decisions. Furthermore they are to be productive, efficient and effective to prove to be assets but not costs for the business and society. A metaphor that comes from mythology like Ulysses or Icarus, knowledge worker is somebody burnt in the process "somebody losing his old identities in this process of constant transformation and of expanding further and exploring further as an ultimate goal (Nicolopoulou & Karatas-Ozkan, 2007).

Education of a Knowledge Worker

One critical feature in Knowledge Worker definition is the high education. Drucker (1989) highlighted this characteristic by emphasizing "the level of qualification acquired during formal and informal learning". This comment changed the programs of high education and encouraged current education experts to suggest a liberal education with the professional qualifications required in a global economy (Rowley, 2000; Johnson, 2006; Stromquist et al., 2007). Quality is to be developed based on goals and content of education.

First goal was the productivity. This is why industrial engineers of Taylor are pointed as the first knowledge workers (Drucker, 2001). Educating knowledge workers was mainly technology focused. As Rowley (2000) identified the high education was requested to include how:

- to create knowledge repositories
- to enhance knowledge access
- to manage knowledge as an asset
- to measure knowledge within intellectual capital

As the e-business and supply chains gained importance, more education is requested on virtual organisations in addition to the team work (Larsen & McInerney, 2002).

The increase of globalisation caused knowledge worker to have an important role in the organisational efficiency. The universities are expected to be both local and global. Implications have been drawn for building up a networked human and technology environment to support formulation of learning communities. The aim is fostering local knowledge and human development pursuing social and organisational values (Cheng, 2004). Research and creativity have become important issues in business schools; while the learning is facilitated as individual learning, and organisational learning improves. The race among the nations has started to educate the talented workforce (Cornuel, 2007).

Improvements in education style changed universities to become learning systems for skill development instead of being profession builders. In order to respond to the goal of global effectiveness, customer oriented approaches in the courses are increased (Nayeri, et al., 2007). Furthermore, new programs are developed consisting of life-long learning schemes, personalisation in education to take into account demands of tutoring and mentoring on an individual basis (Garcia, 2007).

Organisations expected better educated people to give the flexibility needed to switch production, better accommodate innovation, retraining and relocation (Roffe, 2007). In order to respond to these expectations, knowledge workers are to be educated or trained in all the knowledge processes including knowledge acquisition methods (Psarras, 2006), knowledge development context and tools (Magnier-Watanabe & Senoo, 2008) as well as knowledge dissemination algorithms (Norhani, 2008).

APPROACHES TO A KNOWLEDGE WORKER AT WORK

Knowledge-based economy caused the war for talent; companies are battling for those knowledge workers that will take roles in productivity, efficiency and effectiveness of the company. Achievements can only be realised by attracting, motivating and retaining of the high skilled workers with learning ability.

Attracting the Knowledge Worker

Knowledge management blogs and magazines mention the difficulty of employing the knowledge worker. Recruitment of the knowledge worker is less dependent on the professional knowledge and instead depends on a range of factors that build up the reputation and social capital of the applicants (Moore & Taylor, 2009). It is widely known that they cannot be attracted by high salaries or rich benefits alone.

The human resources departments have difficulties to detail the competence searched for. They have to identify product, process and relational skills that will add value to the organisation. Technology related, operations related and market related knowledge is in demand as well as leadership, problem solving, communication and learning capabilities (Ahn & Chang, 2004). Employing the right talents have become an important management skill. Horwitz (et al., 2003) identified the best employers to have three important attributes:

- matching the talent with the business goals;
- finding the ability to grow and adapt in a rapidly changing environment;
- giving the flexibility to balance workplace demands and the needs of business.

Commitment to empowerment, relaxed hierarchy, flexible timing, and decentralised decision making are the recommended features of attractive managers (Magnier-Watanabe & Senoo, 2008). Encouragement for knowledge management and collaboration are the preferences of the most recent winners.

Motivating the Knowledge Worker

Even if the best workers are attracted, it is hard to retain them unless they are motivated. The comfort of the work place, the challenges of the tasks, relations with the peers and rewards form the basis of motivation. High-skilled workers love to share visions and realise thinking together. Developing mental models and learning systems throughout the organisation will help motivation. Specifically, knowledge-enhancing activities must be openly valued and acknowledged, while failure to participate in knowledge sharing must be discouraged (Lee-Kelley, 2007). Individual workers must have the freedom to interact with both internal and external peers. Since knowledge is the only asset that grows when shared (Kayakutlu, 1998), interactions should be rewarded. Sharing organisational mission and business issues to generate revenue will make the result-oriented knowledge sharing more satisfactory (Henard & McFadyen, 2008).

Motivation can also be increased by the behaviour of managers. Several suggestions for managers are summarised as below (Lee-Kelley, 2007; Rusette et al., 2007; Erickson, 2008; Stephen et al., 2008; Davenport & Iye, 2009):

- Managers would allow face-to-face interaction, while being flexible in workplace;

- Dedication to work should not be asked for without being a model;
- Free flow of opinion among the knowledge workers is to be allowed with trust;
- Knowledge workers should be involved in decision processes;
- Quality of the knowledge work should be measured and shared;
- Better insight is to be given to the excitement of creativity;
- Appreciation for self employed attitude must be shown.

Rotation on various responsibilities takes place in the must do list for motivating the knowledge workers.

Retaining the Knowledge Worker

High turnover of knowledge workers is both risky and costly. Job satisfaction is the key to keeping critical employees. It was based on the conditions of work-place, task definitions and communications with the managers and the peers. Classical approaches of giving services like health-related programs or being generous with benefits are not good enough in cases where employees are highly knowledgeable and skilled. Challenging work assignments are accepted more satisfactory than competitive pay packages (Hewitt et al., 2003). Treating any knowledge worker as an individual and making him/her feel unique is only possible with the opportunities given to enhance the skills (Fawcett et al., 2004). The importance of developing critical success factors and using relevant performance factors have always been the lead for retaining the knowledge workers (Terziovski & Morgan, 2006).

These are the employees who know they are distinctive and have an important economic value. They are aware of residing in the core competence of the organisation (Horwitz, 2006). Besides, retaining the knowledge workers means retaining the innovation lead competitiveness. The new organisational culture is to be adaptive to change (Roffe, 2007) by developing the teamwork spirit and collaboration (Lee-Kelly, 2007) to develop existing knowledge. Even in a tough economy as today, organisations are deemed to keep continuous improvement (Hamidizadeh & Farsizani, 2008).

EXPECTATIONS AT DIFFERENT BUSINESS LEVELS

Progression of knowledge worker at work continues at different levels of the organisation. Engestrom's model for the structure of human activity is redesigned for knowledge workers by Gvaramadze (2008). The structure in Figure 1 gave us the lead to define expectations from a knowledge worker at different work levels. Investigation will be held at four work levels defined as operational, team, organisational and inter-organisational levels.

Expectations at Operational Level

Knowledge operations are defined repetitively to be generalised as knowledge acquisition, development and dissemination. Knowledge workers including engineers and medical doctors will start the work life at the operational level where they are expected to accomplish efficient knowledge processes in addition to professional performance. Knowledge-intensive and task-based environments such as research laboratories, consulting firms and high education workers are expected to fully reuse the knowledge assets in process of achieving the goals of business tasks (Liu et al., 2005).

Knowledge acquisition is gaining new knowledge from either inside or outside the organisation .It includes addition of new knowledge to the existing one by making the accumulated knowledge accessible. Explicit knowledge is easier to transmit and efficiently use and therefore it is easy

Figure 1. Structure of interactions for the knowledge worker (Gvaramadze, 2008)

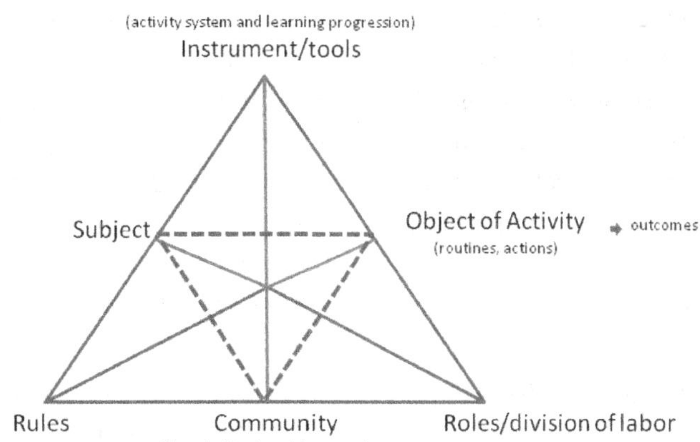

to duplicate and may not always create competitive advantage. In any organisation, the challenge is to accept that not all knowledge is in a form to be readily shared, diffused, or implemented (Magnier-Watanabe & Senoo, 2008).

Knowledge development is the effective use of the knowledge accumulated in order to increase the organisational competence. This is a process that depends on workers' readiness to use and share individual knowledge. Creating knowledge repositories through collaboration of different teams will allow improvements in using the existing knowledge (Delen & Al-Hawamdeh, 2009).

Knowledge dissemination includes knowledge sharing, knowledge diffusion and knowledge marketing. It is the process that changes a lot when the workers change (Huang et al., 2007). Effective knowledge sharing is not only dependent on the skill of knowledge workers; but it requires cultural change, new management practices and investment in network technologies. Knowledge workers however are expected to be well equipped with the appropriate cultural values to facilitate the exploitation of knowledge in line with the business objectives (Norhani, 2008).

Indifferent of the field of work the expectations of knowledge worker in operation are to include the following (Psarras, 2006):

- Transform data or information into knowledge;
- Identify and verify knowledge;
- Capture and secure knowledge;
- Organise knowledge;
- Retrieve and apply knowledge;
- Combine knowledge;
- Create knowledge;
- Learn knowledge;
- Distribute/sell knowledge.

In all the business sectors profit-oriented enterprises show a tendency for limited time employment and decrease the salaries for the knowledge workers which could emerge the "just-in-time knowledge worker" (Stromquist et al., 2007). Yet, observations show a strong positive relationship between the operational and organisational performance (Fugate et al., 2009).

Expectations at Team Level

Knowledge work is typically project based defined by memos, contracts or agreements for different activities. An engineer works in a team to develop a new product; a chirurgical doctor works with a team in each surgery; an information technology expert works in software, hardware or network projects. Knowledge workers are to be leaders as well as team workers simultaneously. That is why they have to be evaluated process specific, team based and firm specific (Swart, 2006). They have to remain self-employed as well as assisting or leading other employees (Fenwick, 2007). They are expected to perform research, analysis, learning, informing, advising and guiding in team processes (Laycock, 2005).

All the team actions, transitions and interactions define and force team effectiveness. Knowledge teams are to create high performance as well as member satisfaction in accordance with the integration power and energy in the team. Members in the team are brought together primarily for their operational expertise, relational skills and contact networks (Le Pine et al., 2008).

Building knowledge teams starts with understanding the team's objectives to complete the requested services for a specific project. Developing a model and structure for the team will enable defining the skills required for the members and the leader. The last step for building a successful team will be to set the right measures to ensure that team members are in the proper job level based on skill and performance (Schell, 2008). One of the unique features of the knowledge teams would be the collaborative thinking process that will need the mindset for each project (Armstrong et al., 2008). Shared visions would allow team practices like brainstorming, improvisation and co-creation by using project management tools and methodologies (Ditkoff & Moore, 2005).

Knowledge teams are expected to be structured with definite purposes within the organisation's business mission (Henard & McFadyen, 2008). To make teams perform well, the following are to be realised (Cabrera & Cabrera, 2005):

- Cross functional interactions- possible by self-driven workers with good communication skills;
- Communication skills- enabled by training programmes geared to articulate and communicate knowledge;
- Communities of practice- caused by formalised orientation and socialisation programmes and events;
- Performance appraisals that recognise knowledge sharing;
- Incentive programmes that reward effective knowledge sharing;
- Group and firm based compensation systems;
- User friendly communication and group sharing technology;
- Open and trusting culture with strong norms of knowledge sharing.

The performance of knowledge teams are measured in the team and among the teams of different projects (Gloor et al., 2007).

Expectations at Organizational Level

Majority of the research is focused on the organisational impact of the knowledge worker. As Liebowitz (2004) stated, an organisation's accumulated value is found in the intellect, knowledge, and experience of its workforce. Firm specific power is the essential basis for sustainable competitive advantage. Required organisational synergy is created only if financial and knowledge investments are combined (Osterloh & Frey, 2006).

The innovation process that is unavoidable for today's industries, need knowledge collaboration of the work force in initiation, development and implementation phases (Gordon and Traftar, 2007). Making knowledge workers collaborators in the work environment will benefit entire organisation (Praner, 2008). Yet, the goal satisfaction by creation of the synergy depends on size, technology, environment, culture and the strategies of the specific organisation (Jafari et al., 2008). In order to measure company performance specific to intellectual capital, employee based factors are to be clarified (Tan et al., 2008). Green (2008) has enlightened the organisational studies by giving a broad list of employee based factors influential on performance. Green's work specifies both features of employees (competencies, education, experience, relationship, productivity, profitability) and organisational drivers for the workers (assignment, retaining position, motivation, training, and turnover) among the intellectual factors. A range of technology applications are used for investigations, collaborations and communications to develop the organisational learning. It is integrated with the knowledge processes, but to be articulated in terms of the business needs and to be designed as embedded with business performance (Roffe, 2007). Organisational effectiveness is provided by the capability development and capacity planning in addition to alignment of knowledge resources with the business strategies (Spratt, 2007). Cultural and personnel controls are to be implemented to increase the firm performance (Teo et al., 2008).

Expectations at Inter-Organizational Level

Strategic alliances in the global supply chains are focused on knowledge based collaborations. Business models are designed to emphasize personal interactions that bind companies in the same industry and other industries together. Ramachandran (2003) analysed the impacts in three levels. Primary impact is defined as the information and technology diffusion to form an information society; secondary impact is the capability and capacity building and improving the knowledge usage to feed into a knowledge society and the tertiary impact is the knowledge based culture development in order to develop a value creating society. Similar interactions are simplified in the model of Arthur et al. (2008) by using knowledge mapping.

No matter what the industry is, the value chain is to create and sustain a culture that fosters innovation, creativity and learning as in any single company today. This new mindset is enabled by pro-active strategies and handling human resources in the chain as an investment (Thite, 2004). Suppliers and buyers are working together to create and transfer knowledge more effectively. Comprehensive and flexible strategies are to be developed to create learning and sharing culture in the value chain (Jafari et al., 2008; Yeh, 2008). Virtual teams of knowledge workers play an important role in trust building. This important role requires the abilities of critical thinking, ethical problem solving, stakeholder analysis, and comprehensive expression (Larsen & McInerney, 2002). Moreover externalisation of the collaborative knowledge worker has to contribute for the society as well as the value chain (Ehin, 2008).

Although multinational companies play the key role to accumulate an immense volume of knowledge, there is more need to expand specialised knowledge customised to the region or industry. That is why independent knowledge workers will have a growing importance for the performance of the value chains even in agricultural industries (Nicolopoulou & Karatas-Ozkan, 2007). Unlike the collaborators in the value chain, independent knowledge workers should accept themselves as connectors. Their activity is generating and linking but not transmitting the knowledge, through which organisations grow (Fenwick, 2007).

KNOWLEDGE WORKER SKILLS

If the innovation cycle is to be managed effectively value of knowledge workers will continue to grow. New challenge for managers and leaders is to take greater risks for the management of new skill set (Terziovski & Morgan, 2006). Wolff (2003) had classified skills for knowledge workers in three groups: substantive like synthesising, coordinating, analysing, verbal and numeric intelligence developed by education and training; interactive, like mentoring, negotiating, instructing,

Figure 2. Interactions binding collaborations (Arthur et al., 2008)

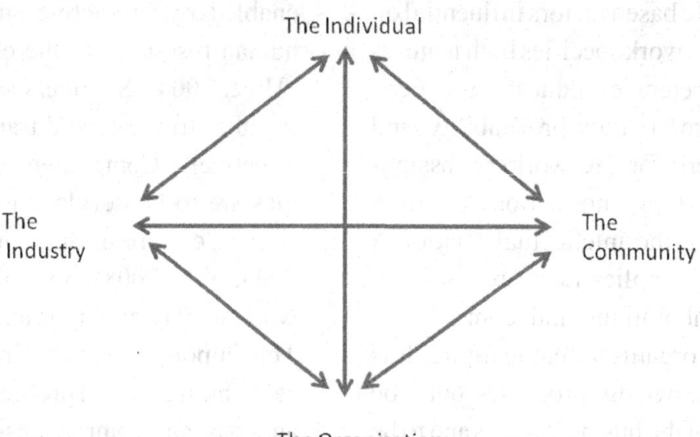

supervising and serving based on organisational culture; motor like coordination, machine operating, materials handling or technology utilisation. Johnson (2005) classified almost the same skills as basic, discipline/profession specific and technology skills. In parallel to the growth of network business and value chains, relational skills have become as important as the rest.

"Business knowledge is practical knowledge, or useful knowledge for management, production, service and innovation in industries, rather than broader social and scientific knowledge" (Gao et al., 2008). This definition gives a general idea about what is the basic professional requirement for any knowledge worker. Professional education is expected to give basic capabilities that will be enhanced by practice in industry. If the critical business issues are defined and knowledge is treated as process rather than product, know-how of activating these processes will be the responsibility for the knowledge worker (Massey et al., 2005). Professional effectiveness will be based on familiarity of the current tasks and amount of progress at the given task (Liu &Wu, 2008).

As knowledge continues to be mobilized, the cost benefit analysis of social ties is given a growing importance. A knowledge worker takes responsibility of tasks which consists of relation with all the stake holders. Hence they have influence and impact on other employees and peers, on customers, on competitors and on partners (Green, 2007). It is business critical to balance the economic values created and to strengthen the social network (Fliaster & Spiess, 2008).

Knowledge is viewed as a multifaceted resource. Management experts note that the ability to create new knowledge is dependent on an individual's ability to recognize and obtain valuable new knowledge and subsequently integrate that knowledge with existing knowledge (Henard & McFadyen, 2008). As an individual who performs in teams, a knowledge worker is expected to accumulate the acquired knowledge, use the creative knowledge, and develop unique knowledge for competitiveness. All thinking styles are to be used to embrace logical and technical skills as well as conceptual, imaginative planning and organisational abilities (Amadi-Echendu, 2007). Unlike the human resource and knowledge experts Johnson (2006) has summarised individual skills of a knowledge worker by abilities to design, to create stories, to show empathy, to play well, to create symphony and learning in order to develop meaning.

Most recently Cobo (2008) defined a knowledge worker in nineteen features:

1. Not restricted to a specific age.
2. Highly engaged, creative, innovative, collaborative and motivated.
3. Uses information and develops knowledge in changing workplaces (not tied to an office).
4. Inventive, intuitive, and able to know things and produce ideas.
5. Capable of creating socially constructed meaning and contextually reinvent meanings.
6. Rejects the role of being an information custodian and the associated rigid ways of organizing information.
7. Network maker, always connecting people, ideas, organizations, etc.
8. Possesses an ability to use many tools to solve many different problems.
9. High digital literacy.
10. Competence to solve unknown problems in different contexts.
11. Learning by sharing, without geographical limitation.
12. Highly adaptable to different contexts/ environments.
13. Aware of the importance to provide open access to information.
14. Interest in context and the adaptability of information to new situations.
15. Capable of unlearning quickly, and always bringing in new ideas.
16. Competence to create open and flat knowledge networks.
17. Learns continuously (formally and informally) and updates knowledge.
18. Constantly experiments new technologies (especially the collaborative ones).
19. Not afraid of failure.

A knowledge worker is a professional who ensures that the gaps between the different levels of an organization are removed, if task is done at his or her most efficient capacity (Scott, 2005).

FRAMEWORK FOR EVALUATING THE SKILLS OF A KNOWLEDGE WORKER

Knowledge worker is always defined to be highly skilled. However the difficulty to define these skills increases as the requests grow. As stated in the literature survey in section 2, the expectations are diverse and immense, as if the managers are looking for a magician. To avoid the expectations to reach a point that a knowledge manager will create a rabbit in an empty hat, the uprising in performance measures should be applied in skill detection. In large companies managerial performance is linked to the business success rather than individual performance as in Toyota (Bryan & McKinsey, 2006). This measure without any doubt includes employing the right person for the right job to ensure the organisational competence.

We designed a new framework for defining the profile of a knowledge worker, to reduce mistakes in engagement, team building, collaboration and success of knowledge workers. The skills requested are to be defined integrating what is needed from the knowledge workers and what can be given to the knowledge workers. As it is shown in Figure 3, the framework combines drivers and requests to determine skills. Literature review helped in specifying all three dimensions in a clear way.

***Requests*:** As detailed in section 2, despite the interactions of different work levels, the knowledge worker needs to know his tasks in detail. Operational, team, organisational and inter-organisational definition of skills will enable both the worker and the manager to recognise the criticality of the tasks. At the operational level, result orientation, knowledge about the processes and ability to access knowledge are requested. In team level, all team features are in demand; worker has to be good in communication skills, knows to co-operate and to add value by co-creation in a team. In the organisational level productivity and profitability are to exist besides the ability to adopt

Figure 3. Framework to determine Knowledge Worker skills

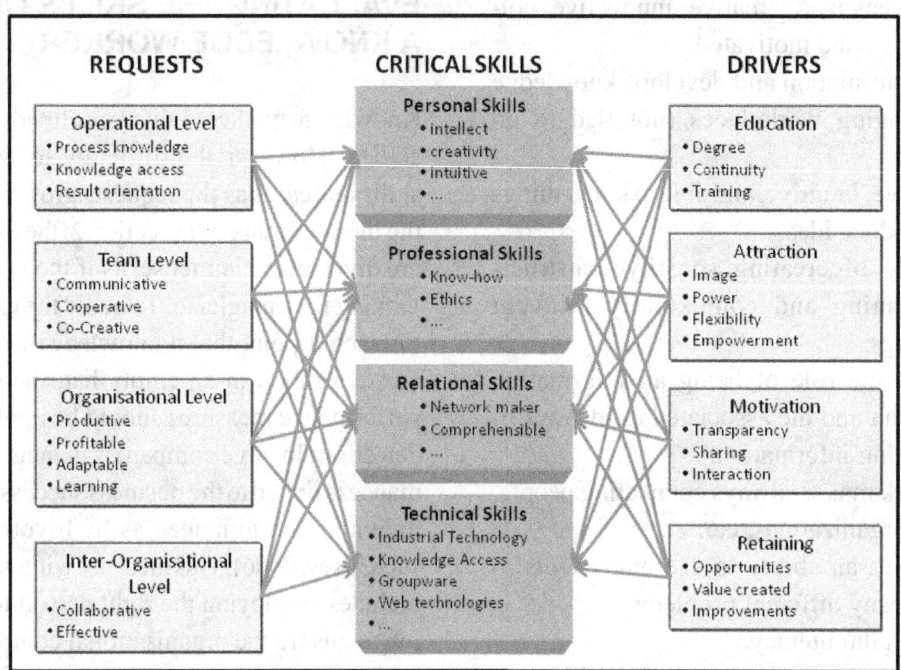

the new culture and changes as well. Learning from organisational operations and achievement is a plus. Knowledge workers are expected to build the trust and collaboration. Therefore they are expected to be ethical and collaborative.

***Drivers*:** Education, attraction, motivation and retaining are considered as the drivers for the knowledge worker, since they will add more to the features brought to the company. Hence, the organisation has to see what they can provide for the high skilled employee to balance the requests. Degree of high level education and lifelong continuity should be considered as a benefit by the organisation as well as on-the-job-training. The worker wants to be impressed by market image, financial power and adoption to change. Structural flexibility with flexible timing and work place allows empowerment and decentralised decision, which are attractive for the knowledge worker. Transparency of the mission and goals will motivate the talented employees as much as encouraging knowledge sharing and managerial interaction. They prefer to work in companies where they have more opportunities to improve and informed about the value they create. Continuous improvements in the company will support sustainability of the work force.

***Critical Skills*:** Competence of a knowledge worker is grouped in personal, professional, relational and technical skills. The personal skills consist of individual abilities that will support his business performance. Professional skills include basic knowledge that is gained in education, industry and operational accumulations obtained through experience. Relational skills comprise of networking, communication, knowledge sharing and collaborative creation. Technical skills will not be limited to utilisation of specific professional technologies (both software and hardware) but the literacy in using groupware and web technologies is required. Continuous follow-up of the technological changes both in information technologies and professional technologies are expected from a knowledge worker.

A good example is determining the requests for a planning engineer. The education is defined to be industrial engineering, information engineering or operational management that brings only basic professional skills. If a planning employee is needed, he is expected to know all the definitions, concepts and methodologies used in planning as well as project planning and scheduling software utilisation. Tasks will be part of a product or service project; hence will interact with other planners. Planning teams are continuously in contact with the production, purchasing, sales and quality teams either internal or external to the organisation. Plans are to be correlated with supplier and customer plans. The requests can already be defined in skills with so much information. However, the organisation has to guarantee that overwhelming candidates do not show up, since they will have a short work life. Therefore, the organisation has to go over what the company specific attractions are, how much motivation can be provided and what retaining strategies should be applied. Only then the organisation is ready to announce for a new post of planning engineer.

Application of this framework will provide benefits in any industry. It is also not specific to technology people and will bring the following benefits for an organisation:

1. Clarify the request hence deal with fewer candidates in recruitment;
2. Ability to determine the salary and the benefits based on critical skills;
3. Balance the critical skills and the performance measures;
4. Reduce turnover by starting retaining strategies in recruitment;
5. Facilitate managerial success.

CONCLUSION

High-performing enterprises are now building their competitive strategies around data-driven insights that in turn generate impressive business results. Their secret weapon is defined to be analytics (Davenport & Harris, 2007). That is why knowledge workers are given an increasing value for the improving role in innovation. New organisations even redesign processes as knowledge workers would carry out, rather than measuring their performance (Bryan & McKinsey, 2006). Leadership, talent and culture are accepted as the basis for knowledge worker skills. In a world where knowledge is a quality introduced, created and developed by the employees, the right person in the right position has more importance. In a tough economy of reducing work durations, income depends on the worker's position relative to the peers in the same knowledge level (Saint-Paul, 2007).

This study proposes a new framework to depict the exact skills requested by any company independent of the company. It was newly stated that the knowledge worker is highly skilled, who is able to convert knowledge into tangible innovative products and services. The firm in search for the talent has to find the right skills and know to keep them in the company for a long enough time to benefit. Intellect, wisdom and ideas of knowledge workers can be converted to economic and competitive values. That is why the integration of the requests are to be combined with the drivers in determination of the skills. Knowledge worker is not only the one who thinks how to work. Knowledge worker can communicate, cooperate and collaborate for the creation of innovative value adding products and services (Daugėlienė, 2007).

Future works will include the application of the framework in different industries. Validation will include utilisation of variety of methodologies like Bayes network, Analytical Network Processing and fuzzy clustering. This new state of thinking integrating both expectations and the drivers to determine the skills will be beneficial for managers, human resource experts and educators.

REFERENCES

Ahn, J. H., & Chang, S. G. (2004). Assessing the Contribution of Knowledge to Business Performance: The KP3Methodology. *Decision Support Systems, 36*, 403–416.

Amadi-Echendu, J. E. (2007). Thinking styles of technical knowledge workers in the systems of innovation paradigm. *Technological Forecasting and Social Change, 74*(8), 1204–1214. doi:10.1016/j.techfore.2006.09.002

Armstrong, D. J., Nelson, H. J., Nelson, K. M., & Narayanan, V. K. (2008). Building the IT Workforce of the Future: The Demand for More Complex, Abstract, and Strategic Knowledge. *Information Resources Management Journal, 21*(2), 63–79.

Arthur, M. B., DeFilippi, R. J., & Lindsay, V. J. (2008). On Being a Knowledge Worker. *Organizational Dynamics, 37*(4), 365–377. doi:10.1016/j.orgdyn.2008.07.005

Arvidsson, A. (2009). The ethical economy: Towards a post-capitalist theory of value. *Capital and Class, 97*, 13–30. doi:10.1177/030981680909700102

Brooks, D. (2008, May 2). The Cognitive Age. *New York Times*.

Bryan, L., & Joyce, C. (2006). Thinking for a living. *Economist*, 1/21/2006, 378(8461)9-12.

Cabrera, E. F., & Cabrera, A. (2005). Fostering knowledge sharing through people management practices. *International Journal of Human Resource Management, 16*(5), 720–735.

Chen, C.-K. (2008). Causal modelling of knowledge-based economy. *Management Decision, 46*(3), 501–519. doi:10.1108/00251740810863915

Cheng, Y. C. (2004). Fostering local knowledge and human development in globalization of education. *International Journal of Educational Management, 18*(1), 7–24. doi:10.1108/09513540410512109

Cobo, C. (2008). *Skills for a Knowledge/Mind Worker Passport (19 commandments)*. Retrieved March 18, 2009, from http://ww.educationfutures.com/2008

Cope, B., & Kalantzis, M. (2009). Signs of Epistemic Disruption: Transformations of the Knowledge. *System of the Academic Journal, 14*(4-6).

Cornuel, E. (2007). Challenges facing business schools in the future. *Journal of Management Development, 26*(1), 87–92. doi:10.1108/02621710710720130

Daugėlienė, R. (2007). The Peculiarities of Knowledge Workers Migration in Europe and the World. *Engineering Economics, 2007*(3), 53.

Davenport, T.H., & Harris, J.G. (2007, March). Competing on Analytics: The New Science of Winning. *Harvard Business School Press*.

Davenport, T.H., & Iye, B. (2009, February). Should you outsource your brain? *Harvard Business School Press*.

Ditkoff, M., Moore, T., Allen, C., & Pollard, D. (2007). *The Ideal Collaborative Team and A Conversation on the Collaborative Process*. Retrieved December 3, 2009, from http://blogs.salon.com/0002007/stories/2005/11/18/theIdealCollaborativeTeamAndAConversationOnTheCollaborativeProcess.html

Drucker, P. (1989). What Business Can Learn from Nonprofits. *Harvard Business Review, 67*(4), 88–93.

Drucker, P. (2001). *Essential Drucker (Classic Drucker Collection)*. New York: Butterworth-Heinemann Ltd.

Drucker, P. F. (1959). *Landmarks of tomorrow*. New York: Harper.

Ehin, C. (2008). Un-managing knowledge workers. *Journal of Intellectual Capital*, *9*(3), 337–350. doi:10.1108/14691930810891965

Erickson, J.T. (2008 February). Task, Not Time: Profile of a Gen Y Job. *Harvard Business Review*.

Fawcett, S. E., Rhoads, G. K., & Burnah, P. (2004). People as the bridge to competitiveness: Benchmarking the ABCs of an empowered workforce. Benchmarking: An International Journal, 11(4), 346–360. Fenwick, T. (2007). Knowledge workers in the in-between: network identities. *Journal of Organizational Change Management*, *20*(4), 509–524.doi:10.1108/14635770410546755

Fliaster, A., & Spiess, J. (2008). Knowledge Mobilization Through Social Ties: The Cost-Benefit Analysis. *Schmalenbach Business Review: ZBF*, *60*, 99–118.

Fugate, B. S., Stank, T. P., & Mentzer, J. T. (2009). Linking improved knowledge management to operational and organizational performance. Journal of Operations Management, 27(3), 247–264. Gao, F., Li, M., & Clarke, S. (2008). Knowledge, management, and knowledge management in business operations. *Journal of Knowledge Management*, *12*(2), 3–17.doi:10.1016/j.jom.2008.09.003

Garcia, B. C. (2007). Working and learning in a knowledge city: a multilevel development framework for knowledge workers. *Journal of Knowledge Management*, *11*(5), 18–30. doi:10.1108/13673270710819771

Gloor, P. A., Paasivaara, M., Schoder, D., & Willems, P. (2007). Finding collaborative innovation networks through correlating performance with social network structure. *International Journal of Production Research*, *46*(5), 1357–1371. doi:10.1080/00207540701224582

Gordon, S. R., & Tarafdar, M. (2007). How do a company's information technology competences influence its ability to innovate? *Journal of Enterprise Information Management*, *20*(3), 271–290. doi:10.1108/17410390710740736

Grech, M. (2008). A school like no other, a leader like no other. *Access*, *22*(4), 9–14.

Green, A. (2007). Business information-a natural path to business intelligence: knowing what to capture. *Vine*, *37*(1), 18–23. doi:10.1108/03055720710741981

Green, A. (2008). Intangible asset knowledge: the conjugality of business intelligence (BI) and business operational data. *Vine*, *38*(2), 184–191. doi:10.1108/03055720810889824

Greene, W. (2006). Growth in Services Outsourcing to India: Propellant or Drain on the U.S. Economy? *Office of Economics Working Paper, U.S. International Trade Commission*, No. 2005-12-A, January 2006.

Gurteen, D. (2006). The Gurteen perspective: Taking responsibility. *Inside Knowledge, 10*(1).

Gvaramadze, I. (2008). Human resource development practice: the paradox of empowerment and individualization. *Human Resource Development International*, *11*(5), 465–477. doi:10.1080/13678860802417601

Hamidizadeh, M. R., & Farsijani, H. (2008). The Role of Knowledge Management for Achieving to World-Class Manufacturing. *Journal of American Academy of Business, Cambridge*, *14*(1), 210–218.

Helbrecht, I. (2004). Bare Geographies in Knowledge Societies – Creative Cities as Text and Piece of Art: Two Eyes, One Vision. *Creative Cultural Knowledge Cities*, *30*(3), 194–203.

Henard, D. H., & McFadyen, M. A. (2008). Making Knowledge Workers More Creative. *Research Technology Management*, *51*(2), 40–47.

Horwitz, F. M., Heng, C. T., Quazi, H. A., Nonkwelo, C., Roditi, D., & van Eck, P. (2006). Human resource strategies for managing knowledge workers: an Afro-Asian comparative analysis. *International Journal of Human Resource Management*, *17*(5), 775–811. doi:10.1080/09585190600640802

Hsiao, H.-D., & Lee, M.-S. (2008). The Comparison of Diagnosis on Business Crisis by Using CART and Logistic Regression. *The Business Review, Cambridge*, *11*(1), 118–124.

Huang, N.-T., Wei, C.-C., & Chang, W.-K. (2007). Knowledge management: modelling the knowledge diffusion in community of practice. *Kybernetes*, *36*(5), 607–621. doi:10.1108/03684920710749703

Johnson, D. (2006). Skills of the knowledge worker. *Teacher Librarian*, *34*(1), 8–14.

Kayakutlu, G. (1998). Knowledge Worker: Essential Resource of the Knowledge Economy, TBD 15. Ulusal Bilişim Kurultayı Bildirileri, İstanbul, 2-6 Eylül 1998, p.222-225.

Larsen, K. R. T., & McInerney, C. R. (2002). Preparing to work in the virtual organization. *Information & Management*, *39*(6), 445–456. doi:10.1016/S0378-7206(01)00108-2

Laycock, M. (2005). Collaborating to compete: achieving effective knowledge sharing in organizations. *The Learning Organization*, *12*(6), 523–539.doi:10.1108/09696470510626739

Lee-Kelly, L., Blackman, D. A., & Hurst, J. P. (2007). An exploration of the relationship between learning organisations and the retention of knowledge workers. *The Learning Organization*, *14*(3), 204–221.doi:10.1108/09696470710739390

LePine, J. A., Piccolo, R. F., Jackson, C. L., Mathieu, J. E., & Saul, J. R. (2008). A Meta-analysis of teamwork processes: Tests of a multidimensional model and relationship with team effectiveness criteria. *Personnel Psychology*, *61*(2), 273–308. doi:10.1111/j.1744-6570.2008.00114.x

Liebowitz, J. (2004). *Addressing the Human Capital Crisis in the Federal Government: a Knowledge Management Perspective*. New York: Butterworth-Heinemann.

Liu, D.-R., & Wu, I.-C. (2008). Collaborative relevance assessment for task-based knowledge support. *Decision Support Systems*, *44*(2), 524–543. doi:10.1016/j.dss.2007.06.015

Liu, D.-R., Wu, I.-C., & Yang, K.-S. (2005). Task-based support systems: disseminating and sharing task-relevant knowledge. *Expert Systems with Applications*, *29*(2), 408–423.doi:10.1016/j.eswa.2005.04.036

Livanage, C., Li, Q., Elhag, T., & Ballal, T. (2008). The Process of Knowledge Transfer and Its Significance in Integrated Environments. *AACE International Transactions*, *2008*, 61–69.

Massey, A. P., Montoya-Weiss, M. M., & O'Driscoll, T. M. (2005). Human Performance Technology and Knowledge Management: A Case Study. *Performance Improvement Quarterly*, *18*(2), 37–56.

Mavrotas, G., Schorrocks, A., & Sen, A. (2007). *Advancing Development: Core Themes in Global Economics*. Basingstoke, UK: Palgrave Macmillan.

McKellar, H. (2005). *The knowledge (worker) economy*. Retrieved May 5, 2009, from http://www.kmworld.com/Articles/Column/From-The-Editor/The-knowledge-(worker)-economy-14264.aspx

Moore, P., & Taylor, P. A. (2009). Exploitation of the self in community-based software productions Workers' freedoms or firm foundations? *Capital and Class*, *97*, 99–119. doi:10.1177/030981680909700106

Nayeri, M. D., Mashhadi, M. M., & Mohajeri, K. (2007). Universities Strategic Evaluation Using Balanced Scorecard. *International Journal of Social Sciences*, *2*(4), 231–236.

Nicolopoulou, K., & Karatas-Ozkan, M. (2007). Practising knowledge workers: perspectives of an artist and economist, PROFESSIONAL INSIGHTS. *Equal Opportunities International, 26*(8), 872–878.doi:10.1108/02610150710836181

Norhani, B. (2008). The Acculturation of *Knowledge* Workers in Malaysian Industries. *International Journal of the Humanities, 6*(1), 63–68.

Osterloh, M., & Frey, B. S. (2006). Shareholders Should Welcome Knowledge Workers as Directors. *Journal of Management & Governance, 10*(3), 325–345.doi:10.1007/s10997-006-9003-4

Psarras, J. (2006). Education and training in the knowledge-based economy. *Vine, 36*(1), 85–96. doi:10.1108/03055720610667390

Ramachandran, R. (2003). Measuring Knowledge Development and Developing Official Statistics for the Information Age. *International Statistical Review / Revue Internationale de Statistique, 71*(1), 83-107.

Roffe, I. (2007). Competitive strategy and influences on e-learning in entrepreneur-led SME. *Journal of European Industrial Training, 31*(6), 416–434.doi:10.1108/03090590710772622

Rowley, J. (2000). Is higher education ready for knowledge management? *International Journal of Educational Management, 14*(7), 325–333. doi:10.1108/09513540010378978

Rusette, J. W., Preziosi, R., Scully, R. E., & de Cossio, F. (2007). A Twenty-First Century Incongruity: Perceptions Regarding Knowledge Worker Didactics. *Journal of Applied Management and Entrepreneurship, 12*(2), 15–44.

Saint-Paul, G. (2007). Knowledge hierarchies in the labor market. *Journal of Economic Theory, 137*(1), 104–126.doi:10.1016/j.jet.2005.09.010

Schell, W. J. (2008). Building a Knowledge Management Framework to Overcome the Challenges of Developing Engineering Teams in Financial Services. *Engineering Management Journal, 20*(1), 3–10.

Scott, P. B. (2005). Knowledge workers: social, task and semantic network analysis. *Corporate Communications: An International Journal, 10*(3), 257–277.doi:10.1108/13563280510614519

Spira, J. B. (2005). Managing The Knowledge Workforce: Understanding The Information Revolution That's Changing The Business World. *Lulu Press*. Retrieved June 6, 2009 from http://www.lulu.com

Spratt, T. (2007). Information Technology Portfolio Management: Search for Business Value. *Futurics, 31*(1/2), 42–45.

Stromquist, N. P., Gil-Antón, M., Colatrella, C., Mabokela, R. O., Smolentseva, A., & Balbachevsky, E. (2007). The Contemporary Professoriate: Towards a Diversified or Segmented Profession? *Higher Education Quarterly, 61*(2), 114–135. doi:10.1111/j.1468-2273.2007.00342.x

Swart, J. (2006). Intellectual capital: disentangling an enigmatic concept. *Journal of Intellectual Capital, 7*(2), 136–150. doi:10.1108/14691930610661827

Tan, H. P., Plowman, D., & Hancock, P. (2008). The evolving research on intellectual capital. *Journal of Intellectual Capital, 9*(4), 585–608. doi:10.1108/14691930810913177

Teo, S. T. T., Lakhani, B., Brown, D., & Malmi, T. (2008). Strategic human resource management and knowledge workers, A case study of professional service firms. *Management Research News, 31*(9), 683–696.doi:10.1108/01409170810898572

Terziovski, M., & Morgan, J. P. (2006). Management practices and strategies to accelerate the innovation cycle in the biotechnology industry. *Technovation*, *26*(5-6), 545–552.doi:10.1016/j.technovation.2004.10.016

Tucker, E., Kao, T., & Verma, N. (2005). Next-Generation Talent Management: Insights on How Workforce Trends are changing the Face of Talent Management. *Business Credit*, *107*(7), 20–27.

Warhurst, C. (2008). The knowledge economy, skills and government labour market intervention. *Policy Studies*, *29*(1), 71–86. doi:10.1080/01442870701848053

Wolff, E. N. (2003). Skills and Changing Comparative Advantage. *The Review of Economics and Statistics*, *85*(1), 77–93. doi:10.1162/003465303762687721

Yeh, H. (2008). A knowledge value creation model for knowledge-intensive procurement projects. *Journal of Manufacturing Technology Management*, *19*(7), 871–892. doi:10.1108/17410380810898796

Chapter 11
Up the Junction? Exploiting Knowledge-Based Development through Supply Chain and SME Cluster Interactions

Tim Donnet
Queensland University of Technology, Australia

Robyn Keast
Queensland University of Technology, Australia

David Pickernell
University of Glamorgan Business School, UK

ABSTRACT

Maximisation of Knowledge-Based Development (KBD) benefits requires effective dissemination and utilisation mechanisms to accompany the initial knowledge creation process. This work highlights the potential for interactions between Supply Chains (SCs) and Small and Medium sized Enterprise Clusters (SMECs), (including via 'junction' firms which are members of both networks), to facilitate such effective dissemination and utilisation of knowledge. In both these network types there are firms that readily utilise their relationships and ties for ongoing business success through innovation. The following chapter highlights the potential for such beneficial interactions between SCs and SMECs in key elements of KBD, particularly knowledge management, innovation and technology transfer. Because there has been little focus on the interactions between SCs and SMECs, particularly when firms simultaneously belong to both, this chapter examines the conduits through which information and knowledge can be transferred and utilised. It shows that each network type has its own distinct advantages in the types of information searched for and transferred amongst network member firms. Comparing and contrasting these advantages shows opportunities for both networks to leverage the knowledge sharing strengths of each other, through these 'junctions' to address their own weaknesses, allowing implications to be drawn concerning new ways of utilising relationships for mutual network gains.

DOI: 10.4018/978-1-61520-721-3.ch011

INTRODUCTION

Knowledge-Based Development (KBD) has become a cornerstone of modern economic activity. Consequently policymakers have increasingly sought ways to encourage activities related to this. Specifically, more and more, knowledge and innovation is a collective rather than an individual activity (Cooke, 1998; Lundvall, 1992; Weick, 1990), for reasons of resource and information intensity and scarcity (i.e. it takes a lot of resources that many firms don't have individually). SMEs for example are often constrained by limited finance, time, and information sources (Gilmore et al., 2006, p.21). For SMEs the resources available for effective KBD are therefore limited at best (Desouza & Awazu, 2006). Due to these deficiencies in resources, SMEs will often look outside of their own boundaries for information and knowledge (Chen, Duan, Edwards, & Lehaney, 2006), exploiting formal and informal network contacts to the firm's advantage (Gilmore et al., 2006, p.21).

The arguments surrounding this condition can also be seen as related to the knowledge spillover theory of entrepreneurship (Acs, Audretsch, Braunerhjelm, & Carlsson, 2004). This theory essentially argues that knowledge developed in one institution may be commercialized by others, and that entrepreneurship is one way in which an economic entity with new knowledge can best obtain returns from that knowledge. The complexity of knowledge intensive entrepreneurship often creates further barriers for firm creation. This may result from:

1. failure of private firms and public institutions to generate new knowledge
2. failure of that knowledge to be disseminated efficiently
3. failure of individuals to exploit new knowledge
4. a range of other factors that make KBD entrepreneurship difficult (also see Audretsch, 2004).

The current focus on KBD therefore needs to supplement analysis of knowledge creation mechanisms with evaluation of the capabilities of knowledge users and effectiveness of knowledge transfer/translation (Braczyk & Heidenreich, 1998; Cooke, Uranga, & Etxebarria, 1997). Of central importance is to link knowledge and innovation in the process of creation and how it is disseminated, with commercialised outcomes in terms of new products, processes and capacities. If, therefore, knowledge generation encompasses the 'triple-helix' elements of Leyesdorff's (2000) government-industry-institutions interactions-based model, it is also important to consider the factors which help stimulate, manage and diffuse created knowledge and encourage KBD as part of an overall knowledge and innovation management framework.

Geographically concentrated cluster-based arrangements can provide a general acceptance between firms for information and knowledge spillover and sharing (Bartlett & Bukvic, 2006), allowing SMEs greater access to relevant information. More importantly, information that is irrelevant to an individual SME is likely to be relevant to another; a point that will be utilised later in exploring the utility of 'junction' firms. These junction firms are simultaneously members of both supply chain and clusters, and can thus act as conduits for two-way flows of information which are beneficial to both types of network. Frenz and Ougthon (2006) argue in particular that proximity facilitates the transfer of tacit knowledge transfer and learning — both of which are important determinants of innovation and thus KBD.

Boschma's (2005) and Frenz and Oughton's (2006) reviews of the theoretical research suggest that the borders of innovation/enterprise systems can be blurred (also see Narula, 2003), particularly as the growing importance of trade and multinational enterprises (Simmie, Sennet, Wood, & Hart, 2002) creates sectoral and technological processes that cross national and regional borders. Together these attributes contribute to building a shared/pooled knowledge base across a range of geographies that can be built on, and leveraged from, for competitive gain.

Importantly, there has also been a dis-integration of supply chains (Bitran, Gurumurthi, & Sam, 2007). Trends to minimise market and economic risk are focusing on developing core business competencies and enhancing the role of outsourcing for strategic benefit (Bertrand & Duhamel, 2003, p.649). As such, previously highly vertically integrated firms are demonstrating the divestment of business risks through the disintegration and externalisation of their internal SCs. This is creating strings of SMEs that fulfil SC needs (Bitran, Gurumurthi, & Sam, 2007). Enhancing competitiveness for firms has thus shifted its focus away from reengineering the internal systems and processes of individual firms, towards the use of collaborative approaches amongst firms to develop sustainable competitive advantages that are mutually beneficial for long term success (Wang & Wei, 2007). This shift to a collaborative approach has meant that, despite the problems with external relationships (in terms of issues of control, knowledge, and power) they have become increasingly important.

The proliferation of SMEs into previously highly integrated SCs enhances the need for effective relationships between all firms in the SC to maintain the competitiveness of the SC as a whole. At the same time, strong regional networks of SMEs demonstrating entrepreneurship and high innovative capacities have also been championed by governments as drivers for economic growth and sustained national competitive advantage from sources globally (Bartlett & Bukvic, 2006; Muscio, 2006; Zhu, Hitt, & Tihanyi, 2006). Failures in such initiatives support the idea, however, that there is still much to be learned about the formation and possible oversight of clustering activities (Smedlund & Toivonen, 2007).

Industry is, therefore, simultaneously increasingly focusing on clustering, particularly for SMEs as well as SCs, in which SMEs are taking a bigger role, for overlapping reasons which can be seen to have direct relevance to KBD (through knowledge creation, dissemination and utilisation). This overlap between SCs and clusters creates three basic sets of issue, related to the synergies that are possible between supply chains and cluster-based arrangements, the impediments / barriers to gaining these synergies, and the enablers (including junction firms) which overcome these barriers and allow the synergies to be realized. Highlighted in Figure 1, these issues form the basis of our subsequent discussion.

SUPPLY CHAIN-CLUSTER OVERLAP ISSUES

Clusters form networks of relationships rich with diverse interactions at the value chain, business-to-business, and social levels that appear to deliver higher value-adding capabilities than other networks (Porter, 2000). Conversely, SCs form networks with interactions focused on meeting the logistics needs of vertically related firms and stakeholders (Murphy & Wood, 2004). A major gap in literature exists, however, in considering how these two types of clusters/networks might work together, particularly when SMEs belong to both types, and are able to lever the most advantage from the situation. Thus, making them a new type of 'hub firm' (e.g. see Dhanaraj & Parke, 2006), perhaps better described as 'junction firms' which combine the role of hub firm in a supply chain whilst simultaneously being a cluster firm, able to utilize and direct knowledge flows in both directions. In particular, questions revolve around the interactions of SCs and clustering, and the mechanisms for facilitating maximisation of their KBD benefits.

Synergies between SCs and SMECs

The first set of issues centre on benefits, requiring an understanding of the transmission and creation of information and knowledge in SCs and SMECs

Figure 1. The supply chain-cluster overlap

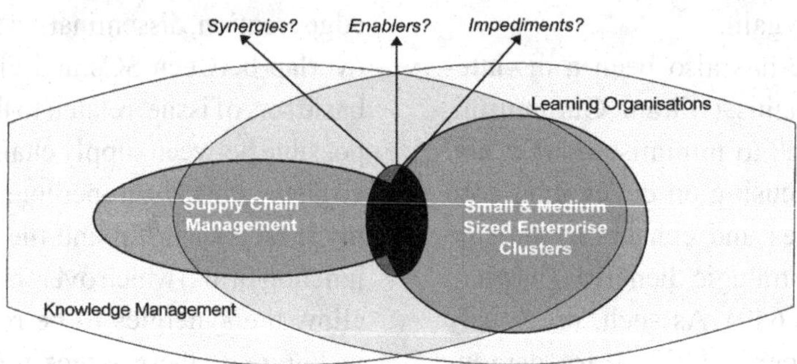

separately, and an evaluation of their strengths and weaknesses in this regard. Different types of learning are possible; codified and tacit (Nonaka & Takeuchi, 1995). As stated previously, tacit learning has been seen as geographically concentrated due to the very nature of the knowledge type; it is learning through doing and the adoption of experience that bounds the spread of tacit knowledge (Nunes, Annansingh, Eaglestone, & Wakefield, 2006). This is being challenged, however, because of the different forms of proximity and the rise of the use of technology to overcome the tyranny of distance (Chen et al., 2006).

For example, SCs exist within and between businesses (Lummus & Vokurka, 1999, p.11), linking goods and services flows from the supplier's supplier to the customer's customer (Quinn, 1997). Contemporary SCs can thus be characterised as functional network structures that facilitate and add value to the flow and creation of products from raw materials through to an end user (Murphy & Wood, 2004). With this functionality in mind, SCs have utilised technologies and processes that have improved market reaction time and reduced time-to-market to streamline products to be in the right place, at the right time, in the right form, at the best possible price. Focusing on the competitive tangibles of speed and efficiency, SCs have delivered innovative ways to improve the delivery of logistical functions through numerous innovations. Many of these innovations have added considerable value to business processes beyond the SC context, often enhancing efficiency and information transfer at all levels of the supply network with such technologies as bar-coding, radio frequency identification (RFID) and electronic database inventory (EDI) systems. Third-Party Logistics providers (3PLs), supplier management, and supplier selection have also been analysed comprehensively in the literature, focusing on the best processes, systems and relationships for both short and long-term SC success (Choy, Tan, & Chan, 2007; Wang & Wei, 2007). In terms of learning, therefore, debates arise over the importance of geographical concentration; codified knowledge being more easily moved across distance, whilst tacit knowledge transfer is more difficult but made increasingly easier by technology.

There is also, however, the issue of social capital and the oscillating strength of organisational ties (Hebbert, Keast, & Mohannak, 2006). That is, clusters with local ties 'get by', clusters with global ties 'get ahead'. Vertical supply chains are also more likely to be formal, and hierarchical in network management, so learning is more likely to be codified and information transferred via formal systems and support agents (e.g. sales agents, electronic database inventories, etc.), but can also transfer information from outside local geographies. In contrast, horizontal SMECs are likely to use more informal structures, relational management, and utilise these structures and relationships for tacit knowledge transfer, giving a knowledge spillover advantage from membership of the cluster, depending on its type.

At the individual firm level, SMEs can obtain a potential network bricolaged advantage (Baker, Miner, & Eesley, 2003) from cluster membership. That is, an advantage individual SMEs may gain from making the best use of resources freely available in and through the cluster network, without requiring additional or significant investment in new or unfamiliar resources. They can look to gain knowledge resources from their network, making them more attractive as a longer-term member of new SC arrangements. Conversely, they can also bring knowledge transfer processes and technology to the cluster/network through its SC membership, improving its efficiency. This also makes the SME a more attractive part of a cluster because they can bring new (though possibly codified) knowledge to the cluster. Such knowledge can also subsequently be used via spillover effects by other cluster members, potentially in different industries, who in turn have the opportunity to pass that knowledge on to their own SCs.

Resilient knowledge growth will crucially depend, of course, on the nature of relationships between sets of firms. Relationships between firms can exist from the most formalised of contractual agreements through to isolated business-to-business interactions and transactions such as purchases or quotations. Firms forming network arrangements can co-operate, co-ordinate or collaborate (Brown & Keast, 2003), with varying levels and types of information shared, creating highly complex systems of interrelationships. As separate network types, SCs and clusters show purposeful behaviours of information and knowledge transfer; unpacking the knowledge systems and tools utilised within SCs and clusters allows for an interrogation of both network types with the aim to highlight underutilised relationships or similarities between these entities.

As much of the literature surrounding SC management emphasises that applying information communication technologies (ICTs) improves SC performance and collaboration (Chang, 2006; Ge, Yang, Proudlove, & Spring, 2003; Wynarczyk, 2000), information flows have expanded rapidly following the subsequent application of ICTs by SC managers. Increased coordination amongst supply chain firms has also uncovered the need for coordination at the SC governance level, in an effort to harvest value from information flows both in and amongst firms (Wang & Wei, 2007).

Information, however, sits separate of knowledge as it is transferred without codification, although it can later be transformed into knowledge when it is appropriated for use by a firm (Lucas, 2006). Organisational learning capabilities must therefore be acknowledged as a primary consideration for firms to achieving strategic competitive advantage, including the capture of tacit knowledge and its codification into the institutions and frameworks of the firm (Graetz, Rimmer, Lawrence, & Smith, 2006). In gaining access to codified and tacit knowledge external of the firm, interpretation of new information should lead to considerations of contextual relevance, adaptability and opportunism to decide on whether an application of knowledge is appropriate for the firm (De Long & Fahey, 2000).

The imperative for learning organisations is, therefore, to successfully and continually access, create and transfer knowledge (Attewell, 1992). McGovern (2006) focuses on learning networks, distinguishing them as cooperative associations of partner firms that share knowledge, physical resources and expertise to improve current performance and advance new business paths. Within a cluster environment, this could be applied to inter-firm coordination for SMEC firms to gain knowledge by accessing other SMEC members' expertise, to further the development of their own resources and capabilities (McGovern, 2006, p.303).

SCs and SMECs can therefore be viewed as separate network structures that both demonstrate an intensification of information and knowledge sharing, acquisition and development through systematic, institutional, formal and informal ties. The increase in the utilisation of technology for communicating and transferring knowledge has led to gains in efficiency and coordination between firms. These adopted technologies continue to evolve to the needs of firms, and the utilisation of technology in networks, particularly information and communication technologies, may thus continue to facilitate increases in collaboration and innovation (Wynarczyk, 2000).

If ICTs are adopted by firms in both networks therefore, SC/SMEC overlap may provide both structures with increased access to readily available information and knowledge; but exposure to information and knowledge is not learning, it is simply a prerequisite. Information may be presented to firms in a form that may be directly attributable to their own business environment, or may be completely irrelevant to the needs of the exposed firm. Firms exposed to new information and knowledge must, however, identify some relevance to themselves or to others in order to implement or pass on the acquired resource to other network members. Without knowing its own information needs, or the information needs of its associated network, a firm may continually be exposed to new information without being able to add value to its exposure in the network. In short, the exposed firm must understand the information and knowledge needs of its network in order to first identify what may be considered relevant, and then have the network capacity to pass this information on to those who may choose to use it; thus capturing value for itself, and/or providing the possibility for other firms in the network to do so.

Where this exists, however, the propagation of SMEs into previously integrated large-scale SCs (Bitran et al., 2007), provides a network intersection of SMEC and SC networks; their inclusion having real potential value to supply chains that re-tool for including SME business processes into their existing systems. Britton (2004) argues therefore that there is a general need for (what we can call 'junction') firms, as part of a network leveraging knowledge, to facilitate external network ties, gaining access to information outside of both the location and scope of the cluster's network horizon in order to draw in new knowledge. Accessing new knowledge also allows the cluster to analyse and review knowledge and technology for integration into existing business processes, and for new market opportunities, providing more avenues for possible product and process development, and innovation (Britton, 2004).

Impediments / Barriers to Synergies between SCs and SMECs

The second set of issues highlighted in Figure 1 relates to impediments, or barriers, to the creation and application of such synergies between SCs and SMECs. Key issues revolve around the importance of knowledge for SCs; importance both as a means of creating and sustaining a competitive advantage and in remaining proactive and agile to emergent shifts in products, markets or technologies. These strategic implications place information and knowledge as critical resources for SCs, where the sharing of developed intellectual property outside of the network may have severe implications for the maintenance of the network's collective sustainable competitiveness.

Not all cluster types, however, will be useful. SMECs most likely to be accepted by SCs for increased information sharing would be those forming loose social network type arrangements, with actors in related processes rather than the more homogenous and highly cooperative product clusters. Porter's (2000) view of clusters acknowledges that they are complex network structures, and constrains them as local infrastructures. As every industry and firm is created and grown with its own contextual differences, however, each definition will fit an individual cluster with varying levels of relevance based on the cluster's context. Industrial districts and technology parks highlight the advantages in geographical agglomeration to knowledge transfer and innovation, and so will be considered too as cluster arrangements. This choice is supported by stark similarities to cluster theories within literature following knowledge and technology transfer, social patterns, and spillover effects from industrial park arrangements (Hebbert et al., 2006; Muscio, 2006). Porter's (2000) definition of clusters is therefore practical for setting network boundaries for the purpose of analysing inter-firm knowledge transfer, but should not preclude the value given by also acknowledging structural (Markusen, 1996), process (Gordon & McCann, 2000) and social (Granovetter, 1992) cluster sub-types. These sub-types allow greater depth of understanding when interrogating existing literature. All three perspectives are used in a balanced framework of contextual lenses to examine firm interactions within cluster environments. Each lens provides valuable insight on how and why firms interact within cluster arrangements to generate a more complete picture of the modes, drivers and agents affecting information and knowledge transfer.

Continuous and stable links between firms, for example, provides trust, shared language and habits that may facilitate the creation of semi-formalised networks (Muscio, 2006, p.292; Smedlund & Toivonen, 2007). In this way firms that deal with one another more regularly are argued to communicate more readily and effectively, reinforcing the strength of both SMEC and external networks of individual firms, depending on their interactions.

Linked to the issues of barriers, are issues arising from information transfer for the firm which sits in both the cluster and the SC simultaneously. Larger Multi-National Enterprises (MNEs) have the internal capacity for information transfer required to be what we have described a 'junction' firm (see Dhanaraj & Parkhe, 2006), but may lack the incentive to share as they have relatively high sunk costs in developing the intellectual property, or may have the capacity to source new information and knowledge through its own resources. This sits in contrast to SMEC firms, who have greater incentive from network bricolage and learning to share information and knowledge, but may lack the internal capacity as individual firms. Mobilising information sharing initiatives within a cluster may therefore highlight the internal knowledge developing and information capturing capabilities of the network. This may provide an incentive for MNEs internal of the cluster to cooperate in information and knowledge sharing initiatives as a means of reducing costs and focusing on the core strengths of the firm, thus enhancing the internal connectedness amongst clustered firms for improved knowledge dissemination. This provides that 'junction' firms need not necessarily be SMEs—essentially any SME or MNE in a cluster could be a 'junction' firm, but information hoarding is likely to preclude a firm from being an effective one.

The very nature of the relationships within each network type do vary, however, with more formalised subscription for SCs, where memberships to the network tacitly requires formalised business-to-business agreements, or the adoption of third party logistics providers. SCs prefer to transfer knowledge and technology by explicit means, set in contracts and producing entry barriers to the SC through technology requisites such as electronic data base inventories (EDI), requisites of product flow infrastructure such as docking facilities, and contractual arrangements such as service level agreements.

By way of contrast, SMEs have, however, previously had difficulty in foreseeing value adding or value creation in knowledge management processes due to a lack of available resources (Nunes et al., 2006). Cluster firms were seen to utilise technology as a process of doing business internal to firms, and through the encouragement of surrounding firms and personal ties (Desouza & Awazu, 2006). It can also be argued that the structure and attributes of a cluster encourage firms to uptake particular technologies due to copy-cat behaviour, limiting the resources to search for new technologies outside of their cluster network boundary (Muscio, 2006). By aiming to produce collective knowledge, rather than individual firm knowledge however, SMEs may then commit more readily to knowledge management strategies to involve the SMEC as a whole.

SMEC/SC 'junction' nodes, through process, therefore become not only a conduit of information but also take on the role of interpreter for highly collaborative SMECs. This was observed in lower collaborative, highly competitive, highly homogeneous industrial parks where technology was implemented but only transferred from spillover and direct contact from other members (Muscio, 2006). In highly collaborative and cooperative SMECs, however, nodes translated the knowledge and passed it on to other members with close social and/or business relational ties and in some cases where knowledge was not deemed of use to the original node itself (Desouza & Awazu, 2006; Wynarczyk, 2000).

These contextual complexities lend issues for the reorganisation of knowledge management by identifying and using new types of links within existing networks. Issues are raised from the differences in the types of firm that will provide the best conduit, becoming a 'junction' firm; for example an SME versus multi-national at different points in a supply chain. There are, however, other enablers of knowledge and innovation flows between the two network types, which can act as both substitutes for, and complements to, 'junction firms'. Issues of network structure and firm inclusion therefore need to be addressed in order to ensure the facilitation of information flows.

Enablers of Synergies between SCs and SMECs

Firms within clusters are more likely to seek information regarding new systems, processes and what their neighbour firms are doing to fulfill their own strategic and competitive needs (Chen et al., 2006; Muscio, 2006). Firm level information regards the information held within each firm's organisational boundary of staff and resource systems — the micro-economic level. As such, this information forms the pool of pragmatically sought information by other members of that network. For example firms in SCs seek information regarding supply and demand for logistical needs, production scheduling and purchasing strategies (Choy, Tan, & Chan, 2007; Tatikonda & Stock, 2003).

The distinct and similar groups of systems, processes and interactions that facilitate information and knowledge transfer within and between SC and cluster structures are termed the agents of information transfer. These agents have the ability to glean, often interpret or codify, and pass on information either automatically or voluntarily from and to their associated networks and information pools. Figures 2, 3 and 4 unpack the roles of agents and their levels of interactions with SMECs and SCs for information sharing; describing the nature of information shared and the likelihood of gleaning meaningful information from each agent.

It is expected that increasing the role of information transfer in everyday business activities would have some effect on the roles within these agents, be it explicitly detailed in new job descriptions or implicitly through the enhancement of relationships. Controlling the role of these agents would likely provide a significant tool for the management of these flows, that is, governing the level of cooperation, coordination or collaboration to directly impact the nature and structure of learning based relationships within the network.

As Figure 2 suggests, shared agents can also form a part of the regular business operations activities for both groups of firms. SCs utilise the shared agents of trade events, sales representatives, and personal associates, as well as business-to-business interactions to hear of new information about both familiar and unfamiliar markets, products, technologies and processes. These agents are

Figure 2. Shared agents for information transfer

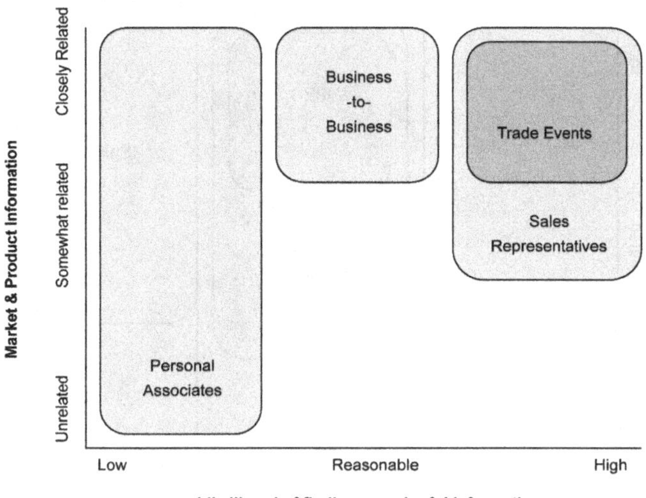

Figure 3. SC agents for information transfer

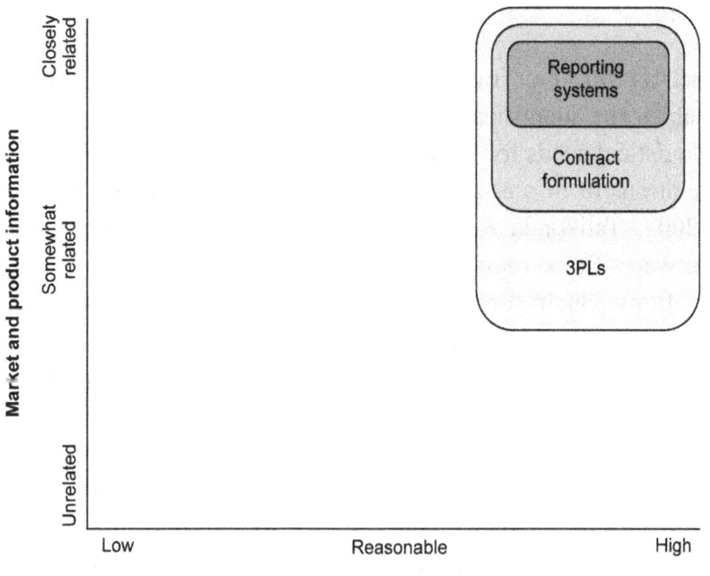

considered shared as both SC and SMEC firms have access to utilise these agents; an SC firm may seek new business opportunities through these avenues, contacting existing business partners or related firms within a region. Likewise an SMEC firm may utilise these agents to learn about competitor behaviour, new systems used in other regions, and new products available.

SC agents form the regular business operations activities utilised by developed SCs, with the expedient coordination and delivery of firm level information driven by these agents. Co-

Figure 4. SMEC agents for information transfer

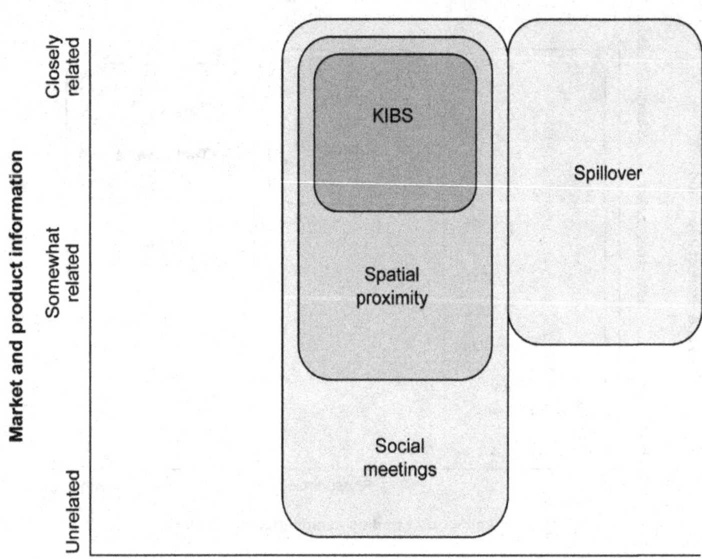

ordinating entities such as 3PLs), or a network of SC managers, enables the identification of product, market and logistical needs for sustainable, competitive operations of SCs as a whole (Murphy & Wood, 2004; Tatikonda & Stock, 2003), interacting between firms regularly to ensure efficient operations. Such coordinated efforts are supported by reporting technologies and systems such as electronic database inventory systems. These technologies are thus designed to regularly and expediently update all firms within an SC network of the supply and demand conditions of every firm for the better management of production and logistics scheduling. Figure 3 highlights the highly task specific role of these technologies, where emphasis is given to existing markets and products. Limiting the exposure of SC firms from more diverse sources and types of information may improve efficiency, but may ultimately impede the ability of SCs to foresee major changes or opportunities in markets and products external of their own.

Relationships between firms in SCs are also typically underwritten by the formulation of contractual arrangements such as service level agreements. In formalising their relationships, SC firms hope to minimise business risks; ensuring adequate trust exists between the parties through transparent processes, but not necessarily requiring an understanding of each others' business processes. Higher levels of formalisation typically demonstrate low trust, cooperative arrangements between parties in products or from markets, often revealing lengthy and prescriptive contracts with little leeway for redress or change (Kwon & Suh, 2004; Spekman, Kamauff Jr., & Myhr, 1998). Lower levels of formalisation often revolve around high levels of trust; trust that opportunistic behaviour has been marginalised, allowing for flex in many or all aspects of the collaborative relationship arrangements (Kwon & Suh, 2004; Spekman et al., 1998).

The formulation of these collaborative agreements often requires the signing parties to consider the contextual nature of the firms, the relationships and the underlying needs of the individual firms and of the SC as a whole, increasing information transferred, minimising uncertainty, and reinforcing trust (Kwon & Suh, 2004; Murphy & Wood, 2004). Where such a contextual appreciation exists, this internal interrogation process may also allow firms greater transparency in business dealings, strengthening trust in relationships and allowing each firm to see the needs of the other. In these circumstances the identification of information pertinent to SC partners' operational activities may be greater than in less highly formalised SCs.

In contrast to the SC agents' highly formalised and coordinated efforts for information sharing, SMEC firms are more likely to be beneficiaries of increased knowledge transfer through human resource spillover effects, with tacit knowledge often transferred from one firm to another through this process (Capello, 1999; Fosfuri & Ronde, 2004). While firms may regularly hire new staff, it is unreasonable to consider this an everyday event for SME firms, making this an intermittent event and a limited route to new information. Adding to these intermittent knowledge transfer events is the use of knowledge intensive business services (KIBS). Businesses can be influenced by functional, not only market and business-to-business interaction; KIBS have shown the benefits of 'bridging' and 'brokering' knowledge between firms through the provision of services to multiple firms in a given region (Smedlund & Toivonen, 2007). For example a mobile accountant may recommend the use of financial planning services outsourced to a local firm. In this example the KIBS provider, the accountant, has identified a need that can be fulfilled through the utilisation of their own tacit knowledge. It is reasonable to assume the intermittent use of KIBS by SMEs, due to inherent deficiencies in internal resources impacting the ability of SMEs to address every business need themselves.

Social meetings and spatial proximity also then play important roles in the information and knowledge transfer for SMECs in particular. Spatial proximity allows for firms close together to learn from each other through observation. Homogeneous firms are likely to copy each other's improvements (Muscio, 2006), while heterogeneous firms may find opportunities to innovate discrete business processes to their own needs (Chen et al., 2006). Due to the need for firms to first identify an opportunity to act upon it, such proximity benefits may take time to reach implementation and are also to be considered intermittent in their transfer of information and knowledge. Social meetings may occur the most frequently of all of the SMEC agents for knowledge and information transfer. This interchange is dependent on the nature of the relationships between neighbouring firms, but may also become somewhat of an institution for some clusters. These interactions can range from impromptu meetings over coffee through to large gatherings of owners on regular occasions. An example of regular organised social meetings is the Hunter Valley wine cluster in New South Wales, Australia (Burgess & Henderson, 2007); viticulturists within the valley meet monthly over wine and cheese at a nominated homestead in the region. This enables the growers and producers to meet in a social environment, stripping away the formality of business relationships and competition between counterparts and intensifying information sharing within the cluster. The central role of social connectivity and place proximity in knowledge sharing and building is depicted in the individual clusters in Figure 5.

THE ROLE OF THE 'JUNCTION' FIRM

Overall, the unpacking of these agents suggests that it is possible to gain synergies in information and knowledge sharing activities between both network types without the necessity of having firms which are simultaneously members of both network types. 'Junction' SMEs who understand the value of the information, how to exploit it, how to transfer it, and why, are however of critical importance for both facilitating sharing initiatives and harvesting value from such undertakings,

Figure 5. Tapping information and knowledge from both SCs and clusters

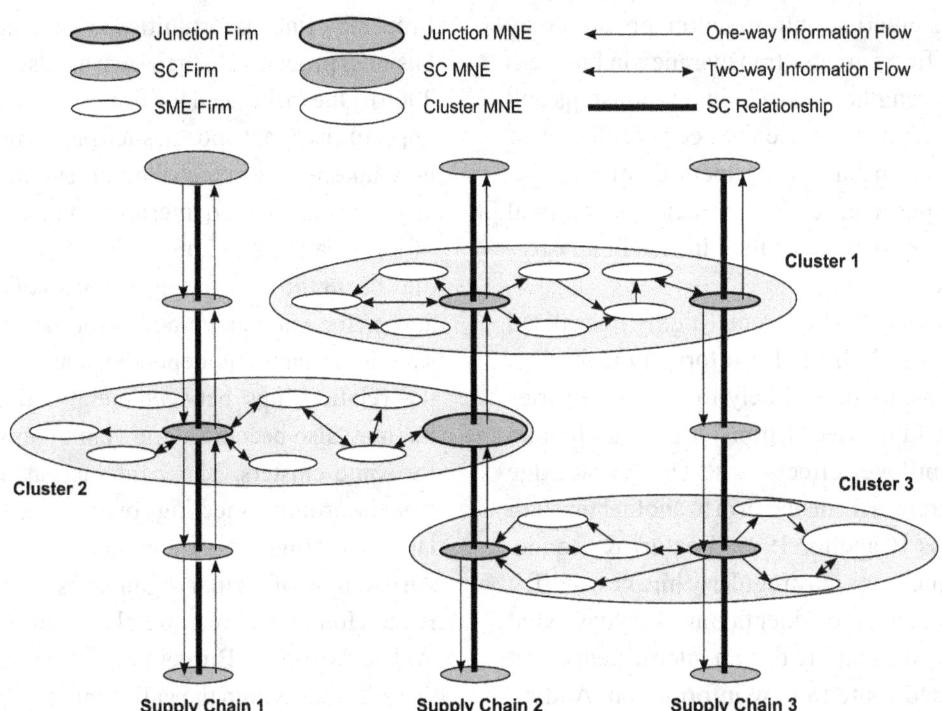

and are therefore of great potential importance in maximising potential KBD.

This is because theories in knowledge management, whilst they have shown benefits to identifying, capturing and codifying knowledge within firms (Nunes et al., 2006; Graetz et al., 2006), have not addressed interactions within and amongst networks of knowledge to extend into firms' knowledge acquisition processes. Both network types discussed can borrow from each others' strengths in information acquisition and sharing to address their own weaknesses in the identification, capture and codification of knowledge. New market or innovation opportunities may thus present themselves to any stakeholder, including the SC, shared and SMEC information transfer agents.

Driven by the need to sustain competitive advantage within the market, however, SCs utilise cooperation, knowledge management, and information sharing methods to compete as entire SCs rather than individual firms (Drickhamer, 2005; Murphy & Wood, 2004). Highly developed SCs maximise these utilities through formalised systems and arrangements, transferring information that is beneficial to all involved SC firms to coordinate supply efforts to meet market demands. SMECs in contrast, while often effective at innovating, transferring knowledge and heightening technology uptake through social and spillover effects, lack the advantages of formalised, regular and transparent information sharing demonstrated within SC structures. Some influence of SCs increasing product specific information, knowledge and technology transfer is apparent (Drickhamer, 2005), but no uptake outside of process driven information is seen flowing from cluster to supply chain.

This existing channel of SMEC knowledge and information could, however, be better utilised by SCs to increase economies of search for new business opportunities and discontinuous innovations. Much like the level of understanding gained between SC firms during the contract formulation process, by simultaneously identifying the mutual needs of both SMEC firms and SC firms, information can be more readily identified and transferred between parties. By knowing the information needs of other cluster firms, a SC/SMEC 'junction' firm may act as an information conduit, identifying relevant information for the SMEC from SC information flows and passing this on to firms that may find the information of use. Likewise, SC relevant information from the SMEC could be of strategic importance to individual SC firms or to the SC as a whole.

By broadening the search horizons for SCs in both scope and scale, without the need to formulate new relationships, SCs can increase their capacity for accessing knowledge without the need to commit significant resources for search activities. SMECs would benefit from the increased levels of information gained from remote knowledge sources, utilising SCs that span multiple clusters to gain generic information of technologies and processes at an increased rate, without affecting the relationships within the cluster.

Clusters glean information from their networks in a typically opportunistic way; the bricolage approach to information gathering and utilisation. SCs are averse to such opportunistic behaviour between its partners due to the detrimental affects this may have on the relationships so dependent on trust and reliability. By utilising SC/SMEC 'junctions', SCs may broaden their information gathering scope without the need for engaging in activities that may damage the trust between its firms. In parallel to the benefits to SCs, clusters may enhance gains in information bricolage effects due to the influx of information tapped from other clusters, through the secondary network relationships of the 'junction' firms.

Figure 5 illustrates the process of cluster tapping. This involves identifying relevant information that may be of use to other firms in related clusters. The use of shared agents, relationships and knowledge transfer systems can then be used to pass this information through the SC to firms in SC linked clusters. This enhanced interaction between SCs and SMEC firms serves both network structures; SMECs for increased innovative and knowledge sharing capacities, hopefully leading to a stronger regional competitive advantage; SCs for heightened market awareness for discontinuous innovations and new business opportunities for increased resilience and competitiveness.

The cluster tapping process highlighted in Figure 5 provides examples of how both SCs and SMECs can benefit each other. By coordinating the use of SC agents and for expedient transmission of information and knowledge gained from SMEC agents, both network types stand to gain from increasing their available catchments for information. Figure 5 also illustrates an ideal process for increasing the information and knowledge sharing capacities of SMECs and SCs; this ideal situation would be limited by the nature of the relationships within clusters and the ability of stakeholders and firms to identify information as worth acting upon. In addition, the uptake of information and knowledge could be interpreted in many different ways depending on the ability of firms to adapt and innovate from the newly available information. It may also be the case, therefore, that a multitude of different vertical/horizontal nodes are possible, depending on the nature of the existing arrangements within each SC and SMEC network.

CONCLUSIONS: SCS, SMECS, JUNCTION FIRMS AND KBD

High capacity entities such as MNEs bring new information to regions through direct linkages with local and non-local actors, providing a 'junction' between socially and spatially separated domains of knowledge. So too, indirectly, do the firms that bridge SC and SME cluster networks provide 'junctions' between remote and local domains of knowledge. If SMEs can learn to tap this information resource effectively, therefore, then they can gain information capacity advantages similar to MNEs. As more SMEs learn to tap this resource, the follow-on effects will increase the KBD potential within both types of networks. In order to facilitate the exchange of information from existing SCs, the collective knowledge gathering, translating and utilising capacity through the cluster network provides an interesting opportunity for the mutual gain of both SCs and SMECs. This demands future attention, both from firms and also policymakers' intent on maximising KBD.

Wynarczyk (2000) warns SMEs that tying their business too closely to large, powerful firms may significantly reduce their ability to scan outside of their immediate business environment due to a lack of human capital. Nevertheless, developed, highly efficient SCs may promise significantly higher levels of business and development for an SME, providing quite a sizeable attraction to subscribe. Building behaviours and processes that promote information sharing between SCs and SMECs may allow SME firms to overcome Wynarczyk's (2000) warnings for their economies of search, while improving the search abilities of SCs: a win-win for both parties. An SME may also be able to mitigate problems in negotiation power dissonance by bringing the value of its associated SMEC network connections to the bargaining table. This would supply greater negotiating power for the SME in the SC, and strengthen relationships with SMEC firms as it would have access to information and knowledge regarding best practices and knowledge flows outside its regular boundaries.

Rather than focusing solely on the internal knowledge management of firms, the implications of this analysis also show value for firms to look outside of their boundaries, not only for knowledge resources but for the mutual benefit of networked firms. Increasing the awareness of the firms' knowledge strengths and resources, and the needs of the networks themselves may create strategic opportunities for firms to become more closely involved with each other, allowing firms to address their knowledge weaknesses through other firms' strengths; networks supporting firms and firms supporting networks, creating networks supporting networks. As such this demonstrates new ways in which the process of knowledge, creation, dissemination and utilisation, and hence KBD potential can be enhanced in an economy.

REFERENCES

Acs, Z. J., Audretsch, D. B., Braunerhjelm, P., & Carlsson, B. (2004). The missing link: The knowledge filter and entrepreneurship in endogenous growth. *Discussion Paper No.4783, December*. London, UK: Centre for Economic Policy Research.

Attewell, P. (1992). Technology diffusion and organizational learning: The case of business computing. *Organization Science*, *3*(1), 1–19. doi:10.1287/orsc.3.1.1

Audretsch, D. (2004). Sustaining innovation and growth: Public policy support for entrepreneurship. *Industry and Innovation*, *11*(3), 167–191. doi:10.1080/1366271042000265366

Baker, T., Miner, A. S., & Eesley, D. T. (2003). Improvising firms: Bricolage, account giving and improvisational competencies in the founding process. *Research Policy*, *32*, 255–276. doi:10.1016/S0048-7333(02)00099-9

Bartlett, W., & Bukvic, V. (2006). Knowledge transfer in Slovenia: Supporting innovative SMEs through spin-offs, technology parks, clusters and networks. *Economic and Business Review*, *8*(4), 337–358.

Bertrand, Q., & Duhamel, F. (2003). Bringing together strategic outsourcing and corporate strategy: Outsourcing motives and risk. *European Management Journal, 21*(5), 647–661. doi:10.1016/S0263-2373(03)00113-0

Bitran, G. R., Gurumurthi, S., & Sam, S. L. (2007). Emerging trends in supply chain governance. *MIT Sloan Management Review, 48*(3), 30–37.

Boschma, R. A. (2005). Proximity and innovation: A critical assessment. *Regional Studies, 39*(1), 61–74. doi:10.1080/0034340052000320887

Braczyk, H.-J., & Heidenreich, M. (1998). Conclusion . In Braczyk, H.-J., Cooke, P., & Heidenreich, M. (Eds.), *Regional innovation systems: The role of governances in a globalized world* (pp. 414–440). London: UCL Press.

Britton, J. N. H. (2004). High technology localization and extra-regional networks. *Entrepreneurship & Regional Development, 16*, 369–390. doi :10.1080/0898562041000167435

Brown, K., & Keast, R. (2003). Citizen-government engagement: Community connection through networked arrangements. *The Asian Journal of Public Administration, 25*(1), 107–131.

Burgess, J., & Henderson, L. (2007). *Mapping the hunter wine cluster. Workshop on industry clusters* (August). New South Wales: University of Newcastle, Graduate School of Business.

Capello, R. (1999). SME clustering and factor productivity: A Milieu production function model. *European Planning Studies, 7*(6), 719.

Chang, H. H. (2006). Technical and management perceptions of enterprise information system importance, implementation and benefits. *Information Systems Journal, 16*(3), 263–292. doi:10.1111/j.1365-2575.2006.00217.x

Chen, S., Duan, Y., Edwards, J. S., & Lehaney, B. (2006). Toward understanding inter-organizational knowledge transfer needs in SMEs: Insight from a UK investigation. *Journal of Knowledge Management, 10*(3), 6–23. doi:10.1108/13673270610670821

Choy, K. L., Tan, K. H., & Chan, F. T. S. (2007). Design of an intelligent supplier knowledge management system – an integrative approach. *Proceedings - Institution of Mechanical Engineers, 221*(b2), 195–211. doi:10.1243/09544054JEM627

Cooke, P. (1998). Introduction: Origins of the concept . In Braczyk, H. J., Cooke, P., & Heidenreich, M. (Eds.), *Regional innovation systems: The role of governance in a globalized world* (pp. 2–27). London: UCL.

Cooke, P., Uranga, M. G., & Etxebarria, G. (1997). Regional innovation systems: Institutional and organisational dimensions. *Research Policy, 26*, 475–491. doi:10.1016/S0048-7333(97)00025-5

De Long, D. W., & Fahey, L. (2000). Diagnosing cultural barriers to knowledge management. *The Academy of Management Executive, 14*(4), 113–127.

Desouza, K. C., & Awazu, Y. (2006). Knowledge management at SMEs: Five peculiarities. *Journal of Knowledge Management, 10*(1), 32–43. doi:10.1108/13673270610650085

Dhanaraj, C., & Parkhe, A. (2006). Orchestrating innovation networks. *Academy of Management Review, 31*(3), 659–669.

Drickhamer, D. (2005). Power partner: Manufacturers-logistics service providers relationship. *Material Handling Management, 60*(4), 22–23.

Frenz, M., & Oughton, C. (2006). *Innovation in the UK regions and devolved administrations: A review of the literature. Final Report for the Department of Trade and Industry and the Office of the Deputy Prime Minister*. London: DTI.

Ge, Y., Yang, J.-B., Proudlove, N., & Spring, M. (2003). System dynamics modelling for supply-chain management: A case study on a supermarket chain in the UK. *International Transactions in Operational Research, 11*(5), 495–509. doi:10.1111/j.1475-3995.2004.00473.x

Gilmore, A., Carson, D., Grant, K., O'Donnell, A., Laney, R., & Pickett, B. (2006). Networking in SMEs: Findings from Australia and Ireland. *Irish Marketing Review, 18*(1&2), 21–28.

Gordon, I. R., & McCann, P. (2000). Industrial clusters: Complexes, agglomeration and/or social networks? *Urban Studies (Edinburgh, Scotland), 37*(3), 513–532. doi:10.1080/0042098002096

Graetz, F., Rimmer, M., Lawrence, A., & Smith, A. (2006). *Managing organisational change* (2nd ed.). Sydney, Australia: Wiley & Sons.

Granovetter, M. (1992). Economic institutions as social constructions: A framework for analysis. *Acta Sociologica, 35*(1), 3–11. doi:10.1177/000169939203500101

Hebbert, W. P., Keast, R., & Mohannak, K. (2006). The strategic value of oscillating tie strength in technology clusters. *Innovation: Management . Policy & Practice, 8*(5), 322–377.

Leyesdorff, L. (2000). The triple helix: An evolutionary model of innovation. *Research Policy, 29*(2), 243–255. doi:10.1016/S0048-7333(99)00063-3

Lucas, L. M. (2006). The role of culture on knowledge transfer: The case of the multinational corporation. *The Learning Organization, 13*(3), 257–275. doi:10.1108/09696470610661117

Lummus, R. R., & Vokurka, R. J. (1999). Defining supply chain management: A historical perspective and practical guidelines. *Industrial Management & Data Systems, 99*(1), 11–17. doi:10.1108/02635579910243851

Lundvall, B.-Å. (Ed.). (1992). *National systems of innovation: Towards a theory of innovation and interactive learning*. London: Pinter.

Nonaka, I., & Takeuchi, H. (1995). *The knowledge-creating company: How Japanese companies create the dynamics of innovation*. Oxford, UK: Oxford University Press.

Nunes, M. B., Annansingh, F., Eaglestone, B., & Wakefield, R. (2006). Knowledge management issues in knowledge-intensive SMEs. *The Journal of Documentation, 62*(1), 101–119. doi:10.1108/00220410610642075

Quinn, F. J. (1997). What's the buzz? *Logistics Management, 36*(2), 43–47.

Smedlund, A., & Toivonen, M. (2007). The role of KIBS in the IC development of regional clusters. *Journal of Intellectual Capital, 8*(1), 159–170. doi:10.1108/14691930710715114

Snow, C. C., Miles, R. E., & Coleman, H. J. Jr. (1992). Managing 21st century network organizations. *Organizational Dynamics, 20*(3), 5–21. doi:10.1016/0090-2616(92)90021-E

Spekman, R. E., Kamauff, J. W. Jr, & Myhr, N. (1998). An empirical investigation into supply chain management. *International Journal of Physical Distribution & Logistics Management, 28*(8), 630–650. doi:10.1108/09600039810247542

Tatikonda, M. V., & Stock, G. N. (2003). Product technology transfer in the upstream supply chain. *Journal of Product Innovation Management, 20*(6), 444–467. doi:10.1111/1540-5885.00042

Wang, E. T. G., & Wei, H.-L. (2007). Interorganizational governance value creation: Coordinating for information visibility and flexibility in supply chains. *Decision Sciences, 38*(4), 647–674.

Weick, K. E. (1990). Organizational culture as a source of high reliability. *California Management Review, 29*(2), 112–127.

Wynarczyk, P. (2000). The role of digital networks in supply chain development. *New Technology, Work and Employment*, *15*(2), 123–137. doi:10.1111/1468-005X.00069

Zhu, H., Hitt, M. A., & Tihanyi, L. (2006). The internationalization of SMEs in emerging economies: Institutional embeddedness and absorptive capacities. *Journal of Small Business Strategy*, *17*(2), 1–26.

Chapter 12
Creativity and Knowledge-Based Urban Development in a Nordic Welfare State:
Combining Tradition and Development in the Helsinki Metropolitan Area

Tommi Inkinen
University of Helsinki, Finland

Mari Vaattovaara
University of Helsinki, Finland

ABSTRACT

This chapter addresses the provision and condition of the knowledge-based development in the Helsinki metropolitan area, Finland. This chapter looks at linkages between regional (urban) development and welfare state elements supported by local and national policies. The authors concentrate on one hand on urban and regional policy tools, and on the other to education, because together they provide a platform for building a knowledge-based society. The authors also explore the current condition of selected creative and knowledge-intensive employment in the Helsinki metropolitan area.

INTRODUCTION

Creativity and knowledge-based regional and urban development have been topical issues of social scientific research for some time now. The works of Florida (2002; 2005) and others (e.g. Bathelt 2005; Cumbers et. al. 2003; Malmberg & Powell 2005; Nonaka & Takeuchi 1995; Schienstock 2004; Simmie 2001) have pointed the way recognizing the role of creativity and personal intuition in the pursuit of new economic growth. In this regard, Park (2001: 50–52) discusses knowledge intensive-industries using a scheme dividing industrial production into contexts of "intensity of knowledge inputs" and "level of technology". He points out that knowledge-intensive companies require a highly skilled and educated labor force in order to conduct the actual research and development (R&D) that is pivotal to knowledge-intensive production. However, creativity is not the only topic in the current regional development debate. In the Nordic context, the other

DOI: 10.4018/978-1-61520-721-3.ch012

is the development and maintenance of a socially coherent welfare state (Esping-Andersen 1992; Heap et al. 1992; Castells & Himanen 2002).

The purpose of this chapter is to examine and discuss linkages between regional (urban) development and welfare state elements supported by local and national policies. We concentrate on one hand on urban and regional policy tools, and on the other on education and creative industries, because together they provide a platform for building a "knowledge-based society". We use statistics to explore the current condition of selected creative and knowledge-intensive employment figures in the Helsinki metropolitan area. Our main questions are:

1) How does creative employment characterize the case of Helsinki?
2) How does education level and system relate to these developments?
3) What policy options have been deployed in order to support knowledge-based regional development?

To take up the task of answering these questions, we present the regional context based on geographical facts and societal conditions. We use the concept of the welfare state as a societal context and Nordic reference. After contextualizing Finland and the Helsinki metropolitan area, we use statistics to provide empirical examples and evidence, including a synthesizing discussion of future trends. We conclude by addressing the main findings of our study.

Finland provides a good case for examination in this study. It has been described as a Nordic welfare state in which the proportion of economic activity accounted for public sector is relatively high. The maintenance of a regionally balanced and stable welfare state is characterized by an effective transfer of resources from urban regions to peripheral areas. These transfers are used to provide welfare services, to build and maintain infrastructure and to attract regional investments.

BACKGROUND

National Pathway Towards a Creative Society

Finland is a Nordic country, with a homogeneous population and almost no flow of foreign immigration until recent decades. Considering the creative class proposition of Florida (2002; 2005), which stresses the importance of multiculturalism and a diversity of cultural talents, the starting point is not particularly promising. However, the traditional Nordic welfare state structures that include free education, affordable health care and wide social security have attracted increasing amounts of immigrants to Finland. The majority of migrants take up residence in the Helsinki metropolitan area.

Finland can not be understood without understanding the welfare state. Relatively small income differences combined with progressive taxation have kept income differences among the smallest in Europe (TÁRKI European Social Report 2005). Thus the homogeneity of the population applies not only to ethnic homogeneity, but also to the rather small income differences. These differences are further diminished by income-related benefits.

A specific characteristic of Finnish society was the welfare state "building era" that begun in the 1950s and continued into the 1970s. During that period the existing institutions that comprise the essence of the "Nordic welfare state" were founded (e.g. Gylfason 1997; Korpi & Palme 1998; in urban context Vaattovaara & Kortteinen 2003). Together with the existence of universities and institutions securing social and welfare policies, the basic structures for an innovative urban development were created (see in detail Bell & Hietala 2002). The combination of the welfare state and a knowledge economy is the main thesis of Manuel Castells and Pekka Himanen (2002), who studied characteristics of the "Finnish model of information society". In other words, the combined structures of the welfare state and knowledge intensiveness are the specifics of the Finnish model.

Finland has a relatively young urban structure. There are few historically traditional towns in Finland. Helsinki is one of them. However, due to the rapid structural changes in the national economy, the agrarian tradition still has a strong impact on the rather thin urban culture. Even as late as in the beginning of the 1960s, almost a third of the population earned its livelihood from agriculture and forestry. Acceleration in the shift from agriculture to urban service industries started in the 1960s. After this late start, the pace has been the fastest in all of Europe. The extensive migration to the cities caused a rapid increase in construction industry. Housing estates were intended to combine the benefits of both rural and urban areas, but the results were not always successful. Urban structures were also scattered. Since the urban areas account for about four-fifths of the total production of the national economy, the competitiveness and expertise exhibited by urban enterprises can be considered the backbone of the entire economy (Vaattovaara & Kortteinen 2003).

In addition to the basic functions of the Nordic Welfare state, there is a profound element in the Finnish model: the specific focus on education. Creativity is closely related to learning and competence, thus also to the factors that are fundamental to education and the educational system. An equal and standardized educational system has been one of the key features of the Finnish welfare state model. Practically all Finnish people have a similar elementary school education, provided by the public sector. This continues to upper educational levels.

From an international perspective, a broad national educational base has been a benefit to Finland and Helsinki, and has provided a basis for its conversion to a knowledge-based society. The educational system and the universities have provided from early on equal opportunities to members of all levels of society. Starting from the 1960's, the university network was expanded from three to twenty and public financing institutions for business-oriented research and development were established. When compared to British, French or German educational systems, the Finnish system has never been selective in a similar manner. Quite the opposite, opportunities have been provided to all social classes in all parts of Finland (Mäkelä 1999: 157). Anthropologists and cultural researchers have noted in their studies the educational ethos that existed already at the beginning of last century. In many European countries the teachers have encountered resistance from disadvantaged societal segments but in Finland the attendance at different educational levels was the same at all socioeconomic strata (Jutikkala 1965; Alapuro 1985; Alestalo 1985; Mäkelä 1999).

Our focus is on macro indicators describing societal segments, such as highly educated and policy target groups. Ennals studied already in the 1980s knowledge transfer from the perspective of competent persons. Creativity can be regarded as one form of competence – as a skill to create and do easily things that are difficult to others. Therefore, competence and creativity should also be understood in relation to the others. Ennals (1987: 69–72) uses the term "skill" in this respect. Skill, creativity and competence are inseparable entities comprising the essence of a knowledge-creating person or organization (e.g. Nonaka & Takeuchi 1995; Florida 2002). This innovativeness is one essential characteristic that is associated with new economic growth theories.

Knowledge creation is commonly based on networks and collaborative arrangements of skilled persons. We propose a triad for this assessment. The first aspect includes an individual component referring to personal capability and characteristics of a "creative" person. In the majority of cases, however, a single person is not enough to manifest the idea and produce an outcome (product, article or process). Therefore, a collection of persons, thus a social network, is needed. The second aspect includes interpersonal networks and the networks of these networks. This is essentially a layered structure that has spatial variations. Lo-

Figure 1. The Metropolitan Area (darker area) and the Helsinki Region (lighter area). Source: Karvinen 2005:2; City of Helsinki Urban Facts 2005

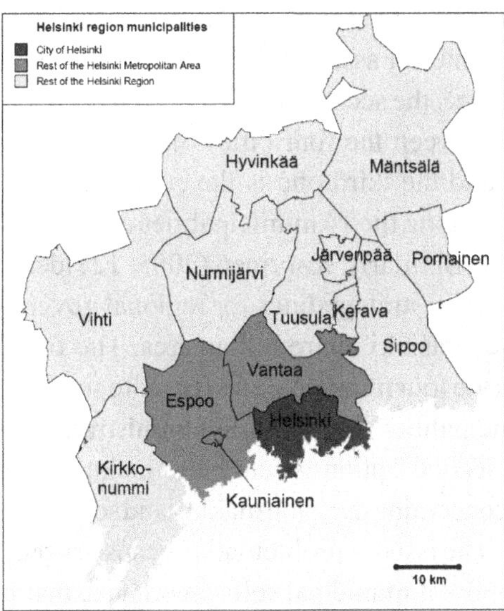

cal networks rapidly expand to the global level in particular fields of expertise. The third aspect is that the institutional setting has relevance. In Finland the egalitarian welfare state has been a considerable factor. Decisions made and options chosen in innovation and regional policy reflect these societal traditions (e.g. Ahlqvist & Inkinen 2007; Conceição & Heitor 2007).

The Context of Helsinki

The development of Helsinki and its surrounding area into a middle-sized European metropolitan area began from its establishment as the capital city in 1812. Capital city status created a platform for growth in population and business and resulted in the creation of the oldest and the most important educational institutions in the country. Helsinki has since been the administrative, educational and cultural center of Finland. There are three geographical entities that are of importance in the Helsinki area: the City of Helsinki, the Metropolitan area of Helsinki and at the largest level the region of Helsinki, including 12 municipalities. A total of approximately 1.2 million people live in the Helsinki metropolitan area (Figure 1). At the moment, the Helsinki region accounts for almost 25% of the national population (5.2 million).

The darkest colored area in Figure 1 is our study area. This metropolitan core has great economic and social impact over a large area. The functional urban areas of Hämeenlinna, shown also on the map of Figure 1, and Lahti (middle-sized cities with 50 000 to 100 000 inhabitants) are included under the definition of the "greater Helsinki region". Thus, they are considered to be under the economic influence of the Helsinki metropolitan area and region. The greater Helsinki region is not an official regional category and it should be considered as a political construction proposed by local municipality executives.

Viewed from European core cities such as London and Paris, the location of Helsinki has been remote. However, the perception of Finland and Helsinki as being on the Nordic periphery has gradually changed from the beginning of the 1990s. The development of communication technologies and modern transport infrastructure allowed distances to diminish in terms of networking and communication. In addition, Finland's location, close to newly established markets of Russia, Poland and the Baltic states, gave (and still gives) locational advantages e.g. in transport logistics and Asian-Europe air-passenger traffic. At the time of the global political changes of the early 1990s, Finland was also hit by severe economic crises in 1990–1991. The subsequent recession is regarded as the worst in OECD countries after World War II. Kautto et al. (2001) showed in their empirical analysis that the Nordic welfare-model adapted rather well to the changing economic circumstances. The severe recession created a motivation for the national administration to rethink its future direction in the development of knowledge society policies and practices.

Policy Options for Knowledge-Based Development in Helsinki

The Helsinki metropolitan area is a unique regional entity in Finland due to its size and economic importance. This means that the relation between national and local policies is problematic. Thus, national policies, such as newly established urban policy, deal to a large extent with the development of the metropolitan area. Moreover, the challenge for national strategies and policies is to find a balance between global networks and local places – the distinction of places of flows and places of places – depicting a well-known schematic of Castells (1996). This refers on the one hand to the status of the Helsinki metropolitan area with respect to global competition and on the other hand to the dispersed and diversified regional needs of Finland. The Helsinki metropolitan area has been one of the fastest growing regions in Europe during recent decades. The European Economic Research Consortium (ERECO) has recently compared 45 major urban areas in western and central Europe (City of Helsinki 2006). They concluded, that in the second half of the 1990's Helsinki was among the three fastest growing cities of the 45 with respect to population, employment and GVA (gross value added) growth.

Urban development policies commonly aim to enhance the characteristics of urban cores to compete on a global level. Finland has not been a frontrunner. For example, Kähkönen (2005) writes that as late as 2005 the issue of urban policy in Finland, referring to Helsinki, was very much an "open question" even though urban development was mentioned in the Finnish Government Programme already in 2003. The long tradition of balancing regional policy has resulted in a lack of policies supporting strong urban regions. Therefore, there has not been an "official" urban policy that would clearly state the support actions for growth areas. In practice, the urban policy is based on co-operation between the six largest cities (Helsinki, Espoo, Vantaa, Tampere, Turku and Oulu) that together started the so-called six-pack co-operation in 2002.

Kähkönen (2005: 8) writes that there are three major collaborative organs in the Helsinki metropolitan area. One of them is driven by the Ministry of the Interior as a part of broader regional policy guidance, the second one is based on the cooperation between the four cities of the metropolitan area and the third one is the cooperation agreement among the 14 municipalities of the Helsinki region. Similarly, Karvinen (2005: 12) identified two major strategy lines for regional governance in the Helsinki metropolitan area. The first is to unite the four municipalities (or more surrounding municipalities) into a single administrative entity. The second option would be to make a national law concerning decision making and service provision. The issue is problematic because of the long tradition of municipal self-governance that leads to conflict of interests between the whole entity (metropolitan area and surrounding region) and single municipalities. The same phenomenon is evident also on larger spatial scales, for example in the European Union. With this recognition Karvinen concludes by suggesting network-based governance for the Helsinki region as whole.

The recognition of the need for urban policy has also started to have visible results at least to some extent. For example, the capital area has a specific urban program that implements joint development projects in the region and develops cooperation procedures amongst its cities and towns. The initial "Urban Programme" was executed in 2002–2004 with an aim to strengthen the knowledge intensiveness, competitiveness and citizen participation. The program was started by an agreement between the Mayors of the four cities forming the metropolitan area (Karvinen 2005).

In the pursuit of knowledge-based regional development, local efforts are generated by public-private partnerships. A good example of such a partnership in the Helsinki region is Culminatum Ltd, which is owned by the three major cities of the metropolitan area (Helsinki, Espoo and Vantaa), the Uusimaa Region Council, universities and other public and private sector organizations. Culminatum executes and manages local development programmes. Considering local strategies implemented during the last ten years, perhaps the most relevant regional development document is the innovation strategy for the Helsinki region published by Culminatum (2005). It presents a "four-pillar strategy" that is built on the following regional areas of emphasis:

1) Improving the international appeal of research and expertise
2) Reinforcing knowledge clusters and creating common development platforms
3) Reform and innovations in public services
4) Support for innovative activities

The strategy (2005: 4) states that the development of the Helsinki metropolitan region will determine the competitiveness of the whole country. The strategy can be regarded as a "typical" development document that provides more general guidelines than practical implementation tools. Thus, the strategy refers to the need for urban policy tools to strengthen the growth of the capital region. The four points presented show the key areas that the strategy is focused on. Essentially, the international appeal and the role of knowledge intensiveness are clearly presented. Reference has been made to national innovation systems and to the need to reform of public service provision.

Another political elite consortium is the Helsinki Metropolitan Area Advisory Board, which presented a vision scheme for the Helsinki metropolitan area (Appendix 1). The vision supports the Culminatum innovation strategy. The vision formulates development targets for the region's co-operative organizations and community structure. The aim is to ensure balanced growth of population and jobs, to supplement the community structure and to create sustainable development. The main objective is to promote a functionally-mixed urban networked structure, and at the same time create the conditions for a high quality of life (also YTV 2003).

An example of an actualized innovation platform in the Helsinki metropolitan area is a "science corridor" that is discussed by the OECD (2003: 65) in a territorial report concerning Helsinki. The traditional university institutions were regarded as nodes of the corridor system within the metropolitan area. The science corridor includes several nodes based on the expertise of educational units. For example, the engineering node is the Helsinki University of Technology located in Otanniemi, Espoo, the medical node is Meilahti (the medical faculty of the University of Helsinki), the social sciences and humanities are located in the centre of Helsinki, natural sciences in Kumpula, agriculture and forestry in Viikki and arts and design in Arabianranta

The Helsinki metropolitan area strategy includes a total of 26 action proposals targeted to increase competitiveness and economic performance in a knowledge-based economy. Proposed actions include issues of organizational co-operation both on vertical and horizontal axes, internationalization and increasing international contacts world-wide, and the role of universities as engines of knowledge creation.

The goals and vision of the strategy can be evaluated according to thesis of Hautamäki (2007: 25) who discusses the relationships between innovation creation and city business development. Hautamäki suggests that Culminatum could be developed as an even stronger organization for regional co-operation. He also sees that a particular entrepreneur forum should be created as a tool to aid business development (also Holstila 2007). Hautamäki presents quite similar tools in the pursuit of regional development to those presented in the Culminatum innovation strategy. He states (2007: 26) that the business development of the city of Helsinki should be targeted especially to creative industries. This illustrates an important connection between public authorities and the private sector.

STATISTICAL EVIDENCE

Statistical characteristics of knowledge industries in the Helsinki metropolitan area

In the following we will move to assess statistical evidence that has been selected in order to represent the condition of "knowledge intensive" industries. Furthermore, industrial structure in Finland has traditionally relied on two major branches, metal engineering and forestry. Since the emergence of Nokia, the world's leading mobile phone manufacturer, a new information and communication (ICT) -based growth sector was born. The impact of the ICT sector has mainly concerned the stock market values of Finnish companies and economic indicators. The ICT sector has contributed significantly to value-adding of the gross domestic product (GDP). Employment figures, the number of employed persons and jobs, are however relatively low compared to the value-adding. The ICT industry can be regarded as a dynamic sector and due to global market pressures, technology companies are in a better position to streamline their operations in the search for efficiency compared with traditional industries having more traditional and hierarchical structures.

The first question of our chapter is answered by looking at the employment statistics collected from the municipalities that collectively form the Helsinki metropolitan area. We use categories that are entitled "creative industries" and "knowledge-intensive industries", which are selected from SIC industrial codes. They exemplify similar industries used by Florida (2002). We present only the most important sectors in terms of growth in 1998–2006 and total employment in Figure 2, which shows sectors employing more than 10 000 workers.

In total, the largest sector is software consultancy and supply. It had almost 17 500 positions in the metropolitan area in 2006. These are the latest official figures currently available. The employment levels indicate that there are four major fields of creative and knowledge-intensive industries: 1) manufacturing of technology (televisions, radios and mobile devices), 2) related software consultancy and supply, 3) legal and financial services and 4) the education sector. Together these fields provide jobs for more than 65 000 people. These segments form the core of knowledge-based development in the Helsinki metropolitan area.

Another influential aspect of development is the growth of industries. There are considerable differences in total growth rates. Software consultancy and supply has experienced the greatest growth. Therefore, it is perhaps the most important single industry. There are two clear groups: industries that have experienced extensive growth and industries that have experienced a state of stagnation. Major growth figures are marked with color in Figure 2.

ICT industries, including manufacturing, consultancy and telecommunications form the most important industrial segment in the Helsinki metropolitan area's economic profile. Suokas has compared the regional economy of Helsinki with other European cities. He provides a description of the service sector structure in Helsinki, which he finds relatively close to the general European average (Suokas 2005: 9). However, there are differences. The relative size of the transportation sector is seven percent higher in Helsinki than the European corresponding average. In addition, the relative size of the financial sector is four percent lower in Helsinki than the European average. The Helsinki metropolitan area requires "new, strong industrial clusters to complement the modern ICT cluster and traditional industries and thereby diversify its economic base" (Suokas 2005: 20). Thus, the importance of the ICT sector in the knowledge-intensive industries is highlighted and also the volatility of the global ICT markets recognized.

Figure 2 shows also the dot-com boom of the ICT sector in the early part of the current decade. The balancing period after 2001 is clearly visible. The ICT sector lost jobs after the peak but the

Figure 2. The total number of jobs and growth rates of the most important branches of creative and knowledge-based industries in the Helsinki metropolitan area 1998–2006. Source: Statistics Finland 2009

Creative industries: the most important sectors in employment

	1998	1999	2000	2001	2002	2003	2004	2005	2
722 Software consultancy and supply	8749	10547	13584	15113	14761	14349	14966	16042	17
742 Architectural and engineering activities and related technical consultancy	12601	13572	13889	14110	14154	14510	14151	14009	14
524 Other retail sale of new goods in specialized stores	11100	11767	12276	12717	12758	13287	13494	14289	15

Knowledge-based industries: the most important sectors in employment

	1998	1999	2000	2001	2002	2003	2004	2005	2
322 Manufacture of television and radio transmitters and apparatus for line telephony and line telegraphy	8541	9757	10673	11988	11433	10679	10693	10917	11
65 Financial intermediation, except insurance and pension funding	12405	12418	12527	12637	12879	12272	12311	12212	13
741 Legal, accounting, book-keeping and auditing activities; tax consultancy, market research and public opinion polling, business and management consultancy	13231	14709	16394	16422	16432	15362	13069	13958	14
803 Higher education	10011	10103	11013	11503	12772	12907	13234	12631	12

recovery took place from 2004 onwards. The most constant growth has been in the higher education sector. Growth has been steady and it has become almost as an important employer as the finance sector, which is the only sector that has experienced stagnant growth in employment. Explanatory factors underlying these development trends are related to structural changes in the economy, thus to pressure from global markets and related streamlining of companies. The finance sector is a clear example of the results of adoption of new technologies. The internet has changed the general way of banking considerably and the reduced need for front-desk services also shows in the total job position numbers (also Vesala 2001).

Another measure of the condition of knowledge intensiveness is GVA to national economy. In Figure 3 we present the relative importance of the ICT sector to the Finnish economy. Figure 3 also shows the importance of selected benchmark industries. We selected paper and pulp production, metal production and chemistry because they are traditional industrial segments for the production of national wealth.

Figure 3 illustrates changes taking place within the national economy of Finland. First, the broadly defined ICT sector provides almost a tenth of national GDP. The largest branch of the ICT segment is manufacturing, in which the predominant business, mobile phone manufacturing, is also included. Second, the old cornerstone of the Finnish economy, paper production, has decreased considerably. An essential factor has been a total growth of the Finnish economy. It has constantly exceeded the European average. The third conclusion that can be drawn is that the ICT sector, either summed together or treated as segments, has become a major component of the Finnish national economy.

The Helsinki metropolitan area and surrounding region is the driving motor of the national economy, particularly in the case of knowledge intensiveness. For example, the Helsinki region accounts for 41.7 percent of national research and development expenditures in 2006. This amounts to 2.4 billion Euros. This figure is 2.5 times higher than the second place R&D region, Tampere. Therefore, regional differences in R&D are great in Finland and this differentiation is the main challenge in the search for a balance between regional (dispersive) and urban (concentrative) policies.

Figure 3. The development of value adding to GDP of selected knowledge-intensive industries in Finland 1998–2006 with comparative data from other major Finnish industries. Source: Statistics Finland 2009

RELATIVE IMPORTANCE IN VALUE ADDING	1998	1999	2000	2001	2002	2003	2004	2005	2006
0 All sectors together (Finland)	100 %	100 %	100 %	100 %	100 %	100 %	100 %	100 %	100 %
32 Manufacture of television and radio transmitters and apparatus for line telephony	3,54 %	4,37 %	5,20 %	4,16 %	4,88 %	4,79 %	4,23 %	4,11 %	4,32 %
642 Telecommunications	1,81 %	2,15 %	2,38 %	2,67 %	2,86 %	2,83 %	2,79 %	2,28 %	2,18 %
72 IT services: hardware consultancy, data processing, maintanance and other computer services	1,38 %	1,51 %	1,53 %	1,85 %	1,75 %	1,75 %	1,92 %	2,00 %	2,01 %
ICT sector combined	**6,72 %**	**8,03 %**	**9,11 %**	**8,68 %**	**9,49 %**	**9,37 %**	**8,94 %**	**8,39 %**	**8,50 %**
COMPARATIVE DATA FROM OTHER MAJOR INDUSTRIES									
21 Production of paper, mass and pulp	4,21 %	4,24 %	4,75 %	4,58 %	3,84 %	3,30 %	3,15 %	2,60 %	2,80 %
29 Machinery production	2,96 %	2,61 %	2,76 %	2,90 %	2,59 %	2,60 %	2,65 %	2,78 %	2,77 %
DG Production of chemicals and chemistry	1,56 %	1,56 %	1,34 %	1,45 %	1,32 %	1,30 %	1,46 %	1,45 %	1,41 %

Higher Education in the Helsinki Metropolitan Area

The educational system plays the essential role in the creation of knowledge. The role of universities is undeniable, particularly in a knowledge-based society. The Helsinki metropolitan area has several well-known universities including the University of Helsinki, Helsinki University of Technology, Helsinki School of Economics and the University of Art and Design Helsinki that are located in the metropolitan area. The two first are consistently ranked among the top 500 universities in the world according to the Shanghai ranking. The University of Helsinki is the highest ranking Finnish university, occupying position 68 in 2007. Among European universities its position is 19th. Helsinki University of Technology ranks among positions 402–503 globally (Shanghai Jiao Tong University 2008).

Educational policy has also followed the general welfare state policy. All citizens should have the possibility to obtain an education on all levels regardless of social background. Another administrative imperative during the last decade highlighted the importance of education. This is evident when reading sector strategies produced by ministries (e.g. Ministry of Education 2003; Ministry of Trade and Industry 2007; Ministry of Transport and Communication 2007). A high level of education and knowledge-intensive occupations with competence are widely used mantras to envision the survival of the Finnish economy in the global competition. In the following, we present statistics of tertiary education in the Helsinki metropolitan area (Table 1).

Table 1 is straightforward to read and it gives a statistical answer to our second question. First, the expansion of graduates is significant. This reflects educational policy having a goal to educate some 50% to 70% of an age cohort with tertiary education. The current situation in the Helsinki metropolitan area is rather good in comparison to other European cities of similar size. However, a central criticism has concerned maintenance of the quality of degrees. The amount of master degree and bachelor degree holders has expanded rapidly during the current decade. The amount of people with university degrees has increased rapidly in three large cities (Helsinki, Espoo and Vantaa) but has actually decreased in the small city of Kauniainen. The Helsinki metropolitan region had approximately 32 percent more highly educated people in 2007 than in 1998. Education levels have continued to grow after the observation period.

An interesting finding is that the relative amount of persons having a PhD degree has actually decreased between 1998–2007 compared to masters and bachelor degree holders. However, the number of PhDs has increased 31 percent during that period. This figure must be considered high

Table 1. Educational groups in the Helsinki metropolitan area according to municipalities 2007. Source: Statistics Finland 2009

Population by education in 2007									
	Polytechnic or bachelor degree			Masters degree			PhD or licentiate		
	Total	Men	Women	Total	Men	Women	Total	Men	Women
City	*Persons*								
Espoo	20658	9807	10851	32001	16777	15224	3858	2521	1337
Helsinki	47316	19560	27756	66419	31101	35318	8272	4987	3285
Kauniainen	791	408	383	1798	1000	798	255	153	102
Vantaa	14037	6441	7596	10905	5359	5546	988	611	377
TOTAL	82802	36216	46586	111123	54237	56886	13373	8272	5101

on all accounts. Among politicians the common argument to support continuing growth of PhD degree production is that the unemployment levels are lower than average for people with doctoral degree. According to the official employment statistics of Statistics Finland, 2.2 percent of PhD degree holders were unemployed in 2006. The corresponding overall unemployment figure was 7.7 percent. However, this argument ignores the costs and individual sacrifices that are commonly needed in order to pursue a degree. A comparison between persons with elementary education and persons with the highest academic education is also a debatable issue.

DISCUSSION AND FUTURE TRENDS

The Helsinki metropolitan area is one of the innovation centers ofNorthern Europe. The statistics presented here suggest that the Helsinki metropolitan area is mainly a technology-driven knowledge city that has good reserves for producing a highly educated workforce for the labor market. Factors such as services and employment opportunities also pull educated professionals from all parts of Finland to the metropolitan area. Majority of international migrants also take up residence in Helsinki metropolitan area. A competition factor for Finnish knowledge-intensive industries is that the Finnish salary levels of highly educated people are in general lower than in several other main competitor European countries (European University Institute 2008).

Finland has had a strong public sector interest in supporting potential growth companies with public sector financing. A pivotal instrument in the Finnish innovation system is TEKES (the Finnish funding agency for technology and innovation), which distributes funding based on competitive applications to private sector. Furthermore, considering our third question, the development paths of the knowledge-intensive industries discussed here are related to the economic success of private sector companies. A central concern regarding future development of the Finnish economy is the aging of the population and the subsequent imbalance between pensioners and the work force. The aging of the population is combined with the question of migration and need for international labor.

The Helsinki region adds one third to the total of the Finnish R&D expenditure (Inkinen 2005). Regional policy has traditionally emphasized balancing between regions and there has not been an urban policy to support growth nodes in global competition. However, the first collaborative efforts to initiate urban-driven development actions have emerged. A tool in this is the development of spearhead projects. Finland has a sophisticated innovation system that includes various actors from public and private sectors (Leppälahti 2000; Harmaakorpi 2006; Suorsa 2007). In addition, several mediating organizations and co-operation systems have been developed during the last 10 years. Finnish society is an example of the fact that a nation can recover relatively fast from a severe economic crisis if there is a political and economic will to drive the required changes. In the case of Finland the global success of Nokia has also made the recovery process easier.

The essential role of the Helsinki region for the whole country means challenges for regional and urban policy. Currently, regional disparities are increasing both in the terms of employment and income as our statistical data indicates (Tables 1 and 2). The situation means balancing the traditional goals of regional policy (all parts of the country equal) with global competitiveness (Helsinki area as the core). One of the key factors that have characterized the development of the Finnish knowledge economy is the ICT cluster. The presence of Nokia and its subcontracting network is a significant single factor affecting the whole economy. Specialization has also been seen as a source of vulnerability. Thus, the economy has been seen as too dependent on one industrial sector (also OECD 2003: 14).

There are several future challenges for research. The first is the societal impact that development actions have had. The projects are still running and there are no assessment materials available. In addition, in most cases, impact assessments are not easily available. The second is that impacts may also require a long time to become apparent and their identification can be difficult. The main point, however, is that creativity issues are on the agendas of cities and local development actors, and there is a considerable amount of work done on these issues.

Moreover, a third research challenge lies in the assessment of the problems presented. Suitable terminology should be developed further to provide a rigid platform for international comparisons. Currently, there are terminological confusions when the "creative knowledge regions" are approached. We consider that geographical concepts such as scale and location need more attention in the analyses and debates surrounding innovation and knowledge creation. In these debates, national and regional categories are usually employed. In order to cope with the dynamics of regional development and growth, it is important to have both a theoretical and empirical understanding of the spatial processes that are taking place in Finland and in Europe.

Future forecasts for Helsinki can be regarded as being positive. The examples presented suggest that Helsinki represents a modern Northern European middle-sized city with a well-trained labor force coupled to a sophisticated R&D environment (e.g. Laakso 2006). Finland has experienced a massive economic change towards an open, globally integrated and ICT- driven economy, together with political stability based on the Nordic welfare state model. This structural mix has led Manuel Castells and Pekka Himanen (2001) to conclude that a special model of an information society has developed in Finland (Vaattovaara & Kortteinen 2003).

CONCLUSION

This chapter presented key statistics and urban policy guidelines of the Helsinki metropolitan area. The metropolitan area vision takes up essential themes common in contemporary urban development efforts around the world. The condition of the environment, the development of land-use and planning for the increasing needs of businesses and inhabitants, and the balance between fragmented and overly compact structures are taken into account. In the case of Finland and Helsinki, welfare policies and creative urban (regional) development seem to support each other rather well. It must be noted that the majority of policies are co-operative efforts. Current co-operative models have a strong market orientation demonstrating a doctrine of new public management. However, the main lesson is that there is an increasing need for joint-project ventures between the public and private sectors.

Current urban development programs have started to recognize the importance of the Helsinki metropolitan area as an international node. Innovation strategy, regional business development, international business marketing and availability of skilled labor together comprise several essentials needed to be addressed by knowledge-driven urban policies. These include proper functioning of physical structures together with social and economic cohesion in various spatial scales. We consider that through these measures general guidelines for knowledge-based urban development are possible to create. This reflects theories of core-and-periphery interaction, in which the competitiveness of a regional core is vital to the entire national economy. Trickle down applies both in an economic and in a social sense. Coordinative and collaborative work over organizational borders is needed to support steady and balanced growth. This applies in Finland and Helsinki as well as other parts of the world.

REFERENCES

Ahlqvist, T., & Inkinen, T. (2007). Technology foresight in multiscalar innovation systems. A spatiotemporal process perspective. *Fennia*, *185*(1), 3–14.

Bathelt, H. (2005). Cluster relations in the media industry: Exploring the 'distanced neighbour' Paradox in Leipzig. *Regional Studies*, *39*(1), 105–127. doi:10.1080/0034340052000320860

Bell, M., & Hietala, M. (2002). *Helsinki, The Innovative City*. Helsinki, Finland: SKS.

Castells, M., & Himanen, P. (2002). *The Information Society and the Welfare State: The Finnish Model*. Oxford, UK: Oxford University Press.

City of Helsinki. (2006). The economic map of urban Europe. Helsinki in the European Urban Network. *Helsinki City Urban Facts Office: Web Publications, 2006*(39). Retrieved January 13, 2009, from http://www.eukn.org/binaries/finland/bulk/research/2007/2/06_12_21_economic_vj39.pdf

Conceição, P., & Heitor, M. V. (2007). Diversity and integration of science and technology policies. *Technological Forecasting and Social Change*, *74*(1), 1–17. doi:10.1016/j.techfore.2006.05.001

Culminatum. (2005). *Innovation Strategy. Helsinki Metropolitan Area*. Culminatum, Espoo. Retrieved August 15, 2008 from http://www.culminatum.fi/content_files/InnovationStrategy.pdf

Cumbers, A., Mackinnon, D., & Chapman, K. (2003). Innovation, collaboration, and learning in regional clusters: a study of SMEs in the Aberdeen oil complex. *Environment & Planning A*, *35*(9), 1689–1706. doi:10.1068/a35259

Ennals, R. (1987). Can skill be transferable? In Göranzon, B., & Josefson, I. (Eds.), *Knowledge, Skill and Artificial Intelligence* (pp. 67–75). London: Springer-Verlag.

Esping-Andersen. (1992). The three political economies of the welfare state . In Kolberg, J. E. (Ed.), *The Study of Welfare State Regimes* (pp. 92–123). New York: Sharpe.

European Social Report, T. Á. R. K. I. (2005). Chapter 3: Income distribution in European countries: first reflections on the basis of EU-SILC 2005. In *Community Statistics on Income and Living Conditions*. Budapest, Hungary: TÁRKI. Retrieved November 29, 2008, from http://www.tarki.hu/en/research/european_social_report/20080701_3.pdf

European University Institute. (2008). *MWP Academic Careers Observatory. Salaries.* Retrieved October 29, 2008, from http://www.eui.eu/MaxWeberProgramme/AcademicCareers/SalaryComparisons.shtml

Florida, R. (2002). *The Rise of the Creative Class and How It's Transforming Work, Leisure, Community and Everyday Life*. New York: Basic Books.

Florida, R. (2005). *The Flight of the Creative Class: The New Global Competition for Talent.* New York: Harper Collins.

Gylfason, T. (ed. 1997). The Swedish model under stress. A view from the stands. In SNS Economic Policy Group Report 1997, Stockholm, Sweden.

Haarmakorpi, V. (2006). Regional development platform method (RDPM) as a tool for regional innovation policy. *European Planning Studies, 14*(8), 1093–1112. doi:10.1080/09654310600852399

Hautamäki, A. (2007). Innovaatioiden ekosysteemi ja Helsingin seutu. Maailmanluokan innovaatioteknologian rakentamisen lähtökohta. *Tutkimuskatsauksia, 1.*

Heap, S., Hollis, M., Lyons, B., Sudgen, R., & Weale, A. (Eds.). (1992). *The Theory of Choice – A Critical Guide*. Oxford, UK: Blackwell.

Holstila, E. (2007). Finland: Towards urban innovation policy . In van den Berg, L., Braun, E., & van den Meer, J. (Eds.), *National Policy Responses to Urban Challenges in Europe* (pp. 125–144). Aldershot, UK: Ashgate.

Inkinen, T. (2005). European coherence and regional policy? A Finnish perspective on the observed and reported territorial impacts of EU research and development policies. *European Planning Studies, 13*(7), 1113–1121. doi:10.1080/09654310500242139

Kähkönen, L. (2005). *Suunta suomalaiselle kaupunkipolitiikalle*. Helsinki, Finland: Suomen Kuntaliitto.

Karvinen, M. (2005). Innovation and creativity strategies in Helsinki Metropolitan Area – Reinvention of regional governance. In *Proceedings of 41st ISoCaRP Congress 2005*, Bilbao, Spain.

Korpi, W., & Palme, J. (1998). The paradox of redistribution and strategies of equality: Welfare states institutions, inequality, and poverty in the Western countries. *American Sociological Review, 63*(5), 661–687. doi:10.2307/2657333

Leppälahti, A. (2000). Comparison of Finnish information surveys. *Science* [Statistics Finland, Helsinki]. *Technology Review, 2000,* 1.

Malmberg, M., & Powel, D. (2005). (How) do (firms in) cluster create knowledge? *Industry and Innovation, 12*(4), 409–431. doi:10.1080/13662710500381583

Ministry of Education. (2003). Ministry of Education Strategy 2015. *Publications of the Ministry of Education, 2003*(35).

Ministry of Trade and Industry. (2007). *Entrepreneurship policy during Prime Minister Matti Vanhanen's term of government 2003-2007: Entrepreneurship Policy Programme. Publications 11/2007.* Helsinki: Edita.

Ministry of Transport and Communication. (2007). *Transport 2030. Major challenges, new directions. Programmes and Strategies 2/2007.* Helsinki: Edita.

Nonaka, I., & Takeuchi, H. (1995) The Knowledge Creating Company. New York: Oxford University Press.

OECD. (2003). *Territorial Reviews, Helsinki, Finland.* Paris: OECD.

Park, S. O. (2001). Knowledge-based industry for promoting growth. In D. Felsenstein & M. Taylor (eds.): Promoting Local Growth. Process, Practice and Policy, 43–59. Aldershot, UK: Ashgate.

Schienstock, G. (2004). Learning competition and business restructuring in the enlarging EU. *European Journal of Vocational Training*, *33*(1), 23–29.

Shanghai Jiao Tong University. (2008). *Academic Ranking of World Universities.* Retrieved January 12, 2009, from http://www.arwu.org/rank2008/en2008.htm

Simmie, J. (2001). *Innovative Cities*. London: Spon Press.

Suokas, J. (2005). *Helsinki Regional Economy. A Dynamic City in the European Urban Network*. Helsinki City Urban Facts Office. Web publications 2005:41.

Suorsa, K. (2007). Regionality, innovation policy and peripheral regions in Finland, Sweden and Norway. *Fennia*, *185*(1), 15–29.

Vaattovaara, M., & Kortteinen, M. (2003). Beyond polarisation versus professionalisation? A case study of the development of the Helsinki region, Finland. *Urban Studies (Edinburgh, Scotland)*, *40*(11), 2127–2145. doi:10.1080/0042098032000123213

Vesala, J. (2001). *Technological Transformation and Retail Banking Competition: Implications and Measurement. Acta Universitatis Oeconomicae Helsingiensis A 184*. Helsinki: Helsinki School of Economics and Business Administration.

YTV. (2003). *Helsinki Metropolitan Area Vision 2025 – Summary*. Helsinki: Helsinki Metropolitan Area Council.

APPENDIX

Figure 4. Common vision for Helsinki metropolitan area. Source: Helsinki metropolitan area advisory board 2007. Retrieved 28.5.2009 from the Internet at http://www.hel2.fi/pks-neuvottelukunta/english/strategia_eng.pdf

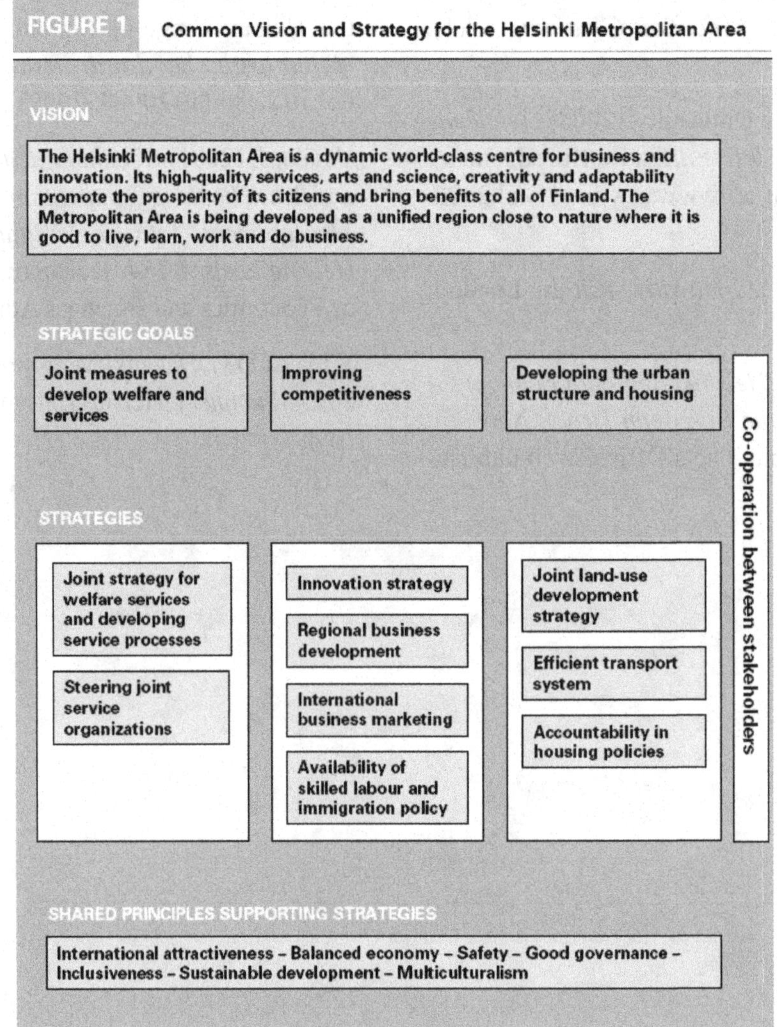

Chapter 13
The Role of the Built Environment in the Creation, Cultivation and Acquisition of a Knowledge-Base

Kristine Peta Jerome
Queensland University of Technology, Australia

ABSTRACT

This chapter explores the role of the built environment in the creation, cultivation and acquisition of a knowledge base by people populating the urban landscape. It examines McDonald's restaurants as a way to comprehend the relevance of the physical design in the diffusion of codified and tacit knowledge at an everyday level. Through an examination of space at a localised level, this chapter describes the synergies of space and the significance of this relationship in navigating the global landscape.

INTRODUCTION

This chapter explores a slice of an integrated multi-level approach of knowledge-based development through an examination of the built environment. Very little research has been directed at understanding the role of the built environment in sustaining everyday action at an everyday level (Franck, 1984; Stimson, 1986; Jobes, 1998; Jerome, 2007). Here, a particular setting is explored in order to comprehend the relevance of the physical domain in operating to create, transfer and use knowledge that appeals to a person in order to secure everyday action. In this instance the setting of McDonald's restaurants is used as a way to demonstrate the importance of micro-spaces in the maintenance of a global economy and how they diffuse codified and tactic knowledge at an everyday level. It does this by describing two different kinds of McDonald's settings. The descriptions illustrate the importance of the physical domain in constructing a common-sense world for participants to manage the task of consuming.

This exploration provides an opportunity to understand the relevance of the built environment in the creation of a knowledge-base at a micro scale. McDonald's restaurants are used as a case to describe this set of relations because these spaces have, and continue to dot the urban landscape across the globe. They are environments that are

DOI: 10.4018/978-1-61520-721-3.ch013

easily recognisable and accessed by a significant percentage of the world's population twenty-four hours a day. It is argued here that an examination of a slice of urban life at a micro scale provides a very interesting reflection of the role of the built environment in the generation and acquisition of a knowledge-base needed to navigate the world environment.

ENGAGING WITH MCDONALD'S RESTAURANTS: THE OLD FACE OF MCDONALD'S

It is at the site of McDonald's restaurants that the physical domain operates for a particular kind of consumer to engage in a particular act of dining with a particular set of products across the globe. Whilst McDonald's recognises that 'diversity' is a key method in its success, evidence suggests that comprehending the extent of diversification manifest in the built environment is crucial for maintaining economic security. This is why the physical environments of McDonald's restaurants have traditionally deviated very little across the globe (Bryman, 2003). They have manufactured and maintained a fast food restaurant 'script' to ensure a standard sequence of events occurs in each location across the globe (Abelson, 1981). The following description reflects the model of traditional McDonald's restaurants and the way the physical design emphasises activities and certain kinds of interaction suitable to the McDonald's experience. It illustrates a design formula intended to homogenise experience and meet the expectations of a clientele seeking the consumption of familiar fast food.

This description is a result of careful observation of a traditional McDonald's restaurant located in Kenmore, a suburb in Brisbane, Australia. The description highlights the way that the interior setting has been carefully planned to standardise experience and engage with the strategy of Westernisation. There are no surprises in this description and there are no surprises in the environment. The absence of surprise is important in enabling participants to engage with the fast food restaurant script with relative ease. This is a traditional McDonald's restaurant, typical of McDonald's restaurants that have populated the urban landscape of Australia.

Prior to entering McDonald's restaurant you are greeted with a square building supporting a tiered roof that supports signage of 'McDonald's'. The building is surrounded by a carpark and access for 'drive-through customers'. A main road sits immediately to the south of the restaurant and a small grassed area separates a footpath from this roadway. A tall yellow 'big M' is located on the grassed area – clearly visible to passing traffic and residents situated opposite the McDonald's restaurant. After moving through the carpark and upon entering McDonald's you are greeted by a tiled floor of muted browns and earth tones. This colouring is repeated on the vinyl panels that cover the wall to dado rail height. Straight ahead of the entrance is a wide corridor that leads directly to the service area. The granite service counter is easily recognizable with counter registers and overhead illuminated signage. This signage displays graphics of consumable items and pricing and, is positioned to the rear of this area. Behind the service area is the food preparation section, barely visible beyond the stainless steel dispensing items.

Situated perpendicular to the service area is another section nominated for the provision of coffee, teas and condiments. On this granite bench is a display cabinet with cakes, muffins and sweet biscuits. Behind the bench area overhead illuminated signage shows imagery of coffee mugs, cakes and milkshakes. In this area the lighting is notably softer - employing downlights as opposed to the fluorescent lighting used elsewhere. Adjacent to this area, in the centre of the restaurant, are timber and vinyl armchairs used for seating around fixed lowest granite tables. A dividing lowset wall of dark blue vinyl tiles and glass mosaic panels of bronze and navy tiles delineates this zone from the other 'less cosy' areas throughout the space.

On the opposite side of this lowest wall are fixed tables and chairs for dining. Here, there are two parallel rows of fixed rectangular tables with fixed stools. The tabletops are granite and the timber swivel stools allow for diners to sit in pairs or groups of four. This area overlooks a fenced and covered play area along with an outdoor eating area. Along the back wall of the restaurant, vinyl bench seating invites larger groups to partake in the ritual of dining. Adjacent to this area are clearly marked toilet facilities. These are serviced through an enclosed communal space, which is screened by glass doors. Throughout this entire space deep blue laminate panels cover the wall to picture rail height. Waste disposal bins are clearly labeled and located at various entrances. At the main entrance, waste disposal bins and fixed furniture housing serviettes, straws and so forth are positioned. These pieces are set beside bench seating which overlooks more outdoor seating. Loud music from the local radio station is consistent throughout the space.

As described here, an efficient thoroughfare, an easily identifiable and accessible service area along with predictable dining arrangements ensure that there are no surprises about the kind of interaction required to consume food and beverage. Different areas are clearly lit and the decor sits as a backdrop to the activities. The spatial environment is familiar and non-descript. This design formula fosters the easy consumption of food and beverage which are seen to be a reflection of a typical American diet. These characteristics remain fairly consistent in McDonald's settings in the hope of consumers recognising and responding to codified and tacit knowledge needed for the economic stability of McDonald's Corporation. Across the globe these kinds of spaces provide a strong script that is underpinned by the concept of 'sameness'. A particular code of conduct is successfully reinforced to ensure that the phenomenon of globalisation is entrenched on a daily basis. It is entrenched through the food and beverages which are accessed through clearly delineated activity zones in the built environment.

As previously highlighted it is at the site of McDonald's restaurants that the physical domain operates for consumers to engage in a particular act of dining with a particular set of products across the globe. It is argued here that the success of operations of McDonald's requires people to accept a code of conduct and acquire tacit knowledge in order to consume its products and comprehend just what the physical environment is attempting to do. Thus, participants must be willing to acquire a set of dispositions in order to act and think in a local context whilst drawing upon global forms of cultural knowledge. Settings that offer standardisation and predictability offer participants a comfort zone in a complex and challenging world.

ENGAGING WITH MCDONALD'S RESTAURANTS: THE NEW FACE OF MCDONALD'S

It is clear that McDonald's restaurants have successfully managed to codify tacit knowledge which is underpinned by codes of conduct founded on the American way of life. Particular built environments have been very important in instituting this code of conduct intent on homogenising experience. In the majority of cases these built environments have offered 'a slice of America'. What is interesting is that McDonald's is currently undergoing a major global change in the way it intends to codify tacit knowledge through the built environment. Across the globe all McDonald's restaurants are now being refurbished under the 'Forever Young Program'. The intention is to maintain existing clients whilst enticing new ones to contribute to the economic growth of the McDonald's Corporation. The description below reflects the model of the "Forever Young Program' McDonald's restaurants are being implemented across the globe. It illustrates a design formula quite different from the traditional one, intending to retain existing customer's familiar with the 'big M' whilst attracting new customers very familiar with the global environment. This new target group is representative of a different generation – one that sits very comfortably with the consumption of technology, media, travel and convenience – all offshoots of the social institution of globalisation and connected to knowledge networks.

The following description is a result of careful observation of a newly built McDonald's restaurant located on the fringes of Sydney's domestic airport in Australia. The description highlights the way that the built environment has again been carefully planned to ensure an experience based on consumption in the global economy. There are many surprises in this description and there are many surprises in the environment. This is a new model of McDonald's restaurant, non-typical of McDonald's restaurants that have traditionally populated the urban landscape of Australia and the rest of the world. This new model challenges the knowledge-base of patrons familiar with the traditional model of standardisation because there is very little that is standard about this space and much of the 'fast food script' is obsolete. New and refurbished models challenge existing 'fast food restaurant scripts' thus disrupting the apparent order of things. The only guarantees are standard food and beverages but even the way these are accessed differs from traditional models.

Prior to entering McDonald's restaurant you are greeted with a red and brown rectangular structure punctuated by white and timber protrusions, which bears no familiar trademarks of traditional environments associated with McDonald's Corporation. A small yellow 'M' that sits on a red vertical wall projecting above the flat roofline is the only indication that this structure is a McDonald's restaurant. The exterior is streamlined, clad in timber and large sections of sheeting coloured in dark grey, red and white. Expanses of glass and timber shade structures frame the building which is surrounded by a carpark and access for 'drive-through customers'. This area is surrounded by main roads heading to Sydney domestic airport. One arterial road runs parallel to it, and this is where cars access the carpark and drive-through facilities.

After moving through the carpark and upon entering McDonald's you are greeted by a tiled floor of mottled terracotta tiles of muted grey tones. Slated timber panels, suspended lighting and bulkhead details denote various zones. Large tabletops are precisely positioned in the centre of the space and are made of freestanding reconstituted stone in tones of white. Loose vinyl ottoman's surround these tables. These are finished in the colours of burgundy and dark grey and they offer an interesting contrast to the large fixed tables. Bench table tops are fixed to the large expanses of glass that run along the periphery and here, timber stools are used for seating. Suspended lighting hangs over the large central tables and spotlights are used elsewhere. Beyond this central area is a small section designated for bench seating. It can comfortably seat eight people and is positioned near a side entrance. This particular area operates as an alcove and is highlighted by a red bulkhead and dividing wall, along with timber paneling. These features offer privacy from the central corridor and side entrance. Immediately behind this area is a section for dispensing softdrinks. A large wall expanse with Warhol style graphics sits beyond the drink dispensing area and adjacent to a contained room for birthday parties. Behind this area the toilets are discretely housed.

It is beside the area designated for dispensing drinks that a small service counter is located. This is not visible from the main entrance and only partially visible from the side entrance. Two cash registers are located on the service counter and a small suspended graphics panel sits in front of the kitchen preparation area. The illuminated panel illustrates a small selection of food and beverages. Prior to arrival at the service counter a series of freestanding and wall mounted 'technology pods' are positioned for easy ordering. Their positioning in front of the small service counter reinforces that this method is a preference for ordering products. Clientele engage with flat screens to select their food and beverage, pay by plastic and then collect their order at the counter. This process means that the service counter operates predominantly as a collection point for orders not as an ordering facility. This area is separated from the main restaurant through vertical and horizontal timber screening that shields booth seating and café patrons.

A large red bulkhead and reconstituted stone counter sits to the right of the main entrance and opposite central seating. This marks the café zone. The service area of the café houses a display cabinet with cakes, muffins and sweet biscuits. It also houses a large coffee machine. A small alcove sits between the counter area and a large expanse of window. This is used for more intimate seating and overlooks the carpark. Bench seating and loose chairs populate the rest of the area designated as the café. Timber sheeting frames the booth seating and acts as a buffer wall to the main corridor. A flat screen television is suspended from the bulkhead in this area, matching the wall-mounted flat screens located in the central seating area. Below these flat screens fitted waste disposal bins are located – discretely flush mounted in the wall paneling and framing large expanses of windows that overlook a screened outdoor seating area. These outdoor areas are large exterior corridors that integrate glass paneling, timber cladding and reconstituted stone with outdoor furniture in a streamlined and linear manner. A section of this exterior area provides views into the indoor party room – which protrudes from the main body of the building and shelters the side entrance. A corner window offers party goers views to the outside area. There is no noticeable music throughout the space.

As previously noted it is at the site of McDonald's restaurants that the physical domain operates for consumers to engage in a particular act of dining with a particular set of products across the globe. Historically, the success of operations of McDonald's has relied upon people accepting a code of conduct and acquiring tacit knowledge in order to consume products whilst comprehending what the physical environment is attempting to do. A fast food script has been offered and followed for generations. As illustrated however, the slick and sophisticated physical domain now operates to service and entice a broader spectrum of consumers who are and will draw upon global forms of cultural knowledge in order to navigate the built environment. In the case of recently refurbished and purpose built McDonald's restaurants this knowledge is underpinned by codes of conduct founded on a global way of life – one framed by consumption, technology, travel, mobility and convenience. In these settings the physical domain operates for consumers to go about their daily business with relative ease. It is the *daily business* of consumers that McDonald's restaurants are now catering for and the physical design is a reflection of this. Arguably, McDonald's Corporation is now servicing a 'mixing of urban activities' through its restaurants (Gencel & Velibeyoglu, 2006, p3). That is, the built environment not only presents opportunities for dining but now offers scenarios for lounging, engaging with technology, meeting with colleagues and other activities that are standard in the lives of a generation that consume technology, media, travel and convenience. It is argued that this new direction is more clearly aligned with the ever-changing social institution of globalisation and relies more heavily on connections to knowledge networks.

KNOWLEDGE AND MICRO SPACES

At a micro scale McDonald's restaurants are indicative of the significance of the built environment in the creation and recreation of knowledge needed to inform daily practice. In these settings Westernisation has been packaged and consumed with relative ease since the mid-twentieth century. The role of the interior and exterior setting has been crucial in establishing and maintaining economic development. The physical domain has also been very important in the creation of a global corporation. It is through the use of codified and tactic knowledge that the American lifestyle has been captured and represented for all to consume through the dining experience at McDonald's. Codified knowledge is defined here as knowledge that is possible to "record or transmit in symbols such as words, drawings or other technical specifications, or that is manifested in some type of concrete form such as a piece of machinery or equipment" (Zook, 2004, p621). It is argued that the physical domain of McDonald's restaurants operates to sustain a codified knowledge that is underpinned by principles of consumerism and informed by the institution of globalisation. It is at the micro level - the physical environment – that the creation and transferral of knowledge about the way to engage with this global setting is managed. Here, the production of an efficient and predictable space that distributes predictable food leads to a predictable experience. In the case of McDonald's restaurants the physical domain has historically clustered activity zones such as dining/servicing and has used non-descript fittings and fixtures and furniture that are functional and forgettable. This process of standardisation means that an encounter with 'sameness' is ensured and the 'fast food script' is operationalised. In this instance, the physical domain reproduces codified knowledge about what to do in any location across the world. This approach has traditionally strengthened economic growth and perpetuated the social institution of globalisation.

When engaging with McDonald's restaurants the provision of a space that operates to standardise the 'act of dining' and homogenisation experience is also critical in the generation of tacit knowledge. Unlike codified knowledge, tacit knowledge is not easily captured in a transferrable form such as the 'big M' synonymous with the McDonald's experience. Tacit knowledge is acquired through experience, be it interaction or observation (Zook, 2005). Inkpen & Ramaswamy (2005) write that "...tacit knowledge is intuitive and unarticulated and not capable of being verbalized". It is knowledge that has been transformed into habit and made traditional, in the sense that it becomes "... the way things are done around here." (p.110). Tacit knowledge is "a form of knowledge that is highly personal and context specific and deeply rooted in individual experiences, ideas, values and emotions" (Gourlay, 2002 in Irick (2007, p.9). In the case of McDonald's, the production of a standard global environment operates to ensure that a standard experience is maintained across the globe. This set of conditions leads to the generation of tacit knowledge. Innovation in the built environment has been quite limited since the mid-seventies leading to a uniform experience of McDonald's and this kind of experience has propagated the embodiment of tacit knowledge by consumers.

Uniformity in the built environment means that consumers are exposed to few surprises and subsequently, they come to expect and rely upon a particular kind of experience when inhabiting McDonald's restaurants. These standardised spaces provide a script – a canvass for interaction - for consumers to learn a particular code of conduct relevant to the global corporation of McDonald's. In these micro spaces tacit knowledge is generated through uniformity and consistency and, it is this formula that has enabled McDonald's to maintain a competitive edge in a globalised economy.

CREATING A NEW KNOWLEDGE-BASE, THE RELEVANCE OF SPACE AND THE DEVELOPMENT OF A CULTURAL HABITUS

The contrast between traditional McDonald's restaurant design models and models reflecting the 'Forever Young Program' is vast. Efficiency is still prevalent but the interaction is not conducive to the experience of homogenisation. The spatial environment is unexpected and it is here that the relevance of previously acquired tacit knowledge is greatly tested. This is because patrons who have frequented traditional models are challenged by an environment that does not provide a recognisable canvass for the cultural habitus to respond to. Instead, it relies upon codified knowledge sustained only through branding and the supply of standard food and beverages. Only this codified knowledge assists participants in knowing what to do.

New restaurant models require *all* consumers to learn another code of conduct in order to navigate the space with relative ease and consume products and a lifestyle partnered with globalisation. Refurbished and newly built restaurants employ 'difference' in order to maintain competitive in a global market place. They also operate to facilitate many different kinds of interaction. The way 'difference' is manifest through the built environment means that participants must 'upgrade' or acquire a cultural habitus that is cognisant of global knowledge and knowledge networks in order to interact and find their raison d'être.

The success of the McDonald's Corporation is again heavily reliant upon daily interaction fostered by the built environment. The built environment must provide a set of conditions that enables tacit knowledge to be transferred into codified knowledge then become embodied and part of the cultural habitus of many participants. The challenge here is that McDonald's restaurants no longer subscribes to a formula of standardisation in order to homogenise experience. There are no longer clearly defined zones of activities to navigate – the servery zone, the dining zone, the play zone and so forth – furnished with durable and non-descript finishes and fixtures. Instead, heterogeneity is injected in the hope of captivating new consumers and retaining old ones. The process of separating functions is blurred and new restaurants operate to assist in the operation of many activities through many multi-purpose zones. What will become apparent over time is whether these new models can provide an acceptable script for the generation of a set of relations necessary for individuals to comprehend what is going on anywhere in the world whilst participating in the consumption of globalisation. This change in direction highlights the great importance of the built environment in the generation of a knowledge-base and the ability to navigate the urban landscape with relative ease. This shift also demonstrates how changes to everyday spaces can disrupt the generation and regeneration of knowledge needed to maintain interaction and the apparent order of things.

This is a dramatic change for the McDonald's Corporation. This change is a wonderful opportunity to further understand the role of the built environment in creating, transferring and using knowledge that appeals to people willing to engage in the urban landscape of everyday spaces. It provides a way to comprehend to what extent the built environment can be manipulated before knowledge required for interaction at an everyday level is lost.

THE IMPORTANCE OF A CULTURAL HABITUS

In order for McDonald's to operate in both the local and global arenas it must provide an environment that fosters the transferral of codified knowledge. This is risky because this process relies heavily on participants willingly engaging with a space where processes of Americanisation have been embedded in daily operations (Ritzer, 1993; 1996). These processes have clearly veer away from more traditional corporate business strategies of diversification (Laux, 2005; Triantis, 2005). This is because 'diversity' in the environment does not guarantee the homogenisation of experience which has been crucial for the transferral and embodiment of a knowledge-base needed to maintain the status quo at McDonald's. The transferral and embodiment of a knowledge-base enables participants to acquire a *cultural habitus* needed to recognise and reproduce a familiar experience anywhere in the world. This process is triggered by a formula of standardisation exemplified at the site of McDonald's. In this particular instance this process also equates with participants actively perpetuating the social phenomenon of globalisation (Ritzer, 1996).

Cultural habitus is a sociological concept that is used to unravel how biographical histories, informed predominantly by family and educational experiences, influence the way individuals participate in daily life and contribute to the construction of an ordered social world (Bourdieu, 1977, pp.72-95). More specifically, cultural habitus is a Bourdivian (1990; 2000) concept that is used to comprehend the way past and present experiences condition the way individuals engage with everyday life and comply with established orders. It provides an opportunity to explain, for instance, why people engage in social interaction in particular ways and often go to great lengths to perpetuate an established order rather than contest the daily rituals of a familiar social world. Thus, the embodiment of cultural and social experiences accounts for why individuals with a particular set of dispositions, are more likely to find their raison d'être in certain places and not in others. In this instance certain individuals with a particular habitus accept the logic of the space of McDonald's restaurants and subsequently contribute to the perpetuation of this little social world and the maintenance of order.

Clearly, as in the case of McDonald's restaurants, some spaces are very successful at providing an environment which appeals to a particular cultural habitus. A formula of standardisation that spans across its services, products and spaces generates a knowledge-base that is consumed by participants. On a micro scale McDonald's restaurants are very good examples of the way a formula setting and formula food and beverages attracts individuals that seek to engage with a 'fast food script'. In this instance, McDonald's Corporation has strategically provided a knowledge-base that is made possible through the multi-level provision of standardised products, including the built environment, in order to provide tacit and codified knowledge that is embodied by participants. Here, participants comply with a set of practices that operate to perpetuate globalisation. McDonald's is a classic case of globalisation and the use of tacit knowledge.

It is through an exploration of the micro components of the urban setting, as exemplified at the site of McDonald's restaurants, that it is possible to understand the relevance of the physical domain in granting people with the opportunity to explore and embody a knowledge-base necessary to navigate this complex world. Through participation in the standardised environments of McDonald's restaurants it is possible for participants to generate a cultural habitus that affords them with the ability to very quickly associate a space with a particular experience. Here, McDonald's restaurants provide a canvass for those who frequent it spaces with the acquisition of a knowledge-base needed to navigate the global environment. This knowledge-base contributes to the development of a cultural habitus, which makes it easy for people to recognise and re-recognise the kind of interaction needed to manage an urban setting.

As previously highlighted however, the built environment of all McDonald's restaurants are undergoing major refurbishments across the globe. Traditional 'canvasses' are being replaced. It is argued here that knowledge-bases acquired through exposure to traditional McDonald's restaurants will require upgrading in order for these participants to navigate refurbished settings with relative ease. In this instance, they will once again be relying upon codified knowledge to engage with this new kind of fast food restaurant experience and, over time, like new clientele, accept the new script and upgrade their cultural habitus in order to interact and manage this micro environment.

DISCUSSION

The success of operations of McDonald's has traditionally required participants to willingly acquire a set of dispositions in order to act and think in a local context whilst drawing upon global forms of cultural knowledge underpinned by the notion of homogenisation. Participants have been able to quite quickly comprehend what the physical environment is attempting to do in order to perpetuate codes of conduct founded on the American way of life. This process has relied heavily on the built environment for its success (Ritzer, 1993, 1998, 2001; Hamilton, 2003; Jerome; 2007). The new model of McDonald's restaurants steers away from the perpetuation of 'sameness' and embraces 'diversity' as a key method of economic growth. It also moves away from Americanisation. It is suggested however, that comprehending the extent of diversification manifest in the built environment is crucial for maintaining economic security. This is because all forms of 'diversity' do not guarantee the homogenisation of experience and this has underpinned McDonald's financial success to date (Bryman, 2003). More specifically, 'diversity' in the built environment challenges a powerful knowledge-base already acquired by many people exposed to the phenomenon of globalisation.

The extent to which this embedded knowledge-base is challenged and its consequences will be reflected through the daily interaction at McDonald's restaurants. The environments of newly refurbished and purpose built restaurants do not offer predictability but contest the traditional way things are done. Codified knowledge embedded in the 'big M' and standard food and beverage items are the only clues that give clientele the opportunity to engage with a script suitable for this setting. Difference and sophistication at this point do not lead to the generation of tacit knowledge, once transformed into codified knowledge and acquired by patrons with relative ease.

Different models of 'Forever Young' schemes also populate the globe whereby up to ten different refurbishment schemes are offered to each different country. This unprecedented level of 'difference' adds another layer of complexity in the provision of tacit knowledge and its transferral into codified knowledge and subsequent creation of a cultural habitus by McDonald's patrons. Perhaps the formula for the generation of a knowledge-base needed to navigate McDonald's restaurants will involve different components of the built environment and not its entirety. Alternatively, these new environments could demonstrate that clientele will easily consume heterogeneity thus reflecting the flexibility of the habitus and its ability to assimilate new forms and experiences in this global world. If successful the new model of McDonald's restaurants could be an example of the need to inject difference into franchised environments across the globe in order to assure a place in the global economy. These new models could provide a formula that responds very clearly to the diverse cultural texture and lifestyle options of people within cities across the world. If unsuccessful, the new model of McDonald's restaurants could demonstrate that restraint is needed in the injection of diversity in the built environment whereby strongly embedded expectations are so clearly challenged and the status quo is disrupted. These new models could be representative of the need for restraint in everyday spaces which are seen to contribute to the socio-cultural atmosphere of the urban landscape.

CONCLUSION

In this chapter McDonald's restaurants have provided an opportunity to describe the relationship between the built environment and the creation, transferral and use of knowledge needed to sustain daily interaction. They have highlighted the role of micro spaces in facilitating interaction between people with different knowledge-bases and described the way a socio-cultural atmosphere is generated at a localised level. Gencel & Velibeyoglu (2006) highlight worldwide trends in urban spaces and the increasing numbers of non-places that decrease interaction between people and the generation of mixed-use buildings intent on housing many activities. As demonstrated through an exploration of McDonald's restaurants these mixed-use places are no longer limited to shopping centres, airports, holiday villages and so forth, but are spilling into once contained settings such as restaurants. This chapter explores a place in the urban landscape at a micro scale in order to demonstrate shifting trends in the design of micro spaces and the relevance of the built environment in the creation, cultivation and acquisition of a knowledge-base needed to navigate urban landscapes. It looks very closely at the synergies of space because this provides an opportunity to understand the way the built environment perpetuates knowledge at an everyday level whilst responding to global cultural knowledge. This chapter raises questions about the degree of appropriateness of injecting change in the built environment and just how much diversity can be managed by participants in a complex global marketplace. It also highlights the importance of the physical domain in the creation of tacit knowledge and how fragile this relationship is.

REFERENCES

Abelson, R. (1981). Psychological Status of the Script Concept. *The American Psychologist, 36*(7), 715–729. doi:10.1037/0003-066X.36.7.715

Bourdieu, P. (1977). *Outline of a Theory of Practice*. Cambridge, MA: Cambridge University Press.

Bourdieu, P. (1990). *The Logic of Practice*. Stanford, CA: Stanford University Press.

Bourdieu, P. (2000). *Pascalian Meditations*. Cambridge, MA: Polity Press.

Bryman, A. (2003, October). McDonald's as a Disneyized Institution: Global Implications. *The American Behavioral Scientist, 47*(2), 154–167. doi:10.1177/0002764203256181

Franck, K. (1984). Exorcising the Ghost of Physical Determinism. *Environment and Behavior, 16*, 411–435. doi:10.1177/0013916584164001

Genzel & Velibeyoglu. (2006). Opportunities & Challenges . In *Public Spaces in the Information Age, 42nd ISoCaRP Congress 2006*. Reconsidering the Planning and Design of Urban Public Spaces in the Information Age.

Hamilton, C. (2001). The Triumph of Ideology: Environment . In Sheil, C. (Ed.), *Globalisation: Australian Impacts* (pp. 187–201). Australia: UNSW Press.

Inkpen, A., & Ramaswamy, K. (2006). *Global Strategy: Creating and Sustaining Advantage Across Borders*. New York: Oxford University Press.

Irick, M. (2007, September). Managing Tacit Knowledge in Organizations. *Journal of Knowledge Management Practice, 8*(3), 8–15.

Jerome, K. P. (2007). An Exploration of the Way the Physical Environment Perpetuates a Moral Code of Conduct Based on Relations of Control: A Case of the McDonald's Restaurant. In *Inhabiting Risk Ideas Conference Proceedings,* Wellington, New Zealand (pp. 71-80).

Jobes, P. (1988). Sociology and Architecture: Excursus and an Example of Planning in Yellowstone National Park. *Design in Education*, 7(2), 8–17.

Laux, C. (2005). Integrating Corporate Risk . In Frenkel, M., Hommel, U., & Rudolf, M. (Eds.), *Risk Management: Challenge and Opportunity* (pp. 437–454). New York: Springer.

Miles, S. (1998). McDonaldization Revisited: Critical Essays on Consumer Culture . In Alfino, M., Caputo, J., & Wynyard, R. (Eds.), *McDonalization and the Global Sports Store: Constructing Consumer Meanings in a Rationalized Society* (pp. 53–66). Santa Barbara, CA: Praeger Publishers.

Ritzer, G. (1993). *The McDonaldization of Society*. Thousand Oaks, CA: Pine Forge Press.

Ritzer, G. (1996). *The McDonaldization of Society* (Rev. Ed.). Thousand Oaks, CA: Pine Forge Press.

Ritzer, G. (1998). *Revolutionizing the Means of Consumption*. Thousand Oaks, CA: Pine Forge Press.

Ritzer, G. (2001). *Explorations in the Sociology of Consumption: Fast food, Credit Cards and Casinos*. London: Sage Ltd.

Stimson, G. (1986). Viewpoint: Place and Space in Sociological Fieldwork. *The Sociological Review*, *34*(3), 64–656.

Triantis, A. (2005). Corporate Risk Management: Real Options and Financial Hedging . In Frenkel, M., Hommel, U., & Rudolf, M. (Eds.), *Risk Management: Challenge and Opportunity* (pp. 591–608). New York: Springer.

Zook, M. A. (2004, September). The Knowledge Brokers: Venture Capitalists, Tacit Knowledge and Regional Development. *International Journal of Urban and Regional Research*, 621–641. doi:10.1111/j.0309-1317.2004.00540.x

Chapter 14
Using Communities of Practice to Share Knowledge in a Knowledge City

Sheryl Buckley
University of Johannesburg, South Africa

Apostolos Giannakopoulos
University of Johannesburg, South Africa

ABSTRACT

In the pre-industrial age, communities existed to connect people. People joined guilds to find mentors who would help them master their crafts. During the industrial revolution, workplace tasks were divided into small chunks to help employers define their employees' roles and responsibilities. With the advent of the knowledge worker, the workplace has undergone another transformation. Now, jobs that involve the most complex type of interactions make up the fastest-growing segments in many industries (Sauve, 2007). A 2005 McKinsey & Company report, titled 'The Next Revolution in Interactions,' examines how workplace tasks are completed in developed economies. It describes a shift from valuing transactional interactions, those that are routine and involve noncreative interaction, to complex interactions, those that require people to deal with ambiguity and solve problems based on experience or tacit knowledge. The phenomenon of the tacit worker is continuing to rise. Gartner, a research institute, estimates that the frequency of non-routine situations that require tacit knowledge will double between 2006 and 2010. The reality is that in many industries in which situations change rapidly, formal learning once or twice a year doesn't provide employees with the experience or knowledge they need to find ongoing success on the job. This means that organisations must revamp their budgets and shift their resources from formal learning settings to informal situations in which the majority of learning actually takes place. While the changing nature of work is central, it is important not to overlook technology trends and how they influence the expectations and requirements of workers. The rise of social computing based on highly innovative new Web 2.0 technologies such as MySpace.com, YouTube.com, Digg.com and Facebook.com, offers a new paradigm for how we approach learning and knowledge sharing and is beginning to have a powerful impact on corporate learning (Sauve, 2007). Business cultures are changing rapidly to take advantage of these new technologies. Today the concept of knowledge sharing through new interac-

DOI: 10.4018/978-1-61520-721-3.ch014

tive online tools is taking hold in more and more public and private organisations. The change from an industrial economy to a knowledge economy forced many organisations to change their modus operandi if they were going to survive in a sustainable way. The introduction of communities of practice (CoPs) by Lave and Wenger in 1991 shed new light on knowledge sharing and dissemination of information. Sharing, interacting, actively participating, collaborating and learning from one another become the central activities in a knowledge society. According to Wenger (1998), CoPs are everywhere. We all belong to a number of them – at work, at school, at home and in our hobbies. In this sense everyone has experienced a CoP. so it can be considered a common experience. Some have a name, some do not. We are core members of some and we belong to others more peripherally. CoPs are informal, naturally occurring, spontaneously evolving groups and the sense of community comes from defining them in terms of practice (Kubiak, 2003). When it comes to a formal CoP, be it face-to-face or virtual, its success or failure will depend on a number of factors. For this reason it is necessary to investigate its nature, functions, aims and reasons for existence. Then the true value of communities, both for the individual participants and the supporting organisation, will come from the ongoing interaction and work of the group. To sustain that value, organisations should quickly move into a sustaining-and-evolving mode to match ever-changing member needs and business goals (Vestal, 2006). In a knowledge based development approach to modern societies as suggested by Ergazakis, Metaxiotis & Psarras (2006), CoPs can be used as the originators of change and innovation for a 'knowledge city'. This chapter will address the role that CoPs can play in the development of a 'knowledge city'.

INTRODUCTION

In any developed or developing country the shift from the industrial era to one of knowledge era has reached a point of no return. It has become now common knowledge that the only way to prosperity of any nation is through the use of knowledge (explicit/hard or implicit/tacit/soft) which is possessed by people. This makes knowledge not only a valuable asset of an enterprise (Nonaka, 1991; Wiig, 1993; Ergazakis, Metaxiotis & Psarras, 2004; Polanyi, 1961) but a prerequisite to any form of change and innovation to a better future of all the citizens of the world. Gartner, a research institute, estimates that the frequency of non-routine situations that require tacit knowledge will double between 2006 and 2010. At the individual level, the "hard worker" is becoming a "smart worker" or a "knowledge worker". At organisational level, once it was realized that intangible assets (human, social, structural capitals) are the key to competitive advantage, organisations have been transformed to knowledge organisations, which necessitated management of knowledge. So the birth of knowledge management (KM) was eminent. In the societal level, the industrial society is changing rapidly to a knowledge society: one which places an explicit and principal value on knowledge as the means to achieve economic and social well being. It is one which features knowledge prominently among the basic needs of all of its citizens and wills all citizens to engage productively with knowledge. In such a society, knowledge represents a core national value: the means through which the citizens achieve (i) greater choice and opportunity (ii) deeper social integration and (iii) longer life expectancy, each across very many dimensions (Mallalieu, 2006). In the national level as more knowledge societies are formed the old industrial cities are transformed to "knowledge cities", where knowledge-based development (KBD) is developed. Carrillo (2002) suggests that KBD is a theoretical and technical field which itself derived from the convergence of a discipline and a movement. According to him, it has three levels: (1) social knowledge infrastructure; (2) human capital development; and (3) development of the social capital system. For Ergazakis et al (2004) "a knowledge city is a city that aims at a knowledge-based development, by encouraging the continuous creation, sharing, evaluation, renewal and update of knowledge." Such development could take place in two ways: a) by developing the individual to a knowledge worker and/or b) the city taking the initiative of becoming a knowledge city which can be achieved "through the continuous interaction between its citizens themselves and at the same time between them and other cities' citizens. The citizens' knowledge-sharing culture as well as the city's appropriate design, IT networks and infrastructures support these interactions" (Ergazakis et al,2004).

The success or failure to build a knowledge city then will depend on two important aspects: a) on the interactions between its citizens themselves and themselves and other cities. Globalisation necessitates such interactios; and b) on the knowledge sharing among them using IT networks and other infrastructures. This new society in a knowledge city then is built on knowledge as capital on the one hand and knowledge as a public good on the other; competitiveness on the one hand and community on the other, all fundamental parameters of a knowledge society. In the new society there are great opportunities: it can mean new employment possibilities, more fulfilling jobs, new tools for education and training, easier access to public services, increased inclusion of disadvantaged people or regions. For Tanedu (2007) a knowledge society is one that creates, shares, and uses knowledge for the prosperity and wellbeing of its people. It is a society where people associate formally having similar interests, who try to make effective use of their combined knowledge about their areas of interest and in the process, contribute to this knowledge (Tanedu, 2007).

However, interactions between people and sharing of their knowledge could happen by mutual need, a mutual goal, a mutual enterprise where they all benefit and more ideally in a voluntary manner. This ideal situation gave rise to Communities of Practice (CoPs), a group of people who share their knowledge voluntarily and they are all active participants. This chapter will address briefly knowledge sharing in a KBD and in detail the role that CoPs play in achieving KM objectives of a "knowledge city" in its narrow sense and the objectives of a "global city" in its broader sense. Existing literature does not address CoPs in the context of a "knowledge city". The authors argue that CoPs can "fill the gaps" in knowledge sharing between the K-agents in implementing KBD policies. Ergazakis, Metaxiotis and Psarras (2006) argue that for KBD policies to be successful "one major challenge is to democratise the processes through which knowledge is created, stored, shared and used in order to ensure the broad participation of the global population in these KM processes." It will be shown that the promotion of CoPs in any organisation, encouragement of CoPs among organisations (locally and globally) is a way (if not the only way) of overcoming the obstacles of the fast changing society and maximize the management of knowledge and subsequent use of it for the prosperity of the organisation and thus of the society as knowledge is a powerful lever in the fight against poverty. The knowledge economy is an opportunity for emerging countries and for their people's welfare.

In a CoP, irrespective of the number of members, knowledge occupies its core business and sharing of such knowledge in a voluntary manner dictates the modus operandi of its members. This paper aims at shedding some light into the role that CoPs can play in the development of a "knowledge city".

KNOWLEDGE, KNOWLEDGE SHARING, KNOWLEDGE CREATING

The role of knowledge (as compared with natural resources, physical capital and low-skill labour) has taken on greater importance. Although the pace may differ, the Organisation for Economic Co-operation and Development (OECD) economies are all moving towards a knowledge-based economy (Smith, 2000 cited by Ergazakis *et al*, 2006). Moreover, Drucker (1998) suggests that "knowledge is now becoming the one factor of production, sidelining both capital and labor." As indicated by Ergazakis *et al* (2006), knowledge sharing is a one of the prerequisites in a knowledge-based developing society if a "knowledge city" is to be developed. But knowledge sharing as an end to itself will not derive the desirable results as knowledge is dynamic and progress of a society depends on change and innovation; and innovation implies creation of new knowledge. Metaxiotis, Ergazakis and Psarras (2005) make this clear when they state that "in the context of the knowledge-based economy, individuals and companies are obliged to focus on maintaining and enhancing their knowledge capital in order to innovate. Their ability to learn, adapt and change, becomes a core competency for survival." Based on Ergazakis *et al* (2004) idea of the "knowledge city" knowledge sharing implies also knowledge creating as a result of knowledge sharing.

'Knowledge' is a complex concept and there is a tendency to be confused with 'information.' Very often information is 'confused' with knowledge and as a result knowledge and information tend to be used interchangeably. This confusion also led to the use of the words "information management" and "knowledge management" interchangeably. Many authors (Bellinger, 2004; Firestone, 1998; Barclay & Murrray, 1997; Polanyi, 1961; Davenport & Prusak, 1998) have formulated their own working definitions which were context dependent. For this study a more generic working definition will be used which suits the KBD perspective. That is, knowledge is information processed by thinking and converted to something permanent in the memory that could be used by the individual to improve his or her way of living by harnessing the world that surrounds him or her. This definition implies that knowledge: a) is possessed by people; b) it is created by people; and c) can be disseminated by people.

Knowledge can be classified as either implicit/ soft/ tacit/individual or explicit/hard (Baumard, 1999; Malone, 2003; Nonaka, 1997; Polanyi, 1961). Explicit knowledge is normally a product of implicit knowledge. It can be coded, stored, reproduced, articulated in language and transmitted. Explicit knowledge is recorded in writing or stored in a computer and includes management information systems (MIS), procedures, rules and regulations, reports and minutes of meetings (Malone, 2003). Tacit knowledge is difficult to define because it is of individualistic nature as it consist of "beliefs, opinions, sensibilities, styles of doing things, and lore that may be expressed in stories and anecdotes, a glance, a nod, body language or go unsaid" (Preece, 2004). Explicit knowledge is more of "common knowledge." Among many authors, Polanyi (1961) and Nonaka (1997) explored the nature of tacit knowledge and both concluded that this type of knowledge possessed by individuals in an organisation is the most important one as it can not be 'copied'. There is consensus among most of the authors on one hand that such knowledge can only be transferred through voluntary sharing on the other hand it contributes to a competitive advantage. However, Geisler (2008, 155) warns us that "tacit knowledge can only be meaningful when it can be measured and useful when it can be accessed and shared."

It was Nonaka and Tekeuchi (1995) who stated that tacit knowledge to be a mode of experience (Malone, 2003), being simultaneous and analog (practical) while for Howells (1996) tacit knowledge is continually being built upon and learnt and it is inherent in people's practice and know-how (Howells, 1996; Preece, 2004). Therefore, it is not possible to transfer tacit knowledge easily or directly as tacit knowledge requires the individual to make changes to their existing behaviour (Howells, 1996). And converting tacit to explicit knowledge is just one way of knowledge creation in any organisation. But this implies that the organisation must create a conducive atmosphere for such a conversion to take place. However, Sun (2002) argued that conversion of, explicit to implicit, implicit to explicit or acquisition of the two in a parallel fashion are also possible. Nonaka and Takeuchi (1995) named these conversions as, socialisation (tacit to tacit), externalisation (tacit to explicit), combination (explicit to explicit) and internalisation (explicit to tacit). And these are the keys to knowledge creation.

Research on knowledge creation and organisational learning is characterised by a recent epistemological shift from an individual and cognitive perspective to knowledge as socially constructed, especially when the level of analysis is the organisation or a community. Research primarily resides in a social constructivist tradition and/or in situative learning theory (Hemetsberger & Reinhardt, 2006). According to social constructivist theory, people construct knowledge as they interact in a social context. Knowledge is dynamic, relational and based on human action. Thus it depends on the situation and people involved rather than absolute truth or hard facts (von Krogh, Ichijo & Nonaka, 2000).

When it comes to sharing of knowledge, it must be borne in mind that the knowledge from the source and the knowledge received cannot be identical as the process of interpretation is subjective and is framed by our existing knowledge and our identity (Miller, 2002). Further more the sharing of information covers a broad spectrum of exchanges and does not necessarily lead to the creation of new knowledge (Van Beveren, 2002). Knowledge-sharing intrinsically implies the generation of knowledge in the recipient.

Knowledge-sharing is the interactive process of making the right information available to people at the right time in a comprehensible manner to enable them to act judiciously – enriching the knowledge base in the entire mechanism. Knowledge-sharing can occur at all levels: between countries, within a country, between communities and among individuals. It can occur from local to global, from poor to rich and vice versa. Systematic, efficient and an open system for sharing of knowledge, in parallel with capacity building, corrects the skew between the knowledge haves and the have-nots for bringing about a better understanding of the causal loop of poverty and ensures inclusion of the poorest individuals and marginalised communities in the change process. And this is what Ergazakis *et al* (2006) see as one of the challenges of KBD. Unrestricted and continuous sharing of global and local knowledge between policymakers, public and private sectors, and the civil society heralds the way forward to an empowered knowledge society which can efficiently manage the development change process. Thus, in a knowledge society, there is not only an efficient transfer of knowledge but also a greater likelihood that such knowledge will be used effectively for empowerment and reducing inequality and poverty. There is no choice, since the growth of knowledge societies is becoming pivotal in the creation of resilient economies. The pertinent question is not whether, but how soon, the developing countries will be able to remove all the barriers to knowledge sharing and harness the potential of all available tools and technologies to transform themselves into knowledge societies for their own growth.

There are a number of factors that can influence knowledge sharing. For example, trust, use of rewards and incentives and availability of technology. Firstly with respect to trust, sometimes people "just trust others", other times it develops over a period of time. Mutual trust encourages reciprocity and thus exchange of knowledge becomes easier. Secondly, Hall (2001, 7) views knowledge-sharing as a social exchange and argues that to 'entice people to share their knowledge … actors need to be persuaded it is worth entering into a transaction in exchange for some kind of resource.' The author further suggests that knowledge-sharing could be included within 'good citizenship' where '[e] mployees who feel that they have been well supported by their organisations tend to reciprocate by performing better and engaging more readily in citizen behaviour' (Wayne et al. 1997, 90 in Hall, 2001, 7). Knowledge-sharing could be motivated by a sense of moral obligation. Indeed, recent studies of CoPs have suggested an association between moral obligation to the community and levels of knowledge-sharing (Ardichvili, Page & Wentling, 2002). This moral obligation either to an individual or an organisation or society is promoted by KBD principles who aim at closing the gap between those that "know" and those that "do not know".

These arguments raise the question of what constitutes an appropriate incentive. Indeed, there is much debate as to the most effective and appropriate incentive in motivating knowledge-sharing activities (Brown & Duguid, 2000; Chung, 2001). Extrinsic rewards such as financial incentives are another method of motivating knowledge sharing (Hall, 2001, 15). However, extrinsic rewards may provide only temporary compliance, rupturing relationships and reducing pro-social behaviour:

"Systems based on extrinsic rewards quickly turn moral obligation into acts of self-interest, and could potentially destroy the open provisioning of knowledge in a community" (Wasko & Faraj, 2000, 170).

O'Dell and Grayson (1998, 2) argue that "if the process of sharing and transfer is not inherently rewarding, celebrated, and supported by the culture, then artificial rewards won't have much effect".

Finally, information communication technologies (ICT's) also contribute to knowledge sharing. IT tools such as knowledge repositories, people finders, bulletin boards and collaborative software help to facilitate sharing beyond face-to-face interaction (Verstal & Lopez, 2004, 147). While technology plays an important role in each community's life, much of the focus and energy is not on the technology but on the personal contact and the development of social capital (Stuckey & Smith, 2004, 156).

In the developed countries, ICT have been the drivers of the knowledge society. They are providing new and faster ways of delivering and accessing information, innovative ways for real-time communication and new ways to do business and create livelihood opportunities. The technology is putting more and more information into the public domain, leading to rearrangement of societal forces and governance structures towards greater efficiency, transparency and accountability in functioning. Ergazakis *et al* (2006) also warn us about the possible inequalities, that good intentions of using ICT technologies to assist with the dissemination of knowledge to the poor and disadvantaged, can bring. They argue that "there is a substantial risk that those without the capacities to access ICTs or to use them effectively ("digital divide"), will be further marginalised ... The management of digital sources of information must be linked to the development of communities of practice and embedded within distinctive organisational styles and politics."

Trust and Knowledge Sharing

The importance of trust in facilitating knowledge sharing is increasingly being recognised, with a lack of trust likely to inhibit the extent to which people are willing to share knowledge with each other (Andrews & Delahaye, 2001; Davenport & Prusak, 1998; Roberts, 2000). To trust someone is to assume that they will honour their obligations, and trusting relations are based on – and developed from – an expectation of reciprocity (Hislop, 2004, 41). Effective cross-community knowledge sharing requires a certain level of trust to exist and consequently requires sensitivity to the character of intercommunity social relations.

The reason for the need for trust and supportive social relations between communities attempting to share knowledge with each other is that, due to the lack of common knowledge and identity between community members, the initial level of trust and mutual understanding may not be high (Hislop, 2004, 42). A growing body of research shows that the character of social relations is likely to be a key factor shaping knowledge sharing dynamics (Andrews & Delahaye, 2001; Robertson, O'Malley & Hammersley, 2000; Storey & Quintas, 2001).

The early 1990s noticed the beginning of a new trend in the work environment, that of the explosion of work teams in manufacturing and service industry (Manz & Sims, 2001). One of the main reasons was that problems were becoming more complex and this required more team work. Team work requires that the members create a cohesive bond which necessitates that the members must be able to respond openly and honestly, without the fear of repercussions, so that in the end the best decision can be made. This can only be possible through the existence of trust between the members (Politis, 2003). Politis (2003) further cites Llivonen and Huotari (2000) who found that trust supports collaboration and knowledge sharing. The author found that trusting co-workers is the chief ingredient for knowledge acquisition and knowledge sharing. It can be argued though that the role of trust in teams (a group of people put together by an organisation), is not necessarily the same when people form groups in a voluntary manner (like a CoP) to achieve a common goal. It can be said that trust is one of the prerequisites for the formation of such a group (Wenger, 1998). Trust in situations like these plays a different role. For McDermott (2001) CoPs thrive on trust. This thriving is one of the ten critical success factors in building CoPs.

This overview of knowledge, knowledge sharing and knowledge creating showed that they form one of the "basic tools" of KBD in developing a "knowledge city." Once the desire exists to share one's knowledge with others, in a voluntary manner, and in an atmosphere of trust, using any means at their disposal a core community is formed, the CoP. The question that arises then is: What role can CoPs play in the development of a "knowledge city" or "regional city" or even a "global city"?

COMMUNITIES OF PRACTICE

It was Skyrme (1998) who said "knowledge sharing is power" and such sharing is possible through CoPs. Politis (2003) adds that modern KM approaches are about "creating a team work environment in which power is equated with sharing knowledge, rather than retaining it." As it was shown in the previous section, knowledge, knowledge sharing and knowledge creation are inextricably linked in a manner that inadvertently knowledge sharing leads to knowledge creation. In the context of a "knowledge city" as indicated by Ergazakis *et al* (2004), a knowledge sharing culture is a prerequisite for a KBD. Therefore, in the same context a CoP can be seen as a very important K-agent. At this point it is necessary to discuss the origin of the CoPs and how they contribute to KM and therefore to KBD.

The term CoP was coined by Lave and Wenger (1991) and is attributed to the Institute for Research on Learning who first used the phrase in their book, Situated Learning (1991). Wenger has since become an internationally recognised expert in the study of how organisations collectively create and share knowledge. Dubbed "Mr Communities of Practice", Wenger has extensively researched, written, consulted and taught the subject. Since the idea of CoPs was accepted as another way of collaborative learning, many authors have tried to add/justify/explain why the formation of CoPs are necessary in any organisation. The aims/functions began to be clearly defined and the benefits derived from them were widely accepted.

As the word "community" has been labelled as one of the most difficult and controversial concepts in modern society. With numerous meanings and interpretations, it stands as an elusive and vague concept and is thought to be the most widely used and abused term in sociology. However, when it comes to gaining or creating knowledge, the word community receives its organic meaning: simply it is "a group of people" coming together with certain aims and predefined goals. So it becomes a "practicing community" where the members act on behalf of themselves and at the same time on behalf of that community. Lave and Wenger (1991, 98) broadened this meaning and combined it with practice to mean "... an activity system about which participants share understandings concerning what they are doing and what that means in their lives and for their community". While a group of CoPs was defined as "... a set of relations among persons, activity and world, over time and in relation with other tangential and overlapping CoPs'"(Lave & Wenger, 1991, 98).

Once CoPs were introduced, they began to evolve. Their functions started being better defined and this definition was accordingly refined by Wenger and Snyder (2000a, 139, 2002). For the authors CoPs are "... groups of people informally bound together by shared expertise and passion for a joint enterprise". Thcy organise themselves, determine their own agendas and establish their own leadership. Members have a personal commitment to the work of the community. At a later stage the authors redefined CoPs as "... groups of people that share a concern, a set of problems or a passion about a topic and who deepen their knowledge and expertise in this area by interacting on an on going basis" (Wenger & Snyder, 2000b). This last definition was an extension and improvement of McDermott's 2001 definition. Schweitzer (n.d.) extends this definition even further when he adds that members of a CoP deepen their knowledge "by utili[s]ing various resources such as tools, documents, routines and common vocabulary". Other authors, Hartnell-Young and McGuiness (n.d.), Barab, Makinster, Moore and Cunningham (2001) and Bilodeau (2003), concur with this definition. van Winkelen (2003) also concurs but he adds the idea of a virtual CoP. It can be argued then that such communities are the epitome of, what Laszlo *et al* (2003) termed, "participatory democracy." CoPs then can be used as the "seeds for a democratic knowledge based developing society".

In order to understand the evolution and foundation of CoPs, one can start with Barab and Duffy (1998) who studied and analysed the functions and challenges that any community in general can be faced with. To the authors, a community is an interdependent system in terms of the collaborative efforts of its members, as well as in terms of the greater societal systems in which it is nested. There are three requisites for communities to exist: (1) a common cultural and historical heritage, including shared goals, negotiated meanings and practices; (2) an interdependent system, in that individuals are becoming a part of something larger than themselves; and (3) a reproduction cycle, through which "newcomers" can become "old-timers" and through which the community can maintain itself. These three criteria for the existence of a CoP are in line with KBD principles of socio-cultural progress and sustainability.

Barab and Duffy (1998) state that, communities go beyond the simple coming together for a particular moment in response to a specific need that needs to be satisfied. Successful communities have a common cultural and historical heritage that partially captures the socially negotiated meanings. This includes shared goals, meanings, belief systems and practices. However, unlike the social negotiation of practice fields that primarily occur on the fly, in CoPs new members inherit many of these goals, meanings and practices from previous community members' experiences in which they were hypothesised, tested and socially agreed upon. They constitute a collective knowledge base that is continually negotiated anew through each interaction.

Second, individuals are becoming a part of something larger as they work within the context and become interconnected to the community, which is also a part of something even larger (the society through which it has meaning/value). It is this part of something larger that allows the various members to form a collective whole, as they work towards the joint goals of the community and its members. It helps to provide a sense of shared purpose, as well as an identity, for the individual and the community in large. It is through the legitimate participation in this greater community, and through the community's legitimate participation in society that communities and identities are formed (Barab & Duffy, 1998; Thorpe, 2003). However, it is not just the community members who are a part of something larger. The community itself functions within a broader societal role that gives it, and the practices of the community members, meaning and purpose. If the community isolates itself from the societal systems of which it is a part, then both the individuals and the community become weaker. The socio-cultural aspect of CoPs therefore can contribute to the local and regional development of the "knowledge city", by aligning CoPs' goals to that of the society they exist.

Thirdly, it is important that communities have the ability to reproduce as new members engage in mature practice with near peers and exemplars of mature practice. This is this line of thinking that led to Lave and Wenger's discussion (1991) of legitimate peripheral participation (LPP). This renewal aspect of CoPs makes it possible for shared knowledge to be renewed and be kept up-to-date with the new developments in the various fields.

Of prime importance for Barab and Duffy (1998) in distinguishing practice fields from community learning contexts are: (1) whether there is a sustainable community with a significant history to become enculturated into, including shared goals, beliefs, practices and a collection of experiences; (2) whether individuals and the community into which they are becoming enculturated are a part of something larger; and (3) whether there is an opportunity to move along a trajectory in the presence of, and become a member alongside, near-peers and exemplars of mature practice – moving from peripheral participant to core member.

It is these three characteristics, which Barab and Duffy (1998) have suggested are central to CoPs, that determine whether there is an opportunity for learning/building identities through LLP. Lave and Wenger used the term LPP to describe the process of moving from one way of being to another. Members in a CoP achieve this state by learning the practice of the community. LLP is complex and composite in character. Each of its three aspects – legitimation, peripherality and participation – is indispensable in defining the others and can not be considered in isolation. Legitimation and participation define the characteristic ways of belonging to a community, while peripherality and participation are concerned with location and identity in the social world. Legitimation is the dimension of CoPs that is concerned with power and authority relations within the group. It is what Laszlo, Laszlo, Campos and Romero (2003) called "participatory democracy."

Furthermore, Lave and Wenger (1991) saw the creation of CoPs as a solution to cope with the knowledge economy, which was taking over the industrial one. The authors were convinced then that an organisation would have to reposition itself in the emerging knowledge society if it was to survive. Learning through knowledge sharing began to emerge as the way to cope with the rate at which information was increasing.

CoPs do not fit comfortably with the notion of work within a formal organisational setting. For Lave and Wenger (1991), legitimacy was gained by being accepted and gaining informal authority through consensus within the group. This notion often sits uncomfortably with the more formal view of a CoP where rank or position in an organisational hierarchy is seen as the principal source of authority. Furthermore, established CoPs are by nature collaborative; and collaboration is for van Winkelen (2003) a cooperative, inter-organisational relationship that does not rely on the market or the hierarchical mechanisms of control, but is negotiated in an ongoing communicative process.

CoPs are a mechanism within which collaboration between organisations can occur. Collaboration between organisations has come into focus in recent years with the recognition that success in a global economy comes through innovation. This is the only way any organisation can keep pace with the rapid developments in technology, increasingly demanding customers and changes in the competitive environment through deregulation, social changes and the actions of competitors. Innovation depends on the exchange of ideas and insights through trusted relationships, which depends on knowing how to collaborate effectively.

People working in the same specialty, the same "practice" – even though they are not usually on the same work team – also develop communications patterns that help spread common understandings about how work is done, what information is relevant and important, and other factors in the work environment (Sharp, 1997). All these different activities that people perform in an organisation in a collaborative manner, networking meaningfully, or working in teams sharing a common goal, necessitates a careful understanding as to what a CoP really is.

Wenger (n.d.) states that communities develop their practice through a variety of activities. Wenger (n.d.) provides typical examples:

Johnson (2001) also provides a historical overview and theory of CoPs. CoPs trace their roots to constructivism (Knowles, Holton & Swanson, 1998; Oliver & Herrington, 2000; Palloff & Pratt, 1999; Persichitte, 2000; Squire & Johnson, 2000), whose main principle shifts control from instructors to learners. Constructivism involves the following concepts for Johnson (2001):

- Ill-structured problems (e.g. open-ended questions). These are authentic and complex problems that learners encounter in the real world.
- Learning in social and physical context of real-world problems, including group activities, collaboration and teamwork. Constructivist learning attempts to recreate a social interdependence.
- Shared goals, which are negotiated between both instructors, learners, and between learners.

Table 1.

Problem-solving	"Can we work on this design and brainstorm some ideas; I'm stuck."
Requests for information	"Where can I find the code to connect to the answer?"
Seeking experience	"Has anyone dealt with a customer in this situation?"
Reusing assets	"I have a proposal for a local area network I wrote for a client last year. I can send it to you and you can tweak it for this new client."
Coordination and synergy	"Can we combine our purchases of solvent to achieve bulk discounts?"
Discussing developments	"What do you think of the new CAD system? Does it really help?"
Documentation projects	"We have faced this problem five times now. Let us write it down once and for all."
Visits	"Can we come and see your after-school program[me]? We need to establish one in our city."
Mapping knowledge and identifying gaps	"Who knows what, and what are we missing? What other groups should we connect with?"

- Cognitive tools, which aid in helping learners organise knowledge, such as methods of categorisation, organisation and planning (Knowles, Holton & Swanson, 1998). These cognitive tools can be aided by processes, procedures and technology (Wenger, 1998).
- An instructor's role as a facilitator or coach, rather than the master.

Wenger et al. (2002) discuss the "downside" of CoPs and Lave and Wenger (1991, 58) emphasise the "contradictory nature of collective social practice" as the dilemma that, while CoP members work together for the benefit of the CoP and most likely seek to achieve a common goal, they also compete with each other for visibility and promotion opportunities. Further, the strong feeling of identity of members belonging to a CoP is mostly regarded as a positive aspect. However, this identity can also lead to a sense of exclusiveness and ignorance towards people who are not part of the CoP and resulting knowledge (Alvesson, 2000). Brown and Duguid (2001, 203) argue that CoPs "can be warm and cold, sometimes coercive rather than persuasive and occasionally even explosive". However, their advantage lies in the fact that they mediate between individuals and large – very often formal – organisations and contribute to organisational learning and knowledge creation.

Soekijad, Huis in 't Veld and Enserink (2004) state other workers like Orr (1990) and Barley (1986) have analysed at great length the interactions of certain groups of professionals using in-depth (ethnographical) studies. Social interaction can be found in the numerous talks and even productive "gossip" among repairmen. The repairmen continuously talked work during lunch or coffee breaks; they posed questions, raised problems, offered solutions and discussed changes in their work. Furthermore, several general characteristics of CoPs can be identified. CoPs consist of people who share a common interest in a certain domain "of human endeavour and engage in a process of collective learning that creates bonds between them" (Wenger, 2001, 2). These groups can be distinguished from teams as a CoP's main (long-term) purpose is to develop capability through the exchange, acquisition and creation of knowledge (Wenger & Snyder, 2000b).

According to Brown and Duguid (1991), in order to be innovative, organisations should focus much more on informal knowledge sharing and informal ways of working, both of which take place in CoPs. Despite their informal and often spontaneous nature, CoPs have been nurtured and encouraged by many organisations. These organisations recognise the key role of CoPs in transferring good practices, solving problems quickly and efficiently, developing professional skills, influencing strategy, and retaining talented employees. They help the individual to be a more productive, effective, and satisfied employee. Many knowledge-intensive organisations seem to search for the "personalised" means to enable employees' knowledge sharing and learning (Hansen, Nohria & Tierney, 1999). Large organisations such as Unilever and BP Amoco have initiated CoPs as tools or instruments in their organisational knowledge–management strategy (de Bruijn & de Nerée tot Babberich, 2000). CoPs "allow a much closer connection between learning and doing, while still providing structures where learning can accumulate" (Wenger, 2001, 3). This innovative function of CoPs can be of great value to the KBD initiative since innovation through knowledge creation is one of its main objectives.

Recently, we have seen contributions which suggest that CoPs can be cultivated and leveraged for strategic advantage (Saint-Onge & Wallace, 2003). Organisations create CoPs as part of their KM strategies and are often viewed as a supplementary organisational form (Swan, Scarbrough & Robertson, 2002). These recent developments about CoPs indicate that they can be responsible for achieving the strategic goals of KM not only of a organisation but regionally and globally as networks of CoPs are formed (Wenger & Snyder, 2000b). And as the link was established between KM and KBD (Ergazakis *et al*, 2006) then KM found application beyond the organisation and into education, government and international agencies in turn KM became the vehicle of achieving the strategic goals of KBD.

CoPs have also been identified as effective loci for the creation and sharing of knowledge (Lave & Wenger, 1991). Such communities are able to retain dynamic and evolving knowledge within a real-time process that adds context to existing static repositories. Members identify and engage each other with a common set of codes and language. The development of a strong network of likeminded individuals who share a common understanding is conducive to the development of an environment typified by high levels of trust, shared behavioural norms, mutual respect and reciprocity (Lesser & Storck, 2001). Such an environment has been identified as being high in social capital, and has been linked directly with the processes of the creation and sharing of knowledge (Nahapiet & Ghoshal, 1998).

Wenger (1998) extended his early work with Lave by emphasising the notion of identity and introduced an important cross-communal perspective to the discussion. Identity often plays a key role in socio-cultural theories on learning. We do not solely learn facts about the world; we develop an ability to act in the world in socially recognisable ways. This turns knowing into complex social processes that involve the acquisition of identities and reflect both how a person sees the world and how the world sees the subject. In Wenger's words:

"We all belong to many CoPs, to some in the past, to some currently; to some as full members, to some in more peripheral ways. Some may be central to our identities; some incidental. Whatever their nature, these various forms of participation all contribute in some ways to the production of our identities" (Wenger, 1998, 165).

Finally, CoPs are many things for many people. For management, they may serve as a locus of knowledge and mentoring. For members, they may serve as a networking forum and answer depot. To the organisation, they provide innovative solutions to problems or reduce turnover by providing "homes" for employees and by strengthening the social fabric of the organisation. On the other hand, CoPs may be seen as irrelevant corporate initiatives, overhead, time wasters or silly exercises in teaming or handholding. People have been organising themselves into communities since the dawn of time; it is a natural state that most individuals will thrive in. Organisations have only begun tapping back into this basic structure, because the break-up into departments, locations and business units has isolated employees (Verstal & Lopez, 2004, 147).

Types of CoPs

For Saint-Onge & Wallace, (2003, 32) there is a wide range of communities: communities of interest, communities of purpose, knowledge networks, communities of commitment, communities of expertise, professional communities, learning communities and so forth.

In a large organisation, according to Denning (2004), it is likely that many different types of communities will emerge, each having different life cycles and pathologies, including:

- discipline-based communities;
- cross-cutting communities;
- time-bound communities which are similar to organisational initiatives and
- umbrella-type communities which embrace a number of different sub communities.

Nevertheless, it is important to recall, in the effort to launch communities, that communities also have a downside. CoPs could be exclusionary (formation of cliques), chaotic, stifle innovation, and be unable to manage their activities.

For McDermott (1999), there are many different kinds of CoPs. Some develop "official" best practices, some create guidelines, some have large knowledge repositories and others simply meet to discuss common problems and solutions. Communities also connect in many different ways. Some meet face-to-face, others have conferences; others share ideas through a website. To decide what kind of community and what kind of connection is best for an organisation, three dimensions need to be understood: what kind of knowledge people need to share, how tightly bonded the community is and how closely new knowledge needs to be linked with people's everyday work. Globalisation is forcing many companies to accelerate their ability both to innovate and to disseminate learning.

The existence of different types of CoPs, evolved by the different purpose they serve, could serve as a catalyst for knowledge sharing in a "knowledge city" whereby CoPs could be created to achieve a particular goal of that community (e.g aliviate poverty) but also contribute to the global community through collaboration with other CoPs that work for the same goal.

But CoPs do not only exist in a face-to-face situation. The last two decades, improvement in communication technologies have eliminated the constraints of time and space in communication. People now can 'meet' also in cyberspace in real time, synchronously, or asynchronously using various communications tools (i.e. email) and create virtual CoPs.

Virtual or Online CoPs

Virtual communities use networked technology, especially the Internet, to establish collaboration across geographical barriers and time zones. In comparison to traditional communities, virtual communities in cyberspace differ in several respects (Johnson, 2001; Schweitzer, n.d). Traditional communities are place-based and have membership according to norms.

Group dynamics often override individual expression. There is a distinct border between membership and differentiation, that is, it is clearly defined who is a member and who is not. In contrast, virtual communities exist according to identification to an idea or task, rather than place. They are organised around an activity, and they are formed as a need arises (Squire & Johnson, 2000). Squire and Johnson (2000) also note that virtual communities do not need formal boundaries for they can be fluid.

Virtual communities have a key characteristic that is especially conducive for CoP to emerge. According to Palloff and Pratt (1999), this includes the lack of traditional group norms caused by the physical presence (e.g., voice, stature, visible reactions, visible approval or disapproval, etc.). For this reason, asynchronous communication is known as the "great equalizer" (Wepner & Mobley, 1998).

LeBaron, Pulkkinen, and Scollin (2000) point out that cultural differences among individual participants can act as barriers to communication. Because virtual community infrastructure can easily be set up across cultures via the WWW, these cultural differences can hinder the desired fluidity of learning in a CoP. In other words, different cultures can hinder the "cultural" development of the CoP itself (i.e., the CoP develops its own culture over time) (Wenger, 1998).

Virtual communities produce a variety of collective goods. They allow people of like interests to come together with little cost, help them exchange ideas and coordinate their activities, and provide the kind of identification and feeling of membership found in face-to-face interaction. In the process they face familiar problems of defection, free-riding and other forms of disruptive behavior although in new and sometimes in very unexpected ways. The novelty of the medium means that the rules and practices that lead to a successful virtual community are not yet well known or set fast in a codified formal system.

Virtual CoPs then could play an important role in knowledge sharing and creation especially where time and space are of essence. For example multinational companies could have CoPs spread all over the world and still function like face-to-face CoPs with the help of Internet technologies. Ardichvili, Page and Wentling (2002) cite a number of authors (Davenport, 1996; Ellis & Amy, 2001; Haimila, 2001) who reported that in multinational companies (such as IBM, Xerox, British Petroleum and Ford to name just a few) virtual CoPs are becoming a KM tool. The authors found that one of the critical factors for not participating in a virtual CoP was the motivation of its members. The authors also cite research by Holtsthouse (1998), De long and Fahey (2000), Szulanski (1996), and Ciborra and Patriota (1998) who found that employees often resist sharing their knowledge, knowledge does not flow easily inspite of the organisation's effort to facilitate knowledge exchange, successful knowledge exchange depends on the organisational KM system's social and technological attributes, and on organisational culture and climate. Ardichivili's *et al* (2002) research confirmed the previous findings and especially the role that organisational culture plays in knowledge sharing. If the employees view knowledge as a public good belonging to the whole organisation, knowledge flows easily but supportive culture and employees moral obligation do not remove all barriers for knowledge sharing. Furthermore the researchers found that security restrictions are barriers for knowledge sharing.

A qualitative study by Buckley (2009) on CoPs at a university of South Africa found that voluntary active participation, encouragement, sufficient free time and trust were the main drivers of the cultivation of CoPs. Furthermore 53% of respondents indicated that they preferred face-to-face communication and 45% preferred online communication which is in line with the findings by Hammond (1998).

CoPs and Knowledge Sharing

One of the most important aspects of CoPs is that a group of people share knowledge, learn together and create common practices. Community members frequently help each other solve problems, give each other advice and develop new approaches or tools for their field. Regularly helping each other makes it easier for community members to show their weak spots and learn together in the public space of the community. As they share ideas and experiences, people develop a shared way of doing things, a set of common practices. Sometimes they formalise these in guidelines and standards, but often they simply remain "what everybody knows" about good practice. Since CoPs focus on topics that people are often passionately interested in, they can become important sources of individual identity.

For Barab, Makinster, Moore and Cunningham (2001), the shared experiences of a community come to constitute a collective repertoire of activities and means of participation (that can include knowledge) that is continually negotiated anew through each interaction. Members interacting with this community have access to this history of previous negotiations. They also have responsiveness from the current members on the functional value of a particular practice, solution or finding. Collaboration among individual community members allows them to view one another as part of a collective whole, working toward the joint goals of the community and its members. As such, a community is an interdependent system defined by the collaborative efforts of its members. Being a member entails being a part of this network.

Members of a community are informally bound by what they do together – from engaging in lunchtime discussions to solving difficult problems – and by what they have learned through their mutual engagement in these activities. A CoP is thus different from a community of interest or a geographical community, neither of which implies a shared practice.

Furthermore, according to Wenger (1998) a CoP defines itself along three dimensions:

- What it is about – its joint enterprise as understood and continually renegotiated by its members.
- How it functions – mutual engagement that binds members together into a social entity.
- What capability it has produced – the shared repertoire of communal resources (routines, sensibilities, artefacts, vocabulary and styles) that members have developed over time.

The fact that members are organising around some particular area of knowledge and activity gives members a sense of joint enterprise and identity. For a CoP to function, it needs to generate an appropriate shared repertoire of ideas, commitments and memories. It also needs to develop various resources such as tools, documents, routines, vocabulary and symbols that in some way carry the accumulated knowledge of the community. This involves practise: ways of doing and approaching things that are shared to some significant extent among members (Smith, 2006; Wesley & Buysse, 2001).

The interactions involved, and the ability to undertake larger or more complex activities and projects through cooperation, bind people together and help to facilitate relationships and trust. Smith (2006) states that CoPs can be seen as self-organising systems and have many of the benefits and characteristics of associational life, such as the generation of what Robert Putnam and others have discussed as social capital.

Hew and Hara (2007) add that conversation is also an important conduit for knowledge sharing among members in CoPs. Batson, Ahmad and Tsang (2002), on the other hand, maintain that individuals are willing to help one another and share knowledge because of egoism, altruism, collectivism and principlism. The ultimate goal in egoism-related motive is to increase one's own personal benefit (e.g. pay, prizes and recognition). Altruism is a motive that increases the welfare of one or more individual(s) other than oneself. Collectivism is a motive that aims to increase the welfare of the group. The difference between altruism and collectivism can be made clearer by viewing altruism as serving the community to benefit a group as a whole. Principlism on the other hand is a motive with the end goal of upholding some moral principles. For example, individuals who have received help from a community in the past feel that they should contribute something they know (Cheung, Shek & Sia, 2004). This principle is commonly referred to in the literature as reciprocity (Nowak & Sigmund, 2000).

Another important aspect for the successful functioning of a knowledge-sharing CoP is active participation of a substantial part (ideally, all) of its members. Dixon (2000) argues that the CoP model allows organisations to overcome barriers to sharing information that conventional technology-based KM systems often encounter. For example, people who are reluctant to contribute when asked to write something up for a database, are willing to share information when asked informally by their colleagues (Dixon, 2000). This sentiment is shared by Hayes and Walsham (2000). For a community to be truly vibrant, there should be an active participation of members in other knowledge-exchange activities; engaging in live chats, Q&A sessions, providing asynchronous feedback on previous postings, etc. (Hayes & Walsham, 2000).

With respect to online sharing of knowledge, research shows that there are numerous reasons individuals could have for sharing their knowledge with other members of a CoP online. These range from boosting self-esteem to altruistic and conformist considerations. Posting of knowledge entries and other active contributions by some members of a community represent only one side of the equation: the supply of new knowledge. For a community to be vibrant, there should also be an active participation on the demand side. The second requirement for a successful CoP is its members' willingness to use the CoP as a source of new knowledge. These two major requirements (willingness to share knowledge and willingness to use a CoP as a source of knowledge) apply to any CoP, be it face-to-face or virtual.

Central to the concept of communities are the "practices" around which communities build, acquire and create their knowledge. Therefore Brown and Duguid (2000, 200) suggest trying to "look at knowledge and organisation through the prism of practice, the way in which work gets done". By focusing on the practice, "peers" are held together by "a common sense of purpose and a real need to know what each other knows". A shared repertoire of resources can be developed such as tools, documents, routines, vocabulary, stories, symbols, artefacts and heroes embodying the accumulated knowledge of the community. This shared repertoire serves as a foundation for future learning (Allee, 2000). The development of such a shared practice may be more or less self-conscious and is usually time consuming. This is not theoretical knowledge, but knowledge related to a common practice such as professional discipline, skill or topic (McDermott, 1999, 3). Sharing knowledge in a community will build or enrich a (set of) common practice(s).

With respect to organisational knowledge, there are many different techniques and practices that can be applied for the capturing and sharing of organisational knowledge. Organisations often fail to recognise that knowledge is created and shared through social interaction between people. These interpersonal relationships form a pattern and are referred to as social innovation capital or social capital (McElroy, 2002, 30). It is in communities that "individuals develop the capacity to create, refine, share and eventually apply knowledge – knowledge that makes an individual a valuable organisational resource" (Thomas, 2002). Although these communities are mainly self-organisational, there needs to be a certain measure of facilitation, encouragement and management in the manner in which knowledge is created, shared and applied, even if it is only to ensure a supportive environment.

In the case of CoPs, groups of people bound together by shared expertise and passion may informally learn from each other and organise themselves to undertake a joint enterprise through a self-selection process (Wenger & Snyder, 2000a). CoPs are often found within a business unit, but they may also stretch across divisional or organisational boundaries.

Dewhurst and Navarro (2004) say CoPs can be seen as useful vehicles for creating shared narratives to transfer tacit knowledge. Nahapiet and Ghoshal (1998) state: "myths, stories and metaphors also provide powerful means in communities for creating, exchanging and preserving rich sets of meanings a view long held by some social anthropologists". Through the use of training courses, internal conferences, and mentoring relationships, new community members can hear and exchange useful tips and anecdotes that are not located in any community archive. Sharkie (2003) recognises that a learning organisation should foster a context to encourage individuals to share their tacit knowledge to facilitate creation of new knowledge, which will also facilitate the distribution and utilisation of knowledge.

The environment, provided by an organisation to facilitate learning among members, has been defined as the organisational context (Szulanski, 1996). Knowledge distribution is enhanced by the conscious knowledge that has been created by external CoPs, such as language, conversation and dialogue, teamwork, polyvalence and social relationships (Brown & Duguid, 1998). The ability to create knowledge and to continue learning from it, according to Zack (1999), becomes a competitive advantage because innovative knowledge developed at present will become the core knowledge of tomorrow and therefore, contribute to the intellectual capital of an organisation. The success of an organisation depends on the degree to which the organisational context fosters and maximizes the organisational competitive advantages (Sharkie, 2003).

With respect to external communities, Adams and Freeman (2000) suggest that external communities are guided by a shared vision that focuses the energies of community members on creating superior value for customers. In order to effectively create and transfer experiences and knowledge within the organisation, Dixon (2000) adds that there are at least two different knowledge activities that external CoPs must be continuously involved in. One is to effectively translate their ongoing experience into knowledge (learning inside the external community) and the other is to transfer that knowledge across boundaries of time and space (learning outside the external community). Furthermore, because CoPs provide a safe forum where people are comfortable in sharing challenges and perspectives around a common topic, they serve as breeding grounds for innovation (Slater & Narver, 2000). In an era where both prospective and existing customers are expecting rapid answers to inquiries, CoPs can help individuals to rapidly identify an individual with the expertise necessary to provide the best answer to a client problem, which is considered to be a significant source of competitive differentiation in the marketplace.

Ardichvili, Maurer, Li, Wentling and Stuedemann (2006) say in recent years CoPs have gained increasing popularity as a way to manage the human and social aspects of knowledge creation and dissemination within organisations, and have also received significant attention in the KM literature (Ardichvili et al., 2006; Gourlay, 2001; Davenport & Prusak, 1998; Walsham, 2001; Wasko & Faraj, 2000; Wenger et al., 2002).

Finally, organisations are supporting and developing CoPs as part of their KM initiatives due to the benefits they provide in facilitating knowledge processes (Hislop, 2004, 38). According to the author, the knowledge literature considers CoPs advantageous for both individuals and organisations, and argues that they provide workers with a sense of collective identity and a social context in which they can develop and utilise their knowledge. For organisations, they can provide a vital source of innovation. The KM literature argues that they can facilitate organisational knowledge processes (Brown & Duguid, 1998; Hildreth, Kimble & Wright, 2000; Lave & Wenger, 1991; McDermott, 1999).

Benefits of CoPs

If one goes back to the creation of CoPs and subsequent refinement, it is clear that the need arose for sharing knowledge as the economy moved to new technological highs, especially with the advent of the Internet. It was no longer possible for individuals in a knowledge organisation to solely possess all the know-how. As CoPs became more sophisticated, organisations and individuals took advantage of that and began to reap the benefits. These benefits can vary from a mere exchange of views and ideas through formal and informal voluntary socialisation to one of sharing the untapped, up-to-now, tacit knowledge.

Van Winkelen (2003) claims that the benefit of investing in developing CoPs is that they offer the opportunity to increase the job satisfaction of knowledge workers and therefore reduce staff turnover. As individuals develop greater awareness of their own worth in the knowledge economy and recognise that inevitably they must take responsibility for their own careers and future (as job security no longer exists), they will increasingly add to their own decision-making process consideration of the opportunity a potential work experience offers to learn and allow them to retain their own market value in the future. Organisations that can offer the opportunity to participate in a leading CoP in the professional knowledge domains of their workers now appear particularly attractive. Being within the company forms the basis for staying ahead in the discipline and this is the source of future individual marketability. The pace of change and the rate of development of new knowledge mean that it has become too difficult for individuals to do this independently.

The organisation, on the other hand, benefits directly from the individual who is involved in a CoP since more explicit knowledge is documented and reused, customer service improves, new employees fit in with the culture of the organisation sooner and more new ideas are developed. However, the organisation will eventually have to assess whether encouraging and supporting a CoP is really to its benefit too; though it is easier to measure the cost, it is more difficult to assess the return on the investment. A way to overcome this difficulty is through systematically collecting anecdotal information from community members.

CoPs are important to the functioning of any organisation, but they become crucial to those that recognise knowledge as a key asset. From this perspective, an effective organisation comprises a constellation of interconnected CoPs, each dealing with specific aspects of the company's competency – from the peculiarities of a longstanding client, to manufacturing safety, to esoteric technical inventions. Knowledge is created, shared, organised, revised and passed on within and among these communities. In a deep sense, it is by these communities that knowledge is "owned" in practice (Van Winkelen, 2003).

A well-functioning CoP can become the centre for the creation, accumulation and diffusion of knowledge in an organisation, according to Wenger (1998). CoPs are the nodes for the exchange and interpretation of information. Since members have a shared understanding, they know what is relevant to communicate and how to present information in useful ways, and can retain knowledge in "living" ways, unlike a database or a manual. CoPs preserve the tacit aspects of knowledge that formal systems cannot capture, can "*steward competencies* to keep the organisation at the cutting edge. Members of these groups discuss novel ideas, work together on problems, and keep up with developments inside and outside a firm" (Wenger, 1998), and provide homes for identities. They are not as temporary as teams, and unlike business units, they are organised around what matters to their members. Identity is important, because in a sea of information, it helps us sort out what we pay attention to, what we participate in and what we stay away from.

Wenger (1998) also warns about the danger of a CoP being a liability if its own expertise becomes insular. Great importance should be placed on the core as well the boundaries of a CoP. For while the core is the centre of expertise, radically new insights often arise at the boundary between communities. CoPs truly become organisational assets when their core and their boundaries are active in complementary ways. CoPs are not good or bad in themselves. They can be a source of problems – such as exclusion, inbreeding and narrowness – as much as a key to solutions. However, if one is concerned with learning, they are a force to be reckoned with (Wenger, 1996).

APQC (2001) asserts that communities are important because in the modern, knowledge-based, global organisation, communities create a channel for knowledge to cross boundaries created by workflow, functions, geography and time.

A less tangible feature of communities is that they strengthen the social fabric of the organisation, a fabric that may have been worn thin by geography and size. People share a common interest, legitimised by business intent, and form relationships that provide social support, excitement and personal validation. Members collaborate, use one another as sounding boards, teach each other and strike out together to explore new subject matter.

As sharing of knowledge (explicit and tacit) is at the centre of a CoP, this shared learning takes place in a collaborative manner. Much of the learning in our lives takes place though informal encounters, be it of a social nature or through personal experience. Increase in the knowledge databank of an individual makes that person feel more confident, more fulfilled and thus more productive.

CoPs contribute to increasing organisational performance in the following ways:

- Faster problem-solving that involves all experts of the company (also, free outside expertise when needed, through the communities' contacts)
- Developing and verifying best practices
- Better grounded, more effective decisions
- Breaking out from knowledge silos, more synergy across units
- Unexpected resources for innovation and implementing strategies
- Reduced turn-over (European Collaborative for Communities, 2005)

Ardichvili, Page and Wentling (2002) state researchers have observed that creating and supporting CoPs is a strong alternative to building teams, especially in the context of new product development and other knowledge work. Further, among the chief reasons why CoPs are efficient tools for knowledge generation and sharing, is the fact that most of a firm's competitive advantage is embedded in the tangible, tacit knowledge of its people and because competencies do not exist apart from the people who develop them. Tacit knowledge is embedded in the stories people tell and skills are discursively produced and disseminated in conversations and networking activities. One of the ways to help people share and internalise tacit knowledge is to allow them to talk about their experiences and to exchange their knowledge while working on specific problems. Since opportunities for face-to-face interactions are rather limited in today's globally dispersed multinational companies, virtual CoPs that are supported by Internet technologies are among few viable alternatives to live conversations and knowledge exchange.

Finally, it is clear that establishing CoPs in an organisation and having the blessing of management leads to a win-win situation for the individual and the organisation.

CoPs and "Knowledge Cities"

In order to see the role that CoPs can play in the development of a "knowledge city", Ergazakis' *et al* (2004) idea of "knowledge city" as depicted in Figure 1, is used.

What makes CoPs ideal for a KBD initiative is that they can contribute to the solutions to a number of challenges that KBD is faced, such as "to help human societal systems to move to an ethical social innovation phase, to promote a simple, meaningful and productive way of life and to support participatory democracy" (Ergazakis *et al*, 2006). Cops are characterised by two important dimensions with respect to development: that of enabling "learning to be seen and analyzed within its social context" and that of "action to promote certain kinds of practice or changes in practice in development requires us to think about the nature of the learning process involved and how it occurs" (Johnson, 2007, 281). The first dimension ensures that learning is embedded in a certain social context while the second ensures that learning is practice oriented. It has been argued that CoPs "may seem to be more about social reproduction and social order than about social change and transformation" (Johnson, 2007, 281). However, Lave and Wenger (1991, 51-52) argued that such a claim is not true as participation is always based in situated negotiation and renegotiation of meaning… understanding and experience are in constant interaction.

Later Wenger (1998) modified the idea of a CoP to one of having three dimensions: mutual engagement, joint enterprise and shared repertoire (see Figure 2):

Mutuality is a key aspect of engagement. Hildreth (2004, 53) explains that practice exists because people engage in actions, and they have to negotiate meanings of these actions with each other. Further practice is not to be found in books or

Figure 1. "A knowledge city"

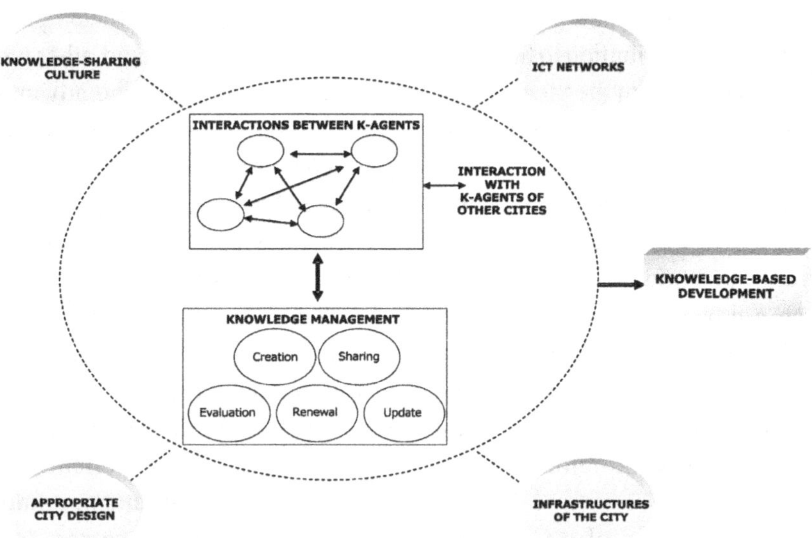

Source: Adapted by Ergazakis *et al.* (2004)

Figure 2. Dimensions of practice as the property of a community (Hildreth, 2004, 53)

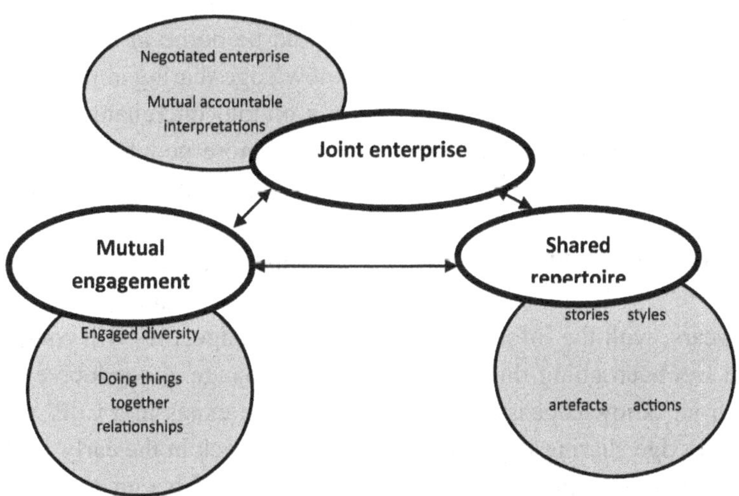

tools. Practice is to be found in a community 'and the relations of mutual engagement by which they can do whatever they do'. Joint enterprise is a key to keeping a community together. The joint enterprise is also defined by the members of the community as they are in the process of pursuing it. In shared repertoire, over time a CoP will create resources for negotiating meaning as the participants pursue the joint enterprise. These resources can include procedures, routines, tools, stories, concepts and artefacts that the community has produced and that have now become a part of the practice.

Furthermore, Wenger (1998) expanded on three other important concepts which contribute to development, that of participation, reification, and identity. Voluntary participation guarantees the member's knowledge contribution to the joint repertoire. Reification deals with the "forms and means of designing, negotiating, agreeing, accounting for and evaluating interventions between donors and beneficiaries" and thus "reifications become part of the repertoire of a community of practice and have the potential to become institutionalized. Such a process can both promote development" (Wenger, 1998). Identity is at the centre of a CoP. Changing identities and new configurations are key issues in current analyses of globalization, movements and relocations of peoples.

These important dimensions of a CoP then become the agents for sharing, creating and disseminating knowledge which are the main drivers in the human development. A CoP thus can be used as the "integrating factor" in the development of the "knowledge city". For this to become a reality though, the idea of CoPs has to be promoted by the various K-agents. As CoPs are formed within the K-agents, they in return interact among themselves and begin to develop a "constellation of CoPs" as Wenger (1998) described them, locally or internationally.

Solutions and Recommendations

For the past fifteen years, with the information explosion, the world has been going through a very important shift, from "knowledge is power" (Allee, 2002) to "knowledge sharing is power", Skyrme's (1997) most famous saying. Readjusting from an industrial era to a knowledge era has been problematic for many organisations, including higher learning institutions which were "the caretakers" as well as the "creators" of knowledge. In a way, higher learning institutions had the monopoly of knowledge. However, with the advent of the Internet, they began to loose that monopoly. Organisations too came to the realisation that, to survive in a knowledge era, they had to concentrate on the intangibles such as the human capital, the employees, rather than the financial capital and other tangibles. In order to sustain a competitive advantage, they had to concentrate on aspects that could not be copied by competitors. One such aspect was the tacit knowledge that employees possess. However, such knowledge is implicit and the employee has ownership over it.

Accepting that for employees to share such knowledge, it can only happen in a voluntary way, a conducive atmosphere for such sharing has to exist. Furthermore, tacit knowledge is created either through experience or by synthesising existing knowledge and new knowledge through various cognitive processes. The minute the individual becomes aware that he or she possesses this new knowledge, on the one hand, can use it as a leverage to make demands on the organisation (knowledge is power) or share that knowledge with others (knowledge sharing is power). Organisations have to be aware of that. What should be borne in mind is that in this context, knowledge sharing implies reciprocity: that there is a mutual interchange of knowledge between two or more people. It has been argued earlier that some individuals prefer not to share their knowledge, out of fear of feeling used and getting nothing in return. However, if a degree of trust exists whereby there will be a mutual exchange of knowledge, they will voluntarily participate in that exchange. A conducive atmosphere for such exchange exists in a CoP. Since the conception of CoPs back in the early 1990s, more and more organisations begun to embrace them as they realized that could be the way to cope in the knowledge society. Those that did and still doing are reaping their benefits. Although most of the CoPs could be informal, once they have the stamp of approval and support by the organisation, the most important capital, the social capital, gives them a competitive advantage.

It is true that some organisations might have the tendency to control existing CoPs or their employees might feel threatened by management or other members of the CoP. However, a CoP is not a team which is appointed by management to solve some problem; it is not an "underground movement" to undermine the organisation; it is not a compulsory participation by its members. It thrives on a win-win situation: mutual benefits, be it among its members or the members and the organisation. It has been stated that "CoPs thrive on passion and they die from lack of it". That is the heart of a CoP. For a CoP to add value to the individual and the organisation, both should adhere to certain rules and perform certain duties. The dilemma though that exists is whether a CoP should operate on formal or informal bases. Formalising it could lead to its demise, since it removes voluntary participation. By keeping it informal, the lack of necessary resources and approval by the organisation could also lead to its demise. The middle road is the solution. On the one hand, the organisation must accept a CoP as an independent body which is there to add value and support it in any way possible when the need arises. On the other hand, the individual must at all times remain a volunteer in a CoP.

It has been argued that using extrinsic rewards and incentives could persuade people to share their knowledge. Moral obligation could be another factor for individuals to share their knowledge. Research has shown that rewards and incentives hold a temporal value to the individual, and can even be counterproductive as there could be competition among the members, giving rise to mistrust. Moral obligation cannot be considered as universal – it has to exist naturally. Some authors argued that career advancement, as an example, could motivate people to share their knowledge. This could be true to some extent but it can also force an individual to withhold his or her tacit knowledge because their job security could be threatened. This is true in situations where the innovator has the original idea and it is taken by another and he or she appears to be the originator.

However, if voluntary sharing of knowledge is the key in a CoP, then neither would achieve permanent results since neither contains the most important ingredient: passion for what you doing. What is suggested by the authors here is that a drive should be initiated to promote the idea of CoPs and make people aware that, by forming CoPs, it will be to their benefit and by default to the benefit of the organisation. But contributing to the organisation over and above what is expected of them, if the organisation flourishes, so will they. One can consider the existence of a CoP in an organisation as an independent group of volunteers who operate according to their rules, who, by sharing their knowledge, improve their practices. One can go as far as to say that the members hold the position of an expert in an interchangeable way, i.e. that in a certain situation one member is the expert and in another situation another member is the expert. In the end, the CoP comprises of a group of experts of equal status.

The problem of knowledge sharing could also be highlighted in the existence or non-existence of CoPs in higher learning institutions. Such institutions' main tasks are dissemination and creation of knowledge. The authors had conducted research at a higher educations institution in 2008 and found that a very small percentage of the 149 respondents (only 18%) are active members of a CoP. Another 54% were not aware of CoPs while a 28% – although they knew about CoPs – preferred not to form one or participate in one. The active members feel that sharing their knowledge makes them better practitioners, while those that are aware of CoPs gave reasons for their non-participation such as mistrust or heavy teaching loads. What was encouraging though, is that most of those who were not aware of CoPs (78%) agreed that they would like to share their knowledge.

Against this background on CoPs their value to the development of a "knowledge city" can not be underestimated. CoPs can become the catalysts in developing knowledge workers through LPP . This is equivalent to the Chinese proverb about giving someone a fish and teaching them how to fish. Thus a CoP can be used as the means of empowering people to close the gap between those that "have" and the "have nots". The CoPs then can be viewed as the micro-knowledge societies who are able to create new ideas and new business. This capacity of CoPs stems out of its ability to transfer not only explicit knowledge, but also tacit knowledge which has been recognized as the most important intangible asset which creates a competitive advantage. In the model of a "knowledge city" as depicted by Ergazakis *et al* (2004) (Figure 1), CoPs can develop initially among the K-agents. The K-agents can be seen as teams with pre-determined goals and functioning according to set rules and regulations. The CoPs on the other hand have their own rules but the same goals. As CoPs are formed among the different K-agents they can form a constellation of CoPs. K-agents of a city can collaborate with K-agents of other cities to solve common problems. This way a global community begins to form.

Summing up, knowledge sharing in an organisation is to the benefit of everyone as a result it can lead to a competitive advantage. As the same principles of knowledge sharing and creating apply to other sectors of society, then the society at large benefits. CoPs are breeding grounds for such sharing and creating of knowledge. Once awareness is created in an organisation about the mutual benefits and the individuals participate in a voluntary passionate manner, then CoPs will flourish.

FUTURE RESEARCH DIRECTIONS

The sharing of knowledge, especially the sharing of tacit knowledge, in a voluntary manner has been recognised as one of the most important prerequisites for the survival of an organisation in a knowledge society. Globalisation, information technologies and telecommunications have forced many organisations to look within themselves and their employees to try and compete in a democratic environment. As the market environment is ever-changing at a very fast pace, organisations have not only to adapt to be reactive but also to be proactive. This requires management of all knowledge.

In order to manage knowledge in any organisation, it is necessary to establish how explicit knowledge is disseminated, how knowledge is created and how knowledge is shared. With respect to dissemination of knowledge, it was stated that various dissemination technologies exist as it was suggested by Gray and Tehrani (2004, 111). Sharing of knowledge can also be done through those technologies, face-to-face in a formal way, or through informal ways such with the use of CoPs. However, dissemination and sharing is preceded by creation of knowledge. It has been suggested that in a knowledge society, it is imperative that the organisation has to be a learning organisation as knowledge is the product of learning. Learning has been approached mostly from a constructivist (cognitive) perspective as well as from a behavioural perspective. Of late it has also been approached from a combination of the two perspectives, the neo-cognitivist perspective (Bandura, 1977). Both theories have shed light on how people learn. However, they have not produced the desired results. The authors propose a new paradigm; the psycho-pragmatic perspective, which is a combination of neo-cognitivist and pragmatic perspectives. The reason for this is that adding the pragmatic perspective to the psychological perspective, highlights the utility of created knowledge rather than creating of knowledge just for the sake of it. Johnson and Onwuegbuzie (2004) discuss the value of pragmatism in a knowledge society where they state (among many) benefits of pragmatism:

- The project of pragmatism has been to find a middle ground between philosophical dogmatisms and scepticism and to find a workable solution (sometimes including outright rejection) too many longstanding philosophical dualisms about which agreement has not been historically forthcoming.

- Rejects traditional dualisms (e.g. rationalism vs. empiricism, realism vs. antirealism, free will vs. determinism, platonic appearance vs. reality, facts vs. values, subjectivism vs. objectivism) and generally prefers more moderate and commonsense versions of philosophical dualisms based on how well they work in solving problems.
- Recognises the existence and importance of the natural or physical world as well as the emergent social and psychological world that includes language, culture, human institutions and subjective thoughts.
- Places high regard for the reality and influence of the inner world of human experience in action.
- Knowledge is viewed as being both constructed *and* based on the reality of the world we experience and live in.

The last point forms the heart of the psycho-pragmatic perspective.

FUTURE RESEARCH

From the conception of CoPs by Lave and Wenger in 1991, research on the value of CoPs in organisations have shed light on one of the most important functions of a CoP and that is the sharing of knowledge, especially the tacit knowledge. Since then, tacit knowledge has been recognized as an important aspect for competitive advantage. Creation of new knowledge and innovation are also interlinked with knowledge sharing. However, the effects of knowledge sharing on the creation of new knowledge and innovation have not been yet established. It can be hypothesized that by sharing knowledge with another person, it can become an activator of thinking processes which otherwise would have been dormant.

Another important aspect that needs to be studied in depth is research on formal creators of new knowledge, namely institutions of higher learning. For centuries, Universities and Colleges have been the curators of knowledge, the creators of new knowledge and the ones entrusted with the dissemination of knowledge for continuity to prevail. The academics find themselves in a precarious situation, since they are considered to be the experts of knowledge in the various fields, and thus they train novices. On the other hand, through research they have to create new knowledge. Forming CoPs then could be problematic. It will be of great interest to the knowledge society to investigate the barriers and factors that promote the establishment of CoPs or why academics share or do not share their tacit knowledge with other academics.

Finally, adding a pragmatic dimension to situated learning which gives rise to a psycho-pragmatic approach to learning and knowledge creation and acquisition opens a new field of research. Concentrating on the utility of knowledge to be acquired, it gives the choice to the individual to decide whether it is worthwhile acquiring such knowledge. In a knowledge society there is no room for "inert" knowledge.

CONCLUSION

In this chapter, the two important types of knowledge that individuals possess, explicit (hard) and implicit (soft) were discussed in the context of a knowledge organisation operating in a knowledge society. Knowledge dissemination within an organisation using modern technologies guarantees that all employees have the knowledge they need at their fingertips. But this is true for explicit knowledge. Tacit knowledge, however, cannot be disseminated but propagated through sharing in an environment characterised by mutual trust. When sharing of knowledge exists, for the recipient it remains information as he or she has to make sense of it through various cognitive processes and the individual takes ownership of that knowledge providing it fits in the existing cognitive structure. As Miller (2002) puts it, the interpretation is subjective and is framed by our existing knowledge and our identity.

Sharing of knowledge in the industrial era and in the current knowledge era is a prerequisite in any organisation if continuity is to be maintained. However, it became apparent that such sharing was directed at the sharing of explicit knowledge which was not sufficient for creating a competitive advantage. Explicit knowledge can be copied and stored. It can also be used by the competitors. It is the tacit, the soft, and the implicit knowledge that creates such advantage. Such knowledge resides only in the mind of the individual. If this is true, and research has shown it to be the case, then once the organisations accept that and the individual is prepared to make a real difference, it becomes a matter of sharing his wealth of tacit knowledge with others. Willingness to share such knowledge in a voluntary manner is the first prerequisite. If such sharing takes place within a CoP, the individual will also benefit from other members who also share their tacit knowledge.

Secondly, in any organisation, if it is accepted that a CoP is a way to tap into individuals' tacit knowledge, the onus could lie on the organisation to create awareness in the employees and encourage them to get involved in CoPs. It will be up to the employee to create or join an existing CoP. Although research has shown that CoPs are formed mostly in a natural way, by creating awareness among the employees and by encouraging them can lead to formation of more CoPs. The organisation though will have to justify such promotion of CoPs and ensure their subsequent support. Whether organisations should use rewards and incentives to promote their formation is inconclusive. Such action should be taken with great care as it could be counterproductive.

Thirdly, sharing of tacit knowledge within a CoP has more benefits than being shared in an isolated, haphazard way. Friendships can be created and developed, which would not otherwise have happened. This social aspect has been highlighted by many authors and it forms a very important aspect in the continuity of the CoP. It has been stated that CoPs occur in a natural way and they also become extinct naturally. If they were created for a specific aim and the goal was achieved, then they cease to exist. Nurturing a CoP is a prerequisite for its continuous existence.

Fourthly, knowledge sharing is directly linked to knowledge creation, in a conscious as well as subconscious way. When tacit knowledge is shared, members become inspired and innovative. This is another important aspect of knowledge sharing. Knowledge is not acquired in a vacuum but is constructed in a certain social environment. It becomes what McElroy (2002) called the social capital.

Finally, sharing of tacit or implicit knowledge in a knowledge society, it can only lead to a competitive advantage if it is converted to explicit knowledge and new knowledge to be created. Knowledge is dynamic and for people to work smarter and not harder, they have to upgrade their knowledge. An organisation has to become a learning community. In a formal as well as informal way (e.g. through CoPs) the organisation must invest on its human capital, its employees, in their development so they can face the ever-changing society with confidence. This way the conversion of a worker to a knowledge worker using CoPs will bring about a total transformation of the work force in the years to come and as a result a "working city" will be converted to a "knowledge city". A CoP then can be conceived as a catalytic agent that speeds up knowledge dissemination and sharing as well as a reagent that coverts tacit knowledge into explicit knowledge.

REFERENCES

Adams, E. C., & Freeman, C. (2000). Communities of practice: bridging technology and knowledge assessment. *Journal of Knowledge Management*, *4*(1), 38–44. doi:10.1108/13673270010315939

Allee, V. (2000). Knowledge networks and communities of practice. *OD Practitioner, 32*(4). Retrieved August 12, 2008, from http://www.odenetwork.org/odponline/vol32n4/knowledgenets.html

Allee, V. (2002). *The future of knowledge: Increasing prosperity through value networks*. New York: Elsevier Science & Technology.

Alvesson, M. (2000). Social identity and the problem of loyalty in knowledge-intensive companies. *Journal of Management Studies*, *37*(6).

American Productivity and Quality Center (APQC). (2001). *Building and sustaining communities of practice*. Retrieved December 7, 2008, from http://www.researchandmarkets.com/reports/40877

Andrews, K., & Delahaye, B. (2001). Influences on knowledge processes in organizational learning: The psychosocial filter. *Journal of Management Studies*, *37*(6), 797–810. doi:10.1111/1467-6486.00204

Ardichvili, A., Maurer, M., Li, W., Wentling, T., & Stuedemann, R. (2006). Cultural influences on knowledge sharing through online communities of practice. *Journal of Knowledge Management*, *10*(1), 94–107. doi:10.1108/13673270610650139

Ardichvili, A., Page, V., & Wentling, T. (2002). Motivation and barriers to participation in virtual knowledge-sharing communities of practice. *Journal of Knowledge Management*, *7*(1), 64–77. doi:10.1108/13673270310463626

Bandura, A. (1977). Self efficacy: Toward a unifying theory of behavioral change. *Psychological Review*, *84*, 191–215. doi:10.1037/0033-295X.84.2.191

Barab, S. A., & Duffy, T. M. (1998). From practice fields to communities of practice. Retrieved December 7, 2008, from http://crlt.indiana.edu/publications/complete.pdf

Barab, S. A., & Makinster, J. G. Moore, J.A., & Cunningham, D.J. (2001). *Designing and building an on-line community: The struggle to support sociability in the inquiry learning forum.* Retrieved December 7, 2008, from http://tiger.coe.missouri.edu/~young/aware/doc/barab.pdf

Barclay, R. O., & Murray, P. C. (1997). *What is knowledge management?* Retrieved August 24, 2008, from http://www.media-access.com/whatis.html

Barley, S. R. (1986). Technology as an occasion for structuring: evidence from observations of CT scanners and the social order of radiology departments. *Administrative Science Quarterly*, *31*, 78–108. doi:10.2307/2392767

Batson, C. D., Ahmad, N., & Tsang, J. (2002). Four motives for community involvement. *The Journal of Social Issues*, *58*, 429–445. doi:10.1111/1540-4560.00269

Baumard, P. (1999). *Tacit Knowledge in Organisations*. London: Sage.

Bellinger, G. (2004). *Knowledge management – emerging perspectives*. Retrieved June 9, 2008, from http://www.systems-thinking.org/kmgmt/kmgmt.htm

Bilodeau, E. (2003). *Using communities of practice to enhance student learning: Examples and issues.* Retrieved December 7, 2008, from http://www.coolweblog.com/bilodeau/docs/2003-10-01-cop-enhancing-student-learning.pdf

Brown, J. S., & Duguid, P. (1991). Organizational learning and communities of practice: Toward a unifying view of working, learning, and innovation . In Cohen, M. D., & Sproull, L. S. (Eds.), *Organizational Learning* (pp. 59–82). London: SAGE Publications.

Brown, J. S., & Duguid, P. (1998). Organizing knowledge. *California Management Review, 40*(3), 90–111.

Brown, J. S., & Duguid, P. (2000). *The social life of information*. Boston, MA: Harvard Business School Press.

Brown, J. S., & Duguid, P. (2001). Knowledge and organization: A social-practice perspective. *Organization Science, 12*(20), 198–213. doi:10.1287/orsc.12.2.198.10116

Buckley, S. B. (2009). *Knowledge-sharing through communities of practice at institutions of higher education.* Unpublished doctoral thesis, University of Johannesburg, South Africa.

Carrillo, F. J. (2002). Capital systems: Implications for a global knowledge agenda. *Journal of Knowledge Management, 6*(4), 379–399. doi:10.1108/13673270210440884

Cheung, C. M. Y., Shek, S. P. W., & Sia, C. L. (2004). Virtual Community of Consumers: Why People are Willing to Contribute? In *proceedings of the Pacific Asia Conference on Information Systems (PACIS 2004),* Shanghai, China (pp. 2100-2107).

Chung, L. H. (2001). 'The Role of Management in Knowledge Transfer', Third Asian Pacific Interdisciplinary Research in Accounting Conference Adelaide, South Australia.

Davenport, T. H., & Prusak, L. (1998). *Working Knowledge*. Boston: Harvard Business School Press.

De Bruijn, H., & de Nerée tot Babberich, C. (2000). *Opposites attract*. Competition values in knowledge management, Lemma, Utrecht.

DeLong, D., & Fehey, L. (2000). Diagnosing cultural barriers to knowledge management. *The Academy of Management Executive, 14*(4), 113–127.

Denning, S. (2004). *Communities for knowledge management*. Retrieved June 12, 2008, from http://www.stevedenning.com/communities_knowledge_management.html

Dewhurst, F. W., & Cegarra Navarro, J. G. (2004). External communities of practice and relational capital. *The Learning Organization, 11*(4/5), 322–331. doi:10.1108/09696470410538224

Dixon, N. (2000). *Common Knowledge: How companies thrive by sharing what they know*. Boston: Harvard Business School Press.

Drucker, P. F. (1998). Management's New Paradigma. Retrieved February 1, 2009, from http://www.forbes.com/forbes/1998/1005/6207152a.html.

Ellis, J. B. B., & Amy, S. (2001). Designing palaver tree online: supporting social roles in a community of oral history in Proceedings of the CHI 2001, Conference on Human factors in computing systems, (Seattle, Washington, 2001), ACM, 474-481.

Ergazakis, K., Metaxiotis, K., & Psarras, J. (2004). Towards knowledge cities: conceptual analysis and success stories. *Journal of Knowledge Management, 8*(5), 5–15. doi:10.1108/13673270410558747

Ergazakis, K., Metaxiotis, K., & Psarras, J. (2006). Knowledge cities: the answer to the needs of knowledge-based development. *Journal of Knowledge Management, 36*(1), 67–84.

European Collaborative for Communities of Practice. (2005). *Creating Value with Communities of Practice.* Retrieved December 7, 2008, from http://www.eccop.com/creatingvalue.htm

Firestone, J. M. (1998). *Basic concepts of knowledge management.* Retrieved September 1, 2008, from http://www.dkms.com/papers/kmbasic.pdf

Geisler, E. (2008). *Knowledge and knowledge systems: Learning from wonders of the mind.* New York: IGI Publishing.

Gourlay, S. (2001). Knowledge management and HRD. *Human Resource Development International, 4*(1), 27–46. doi:10.1080/13678860121778

Gray, P., & Tehrani, S. (2004). Technologies of dissemination knowledge . In Holsapple, C. W. (Ed.), *Handbook on Knowledge Management 2. Knowledge Directions*. Berlin, Germany: Springer-Verlag.

Haimila, S. (2001). *Shell creates communities of practice*. Retrieved January 1, 2009, from http://www.kmworld.com/Articles/News/KM-In-Practice/Shell-creates-communities-of-practice-9986.aspx

Hall, H. (2001). *Social exchange for knowledge exchange. Managing knowledge: conversations and critiques*. University of Leicester.

Hammond, M. (1998). Learning through online discussion. *Journal of Information Technology for Teacher Education*, 7(3), 331–346.

Hansen, M. T., Nohria, N., & Tierney, T. (1999). What's your strategy for managing knowledge . *Harvard Business Review*, *77*(2), 106–116.

Hartnell-Young, E., & McGuinness, K. (n.d.). *Applying a Communities of Practice Model to Research Partnerships.* Retrieved December 7, 2008, from http://www.aare.edu.au/05papc/ha05024y.pdf

Hayes, N., & Walsham, G. (2000). Competing interpretations of computer supported co-operative work. *Organization*, *7*(1), 49–67. doi:10.1177/135050840071004

Hemetsberger, A., & Reinhardt, C. (2006). Learning and Knowledge-building in Open-source Communities. A Social-experiential approach. *Management Learning*, *37*(2), 187–214. doi:10.1177/1350507606063442

Hew, K.F., & Hara, N. (2007). Empirical study of motivators and barriers of teacher online knowledge sharing. Association for Educational communications and Technology.

Hildreth, P., Kimble, C., & Wright, P. (2000). Communities of practice in the distributed international environment. *Journal of Knowledge Management*, *4*(1), 27–37. doi:10.1108/13673270010315920

Hildreth, P. M. (2004). *Going virtual: distributed communities of practice*. Hershey, PA: Idea Group Publishing.

Hislop, D. (2004). The paradox of communities of practice: Knowledge sharing between communities . In Hildreth, P. M., & Kimble, C. (Eds.), *Knowledge Networks: Innovation through Communities of Practice*. Hershey, PA: Idea Group Publishing.

Holthouse, D. (1998). Knowledge management research issues. *California Management Review*, *40*(3), 277–280.

Howells, J. (1996). Tacit knowledge, innovation and technology transfer. *Technology Analysis and Strategic Management*, *8*(2), 91–106. doi:10.1080/09537329608524237

Iivonen, M., & Huotari, M. L. (2000). The impact of trust on the practise of knowledge management. In *Proceedings of the 63rd ASIS Annual Meeting*, Chicago, IL (Vol. 37, pp. 421-29).

Johnson, C. M. (2001). A survey of current research on online communities of practice. *Journal of the Internet and Higher Education*, *4*, 45–60. doi:10.1016/S1096-7516(01)00047-1

Johnson, H. (2007). Communities of Practice and international development. *Progress in Development Studies*, *7*(4), 277–290. doi:10.1177/146499340700700401

Johnson, R. B., & Onwuegbuzie, A. J. (2004). Mixed methods research: A research paradigm whose time has come. *Educational Researcher*, *33*(7). doi:10.3102/0013189X033007014

Knowles, M., Holton, E., & Swanson, R. (1998). *The adult learner: the definitive classic in adult education and human resource development* (5th ed.). Houston, TX: Gulf Publishing.

Kubiak, C. (2003). *A Community of practice perspective on school-based learning communities.* Retrieved December 7, 2008, from http://networkedlearning.ncsl.org.uk/knowledge-base/research-papers/a-community-of-practice-perspective-on-school-based-learning-communities.doc

Laszlo, K. C., Laszlo, A., Campos, M., & Romero, C. (2003). Evolutionary development: an evolutionary perspective on development for an interconnected world. *World Futures: The Journal of General Evolution*, *59*(2), 105–119. doi:10.1080/02604020216075

Lave, J., & Wenger, E. (1991). *Situated learning: Legitimate peripheral participation*. New York: Cambridge University Press.

LeBaron, J., Pulkkinen, J., & Scollin, P. (2000). Promoting cross-border communication in an international Web-based graduate course. *Interactive Multimedia Electronic Journal of Computer-Enhanced Learning, 2*(2). Retrieved September 15, 2008, from http://imej.wfu.edu/articles/2000/2/01/index.asp

Lesser, E. L., & Storck, J. (2001). Communities of practice and organisational performance. *IBM Systems Journal*, *40*(4), 831–841.

Mallalieu, K. I. (2006). *Transforming Trinidad and Tobago into a Knowledge Society.* Retrieved February 3, 2009, from http://www.eclac.cl/socinfo/noticias/noticias/6/26546/ictpol06.pdf

Malone, S. A. (2003). *Learning about learning: an A-Z training and development tools and techniques*. Wiltshire, UK: The Cromwell Press.

Manz, C. C., & Sims, H. P. Jr. (2001). *The New Superleadership: Leading Others to Lead Themselves*. San Francisco, CA: Berrett-Koehler Publishers.

McDermott, R. (1999 May/June). Nurturing Three Dimensional Communities of Practice: How to get the most out of human networks. *Knowledge Management Review*. Retrieved December 6, 2008, from http://home.att.net/~discon/KM/Learning.pdf

McDermott, R. (2001). *Knowing in community: 10 Critical success factors in building communities of practices.* Retrieved May 1, 2009, from http://pages.conversaciones-locales.org-a.googlepages.com/KnowinginCommunity-10CriticalSuccess.doc

McElroy, M. W. (2002). Social innovation capital. *Journal of Intellectual Capital*, *3*(1), 30–39. doi:10.1108/14691930210412827

Metaxiotis, K., Ergazakis, K., & Psarras, J. (2005). Exploring the world of knowledge management: agreements and disagreements in the academic/practitioner community. *Journal of Knowledge Management*, *9*(2), 6–18. doi:10.1108/13673270510590182

Miller, F. J. (2002). Information has no intrinsic meaning. *Information Research*, 8(1). Retrieved September 10, 2008, from http://www.informationr.net/ir/8-1/paper140.html

Nahapiet, J., & Ghoshal, S. (1998). Social capital, intellectual capital, and organizational advantage. *Academy of Management Review, 23*(2), 242–266. doi:10.2307/259373

Nonaka, I. (1991, November). The knowledge creating company. *Harvard Business Review, 69*, 96–104.

Nonaka, I. (1997). A new organizational structure . In *Knowledge in Organizations*. Boston: Butterworth-Heinemann. doi:10.1016/B978-0-7506-9718-7.50009-3

Nonaka, I., & Takeuchi, H. (1995). *The knowledge-creating company: How Japanese companies create the dynamics of innovation*. Oxford, UK: Oxford University Press.

Nowak, M. A., & Sigmund, K. (2000). Cooperation versus competition. *Financial Analysts Journal, 56*, 13–22. doi:10.2469/faj.v56.n4.2370

O'Dell, C., & Grayson, J. C. (1998). If we only knew what we know: identification and transfer of internal best practices. *California Management Review, 40*(3), 154–174.

Oliver, R., & Herrington, J. (2000). Using situated learning as a design strategy for Web-based learning . In Abbey, B. (Ed.), *Instructional and cognitive impacts of Web-based education*. Hershey, PA: Idea Publishing Group.

Orr, J. (1990). S haring Knowledge, Celebrating Identity: War Stories and Community Memory in a Service Culture . In Middleton, D. S., & Edwards, D. (Eds.), *Collective Remembering: Memory in Society*. Beverly Hills, CA: Sage Publications.

Palloff, R., & Pratt, K. (1999). *Building learning communities in cyberspace: effective strategies for the online classroom*. San Francisco: Jossey-Bass.

Persichitte, K. (2000). A case study of lessons learned for the web-based educator . In Abbey, B. (Ed.), *Instructional and cognitive impacts of web-based education*. Hershey, PA: Idea Group.

Polanyi, M. (1961). Knowing and being . *Mind, 70*(280), 458–470. doi:10.1093/mind/LXX.280.458

Politis, J. D. (2003). The connection between trust and knowledge management: What are the implications for team performance? *Journal of Knowledge Management, 7*(5), 55–66. doi:10.1108/13673270310505386

Preece, J. (2004). Etiquette and trust drive online communities of practice. *Journal of universal computer science*.

Roberts, J. (2000). From know-how to show-how: the role of information and communications technology in the transfer of knowledge. *Technology Analysis and Strategic Management, 12*(4), 429–443. doi:10.1080/713698499

Robertson, M., & O'Malley Hammersley, G. (2000). Knowledge management practices within a knowledge-intensive firm: the significance of the people management dimension. *Journal of European Industrial Training, 24*(2-4), 241–253. doi:10.1108/03090590010321205

Saint-Onge, H., & Wallace, D. (2003). *Leveraging Communities of Practice for Strategic Advantage*. Boston, MA: Butterworth-Heinemann.

Sauve, E. (2007). *Informal knowledge transfer*. T+D, American Society for Training and Development, March.

Schweitzer, S. J. (n.d.). *Discussion forums: The core of online communities of practice*. Retrieved December 7, 2008, from http://www.efios.com/kgarden/schweitzer597_project.pdf

Sharkie, R. (2003). Knowledge creation and its place in the development of sustainable competitive advantage. *Journal of Knowledge Management, 7*(1), 20–31. doi:10.1108/13673270310463590

Sharp, J. (1997). *Key hypotheses in supporting communities of practice*. Retrieved December 7, 2008, from http://www.tfriend.com/hypothesis.html.

Skyrme, D. (1998). *Measuring the value of knowledge: Metrics for the knowledge-based business*. New York: Business Intelligence.

Slater, S. F., & Narver, J. C. (2000). Market Oriented is More Than Being Customer-Led. *Strategic Management Journal, 20*, 1165–1168. doi:10.1002/(SICI)1097-0266(199912)20:12<1165::AID-SMJ73>3.0.CO;2-#

Smith, M. K. (2006). *Communities of practice*. Retrieved December 7, 2008, from http://www.infed.org/biblio/communities_of_practice.htm

Soekijad, M., Huis in 't Veld, M., & Enserink, B. (2004). Learning and Knowledge Processes in Inter-organisational Communities of Practice. *Knowledge and Process Management, 11*(1), 3–12. doi:10.1002/kpm.191

Squire, K., & Johnson, C. (2000). Supporting distributed communities of practice with interactive television. *Educational Technology Research and Development, 48*(1), 23–43. doi:10.1007/BF02313484

Storey, J., & Quintas, P. (2001). Knowledge management and HRM . In Storey, J. (Ed.), *Human resource management: A critical text*. London: Thomson Learning.

Stuckey, B., & Smith, J. D. (2004). Building sustainable communities of practice . In Hildreth, P. M., & Kimble, C. (Eds.), *Knowledge Networks: Innovation through Communities of Practice*. Hershey, PA: Idea Group Publishing.

Sun, R. (2002). *Duality of the mind*. New Jersey: Lawrence Erlbaum associates.

Swan, J., Scarbrough, H., & Robertson, M. (2002). The Construction of 'Communities of Practice' in the Management of Innovation. *Management Learning, 33*(4), 477–496. doi:10.1177/1350507602334005

Szulanski, G. (1996). Exploring internal stickiness: Impediments to the transfer of best practice within the firm. *Strategic Management Journal, 17*(1), 27–44.

Tanedu. (2007). *What is a knowledge society*. Retrieved February 3, 2008, from http://www.tanedu.org/index.php?option=com_content&task=view&id=76&Itemid=37

Thomas, B. S. (2002). *Understanding communities of practice*. Retrieved June 10, 2008, from http://www.totalkm.com/knxchanges/cop.html

Thorpe, M. (2003). *Communities of practice and other frameworks for conceptualizing, developing and evaluating NCSL's initiatives in linking staff and school communities.* Unpublished report for the National College of School Leadership.

Van Beveren, J. (2002). A Model of Knowledge Acquisition that Refocuses Knowledge Management. *Journal of Knowledge Management, 6*(1), 18–22. doi:10.1108/13673270210417655

Van Winkelen, C. (2003). *Inter-organisational communities of practice*. Retrieved December 7, 2008, from http://www.elearningeuropa.info/directory/index.php?page=doc&doc_id=1483&doclng=6

Verstal, W. C., & Lopez, K. (2004). Best practices: Developing communities that provide business value . In Hildreth, P. M., & Kimble, C. (Eds.), *Knowledge Networks: Innovation through Communities of Practice*. Hershey, PA: Idea Group Publishing.

Vestal, W. (2006). *Sustaining communities of practice*. Retrieved December 7, 2008, from http://www.kmworld.com/Articles/ReadArticle.aspx?ArticleID=15159&PageNum=4.

Von Krogh, G., Ichijo, K., & Nonaka, I. (2000). *Enabling knowledge creation: How to unlock the mystery of tacit knowledge and release the power of innovation*. New York: Oxford University Press.

Walsham, G. (2001). Knowledge management: the benefits and limitations of computer systems. *European Management Journal, 19*(6), 599–608. doi:10.1016/S0263-2373(01)00085-8

Wasko, M. M., & Faraj, S. (2000). It is what one does: why people participate and help others in electronic CoP. *The Journal of Strategic Information Systems, 9*, 155–173. doi:10.1016/S0963-8687(00)00045-7

Wayne, S., Shore, L., & Liden, R. (1997). Perceived organizational support and leader member exchange: A social exchange perspective. *Academy of Management Journal, 40*(1), 82–111. doi:10.2307/257021

Wenger, E. (1996). *Communities of practice. The social fabric of a learning organisation*. Retrieved December 7, 2008, from http://www.ewenger.com/pub/pubhealthcareforum.htm

Wenger, E. (1998). *Communities of practice. Learning as a social system*. Retrieved December 7, 2008, from http://www.co-i-l.com/coil/knowledge-garden/cop/lss.shtml

Wenger, E. (2001). *Supporting communities of practice. A survey of community-oriented technologies*. Retrieved April 4, 2008, from http://www.ewenger.com/theory/communities_of_practice_intro.htm

Wenger, E. (n.d.). *Communities of practice: a brief introduction*. Retrieved August 23, 2008, from http://www.ewenger.com/theory/communities_of_practice_intro.htm

Wenger, E., McDermott, R., & Snyder, W. M. (2002). *Cultivating communities of practice: A guide to managing knowledge*. United States of America: Library of Congress Cataloging-in-Publication Data.

Wenger, E., & Snyder, W. (2000a). Communities of practice: the organisation frontier. *Harvard Business Review*, 139–145.

Wenger, E., & Snyder, W. (2000b). *Learning in communities*. Retrieved February 12, 2008, from http://www.linezine.com/1/features/ewwslc.htm

Wepner, S., & Mobley, M. (1998). Reaping new harvests: Collaboration and communication through field experiences. *Action in Teacher Education, 20*(3), 50–61.

Wesley, P. W., & Buysse, V. (2001). Communities of practice: expanding professional roles to promote reflection and shared inquiry. *Topics in Early Childhood Special Education, 21*(2). doi:10.1177/027112140102100205

Wig, E. H. (1993). The role of language in learning disabilities. In Spectrum of Developmental Disabilities XIV: ADD, ADHD and LD (pp. 139-154). The Johns Hopkins School of Medicine. Parkton, MD: York Press.

Zack, M. H. (1999). Developing a knowledge strategy. *California Management Review, 4*(3).

Section 3
Global Best Practices of Knowledge-Based Development

Chapter 15
Singapore:
A Model for Knowledge-Based City

Caroline Wong
The University of Queensland, Australia

ABSTRACT

Singapore's commitment to knowledge-based economy (KBE) development in the past decade has enabled it to make a rapid and successful transition to knowledge-based city. This chapter focuses on how Singapore government has forged an environment that is conducive to innovations, new discoveries and the creation of new knowledge. In the process, Singapore has emerged as one of the top knowledge-based cities in the world through various frameworks used globally. In this period, Singapore strengthened its engagement with the global knowledge economy developing a creative industries development strategy which endorsed the importance of creative industries, aiming to position Singapore as a 'new Asian creative hub' (ERC Report, 2002, p.8). The Singapore experience represents one of few examples of how knowledge can become the driving force of economic growth and transformation. It provides valuable insight into how public policies have successfully negotiated the current global network economy to suit economic changes. Although Singapore's developmental model has created benefits in many ways, it had also negatively constrained its development particularly in the area of knowledge creation and application to entrepreneurship and creativity.

INTRODUCTION

Singapore is an interesting case study as its status as a most admired knowledge-based city reflects how government policies have successfully negotiated the current global network economy to suit economic changes. Singapore's commitment to knowledge-based economy (KBE) development has won her recognition for being the most admired knowledge city (MAKCi) in the World Capital Institute and Teleos ranking[1] for the two years running in 2007 and 2008. Singapore relied on many aspects of the capital dimensions listed in the MAKCi framework[2] as a spring board to trigger its knowledge-based

DOI: 10.4018/978-1-61520-721-3.ch015

Figure 1. Global view: Knowledge Economy Index by countries and regions, 1995 and the most recent year 2008

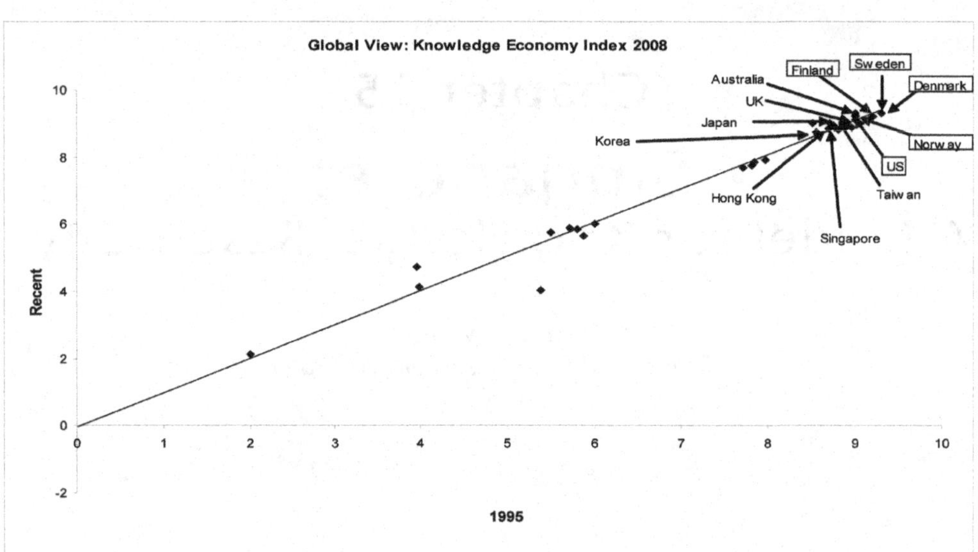

Source: World Bank-Knowledge Assessment Methodology. www.worldbank.org/kam.

development. The MAKCi framework includes eight knowledge capital dimensions that stand as indicators for the MAKCi exercise as the visible drivers of collective capital creation in knowledge-based development city-regions and they include identity capital, intelligence capital, financial capital, relational capital, human individual capital, human collective capital, instrumental-material capital and instrumental-knowledge capital.The details of the indicators in each of the capital dimensions can be located in the 2008 MACKI Report. However, while Singapore ranks high on human capital (which is one of the key traits of a knowledge-based economy) and technical infrastructure in the MAKCI framework, international observers have pointed out that there is a "complete absence of independent media" (Reporters without Borders, *World Press Freedom Ranking 2006*) which reflects on the city's insufficiency of spaces for critical discourse and breath of opinions and views amongst its stakeholders (2008 MAKCI Report).

The Singapore experience, however, represents one of few examples of how knowledge can become the driving force of economic growth and transformation. It has also been ranked amongst the top 25 in the World Bank's Knowledge Economy Index[3] (KEI) in the 2008 World Bank comparisons (See Figure 1).

The KEI is constructed as the simple average of 4 sub-indexes, which represent the following 4 pillars of the knowledge economy[4]:

- Economic Incentive and Institutional Regime (EIR)
- Education and Human Resources
- National Innovation systems
- Information Infrastructure

This framework consists of a set of 80 structural and qualitative variables that benchmark how an economy compares with other countries. Table 1 below shows that the Nordic countries remain among the best performers in the KEI with Denmark, Sweden, and Finland taking up the first three positions followed by Norway taking up the 5th position. Singapore is ranked 24th among the 140 countries covered in the KEI ranking for 2008.

Table 1. Knowledge Economy Index (KEI) 2008 Rankings

Rank	Country	KEI	KI	EIR	Innovation	Education	ICT
1	Denmark	9.58	9.55	9.66	9.57	9.8	9.28
2	Sweden	9.52	9.63	9.18	9.79	9.4	9.69
3	Finland	9.37	9.33	9.47	9.66	9.78	8.56
4	Netherlands	9.32	9.36	9.18	9.48	9.26	9.36
5	Norway	9.27	9.27	9.25	9.06	9.6	9.16
6	Canada	9.21	9.14	9.42	9.43	9.26	8.74
7	Switzerland	9.15	9.03	9.5	9.89	7.69	9.52
8	United Kingdom	9.09	9.03	9.28	9.18	8.54	9.38
9	United States	9.08	9.05	9.16	9.45	8.77	8.93
10	Australia	9.05	9.17	8.66	8.72	9.64	9.16
11	Ireland	8.92	8.82	9.23	9.04	9.08	8.33
12	Austria	8.89	8.76	9.3	8.9	8.53	8.85
13	Iceland	8.88	8.87	8.92	7.98	9.44	9.18
14	Germany	8.87	8.83	8.99	9	8.46	9.04
15	New Zealand	8.87	9	8.48	8.65	9.79	8.56
16	Belgium	8.73	8.7	8.82	8.96	9.14	8.02
17	Taiwan, China	8.69	8.8	8.35	9.24	7.91	9.26
18	Luxembourg	8.65	8.4	9.42	8.91	6.66	9.62
19	Japan	8.56	8.84	7.71	9.15	8.71	8.66
20	France	8.47	8.69	7.82	8.61	9.08	8.38
21	Estonia	8.34	8.22	8.68	7.49	8.27	8.9
22	Slovenia	8.25	8.29	8.11	8.31	8.24	8.33
23	Spain	8.24	8.13	8.58	8.14	8.21	8.04
24	Singapore	8.24	7.75	9.71	9.56	5.19	8.5
25	Israel	8.22	8.24	8.16	9.34	6.72	8.64

Source: World Bank, Knowledge Economy Index Report 2008, KAM 2008 (www.worldbank.org/kam).

Amongst the Asia-Pacific countries, Singapore is ranked 5th after Australia, New Zealand, Taiwan and Japan. It is apparent that Taiwan is leading the Newly Industrialized Economies (NIEs) in the 2008 ranking followed by Japan, Singapore, Hong Kong (ranked 26th) and Korea (ranked 31st).

Taiwan's score of 9.24 in National Innovation Systems and 9.07 in Information Infrastructure surpassed the UK and Germany. This is attributed to the government's vigorous promotion of the information and broadband Internet infrastructure as well as its strengthening of innovation and application services (Council for Economic Planning and Development Website). However, Taiwan's global rankings in the economic incentive regime and education and human resources are lagging behind those of the top tier countries which means that the economic incentive mechanism still needs improvement and with the rapid transformation of the industrial structure, the knowledge workers and creative personnel needed by the new economy are still insufficient (Council for Economic Planning and Development Website).

Of the four major items that make up the KEI's index, Singapore performed very well in Economic Incentive regime with a score of 9.71

Table 2. R&D Expenditure By Area of Research, 2007(in Singapore million dollars)

Areas of research	Total of patents	Private sector	Higher education sector	Government sector	Public research institutes
Total	6,339.1	4,235.0	603.0	770.8	730.3
Agriculture & Food Sciences	70.1	61.9	0.9	7.3	-
Engineering & Technology	4,127.5	3,229.8	232.1	417.5	248.1
Biomedical & Related Sciences	1,057.6	387.4	172.1	124.1	373.9
Natural Sciences (ex biological sciences)	572.9	296.0	117.7	100.3	59.0
Others	511.1	259.9	80.2	121.6	49.4

Source: Agency for Science, Technology and Research in Yearbook of Statistics, Singapore 2009

and Innovation index with a score of 9.56 outpacing Japan, Korea, and Hong Kong amongst the NIEs. This reflects the success of the R&D and innovation policy that the government has implemented in recent years, advocating and promoting the establishment of innovation R&D centres, the reinforcement of patent protection, and the focus on high-value add industries such as engineering and technology, nanotechnology and bio-medical sciences (See Table 2 on page 9 for figures on R&D output in Singapore).

Although Singapore's score of 9.19 in the information infrastructure augurs well for its focus on ICT, its score of 5.16 in the education and human resources item is the lowest amongst the NIEs. This corresponds with the OECD findings where Singapore registers the lowest on knowledge application (See Table 4 on p.11) as entrepreneurship and tertiary education are found to be the weakest links (APEC Economic Committee Report, 2000). Much progress has been made in the area of education, which is now ap-

Table 3. International Comparison of Gross Expenditure on R&D (GERD) in 2005

Country	GERD as % of GDP
Singapore	2.4
EU average	1.9
OECD average	2.3
US	2.7
Japan	3.2
Ireland	1.3
Netherlands	1.8
Denmark	2.4
Israel	4.7
Finland	3.5
Sweden	3.9
Taiwan	2.4
South Korea	3.0

Source: Singapore Department of Statistics Newsletter, Mar 2007

Table 4. Singapore's KBE and Knowledge Economy Index (KEI)

	OECD	Singapore	US	Japan	Korea
Knowledge Creation Index	1.00	1.03	1.69	1.96	0.98
Knowledge Acquisition Index	1.00	1.49	0.86	0.65	0.98
Knowledge Dissemination Index	1.00	1.05	1.24	1.35	0.77
Knowledge Application Index	1.00	0.93	1.52	0.96	0.90
■ **OECD average being set as the base index of one**					

Source: APEC Economic Committee Report (2003)

proaching first world standards. This is, however, moderated by the low level of entrepreneurship in Singapore. With the rapid transformation of the industrial structure, the knowledge workers and creative personnel needed by the new economy are still insufficient.

Singapore has continuously relied primarily on knowledge transfers through MNCs and foreign talents (Toh et al., 2003). It adopts a liberal foreign direct investment (FDI) policy that saw the establishment of 6,000 multinational companies set up their operations in Singapore (EDB Media Releases, 2003). Since the late 1990s, the Singapore government has forged an environment that is conducive to innovations, new discoveries and the creation of new knowledge and one that harnesses the intangibles such as ideas, knowledge and expertise (Ministry of the Arts and Information, Renaissance City Report, 2000). The 1998 Report of the Committee on Singapore's Competitiveness (CSC) and the Economic Development Board (EDB)'s Industry 21 Master Plan set the vision for Singapore to become a globally competitive KBE.

The knowledge-based industries in Singapore have so far contributed to a rising increase in the GDP from 48 percent between 1983 and 1985 to 56 percent in 2001 (APEC Economic Committee Report, 2003). Most of the contributions were in the area of knowledge acquisition and dissemination (Wong, 2004). Although knowledge transfer has provided a significant share of the innovation activities and knowledge spill-over in Singapore, the challenge lies in the creation, ownership and exploitation of new knowledge by the local entrepreneurs. Toh et al's findings (2003) indicated that the mapping of Singapore's KBE has highlighted the need for more entrepreneurs to create new business models and the challenge for existing firms to innovate.

Statistics released by the Global Entrepreneurship Monitor (GEM) 2005 report shows that Singapore lacks behind the OECD countries in starting a business (in general) as a career choice – 46.8 percent versus 55.4 percent and 57.8 percent of Singaporeans believe that new business success is accorded with high status in the country, compared with an average of 66.2 percent in the OECD countries (Wong et al., 2006). Only 29 percent perceived they have the skills to start a business and a low of 17.5 percent who believed that good start-up opportunity exists (Wong et al., 2006). Singapore was ranked 17 among 24 countries with an entrepreneurial established business prevalence rate of 4.8 percent compared to New Zealand's number one ranking of 9.6 percent and the average of 6.2 percent for the 24 OECD countries (Wong et al., 2006).

Overall, the social and cultural attitudes in Singapore towards entrepreneurship are much lower than the overall averages for all the OECD countries (Wong et al., 2006) and this reflects a rather conservative perception where entrepreneurship is concerned. The weak entrepreneurial spirit is attributed to a prevailing culture that seems to discourage creativity, risk taking and failure (Wong et al., 2004). This might have implications for Singapore trying to transit to the creative economy.

In the past decade, the Singapore government is keen to use content and creativity to enter the next wave of development in the so-called 'creative economy'. Emergence of the creative economy paradigm is consistent with the development path laid out by the Government of Singapore in its transformation from port, to industrial park to knowledge economy. The presence of a wide-scale connectivity of capital dimensions listed in the MACKI exercise is not sufficient to make Singapore into a "new Asian creative hub" (ERC Report, 2002, p.8) - a concept which the Singapore government first articulated in its White Paper targeting the creative industries as a growth sector in the 21st century. There is a need to analyze how creativity is located in the knowledge-based economy by examining the ecosystem of creative space and integrating it to the multi-layered knowledge networks and transactions (Jeffcutt, 2005) that are prevailing in the innovation and science sectors of the economy. This boundary-crossing approach helps to develop strategic knowledge in the creative industries (Jeffcutt, 2005, p. 116) and is a multi-disciplinary framework which provides a thorough insight to the challenges facing the creative industries in Singapore.

The value of the chapter lies in the analysis, which concludes that although Singapore's developmental model had created benefits in many ways, it had also negatively constrained its development, particularly in the area of knowledge creation and application to entrepreneurship and creativity. There is seemingly a paradox in the transition from a knowledge-based economy to a creative economy and this might have implications for Singapore's effort towards establishing itself as a renaissance city using culture to re-position its international image as a global city for the arts.

SINGAPORE ECONOMY AND THE DEVELOPMENTAL MODEL

Since independence in 1965, the Singaporean economy has been subjected to interventionist government public policies that have allowed government-linked companies (GLCs) to play a major role in the country's development. The developmental role of the state has contributed to the economic success of the city-state, which had a population of 4.68 million and GDP growth of 8.9 per cent in the third quarter of 2007 (Singapore Statistics Department website).A combination of open trading economy, government-led development and social and political stability are the main underpinnings of its economic development.

Singapore displays many characteristics typical of a knowledge-based economy, such that people, their ideas and capabilities are the key sources of wealth and opportunities (Chia, 2001). Its dynamic business environment spawned a well established IT and telecommunications infrastructure serviced by over 6000 multinational companies (MNCs) and over 100,000 local enterprises comprising small and medium sized enterprises (SMEs) and large local corporations (EDB Singapore, 2003).

According to Mason et al. (1980), the Singaporean developmental model has emphasized government-business relationships. This has resulted in the government not merely being a referee and setting the broad rules of the game but often acting as a major participant in business decisions. It has done this through directly manipulating incentives and disincentives in promoting industrial development (Tan, 1999). It is apt that the term 'Singapore Inc.' has been associated with the directive role played by the state in its political and business economy, culture and ethos (Low, 2005).

The development model took Singapore from an industrialization strategy in the 1970s to a higher, sophisticated manufacturing one that included computer peripherals and software packages (Loo et al, 2003). The manufacturing sector continues to be an important contributor to the economy; its share of GDP has remained above 25 per cent for most years in the last two decades (Wong & Singh, 2004). However, Singapore's manufacturing output is highly dependent on foreign firms (such as multinational corporations, or MNCs) and this has contributed to the lack of a critical mass of indigenous entrepreneurial firms in the global economy (Wong, 2004).

The 1980s in Singapore saw a strategic shift towards technology intensive sectors. By the early 1990s, the focus had moved to knowledge intensive companies (Loo et al, 2003). By the late 1990s, the government acknowledged the need to forge an environment conducive to innovation, new discoveries and the creation of new knowledge. It sought to harness intangibles such as ideas, knowledge and expertise to create and add new value in the knowledge economy (MITA Renaissance City Report, 2000).

It is therefore not surprising that the concept of the knowledge-based economy has generated increased discussion and recognition in the late 1990s. Substantial efforts have also been made in the educational and industry sectors (especially R&D) in the last few years to link learning to knowledge creation and business creativity. Accordingly, the educational and cultural economic policies are tailored to global economic restructuring and reflect the state's ideology of pragmatism and developmentalism (Kong, 2000).

Basis of Singapore's KBE

The Committee on Singapore's Competitiveness was formed in 1997 to address Singapore's competitiveness as a knowledge economy within the next decade. Its vision is for Singapore to become an advanced and globally competitive knowledge economy with manufacturing and services as twin engines of growth (Committee on Singapore's Competitiveness Report, 1998). Singapore continues to attract foreign MNCs, encourage local enterprises to produce high value-added products and provide manufacturing-related and headquarters services to the region. The government also recognises the need to nurture small and medium local enterprises and to build a core of world-class companies with core competencies that can compete in the global economy (Committee on Singapore's Competitiveness Report, 1998).

The Competitiveness Report (1998) laid down the following strategies:

- Manpower 21 plan
    - To help workers increase their productivity; welcome foreign talents to augment it small domestic talent pool
    - To emphasize on skills, knowledge & creativity which are necessary for capabilities in the KBE
- National Science & Technology Plan 2000 and Technopreneurship 21
    - To create world-class firms by developing local entrepreneurs to drive innovation-led growth and capitalize on new business opportunities
    - To attract investments in high growth and high value added areas by encouraging MNCs to locate more key knowledge intensive activities in Singapore and local companies to embrace more knowledge intensive activities and become world-class players
    - To develop a world class workforce through its educational programs

The Singapore Government developed IT2000 which aims to transform Singapore into an intelligent island, where the use of information technology is pervasive in every aspect of its society – at work, home and play (Chew & Suleiman,

2001, p.21). The emphasis was on developing a knowledge infrastructure as well as human and intellectual capital.

Under Technopreneurship 21, a venture capital fund with US$1 billion was pumped in for start-ups in Singapore. Funding is available to both Singaporean entrepreneurs and foreign entrepreneurs who launch start-ups in Singapore.

One of the initiatives is the building of a comprehensive knowledge infrastructure to support the sharing and exchange of information and knowledge. This encompasses Singapore ONE, the legal and policy framework, introduced to support new ways of doing business such as e-commerce, as well as expanding the available resources for our network of educational and research institutes (Chew & Suleiman, 2001, p.22). This knowledge infrastructure will be linked to the major knowledge and business centers of the world. It consists of the physical networks and their interconnections with knowledge or 'thought' centers such as universities, research institutes, and business centers around the world. It is Singapore's nation-wide broadband infrastructure for multimedia applications and services, based on the Automatic Switching Technology (ATM) and was launched in June 1998. This is the result of Singapore's continuing effort to explore emerging technology trends and to exploit the opportunities early (s-one website). Today, Singapore ONE is available for connections in 99% of all homes and is available in all schools, most tertiary institutions, almost all public libraries as well as many community centers throughout Singapore (Chew & Suleiman, 2001, p.22).

To speed up the development of the broadband industry and market in Asia, IDA (Information Development Authority) has taken proactive steps to forge partnerships with leading players in the region; such as Taiwan, China and Korea(Chew & Suleiman, 2001, p.23). IDA has also managed to get Microsoft to use Singapore as the launch site for its Asian Broadband Jump-start Initiative for the deployment of new broadband applications in Asia. IDA with the support of Ministry of Education (MOE) has placed a Fast Track @ School Program, which allowed more than 50 schools to upgrade their broadband facilities and develop interactive broadband education content (Chew & Suleiman, 2001, p.23).

Knowledge-Based Industries (KBI) and Singapore Economy

The size of Singapore's KBE can be estimated by looking at the value added of the knowledge-based industries (KBIs). Within a span of 15 years, the contributions of KBIs to GDP have increased from 48% in 1985 to 56% in 2001(APEC Economic Committee Report, 2003).

Singapore has long depended heavily on foreign MNCs introducing advanced and sophisticated technology and know-how through the FDI process (foreign direct investment). It has now reached a developmental state where it must also develop its own science, technology and innovation capabilities. This was when the National Science and Technology was set up in 1991 to develop public technology infrastructure, support the growth of private R&D, and nurture R&D manpower. This board was subsequently known as A*STAR (Agency for Science, Technology and Research).

Singapore has made good progress towards creating a stronger base for knowledge creation over the last 10 years indicated by the higher GDP spending on R&D and numbers of researchers that have reached the level existing in developed KBE economies. Table 2 shows the growth in R&D spending is spearheaded by the private sector and the R&D output is measured by the number of patents owned and awarded. This measurement has increased significantly over thelast ten years as seen from the latest statistics in 2007.

As illustrated in the figures above, the R&D Expenditure by Area of Research was mainly led by the private sector mainly in agricultural and food sciences, engineering and technology, biomedical and related sciences, natural sciences and others

International Comparison of Gross Expenditure on R&D (GERD)

With gross expenditure of R&D at 2.4% of GDP in 2005, Singapore's R&D intensity was ahead of the EU average of 1.9%, and had surpassed OECD's average of 2.3%; however is lower than that of US (2.7%) and Japan (3.2%).Compared with small advanced countries, Singapore's R&D intensity was ahead of Ireland and the Netherlands and on par with Denmark but fall way behind that of world leaders like Israel (4.7%), Sweden (3.9%) and Finland (3.5%). However amongst the NIEs, Singapore was close to that of Taiwan (2.4%) but behind that of South Korea (3%). [Singapore Department of Statistics Singapore Newsletter, Mar 2007].

Singapore's KBE and World Bank Analysis

The continual success of the KBE will require entrepreneurship and research to create new products, services, markets and opportunities. Investment in skills, knowledge and creativity are necessary to ensure that Singapore's workforce has capabilities for a KBE. Existing literature by World Bank suggests that the strength of a KBE can be measured in terms of four capabilities -Knowledge Creation, Knowledge Acquisition, Knowledge Dissemination and Knowledge Application.

These four capabilities interact with each other in the economy to create the main driver of growth, wealth creation and employment across all industries (APEC Economic Committee Report, 2000). Understanding the production, distribution, and use of knowledge in Singapore allows us to have a systematic overview of Singapore's KBE capabilities.

Knowledge Creation and Acquisition

The production of knowledge is the fundamental driver in the growth of KBE. It provides new ways of increasing efficiency in the production of goods and services. The graph below shows the comparisons made with OECD economies, US and of the newly-industrialized economies (NIEs) to gauge stage of development of Singapore's KBE

Knowledge Dissemination

The ICT revolution has vastly expanded the frontier of possibilities for the KBE by enabling existing and new knowledge to be disseminated at ever-faster speeds, larger volumes and lower costs.

Moreover, the usefulness of knowledge-intensive products such as software for example is subject to network economies, i.e., they become more useful as the user-base increases. The culmination of these developments is the "network effect" which multiplies the benefits of a fixed knowledge base many-fold through dissemination.

Knowledge Application

The economic benefits of an expanding knowledge base and network dissemination are realized when they are adopted and applied by the labor force in the production of goods and services.

The commercial benefits from applying knowledge will provide feedback to the knowledge production community, driving the next round of innovation and absorption.

In the case of Singapore, it continues to rely primarily on knowledge transfers through the attraction of MNCs and foreign talent. However, with the emphasis on science and technology since 1990, Singapore has begun to build a systematic capability in knowledge creation. Hence it is necessary to look at both knowledge creation and acquisition capabilities to measure the extent of the knowledge base in Singapore.

Table 4 above extracted from the APEC Economic Committee Report (2003) illustrates the overall structure of Singapore's KBE relative to the OECD, the US, Japan and Korea. The OECD average is being set as the base index of one. Looking at the table, Singapore's index of 1.03 in knowledge creation seems on par with the OECD average although US and Japan have stronger showing for their innovative ability.

There is a great tendency to rely on knowledge acquisition, as the figure of 1.49 is the highest among the capabilities for Singapore. Singapore has been able to absorb much foreign technology due to the extensive presence of MNCs in their economies. The US and Japan have low acquisition indices as they are the largest producers of new knowledge in the world. Consequently, their dependence on foreign sources of knowledge is low.

Singapore has a comparable index ranking of 1.05 with the OECD economies in knowledge dissemination. Although Singapore has a stronger policy emphasis on ICT infrastructure than many other developed economies, its rating is only slightly higher than the OECD average due to the late liberalization of the ICT sector relative to the OECD as well as the weaker education profile.

It is evident that there is a lot that Singapore has to catch up in the area of knowledge application (with a figure of 0.93) as entrepreneurship and tertiary education are found to be the weakest links (APEC Economic Committee Report, 2000). Much progress has been made in the area of education, which is now approaching first world standards. This is, however, moderated by the low level of entrepreneurship in Singapore.

For example, although Singapore's environment for entrepreneurship was ranked by experts to be above average on all dimensions in the 2004 Global Entrepreneurship Monitor (GEM) report, there is a need to address the institutional and cultural values and the mindsets of the population as many do not regard entrepreneurial activity as a good career choice and therefore do not accord high status to new business success.

Statistics released by the 2004 GEM report shows that Singapore lacks behind the OECD and East Asian countries in starting a business as a career choice - 49.1% versus 59.5% (Wong et al., 2004). The weak entrepreneurial spirit is accrued to a prevailing culture that seems to discourage creativity, risk taking and failure. As such, over the last few years the educational system was re-structured in order to foster greater creativity and instil higher-order (i.e., analytical, creative, and systems) thinking skills amongst its school children.

Education Reforms and Restructuring

Apart from its emphasis on a national innovation system in recent years, many efforts have been channeled to enhance the foundations of the knowledge economy through education and entrepreneurship (Toh et al., 2003). The Singapore government recognizes the need to move away from an MNC-propelled industrialization past to one that embraces an indigenous pool of technological and entrepreneurial expertise (Koh, 2000) – the emphasis on skills, knowledge and creativity. For many years, government in Singapore has utilized education as a means to meet economic goals.

In Singapore there had been an emphasis on preparing the institutions for the knowledge-based economy by the Government of Singapore. This has resulted in introduction of knowledge management programs in public and private sector organizations requiring libraries and information centers to provide corresponding services and products to support these initiatives (Chaudhry, 2005). Accordingly, education providers were expected to introduce new programs for cultivating information and knowledge professionals equipped with competencies required to support knowledge management initiatives. Local universities and professional forums have started a series of professional development activities and academic programs to meet these needs. There is a realization that to make the KM programs more relevant and beneficial understanding of factors that contribute to the success or failure of knowledge management initiatives is important.

As such, the former prime minister, Mr Goh Chok Tong came out with a vision of 'thinking schools and learning nation' way back in 1997 to address the issue. This is where the educational system was re-structured in the last decade or so in order to foster greater creativity and instill higher-order (i.e., analytical, creative, and systems) thinking skills amongst its school children.

There is now a substantial reduction in curriculum content and student assessment in favor of team learning, problem-solving and process skills acquisition (Loh, 1998). This recent quest to restructure and inject critical thinking skills and greater creativity into its educational agenda has been sparked off by the need to reduce reliance on the multinationals and to provide a broader base for future growth.

Efforts at educational restructuring have as their targets, the production of a future intelligent workforce (i.e., today's school children) that is capable of advanced, continuous learning, un-learning, and re-learning (Koh, 2000). This educational restructuring is beginning to pervade the entire spectrum of students ranging from elementary school right through to the university level. In the long term, these efforts aim at having a future workforce that is capable of advanced learning, knowledge creation, and creativity leap-frogging.

Singapore's KBE and Creative Industries

The government also recognised the need to attract global creative talent and even add a few 'bohemians' (Florida, 2002, p.63) to the mix for a culturally vibrant city. The vision for the 21st century includes a 'renaissance city' using culture to reposition its international image and become a global city for the arts (ERC Report, September 2002, p.v). Public policy emphasises human capital, talent, knowledge professionals and the role of cultural and creative endeavours. As such, the economic dividends of culture have become the focus of the state's economic agenda for the arts and creative industries (Kong, 2000).

The Creative Industries Development Strategy was the outcome of a report conducted by the Economic Review Committee (ERC) in 2002 to address Singapore's competitiveness as a knowledge economy within the next decade (ERC Report, 2002). Various recommendations surfaced regarding the creative industries. The creative industries are now considered a growth engine of the Singaporean economy. Targets set by the Creative Industries Working Group (CIWG) for 2012 include:

- Raising the share of the creative industries in GDP to 6 per cent
- Employing 5 to 7 per cent of the national workforce and
- Establishing a reputation for Singapore as a new Asian creative hub (ERC Report, 2002, p.v)

The above targets are ambitious given that the latest economic figures in 2004 indicated that Singapore's creative industries contributed to only 3.6 per cent of GDP (MICA Press Release, August 28, 2007). By focusing on emergent arts and culture, the Singaporean government hopes to expand local creativity in addition to attracting global creative personnel and retaining entrepreneurs for the creative economy. There has been a concerted effort to provide tangible cultural infrastructure in the urban landscape as a means to generate artistic activity. According to Andersson and Andersson (2006), cultural physical (tangible) infrastructure includes museums, palaces, churches, sculptures, paintings and other objects of arts and consists of the aesthetic aspects of the physical infrastructure.

The most tangible iconic cultural infrastructure in Singapore includes the Esplanade, the Theatre on the Bay, which was purpose-built in 2002 as a centre for world-class performing arts. It has a wide range of professional support services and facilities. Even though the Esplanade will not thrust Singapore onto the cutting edge of the creative world in the foreseeable future, the publicity encompassing it will at least make the arts more visible, particularly to local residents.

Singapore has successfully attracted firms to the creative sector. A total of 53 foreign media companies have set up regional headquarters or hubs in Singapore since 2003, providing job opportunities in Singapore's creative sector (MICA Press Release, August 28, 2007). The most notable has been the establishment of the production base of Lucas Film Animation in Singapore. George Lucas, creator of blockbuster films including *Star Wars* (1977) and *Raiders of the Lost Ark* (1981), announced the opening of a digital animation studio in Singapore in August 2004. This is a joint venture with the Economic Development Board (EDB) of Singapore and a consortium of local companies. It is anticipated that the presence of Lucas Film will establish and reposition Singapore as a creative hub in Asia. More importantly, such a reputation will lead to a substantial increase in expected revenues (Andersson & Andersson, 2006) in that it will attract talents within and across the regions to work and stay in Singapore.

It is evident that public policy in relation to the cultural and creative sphere in Singapore has a strong leaning towards an architect model (Hillmand-Chartrand & McCaughey, 1989). The architect model allows government a direct role in shaping the environment and funding the arts and entertainment. This is evident in Singapore's approach to position itself as a cultural renaissance city of the twenty-first century (MITA Renaissance City Report, 2000). Williams (1984) calls this 'a stately sense of cultural policy' (p.5) which is typically about public performances of the state or government power. This is reflected in Singapore's concern with the economic bottom-line in its management of culture whereby government is 'open for businesses in the field of culture and the arts' (Lee, 2004, p.282).

The advantage of this model is that artists and arts organisations are relieved from depending on popular success at the box office (Hillmand-Chartrand & McCaughey, 1989). The weakness of this approach is that artists cannot assert their creative independence. In other words, because government has determined the architecture, this may result in creative stagnation as creatives follow directives.

The volatile, dynamic and risk-taking nature of the creative industries often results in intensive social networking activities among the skilled creative workers (Scott, 2004). According to Bilton (2007), networks of organisations, groups and individuals have become the dominant form of production and the shift is towards social and organisational frameworks through which individuals are connected.

To a large extent, many aspects of Singapore's artistic, cultural and social entrepreneurial activities are still 'bud grafted' by the government rather than left to the free market and individual choice (Low, 2005, p.129). In that regard, Singapore's cultural policies are often tailored according to global economic restructuring and reflect the state's ideology of pragmatism and developmentalism (Kong, 2000).

FUTURE RESEARCH TRENDS AND CHALLENGES

The KBE has become increasingly important to Singapore over the years and like many countries, Singapore is always looking for avenues to develop and grow its KBE. It can be seen from the different frameworks proposed by the World Capital Institute, OECD, APEC and the World

Bank, that various indicators used to measure the Knowledge Economy Index (KEI) place different emphasis on different dimensions. The number of indicators included under the different frameworks, also varies greatly from more than 70 in the World Bank Knowledge Economy Index to about 8 broad capital dimensions in the MAKCI framework. The fact that there is not much overlap among the various frameworks indicates the wide divergence in the selection of indicators.

There are some limitations and challenges in such forms of measurement. First, without an international standard on KBE indicators, it is difficult to benchmark an economy's position as a KBE against other economies. Given that different economies would have different emphasis on the various aspects of a KBE, it is understandable they might choose quite different sets of KBE indicators in their own frameworks. In this aspect, international cooperation in devising a core set of indicators for international comparison would be useful (Leung, 2004). Second, the wide range of indicators might not fully reflect the very substantial achievements in the KBE attributes of an economy especially those resulting from the adoption of a small number of break-through technologies (Leung, 2004, p.10). As such, it is not easy to assess the overall performance of an economy – for example with some indicators improving while some others are deteriorating, it is difficult to assess whether the economy has become more knowledge-based or less. The biggest challenge is to build an appropriate model that links up the various dimensions and indicators and one in which consensus from the international countries has to be sought before any international comparison could be made.

Understandably, Singapore has been able to achieve credible results under the various frameworks due to her strengths in economic, technological and innovation development especially in the science and technology sectors as the government has forged an environment that is conducive to innovations, new discoveries and the creation of new knowledge. In the process, Singapore has emerged as one of the top knowledge-based cities in the world.

In recent years however, the increasing focus on the creative industries has also generated lots of discussion where value creation is based on intellectual content in the form of texts, music, media and script et cetera (Caves, 2000; Scott, 2000) and where the acquisition and creation of new information and knowledge (Inkpen, 2000, p.1037) has become the keys the success. In that regard, the presence of a wide-scale connectivity of capital dimensions listed in the MACKI exercise is not sufficient to make Singapore into a "new Asian creative hub" (ERC Report, 2002, p.8) - a concept which the Singapore government first articulated in its White Paper targeting the creative industries as a growth sector in the 21st century. There is a need to analyze how creativity is located in the knowledge-based economy by examining the ecosystem of creative space and integrating it to the multi-layered knowledge networks and transactions (Jeffcutt, 2005) that are prevailing in the innovation and science sectors of the economy. This boundary-crossing approach helps to develop strategic knowledge in the creative industries (Jeffcutt, 2005, p. 116) and is a multi-disciplinary framework which provides a thorough insight to the challenges facing the creative industries in Singapore.

CONCLUSION

The global market of products and services has become more technology and knowledge-intensive. At the same time, the Singapore economy is maturing. The build-up of capital and labor will slow down and become less important drivers of economic growth. Singapore's ability to create, acquire, disseminate and apply knowledge will be the key to sustaining its economic growth. With its recent emphasis on the creative industries, which are known for its flexible, network-like structure involving complex, non-routine work (DeFillippi & Arthur, 1998), there is a greater need to look at knowledge creation and application.

The network element is an important part of the creative process as 'bright sparks of illumination only catch fire when the right combination of elements is brought together' (Bilton, 2007, p.46). Bilton (2007) outlines the significance of horizontal networks (through peer-to-peer relationships with organisations and individuals) and vertical networks (through supply chain relationships) in the creative industries. There is a shared pool of talent and knowledge through these informal collaborative relationships to bring about idea generation (Bilton, 2007).

It is not sufficient for policymakers to initiate only economic and structural schemes to assist firms in the knowledge-based economy. There is a need to establish an aesthetic and creative milieu for experimentation and exploration of ideas and thinking to produce quality content in different sectors of the economy. It will be a challenge for the government to strike a balance between the structural approach to business with the behavioural and attitudinal dimension of businesses in the creative and knowledge-based industries.

The value of the paper lies in the analysis, which concludes that although Singapore's developmental model had created benefits in many ways, it had also negatively constrained its development, particularly in the area of knowledge creation and application to entrepreneurship and creativity. There is not enough understanding given to the creative process in that creativity is both a complex social process and an individual activity (Csikszentmihalyi, 1996).

There is a need to open the environment to stimulate the development of creative ideas and to analyze how creativity is located in the knowledge-based economy by examining the ecosystem of creative space and integrating it to the multi-layered knowledge networks and transactions (Jeffcutt, 2005) that are prevailing in the innovation and science sectors of the economy. This boundary-crossing approach helps to develop strategic knowledge in the creative industries (Jeffcutt, 2005, p. 116) and is a multi-disciplinary framework which provides a thorough insight to the challenges facing the creative industries in Singapore.

There is a greater need to focus on the wider cultural and aesthetic development of the city-state such that the whole complex system of institutions, agencies, markets and public are involved in the ecology of creativity. For policymakers, this argument may imply a new perspective where economic competitiveness is not just about subsidising business R&D, supporting infrastructures and local spin-offs. Rather, it is about understanding the process of value creation in the creative economy where social and cultural mindsets have to embrace individual creativity, diversity and community-led initiatives. This implies more consultation, research and thinking about the relationships between culture and innovation.

REFERENCES

Andersson, A. E., & Andersson, D. E. (2006). *The economics of experiences, the arts and entertainment*. Cheltenham, UK: Edward Elgar Publishing.

APEC Economic Committee Report. (2003). *The drivers of new economy in APEC – innovation and organizational practices*. Singapore: APEC Secretariat.

Bilton, C. (2007). *Management and creativity: from creative industries to creative management*. Oxford, UK: Blackwell Publishing.

Caves, R. (2000). *Creative industries: contracts between art and commerce*. Cambridge, MA: Harvard University Press.

Chaundhry, A. S. (2005). *Libraries – a voyage of discovery*. Paper presented at the World Library and Information Congress, 71th IFLA General Conference and Council, Oslo, Norway. Retrieved on May 14, 2007 from http://www.ifla.org/IV/ifla71/Programme.htm

Chew, L. L., & Sulaiman, A.-H. (2001). Government initiatives and the knowledge economy: case of Singapore. In W. Kim et al. (Eds.), Human Society@Internet 2001 (LNCS 2105, pp. 19-32). Heidelberg: Springer-Verlag Berlin.

Chia, S. Y. (2001). Singapore: towards a knowledge-based economy . In Masuyama, S., Vandenbrink, D., & Chia, S. Y. (Eds.), *Industrial restructuring in East Asia: towards the 21st Century* (pp. 169–208). Singapore: Institute of Southeast Asia Studies.

Cohen, W. M., & Levinthal, D. (1990). Absorptive capacity: a new perspective on learning and innovation. *Administrative Science Quarterly*, *35*, 128–152. doi:10.2307/2393553

Committee of Singapore's Competitiveness (CSC) Report. (1998). Singapore: Ministry of Trade and Industry. Retrieved March 10, 2005 from www.mti.gov.sg/public/NWS/frm_NWS_Default.asp?sid=42&cid=177

Council for Economic Planning and Development website. (n.d.). *Taiwan tops Asia in knowledge economy index*. Retrieved June 10, 2009 from http://www.cepd.gov.tw/encontent/print.aspx?sNo=0010997

Csikszentmihalyi, M. (1996). *Creativity: flow and the psychology of discovery and invention*. New York: Harper Collins Publishers.

Dahlman, C. (2002). World Bank OECD-IPS-World Bank workshop on promoting knowledge-based economies in Asia. November 21-22, 2002, Singapore.

DeFillippi, R. J., & Arthur, M. B. (1998). Paradox in project-based enterprise: the case of film making. *California Management Review*, *10*(2), 125–139.

EDB (Economic Development Board) Singapore. Media releases. (n.d.). *New headquarters program launched for companies across all industries and geographies*. Retrieved January 7, 2003 from www.sedb.com/edbcorp/browse.jsp?cat=40&type=2&parent=36&root=36

ERC (Economic Review Committee) Report. (2002). *Creative industries development strategy: propelling Singapore's creative economy*. ERC Creative Industries Working Group. Retrieved June 15, 2004 from http://www.mti.gov.sg/public/ERC/frm_ERC_Default.asp?sid=131

Florida, R. (2002). Bohemia and economic geography. *Journal of Economic Geography*, *2*(1), 55–71. doi:10.1093/jeg/2.1.55

Hillman-Chartrand, H., & McCaughey, C. (1989). *The arm's length principle and the arts: an international perspective – past, present and future in cultural economics – collected works of Harry Hillman Chatrand*. Retrieved November 10, 2007 from http://www.culturaleconomics.atfreeweb.com/arm's.htm

Houghton, J., & Sheehan, P. (2000). *A primer on the knowledge economy. Centre for Strategic Studies*. Melbourne: Victoria University.

Hutton, A. T. (2004). Service industries, globalization and urban restructuring within the Asia-Pacific: new development trajectories and planning responses. *Progress in Planning*, *61*, 1–74. doi:10.1016/S0305-9006(03)00013-8

Inkpen, A. C. (2000). Learning through joint ventures: a framework of knowledge acquisition. *Journal of Management Studies*, *37*(7), 1019–1043. doi:10.1111/1467-6486.00215

Jeffcutt, P. (2005). The organisation of creativity in knowledge economies: exploring strategic issues. In D. Rooney, G. Hearn & Ninan (Eds.), Handbook on the knowledge economy. Cheltenham, UK: Edward Elgar.

Knight, R. V. (1995). Knowledge-based development: policy and planning implications for cities. *Urban Studies (Edinburgh, Scotland)*, *32*(2), 225–260. doi:10.1080/00420989550013068

Koh, A. T. (2000). Linking learning, knowledge creation, and business creativity: a preliminary assessment of the East Asian quest for creativity. *Technological Forecasting and Social Change*, *64*(1), 85–100. doi:10.1016/S0040-1625(99)00075-X

Kong, L. (2000). Cultural policy in Singapore: negotiating economic and socio-cultural agendas. *Geoforum*, *31*(4), 409–424. doi:10.1016/S0016-7185(00)00006-3

Lee, T. (2004). Creative shifts and directions: cultural policy in Singapore. *International Journal of Cultural Policy*, *10*(3), 281–289. doi:10.1080/1028663042000312525

Leung, S. (2004). *Statistics to measure the knowledge-based economy: the case of Hong Kong and China*. Paper presented at the 2004 Asia-Pacific technical meeting on information and communication technology (ICT) statistics, Wellington, 30 November – 2 December 2004. Retrieved June 10, 2009 from http://74.125.153.132/search?q=cache:pMolfzT0yH0J:www.unescap.org/stat/ict/ict2004/18

Loh, L. (1998). Technology policy and national competitiveness . In Toh, M. H., & Tan, K. Y. (Eds.), *Competitiveness of the Singapore economy: a strategic perspective*. Singapore: Singapore University Press and World Scientific Publishing Company.

Loo, L. S., Seow, E. O., & Agarwal, A. (2003). Singapore's competitiveness as a global city: development strategy, institutions and business environment. *Cities (London, England)*, *20*(2), 115–127. doi:10.1016/S0264-2751(02)00119-1

Low, L. (2001). The Singapore developmental state in the new economy and polity. *The Pacific Review*, *13*(3), 409–439.

Low, L. (2005). Entrepreneurial development in Ireland and Singapore. *Journal of the Asia Pacific Economy*, *10*(1), 116–138. doi:10.1080/1354786042000309107

MAKCI. *(Most Admired Knowledge City Awards) Report*. (2008). World Capital Institute and Teleos. Retrieved January 4, 2009 from The World Capital Institute website at http://www.worldcapitalinstitute.org/

Mason, E. S., Kim, M. J., Perkins, D. H., Kim, K. S., & Cole, D. C. (1980). *The economic and social modernization of the Republic of Korea*. Cambridge, MA: Harvard University Press.

MITA. *(Ministry of Information and the Arts) Renaissance City Report*. (2000). Retrieved January 5, 2004 from http://www.mita.gov.sg/renaissance

Organization for Economic Corporation and Development (OECD). (1996). *The knowledge-based economy*. Paris: OECD.

Organization for Economic Corporation and Development (OECD). (2002). Towards a knowledge-based economy – recent trends and policy directions from the OECD. Background paper for the OECD-IPS workshop on promoting knowledge-based economies in Asia, 21- 22 November 2002, Singapore.

S-one website. (n.d.). Retrieved June 13, 2007 from http://www.s-one.gov.sg

Scott, A. J. (2000). *The cultural economy of cities: essays on the geography of image-producing industries*. London: Sage Publications.

Singapore statistics department website. (n.d.). Retrieved December 1, 2007 from http://www.singstat.gov.sg/

Tan, K. Y. (1999). Public policies in the Singapore economy . In Adams, F. G., & James, W. E. (Eds.), *Public policies in East Asian development: facing new challenges*. London: Praeger.

Toh, M. H., Tang, H. C., & Choo, A. (2003). *Mapping Singapore's knowledge-based economy in APEC 2003. The drivers of new economy in APEC – innovation and organizational practices*. Singapore: APEC Secretariat.

William, R. (1984). *State culture and beyond: culture and the state* (Appignanesi, L., Ed.). London: Institute of Contemporary Arts.

Wong, P. K. (2004). *The information society and the developmental state: the Singapore model*. Singapore: National University of Singapore (NUS) Entrepreneurship Centre Working Papers.

Wong, P. K., Lee, L., Ho, Y. P., & Wong, F. (2004). *Global entrepreneurship monitor GEM: highlights in Singapore*. Singapore: NUS Entrepreneurship Centre.

Wong, P. K., Lee, L., Ho, Y. P., & Wong, F. (2006). *Global entrepreneurship monitor GEM: 2005 Singapore report*. Singapore: National University of Singapore Entrepreneurship Centre.

Wong, P. K., & Singh, A. (2004). Country survey report: Singapore. Report prepared for ECLAC/IDE (JETRO) joint project, comparative study on East Asian and Latin American IT industries.

World Bank-knowledge assessment methodology. (n.d.). Retrieved January 20, 2007 from http://www.worldbank.org/kam

Yang, L. B. (Minister for Information, Communications and the Arts, Singapore). (2007, August 28). *MICA press release*. Presented at the 2007 creative industries scholarships award ceremony. Retrieved October 10, 2007 from http://www.mica.gov.sg/pressroom/press_070828.htm

Yearbook of Statistics Singapore. 2009. Retrieved 17 January, 2010 from http://www.singstat.gov.sg/pubn/reference/yos.html

ENDNOTES

1 The MAKCi Awards of which Singapore was the top award winner in the last 2 years were created to publicly recognize those cities and regions which are leaders in bringing together intellectual capital and knowledge workers, supported by an advanced ICT infrastructure, in order to create a knowledge-driven global competitive advantage.

2 The MAKCi Framework includes eight knowledge capital dimensions that stand as indicators for the MAKCi exercise as the visible drivers of collective capital creation in knowledge-based development city-regions namely: identity capital, intelligence capital, financial capital, relational capital, human individual capital, human collective capital, instrumental-material capital and instrumental-knowledge capital (2008 MACKI Report).

3 Note: The Knowledge Economy Index (KEI) consists of 80 structural or qualitative variables that benchmark performance of more than 128 countries. KEI is an aggregate of all variables that are normalized from 0 (worst) to 10 (best).

4 Each of the pillar sub-indexes are in turn based on three indicators that proxy the performance of the pillar. For details, please refer www.worldbank.org/kam

Chapter 16
Israel: A Knowledge Region Case Study

Edna Pasher
Edna Pasher Ph.D & Associates, Israel

Sigal Shachar
Edna Pasher Ph.D & Associates, Israel

ABSTRACT

This chapter focuses on knowledge based development in regions, based on Israel's experience. Israel, a small country in the Middle East, is a very unique case of a knowledge based region. The authors have extensively studied Israel as an innovative region in different contexts. Since 1998 they published three Israel Intellectual Capital Reports for the Israeli Government. During 2007 the authors led a study for the European Commission focused on regional innovation systems. This study has aimed to measure the effectiveness of participation in ICT (Information Communication Technology) EU projects on the EU innovation system at the regional level. Israel was selected as a regional best practice though it is a nation state and not a region since it is as small as a region, and since the authors had good relevant data from the previous IC reports and since Israel is consistently recognized as one of the most innovative countries in the world. The authors discovered that an Intellectual Capital audit is a powerful and useful framework to understand the effectiveness of regional innovation systems, offering the possibility for evidence-based future policies rather than retrospective performance analyses. This chapter demonstrates the case of Israel as a knowledge-based region, as well as critical success factors for regional innovation systems.

INTRODUCTION

Innovation leads to productivity and to increased economic growth. This assumption is based on the idea that innovation often relates to technology improvements which enhance the efficiency and effectiveness of production and therefore, increase economic growth (Baumol, 2002). Innovation depends on creativity and on the generation and application of knowledge. Turning knowledge into commercial products demands creating "useful knowledge" that can be disseminated and applied

DOI: 10.4018/978-1-61520-721-3.ch016

by entrepreneurs (Mokyr 2002; Audretesch & Keilbach, 2004).

Today, the global economies are in a phase of transitioning into a knowledge-based structure, where innovation leads to an all-encompassing change in the sectoral composition (Machlup 1962). Therefore, the diffusion of knowledge is more than the transfer of ideas, patents or licenses from person, firms, or departments to other persons, firms, or departments. It often depends on learning and interacting in networks (internal to multi-locational enterprise, external among firms) and on "channels of diffusion" (Pred, 1976). This process is embedded in the social and institutional structure of the region/city/organization.

Castelles and Hall (1994) argue that Regions are being profoundly modified in their structure, and conditioned in their growth dynamic, by the interplay of three major interrelated, historic processes: the first is a technological revolution based on information technologies. The second process is the formation of a global economy that works as a unit in a world wide space for capital management, labor, technology and markets. The third process is the emergence of a new form of economic production and management characterized by the fact that productivity and competitiveness are increasingly based on the generation and distribution of new knowledge. They remark that no region can prosper without some level of linkage to source of innovation and production.

The OECD(1996) defines a Knowledge-Based Economy as one in which the production, distribution, and use of knowledge are the main drivers of growth, wealth-creation, and employment for all industries. In that regard many authors identify information and communication technology (ICT) and globalization as key drivers of knowledge. The European Commission recognized this, and in the recent years has encouraged organizations from different regions in Europe to participate in ICT projects funded through its Framework Programs. These projects have been recognized as a very important and useful factor to increase the innovation dynamics in the EU regions. Because of its reputation as an innovative country, Israel was invited to join these Framework Programs as a full partner and Israeli organizations participate in these projects in a high rate.

Israel is an interesting case of a knowledge-based region because of it's unique story of accomplishments of innovative achievements within a very short period of existence (only 60 years). What are the key success factors? How can we evaluate the intangible assets of a country? What can be learned from an innovative region? In this chapter we will try to answer these questions and to apply the findings to other regions and countries.

KNOWLEDGE MEASUREMENT – THE INTELLECTUAL CAPITAL MODEL

The knowledge in organizations, regions, countries is base on two kinds of deliverables: tangible and intangible. Intangible deliverables, in this sense include all unpaid or non-contractual activities that make things work smoothly and help build relationships. In contrast, tangible deliverables include anything that is contracted, mandated or expected by the recipient as part of the delivery of product, or service. Tangibles typically are directly connected with generating and delivering on revenue or funding. One of the most challenging issues at the organizational network and regional levels today is describing and monitoring the role of intangibles in value creation. At the organizational level pioneers in intellectual capital have demonstrated that intervention and actions must be understood in both tangible and intangible terms. (Sveiby 1997, Edvinsson and Malone 1997, Wallman and Blair 2000, Eccles et al 2001). Intangible assets include brand, employee know-how and competency, the effectiveness of the organization's workgroups and structure, the efficiency of organization's production and service process, and quality of relationships with customers and suppliers.

The Intellectual Capital Assessment by Prof. Leif Edvinsson (the Skandia Nevigator) was first applied in business in the mid 1990s and has been expanded to the national level in countries such as Sweden, Denmark, Finland and Israel.

The IC audit provides a holistic and organized picture of knowledge and intellectual assets. It presents the hidden values that will lead to economic growth and to the country's increased integration in the global market. The Intellectual Capital Report demonstrates these hidden values of the country and its competitive advantage, making the report a vital marketing tool.

Intellectual Capital Assessment *p*rovides a set of indicators based on five focal areas of the model:

- **Financial Capital** – Reflects the organization's history and past achievements. In the case of nations it reflects the tangible economic achievements of the country such as: GDP, structure of industry, workforce, rate of services and products per year, etc.
- **Human Capital** – constitutes the population's total assets and capabilities reflected in learning, knowledge, expertise, experience, motivation, entrepreneurship and many other assets which have a competitive edge in the past and in the present.
- **Process Capital** – reflects the cooperation and flow of knowledge require structural intellectual assets, such as information systems, hardware, software, databases, laboratories, an organizational/ national infrastructure and management focus. This structural capital can increase the output of human resources.
- **Market Capital** – refers to the general assets embodied in the organization/ nation's relationship with the international market. The assets in this focal point include customer/nation loyalty, customer satisfaction, brands, opening to globalization, etc.
- **Renewal and Development Capital** – refers to organization/nation's capabilities and real investments made in an effort to increase its competitive strength in future markets, which, in turn, encourages future growth. Renewal and development assets include investments in research and development, patents, trademarks, start-up companies, etc.

These indicators of the five areas can be used in a predictive way as they show capacity and potential for future innovation of the organization/ nation/ region.

ISRAEL- ECONOMIC BACKGROUND

The State of Israel is located in west Asia, on the southeastern edge of the Mediterranean Sea. It shares a border with Lebanon in the north, Syria and Jordan in the east and Egypt in the southwest. Israel has a diverse population of 7,150,000 citizens, according to the 2007 estimates.

Despite its small size and relatively young age (**60** years of independence), Israel has succeeded in accomplishing great technological achievements. It is at the forefront of a broad range of disciplines such as agro technology, biotechnology, computer-aided education, and data communication. Israel has an open economy, which is fully integrated in the global trading system. Research is performed at each of Israel's seven universities, five technical colleges, and ten specialized research institutes. Furthermore, there is a strong collaboration between universities and the industrial sector, which creates innovative, dynamic and new ideas for future development.

The Israeli government has a very clear strategic policy to encourage innovation. The Law for Encouragement of Industrial Research and Development (1984) acts as the general mandate to the Office of the Chief Scientist (OCS), that is located within the Ministry of Industry, Trade and Labor. Another important policy of this office is to support and to enhance international trade cooperation between nations and between Israeli companies (mainly high-tech companies) and foreign companies.

In addition, the governmental policy aims to support the "infant" companies and start-up's in their early stage in order to encourage them to invest in R&D. One of the key success factors for flourishing start-up companies in Israel (approximately 3000 start-ups) is a targeted policy directed to encourage Venture Capital funds to invest in high-tech start-ups .The governmental policy provides the proper conditions throughout the private infrastructure i.e. VCs as part of the process of generating a generic capability for the development of other new infant industries. The Israeli experience is unique and most successful instance of diffusion of the Silicon Valley model of VCs beyond North America (Avnimelech & Tobal, 2006).

Apart from this policy, Israel has recently been offered membership in the OECD, an organization founded to facilitate development and economic cooperation among the developed countries. This proposal came after impressive economic achievements within Israel in recent years and will make Israel a full member in this exclusive club of 30 developed countries.

VALUING ISRAEL'S INTELLECTUAL CAPITAL

The IC report of Israel was based on data and information collected from international statistics publications, such as OECD, the Human Development Report, IMD, the Global Competitiveness Report, etc., as well from national reports and key figures in the government and the academic world. In these evaluations we have established a base set of Intellectual Capital indicators that can be applied at both the regional and national level, drawing from established practice in the Intellectual Capital field based on the Skandia Navigator model (Edvinsson & Malone, 1997). The audit is a comparative study based upon a comparison of Israel with other developed countries using updated data for the same indicators of the five focal areas of the model.

This IC of Israel shows that Israel has succeeded in accomplishing great technological achievements in diverse fields as bio-technology, nano- technology, sciences, health, communications etc. These accomplishments demonstrated that Israel invest mainly in **Research and Development**, which is part of the most important area in the model (Renewal and Development Capital). As it can be shown in table 1, according to IMD survey in 2004 Israel was placed first out of other developed countries in total expenders in R&D as a percentage of GDP (4.55%). Over the past few years, research and development institutions and start-up high-tech companies have been considered the pioneers of Israel's growth and have come to be viewed as national symbols. Thanks to research and development Israel's enjoys a competitive edge in the global world market and ensures it's potential for future growth. The Israeli government encourages transfer of knowledge from academy to industry, and this activity was translated into growing number of patents registered in the US and Europe.

Israel has chosen to invest mainly in innovation and **Human Capital** in the form of highly educated workforce that is well integrated in the hi-tech sector and in research and scientific activity. In 2004 the Ministry of Finance published that Israel has 135 engineers per 10,000 employees. Another developed area of the model is the process capital – Israel has a **modern infrastructure**: a supportive business environment, a highly advanced financial banking sector, legal protection of foreign trademarks and patents. All of these factors consist a knowledge based ecology which provides Israel with a comparative advantage and

Table 1. The Leading Indicators (The Intellectual Capital of the State of Israel, 2007)

Fig. no.	Source	Indicators	Israel Position
1.1	OECD, 2006	G.D.P Growth Comparison	5
2.2	The Global Competitiveness Report 2006	GCI Indicator (Global Comp. Indicator)	15 (out of 125 countries)
3.6	The Central Bureau of Statistics, 2006	National Expenditure on Education as a Percentage of GDP, 2003	1
4.1	The Global Competitiveness Report 2006-7	Availability of Scientists and Engineers	1
5.9	IMD, 2004	Total Expenditures on R&D (percentage of GDP), 2004	1
5.11	The Global Competitiveness Report 2006-7	Venture Capital Availability	2

high growth potential as one can see from the leading indicators in table 1.

ISRAEL AS A BENCHMARK FOR REGIONS IN EUROPE

In 2007 another study: "Effectiveness of ICT RTD on the EU Innovation System" was conducted for the European Commission, DG INFSO Evaluation and Monitoring Unit, (Pasher et al, 2007). The study aims to assess how effectively EU ICT RTD and deployment initiatives are being exploited in European systems of Innovation at member state and regional levels.

Four methodologies were applied in this study: **Intellectual Capital Assessment** - provides a missing link between ICT RTD and deployment activities and national or regional performance in terms of competitiveness, prosperity and inclusion. At the national level Intellectual Capital is defined as 'potential *for future economic and social growth*', **Value Network Analysis** to understand impact of the networks in terms of actual value creation – at the project, organisation, network and regional levels, the **PACE toolkit** (Project Assets, Core competences and Exploitable items). This methodology visualized the impact of EU-funded ICT-related initiatives on innovation systems within each region by compiling an *Inventory of Regional Assets* that are created by research and deployment projects, and macro-econometric **Multivariate Statistical Methods** – According to this evaluative based approach (Dosi 1988, Young 2003), the economic performance of any territory mainly depends on the combination of socio-cultural and structural factors. This analysis allowed us to identify meaningful correlations between indicators of participation in ICT RTD and deployment projects and the innovative and economic performance for the regions.

This empirical approach combined a quantitative elaboration of data available for EU regions with a more in-depth analysis of 10 regions. In addition, Israel was selected for purposes of comparative benchmarks. Interviews were conducted with project participants and local stakeholders in the 10 regions of Europe: Auvergne-France, Braunschweig-Germany, Crete-Greece, Jihov'ychod-Czech Republic, Kent-UK, Kujasko Promorskie-Poland, Liguria-Italy, Pais Vasco-Spain, Smaaland-Sweden, and Vlaams Brabant-Belgium as well as interviews in the State of Israel which was used as a benchmark for Intellectual Capital evaluation.

Starting from EUROSTAT data, intellectual Capital indicators were developed to profile 10 selected regions and Israel in terms of the local knowledge base, the structure of local industry and the presence of research and innovation networks

Table 2. Regional Indicators of Intellectual Capital used in the study (Effectiveness of ICT RTD Impacts on the EU Innovation System. European Commission, 2007)

Category Intellectual Capital	Indicator
Human Capital	Human resources in Science and Technology (% of population)
Process Capital	Participation in Life-Long Learning (per 100 population aged 25-64)
Process Capital	EPO (Europe Patents Organization)Patents per million population
Market Capital	Employment in Medium-High and High-Tech Manufacturing (% of total workforce)
Market Capital	Employment in High-Tech Services (% of total workforce)
Renewal and Development	Public R&D expenditure (% of GDP)
Renewal and Development	Business R&D expenditure (% of GDP)
Financial Capital	Unemployment (% of total population)
Financial Capital	GDP per Capital

within the region. The assessment was based on statistical data representing the five areas of the IC Framework collected from public sources. See table 2.

According to this in-depth analysis with integration of all the four methodologies, Israel emerges as an innovative region in comparison with the other 10 European regions. This analysis was demonstrated in the Israel profile based on the five focal areas of the IC model (Pasher at el.2007).

In addition in the course of this study, critical success factors for regional innovation systems were annotated. Based on the findings, the following characteristics that would describe an effective regional innovation system began to emerge, as been demonstrated in the case of Israel and in the case of other knowledge-based regions in the study. Besides few factors that refer to the EU projects, most of the critical success factors, based on the intellectual capital assessment, and can be applied on cities, regions and countries for the creation of a knowledge-based ecology that leads to innovation as follow.

Critical Success Factors for Regional Innovation Systems

- **Innovation capacity is systematically tracked and monitored utilizing economic, social and where available, Intellectual Capital, indicators.**

In this study we found that Intellectual Capital audit is a powerful and useful framework to help understand the effectiveness of regional innovation systems, like in the case of Israel that have been applied three times.

- **There is a clear regional government innovation strategy (systems of incentives and innovation funds, etc.) that is integrated with national- innovation policies.**

In this study the most innovative regions (such as in Germany and Belgium) had a clear strategy for increasing the innovation activity, theses regions provide governmental supportive system for investors and private companies to participate in innovation activity.

- **Most of the critical socio-cultural and structural factors for innovation are addressed at the regional policy level.**

The capacity of a regional system to absorb innovation and convert it into economic growth depends on a combination of structural and socio-cultural factors. Increased potential for future growth in European regions has a statistically significant relationship with two factors related to **Human Capital: 1)** the percentage of young people in a status of long term unemployment and **2)** the percentage of total population with higher education. Statistically, a highly skilled labour force and employment in high-tech services are the key success factors explaining the performance of the most "virtuous" regions in terms of innovation. This finding emerges from the Macro-Economic analysis as well as from the Intellectual Capital Audit of the 10 chosen regions.

- **Regional institutions have established science parks, 'virtual districts' or 'technology incubators' involving universities, research centres and private industry to diffuse new ideas in the local context.**

Regional innovation strategies focus on the creation of 'virtual districts' or similar business clusters as a way to improve the take-up of ICT results in the regional industry and society. All the innovative regions in this study provide the environment for knowledge transfer between private companies and research institutes. This infrastructure enables them to create new useful knowledge for hi-tech industry needs.

- **The benefits of participation in ICT RTD projects and deployment activities are tracked and made visible at the levels of organisations, networks, clusters and the region as a whole.**

The EU projects create a demanding environment, often far more advanced than the actual needs of the local, regional, and national markets. In this way, a more knowledge-intensive research environment is created that will ultimately lead to new products and services. The projects also create more experienced academic researchers that will have the capability to apply their theories and experience to real market needs.

- **Policy and institutional frameworks include a system of incentives for the enlargement of intraregional collaboration networks and local take-up of ICT solutions and tools developed as a result of RTD projects.**

Organisations as recipients of both tangible and intangible assets – created through participation in ICT RTD and deployment programmes – redistribute these assets locally to other organisations through expansion of their collaboration networks. According to the Value Network(VNA) analysis the performance of a region in terms of value created from participations in projects depends both on the number of organisations actually taking part in the project consortia, and on the projects themselves being used to increase knowledge sharing, cooperation and connectivity within that region.On the organizational level, participants in EU-funded projects identified gains in both tangible and intangible assets that enhanced their **organisational competitive edge.**These assets contribute to the formation of Intellectual Capital of project participants and to the innovation capacity of the regional system.

CONCLUSION

The results of the studies reviewed in this chapter are consistent with a view of regional innovation as an 'ecology' that converts knowledge and value created locally into long term factors for competitiveness and economic growth. We found out that there are some critical success factors for region to become knowledge based region. From these factors emerge that the link between research and private companies together with policy actions creates a very wide base for innovation dynamics i.e.: collaboration and creating new knowledge as patents, new products and solutions. In Israel, these links exist and allow to create innovation activity between companies, investors and research institutions. The Israeli experience shows that investment in R&D and in Human capital together with a modern infrastructure and above all, clear supportive policy are the key factors for innovation development in the region or the nation.

In addition, we found that an Intellectual Capital audit is a powerful and useful framework to help understand the effectiveness of regional innovation systems, offering the possibility for evidence-based future policies that retrospective performance analysis.

REFERENCES

Audretsch, D. B., & Keilbach, M. (2004). Entrepreneurship and Regional Growth: An Evolutionary Interpretation. *Journal of Evolutionary Economics*, *14*(5), 605–616. doi:10.1007/s00191-004-0228-6

Avnimelech, G., & Tobal, M. (2006). *Microeconomic Insights from Israel's Venture Capital Emergence Towards a Theory of Evolutionary Targeting of Infant Industries*. Haifa, Israel: Neaman Institute.

Baumol, W. J. (2002). *The Free-Market Innovation Machine*. Princeton, NJ: Princeton University Press.

Blume & S. N. Durlauf (Ed.), *The Economy as an Evolving Complex System, Current Perspectives and Future District ions* (*Vol. 3*, pp. 267–282). Oxford, UK: Oxford University Press.

Castells, M., & Hall, P. (1994). *Technopoles of the World*. London: Routledge.

Dosi, G. (1988). Sources, Procedures and Microeconomic Effects of Innovation. *Journal of Economic Literature*, *26*, 1120–1171.

E. Pasher Team. (1998). *The Intellectual Capital of the State of Israel 1998: a Look to the Future*. Herzelia, Israel: Edna Pasher Ph.D and Associates.

Eccles, R. G., Herz, R. H., Keegan, E. M., & Philips, D. M. H. (2001). *The Value Reporting Revoluion*. New York: Pricewaterhouse Coopers.

Edna Pasher Ph.D and Associates. Allee, V., Innocenti, A., Koumpis, A., Mavridis, A., Molinari, F., Pasher, E., Shachar, S., Schwabe, O., Tektonidis, D., Tresman, M. and Vontas, A. (2007). Effectiveness of ICT RTD Impacts on the EU Innovation System: Final Report. Evaluation Study for the European Commission, DG Information Society and Media Directorate C. Lisbon Strategy and Policies for the Information Society. Unit C3 – Evaluation and Monitoring, December 11, 2007.

Edna Pasher Ph.D and Associates. Allee, V., Innocenti, A., Koumpis, A., Mavridis, A., Molinari, F., Pasher, E., Shachar, S., Schwabe, O., Tektonidis, D., Tresman, M. and Vontas, A. (2007). Annex to the Final Report. Evaluation Study for the European Commission, DG Information Society and Media Directorate C. Lisbon Strategy and Policies for the Information Society. Unit C3 – Evaluation and Monitoring, December 11, 2007.

Edvinsson, L., & Malone, M. S. (1997). *Intellectual Capital: Realizing Your Company's True Value by Finding its Hidden Brainpower*. New York: Harper Business.

Lev, B. (2001). *Intangibles: Management, Measurement and Reporting*. Washington, DC: Brookings Institution.

Machlup, F. (1962). *The production and Distribution of Knowledge in the United States*. Princeton, NJ: Princeton University Press.

Mokyr, J. (2002). *The Gifts from Athena: Historical Origins of the Knowledge Economy*. Princeton, NJ: Princeton University Press.

OECD. (1996). *Organization for Economic Cooperation and Development. The Knowledge-Based Economy*. Paris: OECD.

Pasher, E., & Shachar, S. (2004). *The Intellectual Capital of the State of Israel*. Jerusalem, Israel: Ministry of Industry, Trade and Labor.

Pasher, E., & Shachar, S. (2007). *The Intellectual Capital of the State of Israel: 60 Years of Achievements*. Jerusalem, Israel: Ministry of Industry, Trade and Labor.

Pred, A. (1976). The Interurban Transmission of Growth in Advanced Economies. *Regional Studies*, *10*(9), 151–171. doi:10.1080/09595237600185161

Shachar, S. (2002). *Methods For Knowledge And Know-How Measurement.* MA Thesis, Faculty of Management, The Leon Recanati Graduate School of Business Administration. Tel-Aviv, Israel: Tel-Aviv University.

Sveiby, K.-E. (1997). *The New Organizational Wealth: Managing & Measuring Knowledge-Based Assets*. San Francisco, CA: Berrett-Koehler.

Wallman, S., & Blair, M. (2000). *UnSeen Wealth: Report of the Brookings Taskforce on Understanding Intangible Sources of Value*. Washington, DC: The Brooking Institution.

Young, H. P. (2003). The Diffusion of Innovations in Social Networks. In L.E.

Chapter 17
Orchestrating Knowledge-Based Urban Development:
Lessons from Multimedia Super Corridor, Malaysia

Tan Yigitcanlar
Queensland University of Technology, Australia

Muna Sarimin
Queensland University of Technology, Australia

ABSTRACT

In the era of knowledge economy, cities and regions have started increasingly investing on their physical, social and knowledge infrastructures so as to foster, attract and retain global talent and investment. Knowledge-based urban development as a new paradigm in urban planning and development is being implemented across the globe in order to increase the competitiveness of cities and regions. This chapter provides an overview of the lessons from Multimedia Super Corridor, Malaysia as one of the first large scale manifestations of knowledge-based urban development in South East Asia. The chapter investigates the application of the knowledge-based urban development concept within the Malaysian context, and, particularly, scrutinises the development and evolution of Multimedia Super Corridor by focusing on strategies, implementation policies, infrastructural implications, and agencies involved in the development and management of the corridor. In the light of the literature and case findings, the chapter provides generic recommendations, on the orchestration of knowledge-based urban development, for other cities and regions seeking such development.

INTRODUCTION

The 21st century has marked the beginning of the new advancements in the field of information and communication technology (ICT). The rapid development of ICTs has also made a significant impact on the overall socio-economic fabric of cities and thus created an urgent need for urban planners to explore new ways of strategising planning and development that encompass the needs and requirements of the economy and society. The 21st century is also an era that the notion of knowledge economy emerged, where knowledge and ICTs are seen as important

DOI: 10.4018/978-1-61520-721-3.ch017

factors as the classical factors of production (i.e. land, labour, capital) in the creation of jobs and wealth (Cooke, 2001). The era of knowledge economy requires knowledge being the most crucial factor for national, regional and local economic development. Hence, the emergence of a knowledge economy has spawned a new notion of knowledge-based urban development (KBUD) as the latest wave of globalisation that extends over geographical boundaries (Yigitcanlar et. al., 2008a).

Historically cities and metropolitan regions have always been the hubs of knowledge generation and knowledge related activities with highly benefitting from various technologies (Van Doren, 1992). Particularly, advances in ICTs are inevitably making societies and cities increasingly knowledge-based, and responsive and dynamic to answer the needs of residents and to ensure their quality of lives. During the last several decades, following the lead of developed countries, some of the developing countries realised the necessity of starting up their ICT sector in order to compete in an environment of increasing globalisation and emergence of the new knowledge economy. In recent years the nature of the urban development started to change accordingly as activities in the knowledge sector have become more important and they required conditions and environments which are different from the commodity-based manufacturing activities (Knight, 1995). At that instance, KBUD is seen as a new approach in urban planning and development in order to ensure that cities are competitive in the global market of the era of knowledge economy. Hence, in broad sense, KBUD is a new form of urban development for the 21st Century that could potentially bring both economic prosperity and sustainable socio-spatial order to the contemporary city (Yigitcanlar, 2007). In order to realise a KBUD and compete nationally and internationally, Yigitcanlar and Velibeyoglu (2008) suggest that cities need knowledge infrastructure (e.g. universities, research and development institutes), a concentration of well educated people (e.g. knowledge workers), technological, mainly electronic, infrastructure (e.g. ICTs), and connections to the global economy (e.g. international companies and finance institutions for trade and investment).

In the case of Malaysia, the goal of KBUD is taken seriously by policy-makers. Malaysia, being a developing country relies heavily on the manufacturing-led industries for the economic growth due to her rich natural resources and relatively low-cost labour force. However, the structural transformation of the global economy which focuses on knowledge and human capitals has challenged Malaysia to concentrate on activities with a higher level of value addition. In Malaysia, the shift to the knowledge economy is part of a wider plan to achieve the objective of the National Vision for 2020. The Vision 2020 is a 30-year plan to push Malaysia to achieve a level at par with the developed nations in terms of economic performance and technological capability (Mohamad, 1996). With the move towards the knowledge economy and knowledge-based development, Malaysia aims to achieve sustainable gross domestic product (GDP) growth rates in the long run with knowledge playing a dominant role in driving productivity and sustaining economic growth (Economic Research Services Department, 2000). Thus, Malaysia needs to successfully transform herself into a knowledge economy where its growth will be lifted to a new and higher trajectory, which is one of the key requirements for Malaysia to become a developed nation. This shift offers an opportunity for economic growth and prosperity, as well as bringing her faster to the achievement of the Vision 2020 goals. The most significant tangible evidence of Malaysia's commitment to the knowledge economy is the Multimedia Super Corridor (MSC) project, which is the largest KBUD attempt in Malaysia.

This chapter aims to provide an overview of and lessons learned from the MSC project, being the most ambitious KBUD manifestation in South East Asia. Following to this introduction section,

Figure 1. Evolution of factors effecting development (Mohan et al., 2004)

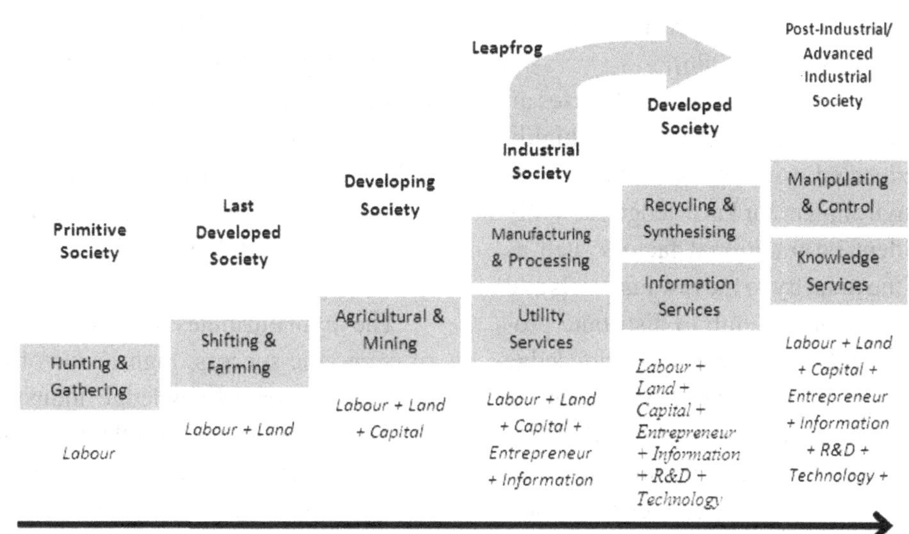

the second section discusses the background, concepts and principles of KBUD. The third section investigates the implementation of the KBUD concept within the Malaysian context. The subsequent section scrutinises the development and evolution of MSC by focusing on strategies, implementation policies, infrastructural implications, and agencies involved in the development and management of the corridor. The final section provides generic recommendations in the light of the MSC experience, on the orchestration of knowledge-based urban development, for other cities and regions seeking knowledge-based development.

BACKGROUND

Knowledge-based urban development (KBUD) is spurred by the growth of knowledge economy, which refers to the generation of income through the creation, production, distribution and consumption of knowledge and knowledge-based products (Yigitcanlar et. al., 2008a; 2008b). The outputs of the knowledge economy are not necessarily raw materials and production of quantified goods, but also highly skilled and educated labour force producing abstract goods such as information, software and management, and transferring skills and knowledge particularly via the internet and other online vehicles. In other words, as Cooke (2001) states the traditional factors of production (i.e. land, labour and capital) are now strongly complemented with information and knowledge in the new knowledge economy. Figure 1 below shows the evolution of the key factors effecting economic development (for more information see Drucker, 1993).

In general, the major elements of knowledge economy are characterised by the non-diminishing resources such as knowledge whereby the knowledge-inputs are rapidly expanding in tandem with technology and innovation. The advancements in internet creates virtual market places and organisations enabling increased mobility of capital and labour, highly educated labour force, high level of per capita wealth, skills and knowledge are key assets, which form a perfect incubator for knowledge generation. ICTs are pillars to the knowledge economy as they provide a well connection to other global nodes and contribute to the formation of an open cosmopolitan society attractive to global talents (Corey and Wilson, 2006).

Since knowledge economy mostly focuses on the creation of abstract goods produced by highly skilled and educated workers, the creation of an ideal work environment for knowledge economy is not dependent on traditional factors such as proximity of the industry to the raw materials and availability of a transport hub to distribute produced goods. Therefore, a shift towards knowledge economy through the creation of KBUD presents significant new opportunities and challenges to the way the government, people and organisations think, operate, and manage their activities. In the knowledge era, KBUD needs to focus on catering and attracting knowledge-based activities and high-technology industries that are expected to contribute significantly to employment, GDP and exports. Factors of production such as labour, capital, raw materials and entrepreneurship remain important but knowledge is the key driving force underlying growth and a valuable commodity, not only as a factor of production but also as a commodity to be traded (Hearn and Rooney, 2008).

KBUD transcends many areas of economic, social and urban policy, and has three broad purposes (Figure 2). Firstly, KBUD is an economic development strategy that codifies technical knowledge for the innovation of products and services, including urban services, market knowledge for understanding changes in the economy, financial knowledge to measure the inputs and outputs of production and development processes, and human knowledge in the form of skills and creativity, within an economic model (Lever, 2002). It aims at a local economic development that is competitive and integrated with global knowledge economy. Secondly, KBUD indicates the intention to increase the skills and knowledge of residents and employees as a means for intellectual, human and social development (Gonzalez et al., 2005). It aims to increase the quality of life by providing necessary services for societal development. Thirdly, KBUD builds a strong spatial relationship among knowledge community precincts for augmenting the knowledge spill-over effect that contributes significantly to the establishment and expansion of creative urban regions and supports linkages and knowledge transfer between these precincts (Yigitcanlar et al., 2008c). It also aims an urban development that is ecologically sensitive, sustainable and safe.

The main attributes of KBUD are high levels of economic success, high levels of knowledge intensity, diverse knowledge industries, strong academic institutions, excellent communications and transport infrastructure, unique offering to investors and individuals, strategies to ensure all benefit from knowledge and economic success (Yigitcanlar et. al., 2008d).

KNOWLEDGE BASED URBAN DEVELOPMENT IN MALAYSIA

Since early 1990s Malaysia's economy has been going through a structural transformation. The transformation has established a transition pace for the economy dominantly dependent on agriculture and primary commodities to move forward to a manufacture-based, export driven economy spurred by high technology and capital-intensive industries (Ramasamy et. al., 2004). Emergence of the knowledge era, where knowledge replacing physical and natural resources as the key ingredient of economic development, has provided a new platform for Malaysia to move forward to achieve a more sustainable economic and socio-spatial growth and become globally competitive. Thus, basic foundations of the knowledge economy have been set in Malaysia's development policies. The foundation is the concentration on the key areas including human resource development, science and technology, research and development, physical info structure, and financing and equity, which are the fundamental elements of building the knowledge economy and minimising the digital

Figure 2. Pillars of knowledge-based urban development (Yigitcanlar, 2008:308)

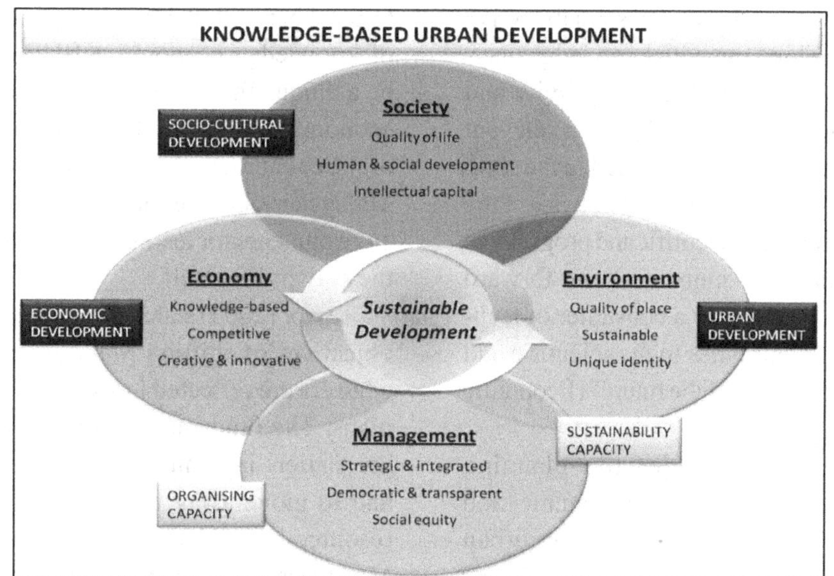

divide (Jaffee, 1998). In Malaysia, the shift to the knowledge economy is also a part of a wider plan to achieve the objectives of the National Vision of 2020. This vision was delineated by the Third Outline Perspective Plan which states that the knowledge economy will provide a platform for Malaysia to sustain a rapid rate of economic growth, enhance global competitiveness, and strengthen Malaysia's capability to innovate, adapt and create indigenous technology. The foundation initiatives for the knowledge economy in Malaysia started in the mid 1990s with the launch of her National ICT Agenda (NITA) and KBUD initiatives (i.e. the Multimedia Super Corridor Project) (Economic Planning Unit, 2001).

While the NITA objectives are very much geared towards the formulation of strategies and promotion of ICT utilisation and development, the KBUD initiatives are aimed at creating an ideal ICT and multimedia environment as well as a global test bed to enable Malaysia to be in the global competition to attract knowledge workers and industries and businesses. The basic physical infrastructures (e.g. telecommunications) for the KBUD initiatives were completed in 1999. In addition to the telecommunications infrastructure, there are also five designated cyber cities (i.e. Kuala Lumpur City Centre, Kuala Lumpur Tower, Technology Park Malaysia, Cyberjaya and Malaysian Technology Development Corporation, University of Putra Malaysia Incubator Centre) which played a critical role on the achievement of KBUD goals. While progressing further towards the knowledge economy, Malaysia has started the experience of such development on the knowledge accumulated from the implementation of the KBUD initiatives since mid 1990s, which has marked the beginning of the era of KBUD in Malaysia. KBUD initiatives are seen as the most significant tangible evidence of Malaysia's commitment to the knowledge economy. The corridor development project along with NITA also serves as a catalyst to expand knowledge economy, in other words, ICT-related industries, by creating an attractive and suitable environment for the development of ICT industry in Malaysia.

The National Vision for 2020 is a 30-year plan to push Malaysia to achieve a level at par with the developed nations in terms of economic performance and technological capability. With the move towards a knowledge economy, Malaysia is moving forward to achieve a sustainable GDP growth rate in the long run with knowledge playing a dominant role in driving productivity and sustaining economic growth. The most relevant context of KBUD has been embedded in the sixth challenge of the Vision 2020 of Malaysia: "the challenge is to establish a scientific and progressive society, a society that is innovative and forward looking, one that is not only a consumer of technology but also a contributor to the scientific and technological civilisation of the future" (Economic Planning Unit, 2006:39).

The Vision 2020 includes the planning and provision of ICT and telecommunication infrastructure in a multi-billion dollar urban mega-KBUD-project (i.e. the Multimedia Super Corridor Project). The Vision 2020 is intended to bring Malaysia to become a united nation, with a confident Malaysian society, infused by strong moral and ethical values, living in a society that is more democratic, liberal and tolerant, caring, economically just and equitable, progressive and prosperous, and in full possession of an economy that is competitive, robust and resilient. Thus, Malaysia needs to successfully transform itself into a knowledge economy where its potential growth will be lifted to a new and higher trajectory (Huff, 2005). This will offer unparalleled opportunity for economic growth and prosperity, as well as bringing the country faster to the achievement of the Vision 2020 goals.

In relation to KBUD, what makes KBUD in Malaysia is so important is that unlike similar projects in other countries, Malaysia is explicitly attaching aspirations for both national development and national identity to it. As envisioned by the Malaysian Government, the mega-KBUD-projects "will not be just a physical location, or just another industrial or technological park, and it is not a far eastern imitation of the Silicon Valley, [but] it represents a new paradigm in the creation of value for the [knowledge era]" (Mohamad, 1998:107). Malaysia envisioned that KBUD initiatives will be the best platform to uplift the nation to be at par with the global aspirations in the era of knowledge economy. KBUD initiatives will be a unique form of KBUD that will incorporate economic goals as well as the socio-spatial vision of the country. As noted by Mohamad (1998) that Malaysian KBUD initiatives are attempts to create environments for testing both the technology and the way of life itself.

Taylor (2003) states that Malaysia's long term objectives of shifting Malaysia into the knowledge era are reflected in the various development plans. The fundamental strategy is to transform the nation into an information-based society, and to move away from the previous focus on resource-based industries. In this respect, the Malaysian government recognises the importance of shifting its investments to intellectual capital and skilled manpower. Malaysia has always placed knowledge as a top priority in economic and social development. These will be translated into the policies incorporated in the national social and economic plans such as the five year Malaysia Plan and Outline Perspective Plan. In the most recent the Ninth Malaysia Plan, which became the economic blueprint for the nation between 2006-2010, knowledge development is placed as the second of five priority development thrusts. Malaysian planning system is very much based on the British plan-led system where future spatial development of the country is directed by policies outlined in the hierarchical order of plans (i.e. National Physical Plan, Structure Plans and Local Plans). These development plans are prepared parallel to the aspirations of Malaysia which are spelt out in the national economic and social plan. As such the direction of future spatial development in Malaysia is foreseen to correspond to the vision of KBUD.

Current policies indicate that Malaysia continues to nurture the elements of knowledge in the future development of the country (Al-Furaih et al., 2007). This future direction was envisioned by the newly elected Prime Minister in his speech at the Symposium of Knowledge Cities which was held in the city of Shah Alam, Selangor, in 2007. He emphasised on the needs to have "the physical infrastructure to cater for greater knowledge acquisition, embarking on initiatives that would attract value added investments into the city through technology transfer and incorporating learning and knowledge culture among the city dwellers". He also added that a "knowledgeable population is a key in fostering a knowledge-based economy which able to bring Malaysia to a greater height in development and progress".

MULTIMEDIA SUPER CORRIDOR

The largest Malaysian KBUD initiative is the Multimedia Super Corridor Project (MSC), which is a hub designed to promote multimedia products and services by bringing together the legislative framework and next generation telecommunications infrastructure. The aim of MSC project is to create a world class urban corridor with state-of-the-art multimedia infrastructure, efficient transportation system and an attractive living environment to attract knowledge workers and industries to invest and operate within the area. The development of MSC contributes to the creation of a high technology environment to enable Malaysia to involve in the mainstream activities necessary to attract knowledge workers, technopreneurs and industries. The first phase of MSC area covers about 750 sq.km. The corridor is a cluster of seven distinctive functional zones within the Klang Valley (Figure 3). There are two intelligent cities (i.e. Putrajaya and Cyberjaya). While the former acts as a new federal administrative centre and electronic government, the latter is a development hub of ICT and multimedia companies, professional and students (Mukhtar, 2008). There is an airport city which serves as a service centre to support Kuala Lumpur International Airport and aeronautical services centre. A nucleus for local ICT small and medium-scaled enterprises (SMEs) is located in the Cyber Village. Tele-Suburb is the residential zones which

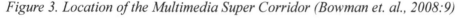

Figure 3. Location of the Multimedia Super Corridor (Bowman et. al., 2008:9)

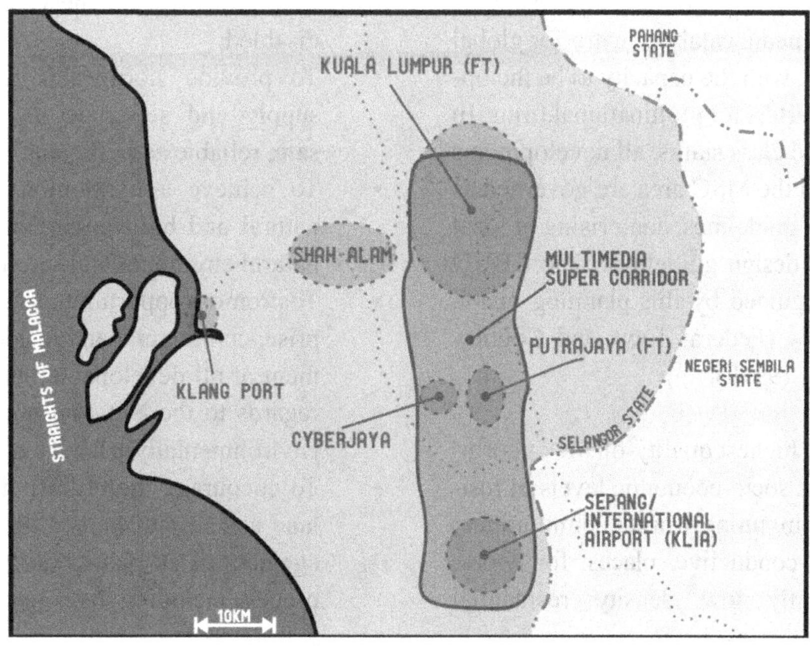

comprises of smart homes, smart schools and smart neighbourhood local centres. High-Technology Park is the location for industrial related activities and they include the high-tech industry, institution and R&D zones. There is also a R&D centre which places a collaborative cluster of academic institutions and corporate R&D Centre at the heart of MSC (MDec, 2008).

Cyberjaya is the core of the MSC and one of the two intelligent cities established within the corridor. While the other intelligent city, Putrajaya, is set to function as the new government headquarters, the development of Cyberjaya is initiated as a Cyberjaya Flagship Zone. Cyberjaya was officially launched in May 1997 and located adjacent to Putrajaya. Cyberjaya covers an area of approximately 7,000 hectares and is designed to provide infrastructure and facilities to support multimedia industries in the MSC. Cyberjaya is planned to accommodate approximately 240,000 residents and a working population of 10,000 foreign knowledge workers. The development components of Cyberjaya consist of designated zones for: housing; enterprise; open space and greenery; institutions, and: commerce and businesses (Federal Department of Town and Country Planning, 2005; 2006). The development aims to create a multimedia catalyst centre for global R&D and design, with the capacity to be the operational headquarters for multinational firms. In achieving a world class status, all developments in Cyberjaya and the MSC area are governed as whole by a set of guidelines, comprising of local plans and urban design guidelines. The KBUD in Cyberjaya is guided by this planning vision outlined as below (Federal Town and Country Planning, 1997a; 1997b):

- To have the highest quality-of-life opportunities for all socio-economic levels of resident and commuting worker communities;
- To create conductive places for work, predominantly low density residential living, and leisure, in safe, attractive, green environments;
- To facilitate the development of a socially and culturally rich community in which residents with a wide diversity of cultural and socio-economic backgrounds have a strong sense of 'civic ownership' and pride in their shared welfare and environment;
- To facilitate the development of a human oriented, intelligent city in harmony with nature;
- To physically facilitate the wide-scale building of an ICT literate population through education and skill development;
- To provide the physical attributes necessary and conducive to the National Strategy for the development of the MSC as a hub of information technological advancement and future economic growth in promoting new industrial sectors;
- To provide advanced telecommunication infrastructure for multimedia and ICT industries, business and residential users;
- To provide road, public transit and pedestrian networks that are convenient, reliable, safe and efficient and provide barrier-free movement for the young, elderly and disabled;
- To provide stormwater drainage, water supply and sewerage networks that are safe, reliable and efficient;
- To achieve a harmonious and balanced natural and built environment, protecting natural environmental resources;
- To promote opportunities for vibrant enterprise, commercial and residential development at all developable land, with having regards to the National policy of creating environmentally friendly entrepreneurs;
- To encourage the orderly development of land and resources, and the efficient management of all phases of the development process including the construction phase.

Multimedia Development Corporation (MDeC), a one stop agency appointed to manage the operation of the MSC, envisions a 20-year time frame for the full implementation and execution of the corridor. There are three phases of activities within the 20-year period as shown in Figure 4. Phase 1 of MSC (1996-2004) has completed and the MDeC has successfully managed to attract a core group of world-class companies, launched seven Flagship Applications, put in place a world-leading framework of cyber laws, and established Cyberjaya as the world's-first intelligent city. Presently, the MSC is at its second phase, which links the corridor to other cities around Malaysia and the globe. Phase 2 of the MSC development is planned to be completed soon (2004-2010) whereby it will link the MSC to other cyber cities in Malaysia and around the world by creating a web of corridors and establishing world class companies. The development will also set global standards in flagship applications, champion cyber laws within the global society, and establish a number of intelligent and globally well-linked cities. Phase 3 (2010-2020) foresees the corridor to be expanded to the whole country by providing a spin for a full transformation into a knowledge economy and society as envisaged in the Vision 2020 (MDeC, 2006; 2008).

In order to make the corridor more attractive to local and international investors, a number of policies are developed. The first policy was focusing on the development of the physical infrastructure including Kuala Lumpur City Centre, Kuala Lumpur International Airport and integrated logistics hubs, rapid rail link to Kuala Lumpur, a smart highway and two intelligent cities (i.e. Cyberjaya and Putrajaya). The second one involves the execution of laws, policies and practices, which are purposely designed to encourage electronic commerce, facilitate the development of multimedia applications. There were also a policy for the development of high-capacity telecommunications and logistic infrastructure, which is built on up to 10 gigabit digital optical fibre backbone and using the ATM switches to provide optic fibre connections to buildings. This

Figure 4. Milestones of the MSC development (Azhar, 2008)

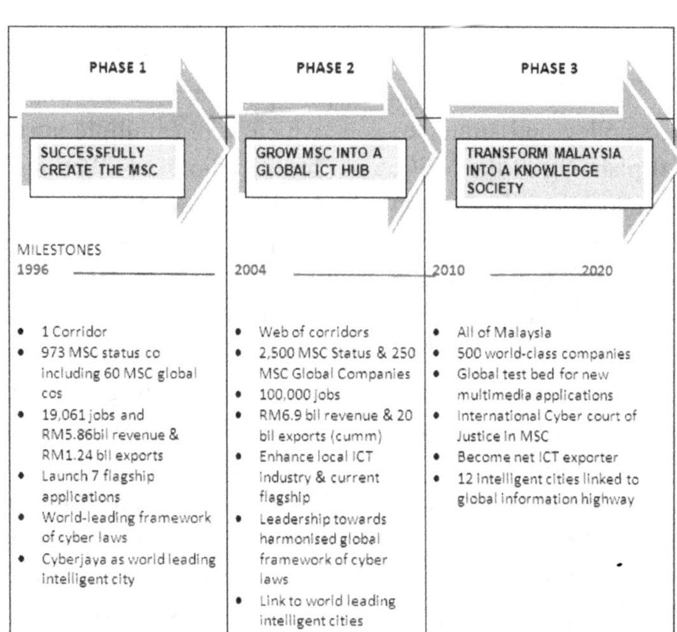

network has a five gigabit international gateway with direct links to the US, Europe and Japan as well as the other nations in South East Asia. The final policy also highlighted the need for a high powered one-stop-shop, the MDeC, to monitor the operation of the MSC. The overall development strategies of the MSC are (MDeC, 2006):

- Leapfrogging Development Stages, which highlighted the transformation from industrial society to knowledge society;
- Flagship Applications, which identified seven main applications to enable Malaysia to achieve a healthy and successful knowledge economy growth. These applications are: multipurpose cards, R&D clusters, electronic government, worldwide manufacturing web, borderless marketing centre, telemedicine and smart schools;
- National Information Technology Council, which drafted the National ICT Agenda and aims to transform the Malaysian society into a civil society in line with the Vision 2020;
- Strategic Policy Thrusts, which concentrated on the development of e-commerce, e-public services, e-learning, e-economy and e-sovereignty.

With abovementioned policy and strategies in mind, for the physical planning of the MSC, ten strategic development locations have been identified: Kuala Lumpur City Centre, Kuala Lumpur Tower, Putrajaya, Cyberjaya, Kuala Lumpur International Airport, High-tech Parks, R&D, Tele-Suburbs, Airport City and Cyber Village. Beyond ICT and multimedia industries the corridor also attracted non-ICT businesses such as finance, insurance and real-estate sectors. In order to encourage the establishment of knowledge industries in the MSC, the Government offers a Bill of Guarantee for "MSC-Status" companies. The Government of Malaysia also commits to (MDeC, 2006):

- Provide a world-class physical and information infrastructure;
- Allow unrestricted employment of local and foreign knowledge workers;
- Ensure freedom of ownership by exempting companies with the MSC Status from local ownership requirements;
- Give freedom to source capital globally for the MSC infrastructure, and the right to borrow funds globally;
- Provide competitive financial incentives, including no income tax for up to 10 years or an investment tax allowance, and no duties on import of multimedia equipment;
- Become a regional leader in intellectual property protection and cyber laws;
- Ensure no Internet censorship is applied;
- Provide globally competitive telecommunications tariffs;
- Tender key infrastructure contracts to leading companies willing to use the MSC as their regional hub;
- Provide an effective one-stop agency – the MDeC.

The MDeC is paying a great attention in attracting and retaining knowledge workers as much as knowledge industries. Companies are to apply through the MDeC for working visas, which permit multiple entries, for their qualifying foreign employees. Working visas for these foreign knowledge workers is granted for initial periods of up to five years. This benefit helps in transfer and understanding of knowledge by working with different people from different parts of the world. Thus, a key factor for the development of MSC is to compete in the global arena (MDEC, 2008).

The MSC status companies are also offered both the financial and non financial incentives. The former includes five years exemption from Malaysian income tax, renewable to 10 years, or a 100% Investment Tax Allowance for up to 5 years on new investments made in MSC cyber cities (provided under the Promotion of Investment Act

1997), duty free import of multimedia equipment as well as R&D grants for local SMEs. Meanwhile there is also non financial incentives given and they include unrestricted employment of foreign knowledge workers, freedom of ownership, freedom to source capital globally, intellectual property protection, execution of cyber laws and a healthy physical environment.

Several agencies played a key role in the development and management of the MSC. These agencies are appointed by the Malaysia government to facilitate and promote the development of MSC.

Multimedia Development Corporation (MDeC) is a government-owned corporation that functions as a 'one-stop agency', focusing on ensuring the success of the MSC and the companies operating in the corridor. The main role of MDeC is to advise the Malaysian Government on legislation and policies, develop MSC specific practises, and set standards for multimedia operations. With a mission to realise Malaysia as a global hub and preferred location for ICT and multimedia innovations, services and operations, MDeC acts as the promoter, developer and manager of the MSC by facilitating the entry of companies and granting MSC status to participating companies as well as realising MSC and Malaysia's overall vision and objectives (MDec, 2008).

Cyberview Corporation is a government owned company and landowner of Cyberjaya. It has been mandated by the Malaysian government to spearhead the development of Cyberjaya. Cyberview's mission is to realise Cyberjaya as a nucleus of the MSC and as global hub and preferred location for ICT, multimedia and services for innovation and operations, and to fulfil specific government initiatives in support of the Vision 2020. Among others, the main Cyberview's roles in the development of Cyberjaya includes ensuring the development of Cyberjaya is achieved in accordance with the MSC guidelines, providing both assistance and support in coordinating joint activities with organisation in Cyberjaya, advising the government on the MSC. In addition, Cyberview is also responsible with the physical development tasks of Cyberjaya including attending to all land administration matters, building enterprise buildings, building supporting amenities as well as undertaking necessary maintenance work (Cyberview Corporation, 2009).

Setia Haruman Corporation acts as the master developer of Cyberjaya. It was entrusted with the role to plan, design and prepare the primary infrastructure for the Cyberjaya Flagship Zone. The area covers 7,000 acres of freehold land consisting of four main zones known as enterprise, commercial, institutional and residential. Each zone is fully equipped with a host of intelligent network services and interactive broadband services. In essence, all aspects of the Cyberjaya development are undertaken by Setia Haruman Corporation. It involves with planning and designing, providing basic infrastructure, marketing and selling of land parcels and other real estate developments to investors and sub developers to design their own premises subject to permitted planning guidelines. In addition, Setia Haruman offers assistance to the MSC status companies in obtaining the right land and approvals for sub division and building plans. It has also been approved to oversee the city's residential development (Setia Haruman Corporation, 2009).

Sepang Municipal Council (SMC) which was previously known as Sepang District Council is the local planning authority for Cyberjaya. In March 2005, Cyberjaya Development Committee approved to upgrading the status of SMC with a total of about 60,000 sq.km developable land. The responsibility of SMC as the local planning authority for Sepang is set out under the Local Government Act 1976, which includes 'planning, development and community services' (MDec, 2006). The function of the local planning authority is crucially vital to deal with any planning applications and to grant planning permissions in Cyberjaya (SMC, 2008).

CONCLUSION

It is evident that ICTs in the knowledge era are continuously shaping the physical and economic developments, including KBUD, which are playing a major role on the development and future expansion of the infrastructure development of cities. The success of Cyberjaya, being the pioneer city in the MSC strategy, has been envied by many. Although there were some criticisms levied pertaining to issues related to social and cultural development, the success can be evaluated from the number of inward investments and the statistics on job creation. Bunnell (2004:148) states that "by the infrastructural and economic criteria of its proponents, [the] MSC is perhaps the qualified success". Lepawsky (2005) highlights that the MSC is unique and interesting as Malaysia is attaching aspirations for both national development and national identity to it, and states that the MSC "is not [only] just another physical location, or just another industrial or technological park – and it is not a far eastern imitation of the Silicon Valley, [but also] represents a new paradigm in the creation of value for the information age" (Mohamad, 1998:107, cited in Lepawsky, 2005:10). Although there are some positive outcomes, still policies on urban development in such large scale and ambitious projects take long time to materialise. Therefore, in terms of urban planning and development of the MSC, it is still early years for a comprehensive evaluation.

Besides project dynamics, physical development of the MSC is also subject to the global economic conditions. Bunnell (2004) reminds us that the physical development of Cyberjaya suffered an inevitable delay of its supporting infrastructure due to economic recession in 1997. However, until recently the overall development of the MSC was progressing quite well when compared to other digital districts such as Boston and Silicon Valley (Indergaard, 2003 cited in Bunnell, 2004). But unfortunately, the current economic crunch beginning of 2008 is foreseen to bring almost similar impact of the 1997 recession to the overall development of the MSC. Nevertheless, the MSC is a long term plan, and it is fully supported by the Malaysian Government and highly regarded as an emerging knowledge corridor. Although the Malaysian government is the architect of and has its overall say of the MSC Vision, its implementation is largely driven by the private sector.

In general, there are a number of lessons that can be learned from the development of MSC being the largest manifestation of KBUD initiative in Malaysia. Firstly, placing MSC as one of the national agendas is perhaps, the best and unique strategy in realising the success of KBUD in Malaysia. While other KBUD initiatives are locally based (e.g. Delft, Barcelona, Silicon Valley), MSC is positioned as part of the Malaysia's national development agenda. The visions of MSC were later translated into series of development plans which guide the direction of the future development for the country. This is a systematic approach in ensuring that elements of KBUD are being continuously embedded in the future socio-spatial development for the whole nation. Secondly, the present success of MSC owes much to the concerted effort by both the public and private sectors. Although the former is the chief architect of the MSC vision and the main provider for the physical and information infrastructure, its implementation is largely driven by the private sector. A high government intervention and its continuous commitment in ensuring the success of this KBUD initiative will increase the confidence of international investors. It indicates a strong commitment given by the Malaysian government against unfavourable market forces. The creation of MDeC, being a one-stop-agency to oversee the operation of MSC is seen as the institutional factor that has contributed to the success. The third lesson learned from the MSC development is that KBUD initiative has to be rightly sited and phased. The first phase of MSC which is located within the Klang Valley Metropolitan Area (KLMA) offers a unique locational advantage. The MSC has a 'unique niche' and it offers a comprehensive package with attractive surroundings and good quality of life (Taylor, 2003). The present pool of the local knowledge workers in Kuala Lumpur, the national capital region plays a big role in the early establishment of the KBUD initiative. KLMA also offer the best urban setting in Malaysia to further enhance the physical environment.

With the steady progress and entering its second phase, the MSC has clearly served as the best platform for the manifestation of KBUD principles and energies to move the country forward to achieve the Vision 2020 and hence, reaching the status of a developed country. The MSC is seen as the best instrument to support Malaysia to be more responsive to the threats and opportunities posed by economic globalisation, which is market driven and technology oriented. In orchestrating a successful KBUD, a comprehensive effort from all levels of government and is required to necessitate the success.

For the case of developing countries, which have similar characteristics like Malaysia, putting the KBUD initiative as part of the national agenda is always regarded as the best strategy. What is presently needed is a continuous and sound policy monitoring in ensuring all of the MSC vision and objectives are achieved and hence making Malaysia to be more competitive in the global market. A particular attention probably is needed in the aspect of intangible factors of MSC such as the attitude and culture of the society (i.e. knowledge communities) that makes up the essence of a successful KBUD. Their input in planning and development of the physical environment is urgently required to further enhance the success of any KBUD initiative. The MSC, being the Malaysia KBUD initiative will certainly equip Malaysia to enter into the global markets by becoming an international centre for knowledge industries and businesses as well as building a knowledge-based society. Future opportunities for research with regards to MSC, being a KBUD initiative in Malaysia is immense. KBUD is a dynamic, participatory and strategic process and it requires a careful and delicate orchestration where the real success cannot happen in a short span of time, and hence a continuous evaluation and assessment are required.

REFERENCES

Al-Furaih, I., Sahab, A., Hayajneh, A., Abdullah, A., Ibrahim, M., & Thalha, M. (Eds.). (2007). Knowledge cities: future of cities in the knowledge economy. Selangor, Malaysia: Scholar Press.

Abu-Anzeh, N., & Ledraa, T. (2007). In Malaysian Institute of Planners, et al. (Eds.), Knowledge Cities, Future of Cities in the Knowledge Economy (pp. 116-139). Kuala Lumpur, Malaysia: Scholar Press.

Azhar, M. K. (2008). *Entrepreneurship and Development*. Powerpoint Slides on AIM Conference Centre, MDeC, MSC Malaysia.

Bowman, B., Nelson, K., Fertjowski, A., Prokuda, L., McCartney, R., & Limb, M. (2008). *Klang Valley Regional Plan 2008 – 2028*. Brisbane: Queensland University of Technology.

Bunnell, T. (2004). *Malaysia, Modernity and Multimedia Super Corridor*. London: Routledge.

Cooke, P. (2001). *Knowledge economies*. New York: Routledge. doi:10.4324/9780203445402

Corey, K., & Wilson, M. (2006). *Urban and regional technology planning*. New York: Routledge.

Cyberview Corporation. (2009). *Cyberview Sdn. Bhd: the landowner of Cyberjaya*. Retrieved May 11, 2009, from http://www.cyberview.com.my/

Drucker, P. (1993). *Post-capitalist society*. New York: Harper Business.

Economic Planning Unit. (2001). *The Third Outline Perspective Plan (2001-2010)*. Putrajata, Malaysia: Economic Planning Unit, Prime Minister's Department.

Economic Planning Unit. (2006). *National Vision 2020*. Putrajata, Malaysia: Economic Planning Unit, Prime Minister's Department.

Economic Research Services Department. (2000). *Special Economic Issue*. Kuala Lumpur, Malaysia: Bumiputra Commerce Bank.

Federal Town and Country Planning. (1997a). Physical planning guidelines for the Multimedia Super Corridor (MSC): *Vol. 1. General Guidelines*. Kuala Lumpur, Malaysia: Ministry of Housing and Local Government.

Federal Town and Country Planning. (1997b). Physical planning guidelines for the Multimedia Super Corridor (MSC): *Vol. 4. Cyberjaya*. Kuala Lumpur, Malaysia: Ministry of Housing and Local Government.

Federal Town and Country Planning. (2005). *National Physical Plan (NPP) 2020*. Kuala Lumpur, Malaysia: Ministry of Housing and Local Government.

Federal Town and Country Planning. (2006). *National Urbanisation Policy (NUP) 2020*. Kuala Lumpur, Malaysia: Ministry of Housing and Local Government.

Gonzalez, M., Alvarado, J., & Martinez, S. (2005). A compilation of resources on knowledge cities and knowledge-based development. *Journal of Knowledge Management*, *8*(5), 107–127.

Hearn, G., & Rooney, D. (Eds.). (2008). *Knowledge policy*. Northampton, UK: Edward Elgar.

Huff, T. E. (2005). Malaysia's Multimedia Super Corridor and its first crisis of confidence . In Baber, Z. (Ed.), *CyberAsia: The Internet and Society In Asia*. Leiden, The Netherlands: Brill.

Jaffee, D. (1998). *Levels of socio-economic development theory*. London: Praeger.

Knight, R. (1995). Knowledge–based development. *Urban Studies (Edinburgh, Scotland)*, *32*(2), 225–260. doi:10.1080/00420989550013068

Lepawsky, J. (2005), Digital Aspirations: Malaysia and the Multimedia Super Corridor. *FOCUS on Geography, 48*(3).

Lever, W. (2002). Correlating the knowledge-base of cities with economic growth. *Urban Studies (Edinburgh, Scotland)*, *39*(5/6), 859–870. doi:10.1080/00420980220128345

MDeC (Multimedia Super Corridor Development Corporation). (2006). *Guide For MSC Malaysia Cybercities and Cybercentres*. Kuala Lumpur, Malaysia: Multimedia Development Corporation.

MDeC (Multimedia Super Corridor Development Corporation). (2008). *MSC Malaysia National Rollout 2020*. Retrieved April 2, 2009, from http://www.mscmalaysia.my

Mohamad, M. (1996). *The way forward Vision 2020*. Kuala Lumpur: Malaysia Business Council.

Mohamad, M. (1998). *Inventing Our Common Future in Mahathir Mohamad: A Visionary and His Vision of Malaysia's Knowledge economy*. Subang Jaya, Malaysia: Pelanduk Publications.

Mohan, A. V., Aliza, A. O., & Kamarulzaman, A. A. (2004). ICT Clusters As A Way To Materlialise A National System Of Innovation: Malaysia's Multimedia Super Corridor Flagships. *Electronic Journal on Information Systems in Developing Countries*, *16*(5), 1–18.

Mukhtar, N. (2008). *Intelligent City of Cyberjaya*. Unpublished MSC Thesis, Cardiff, UK.

Ramasamy, B., Chakrabaty, A., & Cheah, M. (2004). Malaysia's Leap into the Future: An Evaluation of the Multimedia Super Corridor. *Technovation, 24*, 871–883. doi:10.1016/S0166-4972(03)00049-X

Setia Haruman Corporation. (2009). *Setia Haruman Sdn. Bhd: The master developer of Cyberjaya*. Retrieved May 11, 2009, from http://www.cyberjaya-msc.com/

Taylor, R. D. (2003). The Malaysia Experience: The Multimedia Super Corridor . In Jussawalla, M., & Taylor, R. D. (Eds.), *Information Technology Parks of the Asia Pacific*. New York: M.E Sharpe.

Van Doren, C. (1992). *A history of knowledge: past, present and future*. Toronto, Canada: Random House Publishing.

Yigitcanlar, T. (2007). The making of urban spaces for the knowledge economy: global practices . In Al-Furaih, I., Sahab, A., Hayajneh, A., Abdullah, A., Ibrahim, M., & Thalha, M. (Eds.), *Knowledge cities: future of cities in the knowledge economy* (pp. 73–97). Selangor, Malaysia: Scholar Press.

Yigitcanlar, T. (2008). Knowledge-based development of creative urban regions: global perspectives for local actions. In Knowledge International Week, Ibero-American Community for Knowledge Systems, 29-31 Oct. 2008, Manizales, Colombia (pp. 305-324).

Yigitcanlar, T., O'Connor, K., & Westerman, C. (2008c). The making of knowledge cities: Melbourne's knowledge-based urban development experience. *Cities (London, England), 25*(2), 63–72. doi:10.1016/j.cities.2008.01.001

Yigitcanlar, T., & Velibeyoglu, K. (2008). Knowledge-based urban development: local economic development path of Brisbane, Australia. *Local Economy, 23*(3), 197–209. doi:10.1080/02690940802197358

Yigitcanlar, T., Velibeyoglu, K., & Baum, S. (Eds.). (2008a). *Knowledge-based urban development: planning and applications in the information era*. Hershey, PA: Information Science Reference.

Yigitcanlar, T., Velibeyoglu, K., & Baum, S. (Eds.). (2008b). *Creative urban regions: harnessing urban technologies to support knowledge city initiatives*. Hershey, PA: Information Science Reference.

Yigitcanlar, T., Velibeyoglu, K., & Martinez-Fernandez, C. (2008d). Rising knowledge cities: the role of knowledge precincts. *Journal of Knowledge Management, 12*(5), 8–20. doi:10.1108/13673270810902902

Chapter 18
Rising Northern Light:
A Systems Outlook on Manchester's Knowledge-Based Capitals

Blanca C. Garcia
Colegio de la Frontera Norte/Colef., Mexico

ABSTRACT

One of the difficulties in creating and sustaining knowledge cities is the lack of benchmarks to identify those cities and regions that are generating knowledge-driven initiatives, triggering development and collective value. One of such benchmarks is the value-based Generic Capital System (GCS) taxonomy. The rigorous application of GCS to cities in European contexts has already yielded its initial fruits, with Manchester as one of the cities in which a deeper perspective can be gained through the GCS lens. In this chapter, the author aims to introduce GCS as an integrative system of capitals for the case of the Greater Manchester city-region and its journey into developing its knowledge capitals. Through the lens of the GCS generic KC capital system taxonomy, some of Manchester's systems of information, systems of learning and systems of knowledge are expected to emerge as a comprehensive meta system articulated by the extensive life-long learning initiatives implemented by Manchester's development-based Knowledge-City schemes. The GCS lens will be introduced within the different system layers interacting in the city in order to discover how they tie the City's learning, communicating and knowledge-sharing dynamics together in the emerging context of knowledge-based development initiatives. The chapter will attempt to highlight how ICT connectivity systems (managing information) could be viewed as closely linked to skill development (managing learning) and people's management of tacit and explicit knowledge (knowing), with visible regional aspirations for development. Such systems view aims to cover a wider (although still limited) range of the instrumental, human and meta capitals observable in the city in a simultaneously rich mosaic of different layers. The city's traditional and knowledge-intensive hubs, its communications and infrastructure, its identity, traditions and cultural diversity within the Greater Manchester city-region could therefore exemplify the consistent building of a system of capitals in a demanding knowledge-intensive context.

DOI: 10.4018/978-1-61520-721-3.ch018

INTRODUCTION

During the last two decades, the Greater Manchester city-region has deliberately sought to become an economic epicentre in the Northwest of UK. This northern city has unmistakably emerged from industrial decline into Knowledge City (KC) renewal in recent years, especially since its 1990's inner city regeneration push. Seemingly, Manchester's knowledge-intensive elements such as its property-led investments, the strong social capital of its historic movements, its partnerships and long-term city leadership, plus internationally connected ports and increasing connectivity have put Manchester at the threshold of knowledge-based development success.

As the world's first industrial city, Manchester retains a strong manufacturing base, along with its original technological vocation. But the city has also developed a solid service industry of regional and national scope, as well as a retail, leisure and cultural reputation. It has also become the main regional centre for key public services, especially within the higher education sector. In a number of knowledge-based fronts, the city is actively seeking to reach its full post-industrial potential, while at the same time building a unique city brand through its proven resilience capacity for development. The result is a progressively complex tapestry of innovative efforts with long-term consequences that are worth monitoring, recording and evaluating. Indeed a challenging task for research.

Keeping such challenge in mind, this chapter advances an integrative system of capitals perspective in order to facilitate the observation of (some aspects within) the Greater Manchester city-region and its journey into developing its multiple traditional capitals into knowledge-based potential. Through a generic KC capital system lens, the chapter will attempt to create a panoramic view of how Manchester's *systems of information*, *systems of learning* and *systems of knowledge* are articulated within the deployment of a knowledge-based strategy of Manchester under its projected KC scheme.

The first section of the chapter will therefore introduce Manchester as a Knowledge City-region, along with the theoretical frameworks that support such characterization. It will be followed by the introduction of the systemic taxonomy used to observe Manchester as a KC. The second part of the Chapter will present and discuss some of the different system layers interacting in the city, as an example of how they tie the learning, communicating and knowledge-sharing dynamics together in the emerging context of its knowledge-intensive initiatives. The chapter will thus highlight how ICT connectivity systems (*managing information*) could be viewed as closely linked to skill development (*managing learning*) and people's management of tacit and explicit knowledge (*managing knowing*), with visible regional aspirations for development. Such *systems* view aims to cover a range of the instrumental, human and core *meta* capitals to be observed in a rich mosaic of multiple layers.

How is a generic, comprehensive, integrative and systematic account of capitals shaped in the context of the Manchester city-region? This chapter will bring about some clues to such issue: the city-region's mix of traditional and knowledge-intensive hubs, its communications and infrastructure, its identity, traditions and cultural diversity are some of the elements that have seemingly positioned Manchester as a knowledge capital in the European arena, and as a determined player in the knowledge-revolutionary times to come.

1. MANCHESTER AS A CITY-REGION

Researchers and practitioners have agreed that one of the difficulties in creating and sustaining knowledge-based city-regions is the lack of benchmarks to identify those cities and regions that are generating knowledge-driven initiatives, triggering development and collective value (Chase,

2007). In terms of knowledge-based development frameworks, some key notions have emerged to characterise such benchmarks. Cities can now be defined as *Human Capitals* (i.e. Austin, Texas, USA), *Telecommunication Capitals* (i.e. Helsinki, Finland), *Culture* or *Art & Culture Capitals* (i.e. Barcelona, Spain; Melbourne Australia), and/or *Knowledge Capitals* (i.e. One-North, Singapore) according to some emerging knowledge-based criteria (Yigitcanlar, T., et. al. 2008b). In the same line of thought, some other established parallel concepts are *learning regions* (Florida, 1995), *innovation clusters* (Porter, 1995) or *global networks* (World Bank, 2002). Clearly, such rich blend of theory and practice, is finding new theoretical expressions of the generic *Knowledge City* (KC) 'a city purposefully pursuing knowledge as a means for development' (Carrillo, 2004). It also conveys frameworks such as the *Ideopolis*: a city of Ideas and inclusive communities (Work Foundation, 2008); the *Creative City*, as a city driven by the creativity of its creative class and milieu (Landry, 2000; 2006); the *Smart City*, a place that promotes information access, lifelong learning, social inclusion, quality of life, and economic development (Yigitcanlar, T., 2008b), and the *Intelligent City* which heavily relies on social intellect, Intellectual Capital mapping, virtual connectivity and the strong capacities of its citizen story-tellers (PricewaterhouseCoopers, 2005). In considering the different categories for *Knowledge City* cases in terms of size and nature, a few categories seem to have emerged:

- Knowledge Micro-City
- Knowledge Metropolis
- Knowledge Precinct
- Knowledge City-Region
- Knowledge Country
- Knowledge Meta-Community

For the purposes of this chapter, aiming to characterise Manchester's knowledge-based capitals, the specific concept of *Knowledge City-region* has been adopted to exemplify Manchester's capitals. From this perspective, a *K City-region* is usually a medium size city/town, with a population between half a million to three and a half million inhabitants. It acts as regional centre for political, economic or cultural activities. About nine hundred large cities in the world have been identified that qualify as Knowledge City-regions. (Beaverstock, et. al., 2007).

Manchester, extending over 3,111 km² in the heart of the UK's North West region, is home to 3.16m people. It can be therefore considered a Knowledge City-region, as the economic capital of the North West. The Greater Manchester region includes the cities of Manchester and Salford plus the adjoining metropolitan boroughs of Stockport, Tameside and Trafford (Greater Manchester South) and Bolton, Bury, Oldham, Rochdale and Wigan (Greater Manchester North), together with High Peak, Congleton, Macclesfield, Vale Royal, and Warrington Unitary Authority. It is UK's second largest metropolis outside London, and an important central connection between the city regions of Merseyside and Leeds (NWDA, 2003).

Indeed, Greater Manchester is the second largest contributor to UK's output outside London and the south east. In the European context, Manchester has seen steady growth during the 1990s and is only behind Munich and Valencia amongst the EU benchmark cities (Hildreth, 2006). Hence, the role of the Manchester City-region as the dominant force for economic growth in the North of the UK has this far been supported and sustained by a vision of development that integrates inter-regional planning (Work Foundation 2006). A recently integrated inter-regional strategy for transport and connectivity seems to be unlocking not only the potential of the city-region but also the capacity of the parts of the North to access international markets and world class business, ensuring financial and professional services and a cycle for innovation (Garner and Ternouth, 2008). Manchester's links with Liverpool, Leeds and

Sheffield city-regions have also been promoting added capacity and potential for growth for these regions (NWDA, 2003).

On the other hand, although Manchester has the highest concentration of higher education establishments outside London and therefore has the capacity to educate and build up a skilled pool of *knowledge workers*, the HE participation rates across the conurbation remain lower than national averages, at 26%. In order to bridge such gaps, and respond to the challenges of Manchester's particular context, a human capital development initiative under the Lifelong Learning flag has been proposed to tackle some of Manchester's challenges in the skill gap area (GMSA, 2005), discussed later in the chapter.

In such context, the next sections of the chapter will attempt an emphasis on connectivity and the role of the different aspects of capital (human, instrumental and meta-capitals) which will attempt to assess Manchester's capital value base and its relative future human capital development capacities within a knowledge-based framework.

2. A CAPITALS SYSTEM SCOPE

In order to observe such complex tapestry of the Mancunian knowledge-based variables, a systemic accountable base through KC benchmarks seems critical for research. One of such bases is the *Generic Capitals System* (GCS) taxonomy[1]. Inscribed in the third generation of Knowledge Management (KM) models, the GCS adheres to the notion of knowledge as a social construction, where the emergence of knowledge societies adopting knowledge-based frameworks (third generation of KM schemes) is encouraged. In this regard, a number of international bodies such as WB, UNO, OECD and the European Union have pointed out the path to monitoring and developing *human capital* (Carrillo, 2002:379). This path advances development through knowledge-creation and learning schemes as core strategies in the landscape of emerging knowledge-based societies.

Such synergy aims to create a systemic accountable base encompassing human capital with referential, articulation and instrumental capitals. This has been facilitated by third-generation, knowledge-based frameworks that explored alternative focal points to (highly-statistical) CI models. The GCS emerges as a value-based third-generation KM model (Carrillo, 2006:47) that attempts a systemic, global and comprehensive perspective building up on key points from successive generations of Knowledge Management frameworks. It elicits a systematic assessment of a city's capital base (both tangible and intangible) and its capacity to recombine it in innovative ways. The taxonomy considers eight major capital categories, each one eliciting a number of subcategories according to the city it is attempting to characterise (Figure 1).

These correspond to a Taxonomy of Urban Capital deliberately and systematically mapped upon all the resources –both traditional and knowledge-based- required to leverage the balanced and sustainable development of contemporary urban communities such as the Manchester city-region.

The GSC framework is immersed within context (Figure 1), where the value-based background, history and capabilities of a city play a major role. It mirrors the city's historical antecedents and pre-existing knowledge, as well as present knowledge repositories of capital, which in turn will enhance the city's future potential for development.

The underlying rationale for this taxonomy is to satisfy the formal requirements of value production as a complete, consistent and homogeneous system (Carrillo, 1998, 2002). The GSC builds upon other efforts to identify and value collective individual capital at either urban or national or regional levels. This taxonomy identifies the basic capital elements of productive systems and "meta-capitals": those other forms of capital are not productive in themselves but significantly

Figure 1. Generic Capitals System Taxonomy (GCS)

Metacapitals:
1. Identity capital - clarity and differentiation
2. Intelligence capital - external entities and events
3. Financial capital - Economic sustainability
4. Relational capital - Social Integration and cohesion

Human Capitals
5. Human Individual capital
   Health - biological inheritance and physical development
   Education - Holistic personal development
6. Human Collective capital
   Wealth of cultural inheritance
   Cultural Fitness

Instrumental capitals
7. Instrumental-material (tangible) capital
   Natural - existing before the settlement
   Artificial - created or incorporated by the settlers

8. Instrumental-knowledge (intangible) capital
   Production systems in non-electronic repositories
   Production systems in electronic repositories

Source: Adapted from Carrillo, F. J. (2002) and Carrillo, F. J. (2004).

leverage the system's overall capacity. The GSC advances that a global orientation in measurement would "advance accurate achievements, by means of a complete, consistent, systematic and inclusive capital system" (Carrillo, 2002).

Furthermore, the GCS taxonomy is inscribed in the emerging third generation of KM (Carrillo, 2006:47), which advances the generation of capitals systems, articulated within systems. The taxonomy targets the most subtle levels of knowledge, revealing the value structure of the unit; and facilitating the apprehension of its core identity. Such views are advancing an "epistemological shift from matter-centred to relation-centred knowledge" (Carrillo, 2002). The KM3 models aim to find the value blueprint or "soul" of the target city under analysis. (Carrillo, 2006:57). They also seek to convey a creative, generic and systemic view of individuals, cities and societies as living organisms in a constant, perennial process of change. Such framework constitutes an excellent lens to look into Manchester's capitals for research purposes.

3. EMERGING KNOWLEDGE CAPITALS IN MANCHESTER

Indeed, some constant elements of Manchester's "soul" seem to be present when observed through a Knowledge City (KC) lens. In Manchester, as in many emerging KCs, a number of learning spaces reflect its *creativity engine* potential: Universities (Garcia, 2006a), Libraries (Garcia, 2006b), Hospitals, Pubs, Museums and even the Marketplace (Garcia 2004), as innovation engines and gatekeepers trigger knowledge sharing and knowledge creation (Garner and Ternouth, 2008).

Such spaces are used in KC schemes "as creating environments that foster and enable intensive, on going, rich, diverse, and complex *Knowledge Moments*" (Dvir, 2006:245). Knowledge Moments are significant to KC emergence as "spontaneous or planned human experiences in which knowledge is discovered, created, nourished, exchanged and transformed into a new form" (Dvir, 2006:245) and thus intrinsically linked to collective knowledge-creation events. In the specific case of the Greater Manchester city-region, the recording of knowledge moments, their frequency and intensity

Figure 2. Three Layers in the Manchester's KC capital system

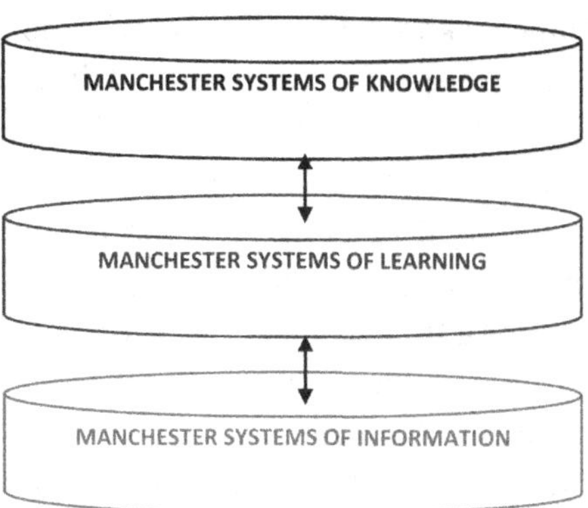

mark their transcendence for the collective building of the city's emerging value capital systems, of which its human capital is paramount. Those knowledge moments might play an important role in understanding how Manchester, a leading urban community during the 1800's Industrial revolution, is arguably reinventing itself into a Knowledge City (KC) pacesetter during the information, learning and knowledge revolutions of the twenty-first century.

Indeed, thriving beyond investments and infrastructure capital to develop its future, the Greater Manchester city-region has progressively relied on its collective engines. Notably, its growing social network of partnerships and its developing capacity for connectivity and dialogue with other cities and regions (Hildreth, P, 2006). Hence, the lens of the GSC taxonomy can be represented as a panoramic view of three *system* layers (Figure 2). Manchester's *systems of information*, *systems of Learning* and *systems of knowledge* are articulated through an extensive life-long learning strategy within the deployment strategy of Manchester as a KC.

Amongst the complex tapestry of knowledge-based initiatives in the city-region, this chapter advances a GCS angle that aims to facilitate the viewing of value capitals system layers, interactions and intersections. The Mancunian capitals system can perhaps be observed and articulated through the extensive life-long learning and skill-development group of initiatives proposed by the various entities responsible for the deployment strategy of Manchester as a KC. Thus, the remaining of this chapter will attempt to group and characterise the different capitals observed in the city through the lens of its key capital assets, articulated by Manchester's human capital developments as identified in the eight main points presented on Figure 1. (NWDA, 2003) and regrouped in Figure 2.

A. MANCHESTER SYSTEMS OF KNOWLEDGE (META-CAPITALS)

Manchester's Referential Capital

Manchester's elements of unique value seem to be favouring the emergence of Knowledge City patterns within its urban community. Although they vary in nature and magnitude as well as in their scale of human capital systems, Manchester relies on (at least) four key ingredients associated with KC attributes and base principles that directly impact human capital development: ***Citizenship, Intelligence, Economy, & Networking.***

Mancunian Citizenship*(Identity: Clarity and Differentiation)* – Manchester is the world's first modern city and home of (once) a large industrial working-class population (MKCP, 2009). Such elements blended in the city making it the cradle of key social processes such as Cooperativism and the modern Labour movement. However, the most prominent attribute of the Greater Manchester city-region is to have been an *ultimate frontier* in UK as one of the last post of the known civilised world for soldiers in Roman Imperial times. Such circumstantial borderland condition conveyed a free, independent and autonomous spirit to Manchester settlers: the Mancunian people. Mancunians thus created an environment both favourable for political and religious radicalism, and for unique open-mindedness, acceptance and liberalism (decidedly divergent to London) in the UK context (Worthington, 2002:3).

The historical vocation of becoming a frontier people was accentuated in Reformation times, when Manchester became one of the last bastions (and home) for persecuted Puritans. Thus receiving the non-conformist worldview of Christian radicals, the city has inherited a profuse legacy of values and beliefs, such as a strong individual sense of identity, equality of opportunity, religious tolerance, and a sense of gender equality (Worthington, 2002:2). Opportunity is indeed a key word in Manchester's identity. Since its textile-town beginnings, as well as an industrial hub, Manchester has been "a place of training with an international perspective; a place where strangers are welcomed and taken in… a city of refuge. Historically, people have come to Manchester from the nations to be trained and sent back…" (Smith, M., 2009). In these post-industrial days, the city seemingly needs to be reminded of such rich heritage: being a bee hive, a powerhouse and an innovation engine is indeed part of Manchester's original nature and spirit.

Even if Manchester 'has always been located at the leading, or bleeding edge of change' (Robson, 2002:3), its relationship with its various epicentres (meaning Rome, Westminster, London, Brussels and beyond) has been accompanied by strong values and collective aspirations for individual and intellectual self-development (Worthington, 2002:2). Such values, present in documents, buildings, urban manners and traditions, draw together the multiple dimensions of the resilient character of Manchester's people.

Mancunian Intelligence*(Intelligence: External Entities and Events)* – Manchester's own vision of its KC assets were described in detail in the 2003 proposal for "Manchester: Knowledge Capital" (MCC,2003), which included: a critical mass of world-class higher education resources; knowledge transfer and skills within its local workforce; innovation, enterprise and creativity within business; ability to channel, connect and communicate knowledge, goods and people at a global scale; a spirit of creativity and diversity; a bold city leadership, with a reputation for building dynamic cross-sector partnerships and an escalating track record of delivery. Such instruments could allow the city to increase its awareness and potential for a true change in its economic drivers through the accumulation of past and present assets; the city's capitals.

Moreover, in 2005, the *Manchester: Knowledge Capital* and *Manchester Enterprises Partnership* were established to lead knowledge-based city initiatives, virtually functioning as the *Future Centre* of the UK Northwest. Its mission is to plan and promote the economic potential of the region, led by its established industries, higher education institutions (HEIs) and creative industries in the North West. The Partnership is presently advancing three core strategies, and an evaluation programme undertaken by a consortium of researchers including the *Manchester Institute for Innovation, SURF* and *Regeneris* (MSC, 2009). Those core strategies are: *Science City*, *Manchester is My Planet*, and *Innovation Investment Fund* (MKCP, 2009, Garner, 2007).

The *Manchester Science City* programme aims to link the latest academic research with industry and the general public to help boost innovation and productivity, and to leverage the city's assets for economic and social value in the region (MSC, 2009). It includes three main lines of activity: A) *Real World Science,* which promotes a larger number of citizen participation on informed debate and decision-making about science issues. B) The *Innovation Ecosystem* which fosters a policy-led city environment for innovation which seeks to attract talented human resources and infrastructure investments, to create networks and partnerships and to promote a creative and cultural buzz in the city. C) *Innovation Partnerships*, which seeks to advance the collaboration between the academy, industry and support agencies in key areas such as healthcare, environment and digital media (MSC, 2009).

The *Manchester is My Planet* programme follows the "Save the planet. Start with Manchester" pledge. It focuses towards the Manchester city-region goal of 20% reduction in carbon emissions in 2010, by increasing energy efficiency, using renewable energy and increasing use of low-carbon transportation (Garner, 2007).

Finally, the *Innovation Investment Fund* programme aims at increasing the rate of innovation across the Manchester city-region, by understanding the opportunities and challenges for innovation, supporting and investing in the innovation ecology, and learning about the role of cities as drivers of innovation (Garner, 2007). Through such MKCP initiatives, Manchester is actively seeking knowledge-based development strategies to create an environment for innovation (MKCP, 2009).

Indeed, Manchester's regeneration and knowledge-based efforts since the early 1990's have started to pay off. For instance, the BBC and Granada in central Manchester form the hub of a growing media sector that is second only to London in size and significance (Collet and Collet, 2004). Major sporting, exhibition and concert venues alongside significant arts, museums and visitor attractions have established Manchester as the second most visited city outside London. Moreover, the re-location of BBC operations from London to Manchester in 2004 were expected to (and likely able to deliver) a significant expansion of the creative sector, and to cascade down into other sectors including the educational one. Manchester has clearly evolved into a centre for knowledge-based activity, media production, sport and culture, with the MKCP partnership aiming to maximise the economic contribution of this sector to the regeneration of the conurbation (Collet and Collet, 2004).

Manchester's Articulation Capital

Mancunian Economy*(Financial: Economic Sustainability)* – Manchester is acknowledged as the largest UK centre for financial, professional and legal services outside London. The city region has achieved both high levels of inward investment in shared services centres while also attracting major legal, insurance and investment businesses. Manchester's financial capital relies today on regional headquarter location for major legal and financial organisations, shared service centres, banking services and investment (MKCP, 2009).

Moreover, property-led initiatives and major research partnerships have given a boost to the higher education sector. In such context, biotechnology is particularly important for the city-region economy and has experienced rapid growth (Garner, 2007). The city region has a number of major pharmaceutical facilities (AstraZeneca at two sites, Aventis and Avecia) and a thriving biotechnology community. AstraZeneca's largest global R&D centre is at Alderley Park Cheshire and there are substantial manufacturing facilities at Macclesfield. Both sites have expanded considerably in the last few years (Work Foundation, 2006). The Aventis site at Holmes Chapel (acquired by Sanofi) is the company's centre for respiratory product research and manufacture. Avecia, a major UK life sciences & biotechnology company, has its global HQ at Blackley, North Manchester. Also a US biotechnology company, Genecor, opened its first UK office in Stockport in late 2002. Clearly, the combined areas of Manchester and Cheshire account for 62% of the regional life science companies (by number), 73% of the employment in the sector and 97% of the commercial R&D spend (MSC, 2009).

On the other hand, the Manchester Biotechnology Incubator has been a significant driver for new company development including Renovo and Intercytex. Both companies are amongst the UK's secured funding projects, drawing from major venture capital international sources. Other major projects include NOWGEN, the NW Genetics Knowledge Park, the NW Institute for Biohealth Informatics, and the Wellcome Clinical Research Facility (NWDS, 2003).

Mancunian Networking – Indeed, Manchester's journey into regeneration initiatives has brought recognition and stronger partnerships, with local, national and international entities. In the last decade, the city-region's partnership network with local public, civic and private stakeholders is already having a positive impact in key areas of its socio-economic infrastructure. Also, by means of its social capital, Manchester's leadership is also building partnerships with other UK cities, the central government, the European Union representatives and other European cities.

However the city-region (with East Manchester in particular), still includes the nation's poorest and most disadvantaged areas, with acute poverty pockets aggravated by the economic recessions of the 1970s and 1980s. The city-region lost 60% of its employment base between 1975 and 1985. In some neighbourhoods, large areas of idle, ex-industrial open space can still be seen: derelict neighbourhoods as well as scenes of high levels of unemployment (Work Foundation, 2006). Seemingly, the historical and existing networks within the Mancunian societal tissue have been fragmented not only by (the lack of) access to education, but also by discrimination based on religious, geographical or ethnic considerations. Manchester's networking capabilities are clearly threatened by (inherited) chronic poverty, crime and the fear of crime, poor health, poor working skills, low educational levels and a lack of educational facilities. These issues are a challenging reality for Manchester's development in terms of social cohesion and consolidation of its multiple relational capitals.

B. MANCHESTER SYSTEMS OF LEARNING

In such context, Manchester's city strategists have highlighted *lifelong learning* as part of a system of systems that can trigger, generate, foster and catalyze knowledge-based development in the city (Carrillo, 2006). Indeed, Manchester has attempted to develop *systems of learning* through complex lifelong learning network relationships that include people, values, processes, tools and technological, physical and financial infrastructure. As mentioned before, close examination of such elements in the Manchester city-region include knowledge-generating public spaces through *learning conversations* (Malik, et. al., 2009). From its universities to its marketplaces, Manchester's organisations and institutions all illustrate how knowledge-based spaces are becoming an essential part of Manchester's (knowledge) city network.

However, not every incubator, library, or Science Park have the capacity to trigger knowledge-based development for its region. In the case of Manchester, a combination of intangible factors including a strategic intention, an explicit vision of Learning as a knowledge-based development engine, a sound leadership, circumstances such as an IRA bomb in 1996 (Holden, 2002:134), and key partnership developments thereafter are but some of the many ingredients combined for a KC profile. Manchester relies on multiple sources of Human Capital, of which two critical ones are highlighted in this opportunity: ***Health*** (Human Capital, collective base), & ***Higher Education*** (Human Capital, individual base).

Manchester's Human (Individual & Collective base) Capital

Mancunian Health – Greater Manchester's health and medical research sector provide a link between the academic facilities within the University of Manchester and major health services, research and teaching facilities at the core of the city region. The sector is also a major employer, with more than 100,000 staff across Greater Manchester (Work Foundation, 2006). With investments including the new UK bio-bank, and bio incubator, research networks across the region on genomics and commercial links with AstraZeneca and GSK. Manchester is actively seeking to become a national leader in biomedical innovation, and to develop its capacity in medical research, life sciences and delivery of health service initiatives (MSC, 2009).

However, the Manchester city-region faces a steep curve in health service delivery, as poor health statistics and inequalities in healthcare provision indicate. Some initiatives launched to bring solutions to such challenges include collaboration between the University of Manchester and its surrounding NHS trusts to conduct high quality health services research. The Greater Manchester Collaboration for Leadership in Applied Health Research and Care (CLAHRC) will insist that knowledge gained from research is translated into improved health care in the NHS. CLAHRC's mission is to also monitor the improving NHS quality of care and support for patient self-management (MKCP, 2009).

Another recent health initiative is the Manchester Academic Health Science Centre (MAHSC). It encompasses a federal partnership of six major teaching hospitals in Greater Manchester and the University of Manchester. MAHSC's mission is to inter-connect existing research activity and research partnerships covering the full spectrum of healthcare, which includes acute, specialist, mental health, primary care and commissioning. (MKCP, 2009).

Mancunian Higher Education – Today, Manchester is home to five HEIs and a combined income of more than £670m per annum, a student population of 90,000 making a contribution of around half a billion pounds to the city-region's economy (NWDA, 2003). Moreover, Manchester started to advance a *UniverCity* model within knowledge city schemes, when in October 2004 the merger of its two major universities in the region created a *super-campus* (Peters and May, 2004). Such initiative, called 'Project Unity' between the Victoria University of Manchester (VUM) and the University of Manchester Institute of Science and Technology (UMIST) expected to raise the profile, scale and research capacity to compete with world-class universities and create an international centre of academic excellence (MKCP, 2009). Such ingredients become observable as capital categories, currently being developed in-house by Manchester's senior stakeholders from business, government and universities, as foreseen by Georghiou and Cassingena-Harper (2003). A prospective set of five key strategies for HEI contributions at different levels were introduced: (Dynamic Infrastructure, Importers of High Quality brains, World Class University Leadership, Massive inward Investment, and Intelligent Networking, as detailed in Garcia, 2006a). Hence, Manchester's human (individual) capital aims to be both a driver of growth and a significant employer and contributor to the wider economy of the Manchester city region.

C. MANCHESTER SYSTEMS OF INFORMATION

Manchester relies on multiple sources of Instrumental Capital, of which two critical ones have been highlighted for the purposes of the chapter: ***Environment/Quality of Life*** (Instrumental Capital, tangible base), & ***Connectivity*** (Instrumental Capital, intangible base).

Manchester's Instrumental (Tangible & Intangible) Capital

Environment/Quality of Life – Manchester boasts a distinctive quality of life and environment, especially in South Manchester and Cheshire. This part of the city-region exhibits a privileged mix of historic towns, a range of country estates and gardens and an extensive network of rural canals and rivers. Such tangible instrumental capital provides substantial benefits for residents and businesses, and plays a significant role in attracting and retaining international inward investment (Work Foundation, 2006). These areas also provide a quality living environment for higher skilled, higher qualified workers. The combination of employment and quality of this living environment has allowed it to attract inhabitants with higher educational qualifications, knowledge-based employment and incomes all well above regional and national averages to this part of the city-region. As well as being an attractive business and residential location, South Manchester and Cheshire also play an important role in tourism, with the region's greatest concentration of parks, gardens, waterways and historic houses (NWDA, 2003). Moreover, although challenged by impoverished and derelict pockets spread across the region, Manchester's successive redevelopment initiatives have made several moves into regeneration and property-led increase of its infrastructure.

For instance, long after the internationally commended City Centre and Hulme Regeneration projects, a proposal from the *Urban Regeneration Company* created expectations around a *new* East Manchester. Indeed, after years of being largely ignored by Manchester's economic and political elite, the deeply rooted economic and social decline of East Manchester was finally addressed. The *Company* is a partnership between Manchester City Council, English Partnerships and the North West Regional Development Agency. However, some scholars consider that as a result of all this policy-based redevelopment activity, with multiple layers of East Manchester representation, the area is beginning to constitute a rather unreal place, reflecting more the imaginations of local and regional politicians rather than that of local communities (Ward, 2003). New East Manchester however, is seemingly one of a number of significant comprehensive regeneration programmes working for Manchester's instrumental capital.

Additionally, current proposals for a Central Salford URC will complement the broad range of such activity taking place in the city core and across elsewhere in the city-region (MKCP, 2009). The Oldham/Rochdale and Manchester/Salford partnerships are promoting comprehensive programmes of renewal of housing stock and their investment programmes will realise c.£2.5 billion over the next ten years (Work Foundation, 2006; MKCP, 2009).

Mancunian Connectivity – Manchester is connected in tangible and intangible forms: with other UK cities and Europe, in clusters and value chains, between institutions and through local relations of trust and reciprocity, in real and virtual networks.

In terms of transportation availability, Manchester's international Airport is the primary international transport hub for the north and a focal point for rapid employment growth. The airport is the third largest in the country with currently c.20mppa (millions of passengers per year). The connectivity provided by the airport is a major asset for the city region and all UK northern regions, and a key to attracting and retaining investment from knowledge based and international businesses (NWDA, 2003).

As of 2008, Greater Manchester had a rail network of 142 miles and 98 stations, offering excellent passenger connections to other UK cities, with a number of stations in Manchester benefitting from extensive refurbishment in recent years. Manchester Piccadilly station has seen over £80m spent on modernisation since 2008 and Victoria station is currently undergoing a £300m redevelopment (MKCP, 2009). The pioneering Metrolink service has a planned £600m investment and extension. Also, one of the most significant regeneration projects supporting the core of the city-region is the phase III expansion of Metrolink light rail system linking Oldham, Rochdale, Ashton and South Manchester and the regeneration areas of North and East Manchester

Table 1. ICT Initiatives in Manchester, 1990-2004

Community based, 'bottom up'			Technology driven, EU based, 'Top down'
1990	Manchester Host	1990	Teleports
1992	Electronic Village Halls (EVHs)	1992	G-MING/ Infocities
1993	Manchester Community Information Network	1993	Telecities / Eurocities
		2003	Manchester Digital Development Agency

Source: Adapted from data in Leach, B. and Copitch G. (2005).

into an integrated network. The existing Metrolink lines are a core element in the development of an integrated transport network built on a more efficient exploitation of the investment resources available to key agencies (NWDA, 2003). A network of line buses connecting most destinations and towns in the region operate around the central hub. Additionally three lines of free, city-centre shuttle buses promote public transport use (MKCP, 2009).

In terms of information and communication technologies (ICTs) infrastructure, Manchester has a number of elements in its favour. In 1991, the Manchester authorities launched the UK's first public access information and communications technologies (ICTs): the Manchester Host (Table 1); followed by the establishment a year later of Manchester's Electronic Village Halls (EVHs).

At the time, some drew parallels between the role Manchester played in the Industrial Revolution, creating sense of Manchester as an *Information City* (Leach and Copitch, 2005). They also compared the Host with other Manchester-based "forward-looking, infrastructure elements and developments which have contributed much to the regional economy". These included the Bridgewater canal (1760's), the first passenger railway service (1830's), the Manchester Ship Canal (1890's) and the first regional airport (1938). These infrastructural developments involved "new ways of moving goods and people around more efficiently. The Host involved new ways of moving information around and it also has the potential to play an important role in the 1990's in the development of the region's economy" (Leach and Copitch, 2005). In fact, the Manchester Host and the EVHs were seemingly focussed on enabling *local*, social and economic regeneration. These development efforts have strongly impacted and influenced one of the city-region's most prominent capital: its universities.

In terms of technology-based (networked) learning, in 1992 the UK Higher Education (HE) sector undertook a ten-year funding cycle of major initiatives concerned with computer-based education (Table 2). The two initiatives which deserved most consideration have been the Computers in Teaching Initiative (*CTI*) and the Teaching and Learning Technologies Project (*TLTP*), as stated by Rosa Michaelson (2002). She brings to mind that in the 1970's, the precursor of the CTI was an initiative called the National Development Programme for Computer Assisted Learning (NDP-CAL) strongly concerned with the pedagogical implications of new technologies. With the *CTI*, established in 1983, a total of 139 computers-in-teaching projects were funded till 1999; and a resulting network of 24 subject-specific centres and one 'service' centre was established to support the use of computers in teaching across the UK higher education sector (Michaelson, 2002:17). In 1999, with new funding rules, the Learning and Teaching Support Network (LTSN) took the place of the CTI support network, and an attempt to decentralise and 'distribute' support centres across the UK was made (Beetham, 1998).

On the other hand the *TLTP*, launched in 1992, became a two-fold initiative. In the context of the new value-oriented policies of the early 1990's, the *TLTP* was originally conceived to make teach-

Table 2. Key Quangos and ICT-based Learning Funding Initiatives

1973	NDPCAL (National Development Programme for Computer-assisted Learning) initiates the ICT wave. http://ifets.ieee.org/periodical/vol_4_2000/scanlon.html	1999	NLN (National Learning Network) aims to increase the uptake of Information Learning Technology (ILT) across the learning & skills sector in the UK. http://www.nln.ac.uk
1983	CTI (Computers in Teaching Initiative) promotes ICTs use, enabling change in HE. CTI is replaced by the LTSN (Learning and Teaching Support Network) in 1999. http://www.cti.ac.uk	2000	JANET (Joint Academic Network) provides UK universities with Internet connectivity, and links academic networks to the rest of the world. http://www.ja.net/development/qos/history.html
1992	TLTP (Teaching and Learning Technologies Project). Learning programme launched by the FE funding councils which has funded the development of courseware for on-line use. http://www.le.ac.uk/tltp/index.html	2002	JISC's Regional Support Centre of the Northwest (RSC NW) is created to pursue connectivity. http://www.rsc-northwest.ac.uk/about/history.asp
1993	JISC (Joint Information Systems Committee) supports He and FE with strategic views and opportunities on ICTs. http://www.jisc.ac.uk/index.cfm?name=about_history	2004	JCIEL, the JISC Committee for Integrated Environments for Learners. It evaluates novel technologies. Now it's the Committee for Learning and Teaching (JCLT). http://www.jisc.ac.uk/index.cfm?name=jciel_home Higher Education Academy. With e-learning as one of the 7 strategies to support the student learning experience, amongst which the e-Learning Initiatives http://www.jisc.ac.uk/programme_elearning.html
1995	FDTL (Fund for the Development of Teaching and Learning) Supports good T&L practice in HE http://www.heacademy.ac.uk/1046.htm		

Source: Adapted from data in Michaelson, 2002, and Website updates.

ing and learning more *productive* and *efficient* by harnessing modern technology through the development of new technology-based materials (Coopers and Lybrand, 1996). With £35.2M funding, 76 projects were launched, of which 67 were subject-specific. By 1998, only 5 items were used widely, and their target groups were first year undergraduate students and pre-university courses. Also, no group-based learning was taken into consideration, as all materials were developed for single-user tasks (Haywood et al, 1999).

With a systems outlook in mind, the chapter has sought to overview a specific range of the instrumental, human and meta capitals within the rich mosaic of different layers conveyed by living, working and learning in Manchester. By undertaking aspects of a systematic account of capitals through the *systems of learning* lens, we had a glimpse into Manchester's journey from a *city that learns* into a *knowledge city*, which by other means would have been nearly impossible to identify for research purposes.

4. IS THERE A KC IN MANCHESTER'S FUTURE?

It can be argued that the resurgence of the city-region core following the IRA bomb in 1996 has clearly triggered a dramatic change in Manchester's partnerships and initiatives, thus contributing to the success of Manchester as an increasingly innovative, dynamic and networked hub. The role of the private sector in promoting significant growth in the tourism/leisure, retail, educational and cultural sectors focusing on the Manchester City-centre is manifest. Today, Manchester genuinely tenders one of the largest business-friendly environments in Europe, thus promoting a new commercial offer in the city-region and in the North West (MKCP, 2009).

Moreover, the city-region has seen massive investment in its sport and cultural facilities as part of a comprehensive strategy for the development of the cultural sector. However, the impact of the *Commonwealth Games* celebrated in 2003 has been ambiguous. Some researchers suggest that the hidden costs of a whole community –the urban poor, is high: they have been removed away from the city centre, placed in a different borough within the city and thus filtered out of view (Stanley, 2005; Peck and Ward, 2002). Some others realize that the *Games* raised Manchester's image and profile, thus relocating the city-region core in the minds of potential investors, which has been fundamental for the generation of over 6,000 full-time equivalent jobs; as well as building investors' confidence in the city-region's ability to deliver results (NWDA, 2003).

In any case, Manchester's partnerships are placing a sound basis for a coherent strategy for the city region. The Greater Manchester Association (AGMA) has led the preparation of a Greater Manchester Strategy that is a significant step towards an integrative city- region framework. The establishment of the *Greater Manchester Forum* provides a further mechanism to co-ordinate the strategic economic objectives for Manchester, thus providing the basis for joint working and to achieve the strategic vision for the region. Also, the Manchester Knowledge Capital partnership shows potential to become a genuine regional force for the delivery of economic growth built around higher added-value knowledge outputs. Clearly, the Manchester city-region is already forging links with others in bringing forward a broader economic renaissance. Some of these efforts include the *Liverpool/ Manchester Vision & Concordat*, the contribution of Manchester to the *Core Cities Group* and to the *Urban Renaissance* initiative, all of which are evidence of the prominent role that the city-region has sought to play in the UK scene.

Although no single organisational or partnership structure covering the city region exists, there are significant public and private partnerships covering different aspects within the Northwest; with MKCP functioning as Future Centre within the city-region. These bodies offer the potential for strategic and political leadership and a vehicle to focus on the key objectives for the city-region.

For instance, as *Regeneris* has reported, along with some success in significant areas of the Capitals System, significant gaps in the areas of human capital (individual and collective) have been identified amongst the most acute needs of the city-region. The skills gap showed 120,000 more people than the England average with no qualifications (Regeneris, 2005). Clearly, the "Manchester city region is not a homogeneous area but a diverse mix of high value and performing economic areas adjacent to some of the most deprived communities in the country" (GMSA, 2005). Such unique human capital configuration highly challenges the city-region social cohesion. In such complex context, the *Greater Manchester Lifelong Learning Network* (GM LNN) initiative aims to increase the number of learners participating in Higher Education (HE) by creating a coherent, and consistent approach to learning. By 2010, the Network aims to become a unified student campus within the whole Greater Manchester city-region under the shape of a holistic learning environment. Focused mainly on vocational and higher education learners, the network aims to become a comprehensive learning club where learners will have a *passport*, giving them access to all the units on the network, thus attempting to encourage learners of all ways of life to embark on their own individual lifelong learning journey (GMSA, 2005).

The vision for the GM LLN required sustained work over the period between February 2006 and July 2009 in its first instance. Alongside funding from the HEFCE of £5.7 million, other partnerships including Aim_Higher, the CONTACT Partnership, the Greater Manchester Higher and Further Education consortium and Manchester: Knowledge Capital Partnership (MKCP), are thought to underpin and strengthen the Network proposal, fostering access to skill development that could meet the needs and aspirations of vocational and work-based programmes at all levels. Skill development from Level 4 to Level 7, has been recognised as a particular challenge by the Network. Hence during its first stages, the programme will address Level 4 (four) skills to enable people to acquire the necessary skills to move into the growing number of jobs in identified skills shortage areas (GMSA, 2005). Such approach aims to provide flexible provision that matches the needs and opportunities of the workplace. Indeed, from a knowledge-based develpment (KBD) standpoint, the emergence of new partnerships such as the *Greater Manchester Lifelong Learning Network* represent a further evolution into Knowledge City models likely to trigger development for city- regions, as cases of recent initiatives aimed to demonstrate.

While further intensive research is needed to identify and characterise a Generic Capitals System for Manchester, the present account of the city's knowledge-based efforts reveals in its first application an integrative, extended effort of a city that has been building its knowledge-based capitals for decades, purposefully seeking knowledge conversion for development. Through the GCS lens, the principles and systemic management of knowledge in the city seem to have provided a firm foundation to the systemic KBD journey that the Manchester city-region has undertaken. It clearly paves the way for people to set off living, working and learning in a potential Knowledge City, in the context of the Greater Manchester city region.

5. SUMMARY AND CLOSING REMARKS

This chapter has aimed to highlight Manchester's knowledge capitals through the lens of the GCS taxonomy (Carrillo, 2004:35). The GCS facilitated an outlook into the city from a KBD angle: the different forms of *capital* existing in Manchester. Such angle brings perspectives on how Manchester has seemingly made an 'entrepreneurial turn' by embracing the KC models that will shape the city-region's economic community in the following years.

It is thought that the application of the GSC model on the Greater Manchester's case has highlighted the relevance of the city-region referential and articulation capitals, and how in recent years Manchester has shaped most of its core human (individual and collective) capital through its partnerships.

However, Greater Manchester exhibits a mixed pattern of growth that accentuates the disparity between affluent and marginalised local people, with different degrees of access to the job and development opportunities created within the cores of the conurbation. Indeed, across the city-region there are serious pockets of deprivation and dereliction, with 25 of the country's 100 most deprived neighbourhoods in Manchester and one third of the city-region containing 20% of the most employment-deprived communities in the country (NWDA, 2003, Work Foundation 2006). Clearly, 'Manchester remains a much divided city; since the 1990's presenting a complex story of poverty characterised by deprivation in tight geographical areas lying in close proximity to relative affluence' (Herd and Patterson, 2002:191). In such context, the disadvantages in the areas of human (individual and collective) capital are highly significant. Therefore, some aspects of the Manchester knowledge-based strategy have recently advanced aspects of skill development, with extensive lifelong learning and education initiatives at all population levels, with clearer targets to tackle.

The chapter has also pointed out the strong points of the city-region's capitals: the referential, articulating and instrumental systems of capitals that combine with the human capital of its citizenship who work, live and learn in the city. By doing so, the application of the GSC taxonomy to the case of Manchester, attempted to underscore how the city's identity, potential and aspirations are being re-invented while advancing new KC initiatives.

Indeed, the strength of the identity and resilience of Manchester people (Mancunians) is indeed regarded as a major human (collective) capital of the city-region, in sheer recognition that 'innovation requires human interaction' (Garner and Ternouth, 2008). In a context that promotes innovation, organisations, institutions (such as HEIs), and the wider communities within the city seem to be immersed in a radical process of re-invention. In a moment in time such as this, Manchester's citizenship is confronted with the possibility of re-conceptualising its regional development, and compelled to minimize the dark side of a globalizing model by radically increasing its human (individual and collective) capital, against the odds of the last two hundred years.

As this chapter advanced practical evidence of the capitals embedded in the micro cosmos of the Mancunian lifelong learning processes, a particular aspect of Manchester's *capital accounts* that constitute the human (individual and collective) capitals of the city were likely to emerge. Most importantly, the chapter has attempted to portray Greater Manchester as a potential knowledge-based city-region, whose initiatives are closely linked to the management of tacit and explicit knowledge of its people. In such context, a glimpse of the role played by *different capital systems*, has revealed them as articulators of knowledge-based urban development within the Mancunian urban communities. Through a systemic outlook, Manchester's capital accounts are likely to emerge and be better monitored. However, as the city-region develops further into KC schemes, the deeper challenges hindering its sustainable development are also more than ever likely to be revealed. This could bring a more balanced and realistic outlook of Manchester as the rising UK Northern Light in the global KBD arena.

6. REFERENCES

Beaverstock, R. G., Smith, J. V., & Taylor, P. J. (2007). A Roster of World Cities. *Cities, 16*(6), 445-458. Retrieved May 18, 2008, from http://www.lboro.ac.uk/gawc/rb/rb5.html#t1

Beetham, H. (1998). *CTI 1997/98: A review of learning and teaching innovation in the UK Higher Education from the Computers in Teaching Initiative (CTI)*. Oxford, UK: Computers in Teaching Initiative Press.

Carrillo, F. J. (2002). Capital systems: implications for a global knowledge agenda. *Journal of Knowledge Management, 6*(4). doi:10.1108/13673270210440884

Carrillo, F. J. (2004). Capital cities: a taxonomy of capital accounts for knowledge cities. *Journal of Knowledge Management, 8*(5), 28–46. doi:10.1108/13673270410558738

Carrillo, F. J. (Ed.). (2006). Knowledge Cities. Approaches, Experiences and Perspectives. Burlington, MA: Butterworth-Heinemann (Elsevier).

Chase, R. (2007). Foreword to the *Most Admired Knowledge City (MAKCi) Report*. World Capital Institute & Teleos. Retrieved April 27, 2009, from http://www.worldcapitalinstitute.org/makci

Collett, M., & Collett, B. (2004 September). *A Snapshot of the Creative Industries in England's North West.* Report prepared for Culture Northwest, Advocate Network Think.

Coopers & Lybrand Consultants. (1996). *Executive Summary of an Evaluation of the Teaching and Learning Evaluation Programme (TLEP)*. Institute of Education/Tavistock Institute.

Dicken, P. (2002). Global Manchester: from globaliser to globalised . In Peck, J., & Ward, K. (Eds.), *City of Revolution. Restructuring Manchester*. Manchester, UK: Manchester University Press.

Dvir, R. (2006). Knowledge City, Seen as a collage of Human Knowledge moments. In F. J. Carrillo (Ed.), Knowledge Cities. Approaches, Experiences and Perspectives. Burlington, MA: Butterworth-Heinemann (Elsevier).

Florida, R. (1995). Towards the Learning Region. *Futures, 27*(5), 527–536. doi:10.1016/0016-3287(95)00021-N

Garcia, B. (2004). Developing Futures: a knowledge-based capital for Manchester in *Journal of Knowledge Management, 8*(5), 47-60.

Garcia, B. (2006a). UniverCities: Innovation and Social Capital in Greater Manchester. In F. J. Carrillo (Ed.), Knowledge Cities. Approaches, Experiences and Perspectives. Burlington, MA: Butterworth-Heinemann (Elsevier).

Garcia, B. (2006b). Learning Conversations: knowledge, meanings and learning networks in Greater Manchester. *Journal of Knowledge Management, 10*(5), 99–109. doi:10.1108/13673270610691215

Garner, C. (2007). *Manchester, Knowledge City*. 7th Key Note Presentation at 1st Knowledge Cities Summit, Monterrey, Mexico. Retrieved from http://www.kbdweek.com

Garner, C., & Ternouth, P. (2008). *Knowledge Cities as Innovation Hubs – the role of gatekeepers in their success*. Paper proposed at the International Conference on Knowledge Management and Intellectual Capital, Ghaziabad, India. Retrieved from http://www.imt.edu/ickmic2009/

Greater Manchester Strategic Alliance (GMSA). (2005). Application and business plan for a Lifelong Learning Network for Greater Manchester. In *Progression through Lifelong Learning Report*. Retrieved January 15, 2008, from http://www.gmsa.ac.uk

Haywood, J., Anderson, C., Day, K., Land, R., MacLeod, H., & Haywood, D. (1999). *Use of TLTP materials in the UK higher education: a HEFCE-commissioned study*. Retrieved October 24, 2003, from http://www.flp.ed.ac.uk/LTRG/TLTP.html

Herd, D., & Patterson, T. (2002). Poor Manchester: old problems and new deals . In Peck, J., & Ward, K. (Eds.), *City of Revolution. Restructuring Manchester*. Manchester, UK: Manchester University Press.

Hildreth, P. (2006). *Roles and Economic Potential of English Medium-Sized Cities: A Discussion Paper*. Working Paper for *SURF*. Retrieved September 13, 2007, from http://www.surf.salford.ac.uk

Holden, A. (2002). Bomb Sites: The politics of opportunity . In Peck, J., & Ward, K. (Eds.), *City of Revolution. Restructuring Manchester*. Manchester, UK: Manchester University Press.

Landry, C. (2006). *The Art of City Making*. London: Earthscan.

Leach, B., & Copitch, G. (2005). Transforming Communities through local Information Networks. The case study of Manchester. *Research Institute for Health and Social Change (RIHSC)/ MMU.* Retrieved November 18, 2005, from http://www.mmu.ac.uk/regional/community/ publications/mcin_paper.pdf

Malik, S., Maryjam, S. S., & Maheshwari, S. (2009). Knowledge Based development and Knowledge Cities paper presented at the *International Conference on Knowledge Management and Intellectual Capital*. (Session Track VI). February 26th and 27th 2009. Ghaziabad, India. Conference URL: http://www.imt.edu/ickmic2009/

Manchester Knowledge Capital Partnership (MKCP). (2009). *Document submitted by The Manchester: Knowledge Capital (M: KC) Partnership to the Most Admired Knowledge City (MAKCi) Report.* World Capital Institute & Teleos. Retrieved from http://www.worldcapitalinstitute.org/makci

Manchester Science City (MSC). (2009). Real work, Real progress, Real Impact. *Report from the MKCP and NWDA.* Retrieved March 18, 2009, from http://www.manchesterknowledge.com

Michaelson, R. (2002). Re-Thinking Laurillard: universities, learning and technology. In . *International Journal of Management Education, 2*(2).

NWDA. North West Development Agency. (2003 February). Northern Way Growth Strategy. Manchester City-Region Profile. *Report from the North West Development Agency (NWDA).* Retrieved June 6, 2004, from http://www.thenorthernway.co.uk/docs/appendices/manchester.doc

Peck, J., & Ward, K. (2002). *City of Revolution. Restructuring Manchester*. Manchester, UK: Manchester University Press.

Peters, M. A., & May, T. (2004). Universities, Regional Policy and the Knowledge Economy. *Policy Futures in Education, 2*(2), 2004. Available at http://wwwords.co.uk/pdf/validate.asp?j=pfie&vol=2&=2&year=2004&article=4_Peters_PFIE_2_2_web&id=130.88.205.96 Accessed 18th January 2004. doi:10.2304/pfie.2004.2.2.4

Porter, M. (1995). The Competitive advantage of the Inner City in *Harvard . Business Review (Federal Reserve Bank of Philadelphia)*, (May-June): 1995.

PriceWaterhouse Coopers. (2005). *Cities of the Future. Global competition Local leadership.* Retrieved February 2007, from http://www.pwc.com

Regeneris Consulting. (2005 March). *North West Economic Baseline: a Report to the North West Development Agency* (NWDA). Retrieved April 18, 2005, from http://www.regeneris.co.uk

Robson, B. (2002). Mancunian Ways: the politics of regeneration . In Peck, J., & Ward, K. (Eds.), *City of Revolution. Restructuring Manchester*. Manchester, UK: Manchester University Press.

Smith, M. (2009 June). The Mancunian Nature. *Manchester Vinelife Newsletter*.

Sperling, B., & Sander, P. (2004). *Cities Ranked and Rated.* Hoboken, NJ: Wiley.

Stanley, D. (2005 April). *Urban Surveillance: The Hidden Cost of Disneyland.* Paper presented at the University of Manchester Conference 'One size fits all?'

Ward, K. (2003). Entrepreneurial urbanism, state restructuring and civilizing 'New' East Manchester. *Area, 35*(2), 116–127. doi:10.1111/1475-4762.00246

Work Foundation. (2006). *Manchester: Creating the Ideopolis.* Knowledge City Consortium Research Project. Retrieved from http://www.theworkfoundation.com/research/ideopolis.jsp

World Bank. (2002). *Global Development Learning Network.* Retrieved from http://www.globalknowledge.org/

Worthington, B. (2002). *Discovering Manchester.* Cheshire, UK: Sigma Press. Retrieved from www.sigmapress.co.uk

Yigitcanlar, T. Velibeyoglu, K., & Baum, S. (Eds.). (2008a). Creative urban regions: harnessing urban technologies to support knowledge city initiatives. Hershey, PA: IGI Global.

Yigitcanlar, T. (2008b). *Knowledge-based development of creative urban regions: global perspectives for local actions*. Keynote Presentation for Latin American Knowledge Week, October 27-Nov 1, Manizales, Colombia. Retrieved from http://www.semanadeconocimiento/info

ENDNOTES

1 The GCS taxonomy is an intellectual property rights reserved item. The application of this taxonomy for Manchester and other

cities has been developed over the last decade by a group of faculty and students doing research at the Centre for Knowledge Systems, the Knowledge Capital Institute, the University of Manchester and MIK-Spain coached by Professor F. J. Carrillo. The GCS and Capital System Framework is a World Capital Institute Copyright. See http://www.worldcapitalinstitute.org/makci

Chapter 19
Knowledge Management Orientation and Business Performance:
The Malaysian Manufacturing and Service Industries Perspective

Baharom Abdul Rahman
Universiti Sains Malaysia, Malaysia

Norizan Mat Saad
Universiti Sains Malaysia, Malaysia

Mahmod Sabri Harun
Universiti Sains Malaysia, Malaysia

ABSTRACT

Even though knowledge has been recognized as a crucial strategic resource in most organizations, Malaysian companies are still at infancy stage of knowledge management. Research and academic writing dealing with knowledge management implementation among Malaysian companies are still scarce. Previous research on the knowledge management efforts among Malaysian companies indicated that these local companies are rather slow in its implementation and still largely rely on the physical aspects of production. This study investigates the level of knowledge management implementation among Malaysian manufacturing and service companies and further explores the effects of such implementation on their overall business performance. The findings suggest that these companies emphasize the dissemination and utilization of knowledge over the creation of new knowledge, thus subjecting them to continuously becoming copiers and adaptors of knowledge.

DOI: 10.4018/978-1-61520-721-3.ch019

INTRODUCTION

The emergence of knowledge-based economy signaled the end of the traditional economic paradigm. The world economy began to lead its life to a knowledge-based direction as boundaries between nations begin to disappear, global competition between international companies become stiff, and technologies change at an unbelievably rapid pace (Clarke, 2001). The knowledge economy, or K-economy was charted by the OECD in their 1996 report as:

"the knowledge-based economy places great importance on the diffusion and use of information and knowledge as well as its creation. The determinants of success of enterprises, and of national economics as a whole, is ever more reliant upon their effectiveness in gathering and utilizing knowledge. Strategic know-how and competence are being developed interactively and shared with sub-groups and networks, where know-how is significant. The economy becomes a hierarchy of networks driven by acceleration in the rate of change and the rate of learning. What is created is a network society, where the opportunity and capability to access and join knowledge and learning intensive relations determines the socio-economic position of individuals and firms" (OECD, 1996, p. 14)

Even though knowledge has been known to be the critical source of progress since the origin of humanity, the most significant change has been in the area of how it is explicitly managed and manipulated as a source of competitive advantage. The shift has forced organizations to realize the importance of managing their knowledge assets rather than the usual land, labor and capital. The major factors of production in the traditional economic paradigm, have now been replaced by what is believed to be the most important factor of all – knowledge (Cliffe, 1988, Hansen et al., 1999; Davenport, 1997).

Zack (1999) argues that knowledge has been viewed as a valuable strategic resource by business organizations, and has therefore emphasized the need to bring that **knowledge** to bear on problems and opportunities. Organizations that know more about its customers, products, and technologies and markets and the linkages should be able to perform better. In many cases, knowledge alone drives the ability of firms to raise capital and acquire the other means of production. Progress in developing a new paradigm is made when the old paradigm is challenged and the old paradigm's explanations no longer are adequate to support the new findings (Kuhn, 1996). This is what is happening in business as new ways of managing innovation replace the old firm methods and strategies. The increasing gap between the book value and the market value of some business entities indicate the increasing importance of knowledge-based intangible assets (Marr, 2003). Firms such as General Electric and IBM have very low percentage of tangible assets – factories, inventories, and property – and most of their market capitalization is in the form of intangible assets (Kluge et al., 2001). Only 5% of Microsoft's market value is explained in is balance sheet (Marr, Mountsen & Bukh, 2003). Their perceived worth is in the knowledge assets that they possess or in their market-perceived capability to create new knowledge.

The dynamic nature of knowledge to identify and find solutions to business problems has eventually undergone another transition as researchers and practitioners realize that the same concept can also be applied to other human organizations. Knowledge management has evolved into a critical and crucial tool to face challenges facing modern societies. Almost every aspect of common thread of technological development possesses knowledge in itself and there is a need to ensure that this knowledge is not only well managed, but new knowledge is constantly being created (Baqir and Kathawala, 2004).

This study is aimed at identifying the level of knowledge management implementation among

Malaysian manufacturing and service companies with particular emphases on how they perceive the importance of knowledge and to what extent these companies gather their resources to acquire, disseminate, and utilize available knowledge in order to improve their business performance.

KNOWLEDGE MANAGEMENT

Knowledge, which is unique, inimitable and valuable, is certainly the best resource and the only sustainable **competitive advantage** a company could have against competitors (Wernerfelt, 1984; Day and Wensley, 1988; Prusak, 1999; Meso and Smith, 2000) and critical to the long term sustainability and success of organizations (Nonaka and Takeuchi, 1995). Lubit (2001) contends that knowledge is one resource that is difficult to replicate and hence is key to achieving advantage over other firms. The question of whether knowledge management fulfills the strategic asset criteria has been the major focus of a few studies (Halawi et al., 2005; Meso and Smith, 2000; Bollinger and Smith, 2001) and with slightly differing results. Looking at organizational knowledge management system (OKMS) from the technical and socio-technical perspectives, Meso and Smith (2000) contend that technology infrastructure of OKMS which may comprise the hardware, software, middle-ware and protocols that allow for the encoding and electronic exchange of knowledge cannot be considered as strategic asset because they are tangible and therefore, easily duplicated by competitors. On the other hand, with the exception of technological infrastructure, other components of the socio-technical perspective, comprising of organizational infrastructure, corporate culture, knowledge, and people, satisfy the conditions of a strategic asset. Bollinger and Smith (2001), on the other hand, argue that collective and cumulative organizational knowledge embodied in wisdom, rather than the knowledge of mobile individuals, meet the characteristics of a strategic asset in that it is:

- Inimitable – each individual in the organization contributes knowledge based on personal interpretation of information. Group interpretations and assimilation of knowledge are dependent on the synergy of the total membership of the group. In addition, organizational knowledge is built on the unique past history of the organization's own experiences and accumulated expertise. Therefore, no two groups or organizations will think or function in identical ways.
- Rare – organizational knowledge is the sum of employee know-how, know-what, and know-why. Since it is dependent on the knowledge and experiences of current and past employees, and is built on specific organizational prior knowledge, it is rare.
- Valuable – new organizational knowledge results in improved products, processes, technologies, or services, and enables organizations to remain competitive and viable. Being the first to acquire new knowledge can help the organization attain a valuable strategic advantage.
- Non-substitutable – the synergy of specific groups cannot be replicated. Thus the group represents distinctive competence which is non-substitutable.

When knowledge is characterized as an intangible resource, it is both ambiguous to competitors and a little more difficult for competitors to imitate, thereby providing a potential source of **competitive advantage** to the innovating firm (Fahey and Smithee, 1999).

Despite the IDC Group (2002) estimation that global corporate spending on knowledge management services will increase from US$4.2 billion in 2003 to US$8.9 billion by 2006, research shows that few organizations have realized benefits from knowledge management initiatives (Murray and Myers, 1997; KPMG, 2000). Lucier and Torsiliera (1997) claim that 84% of all knowledge management programs will fail to have any real impact. They further state, "a disturbingly high proportion of programs initiated with great fanfare are cut back within two or three years." (Lucier and Torsiliera, 1977, p. 15). Sveiby (1997) suggests that one of the reasons knowledge has not been recognized as important and a viable source of competitive advantage is because knowledge is invisible and intangible in nature, in contrast with other financial and capital assets. The wealth of knowledge organizations possess in the form of employees skills and experience or expertise is not quantifiable and therefore cannot be stated in a balance sheet. Therefore, establishing a link between knowledge management and business performance, even after investing huge amounts of resources, will become a daunting task for many managers, causing them to reconsider implementing knowledge management initiatives.

Even though knowledge has been recognized as a crucial strategic resource in most organizations, Malaysian companies are still at infancy stage of knowledge management (New Straits Times, 2003). This is however, in contrast with the other sectors of the Malaysian economy. The practice of knowledge management was evident amongst organizations in the education sector, government owned organizations, and government departments (Abdul Rahman, 2004). Other comparative studies investigating knowledge management adoption between public and private sectors reveal that the public sectors outperform their private counterparts in knowledge management initiatives (Badruddin, 2004; Liebowitz and Chen, 2003; McAdam and O'Dell, 2000). Research and academic writing dealing with knowledge management implementation among Malaysian companies, however, are still scarce despite the government's call for Malaysian public and private sectors to jump onto the knowledge-economy bandwagon.

RESEARCH DESIGN

Data

Data were obtained from a sample of Malaysian **manufacturing** and service organizations listed on the Malaysia 1000 Top Corporate Directory, a listing of prominent and emerging companies developed by the Ministry of Domestic Trade and Consumer Affairs and the Companies Commission of Malaysia. The list is adopted because of the nature of its recency and due to the fact that the majority of these companies are locally grown and serve almost all aspects of the Malaysian business activities. 621 questionnaires were sent to CEOs and other senior managers and officials who are responsible for the implementation of knowledge management programs or those who have sufficient knowledge about their organization's knowledge management activities and as reliable source to get information about business performance (Helfert et al., 2002, Sin et al., 2002). These are the people assumed to have access to the adequate resources of reliable and valid data about the organizational strategy and performance (Sin et al., 2002). Responses were received from 144 companies, yielding a response rate of 24 percent within a period of 3 months.

Definition of Variables

Knowledge Management Orientation – Based on the original scale developed by Darroch and McNaughton (2001) and Gold, Malhotra and Segars (2001), three scales are used to measure the behaviors and practices of each component of knowledge management orientation: **knowledge acquisition,** knowledge dissemination, and responsiveness to knowledge. Results of the factor analysis for the 35 questions related to knowledge management orientation dimensions provided three factors with their relative explanatory power (Eigenvalues) of 6.86, 1.71, and 1.59 respectively. Items related to knowledge dissemination dominated the first factor as it contained 7 out of the 11 items related to the dissemination of organizational knowledge, responsiveness to knowledge dominated the second factor with 5 out of original 10 items related to the process of responding to knowledge and knowledge acquisition dominated the third factor with 8 out of the 14 items related to the activities of acquiring knowledge.

Business Performance – A subjective, multi-dimensional construct consisting of two general dimensions – financial performance and non-financial performance (Venkatraman and Ramanujan, 1986; Wei and Nair, 2006). Financial performance is represented by return on investment (Sin and Tse, 2000; Forker et al., 1996), sales growth (Bontis et al., 2000; Appiah Adu et al., 2001), productivity (Wei and Nair, 2006), and overall financial performance (Sin et al., 2002). Non-financial performance concerns indicators which are measured in general terms and in many instances, operational in nature. Non-financial performances are measured in the form of number of complaints, customer satisfaction, and employee satisfaction (Venkatraman and Ramanujan, 1986; Wei and Nair, 2006). The results of the factors analysis on the 7 items provided 2 factors with their relative explanatory power of 2.90 and 1.17 respectively, cumulatively capturing 58.1% of the variance in the data. Factor 1 consisting of ROI, financial performance, sales growth, and productivity have sufficient items to run reliability analysis, and thus the component is named Business Performance, while items in Factor 2 due to its low reliability, are omitted.

RESULTS AND DISCUSSION

Company Profile

Of the 143 companies with the pertinent information, 60.1% or 86 companies are in the manufacturing sector. Of the other 39.9 percent in the services sector (Table 1), 15.8 percent responses came from the utilities business, 10.5% from transportation companies, 21.1% are from the banking and insurance companies, 22.8% from retail and trade, and 29.8% from other sectors of the services industry.

The majority of the responding companies yield annual revenues exceeding RM201m (43.1%) and more than RM500m (42.4%) respectively as compared to all lower generating income companies combined.

Looking at the number of employees, companies with more than 1000 employees responded the highest (32.6%), followed by what may be considered as a medium sized companies with 100-500 employees (27.1%). An equal balance of responds come from companies with less than 100 employees and those companies having 501-1000 employees.

The table also indicates that companies which have established itself in Malaysia for longer periods of time are more responsive as compared to newly-established companies. This fact is supported by Table 4.3. 50% of responses come from companies which have established itself in this country for more than 20 years, followed by 18.1% of those companies with 16-20 years of establishment, followed by 20.8% from those with 11-15 years of operating age. Companies with less than 10 years of establishment responded the least (1-5 years – 5.6%, 6-10 years – 5.6%).

A wide variety of departments are given the responsibilities of managing organizational knowledge, the most being the Human Resource Department (43.8%). Some companies rely on their Information Technology department (6.3) to manage knowledge, some on their Marketing department (7.6%), and another 9.0% of the responding companies indicate they have no specific department to manage knowledge. Interestingly enough, only 9.0% of the companies admitted having a special Knowledge Management department for all their knowledge activities. The balance 31.8% of the respondents rely on other departments, ranging from the CEO's office to the production department, from a combination

Table 1. Descriptive Analysis of Responding Companies

Demographics		Frequency	Percentage
Type of Industry	Manufacturing	86	60.1
	Services	57	39.9
	Utilities	9	15.8
	Transportation	6	10.5
	Banking and Finance	12	21.1
	Retail and Trading	13	22.8
	Other Services	17	29.8
Annual Revenue	Less than RM10m	3	2.1
	RM11m - RM50m	1	0.7
	RM51m - RM100m	5	3.5
	RM101m - RM200m	12	8.3
	RM201m - RM500m	62	43.1
	More than RM500m	61	42.4
Number of Employees	Less than 100	29	20.1
	101- 500	39	27.1
	501-1000	29	20.1
	More than 1000	47	32.6
No. of Years Operating	Less than 5 years	8	5.6
	6 years - 10 years	8	5.6
	11 years - 15 years	30	20.8
	16 years - 20 years	26	18.1
	More than 20 years	72	50.0
Department Responsible for KM	Human Resource	63	43.8
	Information Technology	9	6.3
	Knowledge Management	13	9.0
	Marketing	11	7.6
	None	13	9.0
	Others	35	31.8
KM Program	Formal	60	41.7
	Informal	68	47.2
	None	16	11.1

Figure 1. Level of Knowledge Management Implementation

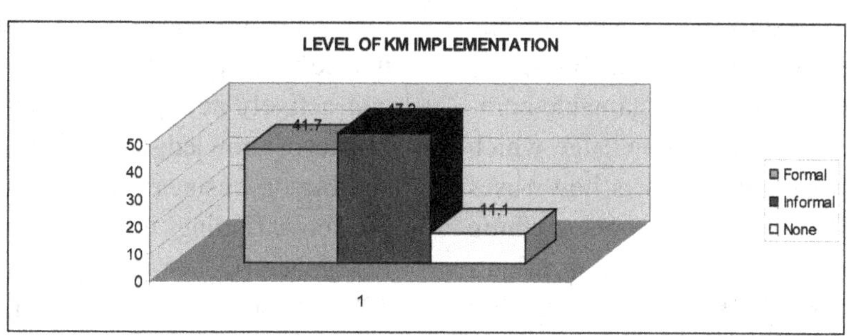

of offices to the research and knowledge departments to look after their knowledge assets. Such a wide continuum of departments given the responsibilities of managing organizational knowledge may indicate that these companies do not have a proper knowledge management program in their respective organization.

Knowledge Management Implementation

By formal knowledge management program, the study refers to whether the companies have specific policies on the subject which manifest in a formal, actual program. Figure 1 indicates that 41.7 per cent of the companies claim to have formal knowledge management program in place, 47.2% have informal programs, and 11.1% admitted to having no knowledge program whatsoever in their organizations.

A cross tabulation analysis between manufacturing and services companies indicate that of the 60 companies which claimed to have a formal knowledge management program in place, 35 of them (40.7%) are from the manufacturing sector and another 24 (42.1%) are from the service sector. A point worth noting is that of the 60 companies with a formal knowledge management program, only 9 (15%) of them have a special knowledge management department to handle organizational knowledge assets. Half of these companies (30), however rely on the Human Resource department to manage their knowledge activities.

Companies with annual revenues exceeding RM100m are more inclined to have a formal KM program as compared to companies with revenues less than RM100m. This indicates that due to the high cost of managing knowledge activities, larger companies are more able to allocate their resource into making their knowledge management efforts succeed. Smaller companies or those with limited resources are more apt to find other means to manage their knowledge assets. The bigger and more established companies have the will to initiate formal KM programs is strengthened by the fact that 90% of these companies have established themselves in this country for more than 10 years and 66.7% of them engage more than 500 employees.

KNOWLEDGE MANAGEMENT AND BUSINESS PERFORMANCE

Knowledge is a critical factor affecting an organization's ability to remain competitive in the new global marketplace. Organizations therefore need to recognize it as a valuable resource and develop mechanism for tapping into the collective intelligence and skills of employees in order to create a greater organizational knowledge base. Most researches (Davenport et al., 1998; Lee and Hong, 2002) agree that knowledge management is an important and necessary component for organizations to survive and as a competitive advantage. In addition, knowledge management is now accepted and widely practiced and utilized in many world-class organizations where its usage has realized benefits (Eldridge et. al., 2006).

Researchers in the field of sustainable competitive advantage contend that knowledge, which includes what the organization knows, how it uses what it knows, and how fast it can know something new, is the only factor that offers an organization a competitive edge (Prusak, 1999). Knowledge and its management are more valuable and more powerful than natural resources, big factories, or fat bankrolls (Stewart, 1997). Such assertions about competitiveness through knowledge management are consistent with results of empirical studies. A survey of 431 US and European organizations conducted by Business Intelligence and the Ernst and Young Center for Business Innovation reports that more active management of knowledge is possible and advisable – indeed that it is critical if a firm is to gain and sustain a competitive advantage (Ernst and Young, 1997).

The association between knowledge management orientation and business performance can be explained by the ability of knowledge-oriented companies to increase profits and improve productivity (KPMG, 1999) and create competitive advantage (Skyrme and Amydon, 1997; Jarrar, 2002). Companies which are actively acquiring and generating knowledge about their business environment, disseminating the knowledge throughout the organization, and finally act upon the knowledge to fulfill organizational objectives stand to achieve and sustain robust and sustainable competitive advantage (Darroch and McNaughton, 2003; Olivares and Lado, 2003). In a surprising contrast to what has been earlier hypothesized, of the three dimensions of knowledge management, only Knowledge Dissemination and Responsiveness to Knowledge are found to have positive and significant impact on Business Performance, which is measured through return on investment, financial performance, sales growth, and productivity.

The result of the analysis of this study indicates that companies can improve their business performance by disseminating organizational knowledge and actively acting upon such knowledge. The impact of knowledge dissemination or knowledge sharing on business performance as depicted in the above findings has been highlighted by some researchers (Cohen and Levinthal, 1990; Hendriks, 1999; Reige, 2005). Lahti and Beyerlein (2000) suggest that firms gain competitive advantage through the value they develop for customers and such value emanates from the construction and communication of important information from employees who engage with the customer to the employees who have the knowledge to create new important information that they can communicate back to the initial employee for action. This implies that the sharing and dissemination process of information among employees of the organization eventually will lead to better customer service, and finally better business performance.

On a similar vein, Bolan and Tenkasi (1995) argued that competitive advantage and product success in organizations results from individuals with diverse knowledge collaborating synergistically toward common outcomes. Bartol and Srivastava (2002) concurred with this idea and posit that knowledge sharing is critical to knowledge creation, organizational learning, and performance achievement. This finding also confirms Darroch and McNaughton's (2003) suggestions that both knowledge dissemination and responsiveness to knowledge represent the greatest potential for creating sustainable competitive advantages to the innovating firm, since in order to disseminate and respond to knowledge, the firm relies on its own peculiar mixture of path dependence, formal structures, informal relationships, skills and experiences of individuals. Knowledge dissemination and responsiveness to knowledge behaviors are unique to the organization and difficult to imitate, and therefore are likely to have a direct relationship with superior financial performance.

Table 2. Knowledge Management and Business Performance

Independent Variable (IV)	Dependent Variable (DV) Overall Business Performance Beta Coefficients and Significance Levels
Knowledge Acquisition	.06
Knowledge Dissemination	.27**
Responsiveness to Knowledge	.29**
R	.53
R^2	.28
Adjusted R^2	.26
F	18.11

** correlation significant at 0.01 level . * correlation significant at 0.05 level

Knowledge acquisition however, is found to have positive but not significant enough impact on business performance. The fact that the process of knowledge generation and creation is not unique to a particular organization and easily imitated may lend support to this finding. In addition to the massive amount of charts, graphs, presentations, voice mail, conversations and customer information that comes in every day, typical management and employees face increasingly large amounts of information in more form than must be processed, understood and acted upon. Unless that information can be transferred into knowledge to improve sales, operations, strategic planning and bottom line results, it can only lead to information overload and confusion (McCampbell et al., 1999).

The descriptive analysis of the three components of knowledge management orientation reveal that knowledge acquisition recorded the lowest mean (3.98) as compared to knowledge dissemination (4.13) and **responsiveness to knowledge** (4.31), which recorded the highest mean of the three components.

This finding implies that Malaysian companies under study believe that in order to improve their business performance, they must actively disseminate information among members of their organization and take appropriate action. This understanding is however contradicts previous research findings about the importance of knowledge acquisition. Previous researches have shown that the new knowledge generated is the principal source of innovation for a firm (Nonaka and Takeuchi, 1995; Grant, 1996). A basic premise has therefore been included in the creation of knowledge: that a firm needs to continuously renovate its knowledge base to ensure that this base does not become obsolete for the development of innovations. New knowledge, the basis for innovation, will constitute the future knowledge base for the organization and will contribute to the regeneration and widening of the existing base. According to some works (Harari, 1994; Nonaka, 1994; West, 1992), organizations that are able to stimulate and to improve the knowledge of their human capital are much more prepared to face today's rapid changes and to innovate in the domain where they decide to invest and to compete.

The importance of knowledge acquisition activities to enhance **innovation** seems to elude the attention of the Malaysian firms under study. The findings of this relationship between knowledge management orientation and business performance is consistent with Shapira et al.'s (2006) Malaysian knowledge economy measurement study which confirms that Malaysian firms are good adopters and adapters of technology rather than innovators. The Shapira et al.'s study found that all Malaysian industries under study performed well in knowledge utilization with almost all of them reaching or exceeding the cross-sectoral average. However, performance in other knowledge process components especially with respect to knowledge generation was generally low.

Malaysian managers should therefore realize that the great challenge in implementing knowledge management initiative is settled on the efforts to innovate, to exploit technological advances, competitors' failures, industry opportunities, and the investment in knowledge processes and knowledge workers. The innovative efforts include the search for, and the discovery, experimentation, and development of new technologies, new products and/or services, new production processes, and new organizational structures. Failure to create new knowledge on the existing knowledge base will render the available knowledge obsolete and an eventual total loss of competitive advantage.

Nevertheless, the R^2 resulted from the regression analysis is .48, indicating that 48% of the variance of the companies' overall performance can be explained by knowledge management. The usage of cross-sectional study and the subjective measures of performance may have affected these findings. Knowledge Management, being a new field of study, and what more, a considerably new phenomenon in Malaysia, needs time to yield performance. A longer period of time is required to truly capture the outcomes of KM by using cross-sectional method in this type of research.

It is further argued that the usage of the subjective measures of business performance can be misleading, in spite of the fact that most companies would prefer to reveal their performance in a subjective rather than objective manner.

CONCLUSION

The purpose of this study is to examine the relationship between knowledge management orientation and business performance among Malaysian manufacturing and service organizations.

Even though research findings linking knowledge management and business performance have been inconclusive, this study provided research evidence to suggest that knowledge management orientation offers performance benefits to organizations. It is however surprising that not enough effort is made among Malaysian companies to acquire new knowledge, or to become innovative for that matter. Emphasis is given towards the dissemination and being responsive to knowledge. Such a strategy may prove fatal in the long run because failure to create new knowledge and becoming innovative may subject these Malaysian companies to an eventual loss of competitive advantage and forever becoming copiers and adaptors of new innovation. To remain competitive and survive in an uncertain economy like Malaysia, these companies should implement strategies which would enable them to not only disseminate information and respond to market trends effectively, but to generate new knowledge and become innovators and leaders in their respective industry.

As knowledge is becoming an organizing principle for the society as a whole, Malaysian business organizations need to develop a knowledge strategy to realize the potential of the storehouse of human and capital knowledge they already possess.

LIMITATIONS

Although this study has been operationalized meticulously according to the generally accepted research guidelines (Churchill, 1979) and (Nunnally, 1978) to maintain its validity and reliability, it may not be totally free from limitations.

First, the perceptual inputs collected from the respondents are likely to have been subject to common method bias, since the picture of the multiple dimensions of practices and performance of a firm was dependent on the responses of one respondent, that is of the management's.

Another limitation comes from the nature of data collection. Knowledge Management is rather a new phenomenon in Malaysia and to be able to gauge the level of implementation among Malaysian companies would require a longitudinal study. A cross-sectional study where data are collected at one point in time may not be able provide a true picture.

The population of this study includes both national and multinational companies as listed in the Malaysia1000 Top Corporate Directory and thereby creating a huge imbalance between established and non-established entities. A comparison between companies of the same level, for example, between SMEs, or those listed in Kuala Lumpur Stock Exchange would provide a better representation of Malaysian companies implementing knowledge management.

The sample used in this study over-represented firms with 1000 or more employees and not completely representative of industry sectors. However, the effect of firm size or industry type on knowledge management is unknown. For example, it might transpire that larger firms or firms in knowledge intensive industries need to manage knowledge more effectively given a greater number of people, divisions or locations or abundance of complex knowledge. Given the importance of knowledge management to knowledge-based societies, it is hoped that a stream of research will emerge that provides further confirmation of the results reported in this study and identifies other consequences, mediators and of course antecedents, of effective knowledge management in the Malaysian context.

FUTURE RESEARCH DIRECTIONS

The fact that knowledge acquisition has little or no positive impact on business performance indicate that Malaysian companies put little emphasis on being innovative or becoming leaders in their respective business areas. Future research may consider the effects of environmental determinants such as market turbulence, technology turbulence, or even economic conditions that may have deterred these companies from acquiring or creating new knowledge.

For a better replication of this study, it is recommended that a longitudinal study be undertaken. This type of study would perhaps provide a better understanding of the importance of knowledge management and the process involved for a successful implementation. The effect of knowledge management on business performance can be better established if data is collected over a period of several years and not on a single point in time.

A better representation of knowledge management implementation among Malaysian companies is better understood if comparison is made between companies of the same level. For example, the implementation of KM between SMEs, or between companies listed on Kuala Lumpur Stock Exchange. The present study flawed because the sampling frame contain both medium size and large multinationals and obviously large companies have all the resources and expertise to implement a knowledge management program as compared to SMEs.

REFERENCES

Appiah-Adu, K., Fyall, A., & Singh, S. (2001). Marketing Effectiveness and Business Performance in the financial Services Industry. *Journal of Services Marketing*, *15*(1), 18–34. doi:10.1108/08876040110381346

Baqir, M. N., & Kathawala, Y. (2004). BA for Knowledge Cities: A Futuristic Technology Model. *Journal of Knowledge Management*, *8*(5), 235–243. doi:10.1108/13673270410558828

Bartol, K. M., & Srivastava, A. (2002). Encouraging Knowledge Sharing: The Role of Organizational Reward Systems. *Journal of Leadership & Organizational Studies*, *9*(1), 64–77. doi:10.1177/107179190200900105

Bolan, R. J. J., & Tenkasi, R. V. (1995). Perspective Making and Perspective Taking in Communities of Knowing. *Organization Science*, *6*(4), 350–372. doi:10.1287/orsc.6.4.350

Bollinger, A. S., & Smith, R. D. (2001). Managing Organizational Knowledge as a Strategic Asset. *Journal of Knowledge Management*, *5*(1), 8–18. doi:10.1108/13673270110384365

Bontis, N., Keow, W. C. C., & Richardson, S. (2000). Intellectual Capital and Business Performance in Malaysian Industries. *Journal of Intellectual Capital*, *1*(1), 85–100. doi:10.1108/14691930010324188

Churchill, G. A. (1979, February). A Paradigm for Developing Better Measures of Market Constructs. *Journal of Marketing*, *16*, 64–73. doi:10.2307/3150876

Clarke, T. (2001). The Knowledge Economy. *Education + Training*, *43*(4/5), 189. doi:10.1108/00400910110399184

Cliffe, S. (1998). Knowledge Management: The Well-Connected. *Harvard Business Review*, *76*(4), 17–21.

Cohen, W. M., & Levinthal, D. A. (1990). Absorptive Capacity: A New Perspective on Learning and Innovation. *Administrative Science Quarterly*, *35*, 128–152. doi:10.2307/2393553

Darroch, J., & McNaughton, R. (2001). *Knowledge Management and Innovation*. Dunedin: Department of Marketing, University of Otago.

Darroch, J., & McNaughton, R. (2003). Beyond Market Orientation: Knowledge Management and the Innovativeness of New Zealand Firms. *European Journal of Marketing*, *37*(3/4), 572–593. doi:10.1108/03090560310459096

Davenport, T., Long, D. W. D., & Beers, M. C. (1998). Successful Knowledge Management Projects. *Sloan Management Review*, *39*(2), 43–57.

Davenport, T. H. (1997). *Information Ecology: Mastering the Information and Knowledge Management*. New York: Oxford University Press.

Day, G., & Wensley, R. (1988, April). Assessing Advantage: A Framework for Diagnosing Competitive Superiority. *Journal of Marketing*, *52*, 1–20. doi:10.2307/1251261

Eldridge, S., & Balubaid, M., & Barber, Kevin D. (2006). Using a Knowledge Management Approach to Support Quality Costing. *International Journal of Quality & Reliability Management*, *23*(1). doi:10.1108/02656710610637569

Ernst & Young. (1997). *Twenty Questions on Knowledge in the Organization*. Retrieved January 2005, from http://www.businessinnovation.ey.com/research/knowle/survey/survey.html

Fahey, J., & Smithee, A. (1999). Strategic Marketing and Resource Based View of Knowledge Management Systems. *Academy of Marketing Science Review*, *99*(10), 1–23.

Forker, L. B., Vickery, S. K., & Droge, C. L. M. (1996). The Contribution of Quality to Business Performance. *International Journal of Operations & Production Management*, *16*(8), 44–62. doi:10.1108/01443579610125778

Grant, R. M. (1996). Toward a Knowledge-based Theory of the Firm. *Strategic Management Journal*, *17*(Special Issue), 109–122.

Halawi, L. A., Aronson, J. E., & McCarthy, R. V. (2005). Resource-based View of Knowledge Management for Competitive Advantage. *Electronic Journal of Knowledge Management*, *3*(2), 75–86.

Hansen, M. T., Nohria, N., & Tierney, T. (1999). What is Your Strategy for Managing Knowledge. *Harvard Business Review*, *77*(2), 106–116.

Harari, O. (1994). The Brain-based Organization. *Management Review*, *83*(6), 57–60.

Helfert, G., Ritter, T., & Walter, A. (2002). Redefining Market Orientation from a Relationship Perspective: Theoretical Considerations and Empirical Results. *European Journal of Marketing*, *36*(9/10), 1119–1139. doi:10.1108/03090560210437361

Hendriks, P. (1999). Why Share Knowledge? The Influence of ICT on the Motivation for Knowledge Sharing. *Knowledge and Process Management*, *6*(2), 91–100. doi:10.1002/(SICI)1099-1441(199906)6:2<91::AID-KPM54>3.0.CO;2-M

Jarrar, Y. F. (2002). Knowledge Management: Learning for Organizational Experience. *Managerial Auditing Journal*, *17*(6), 322–328. doi:10.1108/02686900210434104

Kluge, J., Stein, W., & Light, S. (2001). *Knowledge Unplugged*. Basingstoke, UK: Palgrave.

KPMG. (2000). *Knowledge Management Research Report*. London: KPMG Consulting.

KPMG International, UK. (1999, November). *Knowledge Management Research Report*. London: KPMG Consulting.

Lahti, R. K., & Beyerlein, M. M. (2000). Knowledge Transfer and Management Consulting: A Look at The Firm. *Business Horizons*, *43*(1), 65. doi:10.1016/S0007-6813(00)87389-9

Lee, S. M., & Hong, S. (2002). An Enterprise-wide Knowledge Management System Infrastructure. *Industrial Management & Data Systems*, *102*(1), 17–25. doi:10.1108/02635570210414622

Lubit, R. (2001). Tacit Knowledge and Knowledge Management: The Keys to Sustainable Competitive Advantage. *Organizational Dynamics*, *29*(3), 164–178. doi:10.1016/S0090-2616(01)00026-2

Lucier, C., & Torsiliera, J. (1997). Why Knowledge Programs Fail. *Strategy and Business* (4th Quarter), 14-28.

Marr, B. (2003, February). Known Quantities. *Financial Management*, 25–27.

Marr, B., Mountsen, J., & Bukh, P. (2003). Perceived Wisdom. *Financial Management*, 32.

Meso, P., & Smith, R. (2000). A Resource-based View of Organizational Knowledge Management Systems. *Journal of Knowledge Management*, *4*(3), 224–231. doi:10.1108/13673270010350020

Murray, P., & Myers, A. (1997, September). The Facts about Knowledge. *Information Strategy*, *2*(7), 29–33.

New Straits Times (Malaysia). (2003, March 26). *Be Prepared for Knowledge Era.*

Nonaka, I. (1994). A Dynamic Theory of Organization Knowledge Creation. *Organization Science*, *5*(1), 14–37. doi:10.1287/orsc.5.1.14

Nonaka, I., & Takeuchi, H. (1995). *The Knowledge Creating Company: How Japanese Companies Create the Dynamics of Innovation*. Oxford, UK: Oxford University Press, Inc.

Nunnally, J. C. (1978). *Psychometric Theory* (2nd ed.). New York: McGraw-Hill Book Company.

Olivares, A. M., & Lado, N. (2003). Market Orientation and Business Economic Performance: A Mediated Model. *International Journal of Service Industry Management*, *14*(3), 284–309. doi:10.1108/09564230310478837

Prusak, I. (1999). What's Up with Knowledge Management: A Personal View . In Cortada, J., & Woods, J. (Eds.), *The Knowledge Management Yearbook 1999-2000* (pp. 3–7). Boston: Butterworth-Heinemann.

Shapira, P., Youtie, J., Yogeesvaran, K., & Jaafar, Z. (2006). Knowledge Economy Measurement: Methods, Results, and Insights from the Malaysian Knowledge Content Study. *Research Policy, 35*, 1522–1537. doi:10.1016/j.respol.2006.09.015

Sin, L. Y., Tse, A. C., Yau, O. H., Lee, J. S., & Chow, R. (2002). The Effect of Relationship Marketing Orientation on Business Performance in a Service-oriented Economy. *Journal of Services Marketing*, *16*(7), 656–676. doi:10.1108/08876040210447360

Sin, L. Y. M., & Tse, A. C. B. (2000). How Does Marketing Effectiveness Mediate the Effect of Organizational Culture on Business Performance. The Case of Service Firms. *Journal of Services Marketing*, *14*(4), 295–509. doi:10.1108/08876040010334510

Skyrme, D., & Amidon, D. M. (1997). The Knowledge Agenda.. *Journal of Knowledge Management*, *1*(1), 27–37. doi:10.1108/13673279710800709

Stewart, T. A. (1997). *Intellectual Capital: The New Wealth of Organization*. New York: Doubleday/Currency.

Sveiby, K. E. (1997). *The New Organizational Wealth: Managing and Measuring Knowledge-based Assets*. San Francisco, CA: Berret-Koehler.

Venkatraman, N., & Ramanujan, V. (1986). Measurement of Business Performance in Strategy Research: A Comparison of Approaches. *Academy of Management Review*, *11*(4), 801–814. doi:10.2307/258398

Wei, K. K., & Nair, M. (2006). The Effects of Customer Service Management on Business Performance in Malaysian Banking Industry: An Empirical Analysis. *Asia Pacific Journal of Marketing and Logistics*, *18*(2), 111–128. doi:10.1108/13555850610658264

Wernerfelt, B. (1984). A Resource-based View of the Firm. *Strategic Management Journal*, *5*, 171–180. doi:10.1002/smj.4250050207

West, A. (1992). *Innovation Strategy*. Englewood Cliff, NJ: Prentice-Hall.

Zack, M. H. (1999). *Knowledge and Strategy*. Boston, MA: Butterworth-Heinemann.

Afterword
The Way Forward:
Theorizing Knowledge-Based Development?

J-C Spender
Lund University, Sweden

BACKGROUND

This volume introduces an important new social science - KBD, the knowledge-based development of cities and societies. It arises at the convergence of an urban planning tradition that, as Edvinsson reveals in our Foreword, goes back many centuries, with the economists' concern with knowledge as the factor of production whose predominance characterizes the contemporary world. We live, we are told, in the Knowledge Age, so it is not strange that we are looking for knowledge-based theories to illuminate our situation and guide our actions. History plays its own tricks on us, of course, for this talk of knowledge seems to imply everything previous took place under conditions of ignorance. This is not the point; the term knowledge is simply a label for the change from the 19th century socio-economy dominated by materials, commodities, physical work and tangible products to that of our time, with its predominantly mental and symbolic work, and slippery sense of things valued like Facebook or medical tests. Older economies and societies depended on knowledge and skills too, so the deeper point is to see how the balance of tangibles and intangibles has changed and, with that, the qualitative nature of the human condition.

When such change occurs new socioeconomic theories are needed - KBD is one, a reflection of our new context. The facts are that for the first time in our history more than half the world's rapidly expanding population lives, produces and consumes in urban areas. Farming, mining, fishing, lumbering and hunting, which still engaged the bulk of the world's population in the 19th century, now employ less than 10%, while professional or 'knowledge work' has risen from a whisker to around 40%. Such massive changes imply huge changes in how we engage the world physically - and these changes seem likely to continue, obliging us to pay increasing attention to the relationships between the socio-economy and human geography, and to how we relate to Nature as we occupy the increasingly pressured environment.

Ever since Marshall's thoughtful consideration of 'industrial regions' - where the crucial commercial knowledge was 'in the air' - English-speaking economists have been interested in the spatial analysis of economic activity (Marshall, 1964). This interest was significantly accelerated by the work considered in our volume's chapters - authors such as Castells, Saxenian, Porter, Fligstein, Florida and others - while the focus has shifted from the Sheffield cutlers to Silicon Valley's chipmakers. KBD's impetus is that analyzing human geography's place in economic activity is more than an academic exercise; huge investment, business, tax and social policy decisions turn on it. As we look at the Rust Belt or the Niger Delta or New Orleans it is obvious we have yet to understand sufficiently. The subtlety of the interplay of dimensions Florida has dubbed TAPE (Technology, Arts & Culture, Professionals, Education) has clearly added new richness to our understanding of how the socio-economy, perhaps modeled as a diamond or Triple Helix, might work - but we are still more or less in the dark. KBD embraces all of the above, and adds further with its attention to micro level, the 'built environment' and its interest in what Bourdieu has dubbed '*habitus*', the convergence of the specific actors' past with the specific interactions and structures of the present.

THIS AFTERWORD

Three lines of thought and analysis converge here. First, KBD is positioned as a tool for planners and policy-makers, so it is useful to look to planning's history for some cautions. Attempts to engineer human society and geography go back to time immemorial - to Ragusa, Alexandria and beyond. Many of our book's chapters display a certain historical innocence as they argue governments should take note of interactions that are typical of city life and invest in TAPE-type resources to produce economic innovation and growth - a variation on the 'build it and they will come' approach. This narrative raises unanswered questions about the many hundreds of urban and regional initiatives around the world that, aping Route 128 or Emilia Romagna, have been implemented with little success. Rather than theorize further we might learn more by studying these failures. One response, of course, is that these failing initiatives were policy-deficient and incorrectly architected, too narrow, neglecting one or more of the complex dimensions implied above. Another is that 'social engineering' is an inherently chancy business and that our theorizing is overly prone to lead us into thinking we have grasped the whole of a causal relationship which is, in reality, much more complex - though this throws the planning project itself into doubt. A third view, raised by Jane Jacob's notions of desirable 'urban chaos', is that all central policy is ultimately bound to fail, a view that reflects von Mises's and Hayek's similar attacks on central planning. This kind of reasoning raises parallel questions about the interplay of control and freedom in the realms of the arts and sciences. While patronage seems to have been crucial to many of the exciting periods in the history of art, there have been as many periods in which resource-poor 'outsiders' such as the Impressionists have produced the real paradigm shifts. Big Science has also been no simple route to progress.

The second line of thought is that cities are physical manifestations of the way societies operate and they arise unplanned. We can try to explain them functionally, but can seldom get to the bottom of why they arise in this place rather than that, or why they disappear, suddenly abandoned. Rather than being the outcome of specific plans, such when Caliph Ja'far Al-Mansur founded Baghdad in 762, or the founding of Canberra in 1913, cities like Glasgow emerged from their previous religious and academic identities as local commerce and the Atlantic slave trade grew, necessitating a complex entrepôt and service location. In short, to understand cities we must understand the society of which they are part - and this locates the planners and policy-makers inside them, pulled this way and that, rather than outside, objectively analyzing and pulling levers, insulated by their science from the political and economic systems that already exist. The Romans, for instance, and later the Catalans, developed a sophisticated trading economy throughout the Mediterranean region that extended into North Africa and what we call the Middle East. Their markets were under the control of all kinds of forces, political, religious and military. They had letters of credit, bankers, factories, contracts, lawyers, inventories, production instructions and so forth, administrative instruments just like those we use today. The mix of politics and commerce was intimately articulated in the activities that took place only in cities - Rome and Barcelona, and elsewhere around the Mediterranean. Likewise Genoa's *Banco di San Giorgio*, founded in 1407, that maintained scrupulous records as it helped usher in a history-changing expansion of the credit system, illustrates how the Italian cities of the time set the stage for today's global capitalist economics. Shakespeare's *Merchant of Venice* reveals much about how this worked - and how the city was central to the processes. Likewise in the pre-colonial days of trade in the Indian Ocean - wonderfully illustrated by Chaudhuri's painstaking research (Chaudhuri, 1985) - we see the interplay of power and commerce and see how cities are the nexus of their interaction. No society is without some form of rule and whatever this is, be it a dictatorship, a theocracy or a democracy, it is hungry for the resources that commerce and industry alone produce. Chaudhuri shows us how over and over again across a millennia the merchants' need for security and predictability forced them to come to terms with the taxes, fees and levies the rulers needed equally urgently. Our geography is penetrated by human and social considerations. Delicate and dynamic bilateral arrangements came into place, open to being disturbed by any manner of upset, human or Natural. Today's economic crisis is simply the most recent such disturbance, more obviously global than many before, but inherently city based and shaped even as its effects reach into rural hinterlands in Bangladesh, Brazil or the Bahamas.

Even without being able to predict our socio-economic situation we see the pre-modern era of farming, fishing and so forth, was as dependent on cities for trading, storage, financing, trans-shipment and so on as is the modern economy. Cities existed long before the Industrial Revolution. Likewise Hoselitz's analysis of the classic notions of city function shows that the political economy of ruling and administering must be distinguished from the political economy of commerce and industry - the former giving rise to 'central' cities, the latter to 'industrial' cities (Hoselitz, 1955). We see this today in the separation of, say, Canberra and Sydney, Brasilia and Sao Paulo, Albany and New York. In general we see how the spatial arrangements we create reflect the social and political arrangements and institutions we create - and vice versa, reminding us of the iterations of Giddens's 'structuration theory' (Cassell, 1993). Likewise, while IT and modern communications change much, they do not 'change everything', just as the 'death of distance' turns out to be incorrect (Cairncross, 1997). Our spatial arrangements are neither technologically nor geographically determined. The underlying point being that absent a good understanding of how any particular society works - its ethical, cultural and religious aspects as well as its economic, political and military aspects - we are unlikely to get to the heart of how we inhabit our space and time and why our cities exist.

HOW KNOWLEDGE UNDERPINS KBD

This afterword's third line of thought is KBD's focus on knowledge and in this respect it is path-breaking, leveraging from the knowledge-intensity of modern life to a better understanding of its other dimensions. In addition to understanding cities in terms of their physical structure or economics, places to 'break-bulk', get transportation permits, find buyers or otherwise reduce transactions costs, they are also places to generate new political, social, and technological knowledge that has economic consequences. But knowledge is a complex topic that has occupied philosophers, scientists and educators for centuries - and it is easy to drown in academic debate without getting to any of the key points that might illuminate the KBD project. It is not simply about communication and cities as hubs in a new technologically-facilitated communication network. Indeed given today's technologies, many expected distance and time, and thus human geography itself, to become irrelevant. The opposite seems to be the case. So the challenge is to not merely to find out how the socio-economy works, rather to explore knowledge's specific place in a theory of a knowledge-intensive society - and before we can consider how cities fit in we need some clarification of knowledge itself.

One route into 'knowledge' that avoids the perils of straight philosophy runs via the field of 'knowledge management' (KM). This subject is already familiar to many of our authors and readers. But it is important to be honest about what has been happening here. KM is not strong philosophically (Spender & Scherer, 2007). Nor are its practical implications clear. There is no denying it is tarnished, far from the shiny new coin it seemed three decades ago when Peter Drucker began to bring it - and the underlying social transformation central to KBD - to managers' and policy-makers' attention (Drucker, 1976). Today many wonder what happened to its promise and it is sometimes difficult to recall what all the fuss was about. But KM is no fad; there is substantial achievement beneath the confusion and chatter. 'Knowledge', as KM defines it, is a potentially important route to understanding the modern socio-economy and, thereby, its spatial arrangements. But KM carries a lot of baggage too. On the one hand the information technology (IT) industry capitalized brilliantly and profitably on the new language - knowledge tools, knowledge engineers, knowledge systems, CKOs, KM journals and so on. On the other we see practicing managers using the language of 'tacit' knowledge and 'knowledge sharing' to draw more of their organizations' under-utilized skills and capabilities into play.

To understand knowledge-driven cities and knowledge-driven socio-economies we need to understand something of knowledge's more puzzling aspects. The point about the modern age is not that knowledge has newly become power; rather it is about changes in the processes of generating what we now consider to be wealth. Again, it is not production engineering (recall the Dutch windmills), or consulting (recall Machiavelli) or market research (recall the Silk Road) that is new. Over the last 40 or so years there has been a spectacular rise in productivity worldwide, in manufacturing and agriculture, far outstripping the additional demand from the world's rising population with its lengthening life-span. The result has been an equally staggering rise in standard of living for an increasing proportion of humans - though not all, of course (McCloskey, 2006). The number of hours we in the fortunate group have to work to meet our basic needs has declined to the point where luxuries and discretionary income drive our economies (though also increasing their volatility, as we are presently being reminded).

The structure of the developed economies has changed accordingly, the white-collar component vastly larger, what we have come to regard as 'knowledge workers' (Reich, 1992). Production has always demanded knowledge about how to do the work and, equally important, how to coordinate the extending division of labor that is driving the productivity gains. Coordination between firms, suppliers, and customers through markets and alliances is just as important. The underlying phenomenon is that for every unit of blue-collar work, of direct interaction with materials, be they steel, coffee beans, iPods or the dental patient's teeth, there is a huge and increasing number of units of white-collar 'knowledge work' - designing, planning, measuring, administering, allocating, contracting, directing, etc. Such structural elaboration is what draws new higher productivity equipment and techniques into economic relationship with the processes of consumption. Again, it is not that white-collar work's novelty is different, for clerks, inventory recording, planning and intelligence-collection have always been with us, as the history above notes. The key is the amazing escalation in the relationship between the differentiation, increase and elaboration of knowledge work as it converges on the increased data volume, speed, and availability supporting the new global economy. Finally, the changes in our way of life have led to our developing and consuming services were restricted to the ruling classes alone, which we previously provided ourselves or never knew we needed - restaurants instead of home cooking, TV reality shows, online gaming, insurance instead of impoverishment, medical care instead of suffering, education instead of ignorance, and so on, all of which stand on ever more efficient information handling.

All this seems pretty straightforward, the implication being that managers need to understand how to use IT - ever more powerful for each unit of cost - to squeeze more value from more information, all standing on rising productivity and expanding consumption. This seemed obvious in the 1990s, for example in the rapid rise of outsourcing as the world's economy began to restructure and redistribute the globe's work around a new geographical or regional division of labor - itself contingent on new IT, the Internet, new logistics technologies such as bulk shipping and containerization, and new financing, technology transfer and supply chain management techniques. As a result we began to talk of the world being 'flat', the immediate result of information-intensive management making it possible to move capital, both financial and intellectual, production, and distribution around with rapidity and efficiency as the global infrastructure improved.

What then of 'knowledge cities' as punctuations in this flat distance-less world? Why do cities still exist? Are they no more than vestigial remains of a pre-21st century socio-economy? It has taken the KM community some time, as we absorbed these exciting new capabilities, to discover their limitations, that time and space are still central to the human condition (Spender, 1998). In the process the knowledge management movement morphed and reinvented itself through several phases as it learned that it was not, after all, purveying the magic dust that could address every business problem. Writers such as Larry Prusak, who lived through KM's recent history, point to three phases; first, the immediate feeling of power, of achieving mastery of a new universe of possibilities. Finally we had a way to step behind work's outcomes to assess and control its most crucial input, not capital, land or labor, but knowledge (Prusak, 2001). The possession of resources was not that mattered - be they cash, patents, land, agreements or employees - rather it was the knowledge of how to use them that made for competitive advantage and responsiveness to economic and technological change (Penrose, 1995). We never tired of telling how PARC Xerox invented while Apple profited or Fairchild invented while Intel profited or how Toyota was able to produce autos in America that overpowered the Big Three in the US markets. One result was the dot.com bubble and the accompanying story was that someone working in the business probably knew already what 'the next big thing' was going to be. So management was challenged to set up information collection systems that would mean that none of the corporate knowledge was overlooked, none of its experience in the R&D labs, production or the marketplace would get lost. For KBD the implication is that the city is a place for sharing knowledge of how resources might be best used.

KM's second phase was a corollary of the first. Realizing the firm's strategic knowledge was distributed rather than solely in the hands of the senior executives, we discovered that paying attention to knowledge raised a whole series of problems about the redistribution of organizational power. Subordinates seemed reluctant to share their knowledge, retirees were not happy to be the subjected to knowledge engineers and their expert systems. We discovered that people hung onto their knowledge in different and often devious ways. So KM's second phase was about designing learning, education, and incentive systems designed to 'flatten' the organization, to make it look as if the firm was comprised of people whose interests were fully aligned and that the organization's power differentials did not matter. Many with their heads buried deep in the technology ignored these sociological and psychological issues and blithely worked on 'user-friendly' systems and slick GUI interfaces, attempting to minimize the difficulties confronting those who were prepared to 'share'. Many organizations and KM people are still stuck in this phase, working with intranets, zippy websites and blog-like interactions. For KBD the implication is that a city is a place representing the alignment of actors' interests that lead to knowledge sharing.

The third phase, where some organizations are today, is a sharper change, for it runs against the KM-industry's desires - among other things it reduces their profit margins. Organizations enter this phase as they reclaim their systems from the KM consultants and vendors whose long-term interests are in keeping them in a state of strategic dependency. Organizations learn to 'roll their own' knowledge systems in spite of the trumpeted benefits of outsourcing and facilities management. Senior management eventually learns to question the limits of what IT-based approaches to KM can achieve - and the rest of us learn to reconsider how we think about knowledge and its limits. For KBD the implication is that knowledge can be managed, no matter how ethereal or slippery it seems - and cities, with their defining facilities, seem to be a way in which, through the development of complex social institutions, this actually happens.

Clearly we may be about to get beyond the low hanging KM fruit always visible to those in IT and engage the promise Drucker sensed. In the process we may also get a better understanding of why cities exist and how they work, and of why distance is alive and well and the world is far from flat. One of the events that helped put KM onto executives' radar was the publication of Nonaka & Takeuchi's *The Knowledge-Creating Company* in 1995 (Nonaka & Takeuchi, 1995). On the rare occasions when an academic book influences practicing managers it is often because it provides them with a language and way of thinking about things they are already doing or struggling with. This was the case a century ago when Frederick Taylor and his engineering colleagues began to talk about Scientific Management. Today most managers' notions of measurement and control reflect Taylor's thinking and language. An experienced machinist and foreman himself, Taylor argued the bulk of new production ideas came from the shop floor; so his 'system' began with collecting and analyzing these (Spender & Kijne, 1996). In KM's case Nonaka & Takeuchi's language of explicit versus tacit knowledge, top-down versus bottom-up, and the SECI knowledge-creation cycle, helped managers struggling with dynamic competition to reconnect with innovative capabilities distributed across their organizations. This was not something new, far from it. For decades managers had encouraged suggestion schemes, quality circles and other forms of bottom-up as they also engaged in top-down moves such as 6 Sigma, Baldridge Awards, ISO 9001, business process re-engineering, and so on. The KM approach brought all of this into a new framework - focusing especially on the tacit-explicit interplay that could only take place in the workplace. Here the KM vision was finally pushing beyond the mere collection, collation, storage and distribution of data - valuable as that might be - into a territory that lay outside IT's concerns and probably beyond IT's limits. Thus far KM has paid little attention to limits and we have no widely accepted language for handling knowledge and its impact on economic activity - hence many of the neologisms we see in our book's chapters. Yet knowledge-limits and knowledge-absences are creeping into economic and social theorizing - bounded rationality, transactions costs, principal-agent theory, asymmetric knowledge, and so on. We open up the possibility of thinking about cities as knowledge-limit phenomena as much as they seem to be transaction cost, knowledge-transfer and knowledge-growth phenomena.

THE LIMITS TO KNOWLEDGE

We do not understand a concept if we have no sense of its limits, of its reach. But knowledge is a term without obvious limits. We might contrast it with opinion, but that would only work if we could have 'objective' knowledge, a notion which Descartes and then Kant knocked flat. All knowledge is human rather than objective, determined by 'the real'; opinion is merely a way of disparaging what others claim to know. We might also contrast knowledge with emotion, which only makes sense if we can have knowledge without emotion. This illustrates some of the difficulties of stepping outside knowledge as a way of observing, measuring or analyzing it. Of course we cannot, knowledge refers primarily to our state of consciousness and to understand this better we might contrast the different ways in which we know. This is how the explicit / tacit distinction gathers its considerable power. Another important distinction is between 'data' and 'meaning'. Data is always hostage to the framework in which it is collected, sometimes in terms what can or cannot be measured, but more fundamentally in terms of the meaning attached to the data. Are the clothes sizes US or European, what is the currency, and so on? IT professionals meet this in the design of the system's underlying data structures - the definition of what counts and what does not. Putting this architecture in place makes some computations possible but excludes others for the whole point is to collect data that is relevant, avoiding that which is irrelevant. But data's meaning is outside rather than within the data. Computers do data not meaning. Meaning is about people, and data and meaning are intertwined. Rumsfeld, who had a talent for a felicitous phrase, famously defined meaning problems as 'connecting the dots'. Meaning is always outside the IT system, which is why some speak of IT as mere 'plumbing'.

To the surprise of most IT professionals, KM's vision takes us beyond managing data to the management of meaning. This is much trickier because meaning is subjective; what we humans add to data (Spender, 2007). It is how 'optical illusions' happen - along with 'irrational exuberances' such as tulip-mania, Ponzi schemes and real estate bubbles. Every organization is a system of managed meanings, sometimes suggested in 'mission statements' but more generally floating about in the noisy discussions and interactions that fill the organizational space. Management is about keeping a handle on these meanings, owning them, shaping them, using them to direct the work of others. Many managers are tempted to clamp down on the meanings that develop organically in their organizations - the old battle between the 'formal' and the 'informal' - but doing so also shuts down creative dissent, the contrary or strange view that provides new insight into a problem situation, whether that be on the shop floor or in the Boardroom. We spend so much time in meetings because we are trying to balance being open and flexible against ensuring sufficient control meanings to move towards a shared goal. Yes, decisions get made and performance is reported, but the sub-text is to chew over whether this way of thinking about the situation is productive or not (generally not, we groan, change is slow and too often resisted). Thus KM is not just about data management, it is also about meaning-management - story-telling, reputation management (as when J&J pulled Tylenol), admitting or denying mistakes (the tobacco companies' executives), and so on. One cutting edge for KM, then, is a better understanding of meaning-management, how to theorize or model it and how to practice it. From KBD's point of view cities are places of the stories like Xanadu or Venice that evolve and change men's minds and behaviors.

Managing meaning is not simply about communicating it as if a meaning was another item of data. That is not the way humans work. We tend to have our own views, values, intentions and therefore our own system of meanings. Incompatible meanings are why negotiation is so difficult and exhausting. Meanings change and re-emerge slowly, most effectively and quickly through direct face-to-face interaction. That is why we put parliamentary debate at the center of our democratic system. Meetings can work this way. Direct conversation has breadth and depth computer-mediated communication does not. We have all experienced the difference between email interaction with those who share our views and with whom we can exchange facts (as we think of some data), versus those who do not share the same perceptions, who may be shocked or insulted by our emails. 'No, no' we say, that is not what we meant. Cities then are extensions of the ancient Greek and Roman forums, where politics was done, and the marketplaces of the Dutch Republic, where tulips, textiles and mace were traded. Their emphasis is on the evolving patterns of meaning that determine how goods are valued and therefore how the economy itself functions.

KNOWLEDGE PROCESSES AND HUMAN GEOGRAPHY

The difference between the essential geographically-constrained humanness of meaning-management and the abstract space-less technology of data-management gives us insight into how and why cities work and why geography matters after all - because cities are not passive infrastructures, they are vibrant contexts of human interaction. While data can flow freely - especially when we have appropriate IT systems - meaning is 'sticky', experiencing tremendous frictions. Meanings emerge from the social collective, but they also reflect individual leaders whose ideas are leveraged through the collective. These processes are not simple, because we all know there are times when stories (rumors) fly like wildfire, almost outpacing electronic media. At the micro level, research into the physical layout of R&D labs shows how valuable it can be to create of some neutral shared 'water-cooler' space. This facilitates the flow of ideas too sketchy or radical to be written down in reports - showing we often work in the conceptual spaces 'out of the box' - where the established languages are simply not useful.

A different example is the population distribution in the Great Plains territory (Chorley & Haggett, 1967). While the settlers' homesteads were located according to government edict, the territory changed as 'service centers' grew up - villages, towns and cities. The villages would be separated by half a day's wagon ride - there and back without having to stay over. One would find a church, a school, a barber, a farrier, a grocer, a bar and a rooming house. Towns had a sheriff and a jail, a doctor, a hotel and a theater perhaps, serving multiple villages. Other more complex services were located so they had bigger catchment areas. Where government services were based became a city, being supported by a complex multi-layered infrastructure of lawyers, courthouses, hotels, entertainment facilities, hospitals and so on. Each service has its own pattern of meanings, increasingly specialized and professionalized. Every organization is such pattern and must be constantly reacting to environmental changes - financial, competitive, legal, customer-driven and so on - if it is to remain in viable engagement with its stakeholders and markets. Note this patterning comes about as the synthesis of human desires - to congregate, exchange goods and services, seek justice, enjoy a play, etc. - with the abstract technical possibilities of bringing people together. When the Model T replaces the horse-drawn wagon, the geography changes even though the human desires do not. Thus it is the difficulty of managing meaning that makes the organization's geography important - the need to be visible in Head Office to get promoted, the chance to disappear into the hinterlands and regroup after a defeat. Thus cities (and villages and regional clusters) exist for many reasons, but important among them are reasons to do with trafficking in meaning - just as 19th century artists clustered in Paris and post WWII in New York to be in touch with the latest developments, just as scriptwriters must be in LA. KM as meaning-management is a challenge to the organization's leaders to see and control the organization as a viable city, facilitating the interactions that matter and suppressing those that do not in an over-informationed environment.

But this is not the limit of KM's vision. Seeing the gap between data-management and meaning-management goes back to ancient times and does not distinguish KM from the ancient craft of speech-writing, critical reading, composition, or generally knowing how to harness language to the organization's goals. Messages matter whether they are for employees, shareholders or customers. But the distinction between data and meaning is always worth re-visiting for it reminds us of the differences between facts and values, and the differences between a computer's logical language and the 'natural' and the not-very-grammatical language we humans actually use in our interactions. If every fourth word is 'like', what is really going on? This points to the differences between our ways of knowing and a computer's way of 'knowing' - quite different, as is the implicit notion of 'knowledge', what is known. Humans know meaning as well as data and can appreciate the Epistles as fine examples of meaning management at a distance, revealing both the power of natural language as a way of stepping beyond data into meaning, and its weakness when contrasted with face-to-face conversation (which is why we keep flying to meetings).

KM's most signal contribution was to give a voice to those who knew already that organizations involve more than managing data and meaning (which, melded together, we call information). Organizations are systems of value-adding practice that stand on both information and practical skills - sometimes labeled 'tacit knowledge' (Spender, 1995). The main point of the Nonaka & Takeuchi story is the interplay of information and practice, bridging intention and experience with tacit knowing. KM's full vision lets us separate knowledge-as-data, knowledge-as-meaning and knowledge-as-practice into three universes of understanding and managerial challenges (Spender, 2007). The failure to distinguish between these is one of the principal reasons for the high failure rate of KM projects - and, in a sense, KBD's aspiration is to treat cities (and maybe societies too) as KM projects. If one is engaged in a meaning-management project, putting the IT folks in charge is sure to lead to failure. Cities are not simply 'wired' places. If it the project is about practice, merely providing data will not hack it.

Of the three modes knowledge-as-practice is the most difficult. On the one hand we see the limits of knowledge engineering and expert systems as we seek to capture and model practice, on the other the complexities of 'transferring best practice'. The practice dimension of knowledge management is even less developed than the second meaning-management dimension but, ironically, it is where the greatest gains lie. Securing these clearly demands clarity in understanding how one is not dealing with either data or meaning. At the same time we realize how co-location, contiguity and so on get to matter. If ideas are to be reduced to a new skilled practice the water cooler approach is not enough, we must step inside the lab, as Jobs and Wozniak did, or as Deming did when helping the Japanese. Generally we know we must transfer skilled individuals or teams as viable carriers of best practice, rather than trying to codify the practice, even with lots of graphics and an interactive package. Thus cities are places in which people observe and engage with each others' practice in low cost ways - have meetings, visiting workshops and studios, hearing lectures, and so on. Fashion changes first on the city's streets and in its clubs as imaginative fashionistas strut their stuff. Famously, cubism evolved in a matter of months as Picasso and Braque were in and out of each other's studios daily. Turning this understanding around we see the different forms of knowledge move in very different ways and with different eases. Cities, in this reckoning, are knowledge-efficient systems for parsing the different kinds of knowledge and knowledge-interactions.

CONCLUSION

So what must KBD learn from history, human geography and KM? All disciplines understand their methods and objectives better when they have a grasp of its history and of why it is practiced in the way that it is. In this sense every discipline is more a social institution than an objective scientific endeavor. KBD is part of an attempt to move urban planning as an institutionalized endeavor into the Knowledge Age, proposing that cities and societies should be re-conceptualized around notions of knowledge. Unfortunately this takes us beyond the limits of current theorizing, for we have no knowledge-based theory of either cities or societies. But this should not deter us. Knowledge-based approaches are increasingly important in information technology as well as in economics, sociology and political science. KM's various phases open us up to its truly revolutionary nature as we moved from thinking of knowledge in a naive way - as data to be bundled up and whirled about with computers. This matters, of course, especially to those in the KM industry who are profiting mightily as a result. But it is only the tip of the KM iceberg. Far greater value lies below in the obscurities of managing meaning and practice, and the interactions between all three modes of knowing.

Thinking about 'knowledge cities' reminds us of the gulf separating computer science's logical abstractions and the limitless virtual worlds we can build there - such as SimCity - and how computers are constrained by the way in which they know. Thus Second Life cannot capture the moral complexity and multi-dimensionality of the human condition while the theater with its live actors and live audience can reach towards it. We fight wars over values and practices, not data. Competitive advantage is about connecting new dots and reducing them to novel practice. But as we make progress towards KM's objectives we learn something new about how fragile our cyber-penetrated way of life has become - for our human ways of knowing are increasingly hostage to our IT systems. An effective 'denial of service' attack can bring a hospital, a city, or perhaps even a nation, to a standstill. At the micro-level, this afterword can disappear without trace as my hard drive crashes, just our airplanes will be lost without ATCs and GPSs, and our banks collapsed by a virus. Increasingly we cannot spell or even think without Google to hand. Likewise knowledge cities and societies discover the enormous gains in productivity mentioned at the start of this essay can be reduced to chaos. Right now we are rediscovering the risks of over-leveraged credit; we have yet to discover the even greater risks behind KM's achievements. A KBD analysis is increasingly timely for it can reveal the fragile balance between the gains from our knowledge-driven socio-economy and the risks.

REFERENCES

Cairncross, F. (1997). *The Death of Distance: How the Communications Revolution Will Change Our Lives*. London: Orion Publishing.

Cassell, P. (Ed.). (1993). *The Giddens Reader*. Stanford, CA: Stanford University Press.

Chaudhuri, K. N. (1985). *Trade and Civilisation in the Indian Ocean: An Economic History from the Rise of Islam to 1750*. Cambridge, UK: Cambridge University Press.

Chorley, R. J., & Haggett, P. (1967). *Integrated Models in Geography*. London: Methuen.

Drucker, P. F. (1976). The Coming Rediscovery of Scientific Management: Frederick Winslow Taylor May Prove a More Useful Prohet for Our Times than We Yet Recognize. *Conference Board Record, June*, 23-27.

Hoselitz, B. F. (1955). The City, The Factory, and Economic Growth. *American Economic Review, 45*(2), 166.

Marshall, A. (1964). *Elements of the Economics of Industry*. London: Macmillan & Co. Ltd.

McCloskey, D. N. (2006). *The Bourgeois Virtues: Ethics for an Age of Commerce*. Chicago, IL: University of Chicago Press.

Nonaka, I., & Takeuchi, H. (1995). *The Knowledge-Creating Company: How Japanese Companies Create the Dynamics of Innovation*. New York: Oxford University Press.

Penrose, E. T. (1995). *The Theory of the Growth of the Firm* (3rd ed.). New York: Oxford University Press.

Prusak, L. (2001). Where did Knowledge Management come from? *IBM Systems Journal, 40*(4), 1002-1006.

Reich, R. B. (1992). *The Work of Nations: Preparing Ourselves for 21st Century Capitalism*. New York: Vintage Books.

Spender, J.-C. (1995). Organizations are Activity Systems, Not Merely Systems of Thought. *Advances in Strategic Management, 12B*, 153-174.

Spender, J.-C. (1998). The Geographies of Strategic Competence: Borrowing from Social and Educational Psychology to Sketch an Activity Based Theory of the Firm. In A. D. Chandler, P. Hagstrom & O. Solvell (Eds.), *The Dynamic Firm: The Role of Technology, Strategy, Organization, and Regions* (pp. 417-439). New York: Oxford University Press.

Spender, J.-C. (2007). Data, Meaning and Practice: How the Knowledge-Based View Can Clarify Technology's Relationship With Organizations. *International Journal of Technology Management, 38*(1/2), 178-196.

Spender, J.-C., & Kijne, H. (Eds.). (1996). *Scientific Management: Frederick Winslow Taylor's Gift to the World*. Norwell, MA: Kluwer.

Spender, J.-C., & Scherer, A. G. (2007). The Philosophical Foundations of Knowledge Management: Editors' Introduction. *Organization, 14*(1), 5-28.

Compilation of References

Abelson, R. (1981). Psychological Status of the Script Concept. *The American Psychologist, 36*(7), 715–729. doi:10.1037/0003-066X.36.7.715

Ackoff, R. L. (1978). *The Art of Problem Solving: Accompanied by Ackoff's Fables*. Songs, NY: John Wiley.

Acs, Z. (2002). *Innovation and the growth of cities*. London: Edward Elgar.

Acs, Z. J., Audretsch, D. B., Braunerhjelm, P., & Carlsson, B. (2004). The missing link: The knowledge filter and entrepreneurship in endogenous growth. *Discussion Paper No.4783, December*. London, UK: Centre for Economic Policy Research.

Adams, E. C., & Freeman, C. (2000). Communities of practice: bridging technology and knowledge assessment. *Journal of Knowledge Management, 4*(1), 38–44. doi:10.1108/13673270010315939

Agrawal, A. (2001). University-to-industry knowledge transfer: literature review and unanswered questions. *International Journal of Management Reviews, 3*, 285–302. doi:10.1111/1468-2370.00069

Ahlqvist, T., & Inkinen, T. (2007). Technology foresight in multiscalar innovation systems. A spatiotemporal process perspective. *Fennia, 185*(1), 3–14.

Ahn, J. H., & Chang, S. G. (2004). Assessing the Contribution of Knowledge to Business Performance: The KP3Methodology. *Decision Support Systems, 36*, 403–416.

Albino, V., Carbonara, N., & Messeni-Petruzzelli, A. (2007). Proximity as a communication resource for competitiveness: a rationale for technology clusters. *International Journal of Learning and Intellectual Capital, 4*, 430–452. doi:10.1504/IJLIC.2007.016337

Alcacer, J. (2006). Location choices across the value chain: how activity and capability influence collocation. *Management Science, 52*, 1457–1471. doi:10.1287/mnsc.1060.0658

Alcacer, J., & Chung, W. (2007). Location strategies and knowledge spillovers. *Management Science, 53*, 760–776. doi:10.1287/mnsc.1060.0637

Alcacer, J., & Gittelman, M. (2006). Patent citations as a measure of knowledge flows: the influence of examiner citations. *The Review of Economics and Statistics, 88*, 774–779. doi:10.1162/rest.88.4.774

Al-Furaih, I., Sahab, A., Hayajneh, A., Abdullah, A., Ibrahim, M., & Thalha, M. (Eds.). (2007). Knowledge cities: future of cities in the knowledge economy. Selangor, Malaysia: Scholar Press. Abu- Anzeh, N., & Ledraa, T. (2007). In Malaysian Institute of Planners, et al. (Eds.), Knowledge Cities, Future of Cities in the Knowledge Economy (pp. 116-139). Kuala Lumpur, Malaysia: Scholar Press.

Allee, V. (2000). Knowledge networks and communities of practice. *OD Practitioner, 32*(4). Retrieved August 12, 2008, from http://www.odenetwork.org/odponline/vol32n4/knowledgenets.html

Allee, V. (2002). *The future of knowledge: Increasing prosperity through value networks*. New York: Elsevier Science & Technology.

Allen, T. J. (1977). *Managing the Flow of Technology.* Cambridge, MA: MIT press.

Almeida, P., & Kogut, B. (1999). Localization of knowledge and the mobility of engineers in regional networks. *Management Science*, *45*, 905–917. doi:10.1287/mnsc.45.7.905

Alvesson, M. (2000). Social identity and the problem of loyalty in knowledge-intensive companies. *Journal of Management Studies*, *37*(6).

Amadi-Echendu, J. E. (2007). Thinking styles of technical knowledge workers in the systems of innovation paradigm. *Technological Forecasting and Social Change*, *74*(8), 1204–1214.doi:10.1016/j.techfore.2006.09.002

American Productivity and Quality Center (APQC). (2001). *Building and sustaining communities of practice*. Retrieved December 7, 2008, from http://www.researchandmarkets.com/reports/40877

Amin, A. (2002). Spatialities of globalisation. *Environment & Planning A*, *34*, 385–399. doi:10.1068/a3439

Andersson, A. E., & Andersson, D. E. (2006). *The economics of experiences, the arts and entertainment.* Cheltenham, UK: Edward Elgar Publishing.

Andreasen, A. R. (1995). *Marketing Social Change: Changing Behavior to Promote Health, Social Development, and the Environment.* San Francisco: Jossey-Bass.

Andrews, K., & Delahaye, B. (2001). Influences on knowledge processes in organizational learning: The psychosocial filter. *Journal of Management Studies*, *37*(6), 797–810. doi:10.1111/1467-6486.00204

APEC Economic Committee Report. (2003). *The drivers of new economy in APEC – innovation and organizational practices.* Singapore: APEC Secretariat.

Appiah-Adu, K., Fyall, A., & Singh, S. (2001). Marketing Effectiveness and Business Performance in the financial Services Industry. *Journal of Services Marketing*, *15*(1), 18–34. doi:10.1108/08876040110381346

Arbonies, A., & Moso, M. (2002). Basque Country: the knowledge cluster. *Journal of Knowledge Management*, *6*(4), 347–355. doi:10.1108/13673270210440857

Ardichvili, A., Maurer, M., Li, W., Wentling, T., & Stuedemann, R. (2006). Cultural influences on knowledge sharing through online communities of practice. *Journal of Knowledge Management*, *10*(1), 94–107. doi:10.1108/13673270610650139

Ardichvili, A., Page, V., & Wentling, T. (2002). Motivation and barriers to participation in virtual knowledge-sharing communities of practice. *Journal of Knowledge Management*, *7*(1), 64–77. doi:10.1108/13673270310463626

Armstrong, D. J., Nelson, H. J., Nelson, K. M., & Narayanan, V. K. (2008). Building the IT Workforce of the Future: The Demand for More Complex, Abstract, and Strategic Knowledge. *Information Resources Management Journal*, *21*(2), 63–79.

Arthur, M. B., DeFilippi, R. J., & Lindsay, V. J. (2008). On Being a Knowledge Worker. *Organizational Dynamics*, *37*(4), 365–377.doi:10.1016/j.orgdyn.2008.07.005

Arvidsson, A. (2009). The ethical economy: Towards a post-capitalist theory of value. *Capital and Class*, *97*, 13–30.doi:10.1177/030981680909700102

Ash, J. (2002). Personal Knowledge, analyzing and visualizing Knowledge Domains.

Attewell, P. (1992). Technology diffusion and organizational learning: The case of business computing. *Organization Science*, *3*(1), 1–19. doi:10.1287/orsc.3.1.1

Audirac, I., & Fitzgerald, J. (2003). Information Technology (IT) and Urban Form: An Annotated Bibliography of the Urban Deconcentration and Economic Restructuring Literatures. *Journal of Planning Literature*, *17*(4), 480–511.

Audretsch, D. (2004). Sustaining innovation and growth: Public policy support for entrepreneurship. *Industry and Innovation*, *11*(3), 167–191. doi:10.1080/1366271042000265366

Audretsch, D. B., & Feldman, M. (1996). R&D spillovers and the geography of innovation and production. *The American Economic Review*, *86*, 630–640.

Audretsch, D. B., & Keilbach, M. (2004). Entrepreneurship and Regional Growth: An Evolutionary Interpretation. *Journal of Evolutionary Economics, 14*(5), 605–616. doi:10.1007/s00191-004-0228-6

Augustine, N. (2009, January 7). *America's competitiveness.* Testimony before the Democratic Steering and Policy Committee, U.S. House of Representatives.

Avnimelech, G., & Tobal, M. (2006). *Microeconomic Insights from Israel's Venture Capital Emergence Towards a Theory of Evolutionary Targeting of Infant Industries.* Haifa, Israel: Neaman Institute.

Azhar, M. K. (2008). *Entrepreneurship and Development.* Powerpoint Slides on AIM Conference Centre, MDeC, MSC Malaysia.

Bajracharya, B., & Allison, J. (2008). Emerging Role of ICT in the Development of Knowledge-Based Master Planned Communities . In Yigitcanlar, T., Velibeyoglu, K., & Baum, S. (Eds.), *Knowledge-Based Urban Development: Planning and Applications in the Information Era* (pp. 279–295). New York: Information Science Reference.

Baker, T., Miner, A. S., & Eesley, D. T. (2003). Improvising firms: Bricolage, account giving and improvisational competencies in the founding process. *Research Policy, 32*, 255–276. doi:10.1016/S0048-7333(02)00099-9

Bandura, A. (1977). Self efficacy: Toward a unifying theory of behavioral change. *Psychological Review, 84*, 191–215. doi:10.1037/0033-295X.84.2.191

Baqir, M. N., & Kathawala, Y. (2004). BA for Knowledge Cities: A Futuristic Technology Model. *Journal of Knowledge Management, 8*(5), 235–243. doi:10.1108/13673270410558828

Barab, S. A., & Duffy, T. M. (1998). From practice fields to communities of practice. Retrieved December 7, 2008, from http://crlt.indiana.edu/publications/complete.pdf

Barab, S. A., & Makinster, J. G. Moore, J.A., & Cunningham, D.J. (2001). *Designing and building an on-line community: The struggle to support sociability in the inquiry learning forum.* Retrieved December 7, 2008, from http://tiger.coe.missouri.edu/~young/aware/doc/barab.pdf

Barabasi, A. L. (2002). *Linked: The New Science of Networks.* Cambridge, MA: Perseus Publishing.

Barcelona. (2005). *Metropolitan Strategic Plan of Barcelona Phase 2006/2010.* Retrieved December 9, 2008, from http://www.bcn2000.es/en/publicacions-jornades/publicacions-del-pla-estrategic.aspx?_gIdTema=50&idioma=EN&_gIdContexto=1

Barcelona. (2008). *Barcelona Data Sheet 2008.* Retrieved December 9, 2008, from Ajuntament de Barcelona.Web site: http://w3.bcn.es/V44/Home/V44PublicacionsHomeCanalCtl/0,3729,71420027_75408511_3,00.html

Barclay, R. O., & Murray, P. C. (1997). *What is knowledge management?* Retrieved August 24, 2008, from http://www.media-access.com/whatis.html

Barley, S. R. (1986). Technology as an occasion for structuring: evidence from observations of CT scanners and the social order of radiology departments. *Administrative Science Quarterly, 31*, 78–108. doi:10.2307/2392767

Barth, S. (2000). *The Power of One.* Retrieved March,2009, from http://www.quantum3.co.za/KMM%20Article%20Dec2000.htm

Bartlett, W., & Bukvic, V. (2006). Knowledge transfer in Slovenia: Supporting innovative SMEs through spin-offs, technology parks, clusters and networks. *Economic and Business Review, 8*(4), 337–358.

Bartol, K. M., & Srivastava, A. (2002). Encouraging Knowledge Sharing: The Role of Organizational Reward Systems. *Journal of Leadership & Organizational Studies, 9*(1), 64–77. doi:10.1177/107179190200900105

Bathelt, H. (2005). Cluster relations in the media industry: Exploring the 'distanced neighbour' Paradox in Leipzig. *Regional Studies, 39*(1), 105–127. doi:10.1080/0034340052000320860

Batson, C. D., Ahmad, N., & Tsang, J. (2002). Four motives for community involvement. *The Journal of Social Issues, 58*, 429–445. doi:10.1111/1540-4560.00269

Baum, H. (1996). Practicing planning theory in a political world . In Mandelbaum, I., Mazza, L., & Burchell, R. (Eds.), *Explorations in planning theory*. New Brunswick, NJ: Rutgers.

Baum, J. A. C., Li, S. X., & Usher, J. M. (2000). Making the next move: how experiential and vicarious learning shape the locations of chains' acquisitions. *Administrative Science Quarterly*, *45*, 766–801. doi:10.2307/2667019

Baum, S., Yigitcanlar, T., & O'Connor, K. (2008). Creative industries and the urban hierarchy: the position of lower tier cities and regions in the knowledge economy? In Yigitcanlar, T., Velibeyoglu, K., & Baum, S. (Eds.), *Knowledge-Based Urban Development: Planning and Applications in the Information Era* (pp. 42–57). London: Information Science Reference.

Baum, S., Yigitcanlar, T., Horton, S., Velibeyoglu, K., & Gleeson, B. (2007). *The role of community and lifestyle in the making of a knowledge city*. Brisbane: Urban Research Program.

Baumard, P. (1999). *Tacit Knowledge in Organisations*. London: Sage.

Baumol, W. J. (2002). *The Free-Market Innovation Machine*. Princeton, NJ: Princeton University Press.

Beaverstock, R. G., Smith, J. V., & Taylor, P. J. (2007). A Roster of World Cities. *Cities*, *16*(6), 445-458. Retrieved May 18, 2008, from http://www.lboro.ac.uk/gawc/rb/rb5.html#t1

Beckers, H. L. (1984). The role of industry . In Fusfeld, H. I., & Haklisch, C. S. (Eds.), *University - Industry Research Interactions*. London: Pergamon Press.

Beckstead, D., & Brown, W. M. (2006). *Capacité d□innovation: l□emploi en sciences et en génie dans les villes canadiennes et américaines*. Ottawa, Canada: Statistique Canada.

Beckstead, D., Brown, W. M., & Gellatly, G. (2008). *Villes et croissance: le cerveau gauche des villes nord-américaines: scientifique et ingénieurs et croissance urbaine*. Ottawa, Canada: Statistique Canada.

Beetham, H. (1998). *CTI 1997/98: A review of learning and teaching innovation in the UK Higher Education from the Computers in Teaching Initiative (CTI)*. Oxford, UK: Computers in Teaching Initiative Press.

Bell, G. G. (2005). Clusters, networks, and firms innovativeness. *Strategic Management Journal*, *26*, 287–295. doi:10.1002/smj.448

Bell, M., & Hietala, M. (2002). *Helsinki, The Innovative City*. Helsinki, Finland: SKS.

Bellinger, G. (2004). *Knowledge management–emerging perspectives*. Retrieved June 9, 2008, from http://www.systems-thinking.org/kmgmt/kmgmt.htm

Ben-David, J. (1972). The Profession of Science and its Powers . *Minerva*, 10.

Bennet, A. (2005). *Exploring Aspects of Knowledge Management that Contribute to the Passion Expressed by Its Thought Leaders*. Retrieved from http://www.mountainquestinstitute.com

Bennet, A., & Bennet, D. (2004). *Organizational Survival in the New World: The Intelligent Complex Adaptive System*. Burlington, MA: Elsevier.

Bennet, A., & Bennet, D. (2007a). CONTEXT: The shared knowledge enigma. *VINE . The Journal of Information and Knowledge Management Systems*, *37*(1), 27–40.

Bennet, A., & Bennet, D. (2007b). Knowledge Mobilization in the Social Sciences and Humanities: Moving From Research to Action. Frost, WV: MQIPress.

Bennet, A., & Bennet, D. (2007c). From stories to strategy: Putting organizational learning to work. *VINE: The Journal of Information and Knowledge Systems*, *37*(4), 404–409.

Bennet, A., & Bennet, D. (2008a). The decision-making process for complex situations in a complex environment . In Burstein, F., & Holsapple, C. W. (Eds.), *Handbook on Decision Support Systems 1: Basic Themes* (pp. 3–20). New York: Springer-Verlag. doi:10.1007/978-3-540-48713-5_1

Bennet, A., & Bennet, D. (2008c). The fallacy of knowledge reuse: Building sustainable knowledge. [Special Issue on Knowledge Based Development]. *Journal of Knowledge Management*, 21–33. doi:10.1108/13673270810902911

Bennet, A., & Bennet, D. (2009b). Meta-knowledge: Understanding the knowledge that drives our actions . In Batra, S., & Carrillo, F. J. (Eds.), *Knowledge Management and Intellectual Capital: Emerging Perspectives* (pp. 411–434). New Delhi: Allied Publishers.

Bennet, A., & Bennet, D. (2009c). Managing self in troubled times: Banking on self-efficacy . In *Effective Executive* (pp. 56–82). Hyderabad, India: The ICFAI University Press.

Bennet, A., & Bennet, D. (2009d). Leaders, decisions, and the neuro-knowledge system . In Wallis, S. (Ed.), *Cybernetics and Systems Theory in Management: Tools, Views and Advancements*. Hershey, PA: IGI Global.

Bennet, D., & Bennet, A. (2008a). Engaging tacit knowledge in support of organizational learning. *VINE: The Journal of Information and Knowledge Systems*, *38*(1), 72–94.

Bennet, D., & Bennet, A. (2008c). The depth of knowledge: Surface, shallow or deep? *VINE: The Journal of Information and Knowledge Management Systems*, *38*(4), 405–420.

Bennet, D., & Bennet, A. (2009a). Associative patterning: The unconscious life of an organization . In Girard, J. (Ed.), *Building Organizational Memories* (pp. 201–224). Hershey, PA: IGI Global.

Benneworth, P., & Hospers, G. (2007). Urban competitiveness in the knowledge economy . *Progress in Planning*, *67*, 105–197. doi:10.1016/j.progress.2007.02.003

Bertrand, Q., & Duhamel, F. (2003). Bringing together strategic outsourcing and corporate strategy: Outsourcing motives and risk. *European Management Journal*, *21*(5), 647–661. doi:10.1016/S0263-2373(03)00113-0

Bilodeau, E. (2003). *Using communities of practice to enhance student learning: Examples and issues*. Retrieved December 7, 2008, from http://www.coolweblog.com/bilodeau/docs/2003-10-01-cop-enhancing-student-learning.pdf

Bilton, C. (2007). *Management and creativity: from creative industries to creative management*. Oxford, UK: Blackwell Publishing.

Bitran, G. R., Gurumurthi, S., & Sam, S. L. (2007). Emerging trends in supply chain governance. *MIT Sloan Management Review*, *48*(3), 30–37.

Blakely, E. (2001). Competitive Advantage for the 21st-Century City. *Journal of the American Planning Association. American Planning Association*, *67*(2), 133–145.

Blakely, E. (2005). *Do the Myths: Now is Time to Create the Knowledge City*. Australia: University of Sydney.

Blakely, E., & Bradshaw, T. (2002). *Planning Local Economic Development: Theory and Practice*. Thousand Oaks, CA: Sage Publications.

Blume & S. N. Durlauf (Ed.), *The Economy as an Evolving Complex System, Current Perspectives and Future District ions* (*Vol. 3*, pp. 267–282). Oxford, UK: Oxford University Press.

Bolan, R. J. J., & Tenkasi, R. V. (1995). Perspective Making and Perspective Taking in Communities of Knowing. *Organization Science*, *6*(4), 350–372. doi:10.1287/orsc.6.4.350

Bollinger, A. S., & Smith, R. D. (2001). Managing Organizational Knowledge as a Strategic Asset. *Journal of Knowledge Management*, *5*(1), 8–18. doi:10.1108/13673270110384365

Bontis, N., Keow, W. C. C., & Richardson, S. (2000). Intellectual Capital and Business Performance in Malaysian Industries. *Journal of Intellectual Capital*, *1*(1), 85–100. doi:10.1108/14691930010324188

Borja, J. (2003). *La ciudad conquistada*. Madrid: Alianza Editorial.

Boschma, R. A. (2005). Proximity and innovation: A critical assessment. *Regional Studies*, *39*(1), 61–74. doi:10.1080/0034340052000320887

Boschma, R. A. (2005). Proximity and innovation: a critical assessment. *Regional Studies, 39*, 61–74. doi:10.1080/0034340052000320887

Boschma, R. A. (2005). Social capital and regional development: An empirical analysis of the Third Italy . In Boschma, R. A., & Kloosterman, R. C. (Eds.), *Learning from Clusters: A Critical Assessment from an Economic-Geographical Perspective*. Dordrecht, The Netherlands: Springer-Verlag.

Boschma, R. A., & ter Wal, A. L. J. (2007). Knowledge networks and innovative performance in an industrial district. The case of a footwear district in the South of Italy. *Industry and Innovation, 14*, 177–199. doi:10.1080/13662710701253441

Bounfour, A., & Edvinsson, L. (Eds.). (2005). *Intellectual capital for communities –Nations, regions and cities.* New York: Elsevier Butterworth/Heinemann.

Bourdieu, P. (1977). *Outline of a Theory of Practice.* Cambridge, MA: Cambridge University Press.

Bourdieu, P. (1990). *The Logic of Practice.* Stanford, CA: Stanford University Press.

Bourdieu, P. (2000). *Pascalian Meditations.* Cambridge, MA: Polity Press.

Bowman, B., Nelson, K., Fertjowski, A., Prokuda, L., McCartney, R., & Limb, M. (2008). *Klang Valley Regional Plan 2008 – 2028.* Brisbane: Queensland University of Technology.

Boyd, S. (2001). Rethinking Knowledge Management: This Time It's Personal. *Knowledge Capital Group.* Recuperado Marzo, 2009, de http://www.crmodyssey.com/Documentation/Documentation_PDF/Rethinking_Knowledge_Management.pdf

Braczyk, H.-J., & Heidenreich, M. (1998). Conclusion . In Braczyk, H.-J., Cooke, P., & Heidenreich, M. (Eds.), *Regional innovation systems: The role of governances in a globalized world* (pp. 414–440). London: UCL Press.

Brenner, N. (1998). Global Cities, Glocal States: Global City Formation and State Territorial Restructuring in Contemporary Europe. *Review of International Political Economy, 5*(1), 1–37.

Breschi, S. (2000). The geography of innovation: a cross sector analysis . *Regional Studies, 34*, 213–229. doi:10.1080/00343400050015069

Breschi, S., & Lissoni, F. (2001). Knowledge spillovers and local innovation systems: a critical survey. *Industrial and Corporate Change, 10*, 975–1005. doi:10.1093/icc/10.4.975

Britton, J. N. H. (2004). High technology localization and extra-regional networks. *Entrepreneurship & Regional Development, 16*, 369–390. doi:10.1080/08985620410001674351

Brooks, D. (2008, May 2). The Cognitive Age. *New York Times.*

Brown, J. S., & Duguid, P. (1991). Organizational learning and communities of practice: Toward a unifying view of working, learning, and innovation . In Cohen, M. D., & Sproull, L. S. (Eds.), *Organizational Learning* (pp. 59–82). London: SAGE Publications.

Brown, J. S., & Duguid, P. (1998). Organizing knowledge. *California Management Review, 40*(3), 90–111.

Brown, J. S., & Duguid, P. (2000). *The social life of information.* Boston, MA: Harvard Business School Press.

Brown, J. S., & Duguid, P. (2001). Knowledge and organization: A social-practice perspective. *Organization Science, 12*(20), 198–213. doi:10.1287/orsc.12.2.198.10116

Brown, K., & Keast, R. (2003). Citizen-government engagement: Community connection through networked arrangements. *The Asian Journal of Public Administration, 25*(1), 107–131.

Bryan, L., & Joyce, C. (2006). Thinking for a living. *Economist*, 1/21/2006, 378(8461)9-12.

Bryman, A. (2003, October). McDonald's as a Disneyized Institution: Global Implications. *The American Behavioral Scientist, 47*(2), 154–167. doi:10.1177/0002764203256181

Buckley, S. B. (2009). *Knowledge-sharing through communities of practice at institutions of higher education.* Unpublished doctoral thesis, University of Johannesburg, South Africa.

Buendía, A., Martinez, A., & Martinez, S. (2005). Competencias del Ciudadano en la City de Conocimiento . In Mujica Alberdi, A. (Ed.), *Conocimiento para el Desarrollo* (pp. 215–236). San Sebastián, Spain: Universidad de Deusto.

Bunnell, T. (2004). *Malaysia, Modernity and Multimedia Super Corridor*. London: Routledge.

Burgess, J., & Henderson, L. (2007). *Mapping the hunter wine cluster. Workshop on industry clusters* (August). New South Wales: University of Newcastle, Graduate School of Business.

Burt, R. S. (2004). Structural holes and good ideas. *American Journal of Sociology, 110*, 349–399. doi:10.1086/421787

Cabrera, E. F., & Cabrera, A. (2005). Fostering knowledge sharing through people management practices. *International Journal of Human Resource Management, 16*(5), 720–735.

Camagni, R. (1991). *Innovation Networks. Spatial Perspectives*. London: Bellhaven.

Campbell, J. (1949). *The Hero With a Thousand Faces*. New York: MJF Books.

Cantwell, J., & Piscitello, L. (2005). Recent location of foreign-owned research and development activities by large multinational corporations in the European regions: the role of spillovers and externalities. *Regional Studies, 39*, 1–16. doi:10.1080/0034340052000320824

Capaldo, A. (2007). Network structure and innovation: the leveraging of a dual network distinctive relational capability. *Strategic Management Journal, 28*, 585–608. doi:10.1002/smj.621

Capello, R. (1999). SME clustering and factor productivity: A Milieu production function model. *European Planning Studies, 7*(6), 719.

Carrillo, F. (2004). Capital cities. *Journal of Knowledge Management, 8*(5), 28–46. doi:10.1108/1367327041058738

Carrillo, F. (2004). Capital Cities: A taxonomy of capital accounts for knowledge cities. *Journal of Knowledge Management, 8*(5), 28–46. doi:10.1108/1367327041058738

Carrillo, F. (2006). Knowledge Cities: Approaches, Experiences and Perspectives. Burlington, MA: Butterworth-Heinemann (Elsevier).

Carrillo, F. (Ed.). (2006). *Knowledge cities*. New York: Butterworth–Heinemann.

Carrillo, F. J. (1996). The Ways of Knowledge Management. In *Proceedings of the 1996 National Business Conference: The management of intellectual capital and innovation*. Hamilton, Ontario: McMaster University.

Carrillo, F. J. (2001, January). Meta-KM: A Program and a Plea. *Knowledge and Innovation: Journal of the KMCI, 1*(2), 27–54.

Carrillo, F. J. (2001a). El Futuro de la Gestión del Conocimiento: tres incógnitas, tres fases y tres escenarios . In Arboníes, Á. (Ed.), *Cómo evitar la miopía en la Administración del Conocimiento*. Bilbao, Spain: Cluster de Conocimiento.

Carrillo, F. J. (2001b). Un reporte expedicionario de los nuevos territorios . In *Entorno empresarial del Siglo XXI. Cinco años del Cluster de Conocimiento, Technology park of Zamudio*. Bilbao, Spain: La Evolución de Las Especies de Gestión de Conocimiento.

Carrillo, F. J. (2002). Capital systems: implications for a global knowledge agenda. *Journal of Knowledge Management, 6*(4). doi:10.1108/13673270210440884

Carrillo, F. J. (2004, October). Capital Cities: A taxonomy of capital accounts for knowledge cities. *Journal of Knowledge Management, 8*(5), 28–46. doi:10.1108/1367327041058738

Carrillo, F. J. (2005). Ciudades de Conocimiento: el estado del arte y el espacio de posibilidades. *Transferencia, 18*(69), 26–28.

Carrillo, F. J. (2006). From Transitional to Radical Knowledge-based Development. *Journal of Knowledge Management, 10*(5), 3–5. doi:10.1108/13673270610691125

Carrillo, F. J. (2007). The coming of age of Knowledge-based Development. *Journal of Knowledge Management, 11*(5), 3–5. doi:10.1108/13673270710819753

Carrillo, F. J. (2008). Towards a global Knowledge Based Development agenda. *Journal of Knowledge Management, 12*(5). doi:10.1108/13673270810902894

Carrillo, F. J. (Ed.). (2006). Knowledge Cities. Approaches, Experiences and Perspectives. Burlington, MA: Butterworth-Heinemann (Elsevier).

Castells, M. (1996). *The Information Age: The Rise of the Network Society.* Boston, MA: Blackwell Publishers.

Castells, M. (2004). The information city, the new economy, and the network society . In Webster, F. (Ed.), *The Information Society Reader* (pp. 150–164). London: Routledge.

Castells, M. (Ed.). (2004). *The Network Society (A Cross-Cultural Perspective).* Cheltenham, UK: Edward Elgar Publishing Limited.

Castells, M., & Hall, P. (1994). *Technopoles of the World.* London: Routledge.

Castells, M., & Himanen, P. (2002). *The Information Society and the Welfare State: The Finnish Model.* Oxford, UK: Oxford University Press.

Caves, R. (2000). *Creative industries: contracts between art and commerce.* Cambridge, MA: Harvard University Press.

Centre for International Competitiveness. (2008). *World Knowledge Competitiveness Index 2008.* Cardiff: Cardiff School of Management, University of Wales Institute.

Centro de Sistemas de Conocimiento. (2001). *Manual General de Referencia modalidad electrónica. Documento Integrado de Identidad del CSC. Internal document.* México: Tecnológico de Monterrey.

Centro de Sistemas de Conocimiento. (2002). *Macromodelo Conceptual de los Sistemas de Conocimiento. Internal document.* México: Tecnológico de Monterrey.

Centro de Sistemas de Conocimiento. (2003). *Procesos Clave del KM. Modelo del CSC. Internal document.* México: Tecnológico de Monterrey.

Chang, H. H. (2006). Technical and management perceptions of enterprise information system importance, implementation and benefits. *Information Systems Journal, 16*(3), 263–292. doi:10.1111/j.1365-2575.2006.00217.x

Chase, R. (2007). Foreword to the *Most Admired Knowledge City (MAKCi) Report.* World Capital Institute & Teleos. Retrieved April 27, 2009, from http://www.worldcapitalinstitute.org/makci

Chaundhry, A. S. (2005). *Libraries – a voyage of discovery.* Paper presented at the World Library and Information Congress, 71th IFLA General Conference and Council, Oslo, Norway. Retrieved on May 14, 2007 from http://www.ifla.org/IV/ifla71/Programme.htm

Chen, C.-K. (2008). Causal modelling of knowledge-based economy. *Management Decision, 46*(3), 501–519. doi:10.1108/00251740810863915

Chen, S., Duan, Y., Edwards, J. S., & Lehaney, B. (2006). Toward understanding inter-organizational knowledge transfer needs in SMEs: Insight from a UK investigation. *Journal of Knowledge Management, 10*(3), 6–23. doi:10.1108/13673270610670821

Cheng, Y. C. (2004). Fostering local knowledge and human development in globalization of education. *International Journal of Educational Management, 18*(1), 7–24.doi:10.1108/09513540410512109

Cherry, T. L., & Tsournos, P. T. (2001). Family ties, labor mobility, and interregional wage differences. *Journal of Regional Analysis and Policy, 31*(1), 23–33.

Cheung, C. M. Y., Shek, S. P. W., & Sia, C. L. (2004). Virtual Community of Consumers: Why People are Willing to Contribute? In *proceedings of the Pacific Asia Conference on Information Systems (PACIS 2004),* Shanghai, China (pp. 2100-2107).

Chew, L. L., & Sulaiman, A.-H. (2001). Government initiatives and the knowledge economy: case of Singapore. In W. Kim et al. (Eds.), Human Society@Internet 2001 (LNCS 2105, pp. 19-32). Heidelberg: Springer-Verlag Berlin.

Chia, S. Y. (2001). Singapore: towards a knowledge-based economy . In Masuyama, S., Vandenbrink, D., & Chia, S. Y. (Eds.), *Industrial restructuring in East Asia: towards the 21st Century* (pp. 169–208). Singapore: Institute of Southeast Asia Studies.

Choy, K. L., Tan, K. H., & Chan, F. T. S. (2007). Design of an intelligent supplier knowledge management system – an integrative approach. *Proceedings - Institution of Mechanical Engineers, 221*(b2), 195–211. doi:10.1243/09544054JEM627

Chung, L. H. (2001). 'The Role of Management in Knowledge Transfer', Third Asian Pacific Interdisciplinary Research in Accounting Conference Adelaide, South Australia.

Churchill, G. A. (1979, February). A Paradigm for Developing Better Measures of Market Constructs. *Journal of Marketing, 16*, 64–73. doi:10.2307/3150876

Cincera, M. (2005). Firms' productivity growth and R&D spillovers: an analysis of alternative technological proximity measures. *Economics of Innovation and New Technology, 14*, 657–682. doi:10.1080/10438590500056768

City of Helsinki. (2006). The economic map of urban Europe. Helsinki in the European Urban Network. *Helsinki City Urban Facts Office: Web Publications, 2006*(39). Retrieved January 13, 2009, from http://www.eukn.org/binaries/finland/bulk/research/2007/2/06_12_21_economic_vj39.pdf

City of Melbourne. (2005). *City Plan 2010: Towards a Thriving and Sustainable City. Delft.* (2009). Retrieved January 9, 2009, from http://www.delft.nl/

Clark, T. N. (Ed.). (2004). *The city as an entertainment machine*. Oxford, UK: Elsevier.

Clarke, T. (2001). The Knowledge Economy. *Education + Training, 43*(4/5), 189. doi:10.1108/00400910110399184

Cliffe, S. (1998). Knowledge Management: The Well-Connected. *Harvard Business Review, 76*(4), 17–21.

Clifford, J. S. (2002). *Transcending Locality- Driven Lifestyle: The Potential of the Internet to Redefine our Neighbourhood Patterns.* Cambridge, MA: Harvard University.

Cobo, C. (2008). *Skills for a Knowledge/Mind Worker Passport (19 commandments).* Retrieved March 18, 2009, from http://ww.educationfutures.com/2008

Cohen, W. M., & Levinthal, D. A. (1990). Absorptive capacity: a new perspective on learning and innovation. *Administrative Science Quarterly, 35*, 128–152. doi:10.2307/2393553

Collett, M., & Collett, B. (2004 September). *A Snapshot of the Creative Industries in England's North West.* Report prepared for Culture Northwest, Advocate Network Think.

Colombo, M. G. (2003). Alliance form: a test of the contractual and competence perspective. *Strategic Management Journal, 24*, 1209–1229. doi:10.1002/smj.353

Committee of Singapore's Competitiveness (CSC) Report. (1998). Singapore: Ministry of Trade and Industry. Retrieved March 10, 2005 from www.mti.gov.sg/public/NWS/frm_NWS_Default.asp?sid=42&cid=177

Conceição, P., & Heitor, M. V. (2007). Diversity and integration of science and technology policies. *Technological Forecasting and Social Change, 74*(1), 1–17. doi:10.1016/j.techfore.2006.05.001

Cooke, P. (1998). Introduction: Origins of the concept . In Braczyk, H. J., Cooke, P., & Heidenreich, M. (Eds.), *Regional innovation systems: The role of governance in a globalized world* (pp. 2–27). London: UCL.

Cooke, P. (2001). *Knowledge economies.* New York: Routledge. doi:10.4324/9780203445402

Cooke, P., & Morgan, K. (1998). *The associational Economy. Firms, Regions, and Innovation.* Oxford, UK: Oxford University Press.

Cooke, P., Uranga, M. G., & Etxebarria, G. (1997). Regional innovation systems: Institutional and organisational dimensions. *Research Policy, 26*, 475–491. doi:10.1016/S0048-7333(97)00025-5

Coopers & Lybrand Consultants. (1996). *Executive Summary of an Evaluation of the Teaching and Learning Evaluation Programme (TLEP)*. Institute of Education/ Tavistock Institute.

Cope, B., & Kalantzis, M. (2009). Signs of Epistemic Disruption: Transformations of the Knowledge. *System of the Academic Journal, 14*(4-6).

Corey, K., & Wilson, M. (2006). *Urban and regional technology planning*. New York: Routledge.

Cornuel, E. (2007). Challenges facing business schools in the future. *Journal of Management Development, 26*(1), 87–92.doi:10.1108/02621710710720130

Council for Economic Planning and Development website. (n.d.). *Taiwan tops Asia in knowledge economy index*. Retrieved June 10, 2009 from http://www.cepd.gov.tw/encontent/print.aspx?sNo=0010997

Cozolino, L. (2002). *The Neuroscience of Psychotherapy: Building and Rebuilding the Human Brain*. New York: Norton.

Csikszentmihalyi, M. (1996). *Creativity: flow and the psychology of discovery and invention*. New York: Harper Collins Publishers.

Culminatum. (2005). *Innovation Strategy. Helsinki Metropolitan Area*. Culminatum, Espoo. Retrieved August 15, 2008 from http://www.culminatum.fi/content_files/InnovationStrategy.pdf

Cumbers, A., Mackinnon, D., & Chapman, K. (2003). Innovation, collaboration, and learning in regional clusters: a study of SMEs in the Aberdeen oil complex. *Environment & Planning A, 35*(9), 1689–1706. doi:10.1068/a35259

Cyberview Corporation. (2009). *Cyberview Sdn. Bhd: the landowner of Cyberjaya*. Retrieved May 11, 2009, from http://www.cyberview.com.my/

Dahlman, C. (2002). World Bank OECD-IPS-World Bank workshop on promoting knowledge-based economies in Asia. November 21-22, 2002, Singapore.

Dang, D., & Umemoto, K. (2009). Modelling the development toward the knowledge economy: a national capability approach. *Journal of Knowledge Management, 13*(5). doi:10.1108/13673270910988169

Darchen, S., & Tremblay, D.-G. (2008a). La thèse de la «classe créative»: son incidence sur l'analyse des facteurs d'attraction et de la compétitivité urbaine. *Interventions Économiques*, (37).

Darchen, S., & Tremblay, D.-G. (2008b, May 20-24). *The attraction and retention of students in science and technology, an analysis based on the "Creative Class" thesis: the case of Montreal*. Paper presented at the Annual Meeting of the Association of Canadian Geographers, Quebec City.

Darroch, J., & McNaughton, R. (2001). *Knowledge Management and Innovation*. Dunedin: Department of Marketing, University of Otago.

Darroch, J., & McNaughton, R. (2003). Beyond Market Orientation: Knowledge Management and the Innovativeness of New Zealand Firms. *European Journal of Marketing, 37*(3/4), 572–593. doi:10.1108/03090560310459096

Daugėlienė, R. (2007). The Peculiarities of Knowledge Workers Migration in Europe and the World. *Engineering Economics, 2007*(3), 53.

Davenport, S. (2005). Exploring the role of proximity in SME knowledge-acquisition. *Research Policy, 34*, 683–701. doi:10.1016/j.respol.2005.03.006

Davenport, T. H. (1997). *Information Ecology: Mastering the Information and Knowledge Management*. New York: Oxford University Press.

Davenport, T. H., & Prusak, L. (1998). *Working Knowledge*. Boston: Harvard Business School Press.

Davenport, T., Long, D. W. D., & Beers, M. C. (1998). Successful Knowledge Management Projects. *Sloan Management Review, 39*(2), 43–57.

Davenport, T.H., & Harris, J.G. (2007, March). Competing on Analytics: The New Science of Winning. *Harvard Business School Press.*

Davenport, T.H., & Iye, B. (2009, February). Should you outsource your brain? *Harvard Business School Press.*

Day, G., & Wensley, R. (1988, April). Assessing Advantage: A Framework for Diagnosing Competitive Superiority. *Journal of Marketing, 52*, 1–20. doi:10.2307/1251261

De Bruijn, H., & de Nerée tot Babberich, C. (2000). *Opposites attract.* Competition values in knowledge management, Lemma, Utrecht.

De Long, D. W., & Fahey, L. (2000). Diagnosing cultural barriers to knowledge management. *The Academy of Management Executive, 14*(4), 113–127.

DeBresson, C., & Anesse, F. (1991). Networks of innovators: a review and introduction to the issue. *Research Policy, 20*, 363–379. doi:10.1016/0048-7333(91)90063-V

DeFillippi, R. J., & Arthur, M. B. (1998). Paradox in project-based enterprise: the case of film making. *California Management Review, 10*(2), 125–139.

DeLong, D., & Fehey, L. (2000). Diagnosing cultural barriers to knowledge management. *The Academy of Management Executive, 14*(4), 113–127.

Denning, S. (2004). *Communities for knowledge management.* Retrieved June 12, 2008, from http://www.stevedenning.com/communities_knowledge_management.html

Desouza, K. C., & Awazu, Y. (2006). Knowledge management at SMEs: Five peculiarities. *Journal of Knowledge Management, 10*(1), 32–43. doi:10.1108/13673270610650085

Dewhurst, F. W., & Cegarra Navarro, J. G. (2004). External communities of practice and relational capital. *The Learning Organization, 11*(4/5), 322–331. doi:10.1108/09696470410538224

Dhanaraj, C., & Parkhe, A. (2006). Orchestrating innovation networks. *Academy of Management Review, 31*, 659–669.

Dicken, P. (2002). Global Manchester: from globaliser to globalised . In Peck, J., & Ward, K. (Eds.), *City of Revolution. Restructuring Manchester.* Manchester, UK: Manchester University Press.

Ditkoff, M., Moore, T., Allen, C., & Pollard, D. (2007). *The Ideal Collaborative Team and A Conversation on the Collaborative Process.* Retrieved December 3, 2009, from http://blogs.salon.com/0002007/stories/2005/11/18/theIdealCollaborativeTeamAndAConversationOnTheCollaborativeProcess.html

Dixon, N. (2000). *Common Knowledge: How companies thrive by sharing what they know.* Boston: Harvard Business School Press.

Dolfsma, W., & Soete, L. (2005). Dynamics of a knowledge economy: introduction . In Dolfsma, W., & Soete, L. (Eds.), *Understanding the Dynamics of a Knowledge Economy* (pp. 1–6). Northampton, MA: Edward Elgar.

Dosi, G. (1988). Sources, Procedures and Microeconomic Effects of Innovation. *Journal of Economic Literature, 26*, 1120–1171.

DPNR. (2005). *Metropolitan strategy, economy and employment.* Sydney: Department of Planning and Natural Resources.

Drickhamer, D. (2005). Power partner: Manufacturers-logistics service providers relationship. *Material Handling Management, 60*(4), 22–23.

Drucker, P. (1989). What Business Can Learn from Nonprofits. *Harvard Business Review, 67*(4), 88–93.

Drucker, P. (1993). *Post-capitalist society.* New York: Harper Business.

Drucker, P. (2001). *Essential Drucker (Classic Drucker Collection).* New York: Butterworth-Heinemann Ltd.

Drucker, P. E. (1994). The Age of Social Transformation. *Atlantic Monthly, 274*, 53–80.

Drucker, P. F. (1959). *Landmarks of tomorrow.* New York: Harper.

Drucker, P. F. (1998). Management's New Paradigma. Retrieved February 1, 2009, from http://www.forbes.com/forbes/1998/1005/6207152a.html.

Dublin Chamber of Commerce. (2004). *Dublin 2020: Our vision for the future of the city.* Retrieved January 9, 2009 from http://www.dublinchamber.ie/Uploads/2020%20Vision.pdf

Dublin Chamber of Commerce. (2008). *Developing a Knowledge City Region A TEN POINT PLAN.* Retrieved January 9, 2009, from http://www.dubchamber.ie/uploads/Knowledge_City_Region.pdf

Dumond, M. J., Hirsh, B. T., & MacPherson, D. A. (1999). Wage differentials across labor markets and workers: does cost of living matter? *Economic Inquiry, 37*(4), 577–598. doi:10.1111/j.1465-7295.1999.tb01449.x

Dvir, R. (2006). Knowledge City, Seen as a collage of Human Knowledge moments. In F. J. Carrillo (Ed.), Knowledge Cities. Approaches, Experiences and Perspectives. Burlington, MA: Butterworth-Heinemann (Elsevier).

Dvir, R. (2006). Knowledge city, seen as a collage of human knowledge moments. In Carrillo, F.J. (Eds.), Knowledge Cities: Approaches, Experiences and Perspectives (pp. 245-272). Burlington, MA: Butterworth-Heinemann (Elsevier).

Dvir, R., & Pasher, E. (2004). Innovative engines for knowledge cities: an innovation ecology perspective. *Journal of Knowledge Management, 8*(5), 16–27. doi:10.1108/13673270410558756

Dyer, J. H., & Singh, H. (1998). The relational view: cooperative strategy and sources of interorganizational competitive advantage. *Academy of Management Journal, 23*, 660–679.

E. Pasher Team. (1998). *The Intellectual Capital of the State of Israel 1998: a Look to the Future.* Herzelia, Israel: Edna Pasher Ph.D and Associates.

Eccles, R. G., Herz, R. H., Keegan, E. M., & Philips, D. M. H. (2001). *The Value Reporting Revoluion.* New York: Pricewaterhouse Coopers.

Economic Planning Unit. (2001). *The Third Outline Perspective Plan (2001-2010).* Putrajata, Malaysia: Economic Planning Unit, Prime Minister's Department.

Economic Planning Unit. (2006). *National Vision 2020.* Putrajata, Malaysia: Economic Planning Unit, Prime Minister's Department.

Economic Research Services Department. (2000). *Special Economic Issue.* Kuala Lumpur, Malaysia: Bumiputra Commerce Bank.

EDB (Economic Development Board) Singapore. Media releases. (n.d.). *New headquarters program launched for companies across all industries and geographies.* Retrieved January 7, 2003 from www.sedb.com/edbcorp/browse.jsp?cat=40&type=2&parent=36&root=36

Edna Pasher Ph.D and Associates. Allee, V., Innocenti, A., Koumpis, A., Mavridis, A., Molinari, F., Pasher, E., Shachar, S., Schwabe, O., Tektonidis, D., Tresman, M. and Vontas, A. (2007). Effectiveness of ICT RTD Impacts on the EU Innovation System: Final Report. Evaluation Study for the European Commission, DG Information Society and Media Directorate C. Lisbon Strategy and Policies for the Information Society. Unit C3 – Evaluation and Monitoring, December 11, 2007.

Edvinsson, L. (2003). *Introduction to Issues in Knowledge Management.* Oxfordshire, UK: Henley Knowledge Management Forum.

Edvinsson, L., & Malone, M. S. (1997). *Intellectual Capital: Realizing Your Company's True Value by Finding its Hidden Brainpower.* New York: Harper Business.

Ehin, C. (2008). Un-managing knowledge workers. *Journal of Intellectual Capital, 9*(3), 337–350. doi:10.1108/14691930810891965

Eindhoven. (2006). *Brainport Navigator 2013: Beyond Lisbon!* Brainport. Retrieved January 9, 2009, from http://www.brainport.nl/Brainport_C01/ShowDocument.asp?OriginCode=H&OriginComID=32&OriginModID=2099&OriginItemID=1020&CustID=354&ComID=32&DocID=77&SessionID=~SessionID~&Download=true&Ext=.pdf

Eldridge, S., & Balubaid, M., & Barber, Kevin D. (2006). Using a Knowledge Management Approach to Support Quality Costing. *International Journal of Quality & Reliability Management, 23*(1). doi:10.1108/02656710610637569

Eliasson, G. (2005). The nature of economic change and management in a new knowledge based information economy. *Information Economics and Policy, 17,* 428–456. doi:10.1016/j.infoecopol.2005.02.002

Eller, B. (2006). *Creativity strategies in Munich, Creative Industries – The impact of creative industries on City- Region competitiveness.* Retrieved January 9, 2009, from www.compete-eu.org/events/barcelona1/6_BERNHARD_ELLER.pps

Ellinor, L., & Gerard, G. (1998). *Dialogue: Creating and Sustaining Collaborative Partnerships at Work.* New York: John Wiley & Sons.

Ellis, J. B. B., & Amy, S. (2001). Designing palaver tree online: supporting social roles in a community of oral history in Proceedings of the CHI 2001, Conference on Human factors in computing systems, (Seattle, Washington, 2001), ACM, 474-481.

Ennals, R. (1987). Can skill be transferable? In Göranzon, B., & Josefson, I. (Eds.), *Knowledge, Skill and Artificial Intelligence* (pp. 67–75). London: Springer-Verlag.

ERC (Economic Review Committee) Report. (2002). *Creative industries development strategy: propelling Singapore's creative economy.* ERC Creative Industries Working Group. Retrieved June 15, 2004 from http://www.mti.gov.sg/public/ERC/frm_ERC_Default.asp?sid=131

Ergazakis, K., Metaxiotis, K., & Psarras, J. (2004). Towards knowledge cities: conceptual analysis and success stories. *Journal of Knowledge Management, 8*(5), 5–15. doi:10.1108/13673270410558747

Ergazakis, K., Metaxiotis, K., & Psarras, J. (2005). An Emerging Pattern of Successful Knowledge Cities' Main Features . In Carrillo, F. (Ed.), *Knowledge Cities: Approaches, Experiences and Perspectives.* Amsterdam: Elsevier.

Ergazakis, K., Metaxiotis, K., & Psarras, J. (2006). A Coherent Framework for Building Successful Knowledge Cities in the Context of the Knowledge-Based Economy. *Knowledge Management Research & Practice, 4,* 46–59. doi:10.1057/palgrave.kmrp.8500089

Ergazakis, K., Metaxiotis, K., & Psarras, J. (2006). Knowledge cities: the answer to the needs of knowledge-based development. *Journal of Knowledge Management, 36*(1), 67–84.

Ergazakis, K., Metaxiotis, K., & Psarras, J. (2006). Knowledge cities. *Journal of Information and Knowledge Management Systems, 36*(1), 67–81.

Erickson, J.T. (2008 February). Task, Not Time: Profile of a Gen Y Job. *Harvard Business Review.*

Ericsson, K. A., Charness, N., Feltovich, P. J., & Hoffman, R. R. (Eds.). (2006). *The Cambridge Handbook of Expertise and Expert Performance.* Cambridge, UK: Cambridge University Press.

Ernst & Young. (1997). *Twenty Questions on Knowledge in the Organization.* Retrieved January 2005, from http://www.businessinnovation.ey.com/research/knowle/survey/survey.html

Esping-Andersen. (1992). The three political economies of the welfare state . In Kolberg, J. E. (Ed.), *The Study of Welfare State Regimes* (pp. 92–123). New York: Sharpe.

Etzkowitz, H. (2008). *The Triple Helix: University-Industry-Government Innovation in Action.* London: Routledge.

Etzkowitz, H., & Klofsten, M. (2005). The Innovating Region: Toward a Theory of Knowledge-Based Regional Development. *R & D Management, 35*(3), 243–255.

Etzkowitz, H., & Leydesdorff, L. (1997). (Eds.) Universities and the global knowledge economy. London: Pinter.

Etzkowitz, H., & Leydesdorff, L. (2000). The Dynamics of Innovation: From National Systems and "Mode 2" to a Triple Helix of University–Industry–Government Relations. *Research Policy, 29*(2), 109–123.

European Collaborative for Communities of Practice. (2005). *Creating Value with Communities of Practice.* Retrieved December 7, 2008, from http://www.eccop.com/creatingvalue.htm

European Social Report, T. Á. R. K. I. (2005). Chapter 3: Income distribution in European countries: first reflections on the basis of EU-SILC 2005. In *Community Statistics on Income and Living Conditions*. Budapest, Hungary: TÁRKI. Retrieved November 29, 2008, from http://www.tarki.hu/en/research/european_social_report/20080701_3.pdf

European University Institute. (2008). *MWP Academic Careers Observatory. Salaries.* Retrieved October 29, 2008, from http://www.eui.eu/MaxWeberProgramme/AcademicCareers/SalaryComparisons.shtml

Fagerberg, J., & Srholec, M. (2008). National innovation system, capabilities and economic development. *Research Policy, 37*, 1417–1435. doi:10.1016/j.respol.2008.06.003

Fahey, J., & Smithee, A. (1999). Strategic Marketing and Resource Based View of Knowledge Management Systems. *Academy of Marketing Science Review, 99*(10), 1–23.

Fawcett, S. E., Rhoads, G. K., & Burnah, P. (2004). People as the bridge to competitiveness: Benchmarking the ABCs of an empowered workforce. Benchmarking: An International Journal, 11(4), 346–360. Fenwick, T. (2007). Knowledge workers in the in-between: network identities. *Journal of Organizational Change Management, 20*(4), 509–524.doi:10.1108/14635770410546755

Federal Town and Country Planning. (1997a). Physical planning guidelines for the Multimedia Super Corridor (MSC): *Vol. 1. General Guidelines*. Kuala Lumpur, Malaysia: Ministry of Housing and Local Government.

Federal Town and Country Planning. (1997b). Physical planning guidelines for the Multimedia Super Corridor (MSC): *Vol. 4. Cyberjaya*. Kuala Lumpur, Malaysia: Ministry of Housing and Local Government.

Federal Town and Country Planning. (2006). *National Urbanisation Policy (NUP) 2020*. Kuala Lumpur, Malaysia: Ministry of Housing and Local Government.

Feldman, M. (1994). *The geography of innovation*. Dordrecht: Kluwer Academic Publishers.

Felin, T., & Hesterly, W. S. (2007). The knowledge-based view, and new value creation: philosophical considerations on the locus of knowledge. *Academy of Management Review, 32*, 195–218.

Felsenstein, D. (1994). University-related science parks. *Technovation, 14*(2), 93–110. doi:10.1016/0166-4972(94)90099-X

Firestone, J. M. (1998). *Basic concepts of knowledge management*. Retrieved September 1, 2008, from http://www.dkms.com/papers/kmbasic.pdf

Fliaster, A., & Spiess, J. (2008). Knowledge Mobilization Through Social Ties: The Cost-Benefit Analysis. *Schmalenbach Business Review: ZBF, 60*, 99–118.

Florida, R. (1995). Towards the Learning Region. *Futures, 27*(5), 527–536. doi:10.1016/0016-3287(95)00021-N

Florida, R. (2002). Bohemia and economic geography. *Journal of Economic Geography, 2*(1), 55–71. doi:10.1093/jeg/2.1.55

Florida, R. (2002). *The Rise of the Creative Class and How It's Transforming Work, Leisure, Community and Everyday Life*. New York: Basic Books.

Florida, R. (2002). *The Rise of the Creative Class*. New York: Basic Books.

Florida, R. (2002). *The Rise of the Creative Class: And How It's Transforming Work, Leisure and Community*. New York: Basic Books.

Florida, R. (2002a). The economic geography of talent. *Annals of the Association of American Geographers. Association of American Geographers, 92*(4), 743–755. doi:10.1111/1467-8306.00314

Florida, R. (2002b). *The rise of the creative class and how it's transforming work, leisure, community and everyday life*. New York: Basic Books.

Florida, R. (2005). *Cities and the creative class*. New York, London: Routledge.

Florida, R. (2005). *The Flight of the Creative Class*. New York: Harper Collins.

Florida, R., Mellander, C., & Stolarick, K. (2008). Inside the black box of regional development-human capital, the creative class and tolerance. *Journal of Economic Geography, 8*(5), 615–649. doi:10.1093/jeg/lbn023

Forker, L. B., Vickery, S. K., & Droge, C. L. M. (1996). The Contribution of Quality to Business Performance. *International Journal of Operations & Production Management, 16*(8), 44–62. doi:10.1108/01443579610125778

Franck, K. (1984). Exorcising the Ghost of Physical Determinism. *Environment and Behavior, 16*, 411–435. doi:10.1177/0013916584164001

Frand, J., & Hixon, C. (1999). *Personal Knowledge Management: Who, What, Why, When, Where, How?* Retrieved March, 2009, from http://www.anderson.ucla.edu/faculty/jason.frand/researcher/speeches/PKM.htm

Frenz, M., & Oughton, C. (2006). *Innovation in the UK regions and devolved administrations: A review of the literature. Final Report for the Department of Trade and Industry and the Office of the Deputy Prime Minister.* London: DTI.

Fugate, B. S., Stank, T. P., & Mentzer, J. T. (2009). Linking improved knowledge management to operational and organizational performance. Journal of Operations Management, 27(3), 247–264. Gao, F., Li, M., & Clarke, S. (2008). Knowledge, management, and knowledge management in business operations. *Journal of Knowledge Management, 12*(2), 3–17.doi:10.1016/j.jom.2008.09.003

Garcia, B. (2004). Developing futures: a knowledge-based capital for Manchester. *Journal of Knowledge Management, 8*(5), 47–60. doi:10.1108/13673270410558774

Garcia, B. (2006a). UniverCities: Innovation and Social Capital in Greater Manchester. In F. J. Carrillo (Ed.), Knowledge Cities. Approaches, Experiences and Perspectives. Burlington, MA: Butterworth-Heinemann (Elsevier).

Garcia, B. (2006b). Learning Conversations: knowledge, meanings and learning networks in Greater Manchester. *Journal of Knowledge Management, 10*(5), 99–109. doi:10.1108/13673270610691215

Garcia, B. C. (2007). Working and learning in a knowledge city: a multilevel development framework for knowledge workers. *Journal of Knowledge Management, 11*(5), 18–30.doi:10.1108/13673270710819771

Garner, C. (2007). *Manchester, Knowledge City.* 7th Key Note Presentation at 1st Knowledge Cities Summit, Monterrey, Mexico. Retrieved from http://www.kbdweek.com

Garner, C., & Ternouth, P. (2008). *Knowledge Cities as Innovation Hubs – the role of gatekeepers in their success.* Paper proposed at the International Conference on Knowledge Management and Intellectual Capital, Ghaziabad, India. Retrieved from http://www.imt.edu/ickmic2009/

Garreau, J. (1992). *Edge City: Life on the New Frontier.* New York: Anchor Books.

Ge, Y., Yang, J.-B., Proudlove, N., & Spring, M. (2003). System dynamics modelling for supply-chain management: A case study on a supermarket chain in the UK. *International Transactions in Operational Research, 11*(5), 495–509. doi:10.1111/j.1475-3995.2004.00473.x

Geisler, E. (2008). *Knowledge and knowledge systems: Learning from wonders of the mind.* New York: IGI Publishing.

Genzel & Velibeyoglu. (2006). Opportunities & Challenges . In *Public Spaces in the Information Age, 42nd ISoCaRP Congress 2006.* Reconsidering the Planning and Design of Urban Public Spaces in the Information Age.

Gibbons, M., Limoges, C., Nowotny, H., Schwartzman, S., Scott, P., & Trow, M. (1994). *The new production of knowledge.* London: Sage.

Gilmore, A., Carson, D., Grant, K., O'Donnell, A., Laney, R., & Pickett, B. (2006). Networking in SMEs: Findings from Australia and Ireland. *Irish Marketing Review, 18*(1&2), 21–28.

Gilsing, V., & Nooteboom, B. (2006). Exploration and exploitation in innovation systems: the case of pharmaceutical biotechnology. *Research Policy, 35*, 1–23. doi:10.1016/j.respol.2005.06.007

Giuliani, E., & Bell, M. (2005). The micro-determinants of meso-level learning and innovation: evidence from a Chilean wine cluster. *Research Policy, 34*, 47–68. doi:10.1016/j.respol.2004.10.008

Glaeser, E. L., & Saiz, A. (2003). The rise of the skilled city. *Brookings-Wharton Papers on Urban Affairs,* (5), 47-94.

Glaeser, E. L., Kolko, J., & Saiz, A. (2001). Consumer city. *Journal of Economic Geography, 1*(1), 27–50. doi:10.1093/jeg/1.1.27

Glaeser, E. L., Sheinkman, J. A., & Shleifer, A. (1995). Economic growth in a cross-section of cities. *Journal of Monetary Economics, 36*(1), 117–143. doi:10.1016/0304-3932(95)01206-2

Glaeser, E., & Saiz, A. (2003). *The Rise of the Skilled City.* Discussion Paper Number 2025, Harvard Institute of Economic Research, Harvard University, Cambridge, MA.

Gloor, P. A., Paasivaara, M., Schoder, D., & Willems, P. (2007). Finding collaborative innovation networks through correlating performance with social network structure. *International Journal of Production Research, 46*(5), 1357–1371.doi:10.1080/00207540701224582

Gold Coast City Council. (2008). *Business Precincts: Delivering a Balanced, Connected and Prosperous Economy.* Retrieved March 2, 2008, from http://businessgc.com.au/index.php?page=gc-precincts

Goleman, D. (1995). *Emotional Intelligence: Why it can matter more than IQ.* New York: Bantam Books.

Gomes-Casseres, B., Hagedoorn, J., & Jaffe, A. B. (2006). Do alliances promote knowledge flows. *Journal of Financial Economics, 80*, 5–33. doi:10.1016/j.jfineco.2004.08.011

Gonzalez, M., Alvarado, J., & Martinez, S. (2005). A compilation of resources on knowledge cities and knowledge-based development. *Journal of Knowledge Management, 8*(5), 107–127.

Gonzalez, M., Alvarado, J., & Martinez, S. (2005). A compilation of resources on knowledge cities and knowledge-based development. *Journal of Knowledge Management, 8*(5), 107–127.

Gordon, I. R., & McCann, P. (2000). Industrial clusters: Complexes, agglomeration and/or social networks? *Urban Studies (Edinburgh, Scotland), 37*(3), 513–532. doi:10.1080/0042098002096

Gordon, P., & Richardson, H. W. (1997). Are Compact Cities a Desirable Planning Goal? *Journal of the American Planning Association. American Planning Association, 63*(1), 95–106.

Gordon, S. R., & Tarafdar, M. (2007). How do a company's information technology competences influence its ability to innovate? *Journal of Enterprise Information Management, 20*(3), 271–290.doi:10.1108/17410390710740736

Gourlay, S. (2001). Knowledge management and HRD. *Human Resource Development International, 4*(1), 27–46. doi:10.1080/13678860121778

Graetz, F., Rimmer, M., Lawrence, A., & Smith, A. (2006). *Managing organisational change* (2nd ed.). Sydney, Australia: Wiley & Sons.

Graham, S. (2002). Bridging Urban Digital Divides? Urban Polarisation and Information and Communications Technologies (ICTs). *Urban Studies (Edinburgh, Scotland), 39*(1), 33–56.

Graham, S., & Healey, P. (1999). Relational concepts of space and place. *European Planning Studies, 7*(5), 623–646.

Graham, S., & Marvin, S. (1996). *Telecommunications and the City: Electronic Spaces, Urban Places.* London, New York: Routledge.

Graham, S., & Marvin, S. (2001). *Splintering urbanism.* London: Routledge. doi:10.4324/9780203452202

Granovetter, M. (1973). The strength of weak ties. *American Journal of Sociology, 78*, 1360–1380. doi:10.1086/225469

Granovetter, M. (1992). Economic institutions as social constructions: A framework for analysis. *Acta Sociologica, 35*(1), 3–11. doi:10.1177/000169939203500101

Grant, R. M. (1996). Toward a Knowledge-based Theory of the Firm. *Strategic Management Journal, 17*(Special Issue), 109–122.

Gray, P., & Tehrani, S. (2004). Technologies of dissemination knowledge . In Holsapple, C. W. (Ed.), *Handbook on Knowledge Management 2. Knowledge Directions.* Berlin, Germany: Springer-Verlag.

Greater Manchester Strategic Alliance (GMSA). (2005). Application and business plan for a Lifelong Learning Network for Greater Manchester. In *Progression through Lifelong Learning Report.* Retrieved January 15, 2008, from http://www.gmsa.ac.uk

Grech, M. (2008). A school like no other, a leader like no other. *Access, 22*(4), 9–14.

Green, A. (2007). Business information-a natural path to business intelligence: knowing what to capture. *Vine, 37*(1), 18–23.doi:10.1108/03055720710741981

Green, A. (2008). Intangible asset knowledge: the conjugality of business intelligence (BI) and business operational data. *Vine, 38*(2), 184–191. doi:10.1108/03055720810889824

Greene, W. (2006). Growth in Services Outsourcing to India: Propellant or Drain on the U.S. Economy? *Office of Economics Working Paper, U.S. International Trade Commission*, No. 2005-12-A, January 2006.

Gupta, A. K., Smith, K. G., & Shalley, C. E. (2006). The interplay between exploration and exploitation. *Academy of Management Journal, 49*, 693–706.

Gurstein, M. (Ed.). (2000). *Community Informatics: Enabling Communities with Information and Communication Technologies.* Hershey, PA: Idea Group Publishing.

Gurteen, D. (2006). The Gurteen perspective: Taking responsibility. *Inside Knowledge, 10*(1).

Gvaramadze, I. (2008). Human resource development practice: the paradox of empowerment and individualization. *Human Resource Development International, 11*(5), 465–477.doi:10.1080/13678860802417601

Gylfason, T. (ed. 1997). The Swedish model under stress. A view from the stands. In SNS Economic Policy Group Report 1997, Stockholm, Sweden.

Haarmakorpi, V. (2006). Regional development platform method (RDPM) as a tool for regional innovation policy. *European Planning Studies, 14*(8), 1093–1112. doi:10.1080/09654310600852399

Hagedoorn, J., & Duysters, G. (2002). External sources of innovative capabilities: the preferences for strategic alliances or mergers and acquisitions. *Journal of Management Studies, 39*, 167–188. doi:10.1111/1467-6486.00287

Haimila, S. (2001). *Shell creates communities of practice.* Retrieved January 1, 2009, from http://www.kmworld.com/Articles/News/KM-In-Practice/Shell-creates-communities-of-practice-9986.aspx

Halawi, L. A., Aronson, J. E., & McCarthy, R. V. (2005). Resource-based View of Knowledge Management for Competitive Advantage. *Electronic Journal of Knowledge Management, 3*(2), 75–86.

Hall, H. (2001). *Social exchange for knowledge exchange. Managing knowledge: conversations and critiques.* University of Leicester.

Hamel, G., & Prahalad, C. K. (1994). *Competing For The Future.* Cambridge: Harvard Business School Press.

Hamidizadeh, M. R., & Farsijani, H. (2008). The Role of Knowledge Management for Achieving to World-Class Manufacturing. *Journal of American Academy of Business, Cambridge, 14*(1), 210–218.

Hamilton, C. (2001). The Triumph of Ideology: Environment . In Sheil, C. (Ed.), *Globalisation: Australian Impacts* (pp. 187–201). Australia: UNSW Press.

Hammond, M. (1998). Learning through online discussion. *Journal of Information Technology for Teacher Education, 7*(3), 331–346.

Hammond, S. A., & Hall, J. (1996). *What is Appreciative Inquiry?* Retrieved September 2006, from http://www.thinbook.com

Hampton, K. (2002). Place-Based and IT Mediated 'Community. *Planning Theory & Practice*, *3*(2), 228–231.

Hansen, M. (1999). The search transfer problem: the role of weak ties in sharing knowledge across organization subunits. *Administrative Science Quarterly*, *44*, 82–111. doi:10.2307/2667032

Hansen, M. T., Nohria, N., & Tierney, T. (1999). What is Your Strategy for Managing Knowledge. *Harvard Business Review*, *77*(2), 106–116.

Hansen, S. B., Ban, C., & Huggins, L. (2003). Explaining the «brain drain» from older industrial cities: the Pittsburgh region. *Economic Development Quarterly*, *17*(2), 132–147. doi:10.1177/0891242403017002002

Harari, O. (1994). The Brain-based Organization. *Management Review*, *83*(6), 57–60.

Hargadon, A. B., & Sutton, R. I. (1997). Technology brokering and innovation in a product development firm. *Administrative Science Quarterly*, *42*, 716–749. doi:10.2307/2393655

Hartnell-Young, E., & McGuinness, K. (n.d.). *Applying a Communities of Practice Model to Research Partnerships*. Retrieved December 7, 2008, from http://www.aare.edu.au/05papc/ha05024y.pdf

Haselmayer, S. (2005). *The Intelligent Place: Foundations for a Knowledge City*. Interlace-invent ApS. Retrieved February 5, 2009 from Http://www.localret.net/jornades/materials/gsc/T4_eGovern_Haselmayer.pdf

Hautamäki, A. (2007). Innovaatioiden ekosysteemi ja Helsingin seutu. Maailmanluokan innovaatioteknologian rakentamisen lähtökohta. *Tutkimuskatsauksia, 1*.

Hayes, N., & Walsham, G. (2000). Competing interpretations of computer supported co-operative work. *Organization*, *7*(1), 49–67. doi:10.1177/135050840071004

Haywood, J., Anderson, C., Day, K., Land, R., MacLeod, H., & Haywood, D. (1999). *Use of TLTP materials in the UK higher education: a HEFCE-commissioned study*. Retrieved October 24, 2003, from http://www.flp.ed.ac.uk/LTRG/TLTP.html

He, Z.-L., & Wong, P. K. (2004). Exploration vs. exploitation: An empirical test of the ambidexterity hypothesis. *Organization Science*, *15*, 481–494. doi:10.1287/orsc.1040.0078

Heap, S., Hollis, M., Lyons, B., Sudgen, R., & Weale, A. (Eds.). (1992). *The Theory of Choice – A Critical Guide*. Oxford, UK: Blackwell.

Hearn, G., & Rooney, D. (Eds.). (2008). *Knowledge policy*. Northampton, UK: Edward Elgar.

Hebbert, W. P., Keast, R., & Mohannak, K. (2006). The strategic value of oscillating tie strength in technology clusters. *Innovation: Management . Policy & Practice*, *8*(5), 322–377.

Helbrecht, I. (2004). Bare Geographies in Knowledge Societies – Creative Cities as Text and Piece of Art: Two Eyes, One Vision. *Creative Cultural Knowledge Cities*, *30*(3), 194–203.

Helfert, G., Ritter, T., & Walter, A. (2002). Redefining Market Orientation from a Relationship Perspective: Theoretical Considerations and Empirical Results. *European Journal of Marketing*, *36*(9/10), 1119–1139. doi:10.1108/03090560210437361

Hemetsberger, A., & Reinhardt, C. (2006). Learning and Knowledge-building in Open-source Communities. A Social-experiential approach. *Management Learning*, *37*(2), 187–214. doi:10.1177/1350507606063442

Henard, D. H., & McFadyen, M. A. (2008). Making Knowledge Workers More Creative. *Research Technology Management*, *51*(2), 40–47.

Hendriks, P. (1999). Why Share Knowledge? The Influence of ICT on the Motivation for Knowledge Sharing. *Knowledge and Process Management*, *6*(2), 91–100. doi:10.1002/(SICI)1099-1441(199906)6:2<91::AID-KPM54>3.0.CO;2-M

Henry, N., & Pinch, P. (2000). The industrial agglomeration . In Bryson, J., Daniels, P., Henry, N., & Pollard, J. (Eds.), *Knowledge space economy* (pp. 120–141). London: Routledge.

Herbers, J. (1990). A Third Wave of Economic Development. *Governing, 9*(3), 43–50.

Herd, D., & Patterson, T. (2002). Poor Manchester: old problems and new deals . In Peck, J., & Ward, K. (Eds.), *City of Revolution. Restructuring Manchester*. Manchester, UK: Manchester University Press.

Hew, K.F., & Hara, N. (2007). Empirical study of motivators and barriers of teacher online knowledge sharing. Association for Educational communications and Technology.

Hildreth, P. (2006). *Roles and Economic Potential of English Medium-Sized Cities: A Discussion Paper*. Working Paper for *SURF*. Retrieved September 13, 2007, from http://www.surf.salford.ac.uk

Hildreth, P. M. (2004). *Going virtual: distributed communities of practice*. Hershey, PA: Idea Group Publishing.

Hildreth, P., Kimble, C., & Wright, P. (2000). Communities of practice in the distributed international environment. *Journal of Knowledge Management, 4*(1), 27–37. doi:10.1108/13673270010315920

Hillman-Chartrand, H., & McCaughey, C. (1989). *The arm's length principle and the arts: an international perspective – past, present and future in cultural economics – collected works of Harry Hillman Chatrand*. Retrieved November 10, 2007 from http://www.culturaleconomics.atfreeweb.com/arm's.htm

Hislop, D. (2004). The paradox of communities of practice: Knowledge sharing between communities . In Hildreth, P. M., & Kimble, C. (Eds.), *Knowledge Networks: Innovation through Communities of Practice*. Hershey, PA: Idea Group Publishing.

Hodgkin, R. (1991, September 27). Michael Polanyi—Profit of life, the universe, and everything. *Times Higher Education Supplement*, 15.

Hodgson, G. M. (1998). Competence and contract in the theory of the firm. *Journal of Economic Behavior & Organization, 35*, 179–201. doi:10.1016/S0167-2681(98)00053-5

Holden, A. (2002). Bomb Sites: The politics of opportunity . In Peck, J., & Ward, K. (Eds.), *City of Revolution. Restructuring Manchester*. Manchester, UK: Manchester University Press.

Holstila, E. (2007). Finland: Towards urban innovation policy . In van den Berg, L., Braun, E., & van den Meer, J. (Eds.), *National Policy Responses to Urban Challenges in Europe* (pp. 125–144). Aldershot, UK: Ashgate.

Holthouse, D. (1998). Knowledge management research issues. *California Management Review, 40*(3), 277–280.

Horizon Programme. (2008). Retrieved December 11, 2008, from http://www.programmahorizon.nl

Horwitz, F. M., Heng, C. T., Quazi, H. A., Nonkwelo, C., Roditi, D., & van Eck, P. (2006). Human resource strategies for managing knowledge workers: an Afro-Asian comparative analysis. *International Journal of Human Resource Management, 17*(5), 775–811. doi:10.1080/09585190600640802

Houghton, J., & Sheehan, P. (2000). *A primer on the knowledge economy. Centre for Strategic Studies*. Melbourne: Victoria University.

Howells, J. (1996). Tacit knowledge, innovation and technology transfer. *Technology Analysis and Strategic Management, 8*(2), 91–106. doi:10.1080/09537329608524237

Howells, J. (2006). Intermediation and the role of intermediaries in innovation. *Research Policy, 35*, 715–728. doi:10.1016/j.respol.2006.03.005

Hsiao, H.-D., & Lee, M.-S. (2008). The Comparison of Diagnosis on Business Crisis by Using CART and Logistic Regression. *The Business Review, Cambridge, 11*(1), 118–124.

Huang, N.-T., Wei, C.-C., & Chang, W.-K. (2007). Knowledge management: modelling the knowledge diffusion in community of practice. *Kybernetes, 36*(5), 607–621. doi:10.1108/03684920710749703

Huff, T. E. (2005). Malaysia's Multimedia Super Corridor and its first crisis of confidence . In Baber, Z. (Ed.), *CyberAsia: The Internet and Society In Asia*. Leiden, The Netherlands: Brill.

Hutton, A. T. (2004). Service industries, globalization and urban restructuring within the Asia-Pacific: new development trajectories and planning responses. *Progress in Planning, 61,* 1–74. doi:10.1016/S0305-9006(03)00013-8

Hutton, W. (2007). Building Successful Cities in the Knowledge Economy: The Role of Soft Policy Instruments. In *Proceedings of the OECD International Conference: What Policies for Globalizing Cities? Rethinking the Urban Policy Agenda,* Madrid, Spain.

Huysman, M. H., & Wulf, V. (2005). The role of information technology in building and sustaining the relational base of communities. *The Information Society, 21,* 81–89. doi:10.1080/01972240590925285

Iivonen, M., & Huotari, M. L. (2000). The impact of trust on the practise of knowledge management. In *Proceedings of the 63rd ASIS Annual Meeting,* Chicago, IL (Vol. 37, pp. 421-29).

Illegems, V., & Verbeke, A. (2003). *Moving Towards the Virtual Workplace.* Cheltenham, UK: Edward Elgar Publishing.

INK Research Center at SPRU. (n.d.). Retrieved March 4, 2009, from http://www.sussex.ac.uk/spru/1-4-9-1-1-2.html

Inkinen, T. (2005). European coherence and regional policy? A Finnish perspective on the observed and reported territorial impacts of EU research and development policies. *European Planning Studies, 13*(7), 1113–1121. doi:10.1080/09654310500242139

Inkpen, A. C. (2000). Learning through joint ventures: a framework of knowledge acquisition. *Journal of Management Studies, 37*(7), 1019–1043. doi:10.1111/1467-6486.00215

Inkpen, A. C., & Tsang, E. W. K. (2005). Social capital, networks, and knowledge transfer. *Academy of Management Review, 30,* 146–165.

Inkpen, A., & Ramaswamy, K. (2006). *Global Strategy: Creating and Sustaining Advantage Across Borders.* New York: Oxford University Press.

Irick, M. (2007, September). Managing Tacit Knowledge in Organizations. *Journal of Knowledge Management Practice, 8*(3), 8–15.

Jacobs, J. (2004). *Dark age ahead.* Toronto: Random House.

Jaffe, A. B. (1986). Technological opportunity and spillovers of R&D: evidence from firms' patents, profits, and market values. *The American Economic Review, 76,* 984–1001.

Jaffe, A. B., Trajtenberg, M., & Henderson, R. (1993). Geographic localization and knowledge spillovers as evidence by patent citations. *The Quarterly Journal of Economics, 108,* 577–598. doi:10.2307/2118401

Jaffee, D. (1998). *Levels of socio-economic development theory.* London: Praeger.

Jarrar, Y. F. (2002). Knowledge Management: Learning for Organizational Experience. *Managerial Auditing Journal, 17*(6), 322–328. doi:10.1108/02686900210434104

Jeffcutt, P. (2005). The organisation of creativity in knowledge economies: exploring strategic issues. In D. Rooney, G. Hearn & Ninan (Eds.), Handbook on the knowledge economy. Cheltenham, UK: Edward Elgar.

Jensen, M. B., Johnson, B., Lorenz, E., & Lundvall, B. A. (2007). Forms of knowledge and modes of innovation. *Research Policy, 36,* 680–693. doi:10.1016/j.respol.2007.01.006

Jerome, K. P. (2007). An Exploration of the Way the Physical Environment Perpetuates a Moral Code of Conduct Based on Relations of Control: A Case of the McDonald's Restaurant. In *Inhabiting Risk Ideas Conference Proceedings,* Wellington, New Zealand (pp. 71-80).

Jobes, P. (1988). Sociology and Architecture: Excursus and an Example of Planning in Yellowstone National Park. *Design in Education, 7*(2), 8–17.

Johnson, C. M. (2001). A survey of current research on online communities of practice. *Journal of the Internet and Higher Education, 4,* 45–60. doi:10.1016/S1096-7516(01)00047-1

Johnson, D. (2006). Skills of the knowledge worker. *Teacher Librarian, 34*(1), 8–14.

Johnson, H. (2007). Communities of Practice and international development. *Progress in Development Studies, 7*(4), 277–290. doi:10.1177/146499340700700401

Johnson, L. C. (2003). *The Co-Workplace: Teleworking in the Neighbourhood.* Vancouver, Canada: UBC Press.

Johnson, R. B., & Onwuegbuzie, A. J. (2004). Mixed methods research: A research paradigm whose time has come. *Educational Researcher, 33*(7). doi:10.3102/0013189X033007014

Johnson, S., & Taylor, K. (2006). *The Neuroscience of Adult Learning: New Directions for Adult and Continuing Education.* San Francisco: Jossey-Bass.

Jones-Evans, D., Klofsten, M., Andwerson, E., & Pandya, D. (1999). Creating a Bridge between University and Industry in Small European Countries: The Role of the Industrial Liaison Office. *R & D Management, 29*(1), 47–56.

Joseph, R. (1997). Political myth, high technology and the information superhighway. *Telematics and Informatics, 14*(3), 289–301. doi:10.1016/S0736-5853(97)00004-X

Kähkönen, L. (2005). *Suunta suomalaiselle kaupunkipolitiikalle.* Helsinki, Finland: Suomen Kuntaliitto.

Kalnins, A., & Chung, W. (2004). Resource-seeking agglomeration: a study of market entry in the lodging industry. *Strategic Management Journal, 25*, 689–699. doi:10.1002/smj.403

Kaplan, R. (2000). *Randy Kaplan on PKM, Tools for personal Knowledge Effectiveness.*

Karvinen, M. (2005). Innovation and creativity strategies in Helsinki Metropolitan Area – Reinvention of regional governance. In *Proceedings of 41st ISoCaRP Congress 2005*, Bilbao, Spain.

Katila, R., & Ahuja, G. (2002). Something old, something new: A longitudinal study of search behaviour and new product introduction. *Academy of Management Journal, 45*, 1183–1194. doi:10.2307/3069433

Katz, D., & Kahn, R. (1996). *The Social Psychology of Organizations.* New York: Wiley.

Kayakutlu, G. (1998). Knowledge Worker: Essential Resource of the Knowledge Economy, TBD 15. Ulusal Bilişim Kurultayı Bildirileri, İstanbul, 2-6 Eylül 1998, p.222-225.

Klofsten, M., & Jones-Evans, D. (1996). Stimulation of Technology-Based Small Firms - A Case Study of University-Industry Co-Operation. *Technovation, 16*(4), 187–193.

Klofsten, M., & Jones-Evans, D. (2000). Comparing Academic Entrepreneurship in Europe: The Case of Sweden and Ireland. *Small Business Economics, 14*, 299–309.

Kluge, J., Stein, W., & Light, S. (2001). *Knowledge Unplugged.* Basingstoke, UK: Palgrave.

Knight, R. (1995). Knowledge–based development. *Urban Studies (Edinburgh, Scotland), 32*(2), 225–260. doi:10.1080/00420989550013068

Knight, R. (1995). Knowledge-based Development: policy and planning implications for cities. *Urban Studies (Edinburgh, Scotland), 32*(2), 225–260. doi:10.1080/00420989550013068

Knight, R. V. (1995). Knowledge-based development: policy and planning implications for cities. *Urban Studies (Edinburgh, Scotland), 32*(2), 225–260. doi:10.1080/00420989550013068

Knoben, J., & Oelremans, L. A. G. (2006). Proximity and inter-organizational collaboration: a literature review. *International Journal of Management Reviews, 8*, 71–89. doi:10.1111/j.1468-2370.2006.00121.x

Knowledgboard. (n.d.). Retrieved March 4, 2009, from http://www.knowledgeboard.com/

Knowledge Cities Clearinghouse. (n.d.). Retrieved March 4, 2009, from http://www.knowledgecities.com

Knowles, M., Holton, E., & Swanson, R. (1998). *The adult learner: the definitive classic in adult education and human resource development* (5th ed.). Houston, TX: Gulf Publishing.

Kogut, B., & Zander, U. (1992). Knowledge of the firm, combinative capabilities, and the replication of technology. *Organization Science*, *3*, 383–397. doi:10.1287/orsc.3.3.383

Koh, A. T. (2000). Linking learning, knowledge creation, and business creativity: a preliminary assessment of the East Asian quest for creativity. *Technological Forecasting and Social Change*, *64*(1), 85–100. doi:10.1016/S0040-1625(99)00075-X

Komninos, N. (2002). *Intelligent Cities: Innovation, knowledge systems and digital spaces*. London: Spon-press.

Kong, L. (2000). Cultural policy in Singapore: negotiating economic and socio-cultural agendas. *Geoforum*, *31*(4), 409–424. doi:10.1016/S0016-7185(00)00006-3

Korpi, W., & Palme, J. (1998). The paradox of redistribution and strategies of equality: Welfare states institutions, inequality, and poverty in the Western countries. *American Sociological Review*, *63*(5), 661–687. doi:10.2307/2657333

Kotkin, J. (2000). *The New Geography: How the Digital Revolution Is Reshaping the American Landscape*. New York: Random House.

Kotler, P., & Roberto, W. (1989). *Social Marketing: Strategies for Changing Public Behavior*. New York: The Free Press.

Kotler, P., Roberto, N., & Lee, N. (2002). *Social Marketing: Improving the Quality of Life*. New York: Sage.

KPMG International, UK. (1999, November). *Knowledge Management Research Report*. London: KPMG Consulting.

KPMG. (2000). *Knowledge Management Research Report*. London: KPMG Consulting.

Krackardt, D. (1992). The strength of strong ties . In Nohria, N., & Eccles, R. G. (Eds.), *Networks and Organizations*. Cambridge, MA: Harvard Business School Press.

Krouk, D., Pitkin, B., & Richman, N. (2000). Internet-Based Neighbourhood Information Systems: A Comparative Analysis . In Gurstein, M. (Ed.), *Community Informatics: Enabling Communities with Information and Communication Technologies*. Hershey, PA: Idea Group Publishing.

Ku, Y., Liau, S., & Hsing, W. (2005). The high-tech milieu and innovation-oriented development. *Technovation*, *25*, 145–153. doi:10.1016/S0166-4972(03)00074-9

Kubiak, C. (2003). *A Community of practice perspective on school-based learning communities*. Retrieved December 7, 2008, from http://networkedlearning.ncsl.org.uk/knowledge-base/research-papers/a-community-of-practice-perspective-on-school-based-learning-communities.doc

Kuntz, P. G. (1968). *The Concept of Order*. Seattle, WA: University of Washington Press.

Lacetera, N. (forthcoming). Different mission and commitment power in R&D organization: theory and evidence on industry-university alliances. *Organization Science*.

Lahti, R. K., & Beyerlein, M. M. (2000). Knowledge Transfer and Management Consulting: A Look at The Firm. *Business Horizons*, *43*(1), 65. doi:10.1016/S0007-6813(00)87389-9

Lambooy, J. G. (2004). The transmission of knowledge, emerging networks, and the role of universities: an evolutionary approach. *European Planning Studies*, *12*, 643–657. doi:10.1080/0965431042000219996

Lambooy, J. G., & Boschma, R. (2001). Evolutionary economics and regional policy. *The Annals of Regional Science*, *35*, 113–131. doi:10.1007/s001680000033

Landry, C. (2006). *The Art of City Making*. London: Earthscan.

Larsen, K. R. T., & McInerney, C. R. (2002). Preparing to work in the virtual organization. *Information & Management*, *39*(6), 445–456.doi:10.1016/S0378-7206(01)00108-2

Laszlo, K. C., Laszlo, A., Campos, M., & Romero, C. (2003). Evolutionary development: an evolutionary perspective on development for an interconnected world. *World Futures: The Journal of General Evolution, 59*(2), 105–119. doi:10.1080/02604020216075

Laszlo, K., & Laszlo, A. (2006). Fostering a sustainable learning society through knowledge based development. In *50th ISSS Conference*, 9-14 July 2006, California.

Laux, C. (2005). Integrating Corporate Risk . In Frenkel, M., Hommel, U., & Rudolf, M. (Eds.), *Risk Management: Challenge and Opportunity* (pp. 437–454). New York: Springer.

Lave, J., & Wenger, E. (1991). *Situated learning: Legitimate peripheral participation*. New York: Cambridge University Press.

Lavie, D., & Rosenkopf, L. (2006). Balancing exploration and exploitation in alliance formation. *Academy of Management Journal, 49*, 797–818.

Law, J., & Urry, J. (2004). Enacting the social. *Economy and Society, 33*(3), 390–410. doi:10.1080/0308514042000225716

Laycock, M. (2005). Collaborating to compete: achieving effective knowledge sharing in organizations. *The Learning Organization, 12*(6), 523–539. doi:10.1108/09696470510626739

Leach, B., & Copitch, G. (2005). Transforming Communities through local Information Networks. The case study of Manchester. *Research Institute for Health and Social Change (RIHSC)/ MMU.* Retrieved November 18, 2005, from http://www.mmu.ac.uk/regional/community/publications/mcin_paper.pdf

Learning City/regions resources. (n.d.). Retrieved March 4, 2009, from http://www.learningcities.net/services/Links/displaycat.cfm?CatIdd=340

LeBaron, J., Pulkkinen, J., & Scollin, P. (2000). Promoting cross-border communication in an international Web-based graduate course. *Interactive Multimedia Electronic Journal of Computer-Enhanced Learning, 2*(2). Retrieved September 15, 2008, from http://imej.wfu.edu/articles/2000/2/01/index.asp

Lee, R. G., & Garvin, T. (2003). Moving from information transfer to information exchange in health and health care. *Social Science & Medicine, 56*, 449–464. doi:10.1016/S0277-9536(02)00045-X

Lee, S. M., & Hong, S. (2002). An Enterprise-wide Knowledge Management System Infrastructure. *Industrial Management & Data Systems, 102*(1), 17–25. doi:10.1108/02635570210414622

Lee, T. (2004). Creative shifts and directions: cultural policy in Singapore. *International Journal of Cultural Policy, 10*(3), 281–289. doi:10.1080/1028663042000312525

Lee-Kelly, L., Blackman, D. A., & Hurst, J. P. (2007). An exploration of the relationship between learning organisations and the retention of knowledge workers. *The Learning Organization, 14*(3), 204–221. doi:10.1108/09696470710739390

Leitch, U. K. Review of Skills. (2006). Prosperity for all in the global economy - world class skills. Norwich, UK: Crown.

Lepawsky, J. (2005), Digital Aspirations: Malaysia and the Multimedia Super Corridor. *FOCUS on Geography, 48*(3).

LePine, J. A., Piccolo, R. F., Jackson, C. L., Mathieu, J. E., & Saul, J. R. (2008). A Meta-analysis of teamwork processes: Tests of a multidimensional model and relationship with team effectiveness criteria. *Personnel Psychology, 61*(2), 273–308.doi:10.1111/j.1744-6570.2008.00114.x

Leppälahti, A. (2000). Comparison of Finnish information surveys. *Science* [Statistics Finland, Helsinki]. *Technology Review, 2000*, 1.

Lesser, E. L., & Storck, J. (2001). Communities of practice and organisational performance. *IBM Systems Journal, 40*(4), 831–841.

Leung, S. (2004). *Statistics to measure the knowledge-based economy: the case of Hong Kong and China.* Paper presented at the 2004 Asia-Pacific technical meeting on information and communication technology (ICT) statistics, Wellington, 30 November – 2 December 2004. Retrieved June 10, 2009 from http://74.125.153.132/

search?q=cache:pMolfzT0yH0J:www.unescap.org/stat/ict/ict2004/18

Lev, B. (2001). *Intangibles: Management, Measurement and Reporting*. Washington, DC: Brookings Institution.

Lever, W. (2002). Correlating the knowledge-base of cities with economic growth. *Urban Studies (Edinburgh, Scotland)*, *39*(5/6), 859–870. doi:10.1080/00420980220128345

Lever, W. (2002). Correlating the knowledge-base of cities with economic growth. *Urban Studies (Edinburgh, Scotland)*, *39*(5/6), 859–870. doi:10.1080/00420980220128345

Levinthal, D., & March, J. (1993). The myopia of learning. *Strategic Management Journal*, *14*, 95–112. doi:10.1002/smj.4250141009

Leyesdorff, L. (2000). The triple helix: An evolutionary model of innovation. *Research Policy*, *29*(2), 243–255. doi:10.1016/S0048-7333(99)00063-3

Li, H., Zinand, L., & Rebelo, I. (1998). Testing the neoclassical theory of economic growth. *Economics of Planning*, *32*, 117–132. doi:10.1023/A:1003571107706

Liebowitz, J. (2004). *Addressing the Human Capital Crisis in the Federal Government: a Knowledge Management Perspective*. New York: Butterworth-Heinemann.

Liedloff, J. (1985). *The continuum concept: Allowing human nature to work successfully*. Reading, MA: Addison-Wesley.

Link, A. N., & Scott, J. T. (2005). Universities as partners in U.S. research joint ventures. *Research Policy*, *34*, 385–393. doi:10.1016/j.respol.2005.01.013

Liu, D.-R., & Wu, I.-C. (2008). Collaborative relevance assessment for task-based knowledge support. *Decision Support Systems*, *44*(2), 524–543.doi:10.1016/j.dss.2007.06.015

Liu, D.-R., Wu, I.-C., & Yang, K.-S. (2005). Task-based support systems: disseminating and sharing task-relevant knowledge. *Expert Systems with Applications*, *29*(2), 408–423.doi:10.1016/j.eswa.2005.04.036

Livanage, C., Li, Q., Elhag, T., & Ballal, T. (2008). The Process of Knowledge Transfer and Its Significance in Integrated Environments. *AACE International Transactions*, *2008*, 61–69.

Lloyd, R., & Clark, T. N. (2001). The City as an Entertainment Machine . In Gotham, K. F. (Ed.), *Critical Perspectives on Urban Development* (*Vol. 6*, pp. 357–378). Oxford, UK: Elsevier.

Loader, B. D., Hague, B., & Eagle, D. (2000). Embedding the Net: Community Empowerment in the Age of Information . In Gurstein, M. (Ed.), *Community Informatics: Enabling Communities with Information and Communication Technologies*. Hershey, PA: Idea Group Publishing.

Loh, L. (1998). Technology policy and national competitiveness . In Toh, M. H., & Tan, K. Y. (Eds.), *Competitiveness of the Singapore economy: a strategic perspective*. Singapore: Singapore University Press and World Scientific Publishing Company.

Loo, L. S., Seow, E. O., & Agarwal, A. (2003). Singapore's competitiveness as a global city: development strategy, institutions and business environment. *Cities (London, England)*, *20*(2), 115–127. doi:10.1016/S0264-2751(02)00119-1

Low, L. (2001). The Singapore developmental state in the new economy and polity. *The Pacific Review*, *13*(3), 409–439.

Low, L. (2005). Entrepreneurial development in Ireland and Singapore. *Journal of the Asia Pacific Economy*, *10*(1), 116–138. doi:10.1080/1354786042000309107

Lubit, R. (2001). Tacit Knowledge and Knowledge Management: The Keys to Sustainable Competitive Advantage. *Organizational Dynamics*, *29*(3), 164–178. doi:10.1016/S0090-2616(01)00026-2

Lublinski, A. E. (2003). Does geographic proximity matter? Evidence from clustered and non-clustered aeronautic firms in Germany. *Regional Studies*, *37*, 453–467. doi:10.1080/0034340032000089031

Lucas, L. M. (2006). The role of culture on knowledge transfer: The case of the multinational corporation. *The Learning Organization*, *13*(3), 257–275. doi:10.1108/09696470610661117

Lucier, C., & Torsiliera, J. (1997). Why Knowledge Programs Fail. *Strategy and Business* (4th Quarter), 14-28.

Lummus, R. R., & Vokurka, R. J. (1999). Defining supply chain management: A historical perspective and practical guidelines. *Industrial Management & Data Systems*, *99*(1), 11–17. doi:10.1108/02635579910243851

Lundvall, B. (Ed.). (1992). *National Systems of Innovation*. London: Pinter.

Lundvall, B. A. (1992). *National Systems of Innovations: Towards a Theory of Innovation and Interactive Learning*. London: Printer Publisher.

Machlup, F. (1962). *The production and Distribution of Knowledge in the United States*. Princeton, NJ: Princeton University Press.

MAKCI. *(Most Admired Knowledge City Awards) Report*. (2008). World Capital Institute and Teleos. Retrieved January 4, 2009 from The World Capital Institute website at http://www.worldcapitalinstitute.org/

Malerba, F. (1992). Learning by firms and incremental technical change. *The Economic Journal*, *102*, 845–859. doi:10.2307/2234581

Malik, S., Maryjam, S. S., & Maheshwari, S. (2009). Knowledge Based development and Knowledge Cities paper presented at the *International Conference on Knowledge Management and Intellectual Capital*. (Session Track VI). February 26th and 27th 2009. Ghaziabad, India. Conference URL: http://www.imt.edu/ickmic2009/

Malina, A., & Macintosh, A. (2004). Bridging the Digital Divide: Developments in Scotland . In Mälkiä, M., Anttiroiko, A. V., & Savolainen, R. (Eds.), *eTransformation in governance: new directions in government and politic* (pp. 255–271). Hershey, PA: IGI Publishing.

Mallalieu, K. I. (2006). *Transforming Trinidad and Tobago into a Knowledge Society.* Retrieved February 3, 2009, from http://www.eclac.cl/socinfo/noticias/noticias/6/26546/ictpol06.pdf

Malmberg, M., & Powel, D. (2005). (How) do (firms in) cluster create knowledge? *Industry and Innovation*, *12*(4), 409–431. doi:10.1080/13662710500381583

Malone, S. A. (2003). *Learning about learning: an A-Z training and development tools and techniques*. Wiltshire, UK: The Cromwell Press.

Manchester Knowledge Capital Partnership (MKCP). (2009). *Document submitted by The Manchester: Knowledge Capital (M: KC) Partnership to the Most Admired Knowledge City (MAKCi) Report.* World Capital Institute & Teleos. Retrieved from http://www.worldcapitalinstitute.org/makci

Manchester Science City (MSC). (2009). Real work, Real progress, Real Impact. *Report from the MKCP and NWDA.* Retrieved March 18, 2009, from http://www.manchesterknowledge.com

Maning Thomas, J., & Darnton, J. (2006). Social diversity and economic development in the metropolis. *Journal of Planning Literature*, *21*(2), 153–168. doi:10.1177/0885412206292259

Manz, C. C., & Sims, H. P. Jr. (2001). *The New Superleadership: Leading Others to Lead Themselves*. San Francisco, CA: Berrett-Koehler Publishers.

Marceau, J., Martinez-Fernandez, C., Rerceretnam, M., Hanna, B., Davidson, K., & Wixted, B. (2005). *Stocktake of NSW as a potential knowledge hub*. Sydney, Australia: UWS.

March, J. (1991). Exploration and exploitation in organizational learning. *Organization Science*, *2*, 71–87. doi:10.1287/orsc.2.1.71

Markusen, A. (2006). Urban development and the politics of a creative class. *Environment and Planning, 38*(10), 1921-1940.

Marr, B. (2003, February). Known Quantities. *Financial Management*, 25–27.

Marr, B., Mountsen, J., & Bukh, P. (2003). Perceived Wisdom. *Financial Management*, 32.

Martínez, A. (1999). *Modelo integral de autogestión en grupos de aprendizaje de adultos*. Universidad Virtual. Master's Thesis, Instituto tecnológico y de Estudios Superiores de Monterrey.

Martínez, A. (2001). Un Modelo de Procesos Clave de Administración de Conocimiento. *Transferencia, 14*, 28–29.

Martínez, A. (2005). Knowledge Citizens: A Competence Profile . In Carrillo, F. J. (Ed.), *Knowledge Cities* (pp. 233–244). New York: Elsevier.

Martínez, A. (2006 September). El conocimiento de las personas. Factor clave en la Gestión del Conocimiento. *La Revista Sociedad y Conocimiento.*

Martínez, A. (2007). *Competencias de los integrantes de una comunidad de práctica.* Universidad Virtual. Tesis Doctoral, Instituto tecnológico y de Estudios Superiores de Monterrey.

Martínez, A., & Buendía, A. (2006). Las Competencias del Ciudadano de Conocimiento como base para ejercer sus derechos y responsabilidades . In Mariñez, F. (Ed.), *Ciudadanos, decisiones públicas y calidad de la democracia.* Ciudad de México, México: Limusa Noriega Editores.

Martinez-Fernandez, C. (1998). *Industry clusters.* Newcastle, Australia: HURDO.

Martinez-Fernandez, C., & Martinez-Solano, L. (2006). Knowledge-intensive service activities in software innovation. *International Journal Services Technology and Management, 7*(2), 109–174.

Martinez-Fernandez, C., & Miles, I. (2006). Inside the software firm. *International Journal Services Technology and Management, 7*(2), 115–125.

Martinez-Fernandez, C., & Sharpe, S. (2008). Intellectual assets and knowledge vitality in urban regions . In Yigitcanlar, T., Velibeyoglu, K., & Baum, S. (Eds.), *Creative urban regions* (pp. 48–64). Hershey, PA: Information Science Reference.

Martins, L., & Álvarez, J. M. R. (2007). Towards Glocal Leadership: Taking up the Challenge of New Local Governance in Europe? *Government and Policy, 25*(3), 391–409.

Maruseth, P. B., & Verspagen, B. (2002). Knowledge-spillovers in Europe: a patent citation analysis. *The Scandinavian Journal of Economics, 104*, 531–545. doi:10.1111/1467-9442.00300

Mason, E. S., Kim, M. J., Perkins, D. H., Kim, K. S., & Cole, D. C. (1980). *The economic and social modernization of the Republic of Korea.* Cambridge, MA: Harvard University Press.

Massey, A. P., Montoya-Weiss, M. M., & O'Driscoll, T. M. (2005). Human Performance Technology and Knowledge Management: A Case Study. *Performance Improvement Quarterly, 18*(2), 37–56.

Mavrotas, G., Schorrocks, A., & Sen, A. (2007). *Advancing Development: Core Themes in Global Economics.* Basingstoke, UK: Palgrave Macmillan.

McDermott, R. (1999 May/June). Nurturing Three Dimensional Communities of Practice: How to get the most out of human networks. *Knowledge Management Review.* Retrieved December 6, 2008, from http://home.att.net/~discon/KM/Learning.pdf

McDermott, R. (2001). *Knowing in community: 10 Critical success factors in building communities of practices.* Retrieved May 1, 2009, from http://pages.conversaciones-locales.org-a.googlepages.com/KnowinginCommunity-10CriticalSuccess.doc

McElroy, M. W. (2002). Social innovation capital. *Journal of Intellectual Capital, 3*(1), 30–39. doi:10.1108/14691930210412827

McEvily, B., & Zaheer, A. (1999). Bridging ties: a source of firm heterogeneity in competitive capabilities. *Strategic Management Journal, 20*, 1133–1156. doi:10.1002/(SICI)1097-0266(199912)20:12<1133::AID-SMJ74>3.0.CO;2-7

McKellar, H. (2005). *The knowledge (worker) economy.* Retrieved May 5, 2009, from http://www.kmworld.com/Articles/Column/From-The-Editor/The-knowledge-(worker)-economy-14264.aspx

McNamara, P., & Baden-Fuller, C. (1999). Lessons from the Celltech case: balancing knowledge exploration and exploitation in organizational renewal. *British Journal of Management, 10*, 291–307. doi:10.1111/1467-8551.00140

MDeC (Multimedia Super Corridor Development Corporation). (2006). *Guide For MSC Malaysia Cybercities andCybercentres.* Kuala Lumpur, Malaysia: Multimedia Development Corporation.

MDeC (Multimedia Super Corridor Development Corporation). (2008). *MSC Malaysia National Rollout 2020*. Retrieved April 2, 2009, from http://www.msc-malaysia.my

Melbourne Vice-Chancellors' Forum. (2007). *Melbourne Australia's knowledge capital.* City of Melbourne. Retrieved January 10, 2009, from http://www.melbourne.vic.gov.au/rsrc/Publications/KnowledgeCapital/3030-Uni_study_screen.pdf

Meso, P., & Smith, R. (2000). A Resource-based View of Organizational Knowledge Management Systems. *Journal of Knowledge Management, 4*(3), 224–231. doi:10.1108/13673270010350020

Metaxiotis, K., Ergazakis, K., & Psarras, J. (2005). Exploring the world of knowledge management: agreements and disagreements in the academic/practitioner community. *Journal of Knowledge Management, 9*(2), 6–18. doi:10.1108/13673270510590182

Metropolitan New Economy Index. (n.d.). Retrieved March 4, 2009, from http://www.neweconomyindex.org/metro/

Michaelson, R. (2002). Re-Thinking Laurillard: universities, learning and technology. In . *International Journal of Management Education, 2*(2).

Michaud, P., & Tcheremenska, A. (2003). *Montréal Knowledge City*. Montréal: Report of the Montréal, Knowledge City Advisory Committee.

Miles, S. (1998). McDonaldization Revisited: Critical Essays on Consumer Culture . In Alfino, M., Caputo, J., & Wynyard, R. (Eds.), *McDonalization and the Global Sports Store: Constructing Consumer Meanings in a Rationalized Society* (pp. 53–66). Santa Barbara, CA: Praeger Publishers.

Miller, F. J. (2002). Information has no intrinsic meaning. *Information Research*, 8(1). Retrieved September 10, 2008, from http://www.informationr.net/ir/8-1/paper140.html

Ministry of Education. (2003). Ministry of Education Strategy 2015. *Publications of the Ministry of Education, 2003*(35).

Ministry of Trade and Industry. (2007). *Entrepreneurship policy during Prime Minister Matti Vanhanen's term of government 2003-2007: Entrepreneurship Policy Programme. Publications 11/2007.* Helsinki: Edita.

Ministry of Transport and Communication. (2007). *Transport 2030. Major challenges, new directions. Programmes and Strategies 2/2007.* Helsinki: Edita.

MITA. *(Ministry of Information and the Arts) Renaissance City Report*. (2000). Retrieved January 5, 2004 from http://www.mita.gov.sg/renaissance

Mitchell, W. J. (1996). *City of bits*. Cambridge, MA: The MIT Press.

Mitchell, W. J. (1999). *E-topia*. Cambridge, MA: The MIT Press.

Mohamad, M. (1996). *The way forward Vision 2020.* Kuala Lumpur: Malaysia Business Council.

Mohamad, M. (1998). *Inventing Our Common Future in Mahathir Mohamad: A Visionary and His Vision of Malaysia's Knowledge economy.* Subang Jaya, Malaysia: Pelanduk Publications.

Mohan, A. V., Aliza, A. O., & Kamarulzaman, A. A. (2004). ICT Clusters As A Way To Materlialise A National System Of Innovation: Malaysia's Multimedia Super Corridor Flagships. *Electronic Journal on Information Systems in Developing Countries, 16*(5), 1–18.

Mokyr, J. (2002). *The Gifts from Athena: Historical Origins of the Knowledge Economy.* Princeton, NJ: Princeton University Press.

Montréal. (2002). *Imagining Building Montréal 2025: A World of Creativity and Opportunities.* Retrieved January 10, 2009, from http://ville.montreal.qc.ca/pls/portal/docs/page/montreal2025_en/media/Documents/Montreal_2025_Summary.pdf

Montréal. (2007). *Montréals First Strategic Plan for Sustainable Development 2007- 2009 Phase.* Retrieved January 10, 2009, http://ville.montréal.qc.ca/portal/page?_pageid=4176,4738953&_dad=portal&_schema=PORTAL

Moore, P., & Taylor, P. A. (2009). Exploitation of the self in community-based software productions Workers' freedoms or firm foundations? *Capital and Class, 97,* 99–119.doi:10.1177/030981680909700106

Moulart, F., & Sekia, F. (2003). Territorial innovation models: a critical survey. *Regional Studies, 37,* 289–302. doi:10.1080/0034340032000065442

Mowery, D. C., Oxley, J. E., & Silverman, B. S. (1998). Technological overlap and interfirm cooperation: implications for the resource-based view of the firm. *Research Policy, 27,* 507–523. doi:10.1016/S0048-7333(98)00066-3

Mukhtar, N. (2008). *Intelligent City of Cyberjaya.* Unpublished MSC Thesis, Cardiff, UK.

Munich. (2005). *Munich – City of Knowledge.* Department of Labor and Economic Development. Retrieved January 10, 2009 from http://www.compete-eu.org/publications/Munich_cityofknowledge_2005.pdf

Murray, P., & Myers, A. (1997, September). The Facts about Knowledge. *Information Strategy, 2*(7), 29–33.

Mutius, B. V. (2005). Rethinking leadership in the knowledge society, learning from others: how to integrate intellectual and social capital and established a new balance of value and values. In A. Bounfour & L. Edvinsson (Ed.), Intellectual capital for communities: nations, regions, and cities (pp. 151-163). Tokyo: Elsevier Butterworth-Heinemann. R&B Consulting (Eds.). (2006). Knowledge management Austria, Assess, Wien.

Nahapiet, J., & Ghoshal, S. (1998). Social capital, intellectual capital, and organizational advantage. *Academy of Management Review, 23*(2), 242–266. doi:10.2307/259373

Nathan, M. (2008). Creative class theory and economic performance in UK cities . In Yigitcanlar, T., Velibeyoglu, K., & Baum, S. (Eds.), *Creative urban regions* (pp. 80–94). Hershey, PA: Information Science Reference.

Nathan, M., & Urwin, C. (2006). *City people.* London: IPPR.

National Research Council. (2000). *How People Learn: Brain, Mind, Experience, and School.* Washington, DC: National Academy Press.

Nayeri, M. D., Mashhadi, M. M., & Mohajeri, K. (2007). Universities Strategic Evaluation Using Balanced Scorecard. *International Journal of Social Sciences, 2*(4), 231–236.

Negroponte, N. (1995). *Being Digital.* New York: Knopf.

Nelson, R. (2004). The Market economy and the scientific commons. *Research Policy, 33,* 455–471. doi:10.1016/j.respol.2003.09.008

Nelson, R. R. (Ed.). (1993). *National Innovation Systems: A Comparative Study.* New York: Oxford University Press.

New Straits Times (Malaysia). (2003, March 26). *Be Prepared for Knowledge Era.*

Nicolopoulou, K., & Karatas-Ozkan, M. (2007). Practising knowledge workers: perspectives of an artist and economist, PROFESSIONAL INSIGHTS. *Equal Opportunities International, 26*(8), 872–878. doi:10.1108/02610150710836181

Nonaka, I. (1994). A Dynamic Theory of Organization Knowledge Creation. *Organization Science, 5*(1), 14–37. doi:10.1287/orsc.5.1.14

Nonaka, I. (1997). A new organizational structure . In *Knowledge in Organizations.* Boston: Butterworth-Heinemann. doi:10.1016/B978-0-7506-9718-7.50009-3

Nonaka, I., & Takeuchi, H. (1995). *The Knowledge Creating Company: How Japanese Companies Create the Dynamics of Innovation.* Oxford, UK: Oxford University Press, Inc.

Nooteboom, B. (1999). Innovation and inter-firm linkages: new implications for policy. *Research Policy, 28*, 793–805. doi:10.1016/S0048-7333(99)00022-0

Nooteboom, B. (2000). *Learning and Innovation in Organizations and Economies.* Oxford, UK: Oxford University Press.

Nooteboom, B. (2004). *Interfirm Collaboration, Learning and Networks, an Integrated Approach.* London: Routledge.

Nooteboom, B., Van Haverbeke, W., Duysters, G., Gilsing, V., & van den Oord, A. (2007). Optimal cognitive distance and absorptive capacity. *Research Policy, 36*, 1016–1034. doi:10.1016/j.respol.2007.04.003

Norhani, B. (2008). The Acculturation of *Knowledge* Workers in Malaysian Industries. *International Journal of the Humanities, 6*(1), 63–68.

Nowak, M. A., & Sigmund, K. (2000). Cooperation versus competition. *Financial Analysts Journal, 56*, 13–22. doi:10.2469/faj.v56.n4.2370

Nunes, M. B., Annansingh, F., Eaglestone, B., & Wakefield, R. (2006). Knowledge management issues in knowledge-intensive SMEs. *The Journal of Documentation, 62*(1), 101–119. doi:10.1108/00220410610642075

Nunnally, J. C. (1978). *Psychometric Theory* (2nd ed.). New York: McGraw-Hill Book Company.

NWDA. North West Development Agency. (2003 February). Northern Way Growth Strategy. Manchester City-Region Profile. *Report from the North West Development Agency (NWDA).* Retrieved June 6, 2004, from http://www.thenorthernway.co.uk/docs/appendices/manchester.doc

O'Dell, C., & Grayson, J. C. (1998). If we only knew what we know: identification and transfer of internal best practices. *California Management Review, 40*(3), 154–174.

O'Mara, M. (2005). *Cities of knowledge.* Princeton, NJ: Princeton University Press.

Oakes, J., & Lipton, M. (1999). *Teaching to Change the World.* Boston: McGraw-Hill College.

OECD. (1996). *Organization for Economic Cooperation and Development. The Knowledge-Based Economy.* Paris: OECD.

OECD. (2001). *Benchmarking knowledge-based economies.* Paris: OECD Press.

OECD. (2003). *Territorial Reviews, Helsinki, Finland.* Paris: OECD.

OECD. (2006). *The role of knowledge-intensive service activities in innovation.* Paris: OECD Press.

Olivares, A. M., & Lado, N. (2003). Market Orientation and Business Economic Performance: A Mediated Model. *International Journal of Service Industry Management, 14*(3), 284–309. doi:10.1108/09564230310478837

Oliver, R., & Herrington, J. (2000). Using situated learning as a design strategy for Web-based learning . In Abbey, B. (Ed.), *Instructional and cognitive impacts of Web-based education.* Hershey, PA: Idea Publishing Group.

Organization for Economic Corporation and Development (OECD). (1996). *The knowledge-based economy.* Paris: OECD.

Organization for Economic Corporation and Development (OECD). (2002). Towards a knowledge-based economy – recent trends and policy directions from the OECD. Background paper for the OECD-IPS workshop on promoting knowledge-based economies in Asia, 21-22 November 2002, Singapore.

Orr, J. (1990). S haring Knowledge, Celebrating Identity: War Stories and Community Memory in a Service Culture . In Middleton, D. S., & Edwards, D. (Eds.), *Collective Remembering: Memory in Society.* Beverly Hills, CA: Sage Publications.

Osterloh, M., & Frey, B. S. (2006). Shareholders Should Welcome Knowledge Workers as Directors. *Journal of*

Management & Governance, *10*(3), 325–345. doi:10.1007/s10997-006-9003-4

Otero, B. A. (2000). *The African Past in America as a Bakhtinian and Levinasian other. 'Rememory' as Solution in Toni Morrison's 'Beloved.'* Retrieved March, 2009, from http://dialnet.unirioja.es/servlet/oaiart?codigo=193823 and http://eprints.upc.es/rebiun/index.php/record/view/11860

Palloff, R., & Pratt, K. (1999). *Building learning communities in cyberspace: effective strategies for the online classroom*. San Francisco: Jossey-Bass.

Park, S. O. (2001). Knowledge-based industry for promoting growth. In D. Felsenstein & M. Taylor (eds.): Promoting Local Growth. Process, Practice and Policy, 43–59. Aldershot, UK: Ashgate.

Pasher, E., & Shachar, S. (2004). *The Intellectual Capital of the State of Israel*. Jerusalem, Israel: Ministry of Industry, Trade and Labor.

Pasher, E., & Shachar, S. (2007). *The Intellectual Capital of the State of Israel: 60 Years of Achievements*. Jerusalem, Israel: Ministry of Industry, Trade and Labor.

Pavitt, K. (1985). Patent statistics as indicators of innovative activities: possibilities and problems. *Scientometrics*, *7*, 77–99. doi:10.1007/BF02020142

Peck, J. (2005). Struggling with the creative class. *International Journal of Urban and Regional Research*, *29*(4), 740–770. doi:10.1111/j.1468-2427.2005.00620.x

Peck, J., & Ward, K. (2002). *City of Revolution. Restructuring Manchester*. Manchester, UK: Manchester University Press.

Perry, B. (2008). Academic knowledge and urban development . In Yigitcanlar, T., Velibeyoglu, K., & Baum, S. (Eds.), *Knowledge-Based Urban Development* (pp. 21–41). Hershey, PA: Information Science Reference.

Persichitte, K. (2000). A case study of lessons learned for the web-based educator . In Abbey, B. (Ed.), *Instructional and cognitive impacts of web-based education*. Hershey, PA: Idea Group.

Peters, M. A., & May, T. (2004). Universities, Regional Policy and the Knowledge Economy. *Policy Futures in Education*, *2*(2), 2004. Available at http://wwwords.co.uk/pdf/validate.asp?j=pfie&vol=2&=2&year=2004&article=4_Peters_PFIE_2_2_web&id=130.88.205.96 Accessed 18th January 2004. doi:10.2304/pfie.2004.2.2.4

Plummer, P., & Taylor, M. (2003). Theory and praxis in economic geography. *Environment and Planning C*, 21, 633-649.

Poincare, H. (2001). *The Foundations of Science: Science and Hypothesis, The Value of Science, Science and Method*. New York: Modern Library.

Polanyi, M. (1961). Knowing and being . *Mind*, *70*(280), 458–470. doi:10.1093/mind/LXX.280.458

Polenske, K. R. (2004). Competition, collaboration and cooperation: an uneasy triangle in networks of firms and regions. *Regional Studies*, *38*, 1029–1043. doi:10.1080/0034340042000292629

Politis, J. D. (2003). The connection between trust and knowledge management: What are the implications for team performance? *Journal of Knowledge Management*, *7*(5), 55–66. doi:10.1108/13673270310505386

Porter, D. E., Bennet, A., Turner, R., & Wennergren, D. (2003). *The Power of Team: The Making of a CIO*. Alexandria, VA: U.S. Department of the Navy.

Porter, M. (1995). The Competitive advantage of the Inner City in *Harvard . Business Review (Federal Reserve Bank of Philadelphia)*, (May-June): 1995.

Porter, M. (2001). Regions and the new economics of competition . In Scott, A. (Ed.), *Global city regions* (pp. 139–157). New York: Oxford University Press.

Pouder, R., & John, C. H. S. (1996). Hot spots and blind spots: geographical clusters of firms and innovation. *Academy of Management Review*, *21*, 1192–1225. doi:10.2307/259168

Powell, W. W., Koput, K. W., & Smith-Doerr, L. (1996). Interorganizational collaboration and the locus of innovation: networks of learning in biotechnology. *Administrative Science Quarterly*, *41*, 116–145. doi:10.2307/2393988

Pred, A. (1976). The Interurban Transmission of Growth in Advanced Economies. *Regional Studies, 10*(9), 151–171. doi:10.1080/09595237600185161

Preece, J. (2004). Etiquette and trust drive online communities of practice. *Journal of universal computer science*.

PriceWaterhouse Coopers. (2005). *Cities of the Future. Global competition Local leadership.* Retrieved February 2007, from http://www.pwc.com

Prusak, I. (1999). What's Up with Knowledge Management: A Personal View . In Cortada, J., & Woods, J. (Eds.), *The Knowledge Management Yearbook 1999-2000* (pp. 3–7). Boston: Butterworth-Heinemann.

Psarras, J. (2006). Education and training in the knowledge-based economy. *Vine, 36*(1), 85–96. doi:10.1108/03055720610667390

Putnam, R. D., Leonardi, R., & Nanetti, R. Y. (1993). *Making Democracy Work.* Princeton, NJ: Princeton University Press.

Queensland Government. (2004). *Smart Strategy Progress 2004.* Brisbane: Smart State Council.

Queensland Government. (2005). *Smart Queensland: Smart State Strategy 2005–2015.* Brisbane: Smart State Council.

Queensland Government. (2006). *Smart Regions: Characteristics of Globally Successful Regions and Implications for Queensland.* Brisbane: Smart State Council.

Queensland Government. (2008). *Smart State Strategy 2008-2012.* Brisbane: Smart State Council.

Quinn, F. J. (1997). What's the buzz? *Logistics Management, 36*(2), 43–47.

Ramachandran,R. (2003). Measuring Knowledge Development and Developing Official Statistics for the Information Age. *International Statistical Review / Revue Internationale de Statistique, 71*(1), 83-107.

Ramasamy, B., Chakrabaty, A., & Cheah, M. (2004). Malaysia's Leap into the Future: An Evaluation of the Multimedia Super Corridor. *Technovation, 24*, 871–883. doi:10.1016/S0166-4972(03)00049-X

Ratanawaraha, A., & Polenske, K. R. (2007). Measuring the geography of innovation: a literature review . In Polenske, K. P. (Ed.), *The Economic Geography of Innovation.* Cambridge, UK: Cambridge University Press. doi:10.1017/CBO9780511493386.004

Reagans, R., & McEvily, B. (2003). Network structure and knowledge transfer: the effects of cohesion and range. *Administrative Science Quarterly, 48*, 240–267. doi:10.2307/3556658

Reichert, S. (2006). *The Rise of Knowledge Regions: Emerging properties and Challenges for Universities.* Brussels: European University Association.

Ricardo, S. (2000). *Inteligencia Emocional en la Práctica: Resumen.* CapitalEmocional.com. Retrieved March, 2009, from http://www.capitalemocional.com/articulos/iemo.htm

Ritzer, G. (1993). *The McDonaldization of Society.* Thousand Oaks, CA: Pine Forge Press.

Ritzer, G. (1998). *Revolutionizing the Means of Consumption.* Thousand Oaks, CA: Pine Forge Press.

Ritzer, G. (2001). *Explorations in the Sociology of Consumption: Fast food, Credit Cards and Casinos.* London: Sage Ltd.

Roberts, J. (2000). From know-how to show-how: the role of information and communications technology in the transfer of knowledge. *Technology Analysis and Strategic Management, 12*(4), 429–443. doi:10.1080/713698499

Robertson, M., & O'Malley Hammersley, G. (2000). Knowledge management practices within a knowledge-intensive firm: the significance of the people management dimension. *Journal of European Industrial Training, 24*(2-4), 241–253. doi:10.1108/03090590010321205

Robson, B. (2002). Mancunian Ways: the politics of regeneration . In Peck, J., & Ward, K. (Eds.), *City of Revolution. Restructuring Manchester.* Manchester, UK: Manchester University Press.

Roffe, I. (2007). Competitive strategy and influences on e-learning in entrepreneur-led SME. *Journal of European Industrial Training, 31*(6), 416–434. doi:10.1108/03090590710772622

Romer, P. (1990). Endogenous technological change. *The Journal of Political Economy, 98*(5), 71–102. doi:10.1086/261725

Romer, P. M. (1994). The origins of endogenous growth. *The Journal of Economic Perspectives, 8*(1), 3–22.

Rosenkopf, L., & Almeida, P. (2003). Overcoming local search through alliances and mobility. *Management Science, 49*, 751–766. doi:10.1287/mnsc.49.6.751.16026

Ross, D., & Friedman, R. E. (1990). The Emerging Third Wave: New Economic Development Strategies. *Entrepreneurial Economy Review, 90*, 3–11.

Ross, P. E. (2006, August). The expert mind. *Scientific American*, 64–71. doi:10.1038/scientificamerican0806-64

Rothaermel, F. T., & Thursby, M. (2005). Incubator firm failure or graduation? The role of university linkages. *Research Policy, 34*, 1076–1090. doi:10.1016/j.respol.2005.05.012

Rowlcy, J. (2000). Is higher education ready for knowledge management? *International Journal of Educational Management, 14*(7), 325–333. doi:10.1108/09513540010378978

Rowley, T., Behrens, D., & Krackhardt, D. (2000). Redundant governance structures: an analysis of structural and relational embeddedness in the steel and semiconductor industries. *Strategic Management Journal, 21*, 369–386. doi:10.1002/(SICI)1097-0266(200003)21:3<369::AID-SMJ93>3.0.CO;2-M

Rusette, J. W., Preziosi, R., Scully, R. E., & de Cossio, F. (2007). A Twenty-First Century Incongruity: Perceptions Regarding Knowledge Worker Didactics. *Journal of Applied Management and Entrepreneurship, 12*(2), 15–44.

Ryle, G. (1949). *The Concept of Mind*. London: Hutchinson.

Saint-Onge, H., & Wallace, D. (2003). *Leveraging Communities of Practice for Strategic Advantage*. Boston, MA: Butterworth-Heinemann.

Saint-Paul, G. (2007). Knowledge hierarchies in the labor market. *Journal of Economic Theory, 137*(1), 104–126. doi:10.1016/j.jet.2005.09.010

Santamaria, L., Nieto, M. J., & Barge-Gil, A. (2009). Beyond formal R&D: taking advantage of other sources of innovation in low- and medium-technology industries. *Research Policy, 38*, 507–517. doi:10.1016/j.respol.2008.10.004

Sanyal, B. (2000). Planning's three challenges . In Rodwin, L., & Sanyal, B. (Eds.), *The profession of city planning*. New Brunswick, NJ: Rutgers.

Saul, J. R. (2006, March). The Collapse of Globalism. *Harper's, 308*(1846), 33-43.

Sauve, E. (2007). *Informal knowledge transfer*. T+D, American Society for Training and Development, March.

Saviotti, P. P. (1998). On the dynamics of appropriability, of tacit and of codified knowledge. *Research Policy, 26*, 843–856. doi:10.1016/S0048-7333(97)00066-8

Saxenian, A. (1994). *Regional advantage*. Cambridge, MA: Harvard University Press.

Schamp, E. W., Rentmeister, B., & Lo, V. (2004). Dimensions of proximity in knowledge-based networks: the cases of investment banking and automobile design. *European Planning Studies, 12*, 607–624. doi:10.1080/0965431042000219978

Schell, W. J. (2008). Building a Knowledge Management Framework to Overcome the Challenges of Developing Engineering Teams in Financial Services. *Engineering Management Journal, 20*(1), 3–10.

Schienstock, G. (2004). Learning competition and business restructuring in the enlarging EU. *European Journal of Vocational Training, 33*(1), 23–29.

Schweitzer, S. J. (n.d.). *Discussion forums: The core of online communities of practice*. Retrieved December

7, 2008, from http://www.efios.com/kgarden/schweitzer597_project.pdf

Scott, A. J. (2000). *The cultural economy of cities: essays on the geography of image-producing industries.* London: Sage Publications.

Scott, P. B. (2005). Knowledge workers: social, task and semantic network analysis. *Corporate Communications: An International Journal, 10*(3), 257–277. doi:10.1108/13563280510614519

Searle, G., & Pritchard, B. (2004). *To cluster or not to cluster*? ANZRSAI Annual Conference, Sydney.

Setia Haruman Corporation. (2009). *Setia Haruman Sdn. Bhd: The master developer of Cyberjaya*. Retrieved May 11, 2009, from http://www.cyberjaya-msc.com/

Shachar, S. (2002). *Methods For Knowledge And Know-How Measurement.* MA Thesis, Faculty of Management, The Leon Recanati Graduate School of Business Administration. Tel-Aviv, Israel: Tel-Aviv University.

Shanghai Jiao Tong University. (2008). *Academic Ranking of World Universities.* Retrieved January 12, 2009, from http://www.arwu.org/rank2008/en2008.htm

Shapira, P., Youtie, J., Yogeesvaran, K., & Jaafar, Z. (2006). Knowledge Economy Measurement: Methods, Results, and Insights from the Malaysian Knowledge Content Study. *Research Policy, 35*, 1522–1537. doi:10.1016/j.respol.2006.09.015

Shapiro, J. M. (2005). *Smart cities: quality of life, productivity and the growth effects of human capital.* National Bureau of Economic Research.

Sharkie, R. (2003). Knowledge creation and its place in the development of sustainable competitive advantage. *Journal of Knowledge Management, 7*(1), 20–31. doi:10.1108/13673270310463590

Sharma, R., Ng, E., Dharmawirya, M., & Lee, C. (2008). Beyond the Digital Divide: A Conceptual Framework for Analyzing Knowledge Societies. *Journal of Knowledge Management, 12*(5), 151–164. doi:10.1108/13673270810903000

Sharp, J. (1997). *Key hypotheses in supporting communities of practice*. Retrieved December 7, 2008, from http://www.tfriend.com/hypothesis.html.

Shaver, J. M., & Flyer, F. (2000). Agglomeration economies, firm heterogeneity, and foreign direct investment in the United States. *Strategic Management Journal, 21*, 1175–1193. doi:10.1002/1097-0266(200012)21:12<1175::AID-SMJ139>3.0.CO;2-Q

Sheehan, P., & Tegart, G. (Eds.). (1998). *Working for the future*. Melbourne: Victoria University Press.

Shore, A. (1994). *Affect Regulation and the Origin of the Self: The Neurobiology of Emotional Development.* Mahway, NJ: Erlbaum.

Sidoli, J. (2000). *Think Like an Owner! Personal Knowledge Networking.* Retrieved March, 2009, from http://www.actlikeanowner.com/articles/default.asp

Siggelkow, N., & Levinthal, D. A. (2003). Temporarily divide to conquer: Centralized, decentralized, and reintegrated organizational approaches to exploration and adaptation. *Organization Science, 14*, 650–669.

Simmie, J. (2001). *Innovative Cities.* London: Spon Press.

Simmie, J., & Lever, W. F. (Eds.). (2002). Special Issue on 'The Knowledge-based City.' . *Urban Studies (Edinburgh, Scotland), 39*(5-6).

Simon, C. J. (1998). Human capital and metropolitan employment growth. *Journal of Urban Economics, 43*(2), 223–243. doi:10.1006/juec.1997.2048

Sin, L. Y. M., & Tse, A. C. B. (2000). How Does Marketing Effectiveness Mediate the Effect of Organizational Culture on Business Performance. The Case of Service Firms. *Journal of Services Marketing, 14*(4), 295–509. doi:10.1108/08876040010334510

Sin, L. Y., Tse, A. C., Yau, O. H., Lee, J. S., & Chow, R. (2002). The Effect of Relationship Marketing Orientation on Business Performance in a Service-oriented Economy. *Journal of Services Marketing, 16*(7), 656–676. doi:10.1108/08876040210447360

Singapore statistics department website. (n.d.). Retrieved December 1, 2007 from http://www.singstat.gov.sg/

Singapore. (2009). *Singapore Economic Development Board*. Retrieved January 10, 2009, from http://www.edb.gov.sg/edb/sg/en_uk/index.html

Skyrme, D. (1998). *Measuring the value of knowledge: Metrics for the knowledge-based business*. New York: Business Intelligence.

Skyrme, D., & Amidon, D. M. (1997). The Knowledge Agenda. *Journal of Knowledge Management, 1*(1), 27–37. doi:10.1108/13673279710800709

Slater, S. F., & Narver, J. C. (2000). Market Oriented is More Than Being Customer-Led. *Strategic Management Journal, 20*, 1165–1168. doi:10.1002/(SICI)1097-0266(199912)20:12<1165::AID-SMJ73>3.0.CO;2-#

Small, M. (1995). Rethinking Human Nature (Again). *Natural History, 104*(9), 8–24.

Smedlund, A., & Toivonen, M. (2007). The role of KIBS in the IC development of regional clusters. *Journal of Intellectual Capital, 8*(1), 159–170. doi:10.1108/14691930710715114

Smilor, R., Gibson, D., & Kozmetsky, G. (1988). Creating the Technopolis: High-technology Development in Austin. *Journal of Business Venturing, 4*, 49–67. doi:10.1016/0883-9026(89)90033-5

Smith, M. (2009 June). The Mancunian Nature. *Manchester Vinelife Newsletter*.

Smith, M. K. (2006). *Communities of practice*. Retrieved December 7, 2008, from http://www.infed.org/biblio/communities_of_practice.htm

Smith, W., & Kelly, S. (2003). Science, technical expertise and the human environment. *Progress in Planning, 60*, 321–394. doi:10.1016/S0305-9006(02)00119-8

Snow, C. C., Miles, R. E., & Coleman, H. J. Jr. (1992). Managing 21st century network organizations. *Organizational Dynamics, 20*(3), 5–21. doi:10.1016/0090-2616(92)90021-E

Snowden, D. (1999, November). The paradox of story: Simplicity and complexity in strategy. *Journal of Strategy & Scenario Planning*.

Soekijad, M., Huis in 't Veld, M., & Enserink, B. (2004). Learning and Knowledge Processes in Inter-organisational Communities of Practice. *Knowledge and Process Management, 11*(1), 3–12. doi:10.1002/kpm.191

S-one website. (n.d.). Retrieved June 13, 2007 from http://www.s-one.gov.sg

Spekman, R. E., Kamauff, J. W. Jr, & Myhr, N. (1998). An empirical investigation into supply chain management. *International Journal of Physical Distribution & Logistics Management, 28*(8), 630–650. doi:10.1108/09600039810247542

Sperling, B., & Sander, P. (2004). *Cities Ranked and Rated*. Hoboken, NJ: Wiley.

Spira, J. B. (2005). Managing The Knowledge Workforce: Understanding The Information Revolution That's Changing The Business World. *Lulu Press*. Retrieved June 6, 2009 from http://www.lulu.com

Spratt, T. (2007). Information Technology Portfolio Management: Search for Business Value. *Futurics, 31*(1/2), 42–45.

Squire, K., & Johnson, C. (2000). Supporting distributed communities of practice with interactive television. *Educational Technology Research and Development, 48*(1), 23–43. doi:10.1007/BF02313484

Srivastva, S., & Cooperrider, D. L. (Eds.). (1990). *Appreciative Management and Leadership*. San Francisco: Jossey-Bass.

Stahle, P. (Ed.). (2007). *Five steps for Finland's future*. Helsinki, Finland: TEKES.

Stanley, D. (2005 April). *Urban Surveillance: The Hidden Cost of Disneyland*. Paper presented at the University of Manchester Conference 'One size fits all?'

Sternberg, R. J., & Davidson, J. E. (Eds.). (1995). *The Nature of Insight*. Cambridge, MA: The MIT Press.

Stewart, T. A. (1997). *Intellectual Capital: The New Wealth of Organization.* New York: Doubleday/Currency.

Stimson, G. (1986). Viewpoint: Place and Space in Sociological Fieldwork. *The Sociological Review, 34*(3), 64–656.

Stolarick, K., Florida, R., & Musante, L. (Cartographer). (2005). *Montreal's capacity for creative connectivity: outlook and opportunities.* Catalix.

Stonier, T. (1990). *Information and the Internal Structure of the Universe: An Introduction into Information Physics.* New York: Springer-Verlag.

Stonier, T. (1997). *Information and Meaning: An Evolutionary Perspective.* New York: Springer.

Storey, J., & Quintas, P. (2001). Knowledge management and HRM . In Storey, J. (Ed.), *Human resource management: A critical text.* London: Thomson Learning.

Stromquist, N. P., Gil-Antón, M., Colatrella, C., Mabokela, R. O., Smolentseva, A., & Balbachevsky, E. (2007). The Contemporary Professoriate: Towards a Diversified or Segmented Profession? *Higher Education Quarterly, 61*(2), 114–135.doi:10.1111/j.1468-2273.2007.00342.x

Stuckey, B., & Smith, J. D. (2004). Building sustainable communities of practice . In Hildreth, P. M., & Kimble, C. (Eds.), *Knowledge Networks: Innovation through Communities of Practice*. Hershey, PA: Idea Group Publishing.

Sun, R. (2002). *Duality of the mind.* New Jersey: Lawrence Erlbaum associates.

Suokas, J. (2005). *Helsinki Regional Economy. A Dynamic City in the European Urban Network.* Helsinki City Urban Facts Office. Web publications 2005:41.

Suorsa, K. (2007). Regionality, innovation policy and peripheral regions in Finland, Sweden and Norway. *Fennia, 185*(1), 15–29.

Sveiby, K.-E. (1997). *The New Organizational Wealth: Managing & Measuring Knowledge-Based Assets.* San Francisco, CA: Berrett-Koehler.

Swan, J., Scarbrough, H., & Robertson, M. (2002). The Construction of 'Communities of Practice' in the Management of Innovation. *Management Learning, 33*(4), 477–496. doi:10.1177/1350507602334005

Swart, J. (2006). Intellectual capital: disentangling an enigmatic concept. *Journal of Intellectual Capital, 7*(2), 136–150.doi:10.1108/14691930610661827

Szulanski, G. (1996). Exploring internal stickiness: Impediments to the transfer of best practice within the firm. *Strategic Management Journal, 17*(1), 27–44.

Tallman, S., Jenkins, M., Henry, N., & Pinch, S. (2004). Knowledge, clusters and competitive advantage . *Academy of Management Review, 29*, 258–271.

Tan, H. P., Plowman, D., & Hancock, P. (2008). The evolving research on intellectual capital. *Journal of Intellectual Capital, 9*(4), 585–608.doi:10.1108/14691930810913177

Tan, K. Y. (1999). Public policies in the Singapore economy. In Adams, F. G., & James, W. E. (Eds.), *Public policies in East Asian development: facing new challenges.* London: Praeger.

Tanedu. (2007). *What is a knowledge society.* Retrieved February 3, 2008, from http://www.tanedu.org/index.php?option=com_content&task=view&id=76&Itemid=37

Tapscot, D. (2009). *Grown Up Digital.* New York: McGraw-Hill.

Tatikonda, M. V., & Stock, G. N. (2003). Product technology transfer in the upstream supply chain. *Journal of Product Innovation Management, 20*(6), 444–467. doi:10.1111/1540-5885.00042

Taylor, R. D. (2003). The Malaysia Experience: The Multimedia Super Corridor . In Jussawalla, M., & Taylor, R. D. (Eds.), *Information Technology Parks of the Asia Pacific.* New York: M.E Sharpe.

Teece, D. J., Pisano, G., & Shuen, A. (1997). Dynamic capabilities and strategic management. *Strategic Management Journal, 18*, 509–533. doi:10.1002/(SICI)1097-0266(199708)18:7<509::AID-SMJ882>3.0.CO;2-Z

Teo, S. T. T., Lakhani, B., Brown, D., & Malmi, T. (2008). Strategic human resource management and knowledge workers, A case study of professional service firms. *Management Research News*, *31*(9), 683–696. doi:10.1108/01409170810898572

Terziovski, M., & Morgan, J. P. (2006). Management practices and strategies to accelerate the innovation cycle in the biotechnology industry. *Technovation*, *26*(5-6), 545–552.doi:10.1016/j.technovation.2004.10.016

Thomas, B. S. (2002). *Understanding communities of practice*. Retrieved June 10, 2008, from http://www.totalkm.com/knxchanges/cop.html

Thompson, P., & Fox-Kean, M. (2005). Patent citations and the geography of knowledge spillovers: a reassessment. *The American Economic Review*, *95*, 450–460. doi:10.1257/0002828053828509

Thompson, R. (2000). Re-defining planning. *Planning Theory & Practice*, *1*(1), 126–133. doi:10.1080/14649350050135248

Thornton, W. H. (2000). Mapping the `Glocal' Village: The Political Limits of`Glocalization'. *Journal of Media & Cultural Studies*, *14*(1).

Thorpe, M. (2003). *Communities of practice and other frameworks for conceptualizing, developing and evaluating NCSL's initiatives in linking staff and school communities*. Unpublished report for the National College of School Leadership.

Tijssen, R. J. W. (2006). Universities and industrially relevant science: towards measurement models and indicators of entrepreneurial orientation. *Research Policy*, *35*, 1569–1585. doi:10.1016/j.respol.2006.09.025

Toh, M. H., Tang, H. C., & Choo, A. (2003). *Mapping Singapore's knowledge-based economy in APEC 2003. The drivers of new economy in APEC – innovation and organizational practices*. Singapore: APEC Secretariat.

Torre, A., & Gilly, J. P. (2000). On the analytical dimension of proximity dynamics. *Regional Studies*, *34*, 169–180. doi:10.1080/00343400050006087

Torre, A., & Rallet, A. (2005). Proximity and localization. *Regional Studies*, *39*, 47–59. doi:10.1080/0034340052000320842

Trajtenberg, M. (2001). Innovation in Israel 1968-97: a comparative analysis using patent data. *Research Policy*, *30*, 363–390. doi:10.1016/S0048-7333(00)00089-5

Triantis, A. (2005). Corporate Risk Management: Real Options and Financial Hedging. In Frenkel, M., Hommel, U., & Rudolf, M. (Eds.), *Risk Management: Challenge and Opportunity* (pp. 591–608). New York: Springer.

Tucker, E., Kao, T., & Verma, N. (2005). Next-Generation Talent Management: Insights on How Workforce Trends are changing the Face of Talent Management. *Business Credit*, *107*(7), 20–27.

Tuomi, I. (2004). *Future challenges of the European knowledge society*. Discussion paper presented at Institute for Prospective Technological Studies, IPTS, 11 August 2004. Retrieved from http://www.meaningprocessing.com/personalPages/tuomi/articles/TheFutureOfLearningInThe KnowledgeSociety.pdf

Tushman, M. L. (1997). Special boundary roles in the innovation process. *Administrative Science Quarterly*, *22*, 587–605. doi:10.2307/2392402

Tushman, M. L., & Katz, R. (1980). External communication and project performance: an investigation into the role of gatekeepers. *Management Science*, *26*, 1071–1085. doi:10.1287/mnsc.26.11.1071

Uzzi, B. (1997). Social structure and competition in interfirm networks: the paradox of embeddedness. *Administrative Science Quarterly*, *42*, 37–69.

Vaattovaara, M., & Kortteinen, M. (2003). Beyond polarisation versus professionalisation? A case study of the development of the Helsinki region, Finland. *Urban Studies (Edinburgh, Scotland)*, *40*(11), 2127–2145. doi:10.1080/0042098032000123213

Van Beveren, J. (2002). A Model of Knowledge Acquisition that Refocuses Knowledge Management. *Journal of Knowledge Management*, *6*(1), 18–22. doi:10.1108/13673270210417655

Van Doren, C. (1992). *A history of knowledge: past, present and future*. Toronto, Canada: Random House Publishing.

Van Wezemael, J. (2008). Knowledge creation in urban development praxis . In Yigitcanlar, T., Velibeyoglu, K., & Baum, S. (Eds.), *Knowledge-Based Urban Development* (pp. 1–20). Hershey, PA: Information Science Reference.

Van Winkelen, C. (2003). *Inter-organisational communities of practice*. Retrieved December 7, 2008, from http://www.elearningeuropa.info/directory/index.php?page=doc&doc_id=1483&doclng=6

Vassolo, R. S., Anand, J., & Folta, T. (2004). Non-additivity in portfolios of exploration activities: a real options-based analysis of equity alliances in biotechnology. *Strategic Management Journal, 25*, 1045–1061. doi:10.1002/smj.414

Vence-Deza, X., & Gonzalez-Lopez, M. (2008). Regional concentration of the knowledge-based economy in the EU: towards a renewed oligocentric model? *European Planning Studies, 16*(4), 557–578. doi:10.1080/09654310801983472

Venkatraman, N., & Ramanujan, V. (1986). Measurement of Business Performance in Strategy Research: A Comparison of Approaches. *Academy of Management Review, 11*(4), 801–814. doi:10.2307/258398

Verstal, W. C., & Lopez, K. (2004). Best practices: Developing communities that provide business value . In Hildreth, P. M., & Kimble, C. (Eds.), *Knowledge Networks: Innovation through Communities of Practice*. Hershey, PA: Idea Group Publishing.

Vesala, J. (2001). *Technological Transformation and Retail Banking Competition: Implications and Measurement. Acta Universitatis Oeconomicae Helsingiensis A 184*. Helsinki: Helsinki School of Economics and Business Administration.

Vestal, W. (2006). *Sustaining communities of practice*. Retrieved December 7, 2008, from http://www.kmworld.com/Articles/ReadArticle.aspx?ArticleID=15159&PageNum=4.

Von Krogh, G., Ichijo, K., & Nonaka, I. (2000). *Enabling knowledge creation: How to unlock the mystery of tacit knowledge and release the power of innovation*. New York: Oxford University Press.

Wallman, S., & Blair, M. (2000). *UnSeen Wealth: Report of the Brookings Taskforce on Understanding Intangible Sources of Value*. Washington, DC: The Brooking Institution.

Walsham, G. (2001). Knowledge management: the benefits and limitations of computer systems. *European Management Journal, 19*(6), 599–608. doi:10.1016/S0263-2373(01)00085-8

Wang, E. T. G., & Wei, H.-L. (2007). Interorganizational governance value creation: Coordinating for information visibility and flexibility in supply chains. *Decision Sciences, 38*(4), 647–674.

Wang, Z., & Pan, D. (2005). Framework for Virtual Knowledge City: A Case of City Dalian, China. In *Proceedings of the First World Congress of the International Federation for Systems Research: The New Roles of Systems Sciences For a Knowledge-based Society*, Kobe, Japan.

Ward, K. (2003). Entrepreneurial urbanism, state restructuring and civilizing 'New' East Manchester. *Area, 35*(2), 116–127. doi:10.1111/1475-4762.00246

Warhurst, C. (2008). The knowledge economy, skills and government labour market intervention. *Policy Studies, 29*(1), 71–86.doi:10.1080/01442870701848053

Wartburg, I. V., Teichert, T., & Rost, K. (2005). Inventive progress measured by multi-stage patent citation analysis. *Research Policy, 34*, 1591–1607. doi:10.1016/j.respol.2005.08.001

Wasko, M. M., & Faraj, S. (2000). It is what one does: why people participate and help others in electronic CoP. *The Journal of Strategic Information Systems, 9*, 155–173. doi:10.1016/S0963-8687(00)00045-7

Wayne, S., Shore, L., & Liden, R. (1997). Perceived organizational support and leader member exchange: A social exchange perspective. *Academy of Management*

Journal, *40*(1), 82–111. doi:10.2307/257021

Wei, K. K., & Nair, M. (2006). The Effects of Customer Service Management on Business Performance in Malaysian Banking Industry: An Empirical Analysis. *Asia Pacific Journal of Marketing and Logistics*, *18*(2), 111–128. doi:10.1108/13555850610658264

Weick, K. E. (1990). Organizational culture as a source of high reliability. *California Management Review*, *29*(2), 112–127.

Wenger, E. (1996). *Communities of practice. The social fabric of a learning organisation*. Retrieved December 7, 2008, from http://www.ewenger.com/pub/pubhealthcareforum.htm

Wenger, E. (2001). *Supporting communities of practice. A survey of community-oriented technologies*. Retrieved April 4, 2008, from http://www.ewenger.com/theory/communities_of_practice_intro.htm

Wenger, E. (n.d.). *Communities of practice: a brief introduction*. Retrieved August 23, 2008, from http://www.ewenger.com/theory/communities_of_practice_intro.htm

Wenger, E., & Snyder, W. (2000a). Communities of practice: the organisation frontier. *Harvard Business Review*, 139–145.

Wenger, E., & Snyder, W. (2000b). *Learning in communities*. Retrieved February 12, 2008, from http://www.linezine.com/1/features/ewwslc.htm

Wenger, E., McDermott, R., & Snyder, W. M. (2002). *Cultivating communities of practice: A guide to managing knowledge*. United States of America: Library of Congress Cataloging-in-Publication Data.

Wepner, S., & Mobley, M. (1998). Reaping new harvests: Collaboration and communication through field experiences. *Action in Teacher Education*, *20*(3), 50–61.

Wernerfelt, B. (1984). A Resource-based View of the Firm. *Strategic Management Journal*, *5*, 171–180. doi:10.1002/smj.4250050207

Wesley, P. W., & Buysse, V. (2001). Communities of practice: expanding professional roles to promote reflection and shared inquiry. *Topics in Early Childhood Special Education*, *21*(2). doi:10.1177/027112140102100205

West, A. (1992). *Innovation Strategy*. Englewood Cliff, NJ: Prentice-Hall.

Westlund, H. (2006). *Social capital in the knowledge economy*. Berlin: Springer-Verlag.

Wig, E. H. (1993). The role of language in learning disabilities. In Spectrum of Developmental Disabilities XIV: ADD, ADHD and LD (pp. 139-154). The Johns Hopkins School of Medicine. Parkton, MD: York Press.

Wiig, K. M. (1995). *Knowledge Management Methods: Practical Approaches to Managing Knowledge*. Arlington, TX: Schema Press.

William, R. (1984). *State culture and beyond: culture and the state* (Appignanesi, L., Ed.). London: Institute of Contemporary Arts.

Williamson, O. E. (1999). Strategy research: governance and competence perspectives. *Strategic Management Journal*, *20*, 1087–1108. doi:10.1002/(SICI)1097-0266(199912)20:12<1087::AID-SMJ71>3.0.CO;2-Z

Wilson, E. O. (1998). The Biological Basis of Morality. *Atlantic Monthly*, *281*(4), 53–70.

Wilson, M., & Corey, K. (2008). The alert model . In Yigitcanlar, T., Velibeyoglu, K., & Baum, S. (Eds.), *Knowledge-Based Urban Development* (pp. 82–100). Hershey, PA: Information Science Reference.

Wolff, E. N. (2003). Skills and Changing Comparative Advantage. *The Review of Economics and Statistics*, *85*(1), 77–93.doi:10.1162/003465303762687721

Wong, P. K. (2004). *The information society and the developmental state: the Singapore model*. Singapore: National University of Singapore (NUS) Entrepreneurship Centre Working Papers.

Wong, P. K., & Singh, A. (2004). Country survey report: Singapore. Report prepared for ECLAC/IDE (JETRO) joint project, comparative study on East Asian and Latin American IT industries.

Wong, P. K., Lee, L., Ho, Y. P., & Wong, F. (2004). *Global entrepreneurship monitor GEM: highlights in Singapore*. Singapore: NUS Entrepreneurship Centre.

Wong, P. K., Lee, L., Ho, Y. P., & Wong, F. (2006). *Global entrepreneurship monitor GEM: 2005 Singapore report*. Singapore: National University of Singapore Entrepreneurship Centre.

Woolfolk, E. A. (1990). *Psicología Educativa*. Ciudad de México, México: Prentice Hall Hispanoamericana.

Work Foundation. (2002). *Manchester: Ideopolis?* London: The Work Foundation.

Work Foundation. (2006). *Manchester: Creating the Ideopolis*. Knowledge City Consortium Research Project. Retrieved from http://www.theworkfoundation.com/research/ideopolis.jsp

World Bank. (2002). *Global Development Learning Network*. Retrieved from http://www.globalknowledge.org/

World Bank-knowledge assessment methodology. (n.d.). Retrieved January 20, 2007 from http://www.worldbank.org/kam

World Capital Institute. (2009). Retrieved December 11, 2008, from http://www.worldcapitalinstitute.org/makci.html

Worthington, B. (2002). *Discovering Manchester*. Cheshire, UK: Sigma Press. Retrieved from www.sigmapress.co.uk

Wuyts, S., Colombo, M. G., Dutta, S., & Noteboom, B. (2005). Empirical tests of optimal cognitive distance. *Journal of Economic Behavior & Organization*, *58*, 277–302. doi:10.1016/j.jebo.2004.03.019

Wynarczyk, P. (2000). The role of digital networks in supply chain development. *New Technology, Work and Employment*, *15*(2), 123–137. doi:10.1111/1468-005X.00069

Regeneris Consulting. (2005 March). *North West Economic Baseline: a Report to the North West Development Agency* (NWDA). Retrieved April 18, 2005, from http://www.regeneris.co.uk

Yang, L. B. (Minister for Information, Communications and the Arts, Singapore). (2007, August 28). *MICA press release*. Presented at the 2007 creative industries scholarships award ceremony. Retrieved October 10, 2007 from http://www.mica.gov.sg/pressroom/press_070828.htm

Yearbook of Statistics Singapore. 2009. Retrieved 17 January, 2010 from http://www.singstat.gov.sg/pubn/reference/yos.html

Yeh, H. (2008). A knowledge value creation model for knowledge-intensive procurement projects. *Journal of Manufacturing Technology Management*, *19*(7), 871–892. doi:10.1108/17410380810898796

Yigitcanlar, T. (2007). The making of urban spaces for the knowledge economy . In Al-Furaih, I., & Sahab, A. (Eds.), *Knowledge cities* (pp. 73–97). Selangor, Malaysia: Scholar Press.

Yigitcanlar, T. (2007). The making of urban spaces for the knowledge economy: global practices. In Al-Furaih, I., Sahab, A., Hayajneh, A., Abdullah, A., Ibrahim, M., & Thalha, M. (Eds.), *Knowledge cities: future of cities in the knowledge economy* (pp. 73–97). Selangor, Malaysia: Scholar Press.

Yigitcanlar, T. (2008). Knowledge-based development of creative urban regions: global perspectives for local actions. In Knowledge International Week, Ibero-American Community for Knowledge Systems, 29-31 Oct. 2008, Manizales, Colombia (pp. 305-324).

Yigitcanlar, T. (2008b). *Knowledge-based development of creative urban regions: global perspectives for local actions*. Keynote Presentation for Latin American Knowledge Week, October 27-Nov 1, Manizales, Colombia. Retrieved from http://www.semanadeconocimiento/info

Yigitcanlar, T. Velibeyoglu, K., & Baum, S. (Eds.). (2008a). Creative urban regions: harnessing urban technologies to support knowledge city initiatives. Hershey, PA: IGI Global.

Yigitcanlar, T., & Velibeyoglu, K. (2008). Queensland's Smart State Initiative: A Successful Knowledge-Based Urban Development Strategy? In Yigitcanlar, T., Velibeyoglu, K., & Baum, S. (Eds.), *Knowledge-Based Urban Development: Planning and Applications in the information Era* (pp. 116–131). New York: Information Science Reference.

Yigitcanlar, T., & Velibeyoglu, K. (2008a). Knowledge-based urban development: local economic development path of Brisbane, Australia. *Local Economy, 23*(3), 197–209. doi:10.1080/02690940802197358

Yigitcanlar, T., & Velibeyoglu, K. (2008b). Knowledge-based strategic planning: harnessing (in)tangible assets of city-regions. In *Proceedings of the 3rd International Forum on Knowledge Asset Dynamics*, 26-27 June 2008, Matera, Italy (pp. 296-306).

Yigitcanlar, T., & Velibeyoglu, K. (2008c). Engineering creative urban regions for knowledge city formation: knowledge-based urban development experience of Brisbane, Australia. In *the Proceedings of the 3rd International Symposium on Knowledge Cities*, 17-19 Nov 2008, Istanbul, Turkey.

Yigitcanlar, T., Baum, S., & Horton, S. (2007). Attracting and retaining knowledge workers in knowledge cities. *Journal of Knowledge Management, 11*(5), 6–17. doi:10.1108/13673270710819762

Yigitcanlar, T., OConnor, K., & Westerman, C. (2008). The making of knowledge cities: Melbourne's knowledge-based urban development experience. *Cities (London, England), 25*(2), 63–72. doi:10.1016/j.cities.2008.01.001

Yigitcanlar, T., Velibeyoglu, K., & Baum, S. (2008). *Knowledge-based Urban Development: planning and applications in the information era.* New York: Information Science Reference.

Yigitcanlar, T., Velibeyoglu, K., & Martinez-Fernandez, C. (2008). Rising knowledge cities: The role of urban knowledge precincts. *Journal of Knowledge Management: Towards a global knowledge-based development agenda, 12*(5), 8-20.

Young, H. P. (2003). The Diffusion of Innovations in Social Networks. In L.E.

YTV. (2003). *Helsinki Metropolitan Area Vision 2025 – Summary.* Helsinki: Helsinki Metropolitan Area Council.

Zack, M. H. (1999). Developing a knowledge strategy. *California Management Review, 4*(3).

Zack, M. H. (1999). *Knowledge and Strategy.* Boston, MA: Butterworth-Heinemann.

Zhu, H., Hitt, M. A., & Tihanyi, L. (2006). The internationalization of SMEs in emerging economies: Institutional embeddedness and absorptive capacities. *Journal of Small Business Strategy, 17*(2), 1–26.

Zolnik, E. (2008). Biotechnology and knowledge-based urban development in DNA Valley . In Yigitcanlar, T., Velibeyoglu, K., & Baum, S. (Eds.), *Knowledge-Based Urban Development* (pp. 171–184). Hershey, PA: Information Science Reference.

Zook, M. A. (2004, September). The Knowledge Brokers: Venture Capitalists, Tacit Knowledge and Regional Development. *International Journal of Urban and Regional Research*, 621–641. doi:10.1111/j.0309-1317.2004.00540.x

Zucker, L. G., Darby, M. R., & Armstrong, J. S. (2002). Commercializing knowledge: university, science, knowledge capture, and firm performance in biotechnology. *Management Science, 48*, 138–153. doi:10.1287/mnsc.48.1.138.14274

About the Contributors

Kostas Metaxiotis is Assistant Professor at the University of Piraeus and Senior Advisor to the Secretary for the Information Society in the Greek Ministry of Economy and Finance since 2004. He has wide experience in knowledge management, artificial intelligence, enterprise information systems, inference mechanisms, e-government, e-business. He has published more than 70 scientific papers in various journals and conferences, such as Journal of Knowledge Management, Journal of Information and Knowledge Management, Knowledge Management & Practice, Journal of Intelligent Manufacturing, Applied Artificial Intelligence, Industrial Management & Data Systems, Journal of Computer Information Systems, etc. Dr. Metaxiotis is the Editor-in-Chief of the *International Journal of Knowledge Based Development*. Since 1996 he has been participating in various European Commission (EC)-funded projects within Tacis, Phare, MEDA and IST Programmes as Senior ICT Consultant and Manager. Since 2007 he has been serving as External Evaluator of EC-funded ICT projects.

Francisco Javier Carrillo is an international consultant and Professor of Knowledge Management at Tecnológico de Monterrey, México, he is regarded as a world leader in *Knowledge Cities* and *Knowledge Based Development*. He published in 2005 the book *Knowledge Cities* and is editor since 2002 of the annual Special Issue on *Knowledge Based Development* for the *Journal of Knowledge Management* and general co-editor of the upcoming *International Journal of Knowledge Based Development*. Founder in 1992 and Director of the *Center for Knowledge Systems* www.sistemasdeconocimiento.org where he has lead nearly a hundred contracted projects. President of the *World Capital Institute* www.worldcapitalinstitute.org (organizer of the Most Admired Knowledge City *-MAKCI- Awards*, and the *Knowledge Cities Summit*), founder and Honorary President of the *Iberoamerican Community for Knowledge Systems* www.iberoamericana.org. He holds a Ph.D. in Psychology of Science and Technology (King's Coll., London), an M.Sc. in Logic and Scientific Method (LSE) and an M.Sc, in Experimental Analysis of Behavior (UNAM).

Tan Yigitcanlar is a senior lecturer in urban and regional planning at the Queensland University of Technology in Australia. He has a multi-disciplinary background and extensive work experience in private consulting, government and academia. The focus of his research is promoting knowledge-based and sustainable urban development. He has been responsible for a wide variety of teaching, training and capacity building programmes on urban planning, environmental science, policy analysis and information and communication technologies in Turkish, Japanese and Australian universities. He is the Editor-in-Chief of the International Journal of Knowledge Based Development.

* * *

Tooran Alizadeh is a PhD student at University of Sydney. Her research has focused on the interaction between the new technology and new urban form. Her PhD research concerns with the possibilities that the new telecommunication technologies provide for residential communities to adjust with the different life-style of information-workers and play a productive role in the knowledge-based economy. This study has been based upon her Master thesis in urban design and planning which developed an IT oriented urban design guideline to address the opportunities that the digital revolution has provided to rethink the design of urban environments. She has several years' professional design and planning practice experience, working for the leading firms in her home country Iran, and has been involved with some teaching experience in the University of Sydney regarding local and regional economic development and urban planning.

Alex Bennet is co-founder of the Mountain Quest Institute, a research and retreat center nestled in the Allegheny Mountains of West Virginia focused on achieving growth and understanding through questions for knowledge, consciousness and meaning. She is co-author of the seminal work, *Organizational Survival in the New World: The Intelligent Complex Adaptive System* (Elsevier, 2004), a new theory of the firm based on research in complexity and neuroscience and incorporating networking theory and knowledge management. More recently he worked with the government of Canada to co-author and publish *Knowledge Mobilization in the Social Sciences and Humanities: Moving from Research to Action* (MQIPress, 2007). Dr. Bennet served as the Chief Knowledge Officer for the U.S. Department of the Navy (DON), and was co-chair of the Federal KM Working Group. She is the recipient of the DON Distinguished and Superior Public Service Awards. Dr. Bennet has degrees in Human and Organizational Systems, Human Development, Management for Organizational Effectiveness, English and Marketing.

David Bennet is co-founder of the Mountain Quest Institute, a research and retreat center nestled in the Allegheny Mountains of West Virginia focused on achieving growth and understanding through questions for knowledge, consciousness and meaning. He is co-author of the seminal work, *Organizational Survival in the New World: The Intelligent Complex Adaptive System* (Elsevier, 2004), a new theory of the firm based on research in complexity and neuroscience and incorporating networking theory and knowledge management. More recently he worked with the government of Canada to co-author and publish *Knowledge Mobilization in the Social Sciences and Humanities: Moving from Research to Action* (MQIPress, 2007). Dr. Bennet's experience spans many years of service in the Military, Civil Service and Private Industry, including fundamental research in underwater acoustics and nuclear physics and frequent design and facilitation of organizational interventions. Most recently, he was CEO, then Chairman of the Board and Chief Knowledge Officer of a professional services firm. Dr. Bennet has degrees in Physics, Mathematics, Nuclear Physics, Human and Organizational Systems, Human Development, and Liberal Arts.

Sheryl Buckley is Deputy Head of Department in the Department of Business Information Technology (BIT) at the University of Johannesburg (UJ). Her passion lies in the Information Science discipline. Before joining the University in 2000, Sheryl taught at a High School for ten years and later at a Technical College for ten years. Sheryl is a member of CSSA, IKMS, SAICIT and ISOC-ZA. She is a committee member of a number of international organisations such as ECKM09, ECEI09 and ICICK09 as well as an active peer reviewer. She has presented papers locally, internationally and published in an international journal. Sheryl has recently submitted her doctoral thesis for examination, titled: Knowledge sharing through communities of practice at institutions of higher education.

Sébastien Darchen is professor in Urban and Regional Planning (CLA) at York University (Toronto). He has completed his postdoctoral studies at the Canada Research Chair on the Socio-Economic Challenges of the Knowledge Economy (Montreal) as well as his PhD in Urban Studies at the Institut National de la Recherche Scientifique-Urbanisation, Culture et Société (Montreal). He has also been part-time lecturer at the Department of Geography, Planning and Envrionment (Concordia University) and at the Institut d'Urbanisme (Université de Montréal). His research concerns the field of economic development as well as the study of stakeholders' strategies in the urban development process.

Timothy Donnet is a PhD candidate at Queensland University of Technology's School of Management. His current research on the governance of airport-local urban development is in affiliation to the international research collaboration known as the Airport Metropolis Project, run out of Queensland University of Technology's Faculty for Built Environment and Engineering. His research interests also include knowledge transfer processes within and between clusters of small and medium sized enterprises. He was recently published as a co-author in a research report made on behalf of the Dutch Commission for Spatial Development for Airports (Commissie Raumtelijke Ontwikkeling Luchthavens), and recently had a conference paper on airport privatisation published in a book of selected papers for the 10th Annual TRAIL Congress, Rotterdam.

Emmanouil Ergazakis holds a degree in Mechanical Engineering from the National Technical University of Athens (NTUA). Currently, he is a PhD student at the School of Electrical and Computer Engineering of NTUA. His research interests include decision support systems, artificial intelligence, knowledge management, e-government etc.

Kostas Ergazakis holds a degree in Electrical and Computer Engineering from the National Technical University of Athens (NTUA). He also holds a PhD degree in decision support systems and knowledge management. He is a senior researcher at the School of Electrical and Computer Engineering (NTUA). His research interests include: knowledge-based development, knowledge management, artificial intelligence, management information systems etc.

Blanca Garcia holds a Development Policy Research Fellowship at Northern Borderlands Research College (Colef. Monterrey, Mexico). Blanca is a Human Resources Developer and Learning Technologist dedicated to the facilitation, creation and research of e-learning and knowledge-generative environments through the fostering of networking opportunities in the workplace. She focuses on supporting workplace learners challenged by demanding knowledge-based development (KBD) processes in their institutions and regions. In terms of KBD interests, Blanca presently participates in the international consultation exercise MAKCI (Most Admired Knowledge City Awards) as facilitator and technical secretary, and has contributed with K-Cities case studies for a number of publications on KBD topics, such as the Journal of Knowledge Management, and the seminal Knowledge Cities book, edited by F.J. Carrillo under the Elsevier-Heinemann flag.

Apostolos Giannakopoulos was born in Greece, Pyrgos Ilias, and after matriculating came to South Africa, where he received his B.Sc degree majoring in mathematics. After his diploma in machine design he worked as a designer for more than ten years. In 1980 he joined education. Since then he obtained his B.Ed and M.Ed and currently busy with his D.Ed. He taught in high schools, teachers training college and at the present University of Johannesburg since 1990. He is a believer of pragmatism driven by mathematico-logical passion giving rise to what he calls "a psycho-pragmatic" approach to everything. He has presented his creative ideas to a number of international and national conferences on mathematics, information technology, and knowledge management. He has also written mathematics textbooks and co-authored others.

Tommi Inkinen is currently a Professor of Human Geography at the Department of Geography, the University of Helsinki, Finland. His research interests primarily cover the issues of economic geography, including the regional structuring of innovation systems, technology implementation and networks, as well as logistics and transport. He is a steering group member of the International Geographical Union's (IGU) Information Society Commission and the Secretary of the Finnish Geographical Society.

Kristine Peta Jerome is a Senior Lecturer in the School of Design at the Queensland University of Technology, Australia. Her main research interests explore the way the physical domain contributes to the maintenance of institutional structures and social order. Currently, she is using a case of McDonald's restaurants to investigate how the built environment contributes to the perpetuation of the social phenomenon of globalisation. This includes documenting new and old models of McDonald's restaurants across Australia. Kristine's teaching interests explore these kinds of relationships in the discipline of Interior Design. She has been awarded a number of grants from state and federal governments concerning the relationship between space and social order and these continue to inform social policies.

Gulgun Kayakutlu is an Assistant Professor of Operations Research at Industrial Engineering Department of Istanbul Technical University (I.T.U.). She holds a B.Sc. and M.Sc. in Industrial Engineering from Middle East Technical University (METU) Ankara and a PhD in Engineering Management completed in Marmara University, Istanbul. She has management experiences in Sybase Turkey, Hurriyet Holding Turkey and TES Software Turkey. She has developed the information technology expertise in seven years spent in International Energy Agency/OECD, Paris, France. Dr. Kayakutlu's research interests include knowledge management, intelligent systems, regional innovation, supply chain management and renewable energy fields. She has published in Supply Chain and Energy journals. She has been a visiting Professor in the industrial engineering department of SIUE Edwardsville, IL for the academic year of 2008/09.

Robyn Keast is a Senior Lecturer in the School of Management, Faculty of Business and Director of Research for the Airport Metropolis Project in Built Environment and Engineering Faculty at QUT. She has wide experience having worked across industry sectors including construction, creative industries, business and social services. Her research portfolio is diverse ranging from networks and collaboration, governance arrangements; community engagement; technology parks and innovation clusters and more recently to supply chain relationships, urban governance and social infrastructure. She is widely published in a number of prestigious international journals and texts including Public Administration

Review, Policy and Politics and Construction Engineering and Management. Dr Keast has been the recipient of several research and publication awards.

Christina Martinez-Fernandez is a Policy Analyst at the Organisations for Economic Co-operation and Development (OECD), Centre for Entrepreneurship, SMEs and Local Economic Development, 'LEED' program (Paris) where she is investigating policy implications of skills and development strategies in firms, as it regards to the transition of labour force into the knowledge economy, and in OECD and South-East Asian countries. Prior to this role Dr Martinez-Fernandez was an Associate Professor at the Urban Research Centre, UWS, where she led the research program on Urban and Regional Dynamics focused on the study of processes of growth and shrinkage, and policies and strategies that influence these processes and outcomes. The analysis of industry change, urban performance and socio-economic development in urban areas is strongly anchored within the innovation imperative and the impact of global factors in cities and regions. She is also an invited Professor to the Institute of Geography, University Paris 1 Pantheon-Sorbonne (Paris) and to the University of California (Berkeley).

América Martínez Sánchez has received her Ph.D. in Educational Innovation with a Knowledge Management concentration area at ITESM, Virtual University, 2007. She is Coordinator of Human Capital Technical Area in the Center for Knowledge Systems. She has participated in the design, management and implementation of different projects with a focus on Knowledge Based Value Systems. Her teaching experience has been focused on the area of Knowledge Management at postgraduate and bachelor levels as a professor researcher in Tecnológico de Monterrey. She has also participated in the design of learning courses, workshops and specialized modules on Knowledge Management and Human Capital taught in specialized courses.

Norizan Mat Saad is currently a lecturer in marketing at Universiti Sains Malaysia, Penang, Malaysia. He earned his Ph.D., from the Management Centre, University of Bradford, UK, MBA from the University of Hull, UK and BBA (Hons) in marketing from Coventry University, UK. He has published scholarly papers in internationally refereed journals and proceedings. In summation, there are five journals published including two published under widely cited Emerald journals. It should be noted, that one article has been published in European Journal of Marketing. As an acknowledgement, EJM is one of the most referred international journals in marketing area and is included in ISI Social Sciences Citation Index recently. Dr Norizan has also published about twenty articles in international conferences. These include the presentations in two reputed international marketing conferences; i.e., American Marketing Association (AMA) Educators conference and European Marketing Educators Conference (EMAC).

Antonio Petruzzelli Messeni got the laurea degree in Business Engineering at the Politecnico di Bari. After a two years period as organizational analyst at Eni SpA, he got the PhD in Innovation Management at same university. Visiting scholar at the IESE Business School and research fellow at the Politecnico di Bari, his research interests mainly concern the area of innovation management, including themes such as knowledge creation and transfer, university-industry relationships, proximity, system dynamics modelling, and input-output analysis. In these topics he has published several articles on international journals and presented paper at international conferences.

Edna Pasher earned her Ph.D at New York University in Communication Arts and Sciences from the Media Ecology Program and has served as faculty member at Adelphi University, the City University of New York, the Hebrew University in Jerusalem and the Tel-Aviv University, where she is still teaching. Edna Pasher founded an international strategic management consulting firm in 1978. The firm provides customized consulting services to organizations both in the private and the public sectors. Edna has been a pioneer and leader of the innovation and knowledge management movement in Israel and an active member of the international community of the Knowledge Management and Intellectual Capital Pioneers. She has over 30 years of experience in regional and international ICT R&D projects using a variety of evaluation methodologies, modeling techniques and quantitative and qualitative analysis. Edna is a frequent speaker in national and international conferences and a founding member of the New Club of Paris.

David Pickernell is Head of the Welsh Enterprise Institute and Reader in European and International Business at the University of Glamorgan Business School. He is also Adjunct Professor in the School of Management at Queensland University of Technology in Brisbane Australia. He has had over 50 articles published in refereed journals, given over 30 conference papers and had a number of chapters in edited books. His research areas encompass Foreign Direct Investment and Local-Global interactions, Economic Integration, Clusters and Networks, Regional Economic Development Policy, Construction, Universities and economic development, innovation, festivals and events in social enterprise and capital building, as well as socio-economic effects of gambling. He has also undertaken research and consultancy for a range of organisations, including the OECD, EU, Welsh Assembly Government, Queensland Government, Victorian Government (Australia), Welsh Development Agency, Cardiff Council, Council of Mortgage Lenders, Associated British Ports, Shaw Trust, and the Federation of Small Businesses.

Baharom Abdul Rahman is currently lecturing office and business management at MARA University of Technology, Shah Alam, Malaysia. He earned his PhD. from Universiti Sains Malaysia, MBE from the University of Toledo, USA, and has a Bachelor's Degree in Business Education from Bolwing Green State University, USA. He has presented a number of papers in national and international proceedings.

Rabee Reffat is currently an Associate Professor at the Architecture Department, KFUPM, Saudi Arabia. One of the research interests of Dr. Reffat is knowledge management and e-government. Dr. Reffat's research work is published at various international refereed journals and international refereed conferences held at more than 20 countries worldwide. Dr. Reffat has published one edited book, three book chapters and over 60 refereed journal and conference papers. Dr. Reffat has successfully managed and completed research projects funded by Australian Research Council, University of Sydney and the CRC (Cooperative Research Centers) in Australia; and KFUPM and KACST in Saudi Arabia. Dr. Reffat is an international consultant to both governmental agencies and private businesses in areas related to his diverse expertise.

Mahmod Sabri Haron is currently a lecturer in marketing at Universiti Sains Malaysia, Penang, Malaysia. He earned his PhD. from the University of Bradford, UK. He got his BBA and MBA in International Business from the University of Bridgeport, Connecticut, USA. He has published scholarly papers in internationally refereed journals and proceedings. Dr. Mahmod is also currently undertaking a number of research with the Government of Malaysia.

Muna Sarimin is a lecturer at the Department of Town and Regional Planning, Faculty of Architecture, MARA University of Technology, Shah Alam, Selangor, Malaysia. She graduated with a Bachelor of City and Regional Planning (Hons) in 1996 and MSc in International Planning Practice in 1998; both from the University of Cardiff, Wales, UK. She is also a graduate member of Malaysian Institute of Planners (MIP) since 2005. Presently, she is pursuing her PhD degree at the School of Urban Development, Faculty of Built Environment and Engineering, Queensland University of Technology, Brisbane, Australia. Her research interest lies on the issues related Knowledge Based Urban Development, Knowledge Economy and Urban Planning, Urban Economics and Sustainable Urban Development.

Sigal Shachar earned her MA. in Organizational Behavior at Tel-Aviv University, Israel. Her thesis researched methods for measuring knowledge in organizations. Mrs Shachar is a management consultant and researcher in knowledge measurements projects within regions, states, and organizations. In addition, she is an experienced lecturer and group instructor in the fields of management, innovation, and creativity. She conducted, alongside with Edna Pasher, two Intellectual Capital Assessments for the state of Israel, in 2004 and in 2007. These assessments were based on the Skandia Navigator model of Prof. Leif Edvinsson.

JC Spender is currently Visiting Professor at the School of Economics and Management, Lund University (Sweden) and Visiting Professor ESADE/Universitat Ramon Llull (Spain). His PhD thesis 'Industry Recipes' (Blackwell, 1989), which examined managers' uncertainty handling procedures in three different industries, won the US Academy of Management's 1980 AT Kearney Prize. He has served on the faculties of City University (London), York University (Toronto), UCLA, University of Glasgow, and the Chair of Entrepreneurship and Small Business at Rutgers (New Jersey). His principal work is on Knowledge Management and Corporate Strategy. The focus is on the management and industry responses to uncertainty - meaning (a) the absence of key strategic data, and (b) difficulties with making actionable sense of the data available.

Diane-Gabrielle Tremblay is professor of labour economics at the Télé-université of the University of Québec in Montréal, Canada; she has been appointed Canada Research Chair on the socio-economic challenges of the Knowledge Economy in 2002 (http://www.teluq.uqam.ca/chaireecosavoir/) and is director of the research center CURA on work-life balance over the lifecourse. She has been invited professor at the Sorbonne-Paris I, and Universities of Lille 3, Angers, Toulouse, Lyon 3, Louvain-la-Neuve, in Belgium, University of social sciences of Hanoi (Vietnam) and the European School of Management.

She has published many articles in various journals such as the *Applied Research on Quality of Life, Social Indicators Research, the Journal of E-working, the Canadian Journal of Urban Research, International Journal of Entrepreneurship and Innovation Management, Canadian Journal of Communication, Canadian Journal of Regional Science, Leisure and Society, Women in Management, Géographie, économie et société, Carriérologie, Revue de gestion des resources humaines*, and others.

Mari Vaattovaara is a Professor of Urban Geography at the Department of Geography, the University of Helsinki, Finland. Her research interests cover social segregation in cities, urban development and housing. She is currently involved in numerous research programmes and projects both nationally and internationally. She is a steering group member of the Finnish graduate school of housing.

Caroline Wong teaches at the UQ Business School of the University of Queensland, Australia. The focus of her current research is on managing the intangible resources (such as knowledge and information) and competencies (such as creativity, reputation and experience) that have increasingly become the sources of competitive advantage in the new economy. Her areas of research include sectors in the creative/cultural industries with particular interest in the film industry. She also explores the challenges of new technologies such as digital technology that impact on the value chain of the film industry. Dr. Wong has researched and published widely in the area of creativity management and knowledge management by taking a multidisciplinary approach linking them to human resources management, international business, innovation, entrepreneurship and business strategy.

Index

Symbols

21st century's economy 118

A

agro technology 274
altruism 236
apply knowledge 167
appreciative inquiry 149, 150, 158
Attractiveness Indicators 20

B

bar-coding 182
bio-bank 305
bio incubator 305
biotechnology 274, 275
business environment 103
Business Performance 315, 319, 321, 322, 323, 325, 326, 328
business-to-business agreements 185

C

city-centre 45, 50, 51, 52
cluster environment 183
codified knowledge 63, 79
Collaboration for Leadership in Applied Health Research and Care (CLAHRC) 305
collaborative activities 62
collaborative approach 181
collaborative entanglement 141, 148, 149, 154
collaborative entanglement model 148, 149
collaborative knowledge relationships 61, 62, 63, 64, 68, 69, 70, 71, 72, 74, 75
collaborative relationships 62, 63, 69, 72, 74, 75
collaborative work 207
collectivism 236
Combine knowledge 167
Committee on Singapore's Competitiveness (CSC) 259
communication channels 60
communication technologies 21
communities of commitment 233
communities of expertise 233
communities of practice (CoPs) 223, 224
community development 149
community members 141, 156
community setting 147
community structure 201
complexity and the resulting anxiety (CUCA) 141
complex social processes 233
computer-aided education 274
Computers in Teaching Initiative (CTI) 307, 311
context of innovations 71
contextual lenses 185
contextual relevance 183
co-operation 200, 201, 206
core competencies 134
Create knowledge 167
creativity-related strategies 19
cross-communal perspective 233
cross-cutting communities 233
cultural innovation 122
cultural researchers 198
cultural resource 21

Cyberjaya 281, 285, 287, 288, 289, 290, 291, 292, 293, 294, 295
cyber laws 289, 290, 291

D

data communication 274
decision-makers 143, 148, 155
decision-making 13, 143, 144, 148, 152, 153, 156, 158, 159, 302
Deep knowledge 142, 143, 153, 154, 155, 156, 158
design solutions 164
developmentalism 261, 266
development approach 100
digital divide 83
digital revolution 81
discipline-based communities 233
double helix 92
dual helix 91, 93
dualisms 245
Dublin Institute of Technology (DIT) 22
dynamic blend 119
dynamic nature 316

E

ecology of knowledge 134
economic actors 59, 61, 64, 65, 72, 73, 74, 75
economic benefit 29
economic benefits 120
economic community 310
economic crisis 162
economic development 81, 82, 84, 87, 90, 91, 92, 93, 282, 283, 284, 294, 295
Economic Development Board (EDB) 30, 39, 259, 266
economic development strategy 102
economic geography 100, 101, 114, 116
economic growth 3, 4, 9, 10, 11, 42, 43, 44, 57, 101, 102, 109, 115, 272, 274, 278, 279
economic ladder 22
economic paradigm 316
economic regeneration 307
economic system 2, 3
Economic theory 3
economy 99, 100, 101, 102, 103, 104, 109, 112, 113, 114, 116
ecosystem 260, 267, 268
education community 100
education style 164
egoism 236
egoism-related motive 236
electronic database inventory (EDI) 182, 185
electronic database inventory (EDI) systems 182
employment-deprived communities 310
environmental technology 21
ethnic homogeneity 197
European Economic Research Consortium (ERECO) 200
European Patent Office (EPO) 65
exploitative-explorative nature 59

F

face-to-face 223, 227, 234, 235, 237, 240, 244
face-to-face contacts 62
face-to-face interaction 165, 227, 234
financial capital 256, 271
Finnish economy 203, 204, 205
flexible framework 89
future growth 274, 275, 278

G

Generic Capital System (GCS) 296, 299
Generic Capital System (GCS) taxonomy 296
geographical components 118
global city 118
global democracy 13
global economic crisis 1, 13
global economy 118, 119, 211, 214, 219, 282
Global Entrepreneurship Monitor (GEM) 259, 264
global environment 214, 216, 218
global hierarchy 101
global hub 291
globalisation 213, 214, 215, 216, 217, 218, 219
globalization 273, 274
global KBD platforms 7

global knowledge-based economy 103, 113
global knowledge economy 284
global market 99, 112, 293
global network economy 255
global nodes 284
global R&D agenda 1
global recession 2, 13
global society 289
global talent 281
global trends 138
global warming 13
global world 219
global world market 275
glocal approach 84
government-linked companies (GLCs) 260
Greater Manchester Lifelong Learning Network (GM LNN) 309
gross domestic product (GDP) 202, 282
gross domestic product (GDP) growth 282
growing market 20
Growth Theory (GT) 4

H

HEI contributions 305
heterarchic governance 113
hierarchy of networks 316
Higher Education (HE) 307, 309
higher education institutions (HEIs) 302
historical heritage 229
human activity 2, 3
human capital 132, 136, 137, 299, 301, 309, 310
human-capital model 44
human collective capital 256, 271
human collective experience 12
human environment 102, 116
human experiences 10
human individual capital 256, 271
human knowledge-based 1, 4
human knowledge moments 147, 160
human perspective 135
human resource development 284
human resources 165, 169
hybrid organizational structures 60

I

ICT connectivity systems 296, 297
ICT-related industries 285
ICT revolution 263
industrial economy 223
industrial revolution 222
industrial revolution social production 101
informal learning 164
information and communication (ICT) 202
information and communication technologies (ICTs) infrastructure 307
information and communication technology (ICT) 18, 227, 273, 281, 307
Information and Communication Technology (ICT) tools 18
infrastructural 82, 87
infrastructural development 122
innovation ecology 303
Innovation Ecosystem 302
innovation organizer 91, 92, 93
inquiry approach 149, 150
institutional collaboration 93
instrumental-knowledge capital 256, 271
instrumental-material capital 256, 271
integrative system 296, 297
intellectual property 162
intellectual quality 163
intelligence capital 256, 271
intensive collaboration networks 109
interactive online tools 222
inter-connected 141
internal theory 143
international interaction 91
inter-organisational work 163
inter-organizational knowledge 65
inter-organizational ties 66, 69
inter-organizations knowledge 60
interpersonal networks 198
Israeli government 274, 275
Israel's growth 275
IT infrastructure industry 86
IT systems 27, 37

K

KBD global agenda 10
KBD research 1, 4, 10

KBE indicators 267
KBUD concept 283
KBUD goals 285
KBUD initiative 287, 292, 293
KBVS model 135, 136, 137, 138
KC capital system taxonomy 296
KC concept 20
KC models 310
KC scheme 297
KM emergence 4, 5
KM field 132, 133
KM model 299
KM research 132
KM strategies 232
KM system's social 235
knowledge-as-asset 5
knowledge-as-capability 5
knowledge-as-relation 5
Knowledge Attractor Network Team (KANT) 156
knowledge-base 211, 212, 214, 217, 218, 219, 220
knowledge-based activities 284
knowledge-based activity 303
knowledge-based behavior 2
knowledge-based capital 6
knowledge-based capitals 298, 310
knowledge-based city 255
knowledge-based city-regions 297
knowledge-based community 8, 81, 82, 93
knowledge-based community development 81, 82
knowledge based development 119
knowledge-based development 43, 45, 55, 81, 82, 83, 86, 87, 88, 89, 90, 91, 92, 93, 94, 100, 102, 103, 113, 114, 119, 196, 202
knowledge-based development communicate 81
knowledge-based development engine 304
knowledge-based development (KBD) 17, 18, 20, 21, 28, 29, 31, 32, 34, 35, 37, 39, 223
Knowledge-based Development (KBD) schemes 131, 132
knowledge-based direction 316
knowledge-based economy 11, 225, 255, 256, 260, 261, 264, 267, 268, 269, 270, 271, 316
knowledge-based economy (KBE) 12, 162, 255, 273, 280
knowledge-based economy (KBE) development 255
knowledge-based efforts 303, 310
knowledge-based firms 82, 89
knowledge-based firms/communities 82
knowledge-based frameworks 299
knowledge-based fronts 297
knowledge-based industries (KBIs) 262
knowledge-based intangible assets 316
knowledge-based local development 82, 83, 93, 94
knowledge-based local developments 81, 84
knowledge-based neighborhoods 83, 87
knowledge-based network 65, 66
knowledge-based realities 3, 6, 13
knowledge-based regional 196, 197, 200
knowledge-based regional development 81, 82, 88, 89
Knowledge-based social communities 141
knowledge-based societies 2, 299
knowledge-based society 143, 144, 156, 158, 196, 197, 198, 204, 293
knowledge-based strategy 297, 310
knowledge-based structure 273
knowledge-based urban development 7, 11, 99, 100, 101, 103, 104, 116, 117, 281, 282, 283, 285, 295
knowledge-based urban development concept 281
knowledge-based urban development (KBUD) 281, 282, 283
knowledge-based value dynamics 3
Knowledge-based value generation 12
knowledge-based Value Systems approach (KBVS) 132, 135, 136
knowledge-bases 218, 219
knowledge capital 1, 3, 4, 225
knowledge-centric 31
knowledge cities (KCs) 17, 18, 34, 35, 39
knowledge citizen 131, 132, 135, 136, 137, 138

Knowledge City (KC) 297, 298, 300, 301
Knowledge City-Region 298
knowledge community
99, 100, 101, 109, 110, 111
Knowledge Country 298
knowledge creation 226, 228, 232, 238, 245, 246, 253
knowledge creation process 179
knowledge culture 287
knowledge-driven initiatives 296, 297
knowledge economy 163, 178, 223, 224, 230, 238, 255, 260, 261, 264, 265, 269, 270, 281, 282, 283, 284, 285, 286, 289, 290, 293, 295
Knowledge Economy 23, 23
knowledge economy growth 101
Knowledge Economy Index (KEI) 257, 259, 267, 271
knowledge era 99, 100, 101, 102, 109, 111, 112, 120, 121
knowledge gatekeeper 59, 62, 63, 64, 65, 66, 67, 69, 70, 71, 72
knowledge-generating 304
knowledge-geographers 11
knowledge growth 183
Knowledge (informing) 142
knowledge infrastructure 118
Knowledge-intensive 166
knowledge-intensive activities 30, 39
knowledge-intensive businesses 122
knowledge-intensive business services (KIBS) 104, 189
knowledge-intensive hubs 296, 297
knowledge-intensive industries 202, 204, 205
knowledge-intensive organisations 232
knowledge-intensive production 196
knowledge-intensive service activities (KISA) 105
knowledge-intensive urban economy 21
knowledge management 119, 315, 316, 317, 318, 321, 322, 323, 324, 325
Knowledge Management and Knowledge Based Development 1
Knowledge Management (KM) 4, 131, 223, 299
knowledge management strategies 67
Knowledge Meta-Community 298
Knowledge Metropolis 298
Knowledge Micro-City 298
knowledge mobilization 147, 148, 156
Knowledge mobilization (KMb) 147
knowledge-oriented companies 322
Knowledge Precinct 298
Knowledge (proceeding) 142
knowledge production 81, 99, 100, 101, 102, 104, 105, 106, 107, 108, 109, 110, 111, 113
knowledge-production space 106
knowledge relationships 59, 60, 61, 62, 63, 64, 65, 67, 68, 69, 70, 71, 72, 73, 74, 75
knowledge resources 118, 123, 183, 192
knowledge resulting 109
knowledge-rich-environments 104
Knowledge-sharing 226, 227, 248
knowledge-sharing dynamics 296, 297
knowledge society 21, 22, 28, 31, 33, 35, 36, 37, 38, 39, 199, 223, 224, 226, 227, 230, 242, 244, 245, 246, 252
Knowledge, technologies 12
knowledge worker 42, 43, 45, 53, 54, 55, 100, 107, 108, 109, 110, 119, 162, 163, 164, 165, 166, 167, 168, 169, 170, 171, 172, 173, 176, 282, 285, 287, 288, 290, 291, 293, 299
Knowledge Zone 24

L

Learning and Teaching Support Network (LTSN) 307
learning communities 164
learning conversations 304
learning efficacy 141
learning space 104
Learn knowledge 167

M

macro-econometri 276
macro indicators 198
MAKCi exercise 256, 271
MAKCi framework 256

Malaysian companies 315, 318, 323, 324, 325
management information systems (MIS) 225
managing learning 296, 297
Manchester Is My Planet (MIMP) 29
Manchester: Knowledge Capital Partnership (MKCP) 309
manufacture-based 284
meta capitals 296, 297, 308
micro components 218
micro scale 211, 212, 215, 218, 220
micro-spaces 211
Ministry of Education (MOE) 262
Ministry of University and Research (MIUR) 80
MNEs internal 185
mobile 46, 52, 54
multi-layered knowledge networks 260, 267, 268
multimedia 285, 287, 288, 289, 290, 291
Multimedia Development Corporation (MDeC) 289, 291
multimedia innovations 291
Multimedia Super Corridor 281, 282, 285, 28 6, 287, 293, 294, 295
multinational companies (MNCs) 30, 90, 260
Multi-National Enterprises (MNEs) 185
mutual enterprise 224

N

Nanotechnology 8, 275
National Development Programme for Computer Assisted Learning (NDPCAL) 307
national economy 198, 203, 207
National ICT Agenda (NITA) 285
natural dynamics 3
neo-classical economic 101
Neo-classical theory 101
network-based modes 113
networking forum 233
network interaction 134
network theory 60
neuron connections 142
Next Revolution 222
nomadic societies 2
non collaborative 59, 60, 61, 62, 65, 67, 68, 69, 71, 72, 74, 75
non-contractual activities 273
non-linear perspective 113
non-local actors, 191
non-rivalry 3
non-routine situations 222, 223
Nordic welfare state 197, 206

O

object accumulation 5
Office of the Chief Scientist (OCS) 275
on-line questionnaire 42, 45
organisational efficiency 164
organisational knowledge 232, 237, 238
Organisation for Economic Co-operation and Development (OECD) 225
Organisation for Economic Co-operation and Development (OECD) economies 225
Organise knowledge 167
organizational arrangements 62, 63, 66, 69, 71, 73, 74
organizational context 71
organizational knowledge 317, 319, 321, 322
organizational knowledge management system (OKMS) 317

P

paradigm 82, 84, 89, 90
Personal Knowledge Management (PKM) 131
philosophy 132
physical context 231
physical environment 213, 215, 216, 219
physical infrastructure 22, 33, 108
physical realities 3
PKM approach 136, 138
PKM notions 132
planning paradigm 99, 102, 111, 112
policy-makers 282
pragmatism 244, 261, 266
principlism 236
problem-solving 152, 153, 158, 240
problem-solving arrangements 63
productivity paradox 5
proximity 47, 51
psychological life 2

psychology 132, 135
public-private collaboration 91

Q

Quadruple Helix 81, 82, 92, 93, 94
Quadruple Helix Model 81, 82, 92, 93, 94
quality environments 141
quasi-firm residential communities 84

R

radical approach 1, 4, 9, 10, 15
radical phase 10
radio frequency identification (RFID 182
R&D 100, 101, 105, 275, 276, 277, 279
R&D base 31
R&D collaborations 31, 71
R&D expenditure 205
R&D output 258, 262
R&D sectors 20
real-world problems 231
Real World Science 302
Regeneris 302, 309, 313
regional development 81, 82, 83, 84, 88, 89
regional economy 202
regional policy tools 196, 197
regulatory environment 91
relational capital 256, 271
relationship-based interactions 146
research and development (R&D) 196
research-based economy 31
research community 18
resource-based industries 286
result-oriented knowledge 165

S

scientific organizations 60
sectoral composition 273
secure knowledge 167
self-confidence 135
self-esteem 135, 236
self-evaluation 135
self-knowledge 135, 137
self-management 135, 136
self-sustaining dynamic region 89
self-teaching 135
Sepang Municipal Council (SMC) 291
Shallow knowledge 142, 143
Silicon Valley 103, 107, 111
small and medium-scaled enterprises (SMEs) 260, 287
Small and Medium sized Enterprise Clusters (SMECs) 179
Smart Strategy Plan 89
SMEC network 191, 192
social background 204
social capital 44
social capital systems 7
social community 141, 143, 144, 156
social computing 222
social creatures 145
social development 91, 284, 286
Social development strategy 103
social flows 125
social health 141
social importance 99, 100
social innovation 10, 13
Social interaction 232
social knowledge 135, 138
social knowledge bases 12
social knowledge infrastructure 6
Social learning networks 12
social levels 181
social life 21
Social marketing 150
social network 42, 46, 47, 48, 53, 54, 184, 198
social norms 2
social opportunity 101
social patterns 185
social responsibility 148
social scientific research 196
social security 197
social sense 207
social value 139
social value frameworks 6
social wealth generation 13
socio-cultural 276, 278
socio-cultural atmosphere 219
socio-cultural theories 233
socio-cultural theories on learning 233
socio-economic backgrounds 288

socio-economic development 99, 111, 114
socioeconomic dynamism 27
socio-economic position 316
sociological concept 218
sociology 132
socio-spatial changes 100
socio-spatial development 99, 100, 110, 113, 292
socio-spatial growth 284
spatial consolidation 109
state-of-the-art review 131
strategic decisions 154
strategic framework 17, 18, 39
strategic planning schemes 19
strategic resource 315, 316, 318
strengthened economic growth 216
Supply Chains (SCs) 179
Surface knowledge 142, 143
systemic taxonomy 297
systems of learning 296, 297, 304, 308

T

tacit knowledge 222, 223, 225, 226, 237, 238, 240, 242, 243, 244, 245, 246, 253
Tacit knowledge 216
tacit worker 222
task-based environments 166
Tax Allowance 290
Teaching and Learning Technologies Project (TLTP) 307
technological distance 63, 64
technological opportunities 63, 68, 71, 73
technological proximity 61, 63, 65, 67, 69, 70, 71, 72, 73, 74, 76, 145
technology-based globalization 84
technology-based KM systems 236
technology environment 164
telecommunication 82, 83, 85
theory of human capital 46
time-bound communities 233
transfer knowledge 63, 72
transport network 307
Triple Helix 81, 82, 88, 89, 90, 91, 92, 93, 94, 95, 97

U

umbrella-type communities 233
university-community-government- industry 93
University of Manchester Institute of Science and Technology (UMIST) 305
university research 21
urban-amenities model 44
urban development 196, 197, 200, 206, 207
urban-driven development 205
urban economies 99, 100
urban knowledge spaces 113
urban living environment 50

V

value chain 169
verify knowledge 167
Victoria University of Manchester (VUM) 305
Virtual communities 234
virtual community infrastructure 234
virtual CoPs 234, 235, 240
Virtual CoPs 235
virtual market 283
virtual space 109
Virtual teams 169

W

World Bank Knowledge Economy Index 267
world economic system 2
World Knowledge Competitiveness Index 2008 (WKCI) 19